5 Practice Exams for the
GED® Test

3rd Edition

The Staff of The Princeton Review

PrincetonReview.com

Penguin
Random
House

The Princeton Review
110 East 42nd St, 7th Floor
New York, NY 10017
E-mail: editorialsupport@review.com

Editor: Meave Shelton
Production Editors: Emma Parker and Liz Dacey
Production Artist: Kris Ogilvie
Content Contributor: Josh Nagel

Printed in the United States of America.

10 9 8 7 6 5 4 3 2 1

"Carnegie Libraries," Ontario Ministry of Tourism, Culture, and Sport. © Queen's Printer for Ontario, 2015. Reproduced with permission. The material on the Ministry of Tourism, Culture, and Sport is current to February 28, 2017 and is subject to change. www.mtc.gov.on.ca.

"A Plea for a Coordinated National Water Policy," Gerald E. Galloway Jr., *The Bridge*, Winter 2011, Vol. 41, No. 4. © 2011 by the National Academy of Sciences. All rights reserved. Reproduced with permission of the National Academy of Engineering.

"The Geological Exploration of Tibet and the Himalaya," Nigel Harris, *The Alpine Journal*, Vol. 96, pp. 70–71, 1991. © The Alpine Club. Reprinted with permission of the Alpine Club and Nigel Harris.

The National Organization for Women's Statement of Purpose, October 29, 1966. © 2016 National Organization for Women. All rights reserved. Reprinted with permission of the National Organization for Women. This is a historical document and may not reflect the current language or priorities of the organization.

"Claim That Sea Level Is Rising Is a Total Fraud," *Executive Intelligence Review*, Vol. 34, No. 25, June 22, 2007. © 2007 EIR News Service Inc. All rights reserved. This interview originally appeared in the EIR Magazine of June 22, 2007, and is reproduced here by permission of EIR Magazine.

"Americans in Danger from Rising Seas Could Triple," Marianne Lavelle, National Geographic News, March 14, 2016. © 1996–2015 National Geographic Society. © 2015–2016 National Geographic Partners, LLC. All rights reserved. Reprinted with permission from National Geographic Creative. news.nationalgeographic.com.

"Car-Size Stingray May Be World's Largest Freshwater Fish," Brian Clark Howard, National Geographic News, March 15, 2015. © 1996–2015 National Geographic Society. ©2015–2016 National Geographic Partners, LLC. All rights reserved. Reprinted with permission from National Geographic Creative. news.nationalgeographic.com.

"Climate Change Is Making Your Allergies Even Worse," Becky Little, National Geographic News, April 8, 2016. © 1996–2015 National Geographic Society. © 2015–2016 National Geographic Partners, LLC. All rights reserved. Reprinted with permission from National Geographic Creative. news.nationalgeographic.com.

Every attempt has been made to obtain permission to reproduce material protected by copyright. Where omissions may have occurred the editors will be happy to acknowledge this in future printings.

Editorial

Rob Franek, Editor-in-Chief
David Soto, Director of Content Development
Stephen Koch, Student Survey Manager
Deborah Weber, Director of Production
Gabriel Berlin, Production Design Manager
Selena Coppock, Managing Editor
Aaron Riccio, Senior Editor
Meave Shelton, Senior Editor
Chris Chimera, Editor
Eleanor Green, Editor
Orion McBean, Editor
Brian Saladino, Editor
Patricia Murphy, Editorial Assistant

Random House Publishing Team

Tom Russell, VP, Publisher
Alison Stoltzfus, Publishing Director
Amanda Yee, Associate Managing Editor
Ellen Reed, Production Manager
Suzanne Lee, Designer

Acknowledgments

The Princeton Review would like to thank Josh Nagel for his valuable contributions to the third edition of this book. Thanks also to past contributors: Chris Chimera, Clarissa Constantine, Gina Donegan, Anne Goldberg, Kimberly Beth Hollingsworth, Linda Kelley, Erik Kolb, Sara Kuperstein, and Eliz Markowitz.

Special thanks to Adam Robinson, who conceived of and perfected the Joe Bloggs approach to standardized tests, and many of the other successful techniques used by The Princeton Review.

Our gratitude also goes to the production team—Kris Ogilvie, Emma Parker, and Liz Dacey—for their careful attention to every page.

Contents

Get More (Free) Content

at **PrincetonReview.com/prep**

As easy as 1·2·3

1 Go to PrincetonReview.com/prep and enter the following ISBN for your book:
9780525569251

2 Answer a few simple questions to set up an exclusive Princeton Review account. *(If you already have one, you can just log in.)*

3 Enjoy access to your **FREE** content!

Once you've registered, you can...

- Download printable custom answer sheets for the tests in this book

- Access sample essays for the Extended Response prompts

- Print out the Mathematical Formula Sheet for your reference

- Check to see if there have been any corrections or updates to this edition

Need to report a potential **content** issue?

Contact **EditorialSupport@review.com** and include:

- full title of the book
- ISBN
- page number

Need to report a **technical** issue?

Contact **TPRStudentTech@review.com** and provide:

- your full name
- email address used to register the book
- full book title and ISBN
- Operating system (Mac/PC) and browser (Firefox, Safari, etc.)

Look For These Icons Throughout The Book

 OTHER REFERENCES

 ONLINE ARTICLES

Part I
Introduction

Chapter 1
Your Guide to Getting the Most Out of This Book

GED® Test Prep is The Princeton Review's comprehensive guide to the GED® test. It includes:

- complete review of all 4 test subjects
- guided lessons with sample questions and drills
- 2 full-length practice tests
- 350+ additional practice questions online

WHAT'S INSIDE

Welcome to *5 Practice Exams for the GED® Test*. As the title indicates, this book contains five full-length practice tests, which we at The Princeton Review have created based on the information released by GED Testing Service. We've rigorously analyzed the available tests and sample questions, and our content development team has worked to ensure that our material accurately reflects what you will see in terms of design, structure, style, and most importantly, the content of the official GED® test.

We are confident that if you work through these tests and evaluate your performance with our comprehensive explanations, you'll improve the skills you need to earn your GED® test credential.

HOW TO USE THIS BOOK

Each test is laid out as you'll encounter it on the GED® test. While we recommend that you take each test in full, in accordance with the allotted times and under conditions similar to those that you'll face on the day of the examination, you're welcome to focus on specific sections on which you'd like more practice.

Don't forget to review carefully our detailed explanations! Whether you get the question right or not, carefully reviewing the explanations will help you to identify your strengths and weaknesses or any gaps in your knowledge, which you can then focus your attention on studying.

Please note that this book does *not* provide instruction on the various topics covered on the test. So, if you're unsure whether or not this book is right for you, skim through the four sections in Practice Test 1—Reasoning Through Language Arts, Mathematical Reasoning, Social Studies, and Science. If you have no idea how to solve most of these problems, we highly recommend beginning your study with our comprehensive guide, *GED® Test Prep* (formerly titled *Cracking the GED® Test*), and then using this book for practice once you're feeling more confident.

Online Content

In addition to the tests in this book, we've provided you with some helpful supplements, which you can download and print once you've registered your book online. Flip to the beginning of the book, just after the Table of Contents, for instructions on how to do this. These supplements include the following items:

- Custom answer sheets for all five practice tests. These are particularly useful if you don't want to write in the book itself.
- The Mathematical Formula Sheet that accompanies the Mathematical Reasoning section.
- Sample essays for the Extended Response prompts in the Reasoning Through Language Arts section. These will give you a good idea of what a high-scoring essay looks like.

Online Articles

KEY DIFFERENCES BETWEEN THE GED® TEST AND OUR TESTS

While our practice tests are closely modeled on the types of questions you see on the actual GED® test, the following are some key differences you should know about.

The GED® Test Is Computer Based

You'll be taking the GED® test on a computer. The tests in this book, on the other hand, are in pencil-and-paper format. We've slightly adapted the types of questions that involve using the computer interface so that you can answer them without needing a mouse and keyboard. See the general directions at the beginning of Part II for more information on this.

Scoring

Another key difference is that you will not be able to score your work on these practice tests using GED Testing Service's scoring formula, as it has not been made publicly available. You are welcome to tally up your raw score—the number of questions you answered correctly—which should give you a rough idea of how well you're doing. However, this does *not* translate into a guaranteed measure of readiness to take the GED® test. So we can't promise you that you are likely to pass if you get a certain number of questions right.

> **Experience the Interface for Yourself**
> Test the user interface and familiarize yourself with the different question formats by visiting https://ged.com/study/free_online_ged_test.

GET GED READY®

Fortunately, we *can* point you to the best available indicator of how well you'll do: GED® Ready: The Official Practice Test.

Purchase GED Ready®
https://ged.com/
study/ged_ready

GED Ready® was written by the test creators and gives you the full computer-based experience, as well as an Enhanced Score Report. Although GED Ready® is only half the length of the actual GED® test and doesn't require the same level of endurance, it will give you accurate feedback on your mastery of the content and required skills. You'll be able to access your score report within about an hour of completing the test.

In Chapter 2, we'll give you an overview of what you need to know about the GED® test.

Chapter 2
What You Need to Know for the GED® Test

WHAT IS THE GED® TEST?

The GED® test is actually four tests that you can take in one day or over a series of days. Many people refer to it as a high school equivalency test because when you pass the test, you earn a credential that most colleges and employers recognize as the equivalent of a high school diploma.

The Four GED® Tests

1. **Reasoning Through Language Arts**
   (150 minutes, approximately 51 questions)

   - Section 1 (35 minutes)
   - Section 2: One Extended Response question (45 minutes)
   - Break (10 minutes)
   - Section 3 (60 minutes)

   Sections 1 and 3 will contain a mixture of grammar and reading comprehension questions. There will be six to eight reading passages with approximately six questions each and two language passages with four drop-down questions in each. The questions for the reading passages will be multiple-choice or drag-and-drop. The reading texts will be in this approximate distribution:

Informational Texts	75%
Literature	25%

   In Section 2, you'll be asked to write an essay analyzing two passages that present different views on the same subject. You'll be asked to develop an opinion and support that opinion with specific examples from the text.

2. Mathematical Reasoning
(115 minutes, 46 questions)

- Part 1 (first 5 questions): Calculator not allowed
- Part 2 (remaining 41 questions): Calculator permitted

The Mathematical Reasoning test comes in two parts. In the first, you will not be allowed to use a calculator. In the second, you will have access to the on-screen calculator. (You can also bring your own hand-held calculator—but it must be a TI-30XS Multiview Scientific Calculator.) The first section will test your ability to do basic calculations. In the second section, you will be asked to answer questions common in many work scenarios.

Many of these will be word problems. About one-half of the questions will be based on diagrams or charts. These questions come in several formats including multiple-choice, fill-in-the-blank, drag-and-drop, hot-spot, and drop-down formats. The test will encompass the following mathematical concepts:

Quantitative Problem Solving (arithmetic, averages, ratios, etc.)	45%
Algebraic Problem Solving	55%

3. Social Studies
(70 minutes, approximately 35 questions)

You will find a mixture of passages, charts, graphs, and maps. The questions will be in multiple-choice, hot-spot, drag-and-drop, and fill-in-the-blank formats. The test will cover the following areas of social studies:

Government and Civics	50%
U.S. History	20%
Economics	15%
Geography	15%

4. **Science**
   (90 minutes, 1 section of approximately 34 questions)

The questions will be based on a variety of information ranging from short passages to graphs and charts. The questions will be in multiple-choice, fill-in-the-blank, drop-down, drag-and-drop, and hot-spot formats. The answers to the questions are almost always supplied in the passages or graphic materials. You need only a *general knowledge* of scientific principles. The questions will be about these general areas of science:

Life Science	40%
Physics and Chemistry	40%
Earth and Space	20%

How Is the GED® Test Scored?

For each of the four tests, you will receive a score between 100 and 200. Because each test has a different number of available points, GED Testing Service will standardize your raw scores (or the number of questions you answered correctly for each test) through a scoring metric to yield a score between 100 and 200. It's important to remember that **there is no penalty for wrong answers or questions left blank**, so it is to your advantage to record an answer to every question.

GED® Test Score Levels
145–164: Pass/High School Equivalency
165–174: GED® College Ready
175–200: GED® College Ready + Credit

The minimum score needed to pass any of the four subject tests on the GED® test is 145. In order to get your completion certificate, you must achieve at least this score on each test. A higher score on one test will not make up for a lower score on another. While a passing score is sufficient to obtain your certificate, you may want to strive for a score of at least 165. Such a score entitles you to a GED® College-Ready Score, a distinction that indicates college and career readiness. And if you achieve a score of at least 175, you'll receive the GED® College Ready + Credit designation, which means that in addition to being ready to take college courses, you qualify for up to 10 hours of college credit.

Once you receive a passing score on a test, you do not need to retake that test. If you want to retake the test to receive a higher score, you may do so.

If you do not receive your desired score on a particular test, you can retake that test two more times without any waiting period, subject to scheduling availability. After the third attempt, you will have to wait 60 days to test again. This schedule allows for eight testing opportunities in a year, if you need that many to pass a section.

REGISTERING FOR THE GED® TEST

The best ways to register are to call the information number for your state and/or visit www.ged.com. Once you have registered on the site, you will be emailed a letter with instructions on how to schedule your exam online. If you've been taking a preparation course, your teacher may take care of registration for you, but check to make sure this is the case. The tests are administered year-round, and the new online format allows for a lot more flexibility in scheduling, but in some of the larger states, it may take a while for you to get a test date. It now costs money to take the GED® test—but the cost varies depending on where you live. Visit https://ged.com/policies for your testing location's pricing, rules, and contact information.

> **Whom to Contact**
> For information on registering to take the GED® test and for classes in your area, call 877-392-6433 (877-EXAM-GED).

OTHER RESOURCES

If you are looking for additional support with your preparation, we recommend picking up our other titles: *GED® Test Prep* for comprehensive prep or *Basic Skills for the GED® Test* if you're looking to master the fundamental skills needed to begin your test preparation.

We also recommend spending some time on GED Testing Service's website at www.ged.com—it contains a wealth of useful information, from the thorough FAQ to the sample Enhanced Score Report.

Best of luck with your preparation!

Part II
Practice Tests

DIRECTIONS FOR THE PRACTICE TESTS

The questions in these full-length practice tests are modeled closely on actual GED® test questions in terms of the content they cover, their levels of difficulty, and the various types of questions you should expect to encounter. We have adapted the computer-based format to allow you to answer most of the questions by **writing directly in this book.** If you prefer NOT to write in this book, we have provided **five custom answer sheets,** one for each practice test, which you may download and print when you register your book online.

Here are some guidelines on how to answer questions for each of the six GED® question formats:

- **Multiple choice:** If you are writing directly in the book, circle the letter of the answer choice you select. If you're using an answer sheet, bubble in your choice.
- **Drag and drop:** Write in the correct answer or answers in the space provided. For some questions, you need only write the letter associated with the answer—(a), (b), (c), and so on.
- **Drop down:** Circle or check your selection from the drop-down menu.
- **Fill in the blank:** Write the correct answer in the box or blank provided.
- **Hot spot:** Mark an X or dot on the graphic as indicated.
- **Extended Response:** If you have access to a computer, we recommend typing your response; doing so will give you the closest possible experience of taking the GED® test. Otherwise, you may write your response on a separate sheet of paper.

Before you begin, make sure to have the following items on hand:

- Pencils
- A notepad for scratch paper—and for writing your responses to Extended Response questions, if you will not be using a computer
- A Texas Instruments T1-30XS calculator. You may also use the online calculator at web2.0calc.com
- A clock or watch to help you keep track of time

Good luck!

Chapter 3
Practice Test 1

Reasoning Through Language Arts

Welcome!

Here is some information that you need to know before you start this test:

- You should not spend too much time on a question if you are not certain of the answer; answer it the best you can, and go on to the next question.
- If you are not certain of the answer to a question, you can mark your answer for review and come back to it later.
- This test has three sections.
- You have **35 minutes** to complete Section 1.
- When you finish Section 1, you may review those questions.
- You may not go back to Section 1 once you have finished your review.
- You have **45 minutes** to complete the Extended Response question in Section 2.
- After completing Section 2, you may take a 10-minute break.
- You have **60 minutes** to complete Section 3.
- When you finish Section 3, you may review those questions.

Turn the page to begin.

GO ON TO THE NEXT PAGE

Questions 1 through 8 refer to the following passage.

Excerpt from
Adventures in the Wilderness; or, Camp-Life in the Adirondacks
by William H.H. Murray

1   The Adirondack Wilderness, or the "North Woods," as it is sometimes called, lies between the Lakes George and Champlain on the east, and the river St. Lawrence on the north and west.... The southern part is known as the Brown Tract Region....It lacks the lofty mountain scenery, the intricate mesh-work of lakes, and the wild grandeur of the country to the north....Not until you reach the Racquette do you get a glimpse of the magnificent scenery which makes this wilderness to rival Switzerland. There, on the very ridge-board of the vast water-shed which slopes northward to the St. Lawrence, eastward to the Hudson, and southward to the Mohawk, you can enter upon a voyage the like of which, it is safe to say, the world does not anywhere else furnish. For hundreds of miles I have boated up and down that wilderness, going ashore only to "carry" around a fall, or across some narrow ridge dividing the otherwise connected lakes. For weeks I have paddled my cedar shell in all directions, without seeing a face but my guide's, and the entire circuit, it must be remembered, was through a wilderness yet to echo to the lumberman's axe. It is estimated that a thousand lakes, many yet unvisited, lie embedded in this vast forest of pine and hemlock. From the summit of a mountain, two years ago, I counted, as seen by my naked eye, forty-four lakes gleaming amid the depths of the wilderness like gems of purest ray amid the folds of emerald-colored velvet. Last summer I met a gentleman on the Piacquette who had just received a letter from a brother in Switzerland, an artist by profession, in which he said, that,..."he had not met with scenery which, judged from a purely artistic point of view, combined so many beauties in connection with such grandeur as the lakes, mountains, and forest of the Adirondack region presented to the gazer's eye." And yet thousands are in Europe to-day as tourists who never gave a passing thought to this marvellous country lying as it were at their very floors.

2   Another reason why I visit the Adirondacks, and urge others to do so, is because I deem the excursion eminently adapted to restore impaired health....To such as are afflicted with that dire parent of ills, dyspepsia, or have lurking in their system consumptive tendencies, I most earnestly recommend a month's experience among the pines. The air which you there inhale is such as can be found only in high mountainous regions, pure, rarefied, and bracing....The spruce, hemlock, balsam, and pine, which largely compose this wilderness, yield upon the air, and

GO ON TO THE NEXT PAGE

especially at night, all their curative qualities....Not a few, far advanced in that dread disease, consumption, have found in this wilderness renewal of life and health....

3   There is one sitting near me, as I write, the color of whose cheek, and the clear brightness of whose eye, cause my heart to go out in ceaseless gratitude to the woods, amid which she found that health and strength of which they are the proof and sign....I feel, therefore, that I am able to speak from experience touching this matter; and I believe that, all things being considered, no portion of our country surpasses, if indeed any equals, in health-giving qualities, the Adirondack Wilderness....

4   Gentlemen often ask me to compare the "North Woods" with the "Maine Wilderness."...The fact is, nothing could induce me to visit Maine....I will tell you why. Go where you will, in Maine, the lumbermen have been before you; and lumbermen are the curse and scourge of the wilderness. Wherever the axe sounds, the pride and beauty of the forest disappear. A lumbered district is the most dreary and dismal region the eye of man ever beheld. The mountains are not merely shorn of trees, but from base to summit fires, kindled by accident or malicious purpose, have swept their sides, leaving the blackened rocks exposed to the eye, and here and there a few unsightly trunks leaning in all directions, from which all the branches and green foliage have been burnt away. The streams and trout-pools are choked with saw-dust, and filled with slabs and logs. The rivers are blockaded with "booms" and lodged timber, stamped all over the ends with the owner's "mark." Every eligible site for a camp has been appropriated; and bones, offal, horse-manure, and all the debris of a deserted lumbermen's village is strewn around, offensive both to eye and nose....In the Adirondack Wilderness you escape this. There the lumberman has never been....The forest stands as it has stood, from the beginning of time, in all its majesty of growth, in all the beauty of its unshorn foliage.... The promontories which stretch themselves half across its lakes, the islands which hang as if suspended in their waveless and translucent depths, have never been marred by the presence of men careless of all but gain....There you live in silence, unbroken by any sounds save such as you yourself may make, away from all the business and cares of civilized life.

GO ON TO THE NEXT PAGE

1. What is the main significance of the "gentleman on the Piacquette" (paragraph 1) and the "one sitting near me" (paragraph 3)?

    A. They add credibility to the author's narrative.
    B. Their presence proves that the Adirondack region is not completely devoid of other travellers.
    C. They enable the author to add variety to his descriptions of natural scenes.
    D. They add a non-American perspective to the author's descriptions.

2. What is ironic about the author's purpose? (When something is ironic, it is the opposite of what one would expect or intend, often with a humorous effect.)

    A. His descriptions of the wilderness might end up discouraging people from visiting the Adirondacks.
    B. He is writing for city dwellers who would be lost and uncomfortable in the wilderness.
    C. If he's successful, he'll end up destroying the best features of the region he's describing.
    D. His criticisms of Maine are as vivid as his praise of the Adirondacks.

3. How does the author craft his descriptions of the wilderness to advance his purpose and appeal to his audience?

    A. He makes the natural scenery seem tame and nonthreatening.
    B. He compares the wilderness to desirable things that would be familiar to readers, and contrasts it to undesirable things they would know.
    C. He presents the Adirondack region as difficult and tough, as a challenge to readers who want to test themselves.
    D. He tries to make the wilderness sound as different as possible from anything readers would experience in their everyday lives.

4. What makes the narrator believe that the lumbermen are "careless of all but gain" (paragraph 4)?

    A. The lumbermen destroyed not only the forest but also the mountains, the rivers, and any clearings that could be used for camp sites.
    B. The lumbermen left behind trunks, logs, and booms of timber stamped with marks of ownership.
    C. The lumbermen haven't entered the wild forests of the Adirondacks.
    D. After they took the trees they wanted, the lumbermen started fires to blacken the sides of the mountains.

GO ON TO THE NEXT PAGE

5. What inferences can you make from the author's references to Switzerland and Europe? Write the letters of your selections in the boxes below.

> [   ]

> [   ]

> (a) He thinks people should spend their vacations in their own countries.

> (b) He wishes people would spend the time and energy to discover the world-class destinations available in America.

> (c) He is dismayed that people automatically visit popular destinations.

> (d) He wonders why people go to Switzerland.

> (e) He is critical of people who have no spirit of adventure.

6. Why would the author have chosen a first-person narrator?

   A. to make a nonfiction work read more like a novel
   B. to distance the descriptions of the Adirondacks from his own personal opinions
   C. to add details that he couldn't include in a neutral, non-narrated description
   D. to add credibility to his descriptions

7. Imagine two men visiting the Adirondacks, one of whom read Murray's guidebook first and one who didn't. How are their experiences and impressions of the region likely to differ? Write the letters of the most probable effects of the guidebook into the box representing the corresponding visitor.

The man who read the guidebook first	The man who didn't read the guidebook first

> (a) will have accurate expectations about the general character of the region, but feel the desire to explore specific areas

> (b) will come away with a more personal experience to remember

> (c) will have some preconceived ideas of what benefits he'll gain from the visit

> (d) might have a general idea which lake or area he wants to see first

> (e) will likely plan to return

> (f) will initially be overpowered by the overall wildness and beauty of the scenery, rather than looking to explore specific aspects of the area

GO ON TO THE NEXT PAGE

8. What impact does the description of Maine have on the description of the Adirondacks?

   A. It gives readers more information about the narrator's preferences.
   B. It intensifies the appeal of a natural wilderness unspoiled by people and greed.
   C. It demonstrates the author's talent for descriptions that would influence readers.
   D. It describes a setting that is worse than the cities where many readers live.

GO ON TO THE NEXT PAGE

Questions 9 through 16 refer to the following passage.

Excerpt from *No Steamboats—A Vision*
by James Fenimore Cooper

1   "M. Cooper," continued M. Blouse, "We are *Messieurs de Trois-Idées-Européennes [the gentlemen of the three European ideas]*. The study of the great interests of man constitutes our occupation, their improvement our duty as well as our pleasure; we are true philanthropists devoted to the general interest. We are not like you *Americains* who think only of yourselves;..... But, M. Cooper, what a dreadful picture of your unhappy country has been brought to light by our philanthropic investigations! In America we see the people in possession of powers which naturally belong to the nobility; the consequences are frightful; corruption stalks undisguised; selfishness reigns supreme. A social chaos confounds all classes;...

2   "M. Cooper, my very dear, very esteemed, and too well beloved friend, we are touched to the heart by the danger of a people possessing but *one idea*; an idea so selfish that it confounds an entire nation with itself. We see your perils, moral, social, and pecuniary, and have resolved not to abandon you to your own movements without one effort to show you the gulf into which you are about to fall. We directed our agents in America to send us, without loss of time, the documents necessary for a complete *exposé* of the mournful state of your dear and unhappy country. We can speak with authority; we have just received from New-York a multitude of these documents, by the last steamboat which arrived at Havre."

3   "M. Blouse. I breathe again. As there is no steamboat which navigates the ocean between Europe and America, it is possible that you are deceived with regard to facts more important to my country."

4   "No steamboats!" cried M. Blouse, casting upon me a look of pity mingled with grief. "M. Cooper, your patriotic spirit is too easily alarmed. I had not the slightest intention of making any unpleasant allusion, although these steamboat enterprises are eminently republican. By a moment's reflection you will see the impossibility of disproving a fact recognised by all Europe from the Mediterranean to the White Sea."

5   "It is precisely because the evident falsehood of what you call a fact is seen, so to speak, in your own ports, that I am induced to believe you may be mistaken with regard to things less evident."...

GO ON TO THE NEXT PAGE

6   "We have here," continued M. Blouse, "Proofs, mournful and incontrovertible proofs of the condition of your wretched country. At least one fourth part of these documents is from the United States of North America, themselves."

7   "M. Blouse, there is no country which is called the United States of North America."

8   "You deny facts, so to speak, consecrated in the mind of all Europe! And you think it possible to reason in this strange manner!"

9   "It appears to me that all the merit of our discussion must depend upon facts. You bring forward heavy charges against my country; I think it important to prove that you are misinformed respecting a very familiar subject, and that you are ignorant of its very name."

10   "Monsieur, you attach a very undue importance to facts; you, the champion of rational liberty, to circumscribe the bounds of logic in this manner! However, we are not to be driven from our position by dogmatic assertions...."

11   "It is evident from the interesting documents received by the last steamboat from the United States of North America, that your Republic sleeps upon a volcano, and that you pay in taxes just six dollars and eighty-two cents and a half, each man."

12   "Volcanoes are natural phenomena; and respecting the taxes, as they come from ourselves, it is hardly probable that we pay more than is necessary for our own benefit."

13   "A fatal error! The tendency of every popular movement is to excess; and if we leave with the people the right of taxing themselves, the people will tax themselves to the last cent...."

14   "At the present day there are but two great systems of government—the first, which rests upon the slender and unstable foundation of the people; the other, which depends upon three consequent and well-balanced ideas. It is difficult to believe that you do not see the immense difference between these two categories."

15   "It appears to me to be the same difference as that between a man who stands upon his feet, and a man who stands upon his head."

16   "No North America!" exclaimed M. l'Hérédité.

GO ON TO THE NEXT PAGE

17   "My dear M. l'Hérédité," continued M. Blouse, "All the questions have been decided in our favor. Let us proceed to facts. Behold, M. Cooper, a truly popular oppression. What dreadful tyranny! What a dreadful effect of the supremacy of a people over itself. You chain up the streets on Sunday; and this in a country which calls itself free! Poor streets! How wretched you must be! Would that you were European streets, so clean, so wide, so dry, so well furnished with side-walks; in short, so free! Poor American streets!—how cruelly you are oppressed!"...

18   "Dry your tears, gentlemen, I beseech you; the injury to the streets is not fatal....during certain months of the year, on account of the climate, the windows of our churches are left open, and to prevent the rumbling of carriages, a chain is stretched across the street in places where the noise might create disturbance. But no person is prevented from travelling on foot wherever he pleases; and even carriages draw up to the doors of all without exception."

9. Read the following sentence from paragraph 14.

> At the present day there are but two great systems of government—the first, which rests upon the slender and unstable foundation of the people; the other, which depends upon three consequent and well-balanced ideas.

By "the first" system of government, M. Blouse means

A. monarchy.
B. democracy.
C. dictatorship.
D. anarchy.

10. When he claims, "Your Republic sleeps upon a volcano" (paragraph 11), M. Blouse is using the image of a volcano to signify

A. that America is a young country compared to Europe, since volcanoes are associated with the formation of the Earth.
B. the "social chaos" that he believes "confounds all classes" (paragraph 1) in America.
C. that America is ignoring things to which it should be paying attention.
D. the impending disaster facing America.

GO ON TO THE NEXT PAGE

11. Cooper and the three Europeans have very different views of America. Below are six descriptions of America. Place each one in the column that represents the side of the discussion that holds that view. Write the letters of your selections in the boxes below.

The Three Europeans	Cooper

(a) It claims to be one thing, but is really the opposite.

(b) People are free to do as they please without disturbing others.

(c) It has inverted the natural order.

(d) It is a place of social harmony.

(e) Government decisions are made to benefit citizens.

(f) People think only of themselves.

12. The author's tone can be described as primarily

A. satirical.
B. critical.
C. puzzled.
D. defensive.

13. Cooper and the three Europeans make statements that develop key concepts or themes in the excerpt. Write the letter of the statement that performs this development function into the box with the corresponding concept or theme. You will need to use three of the five statements below.

facts

democracy

America vs. Europe

(a) "an idea so selfish that it confounds an entire nation with itself" (paragraph 2)

(b) "these steamboat enterprises are eminently republican" (paragraph 4)

(c) "the same difference as that between a man who stands upon his feet, and a man who stands upon his head" (paragraph 15)

(d) "It is evident from the interesting documents received by the last steamboat from the United States of North America" (paragraph 11)

(e) "all the questions have been decided in our favor" (paragraph 17)

GO ON TO THE NEXT PAGE

14. For what purpose does the author have the three Europeans confront Cooper with the "dreadful picture of your unhappy country" that "has been brought to light by our philanthropic investigations" (paragraph 1)?

    A. so they can warn Cooper
    B. so they can demonstrate European misconceptions about America
    C. so they can ridicule an American about his country
    D. so they can learn the truth about America from an American

15. Read the following sentences from the description M. Blouse gives in paragraph 17.

    > You chain up the streets on Sunday; and this in a country which calls itself free! Poor streets! How wretched you must be! Would that you were European streets, so clean, so wide, so dry, so well furnished with side-walks; in short, so free!

    Which of the following statements describes the main idea the author intends to convey in this selection from the passage?

    A. America, which calls itself free, keeps its streets in chains while Europe, which Americans would not call free, has streets that are open and free.
    B. America is not really as free as it claims to be, and Europe has more freedom than Americans think it has.
    C. Preconceived ideas prevent us from seeing and understanding the truth of a situation.
    D. Only someone who has direct personal experience can truly understand a situation.

16. Below are three conditions cited by Cooper or the Europeans, and three things they identify as the causes of those conditions. Write the letter for each cause into the boxes in the "Cause" column and beside each one, write the letter of the corresponding result into the "Effect" column.

Cause	Effect

(a) "corruption stalks undis- guised" (paragraph 1)

(b) "tendency of every popular movement is to excess" (para- graph 13)

(c) "you may be mistaken with regard to things less evident" (paragraph 5)

(d) "the people in posses- sion of powers which naturally belong to the nobility" (para- graph 1)

(e) "the people will tax them- selves to the last cent" (para- graph 13)

(f) "there is no steamboat" (paragraph 3)

GO ON TO THE NEXT PAGE

17. The passage below is incomplete. For each "Select" option, choose the option that correctly completes the sentence. For this practice test, circle your selection.

New Company Policy Regarding Visitors

As a result of last week's security incident, we are revising the company's policy regarding visitors. Our aim is to improve the safeguards for employees and corporate assets, while continuing to welcome legitimate visitors who can contribute to the company's business goals.

The new policy is effective immediately.

Select... ▼
Keeping this document for the future.
This document should be kept for you to refer to in the future.
However, if you keep this document, it will be there for your reference in the future.
Keep this document for future reference.

General Principles

Visitors must be controlled at all times until they have left company property. At the same time, they should not be burdened with excessive restrictions which might make them feel less than welcome and valued.

Badges

Employees must wear their employee badges at all times on company property. Visitors will be issued numbered visitor badges when they sign in at the reception desk. The sign-in sheet will record the visitor's name, company, vehicle license number, badge number, purpose of the visit and the company employee | Select... ▼ | the visitor plans to see.

who
that
whom
which

Visitors must wear their visitor badges at all times until they sign out and surrender the badges to a receptionist.

Escorts

If possible, inform Reception in advance that you are expecting a visitor. A receptionist will notify you when your visitor arrives, and ask your visitor to sign in and wait in the lounge until you arrive. Past the Reception entrance, all visitors must be escorted by an employee. If your visitor is meeting with another employee

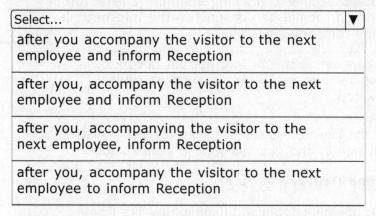

Select... ▼
after you accompany the visitor to the next employee and inform Reception
after you, accompany the visitor to the next employee and inform Reception
after you, accompanying the visitor to the next employee, inform Reception
after you, accompany the visitor to the next employee to inform Reception

that someone else will be signing that visitor out.

VIP Visitors

This new policy applies even if your visitor is a VIP (such as a company CEO or a politician). Visitors at every level will be impressed by the sensible security measures we employ before admitting non-employees to the building.

Groups

If you are expecting a large number of visitors for a meeting, ask other employees to help you escort them in and out. The visitor:employee ratio should not exceed 3:1. Plan group tours with Security well in advance.

Meeting Cubicles

If you have any concerns about the authenticity of a visitor, conduct your meeting in one of the meeting cubicles along the hallway outside the Reception entrance to the main building. Each cubicle is equipped with a meeting table and chairs, a

GO ON TO THE NEXT PAGE

phone, [Select... ▼]

| and a locked cabinet containing a laptop which can connect to the Internet but not to any company systems. |
| and a laptop in a locked cabinet that can connect to the Internet but not to any company systems. |
| and a locked cabinet containing a laptop. The laptop in this locked cabinet can connect to the Internet but not to any company systems. |
| and for connecting to the Internet but not to any company systems. There is a locked cabinet with a laptop. |

You can borrow the key to this cabinet from a receptionist. The visitor must still sign in and out and wear a visitor badge.

Tradespeople and Delivery People

The Facilities Management team will handle all visits from authorized tradespeople. Deliveries can be picked up or dropped off at the delivery kiosk in the visitor parking lot.

By following this policy, you will be making a significant contribution to the company's security and success.

GO ON TO THE NEXT PAGE

Reasoning Through Language Arts, Section 2

Extended Response Answer Guidelines

Please use the guidelines below as you answer the Extended Response question on the Reasoning Through Language Arts test. Following these guidelines as closely as possible will ensure that you provide the best response.

1. **Please note that this task must be completed in no more than 45 minutes.** However, don't rush through your response. Be sure to read through the passage(s) and the prompt. Then think about the message you want to convey in your response. **Be sure to plan your response before you begin writing.** Draft your response and revise it as needed.

2. As you read, think carefully about the **argumentation** presented in the passage(s). "Argumentation" refers to the assumptions, claims, support, reasoning, and credibility on which a position is based. Pay close attention to **how the author(s) use these strategies to convey his or her (their) positions.**

3. When you write your essay, be sure to
   o **determine which position presented** in the passage(s) is **better supported** by evidence from the passage(s)
   o **explain why the position you chose is the better-supported one**
   o **remember, the better-supported position is not necessarily the position you agree with**
   o **defend your assertions with multiple pieces of evidence** from the passage(s)
   o **build your main points thoroughly**
   o **put your main points in logical order** and tie your details to your main points
   o **organize your response carefully** and consider your **audience, message, and purpose**
   o **use transitional words and phrases** to connect sentences, paragraphs, and ideas
   o **choose words carefully** to express your ideas clearly
   o **vary your sentence structure** to enhance the flow and clarity of your response
   o **reread and revise your response** to correct any errors in grammar, usage, or punctuation

GO ON TO THE NEXT PAGE

Instructions

Read

- On the **page 2 tab above**, you will **read two texts** presenting **different views** on the same topic.

- **Both writers argue** that **their position** on the issue is **correct**.

Plan

- **Analyze** the two texts **to determine** which writer presents the **stronger case**.

- **Develop your own argument** in which **you explain** how one position is **better supported** than the other.

- **Include** relevant and specific **evidence** from **both sources** to support your argument.

Write

- **Type** your response in the **box on the right**.

- Your response should be approximately **4 to 7 paragraphs of 3 to 7 sentences each**.

- **Remember** to allow a few minutes **to review and edit your response**.

You have up to **45 minutes** for reading, planning, writing, and editing your response.

Wind Turbines and Birds:
A Guidance Document for Environmental Assessment

1   Wind has been used successfully across the globe to generate electricity, and is generally considered to be an environmentally healthy and viable means of meeting part of our energy demands. However, concerns have been raised about the possible impact of wind turbines on bird populations....

2   As a result, proposals for wind energy projects throughout the United States and Canada have often been accompanied by concerns, scepticism and calls for cautious advancement of the technology and development of wind energy facilities, regardless of a site's attributes with respect to bird populations, scale of facility or siting....A considerable amount of research has been undertaken in assessing the effect of wind turbines on bird populations. In almost all cases, the effect of collision or disturbance on bird populations was minimal. However, any human structure can have an adverse effect on the environment....Appropriate site selection appears to be the key factor in preventing potential significant negative impacts on birds....There is sufficient information currently available that provides general trends which will assist in preventing the problems that have occurred at some wind energy sites.

GO ON TO THE NEXT PAGE

3   Raptors are often cited as the bird group most threatened by wind facilities because of the fatalities that continue to occur at Altamont Pass, but it has been found that in almost all areas, raptors are able to avoid wind turbines, resulting in very few or no collisions. A number of factors contribute to these deaths in California, including unusually high raptor densities, topography and possibly older technology....

4   In North America, the birds most commonly observed to collide with wind turbines are songbirds. Often, these collisions are believed to occur at night during nocturnal migration.... Factors such as topography, turbine lighting and numbers of birds moving through an area on migration can influence the number of collisions observed at a facility, although it is apparent that the operation of the turbines is less important than the lighting and height of the structure and presence of guy wires in contributing to collision risk.

5   The problems that have occurred at some sites need not be duplicated, as the mistakes of the past have provided information that can be used to site wind turbines in such a way as to minimise the effect on bird populations....

Source: Government of Canada Publications, Canadian Wildlife Service

License to Kill: Wind and Solar Decimate Birds and Bats

6   According to a study in the *Wildlife Society Bulletin*, every year 573,000 birds (including 83,000 raptors) and 888,000 bats are killed by wind turbines—30 percent higher than the federal government estimated in 2009, due mainly to increasing wind power capacity across the nation....

7   Over the past five years, about 2.9 million birds were killed by wind turbines. That compares to about 800,000 birds that a *Mother Jones* blog estimated to have been killed by the BP oil spill....Nevertheless, BP was fined $100 million for killing and harming migratory birds....And, wind turbines routinely kill federally protected birds and eagles.

8   Since the study estimating bird and bat deaths was completed based on 2012 wind capacity data, U.S. companies have installed more wind power due to federal and state incentives....

Fines for Killing Birds

9   Besides BP being fined $100 million for killing and harming migratory birds during the 2010 Gulf oil spill, in 2009, Exxon Mobil paid $600,000 for killing 85 birds in five states and PacifiCorp, which operates coal plants, paid more than $10.5 million for electrocuting 232 eagles that landed on power lines at its substations. The first wind farms to be fined took place

GO ON TO THE NEXT PAGE

in November 2013 when Duke Energy paid a $1 million fine for killing 14 eagles and 149 other birds at two wind farms in Wyoming from 2009 to 2013....

10   The Shiloh IV Wind Project in California...received a permit from the U.S. Fish and Wildlife Service allowing it to kill eagles, hawks, peregrine falcons, owls and songs birds while not being subjected to the normal prohibitions afforded under the federal Bald and Golden Eagle Protection Act and the Migratory Treaty Act.

You may take a 10-minute break before proceeding to Section 3.

GO ON TO THE NEXT PAGE

Questions 18 through 25 refer to the following passage.

Excerpt from "Lost Hearts"
by M.R. James

1   The post-chaise [a horse-drawn carriage] had brought him from Warwickshire, where, some six months before, he had been left an orphan. Now, owing to the generous offer of his elderly cousin, Mr. Abney, he had come to live at Aswarby. The offer was unexpected, because all who knew anything of Mr. Abney looked upon him as a somewhat austere recluse, into whose steady-going household the advent of a small boy would import a new and, it seemed, incongruous element. The truth is that very little was known of Mr. Abney's pursuits or temper....It was a matter of great surprise among his neighbours that he should ever have heard of his orphan cousin, Stephen Elliott, much more that he should have volunteered to make him an inmate of Aswarby Hall.

2   Whatever may have been expected by his neighbours, it is certain that Mr. Abney—the tall, the thin, the austere—seemed inclined to give his young cousin a kindly reception. The moment the front-door was opened he darted out of his study, rubbing his hands with delight.

3   "How are you, my boy? —how are you? How old are you?" said he, "That is, you are not too much tired, I hope, by your journey to eat your supper?"

4   "No, thank you, sir," said Master Elliott, "I am pretty well."

5   "That's a good lad," said Mr. Abney. "And how old are you, my boy?"

6   It seemed a little odd that he should have asked the question twice in the first two minutes of their acquaintance.

7   "I'm twelve years old next birthday, sir," said Stephen....

8   "I like to get these things down in my book. Sure it's twelve? Certain?"

9   "Yes, quite sure, sir."

10   "Well, well! Take him to Mrs. Bunch's room, Parkes, and let him have his tea—supper—whatever it is...."

11   Mrs. Bunch was the most comfortable and human person whom Stephen had as yet met at Aswarby. She made him completely at home; they were great friends in a quarter of an hour: and great friends they remained...."

GO ON TO THE NEXT PAGE

12   "Is Mr. Abney a good man?" he suddenly asked....

13   "Good? —bless the child!" said Mrs. Bunch. "Master's as kind a soul as ever I see! Didn't I never tell you of the little boy as he took in out of the street, as you may say, this seven years back? and the little girl, two years after I first come here?"

14   "No. Do tell me all about them, Mrs. Bunch—now, this minute!"

15   "Well," said Mrs. Bunch, "The little girl I don't seem to recollect so much about. I know master brought her back with him from his walk one day, and give orders to Mrs. Ellis, as was housekeeper then, as she should be took every care with. And the pore child hadn't no one belonging to her—she told me so her own self—and here she lived with us a matter of three weeks it might be; and then, whether she were somethink of a gipsy in her blood or what not, but one morning she out of her bed afore any of us had opened a eye, and neither track nor yet trace of her have I set eyes on since. Master was wonderful put about, and had all the ponds dragged; but it's my belief she was had away by them gipsies...."

16   "And what about the little boy?" said Stephen.

17   "Ah, that pore boy!" sighed Mrs. Bunch. "He were a foreigner—Jevanny he called hisself—and he come a-tweaking his 'urdy-gurdy round and about the drive one winter day, and master 'ad him in that minute, and ast all about where he came from, and how old he was, and how he made his way, and where was his relatives, and all as kind as heart could wish. But it went the same way with him. They're a hunruly lot, them foreign nations, I do suppose, and he was off one fine morning just the same as the girl. Why he went and what he done was our question for as much as a year after; for he never took his 'urdy-gurdy, and there it lays on the shelf...."

18   That night he had a curious dream. At the end of the passage at the top of the house, in which his bedroom was situated, there was an old disused bathroom. It was kept locked, but the upper half of the door was glazed, and, since the muslin curtains which used to hang there had long been gone, you could look in and see the lead-lined bath affixed to the wall on the right hand, with its head towards the window.

19   On the night of which I am speaking, Stephen Elliott found himself, as he thought, looking through the glazed door. The moon was shining through the window, and he was gazing at a figure which lay in the bath.

GO ON TO THE NEXT PAGE

20   His description of what he saw reminds me of what I once beheld myself in the famous vaults of St. Michan's Church in Dublin, which possesses the horrid property of preserving corpses from decay for centuries. A figure inexpressibly thin and pathetic, of a dusty leaden colour, enveloped in a shroud-like garment, the thin lips crooked into a faint and dreadful smile, the hands pressed tightly over the region of the heart.

21   As he looked upon it, a distant, almost inaudible moan seemed to issue from its lips, and the arms began to stir. The terror of the sight forced Stephen backwards and he awoke to the fact that he was indeed standing on the cold boarded floor of the passage in the full light of the moon. With a courage which I do not think can be common among boys of his age, he went to the door of the bathroom to ascertain if the figure of his dreams were really there. It was not, and he went back to bed.

GO ON TO THE NEXT PAGE

18. The author builds suspense in the excerpt by giving several indications that something might not be quite as it should be. Some of those indications are listed below. Arrange them in the order in which they appear in the excerpt by writing the letters of your selections in the corresponding empty boxes below.

First indication

Second indication

Third indication

Fourth indication

Fifth indication

(a) A young boy wouldn't fit in with the sedate Aswarby Hall lifestyle.

(b) Two children disappeared without explanation.

(c) Stephen is called an "inmate" (paragraph 1).

(d) Mr. Abney's invitation to live at Aswarby Hall was unexpected.

(e) Mr. Abney asks twice about Stephen's age as soon as he meets him.

19. What is the main characteristic the three children share?

A. They are all happy to be brought to Aswarby Hall.
B. They are all vulnerable.
C. They were all taken by gypsies.
D. They are all young.

20. From the information in the excerpt, what can you infer about Mr. Abney?

A. He might not really be Stephen's cousin.
B. He is lonely.
C. He is kindhearted.
D. He fears growing old.

21. Which characteristics about Stephen can you infer from the information in this excerpt? Write the letters of your selections in the character web below.

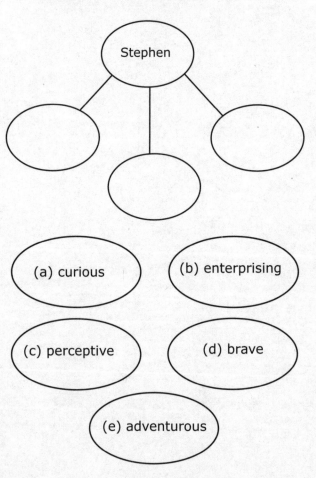

(a) curious
(b) enterprising
(c) perceptive
(d) brave
(e) adventurous

GO ON TO THE NEXT PAGE

22. Read this description from paragraph 18.

> At the end of the passage at the top of the house, in which his bedroom was situated, there was an old disused bathroom. It was kept locked, but the upper half of the door was glazed, and, since the muslin curtains which used to hang there had long been gone, you could look in and see the lead-lined bath affixed to the wall on the right hand, with its head towards the window.

Which aspect of the excerpt does this description support?

A. the atmosphere of suspense
B. the idea that Stephen might not have found the perfect home, but it was better than no home
C. the theme of appearances masking reality
D. the theme of misplaced trust

23. What does Mrs. Bunch's account of the two previous children suggest about her effectiveness as an ally for Stephen?

A. She would not be effective because she's too loyal to Mr. Abney.
B. She would be effective because she's charged with taking care of the children in the house.
C. She would be effective because she and Stephen became friends instantly.
D. She would not be effective because she accepts appearances too readily.

24. Why does the author have Stephen's "curious dream" (paragraph 18) occur on the same night that Mrs. Bunch told him about the missing children?

A. He wants to draw a sharp contrast between Mrs. Bunch and the figure in Stephen's dream.
B. He wants to suggest that Stephen has an overactive imagination.
C. He wants the reader to link the missing children and the figure in the bath.
D. He intends to show that Stephen is already growing uneasy about being at Aswarby Hall.

25. Read the following dialogue from paragraph 3.

> "How are you, my boy? —how are you? How old are you?" said he, "That is, you are not too much tired, I hope, by your journey to eat your supper?"

What inference does this section of dialogue support?

A. Mr. Abney isn't accustomed to welcoming visitors.
B. Stephen has found a good home.
C. Mr. Abney has an ulterior motive in bringing Stephen to Aswarby Hall.
D. Mr. Abney is as good-hearted and kind as Mrs. Bunch believes he is.

GO ON TO THE NEXT PAGE

Questions 26 through 33 refer to the following passage.

Excerpt from "Carnegie Libraries"
Ontario Ministry of Tourism, Culture, and Sport

Note: The British Chartist movement called for greater working class participation in government. Subscription libraries were funded by members' fees and restricted to specific groups.

Carnegie's Early Years

"The man who has the ability to take full possession of his own mind may take possession of anything else too." –Andrew Carnegie

1   Andrew Carnegie was born on November 25, 1835, in Dunfermline, an industrial town in the south of Scotland....His father had a strong influence on Andrew. William's involvement in the British Chartist movement, as well as the Tradesmen's Subscription Library he helped create, exposed Andrew to radical politics and a democratic world view.

2   Andrew Carnegie was required to leave his formal education behind to help support his family. His father's business suffered from the industrialization of the weaving industry in Great Britain, and in 1848, the Carnegies moved from their native Scotland to the United States. The young Carnegie eventually settled in Allegheny, Pennsylvania. He took various industrial jobs before gaining employment at the Pennsylvania railroad.

3   As its assistant to the superintendent, Carnegie learned about the inner workings of the industry and about investment. He made a small fortune by the age of 30 by applying his shrewd business skills to the markets, investing in railroads, oil, and iron. He made the real fortune for which he is best known, however, once he seized hold of the growing steel industry by founding the Carnegie Steel Company in 1889. It became the largest steel manufacturer in the United States.

Carnegie's Philanthropic Initiatives

"People who are unable to motivate themselves must be content with mediocrity, no matter how impressive their other talents."
–Andrew Carnegie

4   Andrew Carnegie poured a great deal of his energies and resources into institutions which would support and further his dedication to free education for all and the notion of a meritocracy. By the age of 35, Carnegie decided to leave his business enterprises behind and concentrate on philanthropy and writing, rather than personal profit. He sold the Carnegie Steel Company in 1901 to J.P. Morgan for $480,000,000 and set up numerous institutions to fund educational projects around the

GO ON TO THE NEXT PAGE

world. Of these, the Carnegie Corporation of New York and the Carnegie Endowment for International Peace still operate today. In his view public libraries, however, were the best way to realize his commitment to free education for all. As his introduction to the opening of one of his free public libraries says: *It is the mind that makes the body rich. There is no class so pitiably wretched as that which possesses money and nothing else. Money can only be the useful drudge of things immeasurably higher than itself....My aspirations take a higher flight. Mine be it to have contributed to the enlightenment and the joys of the mind, to the things of the spirit, to...sweetness and light. I hold this the noblest possible use of wealth.*

Carnegie and Free Public Libraries

"There is not such a cradle of democracy upon the earth as the Free Public Library, this republic of letters, where neither rank, office, nor wealth receives the slightest consideration." –Andrew Carnegie

5   Carnegie believed the best way to provide free education and to foster growing communities was through the establishment of public libraries. These could provide the public with the tools necessary to succeed, regardless of their socio-economic background.

6   In his lifetime, Andrew Carnegie donated $56 million to build 2,509 libraries throughout the world. A typical Carnegie grant was about $10,000—approximately $650,000 in today's dollars. These funds contributed significantly to the development of small communities around the world, providing much needed services, as well as many spectacular buildings for which many towns and cities are known....

7   To realize his vision of free and democratic education, Carnegie and his longtime friend and business partner James Bertram established the *"Carnegie Formula"*—the criteria for any town applying to be a recipient of a Carnegie grant to:

- Demonstrate the need for a public library

- Provide the building site

- Provide 10 percent of the cost of the library's construction annually to support its operation

- Use the building as a library only (building plans could not include other city or recreational facilities)

GO ON TO THE NEXT PAGE

A Vision for a New Public Library System

8   Carnegie's vision of a life filled with a free and lasting education led to the construction of hundreds of libraries around the world as well as many innovations in their functioning.

9   Carnegie public libraries, for instance, had open, rather than closed stacks, to provide a democratic approach to education. Closed stacks require a librarian's assistance. Open stacks readily available to the public, in contrast, encourage and enable people to browse and choose books for themselves.

10   Today Carnegie libraries are recognized for their functionality and their architectural beauty. They have come to represent both the principles of education and those of a man eternally dedicated to it.

Carnegie's Legacy

"Only in popular education can man erect the structure of an enduring civilization." –Andrew Carnegie

11   Over the course of his life, he had contributed more than $350,000,000 to various educational causes around the world, and helped change both people's attitudes toward, and accessibility of, education, as well as the North American landscape....

12   The institutions and trusts he began in his lifetime continue to promote and enhance education and culture around the world. The ideas and causes he fostered and in which he was so heavily involved continue to thrive.

Source: © Queen's Printer for Ontario, 2015. Reproduced with permission. The material on the Ministry of Tourism, Culture, and Sport is current to February 28, 2017 and is subject to change.

26.   How do the four quotes from Carnegie affect this excerpt?

A.   The quotes add authenticity to the biography, making it seem as if Carnegie himself is talking to readers.

B.   The quotes add information that is not found anywhere else in the biography itself.

C.   The quotes function as transitions between paragraphs that describe different stages of Carnegie's life.

D.   The quotes act as subheads, splitting up separate sections clearly for the reader.

27.   What does the *"Carnegie Formula"* (paragraph 7) reveal about Carnegie?

A.   He wanted to limit the number of libraries he would fund.

B.   He wanted to provide a justification for focusing on his favorite communities.

C.   He had other motives besides philanthropy.

D.   He was a shrewd businessman.

GO ON TO THE NEXT PAGE

28. Which details from the excerpt contribute to the irony of Carnegie's "vision of free and democratic education" (paragraph 7)? (When something is ironic, it is the opposite of what one would expect.) Write the letters of the contributing details in the empty boxes below.

> [ ]

> [ ]

> (a) At age 35, Carnegie abandoned his business interests to "concentrate on philanthropy and writing" (paragraph 4).

> (b) "He made a small fortune by the age of 30" (paragraph 3).

> (c) He had to leave school early in order to help support his family (paragraph 2).

> (d) His father's influence exposed him to "a democratic world view" (paragraph 1).

> (e) He founded the Carnegie Steel Company, which became "the largest steel manufacturer in the United States" (paragraph 3).

29. One focus of the present-day Carnegie Corporation of New York (mentioned in paragraph 4) is helping American pre-college students improve their skills for competing in the global economy. If Carnegie were running the corporation today, how would he most likely react to a U.S. tour company's application for a grant to offer grade-school students from lower-income families a free Caribbean cruise, with stops at several islands?

A. He would probably be interested in it, since it would give students exposure to other cultures and economies that their families couldn't afford to provide.
B. He would want the company to offer the free trip to students from all economic backgrounds, not just lower income.
C. He would probably not agree to fund a project from a private company unless the application included specific objectives, some way of measuring whether they were achieved and some contribution from the company.
D. He would likely not think that exposure to Caribbean islands aligned with the Carnegie Corporation's priorities.

GO ON TO THE NEXT PAGE

30. Which three Carnegie quotes best support his "notion of a meritocracy" (paragraph 4)? Write the letters of your selections in the empty boxes below.

┌─────────────────────────────┐
│   │
└─────────────────────────────┘

┌─────────────────────────────┐
│   │
└─────────────────────────────┘

┌─────────────────────────────┐
│   │
└─────────────────────────────┘

┌─────────────────────────────────────┐
│ (a) *"the Free Public Library, this re-│
│ public of letters, where neither rank,│
│ office, nor wealth receives the slightest│
│ consideration"* (before paragraph 5) │
└─────────────────────────────────────┘

┌─────────────────────────────────────┐
│ (b) *"The man who has the ability to│
│ take full possession of his own mind│
│ may take possession of anything else│
│ too."* (before paragraph 1)   │
└─────────────────────────────────────┘

┌─────────────────────────────────────┐
│ (c) *"There is no class so pitiably wretch-│
│ ed as that which possesses money and│
│ nothing else."* (paragraph 4)   │
└─────────────────────────────────────┘

┌─────────────────────────────────────┐
│ (d) *"Only in popular education can│
│ man erect the structure of an enduring│
│ civilization."* (before paragraph 11)│
└─────────────────────────────────────┘

┌─────────────────────────────────────┐
│ (e) *"People who are unable to motivate│
│ themselves must be content with│
│ mediocrity,..."* (before paragraph 4)│
└─────────────────────────────────────┘

31. What does the description of Carnegie's business activities, in relation to the rest of the excerpt, reveal about the author's purpose?

A. The author wants to show that it's possible to have two very different but equally successful careers.

B. The author's focus is Carnegie's libraries, so the description of Carnegie's successful business career is very brief and general compared to the discussion of the libraries.

C. The author's purpose is to highlight Carnegie's philanthropy, not the business career that earned the necessary wealth for him.

D. The author wants to emphasize Carnegie's upbringing and philanthropy, not the business activities that seem out of step with them, so the business section of Carnegie's life is treated only superficially.

GO ON TO THE NEXT PAGE

32. Which characteristics about Carnegie does the author convey in this excerpt? Write the letters of your selections in the character web below.

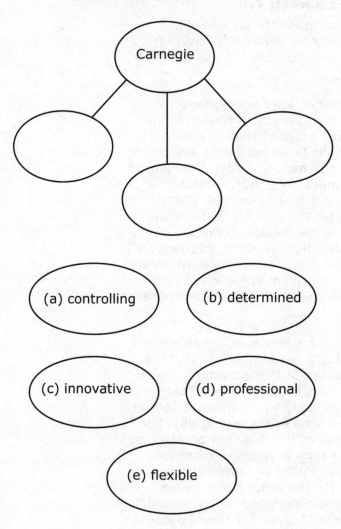

33. Carnegie's preference for open stacks was based on his commitment to democracy. He felt that allowing people to look through the books themselves, instead of asking the librarian to get a specific book, provided "a democratic approach to education" (paragraph 9). From the information given about Carnegie, which of his other beliefs would cause him to favor the open stack system?

A.   self-motivation
B.   strengthening small communities
C.   using wealth for a higher purpose
D.   free education for everyone

GO ON TO THE NEXT PAGE

Questions 34 through 41 refer to the following passage.

Excerpt from "Oddities of Animal Character"
by Edward Burnett Tylor

Notes: John Stuart Mill (paragraph 1) was a British philosopher. "Procrustean" (paragraph 1) refers to violently enforced conformity. Sir John Lubbock (paragraph 2) was a British naturalist. An "incubus" (paragraph 2) is a demon or evil spirit.

1   Mr. J.S. Mill, in his essay on "Liberty," long ago warned us against the stupefying influence of custom upon human beings and held that we ought to encourage eccentricities in each other, and to guard jealously the right to be eccentric, instead of insisting on reducing every one by the hard-and-fast Procrustean standard to a single dead-level of mediocrity. But, whatever our sins may be in this respect toward human beings, surely they are greater still toward the domestic animals. We reduce our horses, so far as possible, to the mechanical condition of locomotive-engines—indeed, eccentric horses might involve very serious dangers to life and limb—our dogs to sentinels, which we drill to a social decorum as rigid as our own; while we regard the eccentricities of a cat with undisguised horror, as the mere prelude to dangerous insanity....

2   What important variations of character, however, might we not promote if we took more pains to foster what a writer of thirty years ago used to call "the individuality of the individual" among our friends of the lower races! Sir John Lubbock thinks that he has partially taught a poodle to read, but, as a correspondent of ours once suggested, that may be a step in the wrong direction—not a development of the true genius of the dog, but an attempt to merge the genius of the dog in habits peculiar to man, and likely rather to result in ingrafting an imitative humanity on a totally different kind of capacity. On the other hand, in his experiments on ants, Sir John Lubbock has gone on the sounder principle of setting the ants problems to solve for themselves—a principle which has resulted in showing that different races of ants have very different resources, and that different individuals, even in the same race, show a very different amount of resource in dealing with the same difficulty. This is confirmed by what we know of our more intimate friends among the domestic animals; and surely we should do more to develop their capacity by stimulating them to meet difficulties by their own resources than we can effect by taking their training so completely under our own care. Is it not possible that, as things go, the companionship of man is rather an incubus on the natural genius of the inferior animals than a help to its development? It is clear that the ants, at least, are more sagacious in proportion as they live more apart from man, and are thrown upon their own resources.

GO ON TO THE NEXT PAGE

3 Certainly there is far too little disposition to allow of eccentricity in the lower animals and for what comes of eccentricity. Half-domesticated birds, however, will occasionally show very remarkable eccentricities, and even appear to be making experiments—though experiments which we should, of course, regard as of a very unscientific kind—in the modification of their own instincts. The present writer knows a pigeon of exceedingly eccentric disposition....He hopes to foster and cultivate the family and parental idea without any corresponding reality, without any aid from outside, indeed, except an apparatus of external ceremony, which feigns the existence of a purely ideal mate, and affects to indulge in the expectation of impossible offspring. Doubtless he thinks that there is nothing so good as the courtly attitude of a pigeon toward his mate, especially if there be no mate to justify it; nothing more touching than the patient preparation for offspring and the education of the young, especially if there be no young to complicate the problem of tenderness and foresight, by requiring a real supply of food and attention....If a human thinker can empty religion of its meaning, and yet justify all its forms and sentiments and external rites, and if he is to receive nothing but praise for his achievement, why may we not regard with interest and admiration the effort of an eccentric bird to retain all the ceremonial forms of chivalrous observance and elaborate parental care and patience, without, in fact, complicating the situation by admitting the neighborhood of either wife or child? To our mind, the idiosyncrasies of such a creature as this deserve the most attentive study. Who knows whether we might not find in the world of eccentric instinct all sorts of anticipations of eccentric intellect? Who knows whether we might not find genius and originality in other races of animals which would throw as much light upon the genius and originality of man as the eccentricities of this pigeon seem to throw on the eccentricities of a most active and confident school of modern thought? If John Stuart Mill were right in thinking it a sacred duty not to discourage the milder lunacies of human beings, might we not with equal advantage extend his exhortation, and make it include the duty of protecting the independent development of the idiosyncrasies of bird and beast, in the hope of finding in them some clew to the various oddities and harmless insanities of human thought and action?

GO ON TO THE NEXT PAGE

34. Below are three conclusions the author reaches and three details that lead him to those conclusions. Write the letter of each detail into the box containing the corresponding conclusion.

> Human intervention diminishes the natural abilities of inferior species.

> Training is sometimes necessary so domestic animals can co-exist with humans.

> Human training can lead to an artificial hybrid capability rather than a more developed example of the species.

> (a) A poodle was partially taught to read.

> (b) Ants display different individual abilities when they are allowed to solve problems for themselves.

> (c) Eccentric horses could be dangerous.

35. The author wants to encourage

A. people to let birds and animals be themselves, without any human intervention to modify their behavior.
B. the development of a certain degree of individuality in both humans and animals.
C. a different approach to training animals.
D. each person to follow his or her impulses to behave oddly and eccentrically.

36. How do the examples of the poodle and the ants (paragraph 2) advance the author's thesis?

A. They show how human intervention can have different effects on the ability of different species to develop their own natural idiosyncrasies.
B. Both examples reveal that humans can accidentally prevent non-humans from expressing their own natural talents.
C. They draw a distinction between negative and positive forms of human intervention in allowing non-humans to develop eccentricities.
D. Both examples of non-human eccentricities can teach us something about human eccentricities.

37. The author's audience is most likely made up of

A. people with an average education and a strong interest in behavior.
B. animal trainers just beginning their careers.
C. readers with advanced education in biology.
D. professional psychologists.

GO ON TO THE NEXT PAGE

38. Which of the following quotes from the excerpt shows how the author is adapting John Stuart Mill's belief in the value of human eccentricity?

    A. "It is clear that the ants, at least, are more sagacious in proportion as they live more apart from man, and are thrown upon their own resources." (paragraph 2)

    B. "...we ought to encourage eccentricities in each other, and to guard jealously the right to be eccentric..." (paragraph 1)

    C. "But, whatever our sins may be in this respect toward human beings, surely they are greater still toward the domestic animals." (paragraph 1)

    D. "Who knows whether we might not find in the world of eccentric instinct all sorts of anticipations of eccentric intellect?" (paragraph 3)

39. The author is acting primarily as

    A. an objective narrator.
    B. a critic.
    C. an advocate.
    D. an alarm.

40. Which of the following best describes the author's attitude throughout the excerpt toward Mill's position that "we ought to encourage eccentricities in each other, and to guard jealously the right to be eccentric" (paragraph 1)?

    A. The author depends on it.
    B. The author agrees with it 100%.
    C. The author can see at least one exception to it.
    D. The author thinks it needs further testing.

41. What functions does the story of the pigeon (paragraph 3) perform in this excerpt? Write the letters of the two correct answers into the empty boxes below.

    ┌─────────────────────────────┐
    │   │
    └─────────────────────────────┘

    ┌─────────────────────────────┐
    │   │
    └─────────────────────────────┘

    (a) It proves that birds, not just animals, are worth studying.

    (b) It illustrates the author's point that idiosyncrasies in animals or birds could increase our understanding of idiosyncrasies in humans.

    (c) It challenges Mill's position.

    (d) It proves the author's claim that birds can develop eccentricities on their own, without any help from humans.

    (e) It demonstrates that eccentric birds can be dangerous, too, like eccentric horses.

GO ON TO THE NEXT PAGE

Questions 42 through 49 refer to the following passage.

Excerpt from *Grace O'Malley, Princess and Pirate*
by Robert Machray

Note: "Arquebusiers" (paragraph 12) refers to fighters armed with an early type of firearm.

1   Seeing that there was a likelihood of the galleon, to which we were giving chase, showing us a clean pair of heels, she ordered Tibbot to the helm of the *Santa Ana*, and, telling him of what she intended, she herself went among the prisoners, who were lying bound in different parts of the ship.

2   Among them she found divers persons who understood the Irish tongue, and them, by both promises and threats, she compelled to bring before her the master of the ordnance and those who assisted him in loading and firing the cannon. Surrounding these men with her own, each of whom had sword, spear, or battle-axe ready in his hand, she marched them to the forecastle and forced them, on pain of instant death, to serve the two great cannon which were in the bow-ports....

3   The balls from these pieces were so ineffective, passing wide of the mark and splashing into the sea a considerable distance from the galleon, that her anger was kindled, and she warned the master of the ordnance that if he were not more successful on a second attempt she would not spare him, being assured that he was merely trifling with her.

4   Whether it was because of the terrifying effect of her words, or because he was determined to give the galleon every opportunity for getting away from us, and was reckless of what became of himself, the succeeding shots flew as wide as before. When Grace O'Malley perceived this she was transported with rage, and, crying that he had brought his fate upon his own head, ran him through with her sword.

5   Had she not quickly interfered, all his companions would have been instantly despatched by the Irish, who were eager to emulate the example she had set them.

6   Aghast at the death of the master of the ordnance, and suspecting that there was no hope of anything else for themselves, they cried out sharply, breathlessly, tremblingly, each protesting and vowing by all the saints that he would undertake to do whatever he was bid, if only his life were promised him.

GO ON TO THE NEXT PAGE

7   Seeing from their look that they were likely to do as they said, but fearing lest they should be unstrung, being so wrought upon by their terror, she agreed that they should not be slain, but commanded them to choose from out of their number him who was the most skilful cannoneer, so that there should be no mistake in regard to the fit service of the ordnance. At the same time she told them that all their lives depended on him, for if he failed at the next discharge to damage the galleon, not only would he be immediately killed, but that all of them would likewise suffer instant death.

8   They chattered for a second together, and then one of them, perhaps bolder or more desperate than the rest, stepped forward, and accepted her offer.

9   Having warned him again, Grace O'Malley had the guns loaded once more, and stood over the man with drawn sword as he applied the burning match to the touch-hole of first one cannon and then of the other. When the smoke had cleared away, it was seen that the mainmast of the galleon had been shot through and had fallen over, so that it lay partly across her waist and partly was in the water....

10   As our vessels approached, we received a broadside from her which did us both no little harm, especially to our hulls and rigging, and a shot tore along the forecastle of the *Capitana* in an oblique direction, killing two of my crew and wounding three or four men before it plunged into the sea.

11   But it was impossible for her to prevent us from coming up alongside of her, and so soon as we had made ourselves fast to her our boarders poured in upon her. And thereupon ensued a battle not more terrible than obstinate, while the faint streaks of a cold and troubled dawn stole upon us, shedding its gleams on the dead and dying as they lay in pools of blood upon her decks.

12   No quarter was asked or given. Whom the sword or the battle-axe or the spear smote not, him the sea received, for many of the Spaniards, crying that all was lost, threw themselves from the galleon into the water and were drowned. There remained, however, towards the end of the fight a small company of arquebusiers and swordsmen upon the deck, and among them was the captain of the ship, his clothing stained and disordered, and a great, red sword in his hand.

13   Seeing that no hope remained, he made signs that he wished to surrender, and begged that his life and the lives of those with him might be spared, to which Grace O'Malley straightway assented.

GO ON TO THE NEXT PAGE

14   As he walked towards her with his sword in his hand, with the purpose apparently of presenting it to her in token of his submission, he seemed to stumble on the planks, which were slippery with blood, and then, suddenly recovering himself, he made a mad, swift rush forward, and would have wounded, perhaps killed, my mistress if his intention had not been guessed by Tibbot, who in the very nick of time dashed aside the point of the captain's sword and brained him with his battle-axe.

15   So incensed were the Irish at this act of treachery that they would show no mercy, and not a soul was left alive.

42.   Read paragraph 7 from the excerpt.

> Seeing from their look that they were likely to do as they said, but fearing lest they should be unstrung, being so wrought upon by their terror, she agreed that they should not be slain, but commanded them to choose from out of their number him who was the most skilful cannoneer, so that there should be no mistake in regard to the fit service of the ordnance. At the same time she told them that all their lives depended on him, for if he failed at the next discharge to damage the galleon, not only would he be immediately killed, but that all of them would likewise suffer instant death.

What does this paragraph reveal about Grace O'Malley's character?

A.   She was utterly ruthless.
B.   She was a keen observer of her crewmembers' characters.
C.   She had an understanding of the human mind.
D.   She cared only about herself.

43.   The phrase "showing us a clean pair of heels" in paragraph 1 means that the ship

A.   would likely escape.
B.   had recently been scraped of barnacles.
C.   was probably lighter and faster than O'Malley's ship.
D.   had not been damaged.

44.   In the empty boxes below, write the letters of the two quotes that reveal something about O'Malley's leadership style.

> [ ]

> [ ]

(a) "Had she not quickly interfered" (paragraph 5)

(b) "her anger was kindled" (paragraph 3)

(c) "No quarter was asked or given." (paragraph 12)

(d) "she was transported with rage" (paragraph 4)

(e) "eager to emulate the example she had set" (paragraph 5)

(f) "telling him of what she intended" (paragraph 1)

GO ON TO THE NEXT PAGE

45. If Tibbot had suggested a different plan to O'Malley (paragraph 1), you would expect that she

   A. would listen, but most likely go ahead with her original plan anyway.
   B. wouldn't let him finish and would definitely proceed with her own plan.
   C. would discuss the merits of both plans with him.
   D. would kill him with her sword for daring to question her.

46. The description, "a battle not more terrible than obstinate," in paragraph 11 supports which ideas? Write the letters of the two correct selections into the empty boxes.

   ```
   ┌─────────────────────────┐
   │                         │
   └─────────────────────────┘

   ┌─────────────────────────┐
   │                         │
   └─────────────────────────┘
   ```

   (a) The crew of the target ship was easily defeated.

   (b) The Spanish crew was determined not to be taken prisoner.

   (c) O'Malley underestimated the fighting ability of the crew she was trying to capture.

   (d) The outcome was not easy to predict.

   (e) O'Malley's crew didn't realize how many men were on the ship they had just boarded.

   (f) The Spanish sailors were angry that one of their own countrymen had destroyed their ship's mainmast.

47. Which of the following would NOT be a reasonable inference to make from O'Malley's quest to find a cannon operator among the prisoners?

   A. Spanish cannons and Irish cannons were not operated in the same way.
   B. Her own men didn't know how to fire a cannon.
   C. Operating a cannon required specialized training.
   D. O'Malley's men didn't want to damage another ship.

48. In his narration, the author intends to

   A. give an objective historical account of a battle between Spanish and Irish sailors.
   B. reveal a historical figure's character through a description of events.
   C. embellish the exploits of a historical figure.
   D. criticize Irish pirates for being overly bloodthirsty and violent.

49. How does the character of Tibbot serve to bring this excerpt full circle, ending it with a theme that was introduced at the beginning?

   A. O'Malley puts him in charge of steering the ship at the beginning, and at the end, they have captured the ship they were pursuing.
   B. Tibbot appears only at the beginning and the end of the excerpt.
   C. At the beginning, O'Malley trusts him with her plan and at the end, Tibbot shows he's worthy of her trust when he prevents the Spanish captain from killing her.
   D. He is the only one of O'Malley's crew who is specifically identified by name, once at the beginning and once at the end.

GO ON TO THE NEXT PAGE

50. The passage below is incomplete. For each "Select" option, choose the option that correctly completes the sentence. For this practice test, circle your selection.

How to Plant and Care for Your New Lilac

Congratulations on choosing to enhance your yard with a beautiful lilac from Magic Grove Nurseries. This is a true old-fashioned lilac that will develop its own shape as its branches stretch toward the sun and reach out for space. It will reward your careful attention and herald the spring with pale mauve flowers in April and May.

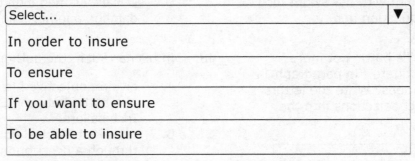

Select... ▼
In order to insure
To ensure
If you want to ensure
To be able to insure

a vigorous, long-lasting bush, simply follow these planting and care instructions.

- Select a location that receives at least four hours of mid-day and afternoon sun. Your new lilac needs strong sunshine in order to flourish.

- Choose a well-drained location with lots of room. Your lilac doesn't like to have its feet constantly wet, and it needs space to spread out as it grows.

- Dig a hole at least 3" wider than the root ball on all sides and 5" deeper. (For example, if your lilac's root ball is 6" wide and 8" deep, the hole should be 12" in diameter and 13" deep.)

- Put about 2" of loose gravel in the bottom of the hole. This will promote good drainage while your lilac is developing new roots. The gravel will not prevent your lilac

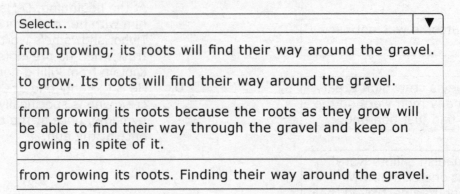

Select... ▼
from growing; its roots will find their way around the gravel.
to grow. Its roots will find their way around the gravel.
from growing its roots because the roots as they grow will be able to find their way through the gravel and keep on growing in spite of it.
from growing its roots. Finding their way around the gravel.

GO ON TO THE NEXT PAGE

- Cut the burlap away from the root ball, and use your fingers to spread out the roots around the edges.

- Put about 1" of Triple Mix on top of the gravel, center your lilac in the hole, and fill the sides of the hole with Triple Mix. This special planting medium contains food to strengthen new plants, peat moss to help them soak up moisture, and rich topsoil to reduce transplanting shock. Pack the Triple Mix down a little, but not too tightly—you want water and air to circulate around the root ball.

- When you're finished, the top of the root ball should be about 2" lower than the surface of your yard. Add a little more Triple Mix, but keep the top of the hole slightly below the

surrounding yard
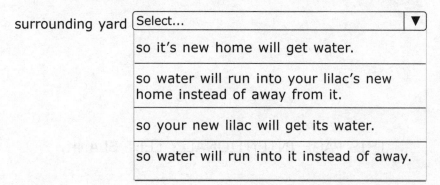

Select... ▼
so it's new home will get water.
so water will run into your lilac's new home instead of away from it.
so your new lilac will get its water.
so water will run into it instead of away.

For the first month, give your new plant some water twice a week and occasionally shovel a bit of flowering shrub food into the surrounding soil. Don't add too much shrub food and don't put it too close to the root ball, though, or else you might burn the roots.

Select... ▼
By following these instructions, your new plant
With these instructions followed, your bush
If you follow these instructions, your lilac
Your new lilac

will beautify your yard for many years to come.

END OF TEST

THIS PAGE INTENTIONALLY LEFT BLANK.

GO ON TO THE NEXT PAGE

Mathematical Reasoning

Welcome!

Here is some information that you need to know before you start this test:

- You should not spend too much time on a question if you are not certain of the answer; answer it the best you can, and go on to the next question.
- If you are not certain of the answer to a question, you can mark your answer for review and come back to it later.
- You have **115 minutes** to complete this test.
- This test has two parts.
- When you finish Part 1, you may review those questions.
- You may not go back to Part 1 once you have finished your review.
- You may not use a calculator in Part 1. You may use a calculator in Part 2.

Turn the page to begin.

GO ON TO THE NEXT PAGE

Mathematics Formula Sheet

Area of a:

square	$A = s^2$
rectangle	$A = lw$
parallelogram	$A = bh$
triangle	$A = \frac{1}{2}bh$
trapezoid	$A = \frac{1}{2}h(b_1 + b_2)$
circle	$A = \pi r^2$

Perimeter of a:

square	$P = 4s$
rectangle	$P = 2l + 2w$
triangle	$P = s_1 + s_2 + s_3$
Circumference of a circle	$C = 2\pi r$ OR $C = \pi d$; $\pi \approx 3.14$

Surface Area and Volume of a:

rectangular prism	$SA = 2lw + 2lh + 2wh$	$V = lwh$
right prism	$SA = ph + 2B$	$V = Bh$
cylinder	$SA = 2\pi rh + 2\pi r^2$	$V = \pi r^2 h$
pyramid	$SA = \frac{1}{2}ps + B$	$V = \frac{1}{3}Bh$
cone	$SA = \pi rs + \pi r^2$	$V = \frac{1}{3}\pi r^2 h$
sphere	$SA = 4\pi r^2$	$V = \frac{4}{3}\pi r^3$

(p = perimeter of base B; $\pi \approx 3.14$)

Data

mean	mean is equal to the total of the values of a data set, divided by the number of elements in the data set
median	median is the middle value in an odd number of ordered values of a data set, or the mean of the two middle values in an even number of ordered values in a data set

Algebra

slope of a line	$m = \dfrac{y_2 - y_1}{x_2 - x_1}$
slope-intercept form of the equation of a line	$y = mx + b$
point-slope form of the equation of a line	$y - y_1 = m(x - x_1)$
standard form of a quadratic equation	$y = ax^2 + bx + c$
quadratic formula	$x = \dfrac{-b \pm \sqrt{b^2 - 4ac}}{2a}$
Pythagorean Theorem	$a^2 + b^2 = c^2$
simple interest	$I = prt$ (I = interest, p = principal, r = rate, t = time)
distance formula	$d = rt$
total cost	total cost = (number of units) × (price per unit)

GO ON TO THE NEXT PAGE

Mathematical Reasoning, Part 1

You may NOT use a calculator in Part 1.

<u>Question 1</u> refers to the following number line.

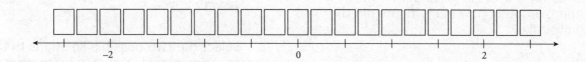

1. Write the numbers below in their correct positions on the number line.

    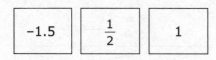

    | −1.5 | $\frac{1}{2}$ | 1 |

    | $-\frac{5}{2}$ | $\frac{3}{4}$ |

2. Subtract.

    $$234.34 - 176.81 =$$

3. What is the value of $\frac{2}{3} \cdot \frac{25}{2} \div \frac{10}{3}$?

    A. $\frac{2}{5}$

    B. $\frac{5}{2}$

    C. $\frac{25}{3}$

    D. $\frac{250}{9}$

4. $\dfrac{\frac{2}{3}}{\frac{5}{6}} =$

    A. $\frac{5}{9}$

    B. $\frac{4}{5}$

    C. $\frac{5}{4}$

    D. $\frac{9}{5}$

5. Which of the following can be used to determine the distance between a point P on the number line and zero?

    A. $|P|$
    B. P
    C. $-P$
    D. $P + 1$

GO ON TO THE NEXT PAGE

Mathematical Reasoning, Part 2

You MAY use a calculator in Part 2.

6. A flight from New York to London travels 3.47×10^3 miles at an average speed of about 4.6×10^2 miles per hour. Approximately how many hours did the flight take?

   A. 0.75
   B. 7.5
   C. 75
   D. 750

<u>Question 7</u> refers to the following equation.

$$x^2 - 3x + 7 = 5$$

7. Select the two possible solutions to the equation above. You may write your selections in the boxes below.

   $x = \boxed{}$

   $x = \boxed{}$

   | −3 | −2 | −1 |

   | 1 | 2 | 3 |

8. A rectangle has a perimeter of 38 and an area of 48. If the length is less than the width, what are the length and width of the rectangle? Write your selections in the boxes below.

   Length $\boxed{}$

   Width $\boxed{}$

   | 2 | 3 | 4 | 6 |

   | 8 | 12 | 16 | 19 |

GO ON TO THE NEXT PAGE

Mathematical Reasoning, Part 2

Question 9 refers to the following table.

Monday	Tuesday	Wednesday
30%	60%	50%

9. Based on the table above, what is the probability that there will be rain on Monday, Tuesday, and Wednesday?

A. 9%
B. 18%
C. 36%
D. 90%

10. Roberta drives from her home to work. As she gets halfway to work, she encounters a traffic jam and her speed slows down significantly before finally arriving at work. Which graph could represent the distance traveled by Roberta?

A.

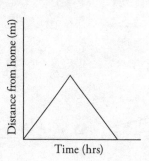

B.

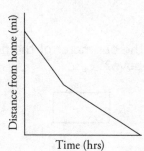

C.

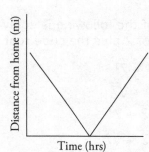

D.

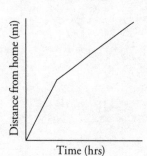

GO ON TO THE NEXT PAGE

Mathematical Reasoning, Part 2

Question 11 refers to the following figure.

Question 13 refers to the following graph.

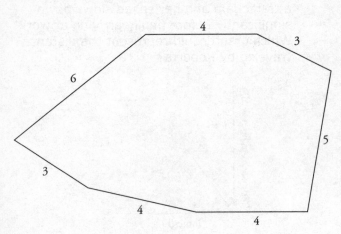

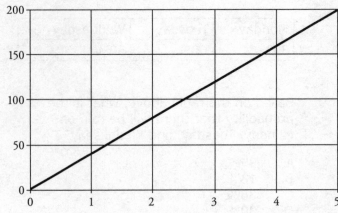

11. What is the perimeter of the figure shown above?

12. Which of the following is equivalent to the square of 2 plus the cube root of 7?

   A. $2^2 + 7^3$

   B. $2^2 + \sqrt[3]{7}$

   C. $\sqrt{2} + 7^3$

   D. $\sqrt{2} + \sqrt[3]{7}$

13. If the line graphed above represents the distance, in miles, traveled by a car over a period of time, in hours, which of the following is the speed, in miles per hour, at which the car is traveling?

   A.   20
   B.   30
   C.   40
   D.   50

GO ON TO THE NEXT PAGE

Question 14 refers to the following figure.

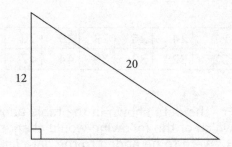

14. What is the perimeter of the triangle shown above?

    A. 32
    B. 48
    C. 55
    D. 96

15. Divide.
$$\frac{3x^2 - 7x + 2}{2x - 4}$$

    A. $1.5x - 2$
    B. $1.5x - 0.5$
    C. $3x - 0.5$
    D. $3x - 2$

Question 16 refers to the following figure.

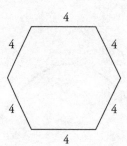

16. The area of a regular hexagon is determined by the equation $A = \frac{3\sqrt{3}}{2}s^2$, where s represents the side of the hexagon. What is the area of the hexagon above?

    A. $12\sqrt{3}$
    B. $16\sqrt{3}$
    C. $24\sqrt{3}$
    D. $48\sqrt{3}$

17. If $2x + 3y = 7$ and $4x - 3y = 5$, what is the value of y?

    A. -3
    B. 0
    C. 1
    D. 2

18. A baker charges $2 for a small loaf of bread and $3.50 for a large loaf of bread. If a customer buys 4 small loves and 6 large loaves, what is the average cost per loaf that the customer pays for the bread?

    A. $2.60
    B. $2.90
    C. $26.00
    D. $29.00

GO ON TO THE NEXT PAGE

Question 19 refers to the following table and figure.

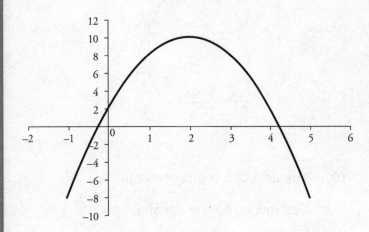

Question 20 refers to the following table.

21	24	26	29	29	30
32	32	32	38	44	47

20. For the data shown in the table above, which of the following would change if a 32 were to be added to the data list?

A.   mean
B.   median
C.   mode
D.   range

21. For which of the following values of x is the expression $\dfrac{x^2 + 7x + 10}{x^2 - 6x + 9}$ undefined?

A.   −5
B.   −3
C.   −2
D.   3

x	$f(x)$
−1	−4
0	−1
1	0
2	−1
3	−4
4	−9
5	−16

19. If the graph above represents the quadratic function g and the table above represents the quadratic function f, what is the average of the y-coordinates of the maximum points of f and g?

A.   0
B.   1.5
C.   5
D.   10

GO ON TO THE NEXT PAGE

Mathematical Reasoning, Part 2

<u>Question 22</u> refers to the following circle graph.

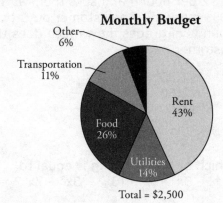

Monthly Budget

Other 6%

Transportation 11%

Rent 43%

Food 26%

Utilities 14%

Total = $2,500

<u>Question 24</u> refers to the following figure.

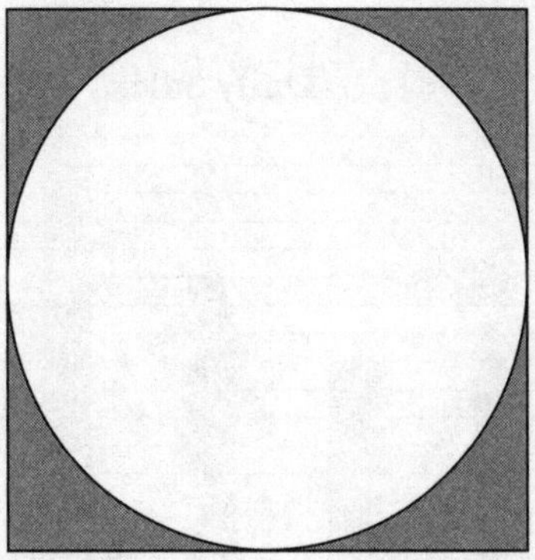

22. Based on the circle graph above, how much more money in the budget was devoted to rent than to transportation?

A. $275
B. $450
C. $800
D. $1,075

23. Which of the following is the equation of a line in the *xy*-plane parallel to the line represented by the equation $20x + 5y = -10$?

A. $-4x + y = 5$
B. $x - 4y = -2$
C. $12x + 4y = 4$
D. $16x + 4y = 12$

24. In the figure above a circle is inscribed in the square with side 8. What is the area of the shaded region shown above?

A. $32 - 64\pi$
B. $32 - 16\pi$
C. $64 - 16\pi$
D. $64 - 64\pi$

GO ON TO THE NEXT PAGE

Mathematical Reasoning, Part 2

Question 25 refers to the following graph.

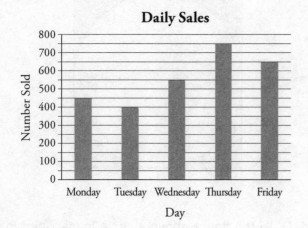

Daily Sales

25. Based on the graph above, what is the approximate percent increase in sales from Monday to Friday?

   A.   10%
   B.   25%
   C.   45%
   D.   65%

26. What is the equation of the line through the points (2, 4) and (1, −3)?

   A. $y = \dfrac{1}{2}x$

   B. $y = \dfrac{1}{2}x + 4$

   C. $y = 7x - 3$

   D. $y = 7x - 10$

27. A basketball has a surface area of approximately 361π in². Which of the following is closest to its volume, in in³?

   A.   530
   B.   3,600
   C.   6,300
   D.   11,000

28. A fruit store buys grapes wholesale at $2 per pound and sells them at a 30% markup. If a customer buys two pounds of grapes, how much does the customer pay?

   A. $2.30
   B. $2.60
   C. $4.60
   D. $5.20

29. Which of the following is equal to $(2x^3 − 3x + 2) − (3x^3 − 5x^2 − 7x)$?

   A. $−x^3 − 5x^2 + 4x + 2$
   B. $x^3 + 5x − 10x − 2$
   C. $5x^3 − 5x^2 + 4x − 2$
   D. $−x^3 + 5x^2 − 10x + 2$

GO ON TO THE NEXT PAGE

30. Which of the following tables does NOT represent a function of x?

A.

x	$f(x)$
−1	3
2	2
4	6
5	−4

B.

x	$f(x)$
−3	−3
−2	−3
4	−3
7	−3

C.

x	$f(x)$
1	3
3	−2
1	4
2	−5

D.

x	$f(x)$
−1	4
2	−3
0	0
−1	4

31. Bailey is packing for her weekend trip. If she packs 3 shirts, 2 pairs of shorts, and 2 pairs of shoes, how many different outfits consisting of one shirt, one pair of shorts, and one pair of shoes can Bailey make?

[ ]

32. If the price of a dress is discounted by 20% to $48, what is the original price of the dress?

A. $38.40
B. $57.60
C. $60.00
D. $68.00

Question 33 refers to the following graph.

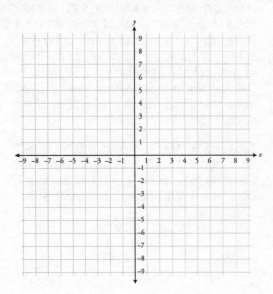

33. On the graph shown above, select the points on the line representing the equation $y = -2x + 4$.

34. Which algebraic expression represents the quotient of the sum of the square of x and y and the product of the cube of z and 2?

A. $\dfrac{(x + y)^2}{2z^3}$

B. $\dfrac{x^2 + y}{8z^3}$

C. $\dfrac{(x + y)^2}{8z^3}$

D. $\dfrac{x^2 + y}{2z^3}$

GO ON TO THE NEXT PAGE

35. David has $300 budgeted for art supplies. He must buy an easel for $41, a canvas for $16.50, and a set of brushes for $53. If he wants to buy as many different colors of paint as possible, and a tube of any color paint costs $5.50, which of the following inequalities can be used to determine the number of colors of paint, c, that David can buy?

   A. $41 + 16.50 + 53c + 5.50 \geq 300$
   B. $41 + 16.50 + 53 + 5.50c \leq 300$
   C. $41c + 16.50 + 53 + 5.5c \geq 300$
   D. $41 + 16.50c + 53 + 5.50 \leq 300$

Question 36 refers to the following table.

85	86	87	88
89	89	92	92

36. In Gail's history course, the final exam is worth 20% of her final score. The rest of her score is determined by the average of her other tests, the results of which are shown in the table above. What is the minimum score she needs on her final exam to get her final score up to 90?

   A. 91.5
   B. 92
   C. 96
   D. 100

37. $\dfrac{a^7 b^3 c}{a^4 b^2 c^5} =$

   A. $a^3 bc^{-4}$
   B. $a^3 b^5 c^4$
   C. $a^3 bc^4$
   D. $a^3 b^5 c^{-4}$

GO ON TO THE NEXT PAGE

Mathematical Reasoning, Part 2

<u>Question 38</u> refers to the following table.

x	f(x)
-2	-3
-1	-1
0	1
1	3
2	5
3	7

38. If $f(x)$ is represented by the table above and $g(x)$ is represented by the equation $g(x) = \dfrac{3}{2}x + 4$, then the rate of change of f is [Select... ▼] that of g.

Select...
greater than
equal to
less than

<u>Question 39</u> refers to the following graph.

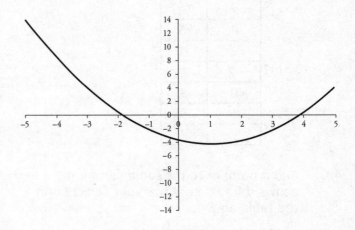

39. For the graph above, which of the following represents the axis of symmetry?

   A. $x = -4$
   B. $x = 1$
   C. $y = -4$
   D. $y = 1$

GO ON TO THE NEXT PAGE

Question 40 refers to the following table.

x	f(x)
4	−3
9	−1
−2	1
0	3
−3	5
	7

40. Add a number to the table so that it shows a function. Write your selection in the table above.

−3	−2	0

2	4	9

Question 41 refers to the following figure.

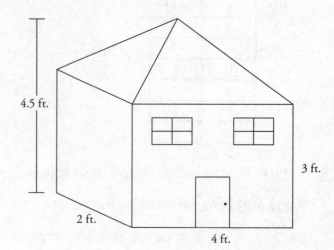

41. The dollhouse shown above is made of a rectangular prism and a right rectangular pyramid. What is the volume, in cubic feet, of the dollhouse?

A. 4
B. 16
C. 24
D. 28

42. What is the slope of the line represented by the equation $3x − 4y = 7$?

A. −4

B. $−\dfrac{7}{4}$

C. $\dfrac{3}{4}$

D. 3

43. What is the sum of the cube of three times x and twice the square of y?

A. $3x^3 + 2y^2$
B. $3x^3 + 4y^2$
C. $27x^3 + 2y^2$
D. $27x^3 + 4y^2$

GO ON TO THE NEXT PAGE

44. If $2x - 3 < 3(x + 1.4)$, which is a possible value of x?

    A. −10
    B. −9
    C. −8
    D. −7

45. Which of the following is equivalent to $x^{-\frac{3}{2}}$?

    A. $-\sqrt{x^3}$

    B. $-\sqrt[3]{x^2}$

    C. $\dfrac{1}{\sqrt{x^3}}$

    D. $\dfrac{1}{\sqrt[3]{x^2}}$

Question 46 refers to the following table.

r	A
4	16π
	36π
1	
	9π
2	4π

46. The table above shows areas with corresponding radii. Select the values below that accurately complete the table. You may write your selections in the table.

3	6	7	9

π	6π	16π	49π

END OF TEST

THIS PAGE INTENTIONALLY LEFT BLANK.

Social Studies

Welcome!

Here is some information that you need to know before you start this test:

- You should not spend too much time on a question if you are not certain of the answer; answer it the best you can, and go on to the next question.
- If you are not certain of the answer to a question, you can mark your answer for review and come back to it later.
- You have **70 minutes** to complete this test.

Turn the page to begin.

GO ON TO THE NEXT PAGE

Questions 1 and 2 refer to the following map.

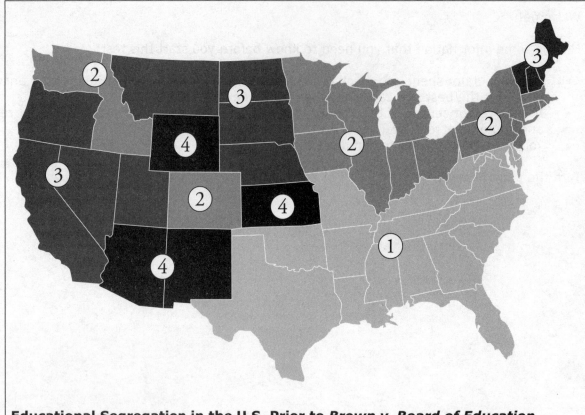

Educational Segregation in the U.S. Prior to *Brown v. Board of Education*

GO ON TO THE NEXT PAGE

1. Which of the following most accurately represents the regional differences in school segregation *prior* to the US Supreme Court case *Brown vs. Board of Education* (1954)?

   A.   Region 1: School segregation is required by state laws.
         Region 2: School segregation is prohibited by state laws.
         Region 3: School segregation is required by state laws.
         Region 4: School segregation is prohibited by state laws.
   B.   Region 1: School segregation is required by state laws.
         Region 2: School segregation is prohibited by state laws.
         Region 3: School segregation is not addressed by state laws.
         Region 4: School segregation is allowed, but not required, by state laws.
   C.   Region 1: School segregation is allowed, but not required, by state laws.
         Region 2: School segregation is required by state laws.
         Region 3: School segregation is required by state laws.
         Region 4: School segregation is prohibited by state laws.
   D.   Region 1: School segregation is prohibited by state laws.
         Region 2: School segregation is required by state laws.
         Region 3: School segregation is not addressed by state laws.
         Region 4: School segregation is allowed, but not required, by state laws.

2. Select the statement that most accurately represents the regional differences in school segregation *after* the US Supreme Court case *Brown vs. Board of Education* (1954).

   School segregation is

Select... ▼
required
prohibited
allowed, but not required
not addressed by federal law

   .

GO ON TO THE NEXT PAGE

Social Studies

Questions 3 through 5 refer to the following source.

1 Washington encouraged the sanctity of the Union with the following exhortation: "The name of American, which belongs to you in your national capacity, must always exalt the just pride of patriotism more than any appellation derived from local discriminations. With slight shades of difference, you have the same religion, manners, habits, and political principles. You have in a common cause fought and triumphed together; the independence and liberty you possess are the work of joint counsels, and joint efforts of common dangers, sufferings, and successes."

2 He also voiced his opinion on political parties: "I have already intimated to you the danger of parties in the State, with particular reference to the founding of them on geographical discriminations. Let me now take a more comprehensive view, and warn you in the most solemn manner against the baneful effects of the spirit of party generally."

3 Washington firmly believed in two items crucial to human thriving: "Of all the dispositions and habits which lead to political prosperity, religion and morality are indispensable supports. In vain would that man claim the tribute of patriotism, who should labor to subvert these great pillars of human happiness, these firmest props of the duties of men and citizens."

4 As for America's role in the world, Washington said: "Observe good faith and justice towards all nations; cultivate peace and harmony with all. Religion and morality enjoin this conduct." And, "It is our true policy to steer clear of permanent alliances with any portion of the foreign world; so far, I mean, as we are now at liberty to do it; for let me not be understood as capable of patronizing infidelity to existing engagements...let those engagements be observed in their genuine sense. But, in my opinion, it is unnecessary and would be unwise to extend them."

–President George Washington, from his Farewell Address delivered in 1796

3. In the context of paragraph 2, what does Washington mean by "discriminations"?

   A. racial prejudices
   B. party loyalties
   C. regional preferences
   D. wise discernments

4. In the third paragraph, what represents the "firmest props of the duties of men"?

   A. religion and morality
   B. patriotism
   C. political prosperity
   D. happiness

5. Each of the following are ideas which Washington supports EXCEPT

   A. fidelity to existing engagements.
   B. religion.
   C. political parties.
   D. national unity.

GO ON TO THE NEXT PAGE

6. Greek political and economic life in the 5th century BCE is often known as the "Golden Age of Athens" and is characterized by the following:

- Equality granted to all citizens

- Work assignments for the poor

- Government land grants

- Public monetary assistance to widows, orphans, and the disabled

- Citizen juries

- Term limits for legislators

Which of the following modern political or economic systems is closest to the political system of 5th century BCE Athens?

A. constitutional monarchy
B. laissez-faire capitalism
C. democratic socialism
D. Marxist communism

GO ON TO THE NEXT PAGE

Social Studies

Questions 7 through 9 refer to the following sources.

Source 1:

"The whites have had us under them for more than three centuries, murdering, and treating us like brutes; and, as Mr. Jefferson wisely said, they have never found us out—they do not know, indeed, that there is an unconquerable disposition in the breasts of the blacks, which, when it is fully awakened and put in motion, will be subdued, only with the destruction of the animal existence. Get the blacks started, and if you do not have a gang of tigers and lions to deal with, I am a deceiver of the blacks and of the whites…if you commence, make sure work—do not trifle, for they will not trifle with you—they want us for their slaves, and think nothing of murdering us in order to subject us to that wretched condition—therefore, if there is an attempt made by us, kill or be killed. Now, I ask you, had you not rather be killed than to be a slave to a tyrant, who takes the life of your mother, wife, and dear little children? Look upon your mother, wife and children, and answer God Almighty; and believe this, that it is no more harm for you to kill a man, who is trying to kill you, than it is for you to take a drink of water when thirsty."

–David Walker, *Appeal*, 1830

Source 2:

"Believing, as we do, that men should never do evil that good may come; that a good end does not justify wicked means in the accomplishment of it; and that we ought to suffer, as did our Lord and his apostles, unresistingly—knowing that vengeance belongs to God, and he will certainly repay it where it is due;—believing all this, and that the Almighty will deliver the oppressed in a way which they know not, we deprecate the spirit and tendency of this Appeal….*We* do not preach rebellion—no, but submission and peace. Our enemies may accuse us of striving to stir up the slaves to revenge but their accusations are false, and made only to excite the prejudices of the whites, and to destroy our influence."

–William Lloyd Garrison, *The Liberator*, 1831

7. David Walker is most likely

   A. a slave-holder.
   B. a black abolitionist.
   C. a white abolitionist.
   D. a Southern legislator.

8. Which of the following best represents Garrison's opinion of the ideas expressed in Walker's *Appeal*?

   A. He agrees with Walker that white slave-holders are murdering brutes.
   B. He agrees with Walker's call for rebellion.
   C. He disagrees with Walker's justification of violence.
   D. He disagrees with Walker's support for abolition.

9. In the context of Garrison's statements what does he mean by "deprecate"?

   A. disapprove of
   B. approve of
   C. moderate
   D. sympathize with

GO ON TO THE NEXT PAGE

10. The following graphic organizer is used to classify systems according to the relationship between economic and social freedom.

In which quadrant did the Nazi regime of World War II Germany belong?

Write an X inside the quadrant you want to select.

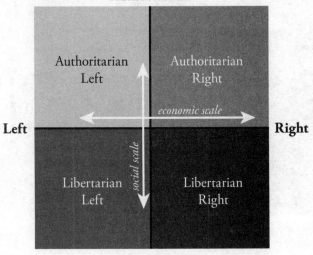

Questions 11 and 12 refer to the following image.

11. Pick the time period that most likely
     includes the year this picture was taken.

     A.   1760–1800
     B.   1800–1850
     C.   1850–1875
     D.   1900–1930

12. "Suffrage" means

     A.   the right to work.
     B.   the right to carry firearms.
     C.   the right to protest.
     D.   the right to vote.

GO ON TO THE NEXT PAGE

Questions 13 and 14 refer to the following source.

> "Under free trade the trader is the master and the producer the slave. Protection is but the law of nature, the law of self-preservation, of self-development, of securing the highest and best destiny of the race of man. [It is said] that protection is immoral....they say, 'Buy where you can buy the cheapest'....Let me give you a maxim that is a thousand times better than that, and it is the protection maxim: 'Buy where you can pay the easiest.' And that spot of earth is where labor wins its highest rewards."
>
> –President William McKinley, 1892

13. President McKinley's "protectionism" is

    A. opposed to free trade.
    B. supportive of free trade.
    C. designed to lower prices on consumer goods.
    D. harmful to labor interests.

14. It can be inferred from the passage that those who are opposed to protectionism believe

    A. it makes workers equivalent to slaves.
    B. it secures the highest and best destiny for mankind.
    C. it promotes higher prices on consumer goods.
    D. it promotes lower prices on consumer goods.

GO ON TO THE NEXT PAGE

Questions 15 through 17 refer to the following map.

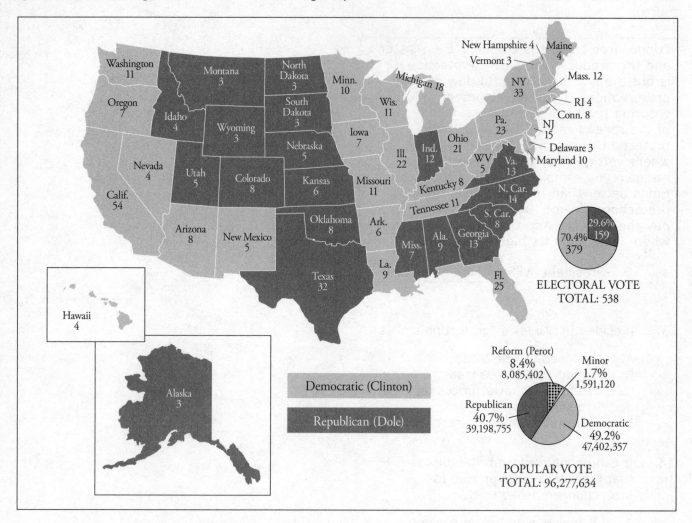

15. The map above supports which one of the following conclusions?

A. Although Candidate Dole won a majority of electoral votes in 1996, he did not win the popular vote.

B. Although Candidate Clinton won a minority of states, he still won the election of 1996.

C. The winner of the popular vote will always take the majority of electoral votes.

D. Candidate Perot did not win a majority of votes in any state in 1996.

GO ON TO THE NEXT PAGE

16. The map on the previous page supports which of the following conclusions?

    A. It is possible for a candidate to win an election without winning the majority of the popular vote.
    B. Candidate Dole lost the election because he did not win votes in the largest geographical areas of the country.
    C. Northerners and Southerners tend to vote in opposing ways.
    D. If Candidate Perot had not run in the election of 1996, Candidate Dole would have won.

17. Based on the map, which of the following is a possibly true, but biased, statement?

    A. Candidate Clinton won the election of 1996 because he secured a majority of the electoral votes.
    B. Candidate Dole won the election of 1996 because he secured a majority of the popular vote.
    C. The votes cast for Candidate Perot prevented either candidate from winning a majority of the popular vote.
    D. 8.4% of the voters in 1996 voted for Candidate Perot in protest of the failed political policies of Democrats and Republicans.

GO ON TO THE NEXT PAGE

Questions 18 through 20 refer to the following quotes from President Theodore Roosevelt.

Source 1:

"I declined to adopt the view that what was imperatively necessary for the Nation could not be done by the President unless he could find some specific authorization to do it. My belief was that it was not only his right but his duty to do anything that the needs of the Nation demanded unless such action was forbidden by the Constitution or by the laws. Under this interpretation of executive power I did and caused to be done many things not previously done by the President and the heads of the departments. I did not usurp power, but I did greatly broaden the use of executive power. In other words, I acted for the public welfare, I acted for the common well-being of all our people, whenever and in whatever manner was necessary, unless prevented by direct constitutional or legislative prohibition."

Source 2:

"The President is merely the most important among a large number of public servants. He should be supported or opposed exactly to the degree which is warranted by his good conduct or bad conduct, his efficiency or inefficiency in rendering loyal, able, and disinterested service to the Nation as a whole. Therefore it is absolutely necessary that there should be full liberty to tell the truth about his acts, and this means that it is exactly necessary to blame him when he does wrong as to praise him when he does right. Any other attitude in an American citizen is both base and servile. To announce that there must be no criticism of the president, or that we are to stand by the president, right or wrong, is not only unpatriotic and servile, but is morally treasonable to the American public."

---

18. Based on President Roosevelt's quotes, he would support all of the following EXCEPT

    A. freedom of the press.
    B. executive orders.
    C. freedom of speech.
    D. executive restraint.

19. Which of the following opinions is closest to the sentiments expressed by President Roosevelt?

    A. Presidential power should override the power of the legislative or judicial branches of government.
    B. Presidential power should be limited and used only in emergency situations.
    C. Presidential power should be used when it is legal to do so, while citizens have a right to protest actions they find objectionable.
    D. Presidential power should be used only when citizens do not find fault with the president's actions.

20. What basic assumption is behind the first quote but not behind the second?

    A. Presidents have a right to take action only when there is specific authorization to do so.
    B. Citizens know when a president's actions are unjustified or unwise.
    C. The judgment of presidents is generally better than that of the general population.
    D. Promoting the public welfare requires direct government action.

GO ON TO THE NEXT PAGE

Questions 21 and 22 refer to the following source.

> "I will build a car for the great multitude. It will be large enough for the family, but small enough for the individual to run and care for. It will be constructed of the best materials, by the best men to be hired, after the simplest designs that modern engineering can devise. But it will be so low in price that no man making a good salary will be unable to own one..."
>
> –Henry Ford, *My Life and Work*

21. Henry Ford's actions led to all of the following results in the 20th century EXCEPT

    A. the invention of the personal computer.
    B. the growth of suburbs.
    C. the Federal Highway Act of 1956.
    D. the growth of the oil industry.

22. Ford's statements rely on which of the following assumptions?

    A. Everyone would want to own a car.
    B. Many of his employees would earn enough money to own one of his cars.
    C. Most of his customers earn a good salary.
    D. Some people would have no interest in owning a car.

GO ON TO THE NEXT PAGE

Questions 23 through 25 refer to the following sources.

Source 1:

1   In the *Third World Water Development Report* (WWAP, 2009),...the governance mechanism for water is divided into two sections....In [one], the so-called "water box," are water-resources professionals who plan, operate, and maintain world water systems. This group deals with myriad problems of managing this fragile, scarce resource and the technical challenges in dealing with water infrastructure, droughts, floods, and other water issues. The people and groups in the water box focus on the specific issues of the day and meeting the needs of the sectors in which they operate. However, their ability to meet these challenges is heavily influenced by the actions of the actors outside the water box—the political and business sectors and the public at large, who may be, but most likely are not, educated in the specifics of water resource issues....

2   For those outside the water box to make sustainable decisions, communication between those in the box and external actors must be dramatically improved. Water professionals must do a better job of getting their messages to principal decision makers and insisting that they understand the full story before they make sometimes irreversible commitments....

3   In *Achieving the Vision for Civil Engineering 2025: A Roadmap for the Profession,* ASCE continues the argument that engineers "have to raise their visibility, becoming proactive within public policy forums and promoting an awareness that their unique background and skills are crucial...engineers cannot just provide engineered solutions; they must define the problems that affect quality-of-life improvements" (ASCE, 2009b).

4   That statement translates into increased participation in local meetings, working with legislatures, delivering testimony, and providing knowledge and expertise when and where it is needed through lobbying and other activities. Those tasks are also crucial to the water community....

5   The time has come for the water community to step up to the challenge and begin to educate and influence those outside the water box about the challenges facing the nation to the efficient, effective, and sustainable management of water resources and what must be done to navigate the uncertainties of the future. No doubt, this mission will make some people uncomfortable—communication is not what we normally do—but it needs to be done, and it needs to be done now!

Source: "A Plea for a Coordinated National Water Policy," Gerald E. Galloway Jr., *The Bridge*, Winter 2011, Vol. 41, No. 4. ©2011 by the National Academy of Sciences. Reprinted with permission of the National Academy of Engineering.

GO ON TO THE NEXT PAGE

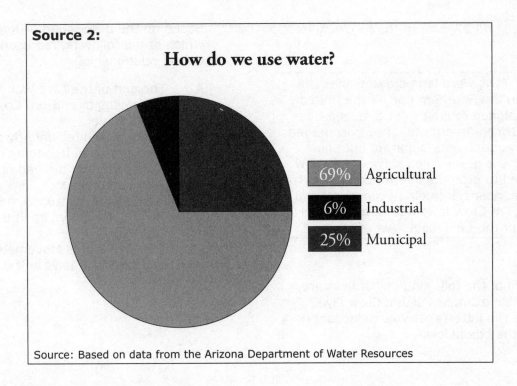

Source 2:

How do we use water?

69% Agricultural

6% Industrial

25% Municipal

Source: Based on data from the Arizona Department of Water Resources

23. According to the passage, the "water box" is

A. a group of experts who manage water systems.

B. those who participate in local meetings related to water systems.

C. a region whose water resources are scarce and must be managed carefully.

D. a group of people who must become more educated about water issues.

24. According to the passage, which of the following requires the most immediate action?

A. solving the problems associated with scarce water resources

B. communicating more effectively with those inside the water box

C. lobbying government officials regarding water resource issues

D. educating those outside the water box regarding water resource issues

25. Which of the following conclusions is best supported by the graph?

A. The state of Arizona spends more money on agriculture than on any other industry.

B. Industrial water use is inside the "water box."

C. Municipal areas utilize fewer public water resources than agricultural areas.

D. Less than one-fourth of Arizona's public water resources are utilized by municipal areas.

GO ON TO THE NEXT PAGE

Questions 26 and 27 refer to the following information.

> "Jim Crow" laws were laws created after the Civil War in the Southern part of the United States, designed to limit the rights and freedoms of African Americans. They encouraged racial segregation and "separate but equal status" for the newly freed slaves. Jim Crow laws tended to promote inferior conditions for African Americans, including economic disadvantages. Jim Crow laws were largely overturned after the Civil Rights Act of 1964.

26. Which of the following law or laws are possible examples of Jim Crow laws? Write the letter(s) of your selection(s) into the box below.

> [ ]

> (a) Segregation of public schools

> (b) Free speech rights for white plantation owners

> (c) Requirement of a literacy test to vote

> (d) Blacks-only public restrooms

> (e) Property taxes for black and white sharecroppers

27. Based on the description of Jim Crow laws, which of the following represents a direct causal relationship?

A. The end of the Civil War motivated Americans to end Jim Crow laws forever.
B. Southern whites unfairly restricted the rights and freedoms of Southern blacks up until the end of the 20th century.
C. Jim Crow laws caused many Northerners to enlist in the Civil War.
D. The Civil Rights Movement helped to end Jim Crow laws in the South.

GO ON TO THE NEXT PAGE

Questions 28 through 30 refer to the following information.

> Article V of the U.S. Constitution spells out the processes by which the Constitution can be amended.
>
> To propose amendments, both the House of Representatives and the Senate must approve by a two-thirds majority vote. Constitutional amendments do not require the signature of the president but are then sent to the states for ratification.
>
> Only 33 amendments to the Constitution have obtained the necessary two-thirds vote in Congress. Of those 33, 27 have been ratified.

28. What does it mean to "amend"?

    A. establish law
    B. change a law
    C. repeal a law
    D. violate a law

29. What does it mean to "ratify"?

    A. change a law
    B. violate a law
    C. approve of a change
    D. provide funding for a law

30. Which of the following represents an important difference between amending the U.S. Constitution and more common methods of creating law?

    A. Amending the U.S. Constitution requires the approval of Congress, while other methods do not.
    B. Amending the U.S. Constitution requires the approval of the president, while other methods do not.
    C. Amending the U.S. Constitution requires state ratification, while other methods do not.
    D. Proposals to amend the U.S. Constitution usually fail, while other methods do not.

GO ON TO THE NEXT PAGE

Questions 31 and 32 refer to the following sources.

Source 1:

Source 2:

"When I say that I am for the square deal, I mean not merely that I stand for fair play under the present rules of the game, but that I stand for having those rules changed so as to work for a more substantial equality of opportunity and of reward for equally good service."

–Theodore Roosevelt, 1910

31. The women in the photo above are exercising which of the following rights?

   A.   1st Amendment, freedom of speech
   B.   19th Amendment, women's right to vote
   C.   24th Amendment, right to vote without tax
   D.   26th Amendment, 18-year-old's right to vote

32. Why does the poster in the photo use the term "square deal"?

   A.   They are supporters of Theodore Roosevelt's campaign for the presidency.
   B.   They are celebrating their new-found right to vote.
   C.   The right to vote would represent greater equality of opportunity for women.
   D.   They are mocking Theodore Roosevelt's opposition to voting rights for women.

GO ON TO THE NEXT PAGE

Questions 33 through 35 refer to the following information.

The Two Branches of the U.S. Congress

	House of Representatives	Senate
Number of members total	435	100
Length of Term	2 years	6 years
Number of members per state	Based on state population	2

33. Of the following choices, which state would likely have the most political influence in the House of Representatives?

    A. Alaska
    B. California
    C. Maryland
    D. New Hampshire

34. What is the most likely reason for a cap of two senators from each state?

    A. Because senators are granted a six-year term, they would likely gain too much power if there were more than two from each state.
    B. States elect both a Republican and a Democrat to represent them in the Senate.
    C. If each state is allowed the same number of senators, it means each one is equally represented in that branch of the Congress.
    D. The Supreme Court has ruled that an unequal representation in Congress is unconstitutional.

35. Select the correct answer from the drop-down menu.

    Since 1929, the total number of representatives in

Select... ▼
the House
the Senate
both the House and Senate
neither the House nor the Senate

    has increased over time.

END OF TEST

THIS PAGE INTENTIONALLY LEFT BLANK.

Science

Welcome!

Here is some information that you need to know before you start this test:

- You should not spend too much time on a question if you are not certain of the answer; answer it the best you can, and go on to the next question.
- If you are not certain of the answer to a question, you can mark your answer for review and come back to it later.
- You have **90 minutes** to complete this test.

Turn the page to begin.

GO ON TO THE NEXT PAGE

Question 1 refers to the following graph.

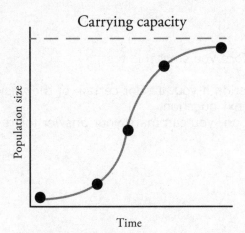

1. A population below its carrying capacity will grow exponentially before slowing and, eventually, stabilizing. On the logistic growth curve, mark an X on the point that represents the point of maximum growth rate.

Questions 2 through 4 refer to the following information.

Chromosomes contain thousands of different genes that form an individual's genotype and phenotype. An individual's genotype is an individual's specific combination of genes, and an individual's phenotype is the physical expression of those genes. A given gene consists of two alleles, which are essentially the instructions for a gene. An allele represented by a capital letter is said to be dominant and an allele represented by a lowercase letter is said to be recessive. A dominant gene is expressed when a dominant allele is paired with either a dominant or recessive allele. However, a recessive gene is only expressed when two recessive alleles are paired.

Consider the chemical phenylthiocarbamide (PTC). When some individuals taste PTC it tastes extremely bitter, while other individuals claim that PTC is tasteless. The ability to taste PTC is a genetic trait that shows a dominant pattern of inheritance. Thus, individuals just need a single copy of the allele T in order to taste PTC.

Geneticists use Punnett Squares to predict the likelihood of specific gene combinations in offspring. The following Punnett Square shows a cross between a heterozygous dominant PTC individual and a homozygous recessive PTC individual.

	T	t
t	Tt	??
t	Tt	tt

GO ON TO THE NEXT PAGE

Science

2. According to the information presented, what genotype should replace the "??" in the Punnett Square?

    A. TT
    B. Tt
    C. tt
    D. t^2

3. If these two individuals have children, what is the likelihood that their second child will not be able to taste PTC?

4. The genotypic ratio of this Punnett Square

    is best expressed as [Select... ▼] ,
    | 1:1 |
    | 1:2:1 |
    | 1:3 |

    while the phenotypic ratio of this Punnett Square is best expressed

    as [Select... ▼] .
    | 1:1 |
    | 1:2:1 |
    | 1:3 |

Question 5 refers to the following chemical equation.

$$6CO_2 + 6H_2O \rightarrow C_6H_{12}O_6 + 6O_2$$

5. The chemical reaction represented by the chemical equation above is

    A. cellular respiration.
    B. ATP creation.
    C. ADP creation.
    D. photosynthesis.

6. Matter exists in one of three states: solid, liquid, or gas. Solids keep their shape, liquids are held together with chemical bonds and can flow into a container, and gases have no shape and disperse unless contained. Matter is affected by temperature. Generally, increasing the temperature of a substance increases the volume of a substance. One major exception to this rule is water, which increases in volume when frozen.

    Ashlee is working in her laboratory. After melting some chocolate, she decides to freeze it. If she freezes the melted chocolate, she should expect the volume

    of the chocolate to [Select... ▼] .
    | decrease |
    | increase |
    | stay constant |

    Ashlee then decides to melt an ice-cube. If she allows the ice-cube to melt, she should expect the volume of the

    liquid to [Select... ▼] .
    | decrease |
    | increase |
    | stay constant |

GO ON TO THE NEXT PAGE

Questions 7 through 9 refer to the following information.

Bacterial meningitis is an infection that can cause permanent disabilities such as brain damage, learning disabilities, and even death. While there are several strains of bacteria that can cause meningitis, some of the leading causes of bacterial meningitis in the United States are the bacteria *Streptococcus pneumoniae*, *Neisseria meningitides*, *Haemophilus influenza*, *Listeria monocytogenes*, and group B *Streptococcus*. In the United States alone, these strains of bacteria are responsible for approximately 4,000 cases of meningitis and 500 deaths per year.

While not as contagious as viruses that cause the common cold or the flu, bacterial meningitis can be spread from person to person through respiratory and throat secretions or by eating contaminated food. However, bacterial meningitis is not contracted through casual contact, such as being in the same room as an afflicted individual.

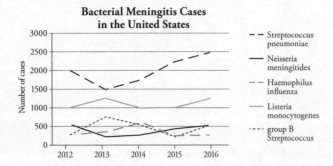

7. Based on the information provided, bacterial meningitis could be contracted by all of the following ways EXCEPT

A. eating meat that is infected with *Listeria monocytogenes*.
B. kissing an individual with group B *Streptococcus*.
C. holding hands with an individual with *Neisseria meningitides*.
D. inhaling the germs when an individual with *Streptococcus pneumoniae* coughs directly on you.

8. Approximately how many individuals died from bacterial meningitis in the United States from 2010–2014? (Include deaths from 2010 and 2014 in your answer.)

9. Which of the following statements is true regarding bacterial meningitis cases in the United States?

A. As the number of *Streptoccoccus pneumoniae* cases has increased, so, too, have the cases of *Haemophilus influenza*.
B. The number of individuals afflicted by *Listeria monocytogenes* in 2012 is half the number of individuals afflicted by *Streptoccoccus pneumoniae* in the same year.
C. The number of individuals afflicted with group B *Streptococcus* has steadily increased since 2012.
D. There were fewer cases of *Neisseria meningitides* in 2016 than there were cases of *Haemophilus influenza* in the same year.

GO ON TO THE NEXT PAGE

10. In order to produce energy, all organisms perform the process of cellular respiration. In cellular respiration, a sugar is combined with oxygen and water to produce carbon dioxide, water, and ATP energy. There are two different types of cellular respiration: one that occurs in the presence of oxygen and one that occurs without the presence of oxygen.

    If ATP is made in the presence of oxygen

    it is called | Select...   ▼ |
                 | aerobic |
                 | anaerobic |
                 | antagonistic |

    respiration, while | Select...   ▼ |
                       | aerobic |
                       | anaerobic |
                       | asymptomatic |

    respiration occurs without the presence of oxygen.

Questions 11 and 12 refer refers to the following information.

In the circulatory system, arteries carry blood away from the heart. As blood travels through the body, it presses against the walls of the arteries. Blood pressure is the measure of how hard the blood is pushing against the walls of the arteries.

	Systolic Pressure (mm/Hg)	Diastolic Pressure (mm/Hg)
Subject 1	112.8	76.0
Subject 2	105.4	70.2
Subject 3	146.8	98.6
Subject 4	132.6	85.8
Subject 5	160.0	112.0

11. What is the average diastolic pressure of the subjects?

    A. 85.8 mm/Hg
    B. 88.52 mm/Hg
    C. 131.52 mm/Hg
    D. 132.6 mmHg

12. What is the median systolic pressure of the subjects?

    [   ] mm/Hg

GO ON TO THE NEXT PAGE

Question 13 refers to the following information.

The Earth's crust is composed of tectonic plates that slowly move over the mantle of the Earth. When the boundaries of tectonic plates interact, friction between them can cause earthquakes and volcanoes. Three types of plate boundary interactions are convergent boundary interactions, which cause the development of mountain ranges; divergent boundary interactions, which cause a gap to form in the Earth's crust; and transform fault interactions, which result in earthquakes.

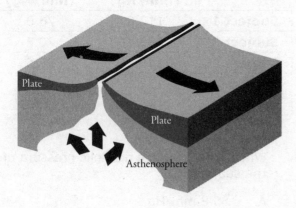

13. The image above depicts a

   A. convergent boundary.
   B. divergent boundary.
   C. transform fault boundary.
   D. volcanic boundary.

14. In order to produce energy, humans draw upon both renewable and nonrenewable resources. Write the letter of each resource into the correct box to show whether it is a renewable or nonrenewable resource.

Renewable	Nonrenewable

(a) coal

(b) wind

(c) geothermal

(d) biomass

(e) solar

(f) nuclear

(g) oil

GO ON TO THE NEXT PAGE

Science

Questions 15 and 16 refer to the following information.

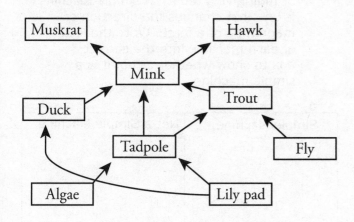

15. Based on the food web above, which of the following organisms is a producer?

    A. algae
    B. duck
    C. mink
    D. hawk

16. The populations of which two organisms would be devastated if the mink were removed from the food web?

    A. algae and lily pad
    B. muskrat and trout
    C. duck and hawk
    D. muskrat and hawk

Questions 17 refers to the following information.

Gravitational potential energy is the amount of energy an object has because of its vertical or horizontal position in a gravitational field. An object's gravitational potential energy is dependent upon the mass of an object and its height in the environment. For example, an object with mass m will have greater gravitational potential energy when dropped from a height of three feet than it will when dropped from a height of three inches.

17. Which of the following has the greatest gravitational potential energy?

    A. a 15-pound cat dropped from a height of two inches
    B. a 20-pound anchor dropped from a height of four feet
    C. a 20-pound brick dropped from a height of three inches
    D. a 90-pound box dropped from a height of ten feet

GO ON TO THE NEXT PAGE

Questions 18 and 19 are based on the following information.

The momentum of an object is the amount of motion of an object, and can be calculated using the equation momentum = mass × velocity.

18. A 12-pound cat is traveling at a velocity of 3 m/s and a 30-pound dog is traveling at a velocity of 6 m/s. How much greater is the momentum of the dog than the cat?

    [   ] lbs × m/s

19. Object A and Object B have the same momentum, but Object A has a greater mass. Object B must be traveling at

    | Select... ▼ | velocity.
    | lesser |
    | the same |
    | greater |

20. In physics, machines are implements that make work easier by redirecting or multiplying forces. A simple machine is one that changes the direction or magnitude of a force. Write the letter of each machine into the correct box to show whether or not it is a simple machine.

Simple Machine	Not a Simple Machine

    | (a) pulley | (f) inclined plane |
    | (b) wedge | (g) engine |
    | (c) gearshift | (h) screw |
    | (d) lever | (i) wheel and axle |
    | (e) drill | (j) funnel |

21. Marble is formed over time when exposed to extreme pressure and heat below the Earth's surface. What type of rock is marble?

    A. fossilized
    B. igneous
    C. metamorphic
    D. sedimentary

22. Which of the following is NOT a potential adverse effect of fossil fuel use?

    A. acid rain
    B. increased biodiversity
    C. greenhouse effect
    D. ozone depletion

GO ON TO THE NEXT PAGE

Science

Questions 23 through 25 refer to the following information.

A wave is a disturbance that carries energy from one point to another through either a medium or space. Waves can be categorized as either electromagnetic, such as light, which does not require a medium to travel, or mechanical, such as sound, which does require a medium to travel. Mechanical waves can be further categorized as either transverse waves, in which the particle motion is perpendicular to the wave motion, or longitudinal, in which particle motion moves in the same direction as the wave motion.

The parts of a wave can be analyzed to find out information about the wave. A single wavelength is equal to the distance between two consecutive crests, or points of maximum height, or troughs, or points of minimum height. The amplitude, or height, of a wave is equal to half the vertical distance between a crest and trough of a wave. The frequency of a wavelength, which is measured in hertz, is equal to the number of times a wave cycles in a second, and the period of a wave is the time it takes for a single wave to cycle. The frequency and period of a wave are inversely related;

i.e., the frequency of a wave is equal

to $\dfrac{1}{period}$ and the period of a wave is equal to $\dfrac{1}{frequency}$.

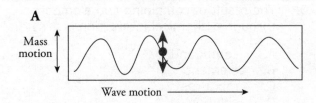

A

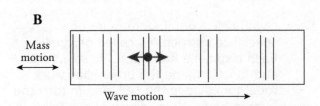

B

23. If a given wave cycles 360 times in a minute, what is the period of the wave?

   A. $\dfrac{1}{360}$

   B. $\dfrac{1}{6}$

   C. 6

   D. 360

24. Diagram A can be classified as a(n)

Select...   ▼
electromagnetic
longitudinal
transverse
sound

   wave, while diagram B

   can be classified as a(n)
Select...   ▼
electromagnetic
longitudinal
transverse
radio

   wave.

25. If the maximum height of a wave occurs at point 15 and the minimum height of a wave occurs at point 5, what is the amplitude of the wave?

GO ON TO THE NEXT PAGE

26. The result of combining two elements through a chemical interaction is a(n)

    A. compound.
    B. element.
    C. mixture.
    D. solution.

27. Living cells contain a number of specialized structures called organelles. Each organelle has a specific structure and function, and the organelles work together to keep the cell, and in turn the human body, alive. Which of the following organelles is responsible for making, processing, and packaging proteins?

    A. nucleus
    B. mitochondria
    C. lysosomes
    D. Golgi apparatus

28. The saturation point of an object is

    A. the temperature at which a solid turns into a liquid.
    B. the point at which no more of a substance can be dissolved into a solution.
    C. the temperature at which a solid turns into a gas.
    D. the point at which the nuclei of an atom breaks down, releasing energy in the form of charged particles.

GO ON TO THE NEXT PAGE

Science

Questions 29 and 30 refer to the following information.

Chemical reactions can be categorized into four main types: combination, decomposition, single displacement, and double displacement. The following chart provides a general example for each type of reaction.

Reaction Types	General Example
Combination	A + B → C
Decomposition	C → A + B
Single Displacement	A + BC → B + AC
Double Displacement	AB + CD → AC + BD

Calcium hydroxide, commonly known as an antacid, is used to neutralize hydrochloric acid, or stomach acid. When calcium hydroxide interacts with hydrochloric acid, calcium chloride, a common salt, and water are produced.

29. A balanced equation is one that has the same number of an element's atoms both before and after a reaction takes place. The balanced chemical equation for the reaction of acetylene and oxygen is $Ca(OH)_2$ + [Select... ▼] HCl →

1
2
3
4

   CaCl [Select... ▼] + $2H_2O$

1
2
3
4

30. What type of basic chemical reaction is the reaction of calcium hydroxide and hydrochloric acid?

   A. combination
   B. decomposition
   C. single displacement
   D. double displacement

Question 31 refers to the following image.

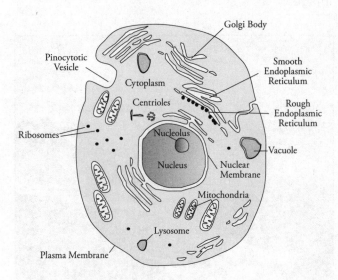

31. The image above is an animal cell. Write an X on the organelle that is composed of a phospholipid bilayer with receptor and transport proteins, and is responsible for maintaining the intracellular environment.

32. Which of the following states that equal volumes of any two gases at identical temperatures and pressures must hold an equal number of molecules?

   A. Avogadro's Law
   B. Law of Conservation of Mass
   C. Newton's Law of Inertia
   D. Planck's Law

GO ON TO THE NEXT PAGE

Questions 33 and 34 refer to the following image.

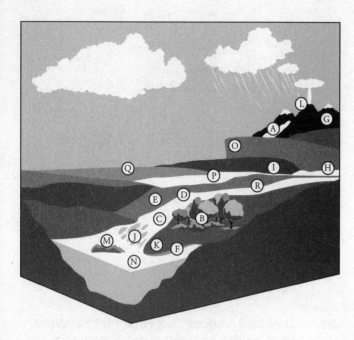

33. The landform labeled "K" is a piece of land that is almost entirely surrounded by water, while the landform labeled "M" is a piece of land that entirely surrounded by water. "K" is referred to as

a(n) [Select... ▼] and "M" is

cape
delta
isthmus
peninsula

referred to as a(n) [Select... ▼].

archipelago
headland
island
tributary

34. Which of the following landforms would best be described as a plain?

A. B
B. E
C. F
D. Q

35. Matthew is working on a science project to determine the relationship between temperature and gas volume. Matthew hypothesizes that the volume of a gas increases as the temperature increases, and wishes to support his hypothesis by designing an experiment using balloons as his primary material.

In order to test his hypothesis most effectively, Matthew should

A. conduct multiple trials, using different types of balloons.
B. conduct only one trial, so that the results will be clear.
C. conduct multiple trials, each using a different gas at a different temperature.
D. conduct multiple trials, using the same gas at different temperatures.

END OF TEST

Chapter 4
Practice Test 1:
Answers and
Explanations

REASONING THROUGH LANGUAGE ARTS

Section 1

1. **A** To some extent, the two people perform the functions outlined in all of the choices. Don't miss the word "main" in the question stem, though. Which function is the most important in the excerpt? That's (A), adding the credibility of another real person who supports the narrator's point. It's not just one man's questionable opinion that the scenery of the Adirondacks surpasses that of Switzerland; the man's brother in Switzerland agrees. The health-enhancing benefits of the wilderness aren't just speculation; the narrator is sitting with a real person whose health has improved after spending time in the woods. Even in this wilderness, it is possible to run into another visitor and to travel with someone besides a guide, (B). The people do break up the narrator's lengthy descriptions of natural scenery, (C). And one person (the man with a brother in Switzerland) shows that the narrator's views aren't simply the result of an American's preference for his own country, (D). While the other choices are valid, they are less important than (A) to an excerpt which rests so heavily on one narrator's personal experiences and opinions.

2. **C** First you need to determine the author's purpose in describing the Adirondacks and his experiences there. He states it at the beginning of paragraph 2: "Another reason why I visit the Adirondacks, and urge others to do so...." That purpose itself is ironic because, if he succeeds in attracting more visitors, the area will no longer be the unspoiled wilderness he enjoys so much. Why would he want to encourage travellers to a region he praises because he can "live in silence, unbroken by any sounds save such as you yourself may make, away from all the business and cares of civilized life" (paragraph 4)? Choice (A) concerns a possible result of trying to achieve his purpose. It doesn't say anything about the author's original purpose itself. Choice (B), while it has some truth to it, deals with audience, not purpose. The descriptions of Maine and the Adirondacks are equally vivid. However, (D) is incorrect because if anything, the criticisms of Maine enhance the author's purpose of encouraging people to visit the Adirondacks by presenting a stark contrast to the natural, unexplored Adirondack wilderness.

3. **B** The author's descriptions strike a skillful balance between conveying the wild, alien character of the Adirondacks and evoking something familiar that would inspire readers to visit the area. The "unvisited" lakes are "like gems" in the "folds of emerald-colored velvet" (paragraph 1). The scenery would "rival Switzerland" (paragraph 1). At the same time, the region offers an escape from undesirable aspects of readers' everyday lives. The natural setting is a stark contrast to "all the business and cares of civilized life" (paragraph 4). The curative quality of the mountain air and trees combat that "dread disease, consumption" (paragraph 2). The author's descriptions are realistic. He doesn't try to downplay the isolated, wild character of the region, (A), nor does he exaggerate its difficulties, (C). He also doesn't go out of his way to emphasize how alien the Adirondacks would seem to readers from more populated areas, (D). Instead, he makes it sound just different enough, yet beneficial and nonthreatening enough, to entice readers to experience it for themselves.

4. **A** The lumbermen's wholesale destruction of Maine's natural environment shows the author that they cared only about what they'd gain from the logs they took. They made no effort to restore the rivers and mountains and no attempt to clean up their campsites before they moved on. If they left valuable logs and timber behind, the lumbermen would be inefficient and lazy, not obsessed with making a gain, (B). The Adirondacks boasts "a wilderness yet to echo to the lumberman's axe" (paragraph 1). If the lumbermen

were driven only by gain, though, they would discover and try to harvest the forests of the Adirondacks, so their absence doesn't show the narrator their greed, (C). The fires, which the narrator thinks might have been started by "malicious purpose" (paragraph 4), suggest deliberate destruction of the environment, not an obsession with gain to the exclusion of everything else, (D).

5.   **(b) and (c)**

The author claims that America offers travel experiences that "the world does not anywhere else furnish" (paragraph 1), and wishes people would make the effort to discover them, (b). The Adirondacks, he believes, boast a "wilderness to rival Switzerland," yet "thousands are in Europe to-day as tourists" (paragraph 1), automatically visiting the same popular places as everyone else, (c). Choice (a) is too general. The author doesn't suggest that people in every country should spend their vacations there, regardless of the travel experiences their own countries can offer. He realizes that people visit Switzerland because of the "magnificent scenery" (paragraph 1), so (d) is incorrect. He does not criticize Americans for having no spirit of adventure when they don't explore their own country, (e). He criticizes them for automatically heading to Europe and not giving "a passing thought to this marvellous country lying as it were at their very floors" (paragraph 1).

6.   **D**   The "rule of thumb" is that a first-person narrator is always suspect until proven reliable. That is because the narrator is part of the story, and the reader sees events, settings, and other people only through the narrator's eyes. He or she could be biased or trying to achieve some hidden purpose or just plain unhinged. In this excerpt, the narrator does show himself to be reliable. He is transparent about his purpose (to urge readers to come to the Adirondacks) and realistic in his descriptions. His presence adds realism and credibility to Murray's work. This isn't just an author in some faraway city rewriting descriptions he read about elsewhere and urging readers to visit a spot he's never seen. This is a real person who has actually been to the Adirondacks several times, who has "boated up and down that wilderness" (paragraph 1), climbed a mountain, and counted the lakes. The impression is that readers can have confidence in his descriptions and trust his recommendation. Choice (A) is incorrect because, although the first-person narrator and his experiences might result in more interesting reading, the work is still a nonfiction travel documentary. There is no suggestion that the author's own opinions differ from the narrator's, (B). The author didn't need a first-person narrator to add details, (C). He could simply have described, for example, the health benefits of the mountain air without having a first-person narrator travelling with someone whose health has improved.

7.   **Read first (a), (c), and (d); didn't read (b), (e), and (f)**

This question asks about the author's secondary purpose. According to the excerpt, his primary purpose is to encourage readers to see the Adirondacks for themselves. He must have assumed he'd succeed with some readers, and written his descriptions partly with those people in mind too. For the visitor who read the guidebook first: While the author gives an accurate general description of the wilderness, the mountains, and the lakes, he doesn't go into much detail about any one area, leaving it up to the visitor to discover specific locations for himself, (a). The visitor would have formed some preconceived ideas of the benefits he'd gain by following Murray's advice to come to the Adirondacks, (c). The author's general descriptions might have fired the visitor's curiosity about a specific area he'd like to explore first, (d). For the visitor who didn't read the book first: Since he is discovering the area for the first time himself, with no prior knowledge about it, his experiences will be entirely his own, (b). Without any previous idea what the area is like, he will likely be overpowered by the general character of the Adirondacks on his first visit, (f), and will want to return to explore specific areas in more depth, (e).

8. **B** This question stem requires careful reading to understand exactly which relationship you're supposed to examine. Only (B) deals with the relationship between the descriptions of the two areas, Maine and the Adirondacks. The picture of Maine—whose natural beauty has been destroyed by the lumbermen, "the curse and scourge of the wilderness"—intensifies the appeal of the Adirondacks, which "have never been marred by the presence of men careless of all but gain" (paragraph 4). Choice (A) refers to the impact on readers' perception of the narrator, not their perception of the Adirondacks. Choice (C) does the same for readers' perception of the author. After reading about Maine, readers might gain a new appreciation for the places where they live, (D), but again, this choice doesn't point to any impact on the description of the Adirondacks.

9. **B** A democracy "rests upon...the people" because the people elect their leaders, who are in turn responsible to the people. The foundation of "the people" seems "slender and unstable" (paragraph 14) to the three Europeans, who are accustomed to an unelected monarch, (A). The people have no role in a dictatorship, (C), and anarchy, (D), is not a system of government.

10. **D** A volcano can appear to be calm and harmless, but could erupt at any time, with disastrous consequences. The volcano image reinforces the impending disaster conveyed in the earlier image of "the gulf into which you are about to fall" (paragraph 2). Since active volcanoes also exist in old, long-established countries, (A) is incorrect. Choice (B) is close—a volcanic eruption is chaotic—but inaccurate because of the time factor. The "social chaos" (paragraph 1) is in the present. The Republic would not be able to sleep on an erupting volcano, though. M. Blouse is referring to a dormant volcano that could erupt in future. Another close choice is (C), but it's not quite accurate, either. The question stem asks specifically about the image of the volcano, not about the action of sleeping as a metaphor [a representation] for ignoring something.

11. **Three Europeans (a), (c), and (f); Cooper (b), (d), and (e)**

    The Europeans highlight America's hypocrisy by citing the example of "a country which calls itself free" practicing the "dreadful tyranny" (paragraph 17) of putting chains across the streets (a). They refer to the chaos, corruption and danger of a country that has inverted the natural order by putting "the people in possession of powers which naturally belong to the nobility" (paragraph 1), (c). In paragraph 1, they describe America as a country where "selfishness reigns supreme," (f). Cooper explains that the chained streets are simply intended to prevent noisy carriages from creating a disturbance, and says "no person is prevented from travelling on foot wherever he pleases" (paragraph 18), (b). From Cooper's determination to "prove that you are misinformed" (paragraph 9), you can infer that he would claim America is a place of social harmony, (d), not "social chaos" (paragraph 1). It is reasonable to extend Cooper's explanation about decisions regarding taxes—"as they come from ourselves, it is hardly probable that we pay more than is necessary for our own benefit" (paragraph 12)—to other government decisions, (e).

12. **A** Careful reading of the question stem will ensure you don't miss "primarily." Each answer choice is true in parts of the excerpt. You're looking for the one that is laced throughout the entire excerpt and leaves an overall impression at the end. That's (A). Throughout the excerpt, the author uses techniques such as humor and exaggeration to satirize current European misconceptions about America. At times he is overtly critical, (B)—for instance, when Cooper says, "I think it important to prove that you are misinformed" (paragraph 9)—but at other times he simply gives a neutral explanation to correct the Europeans' misconception (about taxes in paragraph 12 and about the chained streets in paragraph 18, for example). Cooper reveals that he was initially puzzled, (C), by the Europeans' negative descriptions of America when he says, "I breathe again. As there is no steamboat...it is possible that you are deceived with regard to facts more important to my country" (paragraph 3). However, as the discussion continues

and it becomes obvious that the Europeans are determined to cling to views "recognised by all Europe" (paragraph 4), Cooper's confusion about their criticisms disappears. He is initially defensive, (D), too. In paragraph 9 he says, "You bring forward heavy charges against my country; I think it important to prove that you are misinformed." Again, though, as the discussion progresses, his defensiveness gives way to calm explanations to contradict the Europeans' charges.

13. **(d) facts, (a) democracy, and (c) America vs. Europe**

You'll need to make some inferences in order to answer this question. The statement in (d) develops the concept of facts. Cooper and the three Europeans have different views not only of what the facts about America are, but also of the role of facts in their discussion. When M. Blouse makes the statement in (d), Cooper has just finished explaining that no steamboats cross the ocean and no country is called the United States of North America. Nevertheless, M. Blouse disregards both of the facts Cooper has just stated and claims he has received documents on a steamboat from the United States of North America. Cooper, who has spent most of his life in America, bases his facts on firsthand experience. M. Blouse is so attached to his own preconceived "facts" that he ignores anything that contradicts them. Choice (a) develops the theme of democracy, America's *one idea* (paragraph 2), in contrast to Europe's "three consequent and well-balanced ideas" (paragraph 14). You can infer one of these three ideas from the criticism that "in America we see the people in possession of powers which naturally belong to the nobility" (paragraph 1). That idea is aristocracy. (The other two European ideas of government are monarchy and feudalism.) M. Blouse, accustomed to the balance of power and duties in Europe's three ideas, finds democracy (where the people have the power) to be "selfishness" (paragraph 1) and confusing. A similar theme is developed by (c). Cooper, accustomed to America's system of government, perceives Europe's (where the people have no power) as an unworkable inversion of the American system. American democracy makes sense to him ("a man who stands upon his feet") while Europe's system doesn't ("a man who stands upon his head" paragraph 15). Choices (b) and (e) do not develop the three concepts and themes in the boxes.

14. **B** The author's purpose is to satirize European misconceptions about America. He does this through the images conveyed by the three Europeans and their refusal to listen to any information from Cooper that contradicts their ideas. From the perspective of the three Europeans, (B) is correct. They "have resolved not to abandon you to your own movements without one effort to show you the gulf into which you are about to fall" (paragraph 2). The question asks about the *author's* purpose, though, not the Europeans', so (A) is incorrect. The author's purpose is to ridicule European misconceptions about America, not to ridicule Cooper, (C). The three Europeans ignore every one of Cooper's attempts to correct their misconceptions, (D), so the author does not intend to show that they can learn the truth about America.

15. **C** In this selection, as well as throughout the excerpt, M. Blouse is blinded by his preconceived ideas about America and refuses to change his opinions even when Cooper, with his direct knowledge, gives him facts or explanations. The selection shows how M. Blouse picks examples that reinforce his preconceived ideas, without understanding the reason for the American example he chooses. Choice (A) is fine as a literal summary of the selection. However, it's too literal to answer the question; it doesn't extend to the main idea behind the images of the chained and free streets. From the perspective of M. Blouse, (B) is a good summary. Again, though, this choice doesn't answer the question: What main idea does the *author* (not M. Blouse) intend to convey? Choice (D) pretty well says the opposite of the idea the author intends. M. Blouse has direct personal experience of Europe. The European government system isn't "free" compared with America's, though, so M. Blouse doesn't even have a true understanding of the situation he knows, let alone the one with which he has no direct personal experience (America).

16.   **(b)—(e); (d)—(a), (f)—(c)**

The first cause listed is (b), the tendency of popular movements to excess. The effect is (e), people imposing excessive taxes on themselves. Choice (d) is the next cause: people usurping powers which naturally belong to the nobility. One of the effects identified by the three Europeans is (a), blatant corruption. The third cause is the lack of a steamboat, (f), to bring the documents containing a "complete *exposé* of the mournful state of your dear and unhappy country" (paragraph 2). The effect upon Cooper is (c), the belief that the Europeans are mistaken about other aspects of America.

17.   The option that correctly completes the sentence for each "Select" option:

Drop-Down Item 1: **Sentence construction, awkward wording and transition.**

Option 4 is correct. The wording is crisp, authoritative, and formal, in keeping with the rest of the policy statement. The imperative verb ("keep") reinforces the authoritative tone. The subject (you) of an imperative verb is not stated, but is "understood" to be there.

Option 1 is a sentence fragment. It does not have a subject and verb, and does not stand on its own. The wording is awkward, unclear, and unnecessarily repetitive in option 2. Who is supposed to keep the document, and who besides "you" would refer to it? Option 3 displays similar problems (of course the document will be there if you keep it), as well as an inappropriate transition ("however") from the previous sentence. "However" is a conjunctive adverb used to make a transition from one clause or sentence to a second one that contrasts with the first. A contrast between the policy being effective immediately and keeping the document for future reference doesn't make sense within the meaning of this policy statement.

Drop-Down Item 2: **Pronoun case and pronoun agreement**

Option 3 is correct. "Whom" is the objective case of the personal pronoun. It refers to the object ("the company employee"). A pronoun must agree in case with the noun to which it refers.

Option 1 incorrectly uses the subjective case of the pronoun ("who"). The pronoun should refer to the object ("the company employee"), not to the subject ("the visitor"). Options 2 and 4 incorrectly use "that" and "which"—relative pronouns that refer to things or to groups, not to individual people.

Drop-Down Item 3: **Pronoun agreement**

Option 2 is correct. "Your visitor" is singular, so the pronoun that refers to it must also be singular. The text doesn't specify the visitor's gender, so the accompanying pronoun must allow for either male or female.

The other three options are frequently—and incorrectly—used to avoid an unwieldy (but correct) "him or her." Option 1 is perhaps the most common error. It uses a plural pronoun ("them") to refer to a singular noun ("your visitor"). The pronoun must agree in number and gender with the noun it replaces. Options 3 and 4 reveal gender bias. Not all business visitors are male, nor are they all female.

Drop-Down Item 4: **Misplaced modifier and wordiness**

Option 1 is correct. The modifier ("which can connect...) is placed closest to the noun it describes (the laptop), so the meaning is clear.

Options 2 and 4 illustrate a misplaced modifier. In option 2, the modifier ("that can connect...") is placed closer to the "cabinet" than to the "laptop," which it *should* be describing. The same problem appears in option 4, where the modifier ("for connecting to the Internet...") seems to refer to the locked cabinet, not to the laptop. A misplaced modifier is an easy mistake to make when you're writing quickly. *You* know what you mean, but what about the reader who's seeing the sentence for the first time? Option 3 is unnecessarily wordy. The reader has already been told that there is a laptop in a locked cabinet.

Section 2

Access your Student Tools online to read sample essays representing different score levels for the Extended Response prompts in this book.

Section 3

18.   **(d), (a), (c), (e), and (b)**

You can answer the questions in any order (without, of course, spending too much time skimming the question stems to decide which one to tackle first). This type of question is a good early choice, because answering it will help you learn about the structure of the excerpt and might help you locate details for other questions more easily. The first indication that something might be wrong is the unexpected invitation to live at Aswarby Hall, (d), after Stephen has already been an orphan for six months. Next is the neighbors' surprise at the incongruity of a young boy being invited to the "steady-going household" of the "somewhat austere recluse" (paragraph 1), (a). The author's use of the term "inmate" (paragraph 1), (c), instead of a more neutral term such as "resident," gives the next suggestion that all may not be as it seems. The narrator comments openly on the two questions about Stephen's age, (e)—"It seemed a little odd that he should have asked the question twice in the first two minutes of their acquaintance" (paragraph 6)—drawing attention to the next indication that something is amiss. Mrs. Bunch's vague account of the mysterious disappearance of the two previous children, (b), connects the growing suspense even more directly to Stephen, the third child to arrive.

19. **B** The children are all described as being alone and vulnerable. Stephen is a 12-year-old orphan with no other relatives to care for him. The girl had "no one belonging to her" and just came back with Mr Abney "from his walk one day" (paragraph 15) The boy was from another country and also arrived alone, "a-tweaking his 'urdy-gurdy round and about the drive one winter day" (paragraph 17). There is no indication that any of the children, including Stephen, are happy about coming to Aswarby Hall, so (A) is incorrect. Blaming gypsies for the children's disappearance is simply Mrs. Bunch's guess, and Stephen hasn't been taken by anyone yet, eliminating (C). Yes, the children are all young, but all children are young. This choice is too general. The question stem asks for the main characteristic that these three particular children share, so (D) is incorrect.

20. **A** Neighbors were surprised that Mr. Abney "should ever have heard of his orphan cousin, Stephen Elliott" (paragraph 1). Here is a third child alone in the world, and the pretext of being a relative would provide an acceptable explanation to inviting Stephen to live at Aswarby Hall. Since there are several other indications in the excerpt that things might not be what they seem, it's reasonable to infer that Mr. Abney might not really be Stephen's cousin, either. Mr. Abney is described as an "austere recluse" about whose "pursuits or temper" other people knew "very little" (paragraph 1). His isolation is by choice, eliminating (B). Choice (C) is the appearance Mr. Abney gives by offering a home to children who are alone in the world, and it's

the one Mrs. Bunch accepts without question. However, the disappearance of the previous two children and the ominous signals surrounding Stephen's arrival suggest that Mr. Abney is not the kindhearted person he seems to be. The excerpt doesn't suggest that Mr. Abney wants children in the house because he fears growing old, (D).

21.   **(a), (d), and (e)**

Stephen reveals his curiosity (a) when he hears about the two children and demands "Do tell me all about them, Mrs. Bunch—now, this minute!" (paragraph 14). When Stephen goes back to the door to see if the "figure of his dreams were really there," the narrator comments on the "courage which I do not think can be common among boys of his age" (paragraph 21), (d). It would require an adventurous spirit, (e), to set off for the home of a previously unknown cousin who lived far enough away that the trip had to be made by "post-chaise" (paragraph 1). If Stephen were enterprising, (b), he would have been trying to find a new home for himself. Instead, he seems to have just waited around in "Warwickshire, where, some six months before, he had been left an orphan" (paragraph 1) until the invitation to Aswarby Hall arrived out of the blue. If he were perceptive, he would have realized there must be more to the stories of the missing children and pressed Mrs. Bunch for more details, so (c) is incorrect.

22. **A**   Here's the classic mysteriously locked door. Unlike most classic locked doors, though, it's possible to see what's behind this one. However, its presence does heighten the atmosphere of suspense the author builds throughout the excerpt. Why is such an apparently harmless room kept locked? The reader gets a sense that something is wrong, something is about to happen, raising the suspense level. While the mysteriously locked door might suggest that Stephen has not found the perfect home, that doesn't lead to the inference that it was better than no home, so (B) is incorrect. There is no indication that the locked door appears to be one thing but is really another. Its presence simply heightens the tension and mystery, eliminating (C). The theme of misplaced trust, (D), appears through Stephen and Mrs. Bunch trusting what Mr. Abney tells them. The locked door doesn't lead to that theme.

23. **D**   The sense of foreboding the author builds right from the beginning, with the unexpected invitation to an unsuitable household, suggests that Stephen might wind up needing a more powerful ally. How effective would Mrs. Bunch be? Her account of the two missing children reveals an imperceptive, dull-witted person who accepts appearances too readily and doesn't delve beneath the surface. Mrs. Bunch sees the children's unlikely arrivals as nothing but evidence that Mr. Abney is "as kind a soul as ever I see!" (paragraph 13). When they disappear, she never tries to find them or even questions what happened to them, but simply blames a popular villain of the day, the gypsies. She would likely do the same if Stephen disappeared, too, making her an ineffective ally. It's true that Mrs. Bunch doesn't question Mr. Abney's motives or actions, but there's no indication that it's out of loyalty, (A), instead of simplemindedness. If she's responsible for taking care of the children in Aswarby Hall, (B), she's not doing a very good job when they keep vanishing without a trace. Although Stephen and Mrs. Bunch "were great friends in a quarter of an hour: and great friends they remained" (paragraph 11), such a dull-witted, unquestioning friend, (C), would not be a very effective ally if Stephen needed help.

24. **C**   By connecting the story of the children and the deathly figure so closely in time as well as in the narrative, the author intends to suggest a linkage to the reader. If you were narrowing the choices down to two possible correct answers, (A) was likely the other one you considered. Indeed, there is a strong contrast between the "comfortable and human" (paragraph 11) Mrs. Bunch and the "leaden colour" figure "enveloped in a shroud-like garment" (paragraph 20). The author also contrasts Mrs. Bunch with everyone else "whom Stephen had as yet met at Aswarby" (paragraph 11), though. Linking the mysteriously missing children to the mysterious dream figure, (C), intensifies the atmosphere of foreboding, and is therefore more likely

what the author intended. Stephen doesn't ask any questions or show any other indication that the story of the children has fired his imagination, so an overactive imagination as a result of the story didn't give rise to his dream; (B) is incorrect. The dream alone might show that Aswarby Hall is already making Stephen uneasy, but that doesn't explain the connection to the earlier story of the children, which didn't seem to trouble him at all, so (D) is incorrect.

25. **C** For some hidden reason, Mr. Abney is preoccupied with Stephen's age. He asks about it twice, as soon as Stephen arrives. He seems to want a 12-year-old boy, not his orphaned cousin, indicating a hidden motive in bringing Stephen to Aswarby Hall. Even Mr. Abney realizes how unusual his question about age must sound, though, because he immediately switches to a more normal-sounding question about Stephen's journey and supper. As an "austere recluse" (paragraph 1), Mr. Abney wouldn't be used to welcoming visitors. However, (A) is too general to be the correct answer for this specific piece of dialogue with this specific visitor. The concern about Stephen's journey might make it seem as if he's found a good home, (B), and as if Mr. Abney is as kind as Mrs. Bunch believes, (D). However, these choices ignore the surprising question about his age.

26. **A** This question asks what impact a structural element—the quotes—has on the biography as a whole. The author could just as easily have left them out—why are they there? Let's start by getting rid of clearly wrong answers, using a technique called Process of Elimination (POE). By beginning your search looking for *incorrect* choices, you'll have fewer potentially *correct* choices to consider. The most obvious choice to eliminate is (D). The excerpt already has subheads that split up sections. Next is (C). Each quote appears right after the subhead that marks the beginning of a new section. They don't act as transitions to smooth the flow from paragraph to paragraph. If anything, they interrupt the flow. That leaves (A) and (B). Choice (B) is tempting, but not entirely accurate, since the quotes don't add brand-new information about Carnegie's life. Instead, they illuminate and expand on information that's already suggested in the biography. For instance, the quote about why it's important for people to motivate themselves (so they can rise above mediocrity) casts additional light on Carnegie's aim to provide people with "the tools necessary to succeed" (paragraph 5). After eliminating the other three choices, (A) emerges as the correct answer. It's as if Carnegie himself were agreeing with the biographer's words and expanding upon them, adding explanations such as "this is why I wanted to do that."

27. **D** This question requires you to make an inference based on the biographical information in the excerpt. Carnegie didn't build a successful industrial empire by not carefully considering whether every decision or activity would further his business goals. The "Carnegie Formula" explained in paragraph 7 reveals the same shrewd business instincts at work in his philanthropy. Any town applying for a grant had to demonstrate that it would use the grant money to carry out Carnegie's objectives (points one and four) and that it was committed to his vision (points two and three). The formula doesn't put a blanket limitation on the number of projects to be funded, (A), nor does it suggest that only certain favored towns would succeed, (B). It also doesn't indicate any hidden agenda, (C).

28. **(b) and (e)**

One would not expect someone who became wealthy at an early age, (b), and who built an economic powerhouse, (e), to make an abrupt turn to helping the masses succeed. His vision is ironic for a wealthy, successful member of the industrial elite along with the likes of J.P. Morgan (paragraph 4). On the other hand, there is no irony to the "vision of free and democratic education" (paragraph 7) from someone from a poor background, (c), who was raised according to the principles of democracy, (d), and who chose to dedicate his fortune to philanthropy, (a).

29. **C** This question requires you to make inferences based on the information you can gain from the excerpt about Carnegie's philanthropic goals and his approach to awarding grants. A case can be made for each answer choice. You're asked how he would *most likely* react, though, so you need to decide which answer presents the strongest case. From Carnegie's successful business background and the accountability and contribution demanded in the Carnegie Formula for library grants (paragraph 7), (C) is the most likely choice. Choice (A) covers only the Corporation's interest in the global economy, and there are stronger centers of economic activity than Caribbean islands where students could learn about business in other countries, (D). Choice (B) focuses only on the democratic idea of free knowledge for everyone, and ignores the accountability Carnegie would demand from the project sponsor.

30. **(a), (b), and (e)**

    If you're not familiar with the word, first you need to figure out from the context what a "meritocracy" is. The excerpt provides some clues. Carnegie wanted his libraries to "provide the public with the tools necessary to succeed, regardless of their socio-economic background" (paragraph 5). He insisted on open access to the books "to provide a democratic approach to education" (paragraph 9). Although he had other philanthropic pursuits, he thought libraries "were the best way to realize his commitment to free education for all" (paragraph 4). The word itself provides clues, too: the root "merit" and the similarity to the more familiar word "aristocracy." What do all of these clues add up to? In a meritocracy, those who merit (or deserve) the privilege rise to the top. Social status and wealth don't matter, as (a) makes clear. Those who succeed will be those who merit success because they can focus their minds (b) on gaining the knowledge they need and motivate themselves (e) to take advantage of the free tools available in Carnegie's libraries. Choices (c) and (d) support, respectively, the ideas of using wealth for a higher purpose and educating the people in a democracy. They don't support the notion of a meritocracy.

31. **B** The length and detail of the discussion about the libraries make it clear that the author's purpose is to emphasize that aspect of Carnegie's life. If the author's purpose were to give equal weight to both of Carnegie's careers, (A), his descriptions of them would have equal weight. They don't. The author mentions Carnegie's other philanthropic activities only in passing (paragraphs 4 and 11). His purpose is to highlight the libraries, not Carnegie's philanthropy in general, (C). Carnegie's upbringing is described even more briefly than his business career, so (D) is incorrect.

32. **(b), (c), and (d)**

    The author keeps returning to Carnegie's determination, (b), to provide "free education for all" (paragraph 4) through a nationwide chain of public libraries. Carnegie never wavers from that goal. Although he didn't invent public libraries, Carnegie expanded the concept significantly. His use of public libraries as the vehicle for delivering his vision of "free and democratic education" (paragraph 7) was innovative, (c), as was his development of the Carnegie Formula for forging partnerships and ensuring accountability from his partners. The Carnegie Formula also reveals his professionalism, (d). Instead of simply handing money over to anyone who asked, Carnegie established a clear set of criteria that successful applicants had to meet. Although Carnegie is described as focused and determined, the author doesn't suggest that these characteristics reached the negative level of controlling, so (a) is incorrect. Carnegie's unwavering dedication to his vision eliminates flexibility, (e,) as one of his characteristics.

33. **A** You need to make an inference here, since the only linkage stated directly in the passage is between open stacks and a "democratic approach to education" (paragraph 9). The open stacks mean that people can (or have to) look through the books themselves and make their own selections. One of the Carnegie quotes says, "*People who are unable to motivate themselves must be content with mediocrity*" (before paragraph 4).

His belief in the importance of self-motivation would explain his preference for open stacks. Even if a man who wanted to start a bakery, for instance, were motivated enough to go to the library to learn how, it would be much easier for him to ask the librarian to find books about the bakery business for him. It takes a higher degree of motivation to find the right section in the library, browse through all of the bakery books, and then select the ones with the most useful information. The other three choices apply to libraries themselves, not to open stacks. Carnegie felt that the libraries would help "foster growing communities" (paragraph 5), (B). His commitment to using his wealth for "things immeasurably higher than itself" (paragraph 4) applies to funding the libraries, (C). Public libraries provide "free education for all" (paragraph 4), (D).

34. **Choice (a) leads to the conclusion in the third box.** Instead of developing "the true genius of the dog" (paragraph 2), teaching the poodle to read will likely result in a hybrid capability ("ingrafting an imitative humanity on a totally different kind of capacity," paragraph 2). **Choice (b) results in the conclusion in the first box.** The ants are "more sagacious [clever or knowledgeable] in proportion as they live more apart from man, and are thrown upon their own resources" (paragraph 2). **Choice (c) leads to the conclusion in the second box.** While the author criticizes humans for reducing horses to "the mechanical condition of locomotive-engines" (paragraph 1), he also admits that if horses were allowed to develop their natural eccentricities without any training, they could present "very serious dangers to life and limb."

35. **B** This question asks about the author's main point. It's summed up in the last sentence: Just as we shouldn't discourage individuality and "milder lunacies" (paragraph 3) in humans, so we shouldn't discourage them in animals and birds, either, because animals and birds might teach us something about humans. Choice (A) is too extreme. On the GED® test, it's wise to be suspicious of an all-or-nothing extreme answer choice. The correct answer is usually toned down by some moderating factor. Here, while the author disagrees with hiding a poodle's natural talents under the human skill of reading (paragraph 2), he also acknowledges that horses allowed to follow nothing but their own eccentricities could be dangerous (paragraph 1). Some human intervention is required. Choice (C) is correct as far as it goes. However, it touches on only part of the author's main point. It ignores the relationship to humans. Choice (D), on the other hand, goes farther than the author intends and is again too extreme. He specifies "harmless insanities" (paragraph 3); he wouldn't condone following dangerous impulses that could harm others.

36. **C** On a quick skim, the wording can sound confusingly similar in these answer choices. You need to have a solid understanding of what the author's thesis is, how the two examples relate to it, and then read the answer choices carefully to decide which one helps him advance it. His thesis is that we should encourage animals (including birds and insects) to develop their own idiosyncrasies (as Mill wants us to do with humans) because the animals could deepen our understanding of human eccentricities. The two examples demonstrate very different approaches and results. In the case of the poodle, Lubbock's attempt to superimpose the human skill of reading on a dog had nothing to do with developing "the true genius of the dog" (paragraph 2). That eliminates (A), since this half of the pair of examples doesn't say anything about the effect of human intervention on the development of the dog's natural eccentricities. The dog didn't develop any. Choice (B) is incorrect because it applies only to the poodle, not to both examples. Lubbock's intervention prevents the dog's expression of natural talents. In the example of the ants, his intervention does the opposite and fosters their natural idiosyncrasies. Choice (D) applies only to the example of the ants, not to both. The ants teach us that different individual talents develop in dealing with the same problem; the dog example teaches us nothing about the development of natural eccentricities. That leaves (C). As the author concludes from the two examples, "we should do more to develop their capacity by stimulating them to meet difficulties by their own resources [the ants] than we can effect by taking their training so completely under our own care [the poodle]" (paragraph 2). The right form of human intervention (as illustrated in the example of the ants) will allow non-humans to

develop natural idiosyncrasies that can teach us something about humans, advancing the author's thesis. The wrong form (as shown by the poodle example) will not. In the example of the poodle, the author's thesis isn't wrong; the method of human intervention is wrong.

37. **A** The author focuses on behavior (animal and human), but does not use the kind of technical language and references to specific scientific studies that one would expect in a piece written for specialists with an advanced education in the subject; for example, the article uses common English names for animals, rather than Latin names for genus and species. His language and the details he includes eliminate the professional, well-educated audiences described in (C) and (D). His repeated comparisons to humans leave out readers whose interest is strictly in training animals, (B).

38. **D** The quote in (D) puts the value of human eccentricity (Mill's point) within the framework of the author's main point. The author claims we should also value eccentricity in animals ("eccentric instinct") because, through it, we might learn something about humans ("eccentric intellect). Choice (A) praises the natural instincts of an entire species rather than the eccentricities of individuals within that group. Mill refers to the eccentricities of individual humans. In (B), the author is simply restating Mill's position, not describing his own adaptation of it. The statement in (C) is too general. Here, the author introduces his extension of Mill's point to animals, but this quote doesn't specify what the "sin" is (discouraging valuable eccentricities).

39. **C** This question asks about the author's point of view and tone. Careful reading of the question stem will ensure that you don't miss the key word "primarily." A couple of answers have some validity, and you need to decide which one describes the author's *main* position. By using Process of Elimination (POE) to narrow down your choices by first eliminating answers that are clearly wrong, you can get rid of (A) and (D). The author frequently voices his own opinions, so he is not being objective, (A). He mentions only one possible danger (the "eccentric horses" in paragraph 1), so he is not acting primarily as an alarm, (D). Now you have only two choices to consider, (B) and (C). He does criticize several misguided human attempts to train and develop animals, (B). However, he voices those criticisms in order to strengthen his main point, summed up in the last sentence: we have a duty to protect "the idiosyncrasies of bird and beast." He is acting as an advocate for extending Mill's position "that we ought to encourage eccentricities in each other" (paragraph 1) beyond humans to animals, birds and insects, so the answer is (C).

40. **A** Did you catch the "*best* describes" in the question stem? And did you notice "*throughout* the excerpt"? You're looking for the "best" description of the author's attitude (so there could be more than one that has some validity) as his attitude is displayed in the excerpt as a whole. The excerpt begins with a summary of Mill's view that we should encourage human eccentricities, and then immediately launches into the author's thesis that this view should be extended to animals too. The author discusses his thesis during the entire excerpt, and then wraps up with "If John Stuart Mill were right...," then "might we not...extend his exhortation..." to "protecting the independent development of the idiosyncrasies of bird and beast, in the hope of finding in them some clew to the various oddities and harmless insanities of human thought and action" (paragraph 3). The author depends on Mill's position to launch his own thesis, acknowledges that his theory hinges on Mill being right, and claims that the results of investigating his ideas could circle back and enhance Mill's theory. From his criticism of the result of stifling eccentricities ("a single dead-level of mediocrity," paragraph 1), the author seems to agree completely with Mill's position, (B). However, he does point out an exception, (C), when he extends Mill's position to animals (the dangerous "eccentric horses" in paragraph 1). So while there is some truth to those two choices, the exception, (C), undercuts the complete agreement, (B). In several spots, the author suggests the need for further testing, (D). For instance, in paragraph 2 he wonders what "important variations of character" we could promote if we encouraged individuality in animals. He also claims that the pigeon's idiosyncrasies "deserve the

most attentive study" (paragraph 3). However, the need for further testing applies to his own theory of extending Mill's position to animals, not to Mill's original position regarding humans. So (D) is incorrect.

41.   **(b) and (c)**

The pigeon story allows the author to tie a non-human eccentricity directly to a human one, (b), illustrating his point that animal eccentricities are worth fostering and studying for the light they could shed on the "oddities and harmless insanities of human thought and action" (paragraph 3). However, the parallel human eccentricity he describes is hardly admirable. He likens the pigeon's efforts to "cultivate the family and parental idea without any corresponding reality" to a human who "can empty religion of its meaning": and "receive nothing but praise for his achievement" (paragraph 3). This particular human eccentricity suggests deceit and lack of integrity. The effect is a challenge, (c), to Mill's view that we have a "sacred duty not to discourage the milder lunacies of human beings" (paragraph 3). As the pigeon story illustrates, human eccentricities can also involve socially unacceptable characteristics that should not be encouraged. Choice (a) is incorrect because the author doesn't defend birds against a claim that only animals are worth studying. At times he groups animals, birds, and even insects together as "our friends of the lower races," (paragraph 2), while at other times he refers to one of the three categories individually. The author doesn't make the blanket claim that birds can develop eccentricities on their own, (d). He simply relates the story of one bird that apparently did. The pigeon isn't portrayed as dangerous, (e).

42. **C**   The author is not only narrating an episode in the life of a historical figure, but also developing an understanding of her character by describing what she thought and felt during that episode. There is some truth to each of these answers, and you don't want to spend too long puzzling over one question. What's the trick in a case such as this? Instead of looking for the one "right" answer, start by looking for the answer that is *least* right, narrow your choices by getting rid of that one, look for the next least right answer, and so on. This approach, called Process of Elimination or POE, will lead you to the correct answer choice more quickly and accurately. The first to go is (D). It's clear O'Malley wasn't concerned about the captured sailors, but we're not given enough information to know whether she cared about anyone else. Next is (A). O'Malley was ruthless in promising "instant death" (paragraph 2) to everyone if one man failed to hit the target ship with the next cannon shot, but not "utterly" ruthless because she "agreed that they should not be slain" (paragraph 7) while she gave the cannon operator a second chance. That leaves (B) and (C). O'Malley was a keen observer ("Seeing from their look that they were likely to do as they said..."), but here she is showing her insight into captured prisoners, not her own crewmembers, as (B) specifies. So you can eliminate (B), and you're left with (C), O'Malley's understanding of the debilitating effects of terror.

43. **A**   Choices (C), (D) and even (B) might well be true. However, those choices all describe a possible condition of the target ship. It's a possible event—the ship escaping, (A)—that causes O'Malley to take action and search for a prisoner to operate the cannons.

44.   **(a) and (f)**

Careful reading of the question stem is important here. With the exception of (c), which refers to the battle after O'Malley's crew boarded the target ship, all of the answer choices reveal something about O'Malley's character. The question asks specifically about leadership style, though. Choices (b) and (d) show only that she has difficulty controlling her anger at times. Choice (e) reveals her crew's reaction to her leadership; it does not indicate that she deliberately leads by example. That leaves (a) and (f). As a leader, O'Malley is authoritarian, (a), ordering her crew not to kill the rest of the prisoners. She also demonstrates respect for at least one trusted follower when she shares her plan with Tibbot instead of simply ordering him to the helm without explanation, (f).

45. **B** This question asks you to make an inference about a hypothetical event based on the actual information given in the passage. Details in the passage reveal that O'Malley demanded absolute obedience and took extreme action when she didn't receive it, so she would be unlikely to listen to Tibbot's suggestion, (A), let alone take the time to discuss its merits with him, (C). On the other hand, she trusted him enough to explain her plan to him, so she probably would not think he deserved immediate death, (D), as she thought the disobedient prisoners did. Choice (B) is the most likely. O'Malley simply told Tibbot her plan. She didn't ask for his opinion or ask whether he had a better idea, so she probably wouldn't even have let him finish and would have gone ahead with her original plan.

46. **(b) and (d)**

It's important to read the question stem carefully and understand the task it's setting for you. A GED® test question about ideas and supporting details usually asks you to identify the details that support a specific idea. Here the order is reversed: The question cites a detail and asks which different ideas it supports. The word "obstinate" suggests the idea that the Spanish sailors were determined not to lose the battle, (b). "Terrible" and "obstinate" suggest that O'Malley's crew met their match in the sailors of the ship they boarded, and the outcome wouldn't be easy to predict, (d). A "terrible" and "obstinate" battle doesn't suggest a crew that was easily defeated, eliminating (a). Nothing indicates that the Spanish crew knew who fired the cannon that destroyed their mainmast, (f). There is no indication that O'Malley or her crew were surprised by either the Spanish sailors' fighting ability, (c), or their numbers, (e).

47. **D** Again, you need to read the question carefully so you understand the task and so you don't miss the "not." From the information given about O'Malley's crew—for instance, their eagerness to kill all of the first cannon operator's companions (paragraph 5)—it would *not* be reasonable to infer that they would hesitate to damage a ship they were pursuing, (D). The excerpt doesn't explain why O'Malley needed to search through the prisoners in order to recruit someone to fire the cannon. However, it *is* reasonable to infer that she had to turn to the prisoners because her own men couldn't do the job, (B), perhaps because Spanish cannons were so different from the Irish cannons they knew, (A). After she killed the "master of the ordnance," O'Malley asked for "the most skilful cannoneer" (paragraph 7), which supports the inference that specialized training might be required, (C).

48. **B** This question asks you to determine the author's purpose. In order to do that, you need to consider his tone and point of view, the details he includes, and the way he describes them. The author's focus on O'Malley, together with the details he adds about her reactions to events, the way her men follow her without question, and the fear she inspires in the prisoners are designed to reveal her fearless, ruthless, clever character, (B). This is more than a simple objective account of a historical event, (A). The first-person narrator is easy to miss in this excerpt (paragraph 10). The objectivity of a first-person narrator is always suspect, and his presence provides an additional clue that this isn't simply an objective historical narration. It's possible the author is embellishing historical fact, (C), but the excerpt doesn't contain any evidence to support that inference. There is no hint of a critical tone, or evidence that the Spanish would be any less bloodthirsty and violent than the Irish if their positions were reversed, (D). In fact, the Spanish captain's devious attempt to kill O'Malley (paragraph 14) suggests they might be less honorable.

49. **C** Tibbot ties together the theme of trust, demonstrating that he has O'Malley's trust at the beginning, and that he is worthy of it at the end, when the Spanish captain betrays her trust by pretending to surrender but instead trying to kill her. The author doesn't say whether Tibbot was at the helm until her crew boarded the Spanish galleon, (A); it's not clear whether he is associated with a theme of victory. Choices (B) and (D) are true enough. However, they don't associate Tibbot with anything besides his name.

50.   The option that correctly completes the sentence for each "Select" option:

Drop-Down Item 1: **Frequently confused words and wordiness**

Option 2 is correct. The words "ensure" and "insure" are often confused. "Ensure" means to guarantee or make sure—an appropriate desire for the health of a lilac bush. "Insure," on the other hand, refers to a formal contract to cover the owner's financial loss in case of accident—hardly necessary for a common plant.

That eliminates options 1 and 4, which both use "insure." Option 3 uses the correct word ("ensure"), but is unnecessarily wordy. Since the customer bought the bush and is reading the planting and care instructions, one can assume that he or she "wants to" make sure the plant grows into a healthy specimen.

Drop-Down Item 2: **Sentence structure, punctuation, and verb form**

Option 1 is correct. The semicolon between the two complete thoughts (the gravel not hindering the plant's roots and the roots growing through it) emphasizes the close connection between the two. A period after "growing" would be acceptable, since each thought forms a complete sentence with a subject and a verb. However, a period would disconnect the two thoughts more than the semicolon does.

Option 2 uses an incorrect form of the verb (the infinitive "to grow"). Option 3 is a mind-numbing run-on sentence destined to put readers to sleep. Option 4 includes a sentence fragment ("Finding their way around the gravel"). The fragment has no subject and no verb.

Drop-Down Item 3: **Pronoun antecedent and apostrophe**

Option 2 is correct. It's clear that the lilac is getting the water, and there is an explicit connection between the lower surface and nourishment with water.

Two things are wrong with option 1. First, it contains the common error of putting an apostrophe in the possessive pronoun "its." With an apostrophe, "it's" is a contraction for "it is," not a possessive pronoun. In this correct example—"It's unfortunate the tree lost so many of its leaves"—the first word is a contraction which could be replaced with "It is," while the second instance of "its" is a possessive pronoun referring to the tree, and could not be replaced with "it is." The second problem with option 1 is an unclear antecedent (the noun to which the pronoun "it" refers). Whose new home will get water? The Triple Mix's? The hole's? The yard's? Anything but the lilac, which *should* be the antecedent of "it." In option 3, the possessive pronoun "its" is correct. However, the antecedent isn't clear. Is the lilac getting its own water, or is it taking water that belongs to the Triple Mix, the hole, or the yard? Option 4 is another instance of an unclear antecedent. So water will run into what? As these incorrect options show, an unclear pronoun antecedent can make your writing very confusing for readers.

Drop-Down Item 4: **Dangling modifier, awkward wording, and transition**

Option 3 is correct. It's clear who is following the instructions ("you"), and there is a smooth transition between the instructions and the beautiful plant.

Option 1 is a common error called a dangling modifier, and it makes your writing difficult for readers to follow. The introductory phrase ("By following these instructions...") must modify (describe or refer to) the subject of the main clause. It doesn't here. This dangling modifier has the plant (the subject of the main clause), not the customer, following the instructions. To correct this error, either change the subject of the main clause to match the introductory phrase ("By following these instructions, **you** will have a bush that will beautify...") or change the introductory phrase to an introductory clause with a verb and a subject that takes the action ("If **you follow** these instructions, your new plant will beautify..."). The wording ("With these instructions followed,") is awkward in option 2. The instructions have been followed, but it's not clear by whom. In addition, the wording doesn't match the conversational tone of the rest of the instructions, where the customer is directly addressed as "you." Option 4 lacks a smooth transition from the preceding instructions. There is a cause-and-effect relationship between following the instructions and having a bush that will beautify the customer's yard. Here, a beautiful plant is abruptly introduced with no connection to the planting and care instructions.

MATHEMATICAL REASONING

Part 1

1.

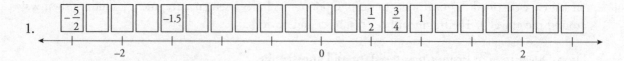

Place the numbers given on the number line. Start by determining the scale of the number line. The number 0 is the in the middle of the number line. The number 2 is placed four intervals to the right of 0. Since four intervals represent a distance of 2, each interval represents a distance of $\frac{2}{4} = \frac{1}{2}$. Place $\frac{1}{2}$ one tick mark to the right of 0. Place 1 one tick mark to the right of $\frac{1}{2}$. Determine the placement of $\frac{3}{4}$. Since the numerator is less than the denominator, it is less than 1. Compare it to $\frac{1}{2}$ using common denominator. Since $\frac{1}{2} = \frac{1 \times 2}{2 \times 2} = \frac{2}{4}$, it is less than $\frac{3}{4}$. Since $\frac{3}{4}$ is between $\frac{1}{2}$ and 1, place it over the interval between the tick marks for $\frac{1}{2}$ and 1. Now place the negative numbers. Since the tick marks are placed $\frac{1}{2}$ apart, $-\frac{5}{2}$ is 5 tick marks to the left of 0. Since $-1.5 = -1\frac{1}{2}$, it is one tick mark to the left of -1. Since 1 is two tick marks to the right of 0, -1 is two tick marks to the left of 0, making -1.5 three tick marks to the left of 0.

2. **57.53**

When subtracting decimals, line up the decimal points, bring down the decimal point, and then treat it like normal subtraction.

$$234.34$$
$$- \underline{176.81}$$

Subtract 1 from 4 to get 3. Since 8 cannot be subtracted from 3, turn 3 into 13 and 4 into 3. Subtract 8 from 13 to get 5. Since 6 cannot be subtracted from 3 turn 3 into 13 and 3 into 2. Subtract 6 from 13 to get 7. Since 7 cannot be subtracted from 2, turn 2 into 12 and 2 into 1. Subtract 7 from 12 to get 5. Subtract 1 from 1 to get 0.

$$\begin{array}{r} {}^{1\ 12\ 13\ 13} \\ 2\ 3\ 4\ .\ 3\ 4 \\ - \underline{1\ 7\ 6\ .\ 8\ 1} \\ 5\ 7\ .\ 5\ 3 \end{array}$$

3. **B** The question asks to multiply and divide fractions. To multiply fractions, just line them up and multiply the numerators together and the denominators together; when you divide fractions, though, you need to rewrite the division as multiplication, by "flipping" (or using the reciprocal) of the final fraction, and then multiplying. Therefore, $\frac{2}{3} \cdot \frac{25}{2} \div \frac{10}{3} = \frac{2}{3} \cdot \frac{25}{2} \cdot \frac{3}{10}$ (because you switched the division to multiplication, and flipped the $\frac{10}{3}$ to get $\frac{3}{10}$). To multiply fractions, multiply the numerators and denominators separately. To simplify this, find ways to cancel. None of the fractions can be reduced normally. However, in multiplication, a numerator of one fraction can be reduced by a denominator of another fraction. Cancel the 2 from $\frac{2}{3}$ with the 2 from $\frac{25}{2}$ and the 3 from $\frac{2}{3}$ with the 3 from $\frac{3}{10}$ to get $\frac{1}{1} \cdot \frac{25}{1} \cdot \frac{1}{10} = \frac{25}{10}$. Divide top and bottom by 5 to get $\frac{5}{2}$. The answer is (B).

4. **B** To divide fractions, flip the bottom and multiply. Therefore, $\frac{\frac{2}{3}}{\frac{5}{6}} = \frac{2}{3} \times \frac{6}{5}$. Multiply straight across to get $\frac{12}{15}$. Divide top and bottom by 3 to get $\frac{4}{5}$. The answer is (B).

5. **A** By definition, the absolute value is the distance a number is from 0. Therefore, the distance between P and 0 on the number line is $|P|$.

Part 2

6. **B** The question provides a rate, so use the rate formula, $d = rt$, where d is the distance, r is the rare or speed, and t is the time. Plug $d = 3.47 \times 10^3$ and $r = 4.6 \times 10^2$ into the equation to get $3.47 \times 10^3 = (4.6 \times 10^2)t$. Divide both sides by (4.6×10^2) to get $t = \dfrac{3.47 \times 10^3}{4.6 \times 10^2}$. Divide 10^3 by 10^2 using the division-subtract rule (when you divide numbers with the same base, subtract the exponents) to get $t = \dfrac{3.47 \times 10}{4.6}$. Simplify the numerator to get $t = \dfrac{34.7}{4.6}$. Divide this using the calculator to get $t \approx 7.5$. The answer is (B).

7. **2 and 1**

   To solve a quadratic, set one side equal to 0. Subtract 5 from both sides to get $x^2 - 3x + 2 = 0$. Factor the left side of the equation. Find two factors of 2 with a sum of -3. To get a positive product and a negative sum, both factors must be negative. The only two negative integer factors of 2 are -1 and -2. Since these do have a sum of -3, the factored form of the equation must be $(x - 2)(x - 1) = 0$. When a product is set equal to 0, set both factors equal to 0 to get $x - 2 = 0$ and $x - 1 = 0$. If $x - 2 = 0$, add 2 to both sides to get $x = 2$. If $x - 1 = 0$, add 1 to both sides to get $x = 1$.

8. **Length: 3, Width: 16**

   The question says that the area of the rectangle is 48. Since area is determined by the formula $A = lw$, find pairs of factors of 48. Determine which ones make the perimeter 38. The pairs of factors of 48 are 1 and 48, 2 and 24, 3 and 16, 4 and 12, and 6 and 8. The perimeter of a rectangle is determined by the formula $P = 2l + 2w$. Plug in each pair of factors, and eliminate any that do not make the perimeter 38. If $l = 1$ and $w = 48$, then $P = 2(1) + 2(48) = 98$. Eliminate this possibility. If $l = 2$ and $w = 24$, then $P = 2(2) + 2(24) = 52$. Eliminate this possibility. If $l = 3$ and $w = 16$, then $P = 2(3) + 2(16) = 38$. Therefore, this is a possible value for the length and width. Since the length is less than the width, the length must be 3 and the width must be 16.

9. **A** In probability, the word *and* translates to multiplication. The question asks for the probability of rain on *Monday, Tuesday, and Wednesday*, so multiply the individual probabilities. The individual probabilities of rain on Monday, Tuesday, and Wednesday are 30%, 60%, and 50%, respectively. Put these in fraction form and multiply to get $\dfrac{30}{100} \times \dfrac{60}{100} \times \dfrac{50}{100} = \dfrac{3}{10} \times \dfrac{6}{10} \times \dfrac{5}{10} = \dfrac{3}{10} \times \dfrac{3}{5} \times \dfrac{1}{2} = \dfrac{9}{100}$. The fraction $\dfrac{9}{100}$ is equal to 9%. The correct answer is (A).

10. **D** The vertical axes are labeled as distance from home. Since Roberta is driving from home to work, the distance from home has to begin at 0. Eliminate (B) and (C), since they don't start at 0. Nothing in the question indicates that Roberta goes back home, but (A) returns to 0 in the end. Eliminate (A). Only one choice remains. To understand why (D) is correct, notice that the graph in always increasing. This is correct since Roberta is going toward work the entire time. Also, notice that the slope in the first portion of the graph is higher than in the second portion of the graph. Since slope corresponds with rate, this is consistent with the information in the graph that says her speed slows down once she's halfway to work. The answer is (D).

11. **29** To find the perimeter, add the length of each side. The sum of the lengths of the sides is 4 + 3 + 5 + 4 + 4 + 3 + 6 = 29.

12. **B** Translate the expression. *The square of 2* translates to 2^2. *The cube root of 7* translates to $\sqrt[3]{7}$. Therefore, the correct answer is (B).

13. **C** Speed is a type of rate: the rate of change in the distance traveled over time. On the line, the rate of change is represented by the slope. Therefore, to get the speed, find the slope using $m = \dfrac{y_2 - y_1}{x_2 - x_1}$. Find two points on the line. The line goes through the origin, which is the intersection of the x- and y-axes. This point has the coordinates (0, 0). The line also goes through the point (5, 200). Plug these into the formula to get $m = \dfrac{200 - 0}{5 - 0} = \dfrac{200}{5} = 40$. Therefore, the slope is 40 and the speed is 40 miles per hour. The correct answer is (C).

14. **B** The question asks for the triangle's perimeter, which is the sum of the lengths of its sides. The triangle shown is a right triangle. Therefore, use the Pythagorean Theorem, which is $a^2 + b^2 = c^2$, where a and b are the length of the two legs (short sides) of the right triangle and c is the length of the hypotenuse (long side). According to the figure, one the of legs is 12 and the hypotenuse is 20. Plug these into the equation to get $12^2 + b^2 = 20^2$. Square 12 and 20 to get $144 + b^2 = 400$. Subtract 144 from both sides to get $b^2 = 256$. Take the square root of both sides to get $b = 16$. Therefore, the perimeter is 12 + 16 + 20 = 48. The correct answer is (B).

15. **B** To divide polynomials, factor the numerator and the denominator and cancel common factors. The denominator is easier to factor, so start there. Since both terms in $2x - 4$ are divisible by 2, factor 2 to get $2(x - 2)$. Now factor the numerator. The numerator is a quadratic expression in the form $ax^2 + bx + c$. Since $a = 3$, the coefficients on the x terms in the factors must have a product of 3. The only positive integer factors of 3 are 1 and 3, so set up $(3x \quad)(x \quad)$. Since $c = 2$, the two constant terms in the factors must have a product of 2. Since b is negative, the two constant terms must be negative. Therefore, the only possible integers are –1 and –2. The sum of the products of the inner and outer terms must be $-7x$.

    To get this –2 must be multiplied by $3x$ and –1 must be multiplied by 1, so the factors are $(3x - 1)(x - 2)$. In factored form, the fraction is $\dfrac{(3x - 1)(x - 2)}{2(x - 2)}$. Cancel $(x - 2)$ to get $\dfrac{(3x - 1)}{2}$. This is not a choice, so divide both terms in the numerator by 2 to get $1.5x - 0.5$. The correct answer is (B).

16. **C** According to the figure, the side of the hexagon is 4. To get the area, plug $s = 4$ into the given formula to get $A = \dfrac{3\sqrt{3}}{2}(4)^2 = \dfrac{3\sqrt{3}}{2}(16) = 3\sqrt{3}(8) = 24\sqrt{3}$. The answer is (C).

17. **C** Since the coefficients on y have the same absolute value, stack and add.

$$
\begin{array}{l}
2x + 3y = 7 \\
\underline{4x - 3y = 5} \\
6x \quad\quad = 12
\end{array}
$$

Divide both sides by 6 to get $x = 2$. The question, however, asks for the value of y rather than x, so plug this value into one of the original two equations and solve for y. Plug $x = 2$ into the first equation to get $2(2) + 3y = 7$. Simplify to get $4 + 3y = 7$. Subtract 4 from both sides to get $3y = 3$. Divide both sides by 3 to get $y = 1$. The correct answer is (C).

18. **B** The question asks for the average cost per loaf. To find the average, divide the total cost by the number of loaves. The customer buys 4 small loaves and 6 large loaves, so there is a total of $4 + 6 = 10$ loaves. To get the total cost, find the total costs of the small loaves and the large loaves separately. The small loaves cost $2 each, so 4 small loaves cost a total of $2 \times 4 = \$8$. The large loaves cost $3.50 each, so 6 large loaves costs $3.50 \times 6 = \$21$. Therefore, the total cost of all the loaves is $\$8 + \$21 = \$29$ and, the average cost per loaf is $\frac{\$29}{10} = \$2.90$. The correct answer is (B).

19. **C** Find the maximum values of both functions. The highest value of $f(x)$, which corresponds with the y-coordinate, on the table is 0, so the y-coordinate of the highest value of f is 0. Go to the graph to find the maximum value of g. Since the graph of g is a downward-facing parabola, the maximum value occurs at the vertex, which is the point at which the graph changes direction. This occurs at the point $(2, 10)$. Therefore, the y-coordinate of the maximum value of g is 10. The question asks for the average of these two, which is the sum divided by the number of numbers. Since there are 2 numbers with a sum of $0 + 10 = 10$, the average is $10 \div 2 = 5$. The answer is (C).

20. **B** To determine which measurement would change, start with the easier measurements. The mode is the number that occurs the most often. According to the table, the number 32 occurs three times and no other number occurs as many times. Therefore, 32 is the mode. Adding another 32 to the data won't change the mode. Eliminate (C). The range is the difference between the greatest and the least element of the list. The greatest element is 47 and the least element is 21. Adding a 32 to the set will change neither the greatest nor the least element, so the range would not change. Eliminate (D). The median is the middle number. If there is an even number of numbers, the median is the average of the middle two. According to the table, the middle two are 30 and 32, so the median is 31. If a 32 were to be added to the list, that would shift the middle number to 32. Therefore, the median would change. There is no need to continue. However, to see why the average would not change, find the average of the original set by adding all the numbers in the table to get 384 and dividing by the number of numbers, which is 12, to get $384 \div 12 = 32$. When a number is added to a list that is equal to the average (mean), the average does not change. Eliminate (A). The answer is (B).

21. **D** A rational expression is undefined when the denominator is 0. Therefore, set the denominator equal to 0 to get $x^2 - 6x + 9 = 0$. Factor the left side. Two factors of 9 must have a sum of -6. These are -3 and -3. Therefore, $(x - 3)(x - 3) = 0$. Set both factors equal to 0. The two factors are the same, so there is only a need for one equation: $x - 3 = 0$. Add 3 to both sides to get $x = 3$. The correct answer is (D).

22. **C** When working with a circle graph, all the percentages listed are of the same total number, so work with the percentages as much as possible. According to the graph, 43% of the budget was devoted to rent and 11% of the budget was devoted to transportation. Therefore, the percent more money spent on rent was $43\% - 11\% = 32\%$ of the total budget. The total budget is $2,500, so 32% of this is $\frac{32}{100} \times 2500 = \frac{32}{100} \times \frac{2500}{1} = \frac{32}{1} \times \frac{25}{1} = 800$. The answer is (C).

23. **D** To find a parallel line, use the fact that parallel lines have equal slopes. To find the slope of a line, get the equation into the form $y = mx + b$, where m is the slope and b is the y-intercept. Start with the original equation, $20x + 5y = -10$. Subtract $20x$ from both sides to get $5y = -20x - 10$. Divide both sides by 5 to get $y = -4x - 2$. Therefore, the slope of the line is -4. Now, go through the answer choices until you find one for which $m = -4$. In (A), add $4x$ to both sides to get $y = 4x + 5$. The slope is $+4$ rather than -4, so eliminate (A). In (B), subtract x from both sides to get $-4y = -x - 2$. Divide both sides by -4 to get $y = 1/4x + 1/2$. Since the slope is $1/4$, eliminate (B). In (C), subtract $12x$ from both sides to get $4y = -12x + 4$. Divide both sides by 4 to get $y = -3x + 1$. Since the slope is -3, eliminate (C). In (D), subtract $16x$ from both sides to get $4y = -16x + 12$. Divide both sides by 4 to get $y = -4x + 3$. Since the slope is -4, the correct answer is (D).

24. **C** To find the area of the shaded region, subtract the area of the unshaded region from the total area. The total area is the area of the square. To find the area of a square, use the formula $A = s^2$ with s representing the side of the square. The question says that the side of the square is 8, so plug in $s = 8$ to get $A = 8^2 = 64$. Now, find the area of the unshaded region, which is the circle. To find the area of a circle, use the formula, $A = \pi r^2$ with r representing the radius of the circle. When a circle is inscribed in a square, the side of the square is equal to the diameter of the circle. Since the side of the square is 8, the diameter of the circle is 8. The radius is always half the diameter, so the radius is 4. Plug $r = 4$ into the formula for area of a circle to get $A = \pi(4)^2 = 16\pi$. Subtract the area of the unshaded region from the total area to get $64 - 16\pi$. The answer is (C).

25. **C** To determine percent increase, use the formula $\dfrac{difference}{original} \times 100$. Because this is a percent *increase*, the *original* is the smaller number, which is the sales number for Monday. Since about 450 were sold on Monday, set this as the *original*. The *difference* is the difference between the number sold on Friday and the number sold on Monday. Since the sales are Friday were about 650, the *difference* is $650 - 450 = 200$. Plug these into the formula to get $\dfrac{200}{450} \times 100 = 44.4$. The question says *approximate*, so select the closest answer choice. The correct answer is (C).

26. **D** The equation of a line can be put into the form $y = mx + b$, where m is the slope and b is the y-intercept. To find the slope, use the formula $m = \dfrac{y_2 - y_1}{x_2 - x_1}$. Let $(x_1, y_1) = (2, 4)$ and $(x_2, y_2) = (1, -3)$ to get $m = \dfrac{-3 - 4}{1 - 2} = \dfrac{-7}{-1} = 7$. Plug this into the equation to get $y = 7x + b$. Now, plug one of the two points into the equation and solve for b. Use $(2, 4)$ to get $4 = 7(2) + b$. Simplify to get $4 = 14 + b$. Subtract 14 from both sides to get $-10 = b$. Substitute this back into the equation to get $y = 7x - 10$. The correct answer is (D).

27. **B** The question gives the surface area of a sphere, so use the formula, $SA = 4\pi r^2$. Plug $SA = 361\pi$ into the formula to get $361\pi = 4\pi r^2$. Divide both sides by π to get $361 = 4r^2$. Divide both sides by 4 to get $90.25 = r^2$. Take the square root of both sides to get $r = 9.5$. The question asks for the volume, so plug $r = 9.5$ into the formula $V = \frac{4}{3}\pi r^3$ to get $V = \frac{4}{3}\pi(9.5)^3 \approx 3{,}591$. The question says closest, so select the closest answer choice. The answer is (B).

28. **D** The markup is the percent increase from the price the store pays for an item to the price at which the store sells the item. The store buys a pound of grapes for $2 and sells them at a 30% markup. Since 30% of $2 is $\frac{30}{100} \times \$2 = \frac{\$60}{100} = \$0.60$, the store sells a pound of grapes for $2.00 + $0.60 = $2.60. The customer, therefore, buy two pounds for 2 × $2.60 = $5.20. The answer is (D).

29. **A** To subtract polynomials, distribute the minus sign and then combine like terms. Distribute the negative to get $2x^3 - 3x + 2 - 3x^3 + 5x^2 + 7x$. Group like terms to get $(2x^3 - 3x^3) + 5x^2 + (-3x + 7x) + 2$. Combine like terms to get $-x^3 + 5x^2 + 4x + 2$. The answer is (A).

30. **C** In order for a relationship to be a function, there must be a unique output for every input. Since the question asks for which table is NOT a function, select the answer for which there is an input with more than one output. In (A) and (B), each input (i.e., x-value) is listed only once. Therefore, there is no possible way for any of them to have more than one output. Eliminate (A) and (B). In (C), $x = 1$ is listed twice. In one case, $f(x) = 3$ and, in the other case, $f(x) = 4$. Since there are two outputs for $x = 1$, this is NOT a function. Check (D) to be sure. In (D), $x = -1$ is listed as an input twice. However, in both cases, the corresponding $f(x)$ is 4. Therefore, there is only one output and this is a function. Eliminate (D). The answer is (C).

31. **12** To get the number of ways that Bailey can make an outfit that consists of one shirt, one pair of shorts, and one pair of shoes, multiply the number of options for each. There are 3 shirts, 2 pairs of shorts, and 2 pairs of shoes, so multiply 3 × 2 × 2 = 12.

32. **C** The question asks for the original price of a dress that has been discounted by 20%. Since the 20% is taken from the original price, plug in the answers. Start with one of the middle choices. Since (C) is easier to work with than (B), start with (C). If the original price of the dress is $60, the price is discounted by 20% of $60, which is $\frac{20}{100} \times \$60 = \$12$. Therefore, the discounted price is $60 − $12 = $48. Since this is consistent with the information in the question, this is correct. The answer is (C).

33.

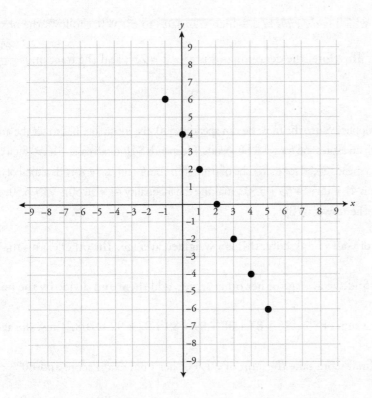

The equation of the line is in the form $y = mx + b$, where m is the slope and b is the y-intercept. The y-intercept is the point at which the line crosses the y-axis and the point at which $x = 0$. Therefore, the line crosses the y-axis at (0, 4). Fill in this point. The slope is –2. The slope is $\dfrac{change\ in\ y}{change\ in\ x}$. Since the slope is negative, the function is decreasing. Since the absolute value is 2, the y-coordinate decreases 2 for every increase of 1 in the x-coordinate. Therefore, also fill in (1, 2), (2, 0), (3, –2), (4, –4), and (5, –6). Also, remember to reverse direction. For every decrease in the x-coordinate by 1, the y-coordinate must increase by 2. Therefore, start from (0, 4) and also fill in (–1, 6). These are the only points that also fit on the graph provided, so stop here.

34. **D** Translate into an algebraic expression. *The quotient* translates to division, so the result will be a fraction. The numerator is the first part, which is *the sum of the square of x and y*. The phrase *the sum of* translates to addition. The first term is what follows, which is *the square of x*, which translates to x^2. The second term is what follows *and*, which is *y*. Therefore, the numerator is $x^2 + y$. The denominator is what follows the next *and*, which is *the product of the cube of z and 2*. The phrase *the product of* translates to multiplication.

The first factor is what follows, which is *the cube of z*, which translates to z^3. What follows the next *and* is the second factor, which is 2. Therefore, the denominator is $z^3 \times 2 = 2z^3$, and the fraction is $\frac{x^2 + y}{2z^3}$. The correct answer is (D).

35. **B** David has $300 budgeted for art supplies. Since the most he can spend is 300, the inequality has to set the amount that he spends ≤ 300. Come up with an expression for what he spends. He spends $41 for an easel, $16.50 for a canvas, and $53 for a set of brushes. He also spends $5.50 for each tube of paint. If he buys c tubes, he spends a total of 5.50c$ on paint. Therefore, the total spent is $41 + 16.50 + 53 + 5.50c$, making the inequality $41 + 16.50 + 53 + 5.50c \leq 300$. This is a choice, so do not simplify. The answer is (B).

36. **C** Since final exam is worth 20% of Gail's final score, this is a weighted average. The other exams make up the other 80% of her score. To find the average of her other scores, add them and divide by the number of scores. The other scores have a sum of $85 + 86 + 87 + 88 + 89 + 89 + 92 + 92 = 708$. Thus, the average is $708 \div 8 = 88.5$. To find the final score take the sum of 20% of her final exam score and 80% of the average of the other scores. This average has to be 90, so set up the equation $\frac{80}{100} \times 88.5 + \frac{20}{100} F = 90$. Since $\frac{80}{100} \times 88.5 = 70.8$, the left side simplifies to $70.8 + \frac{20}{100} F = 90$. Subtract 70.8 from both sides to get $\frac{20}{100} F = 19.2$. Reduce the fraction on the left side by 20 to get $\frac{1}{5} F = 19.2$. Multiply both sides by 5 to get $F = 96$. The answer is (C).

37. **A** Because numbers with same base are divided, subtract the exponents to get $a^{(7-4)} b^{(3-2)} c^{(1-5)} = a^3 b^1 c^{-4} = a^3 b c^{-4}$. The correct answer is (A).

38. **Greater than**

The rate of change of a linear function is equal to its slope. The equation for g is the form $y = mx + b$. In this form the slope is equal to m. Therefore, the slope of $g(x)$ is $\frac{3}{2}$. To determine the slope of f, pick two points from the table and use the slope formula $m = \frac{y_2 - y_1}{x_2 - x_1}$. Two easy points from the table to use are (0, 1) and (1, 3). Plug these into the slope formula to get $m = \frac{y_2 - y_1}{x_2 - x_1} = \frac{3 - 1}{1 - 0} = \frac{2}{1} = 2$, which is greater than the slope of g.

39. **B** The axis of symmetry is the line for which what is to the left of the line is a mirror image of what is to the right of the line. The graph is of a parabola. In a parabola, the axis of symmetry goes through its vertex, the point at which the graph changes from increasing to decreasing (or vice versa). According to the graph, this occurs at $(1, -4)$. The axis of symmetry of a parabolic function is always a vertical line, and vertical lines are represented by $x = c$ for some constant c. Since the x-coordinate of the vertex is 1, the axis of symmetry is $x = 1$. The answer is (B).

40. **2** The question asks for what number can be added to the table so that it shows a function. A function is a relationship for which every input has a unique output. Therefore, the number that is added must not be one for which an input is given multiple outputs. The missing spot on the table is in the input column, so don't repeat an input if it has a different output listed elsewhere. Since the corresponding output to the missing input is 7, an input cannot be repeated if it has an output other than 7. $-3, -2, 0, 4$, and 9 are all listed on the table with outputs other than 7. Therefore, if any of them are added to the table, that input would have more than one output. Eliminate these choices. 2 is not listed elsewhere on the table as an input. Therefore, if it were to be added to the table, it would have a unique output. Thus, the table would show a function. The answer is 2.

41. **D** To find the volume of the dollhouse, find the volumes of the rectangular prism and the pyramid separately, and then get the sum. The volume of a rectangular prism can be found using the formula $V = lwh$. The prism has dimensions 4 ft by 2 ft by 3 ft, so plug these into the formula to get $V = (4)(2)(3) = 24$. The volume of a pyramid can be found using the formula $V = 1/3Bh$, where B is the area of the base and h is the height. According to the figure, the height of the entire dollhouse is 4.5 ft. Since the height of the rectangular solid is 3, the height of the pyramid is 4.5 ft $-$ 3 ft $= 1.5$ ft. The area of the pyramid's base can be found using the formula $A = lw$, with the same length and width as that of the rectangular prism. Plug $l = 4$ and $w = 2$ to get $A = (4)(2) = 8$. Plug this into the volume formula for B to get $V = 1/3(8)(1.5)$ $= 4$. Add the volume of the prism to the volume of the pyramid to get $24 + 4 = 28$. The answer is (D).

42. **C** To find the slope of a line, get the equation into the form $y = mx + b$, where m is the slope and b is the y-intercept. Start with the given equation, $3x - 4y = 7$. Subtract $3x$ from both sides to get $-4y = -3x + 7$. Divide both sides by -4 to get $y = \frac{3}{4}x - \frac{7}{4}$. The question asks for the slope, which is m, which is $\frac{3}{4}$. The answer is (C).

43. **C** Translate the question into an algebraic expression. The phrase *the sum of* translates to addition. *The cube of* translates to $(\quad)^3$, filling the parentheses with whatever comes next. What comes next is *three times* x, which translates to $3x$. Thus, so far, the expression is $(3x)^3 +$. Next is *twice*, which translates to $2(\quad)$, filling the parentheses with whatever comes next. What comes next is *the square of* y, which translates to y^2. Thus, the expression translates to $(3x)^3 + 2(y^2)$. This is not a choice, so simplify it. For $2(y^2)$, simply multiply to get $2y^2$. For $(3x)^3$, apply to exponent to both factors to get $3^3x^3 = 27x^3$. Thus, the simplified version of the expression is $27x^3 + 2y^2$. The answer is (C).

44. **D** To solve an inequality, isolate x. Start by distributing the 3 on the right side of the inequality to get $2x - 3 < 3x + 4.2$. Subtract $3x$ from both sides to get $-x - 3 < 4.2$. Add 3 to both sides to get $-x < 7.2$. Divide both sides by -1. When multiplying or dividing by a negative, flip the inequality sign. Therefore, the result is $x > -7.2$. There is only one choice that is greater than -7.2. The correct answer is (D).

45. **C** To answer this question, you need to understand the rules for negative exponents and fractional exponents.

Negative exponents indicate reciprocals: $a^{-b} = \dfrac{1}{a^b}$. Therefore, $x^{-\frac{3}{2}} = \dfrac{1}{x^{\frac{3}{2}}}$. Fractional exponents relate to

roots. The numerator of the fraction remains as the exponent and the denominator becomes the index of

the root: $a^{\frac{m}{n}} = \sqrt[n]{a^m}$. Therefore, $x^{\frac{3}{2}} = \sqrt{x^3}$ and $x^{-\frac{3}{2}} = \dfrac{1}{x^{\frac{3}{2}}} = \dfrac{1}{\sqrt{x^3}}$. The answer is (C).

46.

r	A
4	16π
6	36π
1	π
3	9π
2	4π
7	49π

The formula for the area of a circle is $A = \pi r^2$. Go find the missing boxes in the table. The first missing box is to the left of 36π. Plug this in for the area to get $36\pi = \pi r^2$. Divide both sides by π to get $36 = r^2$. Take the square root of both sides to get $6 = r$. Fill in 6 for that box. The next missing box is the one next to 1. Plug $r = 1$ into the formula to get $A = \pi(1)^2 = \pi$. Fill in π for that box. The next missing box is the one next to 9π. Plug this in for the area to get $9\pi = \pi r^2$. Divide both sides by π to get $9 = r^2$. Take the square root of both sides to get $3 = r$. Fill in 3 for that box. The next two missing boxes are the ones at the bottom. Find a pair of choices that are consistent with the equation $A = \pi r^2$. As seen above, $r = 3$ and $r = 6$ correspond with $A = 9\pi$ and $A = 36\pi$. Since neither of these is a choice, neither of these can be used. Keep looking. Try $r = 7$. Plug this into the formula to get $A = \pi(7)^2 = 49\pi$. This is a choice, so select 7 for the bottom left and 49π for the bottom right.

SOCIAL STUDIES

1. **B** Hopefully you remembered from your study of the Civil Rights movement that school segregation was practiced in the South. Eliminate (D). Most Northern states (Region 2) not only opposed segregation for moral reasons, but, in fact, prohibited it by law. Eliminate (C). Choice (A) is incorrect, since Western states (Region 3) did not require segregation. (Northern New England would certainly not have had this policy.)

2. **Prohibited**

   Brown vs. Board of Education effectively banned school segregation in all fifty states.

3. **C** When the GED® test asks you to define a word, watch out for obvious "trap" definitions. In this case, we may associate "discrimination" with racial prejudice (A), but that is not the topic of Washington's speech. This paragraph is also not about political parties, (B). Washington says we must "always exalt the just

pride of patriotism *more than* any appellation derived from local discriminations." So, he is not in favor of "discriminations." Rule out (D).

4. **A** "Of all the dispositions and habits which lead to political prosperity, religion and morality are indispensable supports...these firmest props of the duties of men...." Choice (D) may be tempting, but the *pillars* of human happiness are religion and morality.

5. **C** In paragraph 2, Washington warns "you in the most solemn manner against the baneful effects of the spirit of party generally." Even if you aren't sure what "baneful" means (harmful), the fact that he is "warning" the reader gives the sense that Washington believes that political parties are generally negative.

6. **C** The Golden Age of Athens was characterized by government-sponsored job programs and government financial assistance, two aspects of modern-day socialism. It was certainly not a communist society, though, since there was a democratic citizen legislature with term limits. There is no indication that private property ownership would have been banned, which is an essential feature of communism, so you can eliminate (D). A constitutional monarchy, (A), can be eliminated since there is no king or emperor. Laissez-faire capitalism, (B), requires no government interference in economics, so both land grants and public assistance allow you to eliminate this answer choice.

7. **B** David Walker's speech is very passionate. Right from the beginning, you know he is not white: "The whites have had us under them for more than three centuries." When he asks "had you not rather be killed than to be a slave to a tyrant," you know he is opposed to slavery (an abolitionist).

8. **C** Garrison says "We do not preach rebellion," so rule out (B). Choice (A) is not supported by his statements. Choice (D) is likewise unsupported. (Garrison was, in fact, an abolitionist.)

9. **A** Since Walker's Appeal is advocating violence, and Garrison says "We do not preach rebellion," he is clearly disapproving. Choice (D) may be half true, but is not supported as well as (A).

10. **Authoritarian right**

    The Nazis were clearly authoritarian in their tactics (SS officers, concentration camps, etc.). As for Left vs. Right, although the Nazis did implement some government-sponsored programs, they generally allowed private industry to flourish and allowed for private property ownership. Nationalism (promoting German ethnic interests) is often associated with the Right.

11. **D** President Woodrow Wilson was president during World War I, which occurred from 1914–1918.

12. **D** The woman's suffrage movement was dedicated to the effort to grant voting rights to women in all states.

13. **A** McKinley says that the producer is a "slave." He also states that "[It is said] that protection is immoral.... Let me give you a maxim that is a thousand times better than that, and it is the protection maxim: 'Buy where you can pay the easiest.' And that spot of Earth is where labor wins its highest rewards." So, McKinley is in favor of protectionism. It does not lower prices, (C). "They" say 'Buy where you can buy the cheapest', but McKinley offers a counter-argument. Also, according to McKinley, protection "is where labor wins its highest rewards," so (D) contradicts this.

14. **C** As you saw in the previous question, McKinley is an advocate for protectionism. The idea that producers are slaves is McKinley's opinion, not those who oppose protection. Those who claim "that protection

is immoral....they say, 'Buy where you can buy the cheapest'," so they must believe that protectionism encourages *higher* prices. Choice (B) may be tempting, but, remember, the question is about protectionism; certainly those opposed to it would not think that is does something positive. Watch out for answers that contain familiar language taken directly from the passage. They are often traps!

15. **D** Study the map and pie charts carefully before you attempt the questions. Notice that Clinton won 70.4% of the electoral votes. Rule out (A). For (B), count the number of states won by Clinton. He won 31 states, so eliminate (B). Choice (C) is a very broad statement. This map measures the results *only* of the 1996 election. So, (D) must be true. This is because a candidate can only win electoral votes by winning a sizeable number of votes in each state, and according to the pie chart, Perot did not earn any electoral votes.

16. **A** Remember that "majority" means "more than 50%." Clinton did not win more than 50% of the popular vote (though he did win the *plurality*, in other words, more than either Dole or Perot). As for (B), Dole did win many large states in the heartland of America, such as Texas and Montana, and he did win Alaska. Electoral votes are based on the population of a state, though, not on geographical size. Choice (C) is a very broad statement; this map measures only the results of the 1996 election. (Also, some Southern states did vote for Clinton.) Choice (D) is unsupported and hypothetical. The map gives you no way to know whom Perot's voters would have supported had Perot himself not run.

17. **D** A biased statement is one that exhibits a particular opinion, not simply a fact. In (D), you see the word "failed" and also an assertion of causation: "voters in 1996 voted for Candidate Perot in protest of the failed political policies." You simply do not *know* if this is true, and one could believe this statement only if one had a negative view of the two major political parties. It *could* be true, however, so it answers the question adequately.

18. **D** "My belief was that it was not only his [the president's] right but his duty to do anything that the needs of the Nation demanded unless such action was forbidden by the Constitution or by the laws" tells you that Roosevelt believes in the President's right to take action or sign "Executive orders," (B). This is the opposite of "executive restraint." In the second quote, Roosevelt believes "there should be full liberty to tell the truth about his acts," (C). Since the press is an arm of free speech, rule out (A).

19. **C** As with the previous question, the statement "My belief was that it was not only his [the president's] right but his duty to do anything that the needs of the Nation demanded unless such action was forbidden by the Constitution or by the laws" tells you that Roosevelt believes in the president's right to take action. This directly contradicts (B). Choice (A) is too strongly worded, since the latter part "unless such action was forbidden by the Constitution or by the laws" does not give the president absolute power. Choice (D) may be tempting, but, although the second quote does encourage Americans to put presidential power under scrutiny, it does not guarantee that the president will always act in a manner they see fit.

20. **D** Assumptions are ideas that are necessary to an argument, but are unstated. Start by eliminating answers that are not relevant to the first quote. The first quote does not mention the citizens' opinions or judgments, so rule out (B) and (C). If you chose (A), you were being tripped up by deceptive language: "I *declined* to adopt the view that what was imperatively necessary for the Nation could not be done by the President unless he could find some specific authorization to do it." (The key word is *declined*.) Choice (D) is the best choice because, in the first quote, Roosevelt states that he "acted for the public welfare" which implicitly assumes that action is necessary to promote the public welfare, in other words, that the public cannot always act on its own.

21. **A** The invention of the automobile may well be the greatest one of the 20th century. It allowed people much greater mobility and freedom than they had ever had before. It allowed workers to commute to their jobs from some distance away, so many Americans left cities and moved into suburbs, particularly in the 1950s, (B). Automobiles naturally would make large interstate highways more of a necessity, (C). And, since automobiles run on gasoline, a derivative of the oil industry, rule out (D). Personal computers, (A), are not related to automobiles. Although modern cars employ some computerized equipment, Ford's cars did not.

22. **B** Always be suspicious of extreme answers. Choice (A) is too strongly worded, since not *everyone* needs to want a car in order for the "great multitude" to want them. On the other hand, it's quite *possible* that everyone would want a car, so (D) is not the best answer and certainly does not support Ford's statements. The two remaining answers are very tricky, so if you chose (C), you were on the right track. The issue here is which one of the answers is *necessary* to Ford's argument. He says that the price of his car "will be so low in price that no man making a good salary will be unable to own one." That does not mean, however, that those *not* making a good salary couldn't find a way to own one too. Now you're down to (B). At first glance, this may look wrong, but Ford did mention "the best men to be hired." Wouldn't at least some of them make a "good salary"? The word "many" in (B) makes it a safe choice. How many is "many"? Maybe only a few or maybe a lot.

23. **A** Paragraph 1 says "the so-called 'water box,' are water-resources professionals who plan, operate, and maintain world water systems." Choice (B) may sound tempting if you are looking at Paragraph 4, but is not the actual definition of the "water box," nor do we know if water resource professionals are currently attending local meetings. (And some who participate in local meetings may not be water resource professionals.)

24. **D** Paragraph 5 states that "The time has come for the water community to step up to the challenge and begin to educate and influence those outside the water box…it needs to be done, and it needs to be done now!"

25. **C** According to the graph, municipal areas utilize 25% of Arizona's public water supply, while agriculture utilizes 69%. Choice (A) is a trap answer, since the chart is measuring water use, not money spent on or by these industries. Choice (D) is incorrect because 25% *is* one-fourth of 100%, not less. Choice (B) is wrong based on the definition of "water box" in question 23.

26. **Segregation of public schools (a), requirement of a literacy test to vote (c), blacks-only public restrooms (d)**

    The passage specifically mentions segregation. "Blacks-only" is a form of segregation. As for literacy tests, keep in mind that many African Americans were illiterate, particularly in the years following the Civil War. So, being required to take a literacy test would have disqualified many of them from voting, thus limiting their "rights and freedoms." Free speech rights for whites, (b), would not inherently limit the rights of blacks, nor would property taxes, (e), assuming that they were required of all property owners.

27. **D** A causal relationship means that one event caused another. Choice (B) may be true, but does not involve any causation. Choices (A) and (C) are historically inaccurate, since Jim Crow laws were enacted *after* the Civil War. The Civil Rights Movement was largely an effort to end the era of Jim Crow.

28. **B** Constitutional amendments are intended to *change* the Constitution. To "repeal" is to end or reverse a law. Choice (A) is close, but amendments are really changes and not brand-new proposals.

29. **C** When states ratify a law, they affirm that it should be adopted.

30. **C** The passage states, "Constitutional amendments do not require the signature of the president but are then sent to the states for ratification." Choice (B) is directly contradicted by this statement. Choice (A) is incorrect because all law-making is done by Congress. Choice (D) is wrong because many proposed pieces of legislation fail, not just Constitutional amendments.

31. **A** The women in the photo *want* the universal right to vote; therefore, *they do not currently have it*. So, they are not *exercising* any right to vote, but they are exercising freedom of speech by hanging up posters and meeting together to further their political aims.

32. **C** Theodore Roosevelt defines a "square deal" as providing "a more substantial equality of opportunity and of reward for equally good service." Choice (A) may sound tempting, but you really don't know for sure if they support his presidency. You also do not know Roosevelt's position on voting, so rule out (D). Choice (B) cannot be right, since these women do not *yet* have the right to vote; they are hoping to get that right in the future.

33. **B** According to the table, the number of members from each state in the House of Representatives is based on the population of that state (not its geographical size). California is a large state and has a bigger population than any of the other states listed.

34. **C** The Founders of our Republic designed a bicameral legislature (two branches) because they believed that having two legislative bodies subject to different rules would allow for the most fair representation of the people. The House of Representatives assigns a certain number of members based on the population of a state, which fairly allows larger states to have a bigger influence on legislative decisions, but, on the down side, puts smaller states at a disadvantage. So the Senate is designed to balance this out by assigning a set number of two from each state. Choice (A) might seem tempting, but many members of the House serve for many years (multiple terms) too. Choice (B) is not true; voters are free to elect senators from any party. Choice (D) cannot be true, since the House assigns a different number of members to different states.

35. **The Senate**

In 1959, both Alaska and Hawaii were admitted as states. Since each state is represented by two senators, this added four seats to the Senate. Although the population of the United States has certainly increased since 1929, it does not affect the number of members in the House of Representatives, which stays constant at 435. If the population of a state were to drastically change, for instance, there is a mass migration from New York to Vermont, Vermont would gain a Representative and New York would lose one; the total number would stay the same. (In case you're curious, prior to 1929, the number of Representative was allowed to increase with increasing population; that is no longer true.)

SCIENCE

1.   This question requires you to determine the point of maximum growth rate on the logistic growth model. Since the logistic growth model states that a population below its carrying capacity will grow exponentially before slowing and stabilizing, the point that represents the point of maximum growth rate is the last point before the population growth starts tapering off. Thus, the point of maximum growth rate occurs directly in the middle of the logistic growth curve, as shown below.

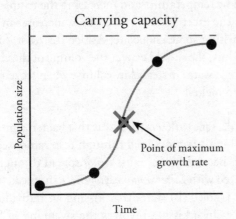

2. **C** In order to determine the unknown genotype, you must cross each column with each row in order to find the possibilities. Here you will combine the allele in the first row, t, with the allele in the first column, t, to find that the unknown genotype is tt. Thus, the answer is (C).

3. **50% or 0.50**

This question requires you to determine the likelihood that this couple's second child will not be able to taste PTC. First, let's consider the importance of the phrase "second child." Note that the genetic makeup of an individual is independent from the genetic makeup of other individuals. Accordingly, this phrase is intended to trick you—all you need to determine is the likelihood that any child of this couple will be unable to taste PTC. The passage states that the ability to taste PTC is a dominant trait, so the only individuals who are unable to taste PTC are those that have a homozygous recessive genotype. The Punnett Square shows that there is a 50% chance of offspring having the genotype Tt and a 50% chance that offspring will have a genotype tt. Accordingly, the probability that the second child will not be able to taste PTC is 50%, or 0.50.

4. **1:1; 1:1**

The genotypic ratio is the expected number of different genotypes produced by the cross of two individuals. In this Punnett Square, the resulting genotypes are Tt, Tt, tt, and tt. Thus, the genotypic ratio is 2:2, which reduces to 1:1. Conversely, the phenotypic ratio is the physical expression of those genes. Since the ability to taste PTC is dominant, individuals having the gene Tt will be able to taste PTC, while those individuals having the gene tt will not be able to taste PTC. Since the cross of our individuals Tt and tt resulted in the genotypes Tt, Tt, tt, and tt, only the individuals with the genes Tt will be able to taste PTC. Thus, the phenotypic ratio is 2:2, which reduces to 1:1.

5. **D** This question requires you to identify the process represented by the chemical equation $6CO_2 + 6H_2O$ → $C_6H_{12}O_6 + 6O_2$. In this reaction, carbon dioxide and water are converted into glucose and oxygen using energy from the Sun. Thus, the correct answer is (D), photosynthesis.

6. **decrease, decrease**

This question requires you to use the information about temperature's effect on matter to complete the sentence. The question tells you that matter is affected by temperature, and increasing the temperature of a substance increases the volume of a substance, with the exception of water, which increases in volume when frozen. First, let's tackle the chocolate. After melting some chocolate, Ashlee freezes it. Since the temperature is decreasing, so too should the volume. Thus, she should expect the volume of the chocolate to decrease when frozen. Next, tackle the ice-cube. Since water increases in volume when frozen, Ashlee should expect the ice-cube to decrease in volume when melted.

7. **C** This question requires you to use the information in the passage to determine a way that bacterial meningitis is *not* spread. According to the passage, bacterial meningitis is contracted through respiratory secretions, throat secretions, and consuming contaminated food. Bacterial meningitis is *not* spread through casual contact. Choice (A) states that eating meat that is infected with *Listeria monocytogenes* can spread bacterial meningitis; this is true, so (A) should be eliminated. Choice (B) states that kissing an individual with group B *Streptococcus* can spread bacterial meningitis; since kissing involves the swapping of bacteria, this could be true and can be eliminated. Choice (C) states that holding hands with an individual with *Neisseria meningitides* can spread bacterial meningitis; this is casual contact, so (C) should be kept. Finally, (D) states that inhaling the germs when an individual with *Streptococcus pneumoniae* coughs directly on you can spread bacterial meningitis; since this is a respiratory secretion, this is a way to spread bacterial meningitis, and (D) can be eliminated. Thus, holding hands with an individual with *Neisseria meningitides* will not spread bacterial meningitis, and the correct answer is (C).

8. **2,500**

This question requires you to determine the number of individuals who died from bacterial meningitis in the United States from 2010–2014, including deaths in 2010 and 2014. The passage states that approximately 500 individuals die from bacterial meningitis each year. Since you need to find the number of individuals who died from 2010–2014, multiply 500 by the number of years, 5. Thus, the number of individuals who died from bacterial meningitis from 2010–2014 is 500 × 5 = 2,500.

9. **B** In order to answer this question, you must use the provided chart to determine the truth of each statement. Choice (A) states that as the number of *Streptococcus pneumoniae* cases has increased, so too have the cases of *Haemophilus influenza*. This is a false statement, because the number of cases of *Haemophilus influenza* has decreased as the number of *Streptococcus pneumoniae* cases has increased; eliminate (A). Choice (B) states that the number of individuals afflicted by *Listeria monocytogenes* in 2012 is half the number of individuals afflicted by *Streptococcus pneumoniae* in the same year. In 2012, the number of individuals affected by *Listeria monocytogenes* was 1,000, while the number of individuals afflicted by *Streptococcus pneumonia* was 2,000; keep (B). Choice (C) states that the number of individuals afflicted with group B *Streptococcus* has steadily increased since 2012. This statement is false, as the number of individuals afflicted with group B *Streptococcus* increased, decreased, and then increased again between 2012–2016; eliminate (C). Finally, (D) states that there were fewer cases of *Neisseria meningitides* in 2016 than there were cases of *Haemophilus influenza* in the same year. This is a false statement because there were 500 cases of *Neisseria meningitides* and 250 cases of *Haemophilus influenza* in 2016; eliminate (D). Thus, the correct answer is (B).

10.   **aerobic; anaerobic**

This question requires you to have some knowledge of cellular respiration. As the passage states, cellular respiration can occur with or without the presence of oxygen. If ATP is made in the presence of oxygen it is called aerobic respiration, while anaerobic respiration occurs without the presence of oxygen.

11.   **B**   In order to find the average diastolic pressure for these subjects, you need to take the sum of the subjects' diastolic pressures and divide it by the number of subjects. Accordingly, the average diastolic pressure for these subjects is $\dfrac{76.0 + 70.2 + 98.6 + 85.8 + 112.0}{5} = \dfrac{442.6}{5} = 88.52$ mm/Hg.

12.   **132.6**

The median is the middle number of an ordered list. So, put the numbers in order (either least to greatest or greatest to least; it works the same either way) and then find the middle number: in this case, 132.6.

Note that because there is an odd number of values, there is just one "middle" number, so that's the median. If you had an even number of values, you'd find the average of the two middle numbers.

13.   **B**   This question requires you to identify the type of boundary depicted in the image. The information given above the image states that convergent boundary interactions cause the development of mountain ranges, divergent boundary interactions cause a gap to form in the Earth's crust, and transform fault interactions cause earthquakes. The boundary depicted in the image shows two plates moving away from each other, creating a gap in the surface of the Earth. Thus, the image depicts a divergent boundary.

14.   Renewable: **(b) Wind, (c) Geothermal, (d) Biomass, and (e) Solar**

Nonrenewable: **(a) Coal, (f) Nuclear, and (g) Oil**

This question requires you to distinguish renewable sources of energy from nonrenewable sources of energy. Recall that a renewable resource is one that can be replenished by natural processes at a sustainable rate. In this example, the renewable resources are biomass, geothermal, solar, and wind. Conversely, a nonrenewable resource is one that exists in limited supply and cannot be naturally replenished at a rate to meet current consumption. In this example, coal, nuclear, and oil are examples of nonrenewable resources.

15.   **A**   This question requires you to analyze the food web and determine which organism is a producer. A producer is an organism that makes its own food. In a food web, plants are the producers, as they create their energy from the Sun. Accordingly, in this food web, algae are the producer.

16.   **D**   Here you need to determine which two organisms would be most devastated if the mink were removed from the food web. In order to answer this question, you need to know how a food web works. In a food web, the arrow moves from the provider of food to the organism that eats the food. In our example, there are arrows from the mink to both the muskrat and the hawk, indicating that minks are food for both muskrats and hawks. Accordingly, if you removed the mink from the food web, the populations of the muskrat and hawk would be most devastated.

17.   **D**   This question requires you to use the information about gravitational potential energy to determine which scenario has the greatest amount of gravitational potential energy. The question tells you that gravitational potential energy is dependent upon the mass of an object and its height in the environment, and that the gravitational potential energy increases as the mass and vertical position increases. In order to select the

item with the greatest gravitational potential energy, compare the answers and eliminate the statement with a lower gravitational potential energy. Choice (A) gives the scenario of a 15-pound cat dropped from a height of two inches, while (B) gives the scenario of a 20-pound anchor dropped from a height of four feet. Between these two options, a 20-pound anchor dropped from a height of four feet will have a greater gravitational potential energy, as both the mass of the object and the vertical position are greater; eliminate (A). Next, compare (B) and (C): a 20-pound anchor dropped from a height of four feet and a 20-pound brick dropped from a height of three inches. While the brick has a mass equal to the anchor, the brick is dropped only from a height of three inches, and therefore has a lower gravitational potential energy than the anchor; eliminate (C). Finally, compare (B) and (D): a 20-pound anchor dropped from a height of four feet and a 90-pound box dropped from a height of ten feet. Since both the mass and the vertical height of the box is greater than that of the anchor, the box has the greatest gravitational potential energy. Thus, eliminate (B) and select (D).

18. **144**

This question requires you to determine the difference between the momentum of the dog and the cat. Accordingly, you will use the given equation *momentum = mass × velocity*. The momentum of the cat will be *momentum* = 12 lbs × 3 m/s and the *momentum* = 36. The momentum of the dog will be *momentum* = 30 lbs × 6 m/s and the *momentum* = 180. Finally, you need to determine how much greater the momentum of the dog than the cat; 180 − 36 = 144.

19. **Greater**

The formula tells us that momentum equals mass times velocity. Objects A and B have the same momentum, but A has a greater mass. That means B must be moving at a greater velocity, in order for the equations to yield the same result. If this is difficult to see without actual numbers, you can just supply your own numbers. For example, let's say Object A has a mass of 100 lbs and a velocity of 10 m/s. According to the formula, that gives a momentum of 1000 lbs × m/s. So, say Object B has a mass of only 20 lbs, but still has a momentum of 1000 lbs × m/s. That means 20 times some velocity equals 1000. Object B's velocity would need to be 50 m/s—in other words, a greater velocity, to make up for its smaller mass.

20. **Simple machines: (a) pulley, (b) wedge, (d) lever, (f) inclined place, (h) screw, (i) wheel and axle Not simple machines: (c) gearshift, (e) drill, (g) engine, (j) funnel**

This question requires you to sort the provided words into the categories of *Simple Machine* and *Not a Simple Machine*. There are six simple machines that you should be familiar with: pulley, wedge, lever, inclined plane, screw, and wheel and axle. The remaining terms, gearshift, drill, engine, and funnel, are not simple machines, and should be sorted as such.

21. **C** This question requires that you have some knowledge about rock formation. You are told that marble is formed over time when exposed to extreme pressure and heat below the Earth's surface. Rocks that are formed due to exposure to extreme heat and pressure are classified as metamorphic rocks. Choice (A), fossilized, is not a category of rock. Choice (B), igneous rock, is rock that is composed of cool magma; basalt is an example of an igneous rock. Choice (D), sedimentary rock, is rock formed by weathering processes, and is composed of layers of pebble, sand, and clay; sandstone is an example of sedimentary rock.

22. **B** In order to answer this question, you need to know the adverse effects of fossil fuel use. Choice (A) is acid rain, which is a direct result of burning fossil fuels, which produces pollutants such as sulfur dioxide and nitrogen dioxide; eliminate (A). Choice (B) is increased biodiversity, which does not result from fossil

fuel use. Rather, fossil fuel use leads to a reduction in biodiversity; keep (B). Choice (C), the Greenhouse Effect, is the increasing atmospheric concentration of carbon dioxide through the burning of fossil fuels; since this is a negative effect, eliminate (C). Finally, (D) is ozone depletion, which occurs when fossil fuels are extracted from the Earth and burned; eliminate (D). Thus, increased biodiversity is NOT an adverse effect of fossil fuel use.

23. **B** This question requires you to find the period of a wave, given that the wave cycles 360 times in a minute.

The passage tells you that the period of a wave is inversely related to the frequency of a wave, which is the number of times a wave cycles per second. Accordingly, you need to determine the number of times the wave cycles per second; $\frac{360 \text{ cycles}}{60 \text{ seconds}} = \frac{x \text{ cycles}}{1 \text{ second}}$, and x cycles/second is 6. Now, find the period of this wave using the formula $period = \frac{1}{frequency}$. Thus, the period of this wave is $\frac{1}{6}$.

24. **transverse, longitudinal**

Here you need to determine the type of wave illustrated in both Diagram A and Diagram B. The passage states that mechanical waves can be further categorized as either transverse waves, in which the particle motion is perpendicular to the wave motion, or longitudinal waves, in which particle motion moves in the same direction as the wave motion. Looking at Diagram A, you see that the mass motion, which moves vertically, is perpendicular to the wave motion, which moves horizontally. Accordingly, Diagram A is an example of a transverse wave. Looking at Diagram B, you see that the mass motion, which moves horizontally, is moving in the same direction as the wave motion, which also moves horizontally. Thus, Diagram B is an example of a longitudinal wave.

25. **5** This question requires you to find the amplitude of a wave if the maximum height of a wave occurs at point 15 and the minimum height of a wave occurs at point 5. The passage tells you that the amplitude of a wave is equal to half the distance between the crest and the trough, or the maximum and minimum heights, of a wave. Accordingly, the amplitude of this wave is $\frac{15 - 5}{2} = \frac{10}{2} = 5$.

26. **A** When two elements are combined via a chemical interaction, the result is a compound. An element is a pure substance that occurs in nature, so combining two elements will not result in another element; eliminate (B). When two elements are combined without a chemical reaction, the result is a mixture; eliminate (C). A solution is the result of dissolving a substance in a liquid; eliminate (D).

27. **D** In order to answer this question correctly, you must know the structure and function of major cell organelles. The nucleus is the epicenter of the cell, contains DNA, and is responsible for directing cell activities. The mitochondria are the powerhouses of the cell, and are responsible for creating ATP. Lysosomes are organelles that contain enzymes created by the cell, and function as the digestion system of the cell, breaking down food and other material. The Golgi apparatus is a major center of protein processing, and is responsible for making, processing, and packaging proteins. Thus, the correct answer is (D).

28. **B** The saturation point of an object is the point at which no more of a substance can be either absorbed or dissolved into a solution. Choice (A), the temperature at which a solid turns into a liquid, is the melting point of a substance. Choice (C), the temperature at which a liquid turns into a solid, is the freezing point of a substance. Choice (D), the process in which the nuclei of an atom is broken down and charged particles of energy are released, is the process of nuclear radiation. Thus, the correct answer is (B).

29. **2, 2**

This question requires you to balance the chemical equation that shows the reaction of calcium chloride and hydrochloric acid. The equation you are given is $Ca(OH)_2$ + ____HCl → $CaCl$____ + $2H_2O$. Start by finding out how many hydrogen atoms are needed in the reactants. The products of the reaction include $2H_2O$, indicating that there are four atoms of hydrogen after the reaction. Accordingly, you need four atoms of hydrogen before the reaction. The first reactant, $Ca(OH)_2$, shows that there are two atoms of hydrogen for every molecule of calcium hydroxide. Thus, you need an additional two atoms of hydrogen in the second reactant, HCl, indicating that the second reactant should be $2HCl$. Now, you can determine how many atoms of chlorine are present before the reaction takes place. Since the reactant is $2HCl$, you know there are two atoms of chlorine present both before and after the reaction. Thus, the first product, calcium chloride, will be properly written as $CaCl_2$.

30. **D** Here you need to determine whether the reaction of calcium hydroxide and hydrochloric acid is a combination, decomposition, single displacement, or double displacement reaction. Since you have multiple reactants and multiple products, you can eliminate (A) and (B), combination and decomposition reactions. Next, consider the process occurring during the reaction. Since calcium is paired with hydroxide in the reactant phase, but paired with chloride in the product phase, you have at least one displacement. Furthermore, since the hydroxide molecules become water after the chemical reaction, there is a second displacement. Thus, this reaction is a double displacement reaction.

31. **Plasma Membrane**

In eukaryotic cells, the plasma membrane is a single-layer membrane that is a phospholipid bilayer with receptor and transport proteins. The plasma membrane is a selectively permeable membrane, controlling the movement of substances into and out of the cell, and is thus responsible for maintaining the intracellular environment.

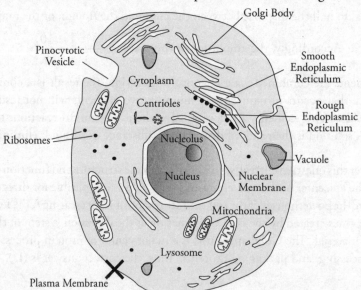

32. **A** This question requires you to identify the law that states that equal volumes of any two gases at identical temperatures and pressures must hold an equal number of molecules. This law is Avogadro's Law, or (A). The Law of Conservation of mass states that matter can neither be created nor destroyed; thus, (B) can be eliminated. Newton's Law of Inertia states that an object at rest will remain at rest, or continue moving in the same direction at the same speed, unless acted upon by external forces; thus, (C) can be eliminated. Planck's Law describes the electromagnetic radiation emitted by a black body in thermal equilibrium at a definite temperature; thus, (D) can be eliminated.

33. **peninsula, island**

This question requires you to be able to match a landform with its definition. First, you are told that the landform labeled "K" is a piece of land that is almost entirely surrounded by water. Consider the answer choices. A cape is a large, high point of land that extends into a body of water; the landform labeled "K" is neither large nor tall, so eliminate (A). A delta is a body of sediment deposited at the mouth of a river or stream where it enters an ocean or lake; the landform labeled "K" is not formed from river sediment, so (B) can be eliminated. An isthmus is a narrow strip of land, surrounded by water on both sides that connects two larger pieces of land; the landform labeled "K" is not connecting two pieces of land and can be eliminated. A peninsula is a piece of land bordered by water on three sides, but connected to the mainland; the landform labeled "K" matches this description, and (D) is the correct option.

Next, the question tells you that the landform labeled "M" is a piece of land that is entirely surrounded by water. An archipelago is an island chain; the landform labeled "M" does not depict an island chain, and (A) can be eliminated. A headland is a cliff or elevated form that overlooks the sea or ocean; the landform labeled "M" does not match this description, so (B) can be eliminated. An island is a piece of land completely surrounded by water; the landform labeled "M" is a landform completely surrounded by water, so keep (C). A tributary is a stream or river than flows into a larger stream, river, or lake; the landform labeled "M" is a piece of land, not a stream, so (D) can be eliminated.

34. **D** This question requires you to identify the plain on the given image. A plain is a flat area that generally occurs in a lowland area. Choice (A) points to the landform marked "B," which is a forested area; this is not a plain, so (A) can be eliminated. Choice (B) points to the landform marked "E," which is a lowland area with a river running through it; this is a river valley, not a plain, so (B) can be eliminated. Choice (C) points to the landform marked "F," which is the area along the coast of the ocean; this is a beach, not a plain, so (C) can be eliminated. Choice (D) points to the landform marked "Q," which is a flat area at a low elevation; this fits the description of a plain, so (D) is the best answer.

35. **D** This passage tells you that Matthew hypothesizes that the volume of a gas increases as the temperature increases, and that he wishes to support his hypothesis by designing an experiment using balloons as his primary material. So, his experiment needs to test how temperature, and temperature alone, affects the volume of the gas. Keeping this in mind, use Process of Elimination to find the best answer choice.

Eliminate (A) because using different types of balloons would not tell him anything about how temperature affects gas volume. Choice (B) can go, too, since experiments always benefit from more trials and more data. As you consider that (C) and (D) correctly include using gases at different temperatures, you can see an important distinction between the two: Matthew should limit his variables to only the one whose effects he is studying—temperature of the gas. Therefore, he should use the same gas and vary only the temperature. This eliminates (C) and makes (D) the best answer.

Chapter 5
Practice Test 2

Reasoning Through Language Arts

Welcome!

Here is some information that you need to know before you start this test:

- You should not spend too much time on a question if you are not certain of the answer; answer it the best you can, and go on to the next question.
- If you are not certain of the answer to a question, you can mark your answer for review and come back to it later.
- This test has three sections.
- You have **35 minutes** to complete Section 1.
- When you finish Section 1, you may review those questions.
- You may not go back to Section 1 once you have finished your review.
- You have **45 minutes** to complete the Extended Response question in Section 2.
- After completing Section 2, you may take a 10-minute break.
- You have **60 minutes** to complete Section 3.
- When you finish Section 3, you may review those questions.

Turn the page to begin.

GO ON TO THE NEXT PAGE

Questions 1 through 8 refer to the following passage.

Excerpt from "Ethics and Standards: More Questions Than Answers" by Jane Kirtley

1   Ethics codes aim not to impose legally enforceable standards but, instead, to offer journalists a framework to help them decide what to report and how to report it. No code of ethics can answer every question, and good ones probably raise more questions than they answer. Reasonable people, even journalists themselves, may disagree about how a specific ethical standard should apply in a particular situation.

2   • For example, should a journalist lampoon a name or image sacred to a particular ethnic or religious group? This is perfectly legal in many countries. But does it contribute to robust public discussion or, instead, foment hatred and promote conflict?

   • Should the press publish classified information, especially where government claims that doing so will damage its efforts to protect the public? Would this be the act of an independent government watchdog or of one needlessly endangering public health and safety?

   • Should a television station air graphic footage of military conflict, including scenes of violence and death? Would this convey to the public the reality of war? Or, instead, undermine morale and needlessly distress surviving family members?

3   Readers and viewers may not agree with every choice a news organization makes. But ethical standards and guidelines can offer guidance toward thoughtful and defensible solutions.

Seeking Truth: The First Principle

4   Most journalism codes emphasize that telling the truth—being accurate—is essential....The one universal ethical principle may be simply this: A journalist never knowingly publishes a falsehood.

5   This is not always an easy standard to uphold. Of course, a journalist should make every effort to verify a story before reporting it. But facts that alter original perceptions may only be learned over time, after publication. Here, a responsible news organization publishes a correction or clarification as quickly as possible.

GO ON TO THE NEXT PAGE

6   News organizations should take great care to assure that headlines, teasers, sound bites, or quotations are not only accurate but do not oversimplify the facts or take them out of context. Photographs, audio, and video may need to be cropped or edited to address considerations of space or time but not in a way that misleads or misrepresents. The staging of photos or reenactments of news events should be avoided or, where absolutely necessary, clearly labeled.

7   Obviously journalists should not fabricate the news, nor should they plagiarize—that is, copy without attribution—another person's work. They should not make up quotations, nor reprint a news story prepared by someone else without first obtaining permission to do so.

Sources

8   A reporter, it is said, is only as good as her sources.....

9   But journalists must be cautious and determine that a source is credible. This includes ascertaining a source's point of view or what his "agenda" might be. Ideally, reporters should consult multiple sources to obtain diverse perspectives on a subject. And they should make every effort to verify the accuracy of a source's information whenever possible.

10   What about anonymous sourcing, the practice of attributing a fact to an unnamed source? It is preferable that all sources be "on the record" and that facts not be linked to "administration sources" or some other imprecise formulation. Sources who stand behind their word are more likely to tell the truth. Attributing information to a named source also helps the reader or viewer evaluate independently the credibility of the source.

11   But sometimes a source has valid reasons to request, or demand, that his identity be kept secret. When possible, a journalist should resist making this promise. But it won't always be possible. Some news organizations require that an editor approve any promise of confidentiality. Although this can frustrate a reporter, the policy makes sense. When an unattributed piece of information is published, the news organization's reputation is at stake along with that of the individual reporter.

12   Reporters should be very clear about their promises. Phrases like "off the record" and "on background" mean different things to different people. Journalist and source should agree on the terms governing the news organization's use of information.

GO ON TO THE NEXT PAGE

13   Once a promise is made, it must be kept. As the British Code of Practice says, "Journalists have a moral obligation to protect confidential sources of information." Should the journalist be called to testify in court about her information, keeping that promise can put the journalist at risk of being held in contempt in nations that do not recognize a legal privilege for journalists. Any reporter must be clear with the source exactly how far he is prepared to go to keep that promise.

Surreptitious and Undercover Reporting Techniques

14   Journalists should avoid deceptive reporting techniques, like using hidden cameras, tape recorders, and microphones, or assuming a false identity. In some jurisdictions, they are illegal. But equally important, they can undermine credibility. Readers and viewers often won't believe that a reporter who essentially lied in order to get a story will tell the truth when he reports it. Generally speaking, a journalist should identify herself as a member of the news media and make clear that she may use whatever she learns in a story.

15   Nevertheless, there are times when a story can be obtained only through subterfuge. Journalists and their news organizations should reserve these techniques for the rare occasion when conventional methods will not work and, only then, when a compelling public interest demands it. News media should then explain their methods when the story is published or broadcast.

Source: *Media Law Handbook*, United States Department of State, Bureau of International Information Programs, 2010.

1. The excerpt identifies some problems with agreeing to let a news source remain anonymous. Which of the following is NOT one of those problems?

A.   News consumers can't evaluate for themselves the credibility of an unnamed source.

B.   The news source might be exposed to danger by going "on the record."

C.   The reporter would be risking her employer's reputation as well as her own if her news organization published or broadcast a false statement from an anonymous source.

D.   The source might be less likely to tell the truth if he doesn't need to worry about his name being connected with the statement.

2. The "British Code of Practice" (paragraph 13) is most likely

A.   a textbook intended only for aspiring journalists.

B.   an explanation of legal rules that determine what journalists can and cannot do.

C.   a professional code that practicing British journalists must swear to uphold.

D.   a framework of ethical standards which journalists can consult for guidance.

GO ON TO THE NEXT PAGE

3. Which quote from the excerpt supports
   the idea that dece...

   ...ause
   ...the

   ...al."

   ...a

   ...ility."

   ...as her

4. Suppose one broadcast news organization airs graphic live video of a battle taking place in a conflict area. It warns viewers that some scenes might be disturbing. Another broadcaster gives a verbal description of the battle, showing only the news anchor and a map of the area. It explains that it has chosen not to air any footage because the images would be too graphic for many viewers. Which principles from the excerpt would support each broadcaster's decision? Write the letter of each principle into the column corresponding to the decision it supports. You will need four of the six principles listed below.

Air battle footage.	Do not air battle footage.

(a) Reporters should not distort facts by taking them out of context.

(b) Media outlets should not intensify the worry of viewers who have family members serving in the conflict area.

(c) Ethical codes are guidelines that allow flexibility in making decisions.

(d) News outlets should not undermine military morale.

(e) Journalists should not present a reenactment as if it were a real event.

(f) News organizations have a responsibility to inform readers about the reality of war.

GO ON TO THE NEXT PAGE

5. Read these sentences from paragraphs 12 and 13.

> Reporters should be very clear about their promises. Phrases like "off the record" and "on background" mean different things to different people. Journalist and source should agree on the terms governing the news organization's use of information (paragraph 12).
>
> Once a promise is made, it must be kept....Should the journalist be called to testify in court about her information, keeping that promise can put the journalist at risk of being held in contempt in nations that do not recognize a legal privilege for journalists. Any reporter must be clear with the source exactly how far he is prepared to go to keep that promise (paragraph 13).

What impact do the sentences from paragraph 13 have on paragraph 12?

A. They add to the information given in paragraph 12 about promises of confidentiality.

B. They add to the criterion of clarity described in paragraph 12.

C. They suggest that, in some cases, journalists are justified in breaking a promise described in paragraph 12.

D. They suggest that, in most cases, journalists should not promise confidentiality.

6. What problems with ethics codes does the author identify? Write the letters of the problems that apply into the empty boxes below.

(a) They differ widely in different countries.

(b) They can raise more questions than they answer.

(c) They can lead to disagreements between a journalist and his or her employer.

(d) They can be interpreted in any way the journalist wants, so they can be used to justify deceptive reporting practices.

(e) They require individual, subjective interpretation.

GO ON TO THE NEXT PAGE

7. From the information in the excerpt, what would the author be most likely to advise news consumers about "citizen journalists"?

   A. She would advise news consumers to verify the credibility of citizen journalists and their stories.

   B. She would say that citizen journalists serve no useful purpose.

   C. She would think citizen journalists always have a hidden agenda that taints the information they provide.

   D. She would see citizen journalists as another source for professional journalists to consult.

8. In which of the following situations might the author agree that "telling the truth"—"the one universal ethical principle"—"is not always an easy standard to uphold" (paragraphs 4 and 5)?

   A. A reporter is so eager to win a journalism award that she copies part of a prize-winning journalist's feature article into her own, without acknowledging the source of the material.

   B. An eyewitness later admits he was nowhere near the scene of an incident about which he volunteered information.

   C. A source who requested anonymity is later revealed not to have access to the information she claimed to be revealing.

   D. At a news conference shortly after a crime, police officials say that they are searching for four suspects. Later that day at another news conference, the same officials say the suspect acted alone.

GO ON TO THE NEXT PAGE

Questions 9 through 16 refer to the following passage.

Excerpt from *King Coal*
by Upton Sinclair

1   Mary Burke it was, for a fact; and she seemed to have the crowd in a kind of frenzy. She would speak one sentence, and there would come a roar from the throng; she would speak another sentence, and there would come another roar. Hal and Jerry pushed their way in, to where they could make out the words of this litany of rage.

2   "Would they go down into the pit themselves, do ye think?"

3   "They would not!"...

4   And Mary swept on: "If only ye'd stand together, they'd come to ye on their knees to ask for terms! But ye're cowards, and they play on your fears! Ye're traitors, and they buy ye out! They break ye into pieces, they do what they please with ye—and then ride off in their private cars, and leave gunmen to beat ye down and trample on your faces! How long will ye stand it? How long?"

5   The roar of the mob rolled down the street and back again. "We'll not stand it! We'll not stand it!" Men shook their clenched fists, women shrieked, even children shouted curses. "We'll fight them! We'll slave no more for them!"

6   And Mary found a magic word. "We'll have a union!" she shouted. "We'll get together and stay together! If they refuse us our rights, we'll know what to answer—we'll have a strike!"

7   There was a roar like the crashing of thunder in the mountains. Yes, Mary had found the word! For many years it had not been spoken aloud in North Valley, but now it ran like a flash of gunpowder through the throng. "Strike! Strike! Strike! Strike!" It seemed as if they would never have enough of it. Not all of them had understood Mary's speech, but they knew this word, "Strike!" They translated and proclaimed it in Polish and Bohemian and Italian and Greek. Men waved their caps, women waved their aprons—in the semi-darkness it was like some strange kind of vegetation tossed by a storm. Men clasped one another's hands, the more demonstrative of the foreigners fell upon one another's necks. "Strike! Strike! Strike!"

8   "We're no longer slaves!" cried the speaker. "We're men—and we'll live as men! We'll work as men—or we'll not work at all! We'll no longer be a herd of cattle, that they can drive about as they please! We'll organise, we'll stand together—shoulder to shoulder! Either we'll win together, or we'll starve and die together! And not a man of us will yield, not a man of us will turn traitor! Is there anybody here who'll scab on his fellows?"

GO ON TO THE NEXT PAGE

9   There was a howl, which might have come from a pack of wolves. Let the man who would scab on his fellows show his dirty face in that crowd!

10   "Ye'll stand by the union?"

11   "We'll stand by it!"

12   "Ye'll swear?"

13   "We'll swear!"

14   She flung her arms to heaven with a gesture of passionate adjuration. "Swear it on your lives! To stick to the rest of us, and never a man of ye give way till ye've won! Swear! Swear!" Men stood, imitating her gesture, their hands stretched up to the sky.

15   "We swear! We swear!"

16   "Ye'll not let them break ye! Ye'll not let them frighten ye!"

17   "No! No!"

18   "Stand by your word, men! Stand by it! 'Tis the one chance for your wives and childer!" The girl rushed on—exhorting with leaping words and passionate out-flung arms—a tall, swaying figure of furious rebellion. Hal listened to the speech and watched the speaker, marvelling. Here was a miracle of the human soul, here was hope born of despair! And the crowd around her—they were sharing the wonderful rebirth; their waving arms, their swaying forms responded to Mary as an orchestra to the baton of a leader.

19   A thrill shook Hal—a thrill of triumph! He had been beaten down himself, he had wanted to run from this place of torment; but now there was hope in North Valley—now there would be victory, freedom!

20   Ever since he had come to the coal-country, the knowledge had been growing in Hal that the real tragedy of these people's lives was not their physical suffering, but their mental depression—the dull, hopeless misery in their minds. This had been driven into his consciousness day by day, both by what he saw and by what others told him. Tom Olson had first put it into words: "Your worst troubles are inside the heads of the fellows you're trying to help!" How could hope be given to men in this environment of terrorism? Even Hal himself, young and free as he was, had been brought to despair. He came from a class which is accustomed to say, "Do this," or "Do that," and it will be done. But these mine-slaves had never known that sense of power, of certainty; on the contrary, they were accustomed to

GO ON TO THE NEXT PAGE

having their efforts balked at every turn, their every impulse to happiness or achievement crushed by another's will.

21 But here was this miracle of the human soul! Here was hope in North Valley! Here were the people rising—and Mary Burke at their head! It was his vision come true—Mary Burke with a glory in her face, and her hair shining like a crown of gold! Mary Burke mounted upon a snow-white horse, wearing a robe of white, soft and lustrous—like Joan of Arc, or a leader in a suffrage parade! Yes, and she was at the head of a host, he had the music of its marching in his ears!

9. When she is speaking to the men, Mary uses different techniques to unite them and gain their support. Arrange the techniques below in the order in which Mary uses them. Write the letter of each technique in the corresponding box below.

(a) Mary gets the men to declare their commitment.

(b) Mary gets the men to agree with her on the problem.

(c) Mary appeals to her listeners' sense of duty.

(d) Mary gets the men to unite behind her and her solution.

(e) Mary displays energy, passion, and anger.

First technique

Second technique

Third technique

Fourth technique

Fifth technique

GO ON TO THE NEXT PAGE

10. Read the following sentences from paragraph 7.

> Not all of them had understood Mary's speech, but they knew this word, "Strike!" They translated and proclaimed it in Polish and Bohemian and Italian and Greek.

What do these sentences explain about why Mary was able to assume a leadership role with the men?

A. Her passion and energy spoke to the men, if not her actual words.

B. The men were used to being followers and to submitting to anyone who seemed to be more powerful.

C. She was able to overcome an underlying barrier to effective action.

D. She was able to confuse most of them by speaking in a language they didn't understand.

11. Which statement from the excerpt gives the first hint that Mary might not be an effective leader in implementing her solution to the men's problems?

A. "For many years it had not been spoken aloud in North Valley." (paragraph 7)

B. "She seemed to have the crowd in a kind of frenzy." (paragraph 1)

C. "How could hope be given to men in this environment of terrorism?" (paragraph 20)

D. "It was his vision come true." (paragraph 21)

12. What does Tom Olson mean when he tells Hal, "Your worst troubles are inside the heads of the fellows you're trying to help!" (paragraph 20)?

A. He means the men don't have enough education to understand how to help themselves.

B. He doesn't think Hal will be able to help people who don't see any point in trying to change their lives for the better.

C. He believes the men are too angry to allow Hal to help them.

D. He doesn't think anyone can help the men improve their situation because they can't reason clearly.

13. What contrasting imagery does the author use?

A. the miners and the gunmen

B. darkness and light

C. the workers and their families

D. men and women

GO ON TO THE NEXT PAGE

14. Which details from the excerpt support the idea that Hal is different from all of the miners and their families in North Valley? Write the letters of the appropriate supporting details into the empty boxes below.

> [ ]

> [ ]

> [ ]

> (a) He comes from a privileged class.

> (b) He considers himself to be free.

> (c) He is trying to help the men.

> (d) He wants to leave the torment of North Valley.

> (e) He wanted to hear Mary's rage-filled speech.

15. Read these sentences from paragraph 14.

> She flung her arms to heaven with a gesture of passionate adjuration. "Swear it on your lives! To stick to the rest of us, and never a man of ye give way till ye've won!

What does "adjuration" mean in this context?

A. pleading
B. defiance
C. desperation
D. anger

16. In the excerpt, what does the author suggest inspired Mary to rally the men into taking action?

A. an incident between the mine owner's gunmen and the miners
B. Mary's character as a natural agitator
C. Hal's vision of her leading the men
D. the nature of life in North Valley

GO ON TO THE NEXT PAGE

17. The passage below is incomplete. For each "Select" option, choose the option that correctly completes the sentence. For this practice test, circle your selection.

Excerpt from "Resident Canada Goose Management"

Numbers of Canada geese that nest and reside predominantly within the...United States have increased exponentially in recent years. These geese are usually referred to as ''resident'' Canada geese. Recent surveys in the Atlantic, Mississippi, and Central Flyways [Select... ▼]

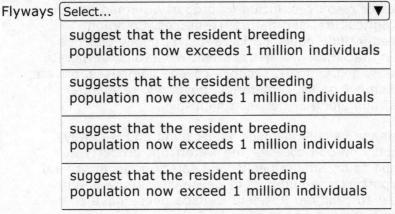

Select... ▼
suggest that the resident breeding populations now exceeds 1 million individuals
suggests that the resident breeding population now exceeds 1 million individuals
suggest that the resident breeding population now exceeds 1 million individuals
suggest that the resident breeding population now exceed 1 million individuals

in both the Atlantic and Mississippi Flyways and is increasing dramatically. Because resident Canada geese live in temperate climates with relatively stable breeding habitat conditions and low numbers of predators, [Select... ▼]

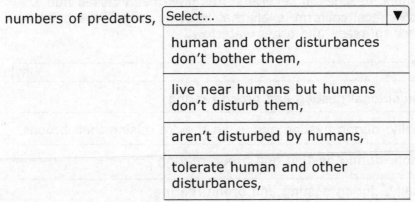

Select... ▼
human and other disturbances don't bother them,
live near humans but humans don't disturb them,
aren't disturbed by humans,
tolerate human and other disturbances,

have a relative abundance of preferred habitat provided by current urban/suburban landscaping techniques, and fly relatively short distances to winter compared with other Canada goose populations, they exhibit consistently high annual production and survival rates. Given these characteristics, the absence of waterfowl hunting in many of these areas, and free food handouts by some people, these urban/suburban resident Canada goose populations are increasingly coming into conflict with human activities in many parts of the country.

GO ON TO THE NEXT PAGE

Conflicts between geese and people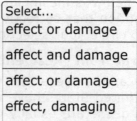

Select... ▼
effect or damage
affect and damage
affect or damage
effect, damaging

several types of resources, including property, human health and safety, agriculture, and natural resources. Common problem areas include public parks, airports, public beaches and swimming facilities, water-treatment reservoirs, corporate business areas, golf courses, schools, college campuses, private lawns, amusement parks, cemeteries, hospitals, residential subdivisions, and along or between highways.

Property damage usually involves landscaping and walkways, most commonly on golf courses and waterfront property.... Negative impacts on human health and safety occur in several ways. At airports, large numbers of geese can create a very serious threat to aviation. Resident Canada geese have been involved in a large number of aircraft strikes resulting in dangerous landing/take-off conditions and costly repairs. As a result, many airports have active goose control programs. Excessive goose droppings are a disease concern for many people. Public beaches in several states have been closed due to excessive fecal coliform levels that in some cases have been traced back to geese and other waterfowl.

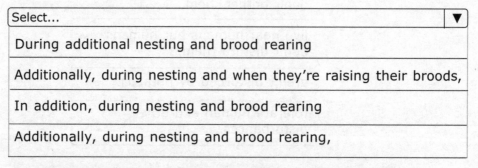

Select... ▼
During additional nesting and brood rearing
Additionally, during nesting and when they're raising their broods,
In addition, during nesting and brood rearing
Additionally, during nesting and brood rearing,

aggressive geese have bitten and chased people. Agricultural and natural resource impacts include losses to grain crops, overgrazing of pastures, and degrading water quality....Overall, complaints related to personal and public property damage, agricultural damage and other public conflicts are increasing as resident Canada goose populations increase.

Source: Department of the Interior, U.S. Fish and Wildlife Service

GO ON TO THE NEXT PAGE

Extended Response Answer Guidelines

Please use the guidelines below as you answer the Extended Response question on the Reasoning Through Language Arts test. Following these guidelines as closely as possible will ensure that you provide the best response.

1. **Please note that this task must be completed in no more than 45 minutes.** However, don't rush through your response. Be sure to read through the passage(s) and the prompt. Then think about the message you want to convey in your response. **Be sure to plan your response before you begin writing.** Draft your response and revise it as needed.

2. As you read, think carefully about the **argumentation** presented in the passage(s). "Argumentation" refers to the assumptions, claims, support, reasoning, and credibility on which a position is based. Pay close attention to **how the author(s) use these strategies to convey his or her (their) positions.**

3. When you write your essay, be sure to
   o **determine which position presented** in the passage(s) is **better supported** by evidence from the passage(s)
   o **explain why the position you chose is the better-supported one**
   o **remember, the better-supported position is not necessarily the position you agree with**
   o **defend your assertions with multiple pieces of evidence** from the passage(s)
   o **build your main points thoroughly**
   o **put your main points in logical order** and tie your details to your main points
   o **organize your response carefully** and consider your **audience, message, and purpose**
   o **use transitional words and phrases** to connect sentences, paragraphs, and ideas
   o **choose words carefully** to express your ideas clearly
   o **vary your sentence structure** to enhance the flow and clarity of your response
   o **reread and revise your response** to correct any errors in grammar, usage, or punctuation

GO ON TO THE NEXT PAGE

Instructions

Read

- On the **page 2 tab above**, you will **read two texts** presenting **different views** on the same topic.

- **Both writers argue** that **their position** on the issue is **correct**.

Plan

- **Analyze** the two texts **to determine** which writer presents the **stronger case**.

- **Develop your own argument** in which **you explain** how one position is **better supported** than the other.

- **Include** relevant and specific **evidence** from **both sources** to support your argument.

Write

- **Type** your response in the **box on the right**.

- Your response should be approximately **4 to 7 paragraphs of 3 to 7 sentences each**.

- **Remember** to allow a few minutes **to review and edit your response**.

You have up to **45 minutes** for reading, planning, writing, and editing your response.

From Live-and-Let-Live to Policeman of the West

1   In 1823, President James Monroe charted an independent U.S. foreign policy course which later became known as the Monroe Doctrine. Eager to sever ties with the Old World and grow in a new direction, free from interference, the republic would stay within its own sphere and urged the European powers to stay within theirs. "It is still the true policy of the United States to leave the parties to themselves, in hope that other powers will pursue the same course," Monroe declared.

2   By the early 1900s, in the light of threatened European intervention to collect debts from Venezuela and later, from the Dominican Republic, President Theodore Roosevelt felt the need to add teeth to the Monroe Doctrine. Instead of a policy of live-and-let-live, Roosevelt asserted America's right to active intervention in the affairs of Latin American countries. "Chronic wrongdoing...may force the United States, however reluctantly, in flagrant cases of such wrongdoing or impotence, to the exercise of an international police power," he declared in his December 6, 1904 annual address to Congress.

3   This position, called the Roosevelt Corollary to the Monroe Doctrine, was a major reversal from the previous passive, defensive stance to active intervention on America's terms. "We do not intend to permit the Monroe Doctrine to be used by any nation on this Continent as a shield to protect it from the consequences of its own misdeeds against foreign nations," he declared a year later, in his

GO ON TO THE NEXT PAGE

December 5, 1905 annual message to Congress. Instead of urging European nations to refrain from colonizing the western hemisphere any further, as the Monroe Doctrine had done, Roosevelt now claimed the right to active intervention if any newly independent Latin American country invited military adventures to the western hemisphere by its former colonial master.

Extending, Not Upending the Monroe Doctrine

4   Contrary to the opinion of some historians, President Theodore Roosevelt's 1904 addition to the Monroe Doctrine—commonly called the Roosevelt Corollary—did not signal a significant shift in U.S. foreign policy. Faced with the possibility that Spain had ambitions in the western hemisphere, President James Monroe had declared decades earlier that "the American continents, by the free and independent condition which they have assumed and maintain, are henceforth not to be considered as subjects for future colonization by any European powers."

5   This position, delivered during an address to Congress on December 2, 1823, was balanced by an offer to stay out of European affairs. "In the wars of the European powers in matters relating to themselves we have never taken any part, nor does it comport with our policy to do so," Monroe said. However, he wasn't advancing a strictly hands-off policy. "It is only when our rights are invaded or seriously menaced that we resent injuries or make preparation for our defense," he continued.

6   Those who see the Roosevelt Corollary as an about-face don't give enough weight to Monroe's pledge to defend America's sovereignty. It sounds quite similar to this declaration from Roosevelt in 1904: "We would interfere with them ["our southern neighbors"] only in the last resort, and then only if it became evident that their inability or unwillingness to do justice at home and abroad had violated the rights of the United States or had invited foreign aggression."

7   Roosevelt even invoked the Monroe Doctrine when he laid out the conditions for abandoning a stance of non-interference. "In the Western Hemisphere the adherence of the United States to the Monroe Doctrine may force the United States, however reluctantly, in flagrant cases of such wrongdoing or impotence, to the exercise of an international police power."

8   The chief difference between the two positions is that, in Monroe's time, the young country did not really have the power to enforce its prohibition against future European colonization of the Americas. By the time Roosevelt's era arrived, it did.

You may take a 10-minute break before proceeding to Section 3.

GO ON TO THE NEXT PAGE

Questions 18 through 25 refer to the following passage.

Excerpt from *The Art of Money Getting*
by P.T. Barnum

Advertise Your Business

1   The whole philosophy of life is, first "sow," then "reap." That is the way the farmer does; he plants his potatoes and corn, and sows his grain, and then goes about something else, and the time comes when he reaps. But he never reaps first and sows afterwards. This principle applies to all kinds of business, and to nothing more eminently than to advertising. If a man has a genuine article, there is no way in which he can reap more advantageously than by "sowing" to the public in this way. He must, of course, have a really good article, and one which will please his customers; anything spurious will not succeed permanently because the public is wiser than many imagine. Men and women are selfish, and we all prefer purchasing where we can get the most for our money and we try to find out where we can most surely do so....

2   A man said to me, "I have tried advertising and did not succeed; yet I have a good article."

3   I replied, "My friend, there may be exceptions to a general rule. But how do you advertise?"

4   "I put it in a weekly newspaper three times, and paid a dollar and a half for it."

5   I replied: "Sir, advertising is like learning—'a little is a dangerous thing!'"

6   A French writer says that "The reader of a newspaper does not see the first mention of an ordinary advertisement; the second insertion he sees, but does not read; the third insertion he reads; the fourth insertion, he looks at the price; the fifth insertion, he speaks of it to his wife; the sixth insertion, he is ready to purchase, and the seventh insertion, he purchases." Your object in advertising is to make the public understand what you have got to sell, and if you have not the pluck to keep advertising, until you have imparted that information, all the money you have spent is lost. You are like the fellow who told the gentleman if he would give him ten cents it would save him a dollar. "How can I help you so much with so small a sum?" asked the gentleman in surprise. "I started out this morning (hiccupped the fellow) with the full determination to get drunk, and I have spent my only dollar to accomplish the object, and it has not quite done it. Ten cents worth more of whiskey would just do it, and in this manner I should save the dollar already expended."

GO ON TO THE NEXT PAGE

7   So a man who advertises at all must keep it up until the public know who and what he is, and what his business is, or else the money invested in advertising is lost....

8   Sometimes a man makes himself popular by an unique sign or a curious display in his window. Recently I observed a swing sign extending over the sidewalk in front of a store, on which was the inscription in plain letters,

"Don't Read The Other Side"

9   Of course I did, and so did everybody else, and I learned that the man had made an independence by first attracting the public to his business in that way and then using his customers well afterwards.

10   Genin, the hatter, bought the first Jenny Lind ticket at auction for two hundred and twenty-five dollars, because he knew it would be a good advertisement for him. "Who is the bidder?" said the auctioneer, as he knocked down that ticket at Castle Garden. "Genin, the hatter," was the response. Here were thousands of people from the Fifth avenue, and from distant cities in the highest stations in life. "Who is 'Genin,' the hatter?" they exclaimed. They had never heard of him before. The next morning the newspapers and telegraph had circulated the facts from Maine to Texas, and from five to ten millions of people had read that the tickets sold at auction for Jenny Lind's first concert amounted to about twenty thousand dollars, and that a single ticket was sold at two hundred and twenty-five dollars, to "Genin, the hatter." Men throughout the country involuntarily took off their hats to see if they had a "Genin" hat on their heads....

11   What was the consequence to Mr. Genin? He sold ten thousand extra hats per annum, the first six years. Nine-tenths of the purchasers bought of him, probably, out of curiosity, and many of them, finding that he gave them an equivalent for their money, became his regular customers. This novel advertisement first struck their attention, and then, as he made a good article, they came again....

GO ON TO THE NEXT PAGE

18. Based on this excerpt, what can you infer about the author's intended audience?

    A. His readers are professional businesspeople.
    B. He is aiming at well-educated entrepreneurs.
    C. He is writing for ordinary people who have or plan to have a small business.
    D. He is addressing owners of retail shops selling products to the general public.

19. What does the story about the drunk (paragraph 6) add to the author's argument?

    A. It provides an example that would be familiar to readers from a mass audience.
    B. It reinforces Barnum's point that if you don't persevere until you reach your goal, you will have squandered all of the resources you've already spent in the effort.
    C. It illustrates that you don't need to spend a lot of money in order to succeed.
    D. It would be more entertaining for readers than the preceding quote from the French writer, and would therefore encourage them to keep reading.

20. Read this part of the sentence from paragraph 9.

    > I learned that the man had made an independence by first attracting the public to his business...and then using his customers well afterwards.

    As it is used in this sentence, the term "made an independence" most likely means that

    A. the man's business grew enough to support him and his family.
    B. he was able to open his own business and become his own boss.
    C. he could pay off his debts and hire more workers.
    D. he was able to buy out his business partners and run the shop on his own.

21. Drag and drop two characteristics that do NOT describe Mr. Genin into the empty boxes below. (For this practice test, you may write the letters of your selections in the boxes below.)

    [ ]

    [ ]

    (a) miserly

    (b) innovative

    (c) ambitious

    (d) timid

GO ON TO THE NEXT PAGE

22. The use of direct dialogue in the story about the man who advertised in the newspaper serves to

    A. convince readers that the author knows what he's talking about because he spoke to a real person.
    B. break up the monotony of the author simply telling readers what they should do.
    C. appeal to poorly educated readers who are more accustomed to watching plays than to reading books.
    D. draw readers in by making the story more immediate and believable.

23. Which of the following best describes the author's purpose?

    A. to inform
    B. to educate and entertain
    C. to teach
    D. to improve skills

24. In each box below, write the letter for a lesson that readers can learn from the results of Mr. Genin's ticket purchase.

    (a) Seven repetitions are required before a customer will buy your product.

    (b) An innovative, unusual advertising technique will attract a new customer only once.

    (c) People prefer to buy from a local business.

    (d) There are better ways to use a newspaper to promote your business than paying for advertising space.

25. Read the following sentence from the first paragraph.

    > He must, of course, have a really good article, and one which will please his customers; anything spurious will not succeed permanently because the public is wiser than many imagine.

    As Barnum uses it in this sentence, the word "spurious" means

    A. outrageous.
    B. common.
    C. shoddy.
    D. luxurious.

GO ON TO THE NEXT PAGE

Questions 26 through 33 refer to the following passage.

Excerpt from
"The Defense Acquisition Trilemma: The Case of Brazil"
by Patrice Franko

Costs of Preserving Autonomy

1   When we type the term *unholy trinity* into Google Translate, "profane trinity" pops up in Portuguese. Indeed profanities might slip out as frustrated defense policymakers navigate the tough tradeoffs between defense modernization and autonomy with a relatively fixed pool of budgetary resources. Sovereignty, or the ability to implement self-rule without being constrained by others, has long been an unsatisfied objective of Brazilian policy. Autonomy can be understood as the means to implement sovereign decision-making in a global system. Powerful nations are able to exercise autonomy in the pursuit of sovereign goals. Although a country may be seen as sovereign in a legal sense, in practice less powerful countries have been unable to control territorial incursions or exclude external actors from domestic interference.

2   Brazil has been characterized as a nation whose strategy is grounded by nationalism in the service of sovereignty.... Brazil's search for autonomy is a guiding concept in its foreign policy. The doctrine articulated by the Escola Superior da Guerra (Superior War College) defines *national power* as the capacity to act independently, supported by an array of men and means, to reach and maintain national objectives. Such national power is expressed through five elements: politics, economics, psychosocial factors, the military, and a scientific and technological base...

3   Yet for Brazil, autonomy has been an elusive quest....

4   Affirming Brazilian national interests involves contesting the asymmetries of power in the global system. Brazil has taken on asymmetries of power through three expressions of autonomy: distance, participation, and diversification. In the first stage, paralleling the economic approach of import substitution industrialization, Brazil turned inward and engaged in a foreign policy that imposed distance between itself and hegemonic powers. It diversified its diplomatic and trade relations and formalized its identity as a representative of the Third World in North-South relations. During this period, which largely dates from the beginning of the military regime in 1964 through the transition to democracy in the early 1980s, the country condemned the control of international trade, finance, and nuclear regimes by the hegemonic North while forging alternative relationships among Southern partners. Autonomy through distance largely opposed the international order of the time,

GO ON TO THE NEXT PAGE

preferring greater autarky from the great powers to preserve sovereignty.

5   The expression of Brazilian autonomy was transformed by changes in the global economy. As the import substitution model was thwarted by the global debt crises of the 1980s, a change in approach became necessary. Reluctantly at first, Brazilian policymakers slowly became convinced of the need to participate in global political and economic institutions in order to acquire power....Brazil edged toward greater participation in multilateral forums as a means of achieving its goal of autonomy. Autonomy came to be seen as the ability to influence world affairs. To become an international force, Brazil perceived that it needed to play within global regimes. Although suspicious of a close embrace with the United States, Brazil began a systematic insertion in global institutions. Rather than rejecting the neoliberal order, it began to use institutions such as the World Trade Organization to gain leverage and policy space. Pragmatism prevailed. In order to be seen as a cooperative player in economic and environmental spheres, Brazil accepted international norms in the security sector. It renounced the right to conduct nuclear tests, even for peaceful purposes, and introduced nuclear safeguards and protection of sensitive military technologies....

6   As U.S. unilateralism became more dominant in the new millennium, Brazil practiced greater assertiveness in international institutions as a counterweight to American power. But rather than retreating into autarky to preserve autonomy, Brazil built strength within global institutions by widening its cooperative base. With the goal of redressing asymmetries in the international arena, Brazil pursued its new foreign policy agenda of human and social rights, environmentalism, technology, and managed financial flows in concert with other developing country partners. Autonomy through diversification therefore embraced South American neighbors through Mercosur (Southern Common Market), amplified South Atlantic ties with Africa, and built frameworks for cooperation with other big emerging markets in the BRICS (Brazil, Russia, India, China, and South Africa) club. Autonomy through diversification does not reject the institution-building and rule-setting agendas of participation; rather, it shifts the locus of engagement from a broader multilateral stage to a South-South approach. In the service of creating a greater equilibrium in global affairs, autonomy intensified relations with emerging market partners to propel a Southern momentum in foreign policy. Attempting to leverage the global economic rebalancing toward the South, Brazil has been pushing for more policy space at the strategic level for developing country partners, thereby enhancing its autonomy at home. Such partnerships with developing countries have been characterized as "consensual hegemony" that rests on shared interests of participating states.

Source: Institute for National Strategic Studies, U.S. Department of Defense

GO ON TO THE NEXT PAGE

26. Below are three initiatives that Brazil undertook as it explored different ways of achieving autonomy. Place these initiatives in chronological order by writing the letters of your selections in the empty boxes below. The earliest initiative is at the top, and the most recent is at the bottom.

> Earliest initiative

> Next initiative

> Most recent initiative

> (a) Brazil became pragmatic and accepted international norms for security.

> (b) Brazil moved toward closer cooperation with partners in emerging markets.

> (c) Brazil turned inward.

27. The term "autarky" (paragraphs 4 and 6) means

    A. hostility.
    B. isolation.
    C. cooperation.
    D. self-sufficiency.

28. Read these sentences from paragraph 1.

> When we type the term *unholy trinity* into Google Translate, "profane trinity" pops up in Portuguese. Indeed profanities might slip out as frustrated defense policymakers navigate the tough tradeoffs between defense modernization and autonomy with a relatively fixed pool of budgetary resources.

How does the "unholy trinity" apply to Brazil?

    A. It suggests that Brazil has been pursuing the wrong strategy.
    B. It explains why autonomy has eluded Brazil.
    C. It highlights the difference between Brazil and its emerging market partners.
    D. It explains why Brazil's foreign policy changed when the country made the transition from military regime to democracy.

29. According to the excerpt, what role did environmental initiatives have in Brazil's pursuit of autonomy?

    A. It pursued them enthusiastically in order to strengthen its economy.
    B. It championed them in order to encourage less developed countries to follow its lead.
    C. It embraced them as a means of reaching out to other countries.
    D. It ignored them because it had more urgent priorities.

GO ON TO THE NEXT PAGE

30. Read the following statement from paragraph 4.

> In the first stage, paralleling the economic approach of import substitution industrialization, Brazil turned inward...

Which of the following would be an example of "import substitution industrialization"?

A. buying grapes from Spain when grapes from Italy become too expensive

B. building a domestic automobile manufacturing industry instead of importing cars from other producing countries

C. expanding electricity generation in order to have a surplus to sell to other countries

D. allowing the country's banks to set below-market interest rates on loans to domestic ship-building companies so those companies can expand their operations

31. Which examples does the author cite to support her claim that "Brazil's search for autonomy is a guiding concept in its foreign policy" (paragraph 2)? Write the letters of the supporting points into the empty boxes below.

```
┌─────────────┐
│             │
└─────────────┘

┌─────────────┐
│             │
└─────────────┘

┌─────────────┐
│             │
└─────────────┘
```

(a) Brazil rejected institution-building and the creation of elaborate sets of rules.

(b) Brazil gave up the right to conduct nuclear tests, even for peaceful purposes.

(c) Brazil developed a scientific and technological base.

(d) Brazil sought a place in international institutions.

(e) Brazil worked within the World Trade Organization.

GO ON TO THE NEXT PAGE

32. Read the following sentences from paragraph 1.

> Sovereignty, or the ability to implement self-rule without being constrained by others, has long been an unsatisfied objective of Brazilian policy. Autonomy can be understood as the means to implement sovereign decision-making in a global system.

As the author defines them, what is the relationship between sovereignty and autonomy?

A. Autonomy requires other countries.
B. Autonomy requires sovereignty.
C. They mean the same thing.
D. Sovereignty is impossible without autonomy.

33. As Brazil experimented with different ways of attaining autonomy, how did it shift the focus for its partnerships?

A. from South-South to North-South, in order to be seen as the most influential representative of southern developing countries
B. from South to North-South grouping, so it could join forces with the more powerful countries in the north during the 1980s financial crisis
C. from former northern partners to southern partnerships, so it could openly criticize northern countries' control of international trade and finance
D. from a broad multi-party focus to a South-South alliance, in order to counteract the weight of the United States

GO ON TO THE NEXT PAGE

Questions 34 through 41 refer to the following passage.

Excerpt from "Hilda Silfverling. A Fantasy"
by Lydia Maria Child

1 Poor Hilda, thankful for any chance to keep her disgrace a secret, gratefully accepted the offer. When the babe was ten days old, she allowed the good Virika to carry it away; though not without bitter tears, and the oft-repeated promise that her little one might be reclaimed, whenever Magnus returned and fulfilled his promise of marriage....

2 It chanced, very unfortunately, that soon after Virika's departure, an infant was found in the water, strangled with a sash very like one Hilda had been accustomed to wear. A train of circumstantial evidence seemed to connect the child with her, and she was arrested. For some time, she contented herself with assertions of innocence....But at last, having the fear of death before her eyes, she acknowledged that she had given birth to a daughter, which had been carried away by Virika Gjetter, to her native place,...Inquiries were accordingly made in Norway, but the answer obtained was that Virika had not been heard of in her native valley, for many years. Through weary months, Hilda lingered in prison,...and at last, on strong circumstantial evidence she was condemned to die.

3 It chanced there was at that time a very learned chemist in Stockholm;...He had discovered a process of artificial cold, by which he could suspend animation in living creatures, and restore it at any prescribed time....A metaphysician suggested how extremely interesting it would be to put a human being asleep thus, and watch the reunion of soul and body, after the lapse of a hundred years. The chemist was half wild with the magnificence of this idea; and he forthwith petitioned that Hilda, instead of being beheaded, might be delivered to him, to be frozen for a century....

4 The subject of this curious experiment was conveyed in a close carriage from the prison to the laboratory. A shudder ran through soul and body, as she entered the apartment assigned her. It was built entirely of stone, and rendered intensely cold by an artificial process. The light was dim and spectral....Around the sides of the room, were tiers of massive stone shelves, on which reposed various objects in a torpid state. A huge bear lay on his back, with paws crossed on his breast, as devoutly as some pious knight of the fourteenth century....

5 The pale face of the maiden became still paler,...She seized the arm of the old chemist, and said, imploringly, "You will not go away?"...

GO ON TO THE NEXT PAGE

6   He replied, not without some touch of compassion in his tones, "You will be sound asleep, my dear, and will not know whether I am here or not. Drink this; it will soon make you drowsy."...

7   The poor girl cast another despairing glance round the tomb-like apartment, and did as she was requested. "And now," said the chemist, "let us shake hands, and say farewell; for you will never see me again."

8   "Why, won't you come to wake me up?" inquired the prisoner; not reflecting on all the peculiar circumstances of her condition.

9   "My great-grandson may," replied he, with a smile. "Adieu, my dear. It is a great deal pleasanter than being beheaded. You will fall asleep as easily as a babe in his cradle."...

10   He handed her up very politely, gathered her garments about her feet, crossed her arms below her breast, and told her to be perfectly still. He then covered his face with a mask, let some gasses escape from an apparatus in the centre of the room, and immediately went out, locking the door after him....

11   The earth whirled round on its axis, carrying with it the Alps and the Andes, the bear, the crocodile, and the maiden.... America took place among the nations; Bonaparte played out his great game, with kingdoms for pawns; and still the Swedish damsel slept on her stone shelf with the bear and the crocodile.

12   When ninety-five years had passed, the bear, having fulfilled his prescribed century, was waked according to agreement. The curious flocked round him, to see him eat, and hear whether he could growl as well as other bears. Not liking such close observation, he broke his chain one night, and made off for the hills....Bears, being more strictly conservative than men, happily escape the influence of French revolutions, German philosophy, Fourier theories, and reforms of all sorts; therefore Bruin doubtless found less change in *his* fellow citizens, than an old knight or viking might have done....

13   At last, came the maiden's turn to be resuscitated....The old chemist and his children all "slept the sleep that knows no waking." But carefully written orders had been transmitted from generation to generation; and the duty finally devolved on a great grandson, himself a chemist of no mean reputation.

14   Life returned very slowly; at first by almost imperceptible degrees, then by a visible shivering through the nerves. When the eyes opened...there was something painfully strange in their marble gaze. But the lamp within the inner shrine lighted up, and gradually shone through them, giving assurance of the presence of a soul....

GO ON TO THE NEXT PAGE

15   The numbers who came to look at her, their perpetual questions how things seemed to her, what was the state of her appetite and her memory, made her restless and irritable....

16   After a few weeks, the forlorn being made her escape from the city...to her native village, under the new name of Hilda Silfverling. But to stand, in the bloom of sixteen, among well-remembered hills and streams, and not recognise a single human face, or know a single human voice, this was the most mournful of all; far worse than loneliness in a foreign land; sadder than sunshine on a ruined city.

34.   Which quotes from the passage are associated with the theme of trust? Write the letters of those that apply into the empty boxes below.

```
┌─────────────────────────────┐
│                             │
└─────────────────────────────┘

┌─────────────────────────────┐
│                             │
└─────────────────────────────┘

┌─────────────────────────────┐
│                             │
└─────────────────────────────┘
```

┌─────────────────────────────────┐
│ (a) "whenever Magnus returned and │
│ fulfilled his promise of marriage" │
│ (paragraph 1)   │
└─────────────────────────────────┘

┌─────────────────────────────────┐
│ (b) "You will be sound asleep, ... and │
│ will not know whether I am here or │
│ not." (paragraph 6)   │
└─────────────────────────────────┘

┌─────────────────────────────────┐
│ (c) "he forthwith petitioned that Hil- │
│ da, instead of being beheaded, might │
│ be delivered to him, to be frozen for │
│ a century" (paragraph 3)   │
└─────────────────────────────────┘

┌─────────────────────────────────┐
│ (d) "the oft-repeated promise that │
│ her little one might be reclaimed" │
│ (paragraph 1)   │
└─────────────────────────────────┘

┌─────────────────────────────────┐
│ (e) "won't you come to wake me up?" │
│ (paragraph 8)   │
└─────────────────────────────────┘

35.   On which character in the excerpt does Hilda depend the most?

A.   on the bear, because his experience of being awakened will be a preview of hers

B.   on the chemist, because his skill in carrying out the suspended animation process will determine whether Hilda wakes up

C.   on Virika, because she is charged with keeping the baby safe until Hilda can reclaim her

D.   on the legal authorities, because they could prevent Hilda from being beheaded by allowing the chemist to have her for his suspended animation experiment

36.   Which quote from the passage supports the idea that the chemist had another motive—besides keeping a promise—for making sure that Hilda would wake up again after 100 years?

A.   "Written orders had been transmitted from generation to generation." (paragraph 13)

B.   "It is a great deal pleasanter than being beheaded." (paragraph 9)

C.   "The chemist was half wild with the magnificence of this idea." (paragraph 3)

D.   "He replied, not without some touch of compassion in his tones." (paragraph 6)

GO ON TO THE NEXT PAGE

37. Which of the following does NOT explain how the description of the chemist's laboratory (paragraph 4) affects the narrative?

    A. It accentuates the contrast between Hilda's two possible fates.
    B. It reinforces the idea that Hilda is fortunate to have the chance to wake up in 100 years.
    C. It deepens the divide between Hilda's previous life and her current situation.
    D. It intensifies the atmosphere of horror.

38. Consider the chronological order of events in the excerpt. What is the main impact of the bear's resuscitation occurring before Hilda's?

    A. It proves that the chemist's suspended animation process works.
    B. It foreshadows the experience Hilda will have.
    C. It shows that the chemist was able to pass the instructions down to his great-grandson.
    D. It lays the foundation for a comment on human progress.

39. Which events highlight the same theme in the excerpt?

    A. Hilda's conviction and the chemist asking to use her in his suspended animation experiment
    B. the birth of Hilda's baby and Hilda's resuscitation from suspended animation
    C. Virika taking the baby and Hilda's admission that she gave birth to a baby
    D. the bear's escape to the hills and Hilda's resuscitation

40. Which of the following is the most likely reason why the legal authorities agreed to let the chemist have Hilda for his experiment?

    A. Hilda would be effectively dead during their lifetimes.
    B. They were hesitant to behead such a young girl.
    C. They wanted the glory of contributing to such a famous scientist's work.
    D. They didn't believe the chemist could really awaken her.

41. Which words best capture an overall description of Hilda as she is portrayed throughout the excerpt? Write the letters of your three selections in the character web below.

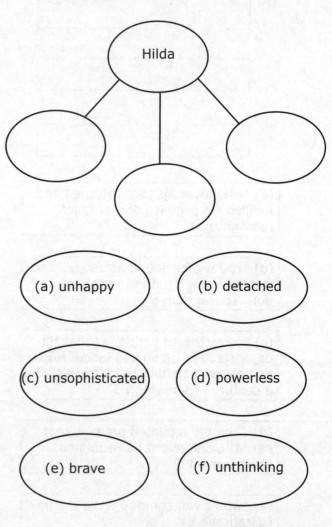

(a) unhappy

(b) detached

(c) unsophisticated

(d) powerless

(e) brave

(f) unthinking

GO ON TO THE NEXT PAGE

Questions 42 through 49 refer to the following passage.

Excerpt from
"The Geological Exploration of Tibet and the Himalaya"
by Nigel Harris

1   Modern understanding of the geology of the highest mountains
on Earth really began with the exploration of the ocean floor and
the formulation of the theory of plate tectonics....Since the early
1960s, earth scientists have realized that oceans were transient
features, growing from sinuous volcanic ridges such as the mid-
Atlantic ridge; these are largely submarine but occasionally form
spectacular volcanic islands, such as Iceland today. Oceans not
only grow but also shrink, due to a process called subduction,
and in the contraction of ocean basins the continents on their
opposing sides converge. The final stage of this process is
collision between two continents. Continental crust is less
dense than oceanic crust, and much less dense than the mantle
beneath it. The low density means that continents cannot be
subducted far beneath the surface. The result is that, although
the processes of the Earth's plates can create crust at subduction
zones, they cannot get rid of it. So after continental collision the
crust crumples and thickens.

2   Professor John Dewey, now at Oxford University, identified the
Himalaya as a possible example of continental collision during
the 1970s. One of the lines of evidence for a collision model
came from geophysical results, from gravity and seismic surveys,
which indicated that the crust beneath the Himalaya is over
60 km thick, twice the normal thickness for continental crust.
A head-on collision between two vast continents will obviously
crumple and thicken the leading edges of the continents. This
explains why the Himalaya is so high—the low density of the
continental crust means that the surface of thickened continents
is uplifted to great altitudes. Like a block of wood floating on
water, the thicker the block the higher it will stand above the
water-line (and the deeper are its roots). So the low density of
the continents means that crust which has been thickened will
be uplifted....

3   Earth scientists have also traced the movement of India before
its impact with the rest of Asia. About 100 million years ago,
India lay in the southern hemisphere where it fragmented from
a vast southern landmass, rifting from Madagascar along its
western coast and from Antarctica along its eastern coast. India
drifted north at a velocity of about 20 cm per year. Impact with
the rest of Asia occurred 50 million years ago. The fragments
of oceanic crust found by Augusto Gansser in the Indus valley
are the remains of a vast ocean floor which was folded and
crumpled within the suture zone that now separates the former
continental masses.

GO ON TO THE NEXT PAGE

4   This simple model of collision between two continents explains the formation of a narrow high mountain range such as the Himalaya, but does not obviously explain the Tibetan Plateau. Like the Himalaya, Tibet is supported by an unusually thick crust. A related problem is the continued northern movement of India. Since the initial collision the two continents have not simply fused into a single supercontinent. India and the rest of Asia have continued to converge at an average rate of 5 cm a year, amounting to over 2,000 km since the ocean was first closed by subduction. Three models have been proposed to account for such a staggering convergence between continents in the absence of an intervening ocean.

5   Firstly, the crust can be squeezed out sideways. The idea was first put forward in 1975 by Peter Molnar of MIT and Paul Tapponier of the University of Paris. On satellite images they spotted long faults dissecting the Earth's crust in northern, eastern and western Tibet. From analysing the seismic waves associated with earthquake activity that result from movement along the faults they determined that the Earth's crust is moving sideways across them. Such faults are called strike-slip faults.... The Molnar-Tapponier model for crustal deformation in Tibet predicts that movement across these strike-slip faults allows wedges of continent to move out sideways, particularly to the east, clearing the path of the converging continents.

6   Secondly, the Indian crust may be thrust under Tibet by a series of faults which dip towards the north; such faults which result from compression of the crust are known as thrust-faults....Field-work in the Himalaya has identified a series of such faults. The devastating earthquakes that plague the lives of inhabitants along the southern slopes of the Himalaya result from movement along these thrust-faults. Although no single fault carries a slice of continental crust more than a few tens of kilometres beneath another, their combined effect is to thicken up the crust. Some mountains owe their altitude to movement on such faults. Nanga Parbat, for example, is an extraordinary mountain in that it is a long way from any other 8000-metre Himalayan peak and stands proud of its neighbours by several thousand metres. This is partly because it lies on a finger of the Indian plate which points north into the Asian landmass, and is riding upwards on thrust-faults to the north, east and west.

7   A third theory for the mechanism of India's northward movement suggests that the crust may shorten by stretching vertically, as a piece of plasticine is lengthened when squashed from the side. The vertical stretching model is not needed in the Himalaya because much of the convergence can be explained by the major thrust-faults, but it could account for crustal shortening across the Tibetan Plateau.

Source: *The Alpine Journal*, Vol. 96, pp. 70–71, 1991. © The Alpine Club. Reprinted with permission of the Alpine Club and Nigel Harris.

GO ON TO THE NEXT PAGE

42. Which of the following is the most likely definition of "subduction" (paragraph 1)?

    A. a process that explains the formation of high mountains
    B. movement in which one of the Earth's plates is forced underneath another plate
    C. a property of the Earth's crust that prevents continents from converging
    D. the interaction of the Earth's plates

43. Which of the following is a characteristic of the passage supporting the idea that the author was writing primarily for people involved in mountaineering rather than for geologists?

    A. The author refers readers to other mountaineering sources rather than giving references to works by geologists.
    B. The author focuses on the geology of mountains that mountaineers find the most technically challenging.
    C. The author explains the process behind the formation of the world's highest mountains.
    D. The author defines technical terms used by geologists.

44. In paragraphs 1 and 2, the author describes several events that led to the formation of the Himalayas. Place the following events in sequence by writing their letters in the corresponding boxes below.

    First event

    Second event

    Third event

    Fourth event

    Fifth event

    Sixth event

    Seventh event

    (a) The two continents collide.

    (b) The crust at the leading edge of the continents crumples and thickens.

    (c) Subduction occurs on the ocean floor.

    (d) The continents on opposing sides of the ocean basin converge.

    (e) The surface of the thickened crust is uplifted.

    (f) A crust is created.

    (g) The ocean basin contracts.

GO ON TO THE NEXT PAGE

45. From the overall tone and content of the passage, you can infer that the author's main purpose is to

    A. inspire.
    B. entertain.
    C. educate.
    D. interest.

46. According to the passage, why did geologists first need to understand plate tectonics and subduction in the ocean before they could understand "the geology of the highest mountains on Earth" (paragraph 1)?

    A. so they would understand the cause and the effect of continental collision
    B. as a contrast to the results of movement of the Earth's plates on land
    C. so they would understand the impact of faults on the movement of the Earth's plates
    D. because subduction in the ocean works the same way as subduction in colliding continents on land

47. The author presents three theories for the continuing convergence of India and Asia. What can you infer about his reason for the order in which he arranged those three theories?

    A. He went from the most well-known theory, to a similar theory involving a different kind of fault line, to a theory which does not concern faults.
    B. He arranged the theories in decreasing order of supporting evidence, from the best supported to the most speculative.
    C. He started with the theory he considers the most likely and ended with the one he thinks is least likely.
    D. He arranged them according to when each theory was developed, beginning with the earliest.

48. The author would likely agree with which of the following statements?

    A. If only there were more money and scientific minds, we would have more certainty about the forces and processes that are operating on the Earth.
    B. Theories about geological processes can all be verified by observation and analysis, allowing us to eliminate incorrect theories.
    C. Scientists should be encouraged to work together if they're investigating the same phenomenon, in order to minimize the development of conflicting theories.
    D. After so many years of scientific discovery, we are still learning about the processes at work on the Earth.

49. What evidence leads the author to conclude that a "simple model of collision between two continents" (paragraph 4) does not explain the high, vast Tibetan plateau?

    A. "Nanga Parbat...is a long way from any other 8000-metre Himalayan peak and stands proud of its neighbours by several thousand metres." (paragraph 6)
    B. "Fragments of oceanic crust found...in the Indus valley are the remains of a vast ocean floor which was folded and crumpled." (paragraph 3)
    C. "Tibet is supported by an unusually thick crust." (paragraph 4)
    D. "A head-on collision between two vast continents will obviously crumple and thicken the leading edges of the continents." (paragraph 2)

GO ON TO THE NEXT PAGE

50. The passage below is incomplete. For each "Select" option, choose the option that correctly completes the sentence. For this practice test, circle your selection.

Frequently Asked Questions About the Adventure Experience Card

With the Adventure Experience Card, you'll earn 3% on adventure trip purchases and 0.5% on everything else.

If you're wondering about some other features of the Adventure Experience Card, you might find the answer in the Frequently Asked Questions below. If you still have questions, our knowledgeable customer care agents are ready to help. Simply call 555-555-1111 or click "Chat now."

Which trips qualify as adventure experiences?

Are you trekking through Annapurna? Whitewater rafting on the Futaleufu River? Extreme skiing in the Alps? On safari in Kenya? Hang-gliding over Costa Rica? Then the experience will likely qualify as an adventure and earn a 3% reward. On the other hand, if you're cruising the Caribbean or seeing the sights of Europe with a guided bus tour,

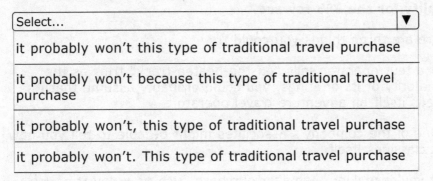

Select... ▼
it probably won't this type of traditional travel purchase
it probably won't because this type of traditional travel purchase
it probably won't, this type of traditional travel purchase
it probably won't. This type of traditional travel purchase

earns a 0.5% reward.

GO ON TO THE NEXT PAGE

Do you publish a list of companies that call themselves adventure travel operators?

There are many companies offering short-term and long-term adventure experiences, with new ones popping up all the time,

Select... ▼
however, it would be impossible to maintain an up-to-date list.
so it would be impossible to maintain an up-to-date list.
it would be impossible to maintain an up-to-date list.
which would make it impossible to maintain an up-to-date list because there are too many and they change too often.

We rely on your chosen suppliers to classify themselves as adventure travel operators when they submit your purchase for payment through our system.

How can I find out in advance if a trip purchase will qualify for the 3% reward?

There are three things you could try.

- If a tour operator sells "off-the-beaten-track" trips as the majority of its offerings, you could probably assume that it calls itself an adventure travel operator.

- One of the company's associates might be able to tell you how it classifies itself.

- If you're making a smaller purchase such as a day trip, you could treat that as an experiment

Select... ▼
to see if it earns the 3% reward
and try and see if it earns the 3% reward
to see that it earns the 3% reward
to try seeing whether it could earn the 3% reward

before making a larger purchase from that company.

GO ON TO THE NEXT PAGE

How do I redeem rewards?

Once your reward reaches $50 or more, simply contact us to redeem your reward. You can choose to receive your reward as a credit on your next purchase, as a deposit to your linked bank account, or as a mailed check.

Is there any limit to the amount of rewards I can earn?

You will earn 3% on the first $5,000 of adventure experience purchases in a year.

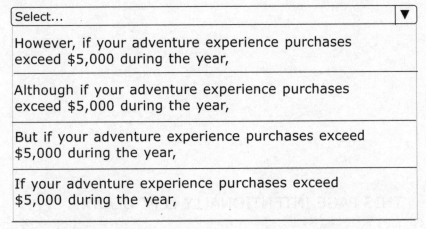

Select... ▼
However, if your adventure experience purchases exceed $5,000 during the year,
Although if your adventure experience purchases exceed $5,000 during the year,
But if your adventure experience purchases exceed $5,000 during the year,
If your adventure experience purchases exceed $5,000 during the year,

the balance will earn rewards at the rate of 0.5%.

Can I use the Adventure Experience Card for other types of purchases?

You certainly can! Use the Adventure Experience Card when you do all of your regular shopping. Any purchase from a business that accepts the Adventure Experience Card qualifies for a 0.5% reward.

END OF TEST

THIS PAGE INTENTIONALLY LEFT BLANK.

Mathematical Reasoning

Welcome!

Here is some information that you need to know before you start this test:

- You should not spend too much time on a question if you are not certain of the answer; answer it the best you can, and go on to the next question.
- If you are not certain of the answer to a question, you can mark your answer for review and come back to it later.
- You have **115 minutes** to complete this test.
- This test has two parts.
- When you finish Part 1, you may review those questions.
- You may not go back to Part 1 once you have finished your review.
- You may not use a calculator in Part 1. You may use a calculator in Part 2.

Turn the page to begin.

GO ON TO THE NEXT PAGE

Mathematics Formula Sheet

Area of a:

square	$A = s^2$
rectangle	$A = lw$
parallelogram	$A = bh$
triangle	$A = \frac{1}{2}bh$
trapezoid	$A = \frac{1}{2}h(b_1 + b_2)$
circle	$A = \pi r^2$

Perimeter of a:

square	$P = 4s$
rectangle	$P = 2l + 2w$
triangle	$P = s_1 + s_2 + s_3$
Circumference of a circle	$C = 2\pi r$ OR $C = \pi d$; $\pi \approx 3.14$

Surface Area and Volume of a:

rectangular prism	$SA = 2lw + 2lh + 2wh$	$V = lwh$
right prism	$SA = ph + 2B$	$V = Bh$
cylinder	$SA = 2\pi rh + 2\pi r^2$	$V = \pi r^2 h$
pyramid	$SA = \frac{1}{2}ps + B$	$V = \frac{1}{3}Bh$
cone	$SA = \pi rs + \pi r^2$	$V = \frac{1}{3}\pi r^2 h$
sphere	$SA = 4\pi r^2$	$V = \frac{4}{3}\pi r^3$

(p = perimeter of base B; $\pi \approx 3.14$)

Data

mean	mean is equal to the total of the values of a data set, divided by the number of elements in the data set
median	median is the middle value in an odd number of ordered values of a data set, or the mean of the two middle values in an even number of ordered values in a data set

Algebra

slope of a line	$m = \dfrac{y_2 - y_1}{x_2 - x_1}$
slope-intercept form of the equation of a line	$y = mx + b$
point-slope form of the equation of a line	$y - y_1 = m(x - x_1)$
standard form of a quadratic equation	$y = ax^2 + bx + c$
quadratic formula	$x = \dfrac{-b \pm \sqrt{b^2 - 4ac}}{2a}$
Pythagorean Theorem	$a^2 + b^2 = c^2$
simple interest	$I = prt$ (I = interest, p = principal, r = rate, t = time)
distance formula	$d = rt$
total cost	total cost = (number of units) × (price per unit)

GO ON TO THE NEXT PAGE

Mathematical Reasoning, Part 1

You may NOT use a calculator in Part 1.

1. For which of the following values of y does the expression $\sqrt{y-3}$ have no real number solution?

   A. 2
   B. 3
   C. 4
   D. 5

2. Add.

   $$\frac{7}{2} + \frac{4}{3} =$$

   A. $\dfrac{10}{5}$

   B. $\dfrac{11}{5}$

   C. $\dfrac{28}{6}$

   D. $\dfrac{29}{6}$

3. If $a = 2$ and $b = -3$, what is the value of $-4a + 2b$?

Question 4 refers to the following number line.

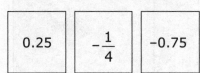

4. Place the numbers below in their correct places on the number line.

   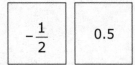

Question 5 refers to the following dot plot.

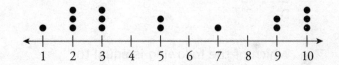

5. Add to the dot plot above, so that 3 is the only mode. Draw an X as many times as is needed.

GO ON TO THE NEXT PAGE

Mathematical Reasoning, Part 2

You MAY use a calculator in Part 2.

Question 6 refers to the following figure.

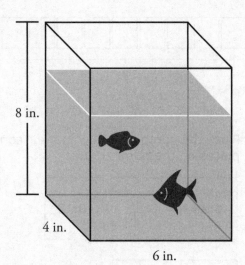

8 in.

4 in.

6 in.

Question 8 refers to the following graph.

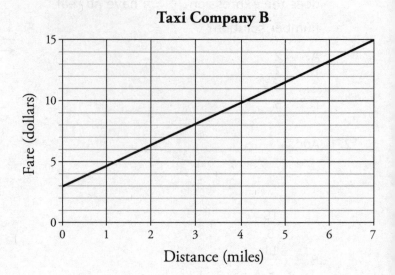

6. The figure above represents a fish tank. If there are 120 cubic inches of water in the fish tank, what is the height of the water, in inches?

   A. 4
   B. 5
   C. 6
   D. 7

7. Which of the following is equal to $x^2 - 2x - 15$?

   A. $(x - 3)(x - 5)$
   B. $(x - 3)(x + 5)$
   C. $(x + 3)(x - 5)$
   D. $(x + 3)(x + 5)$

8. Two taxi companies charge on initial fee and a rate per mile. Company A's fare can be modeled by the equation $A(m) = 3.50 + 1.5m$, where m represents the number of miles in the trip. Company B's fare can be modeled by the graph above. The rate per mile for Company A

is [Select...   ▼] that of Company B.
   | greater than |
   | equal to |
   | less than |

GO ON TO THE NEXT PAGE

Question 9 refers to the following graph.

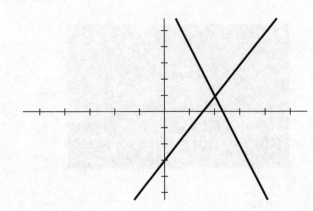

9. If the two lines in the graph above represent $y = 2x - 3$ and $y = -3x + 7$, respectively, select the point that represents the solution to the system of equations.

10. If $(x + 3)^2 = 16$, which of the following is a possible value of x?

   A. −7
   B. −4
   C. −1
   D. 4

11. Which of the following graphs does NOT represent a function of x?

   A.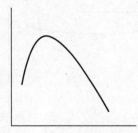

   B.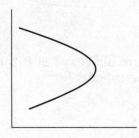

   C.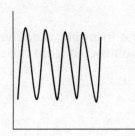

   D.

12. A concert promoter has to determine the order of four bands for a concert. How many different orderings of the four bands can the promoter make?

   A. 4
   B. 8
   C. 16
   D. 24

GO ON TO THE NEXT PAGE

Mathematical Reasoning, Part 2

Question 13 refers to the following figure.

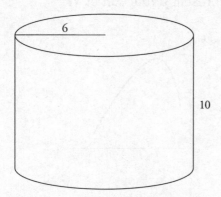

Question 15 refers to the following figure.

13. In the figure above, what is the surface area of the cylinder?

 A. 120π
 B. 156π
 C. 192π
 D. 360π

14. Which of the following is equivalent to the cube of 5 subtracted from the square root of 16?

 A. -121
 B. -95
 C. 95
 D. 121

15. The figure above represents a plot of soil that a gardener plans to sod. If the type of sod she will use costs 35 cents per square foot, which of the following expressions could be used to determine the cost, in dollars, of the sod?

 A. $(0.35) + (10) + (15)$
 B. $(0.35)(10 + 15)$
 C. $(0.35)(10) + (15)$
 D. $(0.35)(10)(15)$

GO ON TO THE NEXT PAGE

Mathematical Reasoning, Part 2

Question 16 refers to the following figure.

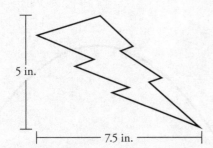

Question 18 refers to the following triangle.

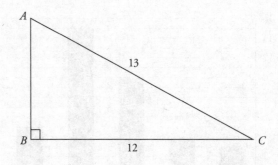

16. An artist sketches a scale drawing of a sculpture she intends to create. If the actual sculpture will be 3 feet high, what will be its width, in feet?

   A. 4.5
   B. 5.5
   C. 17.5
   D. 22.5

17. Mercedes has three blocks of cheese that weigh 5 ounces, 3 ounces, and 6 ounces, respectively. If an ounce is about 28.35 grams, which of the following expressions could be used to determine the total weight of the three blocks in grams?

   A. $(5)(3)(6) + 28.35$

   B. $\dfrac{(5)(3)(6)}{28.35}$

   C. $(5 + 3 + 6)(28.35)$

   D. $\dfrac{5 + 3 + 6}{28.35}$

18. In right triangle *ABC* shown above, what is the length of side *AB*?

   A. 1
   B. 5
   C. 11
   D. 18

19. If $p = 4$ and $q = -3$, what is the value of $\dfrac{p^2 + 2pq}{p + 2q}$?

   A. −20
   B. −4
   C. 4
   D. 20

GO ON TO THE NEXT PAGE

Mathematical Reasoning, Part 2

Question 20 refers to the following graph.

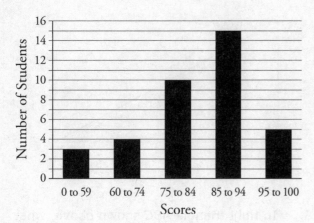

Question 21 refers to the following graph.

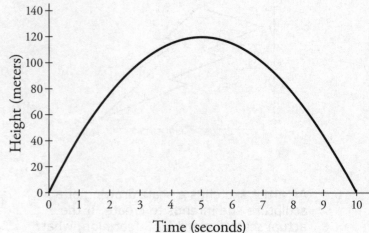

20. Students' scores on a recent biology exam are displayed in the histogram shown above. Which of the following could be the median of the scores?

   A. 61
   B. 78
   C. 86
   D. 97

21. A ball is thrown vertically upward from level ground. Its height, h, in meters t seconds after it is thrown is graphed above. Select the point on the graph indicating the time and the position of the ball when it reaches its maximum height.

22. Multiply.

$$(x^2y)^2(x^{-3}y^3)^4$$

   A. $\dfrac{y^{14}}{x^8}$

   B. $\dfrac{x^8}{y^{14}}$

   C. $\dfrac{y^{24}}{x^{48}}$

   D. x^8y^{14}

GO ON TO THE NEXT PAGE

Question 23 refers to the following table.

34	31	29
27	30	39
24	33	41

23. Based on the data in the table above, select the median and the mean. You may write your selections in the boxes below.

Median [   ]

Mean [   ]

30	31	32

33	34

Question 24 refers to the following graph.

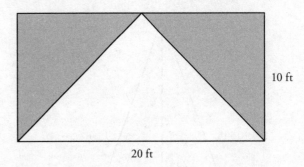

20 ft

10 ft

24. What is the area, in square feet, of the shaded region shown above?

A.   50
B.   100
C.   150
D.   200

25. If $f(x) = 2x - 3$, what is the value of $f(-4)$?

A.   −11
B.   −5
C.   5
D.   11

GO ON TO THE NEXT PAGE

Question 26 refers to the following figure.

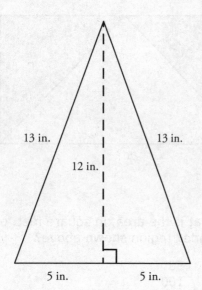

Question 28 refers to the following coordinate plane.

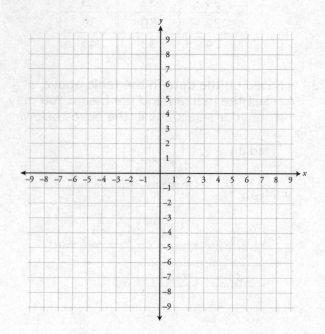

26. What is the area, in square inches, of the triangle shown above?

    A.   30
    B.   32.5
    C.   60
    D.   65

27. What is the perimeter of a square with an area of 25?

    A.   20
    B.   80
    C.   100
    D.   625

28. Select the point (5, −4) on the coordinate plane above.

GO ON TO THE NEXT PAGE

Mathematical Reasoning, Part 2

Question 29 refers to the following number line.

A ———— B
-1 0 1

29. Which of the following represents the distance between point A and point B on the number line above?

    A. $|A| - |B|$
    B. $A - B$
    C. $|A - B|$
    D. $A + B$

30. Which of the following is the area of the region enclosed by the lines represented by the equations $y = x + 2$, $x = 4$, and $y = -\frac{1}{4}x + 2$?

    A.   10
    B.   20
    C.   30
    D.   40

Question 31 refers to the following graph.

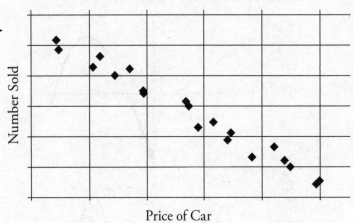

Price of Car

31. According to the scatterplot above, as the price of a car increases, the number sold

    | Select...   ▼ | .
    | increases |
    | decreases |
    | is unaffected |

32. A grocer sells bananas by the bunch, each of which contains 6 bananas. If a bunch of bananas costs $2.25 and a customer wants at least 20 bananas, what is the least amount of money that the customer can spend?

    A. $3.33
    B. $4.00
    C. $6.75
    D. $9.00

33. If $g(x) = 3x^2 + 4x - 7$, which of the following is the value of $g(-3)$?

    A.   8
    B.   16
    C.   24
    D.   32

GO ON TO THE NEXT PAGE

34. Which of the following graphs has a relative minimum at (3, −4)?

A.

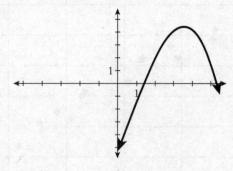

B.

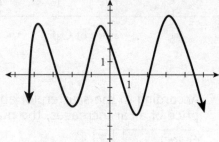

C.

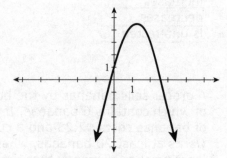

D.

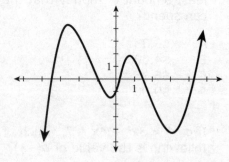

35. If a line through the point (3, 0) has a slope of 4, which of the following represents the equation of the line?

A. $y = 4x - 12$
B. $y = 4x - 3$
C. $y = 4x + 3$
D. $y = 4x + 12$

36. If Fergal has 4 blue marbles, 10 black marbles, 5 green marbles, and 9 red marbles, what is the probability that a marble selected at random will be blue?

A. $\dfrac{1}{7}$

B. $\dfrac{1}{6}$

C. $\dfrac{1}{5}$

D. $\dfrac{1}{4}$

37. Multiply.

$$\left(2x^2 - \frac{1}{2}\right)(6x^3 + 3x)$$

A. $12x^5 + 3x^3 - \dfrac{3}{2}x$

B. $12x^5 - 3x^3 + \dfrac{3}{2}x$

C. $12x^6 - 3x^3 - \dfrac{3}{2}x$

D. $12x^6 + 3x^3 + \dfrac{3}{2}x$

GO ON TO THE NEXT PAGE

Question 38 refers to the following table.

x	y
−1	2
1	5
3	8
5	11

38. The table above represents a linear of function of x. If the function is graphed on the xy-plane, which of the following represents the graph of the function?

A.
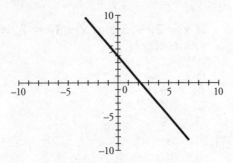

B.
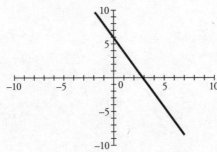

C.
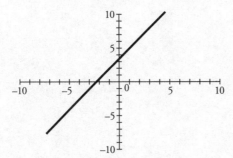

D.
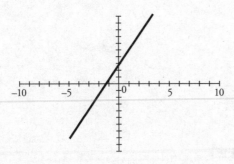

39. Chelsea opens a bank account that earns 2% simple annual interest. If her initial deposit is $400 and she makes no other deposits or withdrawals, how much money will be in her account after 5 years?

A. $8
B. $40
C. $408
D. $440

40. What is the solution to the equation $2(x + 1.5) = 4x + 2(x − 3)$?

A. 1

B. $\dfrac{3}{2}$

C. 2

D. $\dfrac{9}{4}$

41. If a circle has a circumference of 16π, which of the following represents the area of the circle?

A. 8π
B. 16π
C. 64π
D. 256π

42. If $1.5x^2 − 4x + \dfrac{5}{3} = 0$, which of the following expresses all possible values of x?

A. $x = \dfrac{-4 \pm \sqrt{6}}{3}$

B. $x = \dfrac{-4 \pm \sqrt{26}}{3}$

C. $x = \dfrac{4 \pm \sqrt{6}}{3}$

D. $x = \dfrac{4 \pm \sqrt{26}}{3}$

GO ON TO THE NEXT PAGE

43. Harriet eats at a restaurant and receives a bill for $81.30. If she leaves a 20% gratuity, how much in total does Harriet pay for the meal?

   A. $16.26
   B. $65.04
   C. $97.56
   D. $101.30

44. The area of a regular octagon can be determined by the equation $A = 2(1 + \sqrt{2})s^2$, where s represents a side of the octagon. If the area of a regular octagon is $6 + 6\sqrt{2}$, what is its perimeter?

   A. $8\sqrt{2}$
   B. $8\sqrt{3}$
   C. $16\sqrt{2}$
   D. $16\sqrt{3}$

Question 45 refers to the following box plot.

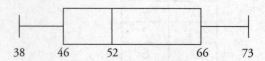

45. According to the box plot show above, what is the difference between the maximum and the median?

   A. 13
   B. 14
   C. 17
   D. 21

46. If $x = 2y - 3$ and $x - 3y = 7$, what is the value of x?

   A. −23
   B. −10
   C. 4
   D. 9

END OF TEST

Social Studies

Welcome!

Here is some information that you need to know before you start this test:

- You should not spend too much time on a question if you are not certain of the answer; answer it the best you can, and go on to the next question.
- If you are not certain of the answer to a question, you can mark your answer for review and come back to it later.
- You have **70 minutes** to complete this test.

Turn the page to begin.

GO ON TO THE NEXT PAGE

Questions 1 and 2 refer to the following graphs.

Source 1:

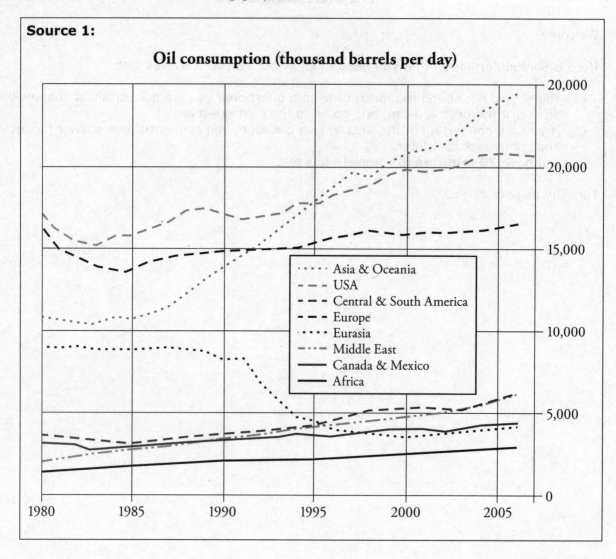

Oil consumption (thousand barrels per day)

Legend:
- Asia & Oceania
- USA
- Central & South America
- Europe
- Eurasia
- Middle East
- Canada & Mexico
- Africa

Source 2:

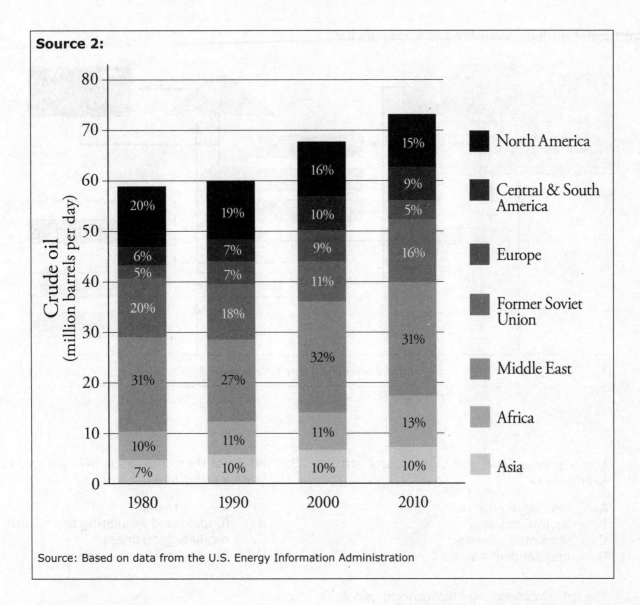

Source: Based on data from the U.S. Energy Information Administration

1. The graphs support which of the following statements?

    A. Due to increased conservation efforts, the United States made dramatic cuts to its oil consumption throughout the time period measured.

    B. Increased oil consumption by Asia and Oceania caused drastic cuts in the oil consumption in Eurasia.

    C. Both the United States and Europe had similar energy policies throughout the time period measured.

    D. Oil consumption in Asia and Oceania increased by a larger percentage than any other region in the time period measured.

2. An oil surplus can be defined as occurring when a region produces far more oil than it consumes.

    | Select...   ▼ | had the largest oil
    | North America |
    | Europe |
    | The Middle East |
    | Africa |
    | Asia |

    surplus throughout the years 1980–2005.

GO ON TO THE NEXT PAGE

Questions 3 through 5 refer to the following chart.

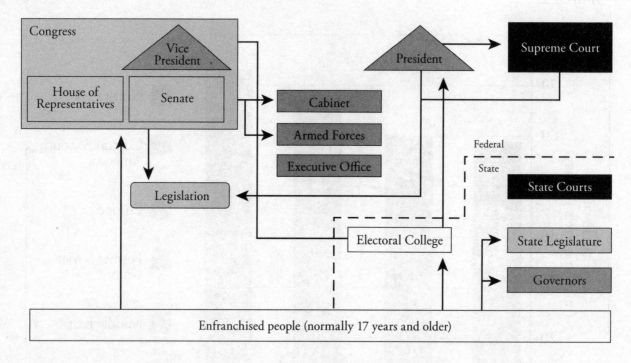

3. The Supreme Court and State Courts are examples of

    A. executive powers.
    B. judicial powers.
    C. legislative powers.
    D. independent powers.

4. The arrow connecting enfranchised people with the Congress most likely means

    A. voters elect members of Congress directly.
    B. voters elect members of the electoral college, who then elect members of Congress.
    C. voters elect members of their state legislatures, who then elect members of Congress.
    D. voters elect a president and vice president, who then appoint members of Congress.

5. Which of these powers is NOT granted to state legislatures?

    A. levying taxes
    B. funding and regulating the military
    C. regulating business
    D. funding public education

GO ON TO THE NEXT PAGE

Social Studies

Questions 6 and 7 refer to the following map.

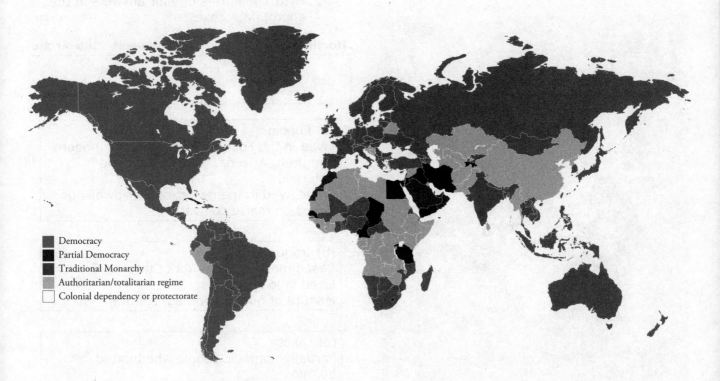

Democracy
Partial Democracy
Traditional Monarchy
Authoritarian/totalitarian regime
Colonial dependency or protectorate

6. Modern Africa is largely made up of

A. democracies.
B. colonial dependencies.
C. partial democracies.
D. a mixture of authoritarian regimes and democracies.

7. If a map similar to the one above had been created to reflect world politics in 1965, the map would have been different from the one above in which of the following ways?

A. Most of Asia would have been controlled by authoritarian regimes.
B. Most of Europe would have been controlled by traditional monarchies.
C. Most of North America would have been democratic.
D. Most of Africa would have been democratic.

GO ON TO THE NEXT PAGE

Questions 8 through 10 refer to the following map.

9. Match the following historic Native American tribes to their regions. Write the letters of your answers in the appropriate boxes.

Northeast	Plains	Southwest	Sub-Arctic

(a) Pueblo
Lived in the Four Corners region of modern-day Utah, Arizona, New Mexico, and Colorado
Some lived in the desert on cliff-dwellings
Relied on maize cultivation

(b) Iroquois
Based mostly in New York State
Lived in long-houses
Mixture of hunting and agriculture

(c) Lakota
Partially nomadic people who hunted buffalo
Often hunted with horses
Many surviving members have large reservations in modern United States

(d) Inuit
Lived in the coldest regions of North America in ice houses
Relied almost entirely upon whaling
Live in modern-day Canada

8. All of the following European powers first settled in the Northeast EXCEPT

A. France.
B. Great Britain.
C. The Netherlands.
D. Spain.

GO ON TO THE NEXT PAGE

10. From the early 1830s onward, the Oregon Trail and other routes were used by hundreds of thousands of ranchers, farmers, and entrepreneurs to settle the West. This would have had the LEAST impact on which TWO of the tribes listed in question 9? Write the letters of your answers in the boxes below.

```
┌─────────────────────────┐
│                         │
│                         │
└─────────────────────────┘

┌─────────────────────────┐
│                         │
│                         │
└─────────────────────────┘
```

11. Read each description and write the letter of each one into the correct column.

Legislative Branch	Executive Branch	Judicial Branch

(a) Passes bills, has power to tax, controls the federal budget

(b) Has veto power, can declare a state of emergency, appoints judges

(c) Decides upon the constitutionality of a law, is not elected, not subject to term limits

Question 12 refers to the following list of rights enumerated by the first five Amendments to the Constitution.

First—Free exercise of religion, freedom of speech, freedom of the press, freedom to peaceably assemble, the right to petition the government for redress of grievances
Second—Right to bear arms
Third—Prohibits the quartering of soldiers in citizens' homes
Fourth—Prohibits the search and seizure of citizens' property without probable cause
Fifth—Gives defendants the right to abstain from testifying against themselves in a court proceeding

12. Which of the first five amendments has been LEAST challenged in federal and local courts in modern times?

   A. First Amendment
   B. Second Amendment
   C. Third Amendment
   D. Fourth Amendment

13. Suppose that a case came before a judge claiming that federal agents in airports should not have the right to screen the baggage of airline passengers. Which Amendment of the Constitution would best support this and why?

   A. the First Amendment, since it protects the right to peaceably assemble
   B. the First Amendment, since it allows citizens to petition the government for redress of grievances
   C. the Second Amendment, since it allows citizens to carry firearms
   D. the Fourth Amendment, since it prohibits unwarranted search and seizure

GO ON TO THE NEXT PAGE

Social Studies

Questions 14 and 15 refer to the following source.

"Every Bill which shall have passed the House of Representatives and the Senate, shall, before it become a Law, be presented to the President of the United States; If he approve he shall sign it, but if not he shall return it, with his Objections to that House in which it shall have originated, who shall enter the Objections at large on their Journal, and proceed to reconsider it. If after such Reconsideration two thirds of that House shall agree to pass the Bill, it shall be sent, together with the Objections, to the other House, by which it shall likewise be reconsidered, and if approved by two thirds of that House, it shall become a Law....If any Bill shall not be returned by the President within ten Days (Sundays excepted) after it shall have been presented to him, the Same shall be a Law, in like Manner as if he had signed it."

–Presentment Clause, Article I, U.S. Constitution

14. If the president does not sign a bill within five days it

    A. fails to become law.
    B. immediately reverts back to Congress for a vote.
    C. immediately becomes law.
    D. may or may not become law depending on the president and Congress's subsequent actions.

15. When a president returns the law to Congress "with his Objections," this is known as a(n)

    A. impeachment.
    B. ratification.
    C. repeal.
    D. veto.

16. At the federal level, Article II of the United States Constitution states in Section 4 that "the President, Vice President, and all civil Officers of the United States shall be removed from Office on Impeachment for, and conviction of, Treason, Bribery, or other High Crimes and Misdemeanors."

    "Impeachment" means

    A. removal from office.
    B. treason.
    C. formal charges of wrongdoing.
    D. resignation from office.

GO ON TO THE NEXT PAGE

Social Studies

Questions 17 and 18 refer to the following tables, which measure the results of elections for Speaker of the House of Representatives in the years noted. (R) indicates a Republican candidate. (D) indicates a Democrat candidate.

January 2003

Candidate	Votes	%
Dennis Hastert (R)	228	52.4%
Nancy Pelosi (D)	201	46.4%
Jack Murtha (D)	1	0.2%
"Present"	4	0.8%
Not voting	1	0.2%

January 2007

Candidate	Votes	%
Nancy Pelosi (D)	233	53.6%
John Boehner (R)	202	46.4%
Total	435	100.0%

January 2011

Candidate	Votes	%
John Boehner (R)	242	55.6%
Nancy Pelosi (D)	173	40.0%
Heath Shuler (D)	11	2.5%
John Lewis (D)	2	0.5%
Dennis Cardoza (D)	1	0.2%
Jim Costa (D)	1	0.2%
Jim Cooper (D)	1	0.2%
Steny Hoyer (D)	1	0.2%
Marcy Kaptur (D)	1	0.2%
Total	433	100.0%
"Present"	1	0.2%
Not voting	1	0.2%

17. Who is directly responsible for electing the Speaker of the House of Representatives?

    A. the American people
    B. the Senate
    C. other members of the House of Representatives
    D. circuit judges

18. Which of the following most accurately explains why the Speaker of the House changed every four years in the time period 2003–2011?

    A. 2003, 2007, and 2011 were all years that the American people elected a new president.
    B. Both Dennis Hastert and Nancy Pelosi were unpopular with the American people.
    C. Members of the House tend to vote for a Speaker who is a member of their own party and the House party majority changed in all three of the years listed.
    D. In 2011, Nancy Pelosi was challenged by several other Democrats who undermined her ability to retain the position of Speaker.

GO ON TO THE NEXT PAGE

Question 19 refers to the following sources.

Source 1:

"No freeman shall be taken, imprisoned, dis-seized, outlawed, banished, or in any way destroyed, nor will we proceed against or prosecute him, except by the lawful judgment of his peers or by the law of the land."

–*Magna Carta*, 1297

Source 2:

"No person shall be held to answer for a capi-tal, or otherwise infamous crime, unless on a presentment or indictment of a Grand Jury, except in cases arising in the land or naval forces, or in the Militia, when in actual ser-vice in time of War or public danger; nor shall any person be subject for the same offence to be twice put in jeopardy of life or limb; nor shall be compelled in any criminal case to be a witness against himself, nor be deprived of life, liberty, or property, without due process of law; nor shall private property be taken for public use, without just compensation."

–Fifth Amendment, U.S. Constitution

19.   The quotes above support the idea that both the *Magna Carta* and the Fifth Amendment

   A.   guarantee the right to a jury trial.
   B.   guarantee the right to a speedy trial.
   C.   ban the use of capital punishment.
   D.   ban the taking of private property.

Questions 20 through 22 refer to the following sources.

Source 1:

"Your principles will conquer the world. By the glorious example of your freedom, welfare, and security, mankind is about to become conscious of its aim. The lesson you give to humanity will not be lost. The respect for State rights in the Federal Government of America, and in its several States, will become an instructive example for universal toleration, forbearance, and justice to the future states and republics of Europe."

–Lajos Kossuth, Hungarian politician, 1852

Source 2:

"We shall rejoice to see our American model upon the Lower Danube and on the moun-tains of Hungary….That first prayer shall be that Hungary may become independent of all foreign power….I limit my aspirations for Hungary, for the present, to that single and simple point—Hungarian independence, Hun-garian self-government, Hungarian control of Hungarian destinies."

–Secretary of State Daniel Webster, 1852

20.   Lajos Kossuth is most likely speaking to

   A.   the people of Hungary.
   B.   Daniel Webster.
   C.   the United States of America.
   D.   the republics of Europe.

GO ON TO THE NEXT PAGE

21. Based on the comments of Daniel Webster, it can be inferred that Lajos Kossuth is seeking

   A. independence for Hungary.
   B. greater unity among European nations.
   C. to conquer the world.
   D. states' rights in Hungary.

22. Based on the quotes above, Lajos Kossuth and Daniel Webster most clearly agree that

   A. American political principles should spread around the world.
   B. European countries will inevitably live in greater harmony.
   C. the American model of government is worthy of imitation.
   D. Hungary should submit to the will of its neighbors.

GO ON TO THE NEXT PAGE

Questions 23 and 24 refer to the following map.

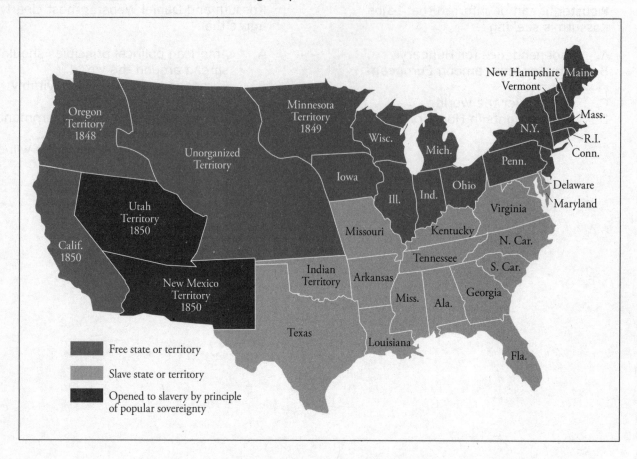

The Compromise of 1850

23. The map above supports which of the following conclusions?

   A. Most new territories acquired in the 1800s allowed the practice of slavery.

   B. By 1850, the United States was divided clearly between North and South in its acceptance of slavery.

   C. More free people lived in Northern states than in Southern states.

   D. The Civil War occurred solely due to controversy regarding the acquisition of slave territories in the 1840s and 1850s.

24. The region labeled "Indian Territory" is now the modern state of

   [   ] .

GO ON TO THE NEXT PAGE

Social Studies

Questions 25 and 26 refer to the following quote.

> "My friends, I must say to you that we have not made a single gain in civil rights without legal and nonviolent pressure. History is the long and tragic story of the fact that privileged groups seldom give up their privileges voluntarily. Individuals may see the moral light and give up their unjust posture; but as Reinhold Niebuhr has reminded us, groups are more immoral than individuals."

25. Which advocate for Civil Rights is most likely to have said these words?

   A. Malcolm X, leader of the Black Panthers
   B. Martin Luther King, Jr., after being confined in a Birmingham jail
   C. Rosa Parks, after refusing to give up her seat on a bus
   D. Nelson Mandela, President of South Africa, after receiving the Nobel Peace Prize

26. Which of the following is an assumption behind the quote above?

   A. Groups and individuals sometimes behave differently.
   B. Privileged individuals are usually slow to change their positions on issues.
   C. Civil rights cannot be achieved without some use of violence.
   D. Individuals often hold views more immoral than the groups with which they are associated.

GO ON TO THE NEXT PAGE

Questions 27 and 28 refer to the following photograph of Charleston, South Carolina, in 1865.

27. Which of the following best explains the scene in the picture above?

   A. The severe economic depression of the 1860s forced many businesses to close in the South, leading to the abandonment of major cities.
   B. The Gold Rush motivated many Americans to leave the South and seek their fortunes in the West.
   C. During the Civil War, several major Southern cities were in ruins after military actions carried out by the Union Army.
   D. A drought in the South caused fires to sweep through many major cities, devastating their infrastructure.

28. Fill in the blank.

   The [_____] Era of the 1860s and 1870s included laws designed to provide federal money to help rebuild cities in the South such as Charleston, South Carolina.

GO ON TO THE NEXT PAGE

29. The Nineteenth Amendment to the U.S. Constitution states that "the right of the citizens of the United States to vote shall not be denied or abridged by the United States or by any State on account of sex."

Which of the following historic persons was most likely a vocal advocate for the Nineteenth Amendment?

A. Abigail Adams, 2nd First Lady to the United States
B. Abraham Lincoln, 16th President of the United States
C. Carrie Chapman Catt, suffragette
D. Eleanor Roosevelt, 1st Chairperson of the United Nations Commission on Human Rights

30. "Sutter's Mill" is the name of a famous sawmill owned by 19th-century pioneer John Sutter. When gold was found in this location, it sparked the Gold Rush of 1849. Sutter's Mill is most likely located in

A. Alaska.
B. California.
C. Texas.
D. Yukon Territory.

31. Use the drop-down menus to choose the best words to fill in the blanks. Circle your selections.

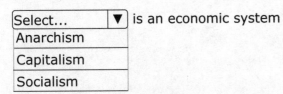

is an economic system

Select... ▼
Anarchism
Capitalism
Socialism

that favors a planned economy and the public ownership of utilities, land, and some industry. It is most opposed to

Select... ▼
capitalism
communism
monarchy

.

Question 32 refers to the following map representing the ancient Egyptian empire around the 15th century BCE.

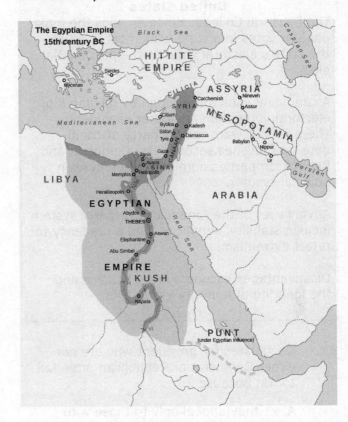

32. The map above supports which of the following conclusions?

A. The Ancient Egyptian Empire was contained within the continent of Africa.
B. The Ancient Egyptians were often in conflict with their neighbors due to their tendency to acquire more and more territory.
C. The Red Sea was the most important waterway used in trade between ancient Egypt and its neighbors.
D. Ancient Egyptian cities were built near water in order to irrigate crops and allow for trade among neighboring peoples.

GO ON TO THE NEXT PAGE

Question 33 refers to the following information.

Outline of the Electoral System in the United States

The Electoral College: Whoever wins the most popular votes in a state wins most or all of the state's electoral votes in the presidential election.

A candidate wins the election by gaining more electoral votes than any other candidate. There is no reward for the party or candidate that finishes second. The Democrat and Republican parties dominate the American political system.

Advantages of the American two-party system include stability, simplicity, and a tendency to reject extremism.

Disadvantages include a lack of choice and the ignoring of minority viewpoints.

---

33.   Candidates for president who are not either Democrat or Republican often fail to win because

   A.   they appeal only to those with extreme political views.
   B.   they fail to acquire enough electoral college votes to win the election.
   C.   their names do not appear on the ballots in all fifty states.
   D.   they usually ignore the viewpoints of minority groups.

GO ON TO THE NEXT PAGE

Questions 34 and 35 refer to the following political cartoon.

THE GAP IN THE BRIDGE.

34. Which of the following is closest to the meaning being conveyed by the author of cartoon?

A. The United States was lazy for not participating in the design of the League of Nations.

B. The United States sided with England and Italy in their opposition to Belgium and France in the League of Nations.

C. The United States held together the League of Nations by bridging the gap between opposing European nations.

D. Although the United States helped to design the League of Nations, it did not join, thus leaving a gap in leadership.

35. The League of Nations was eventually replaced by the Select... ▼ .

European Union

United Nations

Warsaw Pact

END OF TEST

THIS PAGE INTENTIONALLY LEFT BLANK.

GO ON TO THE NEXT PAGE

Science

Welcome!

Here is some information that you need to know before you start this test:

- You should not spend too much time on a question if you are not certain of the answer; answer it the best you can, and go on to the next question.
- If you are not certain of the answer to a question, you can mark your answer for review and come back to it later.
- You have **90 minutes** to complete this test.

Turn the page to begin.

GO ON TO THE NEXT PAGE

Science

Questions 1 and 2 refer to the following information.

Rocks are naturally occurring masses of one or more minerals. There are three types of rocks: sedimentary, igneous, and metamorphic. Layers of minerals and organic matter that have been compressed over time are sedimentary rocks. Igneous rocks are formed through the cooling and solidification of magma or lava. Metamorphic rocks are formed below the surface of the Earth, when existing rocks are exposed to extreme heat and pressure.

1. Pumice is formed when molten rock is quickly expelled from the mouth of a volcano, while marble is formed when limestone is exposed to both high temperature and pressure. Accordingly, pumice is a(n) Select... ▼

   | igneous |
   | metamorphic |
   | sedimentary |

   rock, while marble is a(n)

   Select... ▼ rock.

   | igneous |
   | metamorphic |
   | sedimentary |

2. Which type of rock would most likely be on the ocean floor?

   A. igneous
   B. metamorphic
   C. sedimentary
   D. hard

3. An object's speed refers to how fast the object moves. The speed of an object, S, is equal to the distance travelled, D, divided by the amount of time travelled, T:

   $$S = \frac{D}{T}$$

   If a kitten were to run at a speed of 8 miles per hour for 5 miles, for how many minutes did the kitten run?

4. The river Zhang travels through the town of Bahn. A few years ago, Mystify Power Inc. built a coal mine along the river. Jiajie wants to show that the coal mines has adversely affected the water quality of the river Zhang. Jiajie hypothesizes that the acidity of the water will be highest near the coal mines, and wishes to support his hypothesis by designing, and conducting, an experiment.

   Which of the following would NOT be important for Jiajie's experiment?

   A. water from the Zhang River collected near the coal mine
   B. water from the Zhang River collected upstream from the coal mine
   C. water from a different river that is known to be polluted by a coal mine
   D. water from a different river that is known to be unpolluted by any mining pollution

GO ON TO THE NEXT PAGE

Questions 5 and 6 refer to the following information.

In order to survive, mammals must find and consume food, either in the form of plant or animal matter. Unlike mammals, however, plants can make their own food. When chlorophyll in a plant's leaves is activated by the sunlight, the process of photosynthesis begins. Photosynthesis is the process by which plants convert carbon dioxide, water, and energy from the Sun into glucose and oxygen.

5. Which of the following is the chemical equation for photosynthesis?

A. $6CO_2 + 6H_2O \rightarrow C_6H_{12}O_6 + 6O_2$
B. $6HO_2 + 6C_2O + ATP \rightarrow C_6H_{12} + 12O_2$
C. $6CO_2 + 6H_2O + ADP \rightarrow C_6H_{12}O_6 + 6O_2$
D. $6C + 6H_2 \rightarrow C_6H_{12}$

6. Which of the following statements is NOT true?

A. Only organisms with chlorophyll can make their own food through photosynthesis.
B. Photosynthesis depends upon energy from the Sun.
C. The products of photosynthesis are glucose and oxygen.
D. Both plants and mammals have chlorophyll.

Question 7 refers to the following information.

Deoxyribonucleic acid is a double helix structure and is comprised of nucleotides. Each nucleotide consists of a phosphate group, a five-carbon sugar molecule, and a nitrogen-containing base, which can be adenine, thymine, cytosine, or guanine. There are rules governing the pairing of nucleotide bases; e.g., adenine pairs only with thymine, and cytosine pairs only with guanine.

7. If one strand of DNA had nucleotide bases of CGATCG, the complementary strand of DNA would have nucleotide bases of G

Select... ▼	T	Select... ▼	GC.
adenine		adenine	
cytosine		cytosine	
guanine		guanine	
thymine		thymine	

GO ON TO THE NEXT PAGE

8. The skeletal system supports and protects the body and its organs, as well as aiding in motor skills. The skeletal system consists of bones, or hard connective tissues that form the structure of most vertebrates, that are connected together with tendons and ligaments. Tendons are fibrous cords of connective tissue that attach muscle to bone, cartilage, or other muscles, while ligaments are short, tough bands of connective tissue that connect two bones together, sometimes forming a joint. Mark an X on the line pointing to the ligament in the image below.

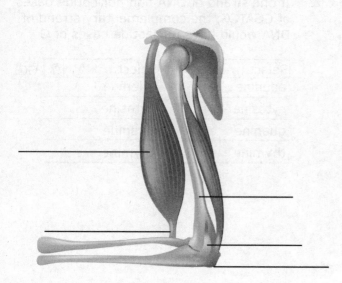

Questions 9 through 11 refer to the following information.

Of the eight major planets in our solar system, half of them are inner planets and half of them are outer planets. The inner planets, or those closest to the Sun, have metallic cores and are formed primarily of rock. Conversely, the outer planets, or those farthest from the Sun, are known as gas giants and ice giants, as they are formed primarily of either gas or ice.

Mean Distances of the Terrestrial Planets From the Sun
(Orbits drawn approximately to scale)

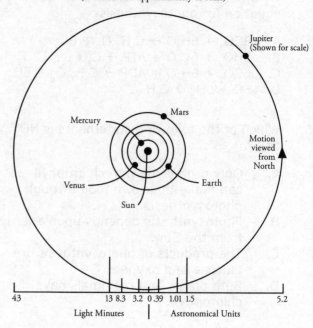

9. Of the following planets, which is the fewest light minutes from Jupiter?

A. Mercury
B. Mars
C. Venus
D. Earth

GO ON TO THE NEXT PAGE

10. Write the letter of each planet into the correct box to show whether it is an inner planet or an outer planet. (You may not use each item twice.)

Inner Planet	Outer Planet

(a) Mars	(f) Mercury
(b) Uranus	(g) Earth
(c) Gandolf	(h) Venus
(d) Saturn	(i) Neptune
(e) Sun	(j) Jupiter

11. Approximately how many astronomical units is Mercury from Mars? (Round your answer to the nearest integer.)

12. The nucleus of an atom is composed of protons and neutrons, and electrons orbit around the nucleus. With the exception of hydrogen, an atom must have at least one neutron for every proton. If the element Dubnium has 105 protons, how many neutrons can it NOT have?

A. 102
B. 105
C. 157
D. 163

13. The Law of Conservation of Mass states that matter can neither be created nor destroyed. The Law of Conservation of Energy states that

A. energy can be created, but not destroyed, in a closed system.
B. energy can be destroyed, but not created, in a closed system.
C. energy can be neither created nor destroyed in a closed system.
D. energy can both be created and destroyed in either an open or closed system.

GO ON TO THE NEXT PAGE

Science

Questions 14 through 16 refer to the following information.

The chart below details the history of the Earth in terms of eons, eras, periods, and epochs.

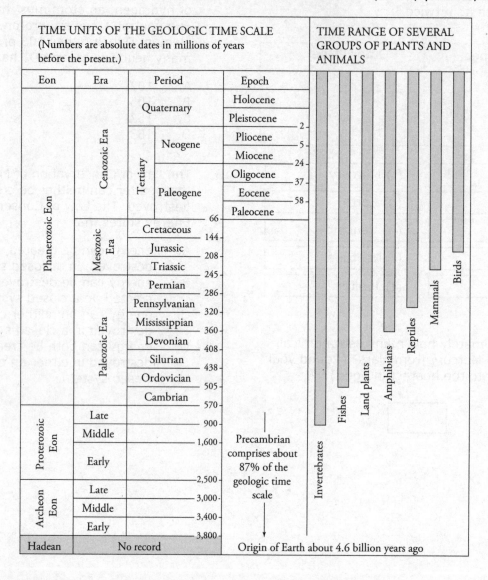

14. Which of the following statements is NOT supported by the information provided?

   A. The beginning of the Archeon Eon was approximately 3.8 million years ago.
   B. The Cambrian Period was the first period of the Paleozoic Era.
   C. There is no record regarding the eras and periods of the Hadean Eon.
   D. The Protocambrian period comprises about 87% of the geologic time scale.

15. Approximately how old is the Earth? (Round your answer to the nearest tenth.)

   ☐ billions of years

GO ON TO THE NEXT PAGE

16. The Phanerozoic Eon is comprised of the Paleozoic, [Select... ▼], and

Select... ▼
Archeon
Mesozoic
Proterozoic

Cenozoic Eras. Each of these eras is further broken into periods and epochs. The Mesozoic Era is comprised of the Cretaceous, Jurassic, and Triassic Periods, which spanned from 245 million years before present to [Select... ▼]

Select... ▼
66
144
208

millions of years before present.

17. pH is the hydrogen ion concentration of a solution. Chemists use a numeric scale that ranges from 0–14 to measure the pH of a solution. A pH less than seven indicates an acidic solution, a pH of seven indicates a neutral solution, and a pH greater than seven indicates an alkaline solution.

Write the letter of each item into the correct box to show whether it is acidic, neutral, or alkaline.

Acidic	Neutral	Alkaline

(a) Bleach (pH = 12)   (e) Urine (pH = 6)

(b) Pure Water   (f) Soda (pH = 3)

(c) Lemon Juice (pH = 2)   (g) Antacid Tablets

(d) Soap (pH = 11)   (h) Battery Acid

18. How many pairs of chromosomes do humans have?

A. 22
B. 23
C. 44
D. 46

GO ON TO THE NEXT PAGE

Science

Question 19 refers to the following information.

Magnets are objects with strong magnetic fields that attract or repel other objects. A magnet has both a north pole and a south pole, and like poles repel each other, while unlike poles attract one another. Magnets can be categorized as either permanent, which are made from highly magnetic materials such as iron, or temporary, which can function only through the use of electricity.

19.   Write an X on all of the temporary magnets in the group below.

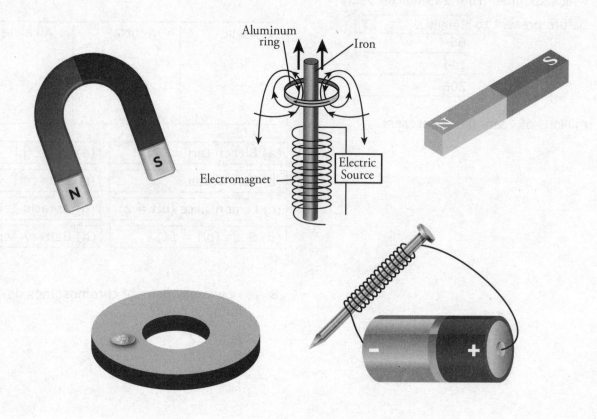

GO ON TO THE NEXT PAGE

Questions 20 through 22 refer to the following information.

In the 19th century, Gregor Mendel studied the effects of breeding on different strains of pea plants. Mendel decided to study how pea plants passed the trait of height to offspring. Height (H) is expressed in offspring who have at least one dominant allele; i.e., individuals who have two dominant alleles, HH, or one dominant and one recessive allele, Hh, will be tall. In order to determine the inheritance of potential offspring, Mendel used Punnett Squares. Punnett Squares are used to predict the offspring of two individuals, and monohybrid crosses are used to study a specific trait.

Mendel found that the offspring of two homozygous dominant pea plants (HH) would always produce tall pea plants, the offspring of two homozygous recessive pea plants (hh) would always produce short pea plants, and the offspring of a homozygous dominant (HH) and a homozygous recessive (hh) pea plant would all be tall, having alleles of Hh.

Long tails are present in cats that have at least one dominant allele for a long tail (L). Lincoln is interested in how the trait for tail length is passed to offspring.

20. Consider the cross between a heterozygous dominant cat with a long tail and a homozygous recessive cat with a short tail. The likelihood that they will have offspring with a long tail is

Select... ▼
0%
25%
50%
75%
100%

, while the probability that they will have offspring with a short tail is

Select... ▼
0%
25%
50%
75%
100%

.

21. Mendel noted that pea plants with a single dominant allele for height led the pea plant to express the trait for height. This exemplifies Mendel's Law of

A.   Dominance.
B.   Segregation.
C.   Independent Assortment.
D.   Engendered Production.

22. What is the probability that two homozygous recessive cats will have a cat with a long tail?

[   ] %

GO ON TO THE NEXT PAGE

23. Which of the following statements is NOT expressed by Newton's Laws of Motion?

    A. An object at rest will remain at rest, unless acted upon by some outside force.
    B. The work of an object is equal to the product of the force upon that object and the distance the object travels.
    C. When acted upon by an external force, an object will accelerate in proportion to that force.
    D. For every action, there is an equal and opposite reaction.

24. The cell life cycle consists of two stages: interphase and mitosis. Interphase is the time between cell divisions, and is the first stage of a cell's life cycle. Interphase consists of three phases: G1, when replication enzymes are produced, S, when chromosomes are replicated, and G2, when the cell readies itself for mitosis.

    Mitosis consists of four stages: prophase, metaphase, anaphase, and telophase. During prophase, the cell's nucleolus disappears, chromosomes become visible, and centrioles, including their spindle fibers, move towards opposite ends of the cell. During metaphase, chromosomes line up along the metaphase plate, and during anaphase, the cell elongates as sister chromatids of each chromosome separate and migrate to opposite poles. Finally, during telophase, a nuclear membrane forms around each set of chromosomes, the nucleoli reappear, the cytoplasm splits through a process called cytokinesis, and two daughter cells are formed.

    Which phase of mitosis is illustrated in the following image?

    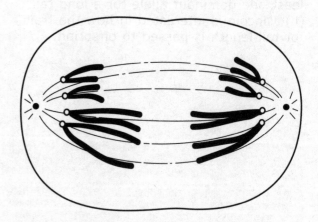

    A. prophase
    B. metaphase
    C. anaphase
    D. telophase

GO ON TO THE NEXT PAGE

Questions 25 through 27 refer to the following information.

Scale	Convert to Fahrenheit	Convert to Celsius	Convert to Kelvin
Fahrenheit (F)		(F –32) × 1.8	(F –32) × 1.8 + 173.15
Celsius (C)	(C × 1.8) + 32		C + 273.15
Kelvin (K)	(K –273.15) × 1.8 + 32	K –273.15	

The scale for measuring heat is temperature, or the kinetic energy of the molecules in an object. Temperature can be measured in Celsius, in which the freezing point is 0° and the boiling point is 100°, or in Fahrenheit, in which the freezing point is 32° and the boiling point is 212°. Kelvin is the Standard International (SI) unit of thermodynamic temperature, in which 0°K is absolute zero, or the point at which all molecular movement stops.

25. Robert is measuring the temperature of a steel ball across a variety of environmental conditions. All of the following are possible temperatures of the ball EXCEPT

    A. –45°C.
    B. –1°K.
    C. 20°F.
    D. 450°F.

26. 42° Celsius is equivalent to what Fahrenheit temperature?

    [ ] °F

27. 0°K is [Select... ▼] than 0°F,
    warmer
    colder

    and 0°C is [Select... ▼] than 0°F.
    warmer
    colder

GO ON TO THE NEXT PAGE

28. Heat is the transfer of energy from the particles of one object to another due to the different temperatures of each object. An exothermic reaction occurs when heat is generated in a system and released to its surroundings, while an endothermic reaction is one that absorbs heat from its surroundings.

When Liz lights a candle, an

Select... ▼
endothermic
exothermic

reaction occurs, while

an

Select... ▼
endothermic
exothermic

reaction occurs

when she cooks an egg.

GO ON TO THE NEXT PAGE

Questions 29 through 31 refer to the following information.

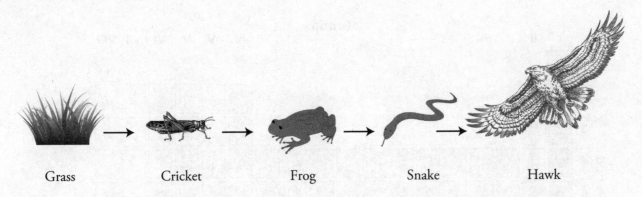

Grass   Cricket   Frog   Snake   Hawk

29. The diagram provided is best described as a

   A. food chain.
   B. food web.
   C. food pyramid.
   D. phylogenetic tree.

30. Which of the following is a secondary consumer?

   A. grass
   B. cricket
   C. frog
   D. hawk

31. In a linear network such as the one shown above, approximately 10% of energy is transferred from one level to the next—this is known as the 10% Rule. If a cricket consumes 500 Units of Energy,

   | Select...   ▼ | Units of Energy are
   | 500 |
   | 50 |
   | 5 |

   passed to the frog, and | Select...   ▼ |
   | 50 |
   | 5 |
   | 0.5 |

   Units of Energy are passed to the Snake.

GO ON TO THE NEXT PAGE

Questions 32 and 33 refer to the following information.

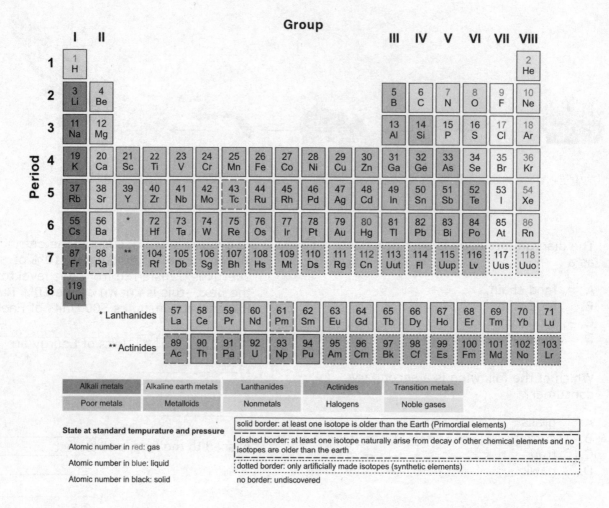

In the periodic table, chemical elements are ordered by their atomic number, electron configurations, and recurring chemical properties. As shown in the diagram above, from left to right and top to bottom, elements are listed in order of atomic number, which is the number of protons in each atom. Furthermore, elements in the same group, or column, share similar properties.

32. Which of the following is NOT an alkali metal?

   A.   lithium (Li)
   B.   sodium (Na)
   C.   potassium (K)
   D.   hydrogen (H)

33. Which element has two protons per atom?

   A.   hydrogen (H)
   B.   helium (He)
   C.   beryllium (Be)
   D.   iron (Fe)

GO ON TO THE NEXT PAGE

Science

Questions 34 and 35 refer to the following information.

mRNA contains a sequence of nucleotide bases that are translated into codons and, in turn, code for the amino acids to make protein chains. A codon is a set of three nucleotide bases that together form a unit of genetic code. For example, a string of RNA that contains a string of nucleotide bases "AUGCAUUGU" has an initial codon, known as the start codon, of AUG. Based on the following codon chart, the start codon for the previous string is Methionine.

Second base

	U	C	A	G	
U	UUU ⌐ Phenyl-alanine F / UUC ⌐ alanine / UUA ⌐ Leucine L / UUG ⌐	UCU / UCC ⌐ Serine / UCA / UCG ⌐ S	UAU ⌐ Tyrosine Y / UAC ⌐ / UAA Stop codon / UAG Stop codon	UGU ⌐ Cysteine C / UGC ⌐ / UGA Stop codon / UGG Tryptophan W	U C A G
C	CUU ⌐ / CUC ⌐ Leucine L / CUA / CUG ⌐	CCU / CCC ⌐ Proline / CCA / CCG ⌐ P	CAU ⌐ Histidine H / CAC ⌐ / CAA ⌐ Glutamine / CAG ⌐ Q	CGU ⌐ / CGC ⌐ Arginine / CGA / CGG ⌐ R	U C A G
A	AUU ⌐ I / AUC ⌐ Isoleucine / AUA / AUG M Methionine start codon	ACU / ACC ⌐ Threonine / ACA / ACG ⌐ T	AAU ⌐ Asparagine / AAC ⌐ N / AAA ⌐ Lysine / AAG ⌐ K	AGU ⌐ Serine S / AGC ⌐ / AGA ⌐ Arginine / AGG ⌐ R	U C A G
G	GUU ⌐ / GUC ⌐ Valine V / GUA / GUG ⌐	GCU / GCC ⌐ Alanine / GCA / GCG ⌐ A	GAU ⌐ Aspartic acid D / GAC ⌐ / GAA ⌐ Glutamic acid / GAG ⌐ E	GGU ⌐ / GGC ⌐ Glycine / GGA / GGG ⌐ G	U C A G

First base ← (left) · Third base → (right)

34. The second codon in the string of RNA with bases AUGUACCGUAGU is

   A. methionine.
   B. tyrosine.
   C. arginine.
   D. serine.

35. Which of the following is NOT a nucleotide base associated with RNA?

   A. adenine
   B. guanine
   C. thymine
   D. uracil

END OF TEST

Chapter 6
Practice Test 2:
Answers and
Explanations

REASONING THROUGH LANGUAGE ARTS

Section 1

1. **B** Did you read the question stem carefully enough to catch the "not"? All of the choices except one describe problems that *could* arise if a correspondent allows a news source to remain anonymous. You're looking for the one that doesn't apply. That's (B): Potential danger would be a reason for allowing a news source to remain anonymous, not a problem with allowing it. The remaining three all apply, so those choices are incorrect answers for this question. Giving the source's name "helps the reader or viewer evaluate independently the credibility of the source" (paragraph 10), (A). If a published anonymous statement turns out to be wrong, "the news organization's reputation is at stake along with that of the individual reporter" (paragraph 11), (C). "Sources who stand behind their word are more likely to tell the truth" (paragraph 10), (D).

2. **D** Since the excerpt doesn't explain specifically what the British Code of Practice is, you'll need to make an inference from the information given. When you're looking for information to support an inference, often the easiest place to start is to eliminate clearly wrong answers first using the technique of Process of Elimination (POE). Eliminate the wrong answers until you're left with the right one (or, at the least, a couple of possible right answers instead of four). Choice (A) is too extreme. A "practice" code would not apply "only" to people who haven't yet entered the practice of journalism. Be suspicious of answer choices that use all-or-nothing words such as "only," "never," or "always." The sentence that mentions this code talks about a "moral obligation" (paragraph 13) of journalists, which tells you two things: that the code applies to journalism and that (B) is wrong. A "moral obligation" suggests a standard that is less clear-cut than a legal rule, and also less enforceable. The excerpt gives no information to support the idea that British journalists must swear to uphold the code, so (C) is incorrect. That leaves (D), which corresponds to the section of the excerpt that explains the status of ethics codes. These codes "offer journalists a framework to help them decide what to report and how to report it" (paragraph 1).

3. **C** The author points out that getting a story by deceptive means—such as "hidden cameras, tape recorders, and microphones, or…a false identity" (paragraph 14)—undermines the credibility of the reporter and the story. "Readers and viewers often won't believe that a reporter who essentially lied in order to get a story will tell the truth when he reports it" (paragraph 14). An action that damages the credibility of one can, in the public's mind, cast doubt on the whole profession. How many other reporters use those tactics? How did the reporter get this story? News consumers don't know. They could assume that if one reporter relies on deception, many more are probably doing the same thing, causing widespread damage to the reputation of the entire profession. The other three quotes refer to something other than the damage caused by deceptive practices. The quote in (A) refers to "the one universal ethical principle" (paragraph 4). Choice (B) refers to the latitude for individual interpretation of ethics codes. Choice (D) concerns the need to verify sources.

4. **air footage (c) and (f); not air footage (b) and (d)**

   Since the question stem tells you that you'll need to get rid of two choices, let's start there and eliminate the principles that don't apply to this situation. This Process of Elimination (POE) technique results in a narrower field of choices to consider. There is no suggestion that the battle footage has been taken out of context, (a), and the question stem states that the footage is live, so it is not a reenactment, (e). With those two choices gone, you now need to decide into which column you should place the remaining four choices. Starting with the next available choice, (b), consider which decision this principle would support. Seeing graphic footage of an intense battle could distress viewers who have family members serving in *any* conflict area, so (b) supports the decision not to air the footage. The next choice, flexibility within the guidelines of ethical codes, (c), could actually support either decision, so let's leave that one until you see which column ends up needing another principle. Graphic footage of a violent battle could undermine morale among members of the military, whether they are currently serving in conflict areas or not, so (d) also belongs under the decision not to air the footage. Since you have two specific choices—(b) and (d)—that belong in the "don't air footage" column, you know that the remaining two fit under the decision to air. A responsibility to convey the harsh reality of war, (f), supports the decision to show the video. That column needs one more principle, so that's where (c) goes.

5. **B** In addition to the terms described in paragraph 12—what "off the record" means and how the news outlet can use the confidential information—the paragraph 13 sentences add another specific provision: Under what conditions might the journalist refuse to continue protecting the identity of a source? This addition to the terms could be more serious for the source, and might make him or her reconsider divulging any information, even if the journalist promises confidentiality. Choice (A) is too general when a more specific choice, such as (B), is available. Add what? It could be anything. Choice (C) twists the meaning of the paragraph 13 sentences. They don't suggest that a journalist is justified in breaking a promise when threatened with a contempt citation. Instead, those sentences tell journalists to be honest with the source about any conditions that might lead them to break a promise of confidentiality, so the source can agree to those terms up front, before the situation arises. Choice (D) goes too far. The penalties for being held in contempt vary in different areas. Depending on the importance of the anonymous information, a journalist might be willing to accept a fine or even a night in jail if that's what a contempt citation means. Most journalists aren't working in areas where they could face lengthy jail terms or even torture for refusing to reveal a source.

6. **(b), (c) and (e)**

    The author cautions that good ethics codes "probably raise more questions than they answer" (paragraph 1), (b). She also warns that, since ethics codes don't contain hard-and-fast rules, journalists "may disagree about how a specific ethical standard should apply" (paragraph 1). That disagreement could expand to include a journalist and the news organization that employs him or her, (c). The codes provide journalists with a "framework to help them decide what to report and how to report it" (paragraph 1), so interpretation is an individual, subjective affair, (e). The remaining two choices are incorrect. There is no evidence in the passage to support the idea that ethics codes for journalists vary widely in different countries, (a). Although ethics codes are guidelines and allow for flexibility in interpretation, they are not described as being so loose that they could be twisted into an endorsement of deceptive reporting practices, (d).

7. **A** This question requires you to create a quick summary in your head of the author's arguments and point of view, and then apply that summary to a different situation. The author is writing about a profession governed by codes of ethics and one firm rule, "a journalist never knowingly publishes a falsehood" (paragraph 4). Although she acknowledges that ethics codes are open to interpretation, she believes they provide good guidance to all journalists in difficult situations such as requests for anonymity or questions about making classified information public. "Citizen journalists" operate in a different world. For the most part, they control their publication outlets (such as blogs or social media platforms) and don't recognize any uniform ethics code. They can augment the work of professional reporters (for example, when someone who is trapped in an inaccessible area describes events over the phone to a reporter) or, worst case, they can publish whatever they want under the guise of facts, subject only to libel laws. The author's tone is not dogmatic; she recognizes that flexibility is sometimes necessary to

adapt to unusual situations. Nevertheless, she is more comfortable in a world where professional journalists are guided by ethics codes. Given her flexibility and her orientation to professionalism and ethics codes, (A) is the author's most likely position. Just as she advises professional journalists to "determine that a source is credible," to discover "what his 'agenda' might be," to "consult multiple sources," and to "verify the accuracy of a source's information" (paragraph 9), she would most likely advise news consumers to do the same with citizen journalists. Choice (B) is unlikely in view of the author's willingness to consider exceeding the usual bounds of professional journalism, such as when she allows for "times when a story can be obtained only through subterfuge" (paragraph 15). That type of flexibility makes (C) unlikely too. That choice is too extreme for this author's tone and point of view. The author's willingness to consider situations and sources on a case-by-case basis also makes (D) unlikely. In some cases, citizen journalists might be a useful source and in some cases, they might not.

8. **D** Developments in an investigation or simply the passage of time can make it clear that the initial "facts" were incorrect. The author acknowledges that this can make it difficult to tell the truth at first. News consumers are waiting for information; the reporter has deadlines. In the midst of an active situation, it's not always possible to wait until final, verified, accurate facts are available. In that situation, the best a responsible news outlet can do is correct the initial information as quickly as possible. None of the other choices describe a situation in which it's difficult to tell the truth. Choice (A) is plagiarism, plain and simple. There is no reason for the reporter not to tell the truth about the source of her material. Choices (B) and (C) describe similar situations. In both cases, the author would say that the reporter should have verified the sources and their access to the information they claimed to have before publishing the story.

9. **(e), (b), (a), (c), and (d)**

Mary initially displays an energy, passion, and "litany of rage" that "seemed to have the crowd in a kind of frenzy" (paragraph 1), (e). She then seizes upon this mob mentality to get the men to agree with her about the problem they need to solve, (b). "Would they go down into the pit themselves, do ye think?" (paragraph 2), she asks..."They would not!" (paragraph 3), her listeners agree. "They buy ye out! They break ye into pieces" (paragraph 4) she continues, describing the sorry state to which the men have allowed themselves to be reduced. After she gains the men's agreement on the problem, Mary gets them to commit to the solution, (a): "stand together" (paragraph 4) and refuse to submit any longer. They swear "on your lives" (paragraph 14) to stick together, back the union, and not "give way till ye've won" (paragraph 14). As if the men's duty to themselves and to one another wasn't enough to convince them to fight the oppression that plagues their lives, Mary then invokes her listeners' duty to "your wives and childer!" (paragraph 18), (c). Finally, with "leaping words and passionate out-flung arms" she carries her listeners to the point where they unite behind her "as an orchestra to the baton of a leader" (paragraph 18), (d).

10. **C** The sentences reveal a communication barrier among men who speak several different languages and who don't all understand English. You need to make an inference in order to answer this question, since the author doesn't explain why the language issue is important. That underlying communication barrier would prevent the men from organizing themselves into an effective group, even if they do all have the same complaints. Mary hits upon one word that slices through the barrier. Her listeners can all understand "Strike!" as a solution that promises action and control, and they accept the leadership of the person who offers that solution. They put "Mary Burke at their head" (paragraph 21). Mary's passion and energy might attract an audience and get the men to listen to her out of curiosity, but that wouldn't be enough to get them to accept the speaker's leadership, so (A) is incorrect. The men were used to being "slaves," forced to resign themselves to being driven by someone else like "a herd of cattle" (paragraph 8). However, that doesn't suggest that they would willingly accept the leadership of just anyone who wasn't using force and power to compel them, (B). Confused listeners wouldn't be able to figure out that Mary wanted to become their leader, (D).

11. **A** Did you catch the "first hint" in the question stem? Even if more than one answer suggests that Mary might not be effective in implementing the solution of getting the men to stand together and refuse to submit, you're looking for the first one. Since the choices give the locations of the quotes, you can use that information to help find the answer. Start at the beginning, with the paragraph 1 quote. A crowd in a frenzy, (B), might be difficult to control and to maintain at that level, but that doesn't suggest Mary wouldn't be able to do it. Moving on to paragraph 7, Mary reached the crowd with the word "strike!" (paragraph 6). Why had that word "not been spoken aloud in North Valley" for "many years" (paragraph 7), though? It seems an obvious solution; why had no one tried it or even suggested it recently? This is the first hint, (A), that Mary might not have all of the information she needs in order to implement her solution effectively, or that she could simply be too naïve to be an effective leader and overcome the obstacles ahead. Since (A) is the first suggestion, you can discard the other two choices. Choice (C) does indicate that Mary might have taken on an impossible task. However, it's in paragraph 20, so it's not the "first" hint that the question stem asked you to find. If Mary were fulfilling someone else's vision instead of her own, (D), she might not be effective, but then again, she might. In any case, this quote occurs in paragraph 21, so it's not the first hint, either.

12. **B** You'll need to make an inference from the quote in the question stem, because the author doesn't explain what Tom means. The author makes a similar claim when he says, "the real tragedy of these people's lives was not their physical suffering, but their mental depression" (paragraph 20). He doesn't explain the significance of that claim, either; however, the reference to "mental depression" does help clarify what Tom means. The problem "inside the heads" of the "mine-slaves" (paragraph 20) is lack of hope that they could ever improve their situation. These men "were accustomed to having their efforts balked at every turn" (paragraph 20), so they would see no point in uniting and fighting to change their lives. That's the problem facing Hal or anyone who tries to help them. Lack of education, (A), wouldn't prevent the men from trying to bring about improvements. Anger and rage might actually prompt them to act, not prevent them from taking action, (C). Depressed, hopeless people might not be reasoning clearly, but depression and lack of hope are the root of the problem, not the impaired reasoning that results from them, (D).

13. **B** All four choices describe contrasting pairs in the excerpt. If you read the question stem carefully, though, you noticed that you're looking for contrasting *imagery*, not characters. Only (B) deals with imagery. On the one hand, the author evokes the black coal, the dark pits, the men's hopeless lives, like dark tunnels with no light at the end. On the other hand is Mary, igniting the crowd with the word "Strike!" like a "flash of gunpowder" (paragraph 7). By the time she gains the crowd's commitment, she is "mounted upon a snow-white horse, wearing a robe of white" (paragraph 21). The other three choices all deal with contrasting characters and roles.

14. **(a), (b), and (d)**

Hal came from a privileged "class which is accustomed to say, 'Do this,' or 'Do that,' and it will be done" (paragraph 20), (a). The miners and their families in North Valley "had never known that sense of power, of certainty" (paragraph 20). Hal is "young and free," different from the "mine-slaves" in North Valley (paragraph 20), (b). Hal "wanted to run from this place of torment" (paragraph 19) to escape the hopeless life there. The miners and their families, on the other hand, seem powerless to leave, (d). Instead, they vow to make their stand in North Valley: "Either we'll win together, or we'll starve and die together!" (paragraph 8). The remaining two choices don't differentiate Hal from all of the miners and their families. Tom Olson refers to Hal's desire to help the miners. However, Mary is trying to help them too, (c), so Hal isn't different from at least one other person in North Valley. In wanting to "make out the words" of Mary's "litany of rage" (paragraph 1), Hal is behaving like the rest of the crowd, (e).

15. **A** Mary is making an urgent plea to these depressed, downtrodden people to find the courage to unite and fight the mine owners who "break ye into pieces" and "do what they please with ye" (paragraph 4). She wants the men to commit to joining her, so a gesture of "defiance" would be the opposite of what she intends, eliminating (B). "Desperation" describes the miners' current situation, not the hope and power that Mary is offering them with the ideas of a union and a strike, so (C) is incorrect. Although Hal describes Mary's speech as a "litany of rage" (paragraph 1), at this point she has finished describing the conditions that make her angry and is, instead, offering the people a solution, so (D) is incorrect.

16. **D** The excerpt doesn't explain the background to Mary's fiery speech; however, it does give enough information for you to make an educated guess. A question like this, which doesn't link back to much detail in the excerpt, is a good place to use Process of Elimination (POE) technique. Start by looking for *wrong* answers. After eliminating those, you'll have fewer choices for an educated guess. The excerpt doesn't describe an incident that might have triggered Mary's speech, so (A) is gone. If Mary were a natural agitator, (B), she would have tried to rally the men long before their situation became so desperate. Yet the author says the word "Strike!" hadn't even been spoken in North Valley "for many years" (paragraph 7). That eliminates (B). "The people rising—and Mary Burke at their head" was Hal's "vision come true" (paragraph 21), (C). There is no indication that Hal had shared his vision with Mary or that she was trying to fulfill it, though, so (C) is gone too. That leaves (D) as the only possible correct answer. Is it a reasonable one? As Hal watched Mary and listened to her speech, he saw "hope born of despair" (paragraph 18). It's reasonable to think that the nature of life in North Valley—this "place of torment" (paragraph 19) and "environment of terrorism" (paragraph 20)—might have finally become too much for Mary and galvanized her into an attempt to bring about a change for the better.

17. The option that correctly completes the sentence for each "Select" option:

Drop-Down Item 1: **Subject-verb agreement in complicated sentences with interceding phrases and collective nouns**

Option 3 is correct. Skip back over the interceding phrase—"in the Atlantic, Mississippi, and Central Flyways"—and you'll find that the subject is plural ("surveys"), so the verb ("suggest") must agree with that plural noun. The next subject ("population") is a collective noun. It represents many individuals; however, it is still singular and the verb ("exceeds") must agree with it. Other examples of singular collective nouns are flock and wildlife.

This question illustrates the importance of reading each answer choice carefully. If you skim through them, you could easily miss the small differences that make the other three options incorrect. Don't spend too much time on any one question, though. If the differences aren't obvious to you immediately, guess using your "option number of the day" (the number you've decided to use for every guess in order to maximize the chance that it will be correct for at least one question), mark the question for review and move on. Option 1 has a plural collective noun ("populations") but a verb ("exceeds") that agrees with a singular noun. Option 2 has a verb ("suggests") that would agree with a singular noun, not with the plural noun "surveys." Option 4 treats the singular collective noun ("population") as if it were plural by using the verb "exceed."

Drop-Down Item 2: **Parallelism**

Option 4 is correct. This long (but not run-on) sentence lists four conditions that lead to the high reproduction and survival rates of resident geese. You need to read the whole sentence in order to select the option that matches the structure of the other three conditions so all four have parallel (or matching) construction. You can understand this sentence better if you omit the descriptive words and focus on the structure: "Because...Canada geese (1) live [where?], 3. have {what?} and 4. fly [where?], they exhibit..." Drop-down item 2 concerns the second condition. Only option 4—tolerate [what?]—is parallel because it matches the structure of the other three.

Option 1 is incorrect because it emphasizes a noun ("disturbances,") not a verb. Option 2 at first seems as if it might be correct ("live [where?]"). However, then it launches into a complete thought with a subject and verb ("humans don't disturb them), which does not match the structure of the other three conditions. Option 3 is incorrect because it begins with an intransitive verb ("aren't") rather than a transitive (action) verb, as the other three conditions do.

Drop-Down Item 3: **Frequently confused words, words supporting logic and clarity, and sentence structure**

Option 2 is correct. "Affect" and "effect" are often confused. "Affect" is the verb form, which is what you want here: "Conflicts...affect...resources." "Effect" is the noun, the end result: "The effect of conflicts includes damage to resources."

Options 1 and 4 incorrectly use the noun, "effect." In addition, option 4 uses "and" instead of "or" to connect the two words, which essentially equates them. However, something can be affected without necessarily being damaged in the process. Option 3 is an awkward incomplete sentence: "Conflicts...affect [what?], damaging several types of resources." The verb "affect" needs an object to specify what was acted upon, but it doesn't have one here.

Drop-Down Item 4: **Transitional words, comma use, illogical word order, and parallelism**

Option 4 is correct. The transitional word "Additionally" is correctly set off by a comma and carries readers smoothly from the danger for swimmers to the danger for people who venture too close to a nest. The descriptive phrase "during nesting and brood rearing" is correctly set off from the main part of the sentence.

Option 1 is an instance of illogical word order. If the attacks on people occur during "additional" nesting and brood rearing, are there no attacks during the first round of nesting and brood rearing? Option 2 lacks proper parallel construction. It begins with a phrase, "during nesting," and then switches to a clause with a subject and verb ("when they're raising"). Correct parallel construction would match either the phrase construction ("during nesting and brood raising,..") or the clause construction ("when they're nesting and raising their broods,.."). Option 3 needs a comma after "rearing" to set off the descriptive phrase from the main part of the sentence.

Section 2
Access your Student Tools online to read sample essays representing different score levels for the Extended Response prompts in this book.

Section 3

18. **C** This question asks you to make an inference based on the evidence given in the excerpt. You won't find an explicit answer in the passage; instead, you'll need to make assumptions based on the author's tone, the content he conveys and the way he conveys it. If you recognized the author's name, you've found another good clue: He is indeed the P.T. Barnum of circus fame, the successful promoter of "The Greatest Show on Earth." Ordinary people—the kind of people who go to the circus—would be most receptive to Barnum's friendly, conversational tone and to his simple principles and the entertaining stories that support them. These are the small shopkeepers and service providers, blacksmiths and carpenters without a lot of formal education but with a desire to prosper. If Barnum were writing for professional businesspeople, (A), he wouldn't need to advise them to advertise, let alone tell entertaining stories to convince them. His casual, conversational tone is also out of step with the more formal language a professional business audience would expect. For a well-educated audience with an entrepreneurial streak, (B), you would expect more technical terms, and solid facts and figures to support Barnum's point about the effectiveness of advertising. While the example of Genin the hatter does deal with a retail shop, (D), Barnum says his principle of sowing advertising and then reaping sales "applies to all kinds of business" (paragraph 1). In addition, nothing in the passage eliminates people who are planning to open a business but don't yet own one.

19. **B** This question asks you to identify and evaluate how the author presents his argument that "advertising is like learning—'a little is a dangerous thing!'" (paragraph 5). He makes that argument in three steps: the story of the man who advertised three times and failed, the quote from the French writer explaining why seven ads are required, and finally, this example of the drunk who, like the man, stopped too soon and therefore didn't reach his goal. The story about the drunk therefore reinforces Barnum's point about perseverance. Another 10 cents for whiskey, like another $2 for four more ads, would bring success and preserve the value of the money already spent. Choice (A) is wrong because you can't assume that all readers are familiar with the quest to get drunk. Choice (C) is only partly true. It doesn't take much money to succeed provided you have already invested in reaching your goal and just have a little bit farther to go. There is some truth to (D). However, entertainment isn't the primary function of the drunk's story. Its main purpose is to provide another example that reinforces the author's point, (B).

20. **A** This question asks you to determine the meaning of an unusual term from the context. You need to consider not only the sentence itself, but also the audience and the author's message to them. At first glance, the correct answer might not be obvious. The "most likely" in the question stem gives you a hint that more than one answer could seem to be correct. In a case like this, the best approach is to look for answers that are definitely wrong and eliminate those first; then chose the correct answer from a smaller number of possibilities, using a technique called Process of Elimination (POE). Here (B) is clearly wrong. The sentence refers to the shop as "his business," so he already has his own. You can eliminate (D) next. If the shop is "his business," there are no partners to buy out. Process of Elimination will often allow you to eliminate two choices, as it does here, leaving just two to consider instead of four. Both (A) and (C) are plausible; however, (C) is too specific for the information given in the passage. You're not told if the man has debts or needs more workers to serve the new customers he attracts. That leaves (A), which would surely appeal to Barnum's audience of ordinary people who don't aspire to build an empire. They simply want to have a small business that will support them and their families.

21. **(a) and (d)**

    This tricky character development question asks you to consider what characteristics Mr. Genin's advertising technique (described in paragraph 10) reveals about him, and then select the ones that do NOT apply. This example illustrates how important it is to read the question stem carefully, so you understand the task it sets for you. If you just skimmed the question stem quickly, you might miss the "not" and select the two incorrect answers. For this question, you need to eliminate the characteristics that Mr. Genin's advertising technique *does* reveal. His technique of placing a high bid for a concert ticket was certainly innovative, (b), in an era when the usual methods of advertising were buying a newspaper ad or hanging a sign. And his calculated attempt to spread his name far and wide reveals his ambition, (c), for expanding his business. Therefore, the correct answers are the two remaining characteristics. He is not miserly, (a); he bid the high sum of $225 when the author's earlier story reveals that three newspaper ads cost only $1.50. Mr. Genin is not timid, (d), either. He took a big risk that the publicity generated by his $225 bid would pay off (as it did).

22. **D** After a brief introductory paragraph describing, in general terms, the value of advertising in building sales and the importance of having a good product to sell, Barnum launches into a dialogue that says, in effect, "OK, now I'm going to tell you a true story." The focus narrows to one man and his experience with placing newspaper ads. The writing becomes more direct, more concrete, more specific, drawing readers in and making them want to find out what happens. The "real person" is simply described as "a man," too vague to function as an authority that would convince readers of the author's credibility, (A). In any case, Barnum's well-known success gave him enough credibility that readers bought his book. The writing style is easy to read and entertaining for a mass audience. It's not a monotonous set of instructions that would need some relief, (B). Granted, most of Barnum's readers wouldn't be very well educated. However, the dialogue section is very brief in this passage. There is no indication that the author is trying to turn his writing into a play, (C).

23. **B** This question poses a dilemma because there's some truth to each answer. The best tactic in a case such as this is to use Process of Elimination (POE). Start by looking for the most *in*correct answer, eliminate that, compare the remaining three, strike the most incorrect choice from that set, and so on until you're left with the most correct answer. The first choice to go is (A). Yes, Barnum does inform the audience about the value of advertising and how well unconventional methods can work. But consider his conversational tone, his use of stories and examples. "Inform" could easily mean using very formal language to let people know about a new law. Next to go is (D). The author first tries to convince readers about the value of advertising before he describes some skills. Choice (C) ignores the entertainment value of the anecdotes and examples. That leaves (B). The author is trying to educate readers about building a business, and astutely chooses to do it in an entertaining way that will interest his audience of ordinary people.

24. **(d) and (b)**

One lesson is fairly obvious. Mr. Genin made news with the high price he paid for the first Jenny Lind ticket, gaining exposure to millions of people across the country. His technique of making news turned out to be a much more effective way to use newspapers than buying advertising space would have been, (d). The second lesson is a little less obvious. In the last paragraph, the author says that "This novel advertisement first struck their attention, and then, as he made a good article, they came again." Mr. Genin's innovative technique would attract a new customer only once, (b). To gain repeat business from that customer, he had to offer a good product. The lesson about seven repetitions, (a), applies to buying advertising space, not to the technique of making news. Mr. Genin sold thousands of hats to customers across the country, demonstrating that people don't necessarily prefer a local business, (c).

25. **C** The usual meaning of "spurious" is counterfeit or fake, as in an imitation of a famous designer's coat or handbag. However, in this case the author simply means a product which is not really good and which will not please the customer. The product is shoddy (inferior or substandard), but is not a counterfeit (falsely presented as a genuine article produced by a well-known expert). An outrageous product, (A), could still

be good and well made. Likewise, a common product, (B), (such as a hammer or an umbrella) could still be good and please the customer, and so could a luxurious item, (D).

26.   **[in order] (c), (a), and (b)**

This question asks you to unearth the chronological structure underlying the author's discussion of Brazil's pursuit of autonomy. Understanding this overall structure will provide a helpful foundation for answering more detailed questions about parts of the passage. The author says that Brazil has "taken on asymmetries of power through three expressions of autonomy: distance, participation, and diversification" (paragraph 4). She then goes on to discuss, in chronological order, each of those three stages of Brazil's pursuit of autonomy, and gives examples of the initiatives the country undertook during each stage. So you need to order the initiatives (the examples) according to which one represents first, the distance stage; second, the participation stage; and third, the diversification stage. During the first (distance) stage, "Brazil turned inward" (paragraph 4), (c). During the second (participation) stage, Brazil "became convinced of the need to participate in global political and economic institutions." The author says that "pragmatism prevailed" and "Brazil accepted international norms in the security sector" (paragraph 5), (a). During the third (diversification) stage, Brazil "intensified relations with emerging market partners" (paragraph 6), (b).

27. **D** This question gives you good practice in guessing the meaning of a pretty obscure word from the excerpt's context and meaning. First, to situate the word in a general subject area, look at what the excerpt is about. It concerns a country and, as the title says, that country's efforts to preserve its autonomy. Next, look at the subject matter in the sentences that use the word and a couple of sentences before and after. In paragraph 4, "autarky" is a way for Brazil to protect itself from more powerful international players in order to preserve its autonomy. In paragraph 6, Brazil abandons "autarky" for the opposite tactic. Instead of building walls to keep powerful nations away, it "built strength within global institutions" to protect its autonomy. So the word concerns one way of protecting autonomy from more powerful countries. Now narrow down the choices by getting rid of those that are clearly wrong, using Process of Elimination (POE). Hostility, (A), wouldn't do much good when you're out-gunned by stronger players, so that's the first choice to go. "Cooperation," (C), might fit with the context in paragraph 6, but not with the context in paragraph 4, where Brazil is in its "distance" stage and not cooperating with anyone. By starting with a search for *wrong* answers, you now have only two choices to worry about, (B) and (D). "Isolation," (B), is tempting (especially because of the use of "retreating" in paragraph 6), and it sounds as if it fits into the two sentences grammatically as a replacement word. How would isolation "from the great powers" help Brazil "preserve sovereignty" (paragraph 4), though, especially if it needed those countries as customers for its exports and suppliers for its imports? So (B) is gone, too, leaving (A), self-sufficiency. During its first, inward-turning stage, Brazil focused on becoming self-sufficient so it could distance itself from powerful countries. Later, during its diversification stage, it abandoned self-sufficiency as a means of protecting its autonomy from the growing power of the United States and instead turned to other developing countries to broaden its base of support (paragraph 6). Incidentally, another word in the excerpt that might be unfamiliar—"hegemonic" (paragraph 4)—means supreme or dominant.

28. **B** Imagine a triangle with "defense modernization" (the means to prevent another country from interfering in your affairs), on one point, "autonomy" on a second and "fixed budget resources" on the third. Now imagine constant tension within the triangle. The author highlights the "tough tradeoffs" (paragraph 1) among those three points. Brazil needs the means (defense modernization) to attain and preserve its autonomy in a global system; however, fixed budget resources don't allow it to do that. So for Brazil, "autonomy has been an elusive quest" (paragraph 3). The author describes three different strategies Brazil pursued in its quest for autonomy, so it wasn't clinging to one wrong strategy, eliminating (A). Tradeoffs in the unholy trinity confront any country: Should it direct more of its fixed amount of resources toward

defense, strengthening its autonomy at the expense of other national priorities (such as education or infrastructure)? Or should it let its autonomy suffer while investing in other needs? Brazil and its emerging market partners all face these choices, making (C) incorrect. Brazil did change its foreign policy tactics between the military regime and democracy. However, the author attributes the change to "the global debt crises of the 1980s" (paragraph 5) that made Brazil's military-era policy of autarky impossible, so (D) is incorrect.

29. **C** Here's the type of question where mapping out the structure of the excerpt pays off. During its distance stage of trying to preserve its autonomy, Brazil turned inward and concentrated on becoming self-sufficient. It reached out to major international players during its participation phase. As the power of the United States grew, it turned to other emerging markets during its diversification phase in order to build a broader base of support for itself. Among those three areas of focus, where would the pursuit of environmental initiatives be an advantage? In gaining acceptance from other countries and in building partnerships with them (during its participation and diversification phases, respectively). When it was trying to gain entry to "global political and economic institutions," Brazil needed to "be seen as a cooperative player in... environmental spheres" (paragraph 5). Later, when it was trying to strengthen its base of support, it "pursued its new foreign policy agenda of...environmentalism...with other developing country partners" (paragraph 6). Environmental initiatives became a means of reaching out first, to major international countries and later, to other emerging countries. A focus on the environment would not have helped Brazil strengthen its economy and become more self-sufficient (during its distance stage), (A). It used environmentalism with powerful international players too, not only with less developed countries, (B). Choice (D) might well be true when Brazil was concentrating on becoming self-sufficient during the distance phase, but that's only speculation; the excerpt doesn't provide that information, so this choice is incorrect too.

30. **B** When you run into a term that sounds complicated and technical, such as "import substitution industrialization," you'll sometimes find that you can decipher it fairly easily by looking at each word individually and rearranging them. Here, the author is talking about industrializing in order to produce something that was previously imported—in other words, producing a domestic substitute for that import. This was one way Brazil attempted to become self-sufficient and distance itself from more powerful countries. Choice (B) uses automobiles as an example of that process. Two things make (A) incorrect: The grapes are still being imported, whether they come from Spain or Italy, and grapes don't involve an industrial process. Choice (C) involves exporting to other countries, not building domestic capacity. Choice (D) doesn't replace a product that was previously imported.

31. **(b), (d), and (e)**

According to the author, Brazil initially sought autonomy—the power to implement its own decisions, free from interference—by becoming self-sufficient. Following the 1980s global economic crisis, "Brazilian policymakers slowly became convinced of the need to participate in global political and economic institutions in order to acquire power" (paragraph 5), (d). This about-face in foreign policy shows up in the nuclear test concession (b), which Brazil made "in order to be seen as a cooperative player" (paragraph 5). Where it had previously tried to avoid international trade by turning to self-sufficiency, and previously condemned the control that powerful northern countries exerted over international trade, Brazil "began to use institutions such as the World Trade Organization to gain leverage and policy space" (paragraph 5), (e). All of these foreign policy examples were inspired by Brazil's search for autonomy. The author explains that "autonomy through diversification [the third stage of Brazil's pursuit of autonomy] does not reject the institution-building and rule-setting agendas of participation [the second stage]" (paragraph 6). Rejecting "institution-building and rule-setting agendas" is not one of Brazil's foreign policy initiatives, (a). In fact, Brazil embraced them when its quest for autonomy led it to seek membership in international institutions.

A "scientific and technological base" (paragraph 2) is cited as one element of an expression of national power, not as a foreign policy initiative that Brazil undertook in its quest for autonomy, (c).

32. **A** Careful reading is required here, since both the two definitions and the four choices are quite close. "Self-rule" can be implemented without constraint if there are no other countries to act as forces of constraint. That is sovereignty. It is only within the context of a "global system"—in other words, in the context of other countries—that autonomy is necessary in order to exercise sovereignty. The author points out the "asymmetries of power" (paragraph 4) in the global system. Less powerful countries do not have the means to implement their sovereign decisions when faced with a threat to their autonomy. More powerful countries have autonomy because they have the means to deter an attempt by less powerful countries to interfere with their actions. Choices (B) and (D) are deceptively close to being correct, but not entirely accurate. The reason is the same as the reason that (A) is correct. Autonomy is not an issue unless there is a risk of "territorial incursions" or "domestic interference" (paragraph 1) from other countries. Choice (C) is incorrect because sovereignty focuses inward (on "self-rule" and national priorities), while autonomy focuses outward (on defending the nation's capacity to implement its sovereign decisions).

33. **D** You need to read the answer choices carefully in this question. Each choice has two parts: the shift in partnership focus and the reason for that shift. *Both* of those parts need to be correct. These practice answer choices contain some examples of "part wrong is all wrong." If you just skim the choice and the first part happens to be correct, you could miss a trick answer where the second part is wrong, making the entire choice wrong. Start with (A). During its distance stage, Brazil "formalized its identity as a representative of the Third World in North-South relations" (paragraph 4). There is no indication in the excerpt that it abandoned a former South-South alliance in a deliberate attempt to do this, though, as (A) says it did. When (A) is part wrong, it's all wrong. During the global financial crisis, Brazil "edged toward greater participation in multilateral forums" (paragraph 5) because self-sufficiency was no longer a viable way of preserving autonomy. This was a move to reach out to a broad, multi-party group, not a deliberate attempt to align itself with powerful northern countries, so (B) is wrong. During its distance stage, Brazil "condemned the control of international trade, finance, and nuclear regimes by the hegemonic North" and forged "alternative relationships among Southern partners" (paragraph 4). However, these powerful northern countries were not its former partners, as (C) incorrectly says. Again, part wrong is all wrong. The correct answer is (D), where both the change in focus and the reason for it are correct. During its diversification stage, Brazil shifted "the locus of engagement from a broader multilateral stage to a South-South approach" in order to broaden "its cooperative base" because it saw the need for "a counterweight to American power" (paragraph 6).

34. **(a), (d), and (e)**

The theme of trust—both wisely and unwisely placed—echoes throughout the excerpt. Both (a) and (d) concern misplaced trust: Magnus didn't return and Virika didn't take the baby "to her native place" (paragraph 2) where Hilda could reclaim her. Choice (e) suggests one time when Hilda asks, "Can I trust you?" instead of unquestioningly placing her trust in the wrong people. In (b), the chemist is giving the frightened Hilda a factual explanation for why it doesn't matter whether he leaves or not. The statement is not designed to earn or regain her trust. Choice (d) describes the chemist's attempt to get a human subject for his experiment. Again, it is not related to the theme of trust.

35. **C** You need to replay the sequence of events in order to answer this question correctly. Yes, Hilda depends on the chemist's skill in order to wake up in 100 years, (B). Choice (A) says essentially the same thing; if the chemist's process works well enough that the bear wakes up, then so will she. But why is Hilda in a

position of depending on the chemist? Because the legal authorities agreed that he could use Hilda in his experiment, (D). And why was Hilda controlled by the legal authorities and facing death? Rewind the plot line even further and you'll reach, (C). Hilda depended on Virika to keep the baby safe, as she offered to do. If Virika hadn't strangled the baby with Hilda's sash, then Hilda would not have been arrested and condemned to death, the legal authorities would not have had control over her fate, and she would not have become an ideal human subject for the chemist's experiment. The chain of dependencies ultimately reaches back to Virika, who started the sequence of events and who is therefore the character on whom Hilda depended the most.

36. **C** The chemist goes "half wild" (paragraph 3) with excitement at the idea of trying his recently discovered suspended animation process on a human. Putting Hilda to sleep was only half of the process, though. A successful experiment required waking her up again in 100 years too. His reason for making sure Hilda would wake up was completing the entire process successfully, not keeping a promise to her or to the authorities. Choice (A) describes how the chemist tried to ensure that Hilda would wake up in 100 years, not what his motive was. There is no evidence in the excerpt that the chemist's motive was to save Hilda from being beheaded, (B). When he makes this statement, he is simply trying to calm her fears so he can get on with putting her into a state of suspended animation. The chemist's compassion because of Hilda's fear, (D), doesn't necessarily reveal anything about his reason for making sure she wakes up again.

37. **B** You need to notice the "not" in the question stem to avoid heading in the wrong direction when you answer. If Hilda thought she was fortunate to escape being beheaded, the "tomb-like " (paragraph 7) chemist's laboratory changed her mind. The narrator says "a shudder ran through soul and body, as she entered" (paragraph 4), and she shows her fear when she is talking to the chemist. The description of the laboratory conveys the impression that Hilda has gone from one horrible fate to a very different, but equally horrible one. It does not suggest that she was fortunate. The other three choices all deal with how the laboratory setting *does* affect the narrative, so they are not correct answers to this question. In contrast to a public beheading—a crowded, noisy, chaotic scene—the laboratory is private, quiet, cold, shared only with a dispassionate scientist and "the bear" and "the crocodile" (paragraph 11) asleep on their stone shelves, (A). In her previous life, Hilda knew people in "her native village" (paragraph 16), and had a lover and a baby. In the laboratory, on the other hand, she is alone except for a clinical chemist who sees her only as a scientific experiment. The setting is cold and austere, far from the "well-remembered hills and streams" (paragraph 16) she knew before, (C). From the terror of execution by beheading, the description of the laboratory—with its harsh, otherworldly environment and sleeping beasts—intensifies the atmosphere of horror surrounding Hilda's situation, (D).

38. **D** After 100 years, neither the bear nor Hilda would find anyone they knew when they returned to their former lives. However, "bears, being more strictly conservative than men, happily escape the influence of French revolutions, German philosophy, Fourier theories, and reforms of all sorts; therefore, Bruin doubtless found less change in *his* fellow citizens" (paragraph 12). The author uses the contrast between the bear and the human to comment on the less conservative aspects of the human spirit, which lead people to experiment with new things, pursue new discoveries, and struggle for power. Yes, the bear's successful resuscitation does prove that the chemist's process works, (A) and that the chemist's great-grandson received instructions, (C), therefore suggesting that Hilda will wake up too. However, the question asks for the *main* impact. These answers are too general. Anything—or anyone—could have been resuscitated first. There is more to the bear's experience than waking up successfully, and there is a reason why the first subject of the experiment was not a person. The bear's resuscitation does foreshadow Hilda's experience with curious onlookers and the subsequent desire to escape from them, (B). However, their attempts to return to an old life are very different for the bear and for Hilda.

39. **B** Hilda's baby and her resuscitation highlight the theme of birth and rebirth. There is a cause and effect relationship between Hilda's conviction and her availability as a subject for the chemist's experiment, (A). The two events do not point to the same theme, however. The events in (C) aren't connected to the same theme; neither are the events in (D).

40. **A** The author doesn't answer this question directly in the excerpt. You can find some clues to help you make an educated guess, though. This is a society that made Hilda feel she had to "keep her disgrace a secret" (paragraph 1) when she had a child but no husband. It's a legal system that would behead a 16-year-old for infanticide based only on "strong circumstantial evidence" (paragraph 2). These people were serious about demanding adherence to a moral code. So why would they give up their condemned prisoner to a chemist who claimed the prisoner would be alive again in 100 years? With an "educated guess" question such as this, the best place to start is by eliminating choices that clearly have no support at all in the passage, using the Process of Elimination (POE) technique. After getting rid of those, you'll be left with an answer that is the best guess. There is no suggestion in the excerpt that the authorities felt any hesitation about beheading a 16-year-old, (B), or had any desire to make a contribution to science, (C). There is also no indication that they didn't believe the chemist could do what he claimed, (D). That leaves (A) which is a fact, not speculation as the other three choices are. For all practical purposes, Hilda would be dead and the state would have its justice. If she really did awaken in 100 years, the legal authorities who condemned her would be long gone by then, so they didn't need to worry about the possibility.

41. **(a), (c), and (f)**

From the beginning of the excerpt, when she lets Virika take her baby "though not without bitter tears" (paragraph 1) until the end, when she realizes she doesn't know anyone in her native village and finds it "sadder than sunshine on a ruined city" (paragraph 16), Hilda is unhappy, (a). She is unsophisticated, (c), in her response to every situation. Her simple, childlike nature leads her to take the easiest way out (accepting Virika's offer, admitting her guilt, escaping to the familiar place of her childhood). She doesn't have the experience to navigate her way through the difficulties she faces. In a similar way, Hilda is unthinking, (f). It never occurs to her that she should investigate Virika before accepting her offer of taking the baby. She doesn't realize that confessing won't help her escape the death penalty. In the lab, she is "not reflecting on all the peculiar circumstances of her condition" (paragraph 8) when she asks why the chemist won't be there in 100 years to wake her up. None of the people she knew in her native village are there anymore, either, yet that's where she automatically runs without thinking through the plan: The remaining three choices are not true throughout the excerpt, as the question stem specifies. Hilda shows at least some awareness of her various predicaments (the baby, her arrest, the chemist's lab and experiment) and takes some action (giving the baby to Virika, admitting her guilt) or displays some emotion (fear) in response to them, so she is not completely detached, (b). Choice (d) is tempting, but not entirely accurate. After she is resuscitated and finds herself surrounded by curious onlookers with their "perpetual questions" (paragraph 15), Hilda finally does take some control and escapes "from the city...to her native village" (paragraph 16) under a new name. The fear that Hilda displays in the laboratory and earlier, when "the fear of death before her eyes" (paragraph 2) leads her to admit she had a baby, eliminates (e).

42. **B** It's a word you likely never heard before, but you can figure out the most probable meaning of "subduction" from the context in paragraph 1. The author explains that "oceans not only grow but also shrink" as a result of subduction, and he refers to the "contraction of ocean basins" (paragraph 1). What's going on? The earlier reference to "the theory of plate tectonics" provides a clue. The interaction of the Earth's plates can shrink the surface of ocean basins to such an extent that "continents on their opposing sides converge" (paragraph 1) and collide. Another clue comes from the prefix "sub-," which you likely already associate with a position such as "underneath" or "below." Put those clues together and you end up with

a word that refers to one of the Earth's plates being forced underneath another one. Subduction works differently on land, the author explains, because "continental crust is less dense than oceanic crust" and therefore "continents cannot be subducted far beneath the surface" (paragraph 1), so (A) is incorrect. The author doesn't say that continents can be prevented from converging, (C). Choice (D) is incomplete. Yes, subduction does involve the interaction of the Earth's plates, but the definition must include the fact that one plate ends up being forced beneath another one.

43. **C** This is the only choice that describes a characteristic of the passage. Geologists would already know the process that formed the Himalayas. Mountaineers might not, but this audience would likely be interested in how the world's highest, most spectacular mountain range was formed. The author mentions researchers in the field, but does not refer readers to any particular works, so references are not a characteristic that identifies the intended audience, (A). The author mentions only one specific mountain: Nanga Parbat in paragraph 6. Otherwise he talks about the Himalayas as a group, so a focus on specific mountains does not help identify the audience, (B). He does not define technical terms (such as "subduction" in paragraph 1 and "suture zone" in paragraph 3), so this characteristic doesn't point to the intended audience, either, (D). He could be writing for geologists who are already familiar with the terms, or he could be assuming that professional mountaineers already know what the terms mean.

44. **(c), (g), (d), (a), (f), (b), and (e)**

You can answer questions in any order. After you've done the easy questions, one like this—which helps you uncover a sequence of events and learn how the passage is constructed—is a good next step. In this case, the answer will help you understand processes the author describes later in the passage. First, subduction occurs, (c), leading to contraction of the ocean basins, (g), which causes a convergence of "the continents on their opposing sides" (paragraph 1), (d). Next comes "collision between two continents" (paragraph 1), (a), which creates a crust, (f). Because of its low density, this continental crust cannot be forced underneath another plate (it "cannot be subducted"), so "after continental collision the crust crumples and thickens" (paragraph 1), (b). Finally, "the surface of thickened continents is uplifted to great altitudes" (paragraph 2), (e).

45. **D** These four choices are fairly close; however, you need to decide which one is the author's *main* purpose. Start by getting rid of the least likely choices, using the Process of Elimination (POE) technique. (Look for the wrong choices first in order to narrow down the field of possible correct choices.) The author doesn't include harrowing accounts of ocean floor exploration or scientific climbing expeditions, and his tone is neutral, so (B) is a good choice to eliminate first. There is no indication that he wants readers to do anything in particular after reading the passage, so (A) can go too. Now you're left with two similar choices, (C) and (D). If the author wanted to educate readers, how would the passage be different? It would probably include more detail about the discoveries, processes, and theories he describes, and it would point readers to credible sources of additional information. Of the two remaining choices, (C) is the best one to eliminate. Do the tone and content of the passage support, (D), as a good inference? In a neutral tone, the author gives fairly thorough, but not overly detailed or technical, explanations. He focuses on a mountain range and puzzling high plateau that would intrigue mountaineers. It's reasonable to infer that he is trying to interest his readers without trying to turn them into geologists.

46. **A** Answering this question will help you follow the sequence of discoveries that the author builds into an explanation of how the Himalayan range was formed. First, scientists needed to realize that the Earth's crust is composed of plates which move and interact (plate tectonics). Then they needed to understand one result of plate interaction (subduction) for two reasons: to know why continents collide in the first place,

and to recognize that the process is different on land. Choice (B) is incomplete. Half right is all wrong. Yes, the lower density of the continental crust causes it to crumple and thicken instead of one plate being forced under another, as occurs in subduction. However, this choice ignores the importance of first understanding that the Earth's crust is broken up into plates (the theory of plate tectonics). A knowledge of plate tectonics and subduction is necessary to understand a "simple model of collision between two continents" which "explains the formation of a narrow high mountain range such as the Himalaya" (paragraph 4). Faults are not part of that simple model, so (C) is incorrect. The author explains that, because of the lower density of the continental crust, subduction does not occur on land when continents collide, eliminating (D).

47. **B** The author is listing scientific theories to explain a geological process. He would therefore consider research and confirming evidence to be important in evaluating the value of a particular theory. Here, he has arranged the three theories according to the amount of evidence supporting each one. The first is supported by "satellite images" showing "strike-slip faults," and by analysis of "seismic waves associated with earthquake activity" showing that "the Earth's crust is moving sideways across them" (paragraph 5). The second theory is supported only by "field-work in the Himalaya," which identified thrust-faults that "result from compression of the crust" (paragraph 6). Finally, he mentions the third theory, which is only conjecture. It "could account for crustal shortening across the Tibetan Plateau" (paragraph 7), but it is not supported by any evidence. Choice (A) could be factually correct. The first theory may indeed be the best known. It even has a label: "the Molnar-Tapponier model" (paragraph 5), named after the two scientists who developed it. The second theory does deal with a different type of fault, while the third theory concerns only the Tibetan plateau and doesn't depend on faults at all. However, this choice doesn't present a compelling reason why the author would chose this particular order. Consider the subject matter. For a scientific discussion of different theories concerning a geological process, (B), with its emphasis on research and evidence, is a better match. Choice (C) is too general. It doesn't specify what characteristic of the theory makes the author believe one is more likely than another. Only the first theory is dated. There is no evidence in the passage that the other two theories came later, eliminating (D).

48. **D** This question asks you to "read between the lines" of the excerpt as a whole to gain a sense of the author's approach to geological investigation and then test that approach against positions that are not stated in the passage. As he explains in paragraph 1, in some cases we need to discover one process or principle before we can understand others that result from it. And we have only theories, not certainty, about some processes, as is evident in his discussion of the three theories to explain the same process (the continuing convergence of India and Asia). We are still learning. Clues in the excerpt suggest that the author would not agree with the remaining three choices. His list of three theories makes it doubtful he would believe we can have certainty about the Earth's processes, regardless of the amount of resources thrown at the effort, so (A) is incorrect. The author lists different research tools (for example, "gravity and seismic surveys" in paragraph 2, "satellite images" in paragraph 5 and "field-work" in paragraph 6) which underlie different theories, so observation and analysis don't necessarily lead to fewer theories, (B). There is no evidence that the author would agree with (C), which would undermine the independent lines of inquiry that can lead to breakthroughs such as the "formulation of the theory of plate tectonics" (paragraph 1).

49. **C** Like the Himalayas, the Tibetan plateau rests on "an unusually thick crust" (paragraph 4). Why, then, is it a plateau instead of a "narrow high mountain range such as the Himalaya" (paragraph 4)—which the author does attribute to continental collision. He concludes that something else must account for the Tibetan plateau. The isolated location of Nanga Parbat, (A), is explained as the result of thrust faults and the mountain's position on the Indian plate. It does not lead to the conclusion that factors other than simple continental collision explain the high Tibetan plateau. The remains of the ocean floor are evidence of the northward movement of India, (B), not directly connected to the difference between the formation the Himalayas and of the Tibetan plateau. Choice (D) describes the "simple model of collision

between two continents" (paragraph 4) that explains the formation of the high Himalayan mountains. On its own, this model does not lead to the author's conclusion that other factors must explain the high Tibetan plateau.

50.   The option that correctly completes the sentence for each "Select" option:

Drop-Down Item 1: **Fused sentence, comma splice, and words that support logic and clarity**

Option 4 is correct. The two complete sentences are correctly separated by a period at the end of the first sentence (after "won't") and a capital letter at the beginning of the second ("This").

Option 1 is a fused sentence. Two independent clauses (complete sentences that can stand on their own, each with a subject and verb) are just run together without any punctuation (such as a period or semicolon) or conjunction (a joining word, such as "and" or "but") to separate them. Option 3 is a similar error called a comma splice. The two independent clauses are separated by nothing but a comma. A comma can be used for many things, but separating two independent clauses isn't one of them. That task demands more robust punctuation, such as a period or semicolon. The error in option 2 is more difficult to identify. Grammatically it is almost correct: The two independent clauses are separated by a conjunction ("because"). The only thing missing is a comma before the conjunction. Notice the subtle change in meaning this option creates, though. The implication in option 2 is that the card's rules define what type of travel purchase earns a 0.5% reward, which isn't quite accurate. The only travel purchase defined by the card's rules (explained in the first sentence) is "adventure trips," for a 3% reward. The rules just specify one other category—"everything else," whether it's groceries or gas or traditional travel—that gets 0.5%. This question illustrates the importance of considering context and meaning, as well as correct language usage, when you're evaluating answer options.

Drop-Down Item 2: **Sentence construction and words indicating relationship**

Option 2 is correct. It correctly uses the conjunctive adverb "so," preceded by a comma, to join the two independent clauses ("There are many..." and "it would be impossible..."). A conjunctive adverb is simply an adverb that acts as a conjunction (a joining word) between two independent clauses (complete sentences that could stand alone). In this option, the conjunctive adverb shows the cause-and-effect relationship between the large number of companies and the difficulty of keeping an up-to-date list.

Option 1 also uses a conjunctive adverb ("however"). The punctuation is wrong, though: There should be a semicolon before "however" and a comma after it. More important is the inaccurate relationship that "however" indicates. This relationship is not one of cause and effect, as it should be. The implication here is that the large number of companies should make it easy to maintain a list, but for some other reason it's impossible to do so. Option 3 is a comma splice—the incorrect use of a comma to separate two independent clauses without an accompanying conjunction. Option 4 is a repetitive run-on sentence. It would be correct, although rather wordy, if it ended after "list."

Drop-Down Item 3: **Non-standard or informal language usage and wordiness**

Option 1 is correct. This option correctly uses the infinitive form of the verb ("to see") and reinforces the unknown result of an experiment by using the term "if."

Option 2 illustrates informal language usage with "try and see." "Try" should take the infinitive here ("try to see"). Moreover, adding "try" just makes this option unnecessarily wordy. The small purchase has already been defined as an experiment (a trial or test). Option 3 undercuts the meaning of "experiment" by using the word "that." This option implies that the 3% reward is already a known result, making the small purchase merely an additional test to confirm that conclusion. In addition to being unnecessarily wordy, option 4 anthropomorphizes (gives life to) the inanimate small purchase by suggesting that it would be capable of doing something (earning the 3% reward).

Drop-Down Item 4: **Coordination and subordination, words supporting logic and clarity, and punctuation and capitalization**

Option 4 is correct. It is a straightforward, neutral explanation of the rules, with the same tone and weight as the preceding sentence about earning 3% on the first $5,000 of annual adventure trip purchases. It is a separate sentence, so it does not encourage a comparison between the two rates.

You need to consider the context—the author, audience, and purpose—to recognize the overall problem with the other three options. The company offering the card is trying to attract new customers with the information in these Frequently Asked Questions. The 3% reward rate is a good deal; the 0.5% rate definitely is not. The company would not want to undercut its appeal by emphasizing the low-end rate, but that's just what the other three options do. Option 1 stresses the stark contrast between the high and the low reward rates by using "however" to make the transition from 3% to 0.5%. Option 2 uses the subordinating conjunction "although" to emphasize that the reward on adventure purchases in excess of $5,000 is inferior to the main reward on the first $5,000. A subordinating conjunction joins a dependent clause ("if your adventure experience purchases exceed...") to the main, independent clause ("You will earn 3%..."). Since there is a period at the end of the independent clause, option 2 should also start with a capital letter on "although." Option 3 does the same thing as option 1, using "but." The punctuation is also incorrect in option 3: "But" should be followed by a comma.

MATHEMATICAL REASONING

Part 1

1. **A** A radical expression has no real number solution if there is a negative under the square root sign, because there is no real number that can be multiplied by itself to produce a negative. So, which choice for y would give a negative number under the root sign? If you insert 2 for y, you get -1 under the root sign, which has no real number solution. Only one choice is less than 3. The correct answer is (A).

2. **D** To add (or subtract) fractions, both fractions need to be in the same terms—in other words, they need to have a common denominator. Here our original denominators are 2 and 3, so you can use 6 as the lowest common denominator. Multiply the numerator and denominator of the first fraction by 3 to get $\frac{7}{2} = \frac{21}{6}$. Similarly, multiply the numerator and denominator of the second fraction by 2 to get $\frac{4}{3} = \frac{8}{6}$.

   Now add the fractions, by adding the numerators and keeping the denominator. $\frac{21}{6} + \frac{8}{6} = \frac{29}{6}$.

3. **–14**

   Substitute $a = 2$ and $b = -3$ to get $-4a + 2b = -4(2) + 2(-3) = -8 - 6 = -14$. The answer is -14.

4.

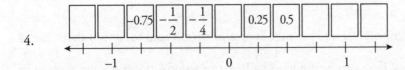

To place the numbers on the number line, first determine the scale of the number. There are four intervals between 0 and 1, so each interval is $\frac{1}{4}$. Start with the fractions. Since each interval is $\frac{1}{4}$, $-\frac{1}{4}$ must be one interval to the left of 0. Since $-\frac{1}{2} = -\frac{2}{4}$, $-\frac{1}{2}$ must be two intervals to the left of 0. Now, go to the decimals. Since $0.25 = \frac{25}{100} = \frac{1}{4}$, 0.25 is one interval to the right of 0. Since $0.5 = \frac{50}{100} = \frac{1}{2}$, 0.5 is two intervals to the right of 0. Since $-0.75 = -\frac{75}{100} = -\frac{3}{4}$, -0.75 is three intervals to the left of 0.

5.

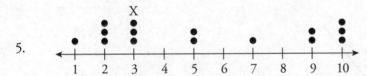

A dot plot is a figure that puts a dot above a number for every instance of that number in a list. In a list of numbers, the mode is the number with the most instances. Therefore, the mode is the number with the most dots above it. In the figure, there are three dots above 2, 3, and 10. Since no number has more than three dots, 2, 3, and 10 are all considered to be modes of the list. The question asks for 3 to be the only mode. To make it the only mode, put another dot above 3, so that it is the only one with at least 4.

Part 2

6. **B** The question asks for the height of the water in the fish tank. When the water is poured into the tank, it will take the shape of the tank. Since the fish tank is a rectangular prism, the water will be too. The volume formula for a rectangular prism is $V = lwh$. The length and width of the water is the same as those of the tank, which is 6 in. and 4 in., respectively. The volume of the water is 120 cubic inches, so plug $V = 120$, $l = 6$ and $w = 4$ into the volume formula to get $120 = (6)(4)h$. Simplify the right side to get $120 = 24h$. Divide both sides by 24 to get $h = 5$. Notice that the height of the tank is irrelevant, since it is not the same as the height of the water. The correct answer is (B).

7. **C** To factor a quadratic in the form $x^2 + bx + c$, find two factors of c with a sum of b. Since the c term is negative, there will be one positive and one negative factor. Since the b term is also negative, the factor with the larger absolute value will be negative. Find the factors of the c term, which is 15. There are two pairs of factors of 15. One pair is 1 and 15. The sum of 1 and -15 is not -2, so these are not the needed factors. The other pair of factors is 3 and 5. Since the sum of 3 and -5 is -2, these are the needed factors. Therefore, $x^2 - 2x - 15$ factors to $(x + 3)(x - 5)$. The correct answer is (C).

8. **Less than**

The question asks for whether Company A's rate per mile is greater than, equal to, or less than that of Company B. Since both companies' fares can be modeled by linear functions, the rate is represented by the slope. $A(m)$ is a linear function in the form $y = mx + b$. In this form, the rate is represented by m, the coefficient on x. In this case, $m = 1.5$, so the rate per mile is 1.5. To find the rate per mile for Company B, find the slope of the line in the graph. Find two points on the graph and use the slope formula, $m = \dfrac{y_2 - y_1}{x_2 - x_1}$. The points $(3, 8)$ and $(7, 15)$ are easy to identify, so use these two points. Plug these into the slope formula to get $m = \dfrac{y_2 - y_1}{x_2 - x_1} = \dfrac{15 - 8}{7 - 3} = \dfrac{7}{4} = 1.75$. Therefore, the rate per mile for Company B is 1.75. Since Company A's rate is 1.5, its rate is less than that of Company B.

9.

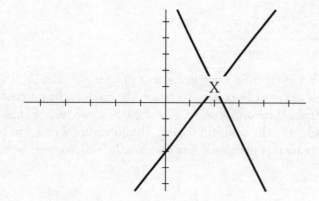

To the find the solution to a system of equations graphed on the xy-plane, find the point of intersection between the two lines. Select that point.

10. **A** Because the square of an expression is isolated, solve by inspection. Take the square root of both sides to get $x + 3 = \pm 4$. The $\pm$ sign is necessary because the square of a negative is positive, so the positive and negative must both be considered. Create two separate equations: $x + 3 = 4$ and $x + 3 = -4$. Subtract 3 from both sides in both equations to get $x = 1$ and $x = -7$. Only one of these is a choice. The correct answer is (A).

11. **B** In order to be a function, a graph must pass the vertical line test, meaning that no vertical line can be drawn so that it touches the graph more than once. In the case of (A), (C), and (D), no such vertical line can be drawn, so these are functions. In the case of (B), a vertical line can be drawn to touch the graph twice as shown below:

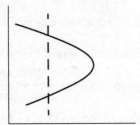

The answer is (B).

12. **D** There are four bands to order. Determine the number of possibilities for each position and then multiply. There are 4 possibilities for the first band. Once this band is selected, there are 3 remaining possibilities for the second band, 2 remaining possibilities for the third band, and 1 remaining possibility for the fourth band. Therefore, there are $4 \times 3 \times 2 \times 1 = 24$ different orders. The answer is (D).

13. **C** To find the surface area of a cylinder, use the formula $SA = 2\pi rh + 2\pi r^2$. According to the figure, the height of the cylinder is 10 and the radius is 6. Plug $h = 10$ and $r = 6$ into the formula to get $SA = 2\pi(6)(10) + 2\pi(6)^2 = 120\pi + 72\pi = 192\pi$. The answer is (C).

14. **A** Translate the question into an expression. *The cube of 5* translates to 5^3. *Subtracted from* translates to minus with the first term following the second. Therefore, the question up to this point translates to "___ $- 5^3$" with whatever comes next filling in the blank. What comes next is *the square root of 16*, which translates to $\sqrt{16}$. Therefore, the question translates to $\sqrt{16} - 5^3$. Simplify the expression to get $4 - 125$, which is -121. The correct answer is (A).

15. **D** The question asks for the total cost of the sod, which is 35 cents per square foot. Therefore, the total cost is the cost per square foot times the number of square feet. To determine the number of square feet, use the formula $A = lw$. According to the figure, the plot has a length of 10 ft and the width of 15 ft, so the area is $A = (10)(15)$. Look at the answer choices to realize that this doesn't need to be multiplied out. Multiply this expression by the cost per square foot to get $(0.35)(10)(15)$. The answer is (D).

16. **A** Because the drawing is a scale drawing, set up a proportion. The actual sculpture will be 3 feet high, and the scale drawing has a height of 5 inches, so set up $\dfrac{3 \text{ ft}}{5 \text{ in}}$. The question asks for the actual width, so call it w. The scale drawing has a width of 7.5 inches, so set up $\dfrac{3 \text{ ft}}{5 \text{ in}} = \dfrac{w \text{ ft}}{7.5 \text{ in}}$. Cross-multiply to get $5w = 22.5$. Divide both sides by 5 to get $w = 4.5$ The correct answer is (A).

17. **C** Look at the answer choices to see that there is no need to complete the calculation but only to set up the calculations. The question asks for the total weight of the three blocks in grams. To determine the total weight in grams, find the total weight in ounces and do a unit conversion, using proportions. The total weight is (5 oz + 3 oz + 6 oz). Since these numbers appear in the choices, leave this expression in this form rather than going through the addition. To set up a ratio, set the known relationship equal to the unknown relationship. The question says that an ounce is about 28.35 grams. Set up $\frac{1 \text{ ounce}}{28.35 \text{ grams}}$. Set this equal to the unknown relationship, which is the number of grams that makes up (5 + 3 + 6) ounces, to get $\frac{1 \text{ ounce}}{28.35 \text{ grams}} = \frac{(5 + 3 + 6) \text{ ounces}}{x \text{ grams}}$. Make sure that the units in both numerators are the same and that the units in both denominators are the same. Cross-multiply to get $x = (5 + 3 + 6)28.35$. The correct answer is (C).

18. **B** To find the length of a side in a right triangle, use the Pythagorean Theorem: $a^2 + b^2 = c^2$. In this formula, c represents the hypotenuse, which is the longest side and the side opposite the right angle. In this case, the length of the hypotenuse is 13. Also, a and b represent the lengths of the other two sides of the triangle. One of the other sides has length 12, so let $a = 12$. Plug $a = 12$ and $c = 13$ into the formula to get $12^2 + b^2 = 13^2$. Solve for the missing side. Substitute $12^2 = 144$ and $13^2 = 169$ to get $144 + b^2 = 169$. Subtract 144 from both sides to get $b^2 = 25$. Take the square root of both sides to get $b = 5$. The answer is (B).

19. **C** Plug $p = 4$ and $q = -3$ into the expression to get $\frac{p^2 + 2pq}{p + 2q} = \frac{4^2 + 2(4)(-3)}{4 + 2(-3)}$. Simplify to get $\frac{16 - 24}{4 - 6}$. Subtract to get $\frac{-8}{-2}$. Divide to get 4. The answer is (C).

20. **C** The median is the middle number when listed in order. The histogram does not give the exact scores, so there is no way to list them all. However, the median (or in this case possible range of the median) can also be found by using the total number of scores to determine where the middle number would be. To get the total number, go through each column of the histogram and add all the numbers. There are 3 scores from 0 to 59, 4 scores from 60 to 74, 10 scores from 75 to 84, 15 scores from 85 to 94, and 5 scores from 95 to 100. Therefore, there are a total of 3 + 4 + 10 + 15 + 5 = 37 scores. Since there is an odd number of numbers, the median is a particular score in the list rather than the average of two scores. To find the number, divide the total number of scores by 2 and round up. Since 37 ÷ 2 = 18.5, the median is the 19th score. Confirm this by using the fact that there are 18 scores below the 19th score and 18 scores above the 19th score. Find the range of the 19th score. There are 3 scores from 0 to 59 and 4 scores from 60 to 74, so there are 3 + 4 = 7 scores from 0 to 74. The median is still higher than this. There are 10 scores from 75 to 84, to there are a total of 7 + 10 = 17 scores from 0 to 84. The median is still higher. There are 15 scores from 85 to 94, so there are a total of 17 + 15 = 32 scores from 0 to 94. Since the total number of scores passed 19 in the 85 to 94 range, this must be the range of the median. Only one answer choice is in this range, so this is the only possible answer. The correct answer is (C).

21.

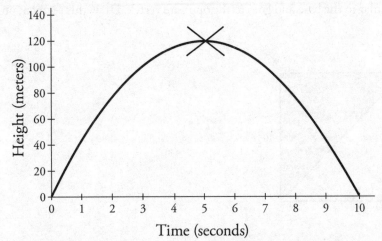

The question asks for the point at which the ball reaches its maximum height. The graph is a parabola opening downward, with the height represented by the y-axis. A downward parabola has its maximum y-value at its vertex, which is the point that the parabola changes direction. Mark the vertex, which occurs at about (5, 120).

22. **A** Each factor in the expression is raised to an exponent. Because the operation inside the parentheses is multiplication, apply the exponent to each factor inside the parentheses to get $(x^2)^2 y^2 (x^{-3})^4 (y^3)^4$. Because numbers with exponents are raised to other exponents, multiply the exponents to get $(x^4)(y^2)(x^{-12})(y^{12})$. Group factors with like bases to get $(x^4)(x^{-12})(y^2)(y^{12})$. Because numbers with the same bases are multiplied, add the exponents to get $(x^{-8})(y^{14})$. Because x has a negative exponent, move it to the denominator as a positive exponent to get $\dfrac{y^{14}}{x^8}$. The correct answer is (A).

23. **Median: 31. Mean: 32.**

To find the median, rewrite the numbers in the list in order. The numbers in order are 24, 27, 29, 30, 31, 33, 34, 39, 41. The median is the middle number, which is 31. Therefore, 31 is the median. To find the mean, or average, get the sum of the numbers and divide by the number of numbers. There are nine numbers with a sum of $24 + 27 + 29 + 30 + 31 + 33 + 34 + 39 + 41 = 288$. Divide this by 9 to get 32. Therefore, the mean is 32. Fill in 32 for the mean.

24. **B** To find the area of a shaded region, subtract the area of the unshaded region from the total area. The total area is a rectangle. The area of a rectangle can be found using the formula $A = lw$. According to the figure, the length is 20 ft and the width is 10 ft, so the area is $A = (20)(10) = 200$. Now determine the area of the unshaded region, which is a triangle. The area of a triangle can be determined using the formula $A = 1/2bh$. The base of the triangle is the same as the length of the rectangle, which is 20 ft. The height is

a segment that is perpendicular to the base and goes to the opposite vertex. Draw this segment on scratch paper like below.

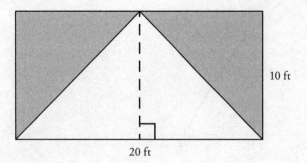

Notice that this segment divides the rectangle into two smaller rectangles. Since the segment is opposite the width of the rectangle, they are congruent. Therefore, the height of the triangle is also 10. Plug the base and height into the area formula to get $A = 1/2(20)(10) = 100$. To get the area of the shaded region, subtract this from the total area to get $200 - 100 = 100$. The answer is (B).

25. **A** When a function is written using function notation, anything inside the parentheses replaces x. Since the question asks for $f(-4)$, replace x with -4 to get $f(-4) = 2(-4) - 3 = -8 - 3 = -11$. The answer is (A).

26. **C** To find the area of a triangle, use the formula $A = 1/2bh$, where b is the base and h is the height. The base is any side of the triangle, and the height is the length of a segment perpendicular to the base and going to the opposite vertex. In the triangle shown in the figure, the base is 10 and the height is 12. Make sure to use the entire base and not just one of the two portions split by the height. Also, ignore the two sides that are not the base. They are not perpendicular to the base and, therefore, cannot be the height. Plug $b = 10$ and $h = 12$ into the area formula to get $A = 1/2(10)(12) = 60$. The correct answer is (C).

27. **A** The question provides the area of a square. Plug this into the area formula $A = s^2$ to get $25 = s^2$. Take the square root of both sides to get $5 = s$. (Since there are no negative sides, don't worry about the negative of the square root.) The question asks for the perimeter, so use the formula $P = 4s$ to get $P = 4(5) = 20$. The correct answer is (A).

28.

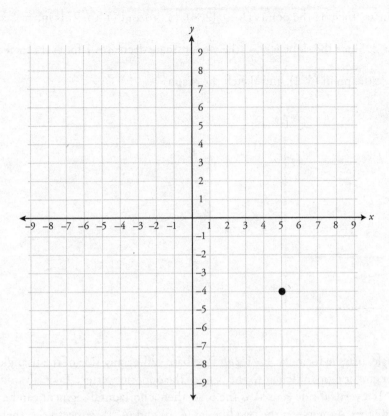

In an ordered pair, the first coordinate is the *x*-coordinate and the second coordinate is the *y*-coordinate. Therefore, the *x*-coordinate is 5, and the *y*-coordinate is –4. The *x*-axis is the horizontal axis. Since the *x*-coordinate is positive, count 5 units to the right on the *x*-axis. Since the *y*-coordinate is negative, count 4 units down. Select this point.

29. **C** Distance is always represented by a difference, so eliminate (D). Furthermore, distance cannot be negative, so there must be an absolute value. Eliminate (B). Although (A) has absolute values, it is negative if $|B| > |A|$. Eliminate (A). Only one answer choice remains. As an alternative, find the values for *A* and *B*. Since *A* is three units to the left of 0, $A = -3$. Since *B* is 4 units to the right, $B = 4$. Count units from *A* to *B*. There are 7, so the distance is 7. Plug $A = -3$ and $B = 4$ into the answer choices and eliminate any that are not 7. Choice (A) is $|-3| - |4| = -1$, so eliminate (A). Choice (B) is $-3 - 4 = -7$, so eliminate (B). Choice (C) is $|-3 - 4| = 7$, so keep (C). Choice (D) is $-3 + 4 = 1$, so eliminate (D). The correct answer is (C).

30. **A** The question provides the equations of three lines, so sketch out a figure. The simplest line is the line $x = 4$. Any line in the form $x = c$, where *c* is a constant, is a vertical line that crosses the *x*-axis at *c*. Therefore, $x = 4$ is a vertical line that crosses the *x*-axis at 4. Now look at the other two lines. A line in the form $y = mx + b$ has a slope of *m* and a *y*-intercept of *b*. Since both lines have a *y*-intercept of 2, they intersect at (0, 2). To find the triangle, sketch enough of the graph to find their intersections with the line $x = 4$.

The line $y = x + 2$ has a slope of 1. Begin the sketch at (0, 2). Increase the *y*-coordinate by 1 for every increase of 1 in the x-coordinate. Include the points $(1, 3)$, $(2, 4)$, $(3, 5)$, and $(4, 6)$. This intersects with $x = 4$. Now sketch $y = -\dfrac{1}{4}x + 2$. Since the slope is $-\dfrac{1}{4}$, the y-coordinate decreases 1 for every increase of 4 in the x-coordinate. Include the point $(4, 1)$, and sketch the graph.

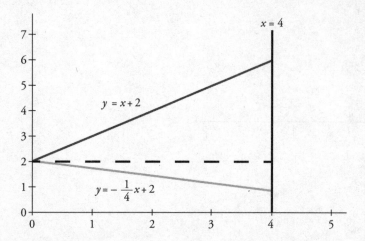

To find the area of this triangle, use the formula $A = 1/2bh$. The base can be any side of the triangle and the height is the length of a segment perpendicular to the base to the opposite vertex. Take advantage of the fact that $x = 4$ is vertical. If a vertical side is used as the base, then a horizontal segment can be used to represent the height. The line $x = 4$ intersects the two lines at $(4, 6)$ and $(4, 1)$, respectively. Therefore, the length of the base is the distance between these two points, which is $6 - 1 = 5$. The height is the horizontal line from $(0, 2)$ to the line $x = 4$. Since horizontal lines have a constant y-coordinate, the height must intersect the base at $(4, 2)$. Therefore, the height is the distance between $(0, 2)$ and $(4, 2)$, which is $4 - 0 = 4$. Plug $b = 5$ and $h = 4$ into the formula to get $A = 1/2(5)(4) = 10$. The correct answer is (A).

31.   **decreases**

Look at the trend on the scatterplot. The points on the scatterplot seem to approximate a line going from the top left to the bottom right. This indicates a decreasing relationship, so select decreases.

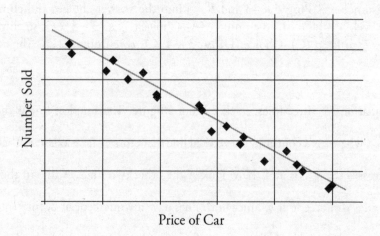

32. **D** The question asks for the least amount of money a customer can spend on at least 20 bananas. Bananas are sold by the bunch, so determine the least number of bunches the customer can buy. Since there are 6 bananas in a bunch, divide 20 by 6 to get $\dfrac{20}{6} = 3.\overline{33}$. Since 3 bunches would be only $3 \times 6 = 18$ bananas, round up to get 4 bunches. Since each bunch costs $2.25, four bunches would cost $4 \times \$2.25 = \$9.00$. The correct answer is (D).

33. **A** When a function is written using function notation, anything inside the parentheses replaces x. Since the question asks for $g(-3)$, replace x with -3 to get $g(-3) = 3(-3)^2 + 4(-3) - 7 = 3(9) - 12 - 7 = 27 - 12 - 7 = 8$. The answer is (A).

34. **D** A relative minimum is a point for which the y-coordinate is less than those on all the points immediately surrounding it. A relative minimum does not have to be the lowest point on the graph. Go through the choices, find the point $(3, -4)$, and determine whether each is a relative minimum. Choice (A) and (B) do not even contain the point $(3, -4)$, so eliminate these choices. Choice (C) does contain the point $(3, -4)$. However, the curve continues to decrease to the right of this point, so this is not a relative minimum. Eliminate (C). Choice (D) contains the point $(3, -4)$. The graph is increasing to the left and to the right of the point $(3, -4)$. Although there are points to the far left side of the graph that are lower, the points in the immediate vicinity are all higher, so this is a relative minimum. The answer is (D).

35. **A** The equation of a line can be put into the form $y = mx + b$, where m is the slope and b is the y-intercept. Since the question says that the slope is 4, plug $m = 4$ into the equation to get $y = 4x + b$. To find b, plug the point the question provides into the equation. Since $(3, 0)$ is on the line, plug $x = 3$ and $y = 0$ into the equation to get $0 = 4(3) + b$. Simplify to get $0 = 12 + b$. Subtract 12 from both sides to get $-12 = b$. Therefore, the equation of the line is $y = 4x - 12$. The correct answer is (A).

36. **A** The question asks for the probability that a randomly selected marble will be blue. To determine this, put the number of blue marbles over the total number of marbles. There are 4 blue marbles, and in total there are $4 + 10 + 5 + 9 = 28$ marbles. Therefore, the probability is $\dfrac{4}{28}$. This is not an answer choice, so reduce the fraction by 4 to get $\dfrac{1}{7}$. The correct answer is (A).

37. **A** To multiply binomials, use FOIL. Start by multiplying the first terms. Multiply the coefficients normally to get $2 \times 6 = 12$. To multiply x^2 by x^3, add the exponents to get x^5. Therefore, $(2x^2)(6x^3) = 12x^5$. Similarly, multiply outer terms to get $(2x^2)(3x) = 6x^3$. Multiply inner terms to get $\left(-\dfrac{1}{2}\right)(6x^3) = -3x^3$. Multiply last terms to get $\left(-\dfrac{1}{2}\right)(3x)$ to get $-\dfrac{3}{2}x$. Add these four products to get $12x^5 + 6x^3 - 3x^3 - \dfrac{3}{2}x$. Combine like terms to get $12x^5 + 3x^3 - \dfrac{3}{2}x$. The answer is (A).

38. **C** Start by determining whether the slope is positive or negative. Because, on the table, y increases as x increases, this is a positive slope. Eliminate (A) and (B), which have a negative slope. To choose between the two remaining choices, find a point on the table and eliminate any choice that doesn't include it. Both graphs include the point $(1, 5)$, so use a different point from the table. Try $(3, 8)$. Choice (C) includes the point $(3, 8)$, while (D) does not. Eliminate (D). The answer is (C).

39. **D** The question states that Chelsea gains simple annual interest. Simple interest means that the interest is gained only on the initial deposit and not on any money gained from past interest (which would be compound interest). Since Chelsea gained 2% interest per year on $400, each year she gained $\frac{2}{100} \times \$400 = \$8$. Since she gained $8 each year, after 5 years, she gained 5 × $8 = $40. Therefore, she will have $400 + $40 = $440 in her account after 5 years. The answer is (D).

40. **D** To solve the equation, first distribute both the 2 on the left side and the 2 on the right side to get $2x + 3 = 4x + 2x - 6$. Combine like terms on the right to get $2x + 3 = 6x - 6$. Subtract $6x$ from both sides to get $-4x + 3 = -6$. Subtract 3 from both sides to get $-4x = -9$. Divide both sides by 4 to get $x = 9/4$. The correct answer is (D).

41. **C** The question asks for the area of the circle, which can be determined using the formula $A = \pi r^2$. To determine the radius, use the fact that the circumference is 16π. The circumference formula is $C = 2\pi r$. Plug in $C = 16\pi$ to get $16\pi = 2\pi r$. Divide both sides by 2π to get $r = \frac{16\pi}{2\pi}$. Cancel the πs to get $r = \frac{16}{2} = 8$. Plug this into the area formula to get $A = \pi r^2 = \pi(8)^2 = 64\pi$. The correct answer is (C).

42. **C** The equation involves decimals and fractions, so it is likely difficult to factor. Furthermore, the answer choices resemble the quadratic formula: $x = \frac{-b \pm \sqrt{b^2 - 4ac}}{2a}$, where $ax^2 + bx + c = 0$. Use the quadratic formula with $a = 1.5$, $b = -4$, and $c = \frac{5}{3}$ to get $x = \frac{-(-4) \pm \sqrt{(-4)^2 - 4(1.5)\left(\frac{5}{3}\right)}}{2(1.5)}$. Simplify to get $x = \frac{4 \pm \sqrt{16 - 10}}{3}$ and $x = \frac{4 \pm \sqrt{6}}{3}$. The answer is (C).

43. **C** Harriet leaves a 20% gratuity on a $81.30 bill. Therefore, she leaves $\frac{20}{100} \times \$81.30 = \$16.26$ as a gratuity. Therefore, she leaves a total of $81.30 + $16.26 = $97.56. The answer is (C).

44. **B** Plug the given area into the area formula to get $6 + 6\sqrt{2} = 2(1 + \sqrt{2})s^2$. Since both terms on the left side have 6 as factors, factor 6 to get $6(1 + \sqrt{2}) = 2(1 + \sqrt{2})s^2$. Divide both sides by $(1 + \sqrt{2})$ to get $6 = 2s^2$. Divide both sides by 2 to get $3 = s^2$. Take the square root of both sides to get $s = \sqrt{3}$. The question asks for the perimeter, which is the sum of the sides. Since this is a regular octagon, it is made up of 8 equal sides. Therefore, $P = 8s = 8\sqrt{3}$. The answer is (B).

45. **D** In a box plot, the maximum is indicated by the number on the far right on the whisker, and the median is indicated by the number at the line inside the box. Therefore, the maximum is 73 and the median is 52. Thus, the difference is 73 − 52 = 21. The correct answer is (D).

46. **A** Because x is isolated in one of the equations, use the substitution method. Substitute $2y - 3$ from the first equation into the second equation for x to get $2y - 3 - 3y = 7$. Combine like terms to get $-y - 3 = 7$. Add 3 to both sides to get $-y = 10$. Divide both sides by -1 to get $y = -10$. The question, however, asks for the value of x rather than y. Plug $y = -10$ into the first equation to get $x = 2(-10) - 3 = -20 - 3 = -23$. The correct answer is (A).

SOCIAL STUDIES

1. **D** The first graph measures oil consumption, while the second graph measures oil production. Choice (A) cannot be true, since the United States line has increased, not decreased, in the time period measured by the first graph. Choice (B) establishes a causal relationship that is not known. Choice (C) might look tempting, since the United States and Europe lines do seem to parallel each other, but you do not know if this has anything to do with similar energy policies.

2. **The Middle East**

    An oil surplus occurs when there is more oil produced than consumed. This is really a math question. Which country had the highest rate of production (second graph)? The Middle East, since its percentages are consistently higher than all other regions. Now look at the first graph. Whose usage is lowest? Africa, but the Middle East is not much higher. Since Africa produced only about a third of the oil (about 10% versus 30%) that the Middle East did, and the Middle East's usage is not much higher than Africa's, the Middle East must have had a bigger oil surplus.

3. **B** Courts are considered part of the judicial branch of government. The president and his appointed heads are members of the executive branch. Congress is the legislative branch.

4. **A** Enfranchised people are voters. The arrow in the diagram is pointing directly from the enfranchised people to the Congress, meaning that they elect them directly. The other answers are not supported by the flow chart, since there are no arrows going to Congress other than the one from the enfranchised people.

5. **B** States do all sorts of things, including many of the things that the federal government does: impose taxes, fund public education, and create regulations. But no state maintains its own military. That is entirely a function of the U.S. Department of Defense.

6. **D** Africa is the large horn-shaped continent in the middle of the map. As you know, the United States and Canada are democracies, but the numbers in Africa are a combination of 1s, 2s, and 4s. According to the map key, this is closest to (D). If you chose (B), you forgot that European colonialism in Africa ended in the 20th century.

7. **A** Africa has never been mostly democratic, so rule out (D). Europe used to contain many monarchies, (B), but that was hundreds of years ago, not as recently as 1965. Choice (C) might look like a tempting answer, but remember, the question is asking you for a difference. Choice (A) is the best choice. You may remember that the Soviet Union was an authoritarian communist country up until about 25 years ago, and it controlled a vast territory within Asia and parts of Europe.

8. **D** Spain settled areas of the United States largely in Florida, Texas, and the Southwest. They had no settlements of any kind in the Northeast. The British settled mostly in New England. The Dutch settled parts of the mid-Atlantic region. France settled parts of the Ohio Valley, Canada, and northern New England.

9. **(b) Northeast = Iroquois, (a) Southwest = Pueblo, (c) Plains = Lakota, (d) Sub-Arctic = Inuit**

   If you're good with geography, this one is a slam dunk. Just base your answers on the locations mentioned: New York is in the Northeast. Arizona and New Mexico are in the Southwest (Great Basin is not an option). The "coldest regions" must be the Sub-Arctic. That leaves you with Lakota in the Plains. If your geography is a little fuzzy, you may still have been able to make some matches based on the descriptions mentioned. For instance, buffalo were found mostly in the Plains states and the desert is in the Southwest.

10. **Iroquois, Inuit**

    This one is also about geography. It is talking about settling the West, and the Iroquois and Inuit live nowhere near this region. In fact, perhaps the Iroquois celebrated the white man's departure for the West!

11. **Legislative branch (a) = "passes bills, etc."**
    Executive branch (b) = "has veto power, etc."
    Judicial branch (c) = "decides upon the constitutionality, etc."

12. **C** "Quartering" of soldiers in citizens' homes (Third Amendment) means the military requiring citizens to provide a home to soldiers. This is a throwback to the times before the American Revolution when the British military required colonists to take in British soldiers. As you may imagine, this was not popular. Thankfully, though, our federal government has not tried to violate this amendment to the Constitution in modern times and you are unlikely to hear of any Supreme Court cases involving the Third Amendment. The others, though, regarding freedom of speech (First Amendment), the right to bear arms (Second Amendment), and government surveillance and searches (Fourth Amendment) are frequently controversial and are challenged in the courts.

13. **D** Screening the baggage of airline passengers would be an example of the search (and possible seizure) of a citizen's property without a warrant. This could be interpreted as a violation of the Fourth Amendment, (D). Choice (A) does not involve any deliberate "assembling" on the part of passengers, and firearms, (C), do not apply to this situation. Choice (B) may look tempting, but this has no specific connection to searching baggage; "redress of grievances" is fairly broad and could apply to almost any situation.

14. **D** Notice that the Presentment Clause gives the president a window of ten days to make a decision. So, if the president does not sign a bill within five days, no particular part of the law would apply.

15. **D** The key word in this question is "returns." A president would have the opportunity to return a bill to Congress only if it had already been voted on and passed. If he returns it with objections, it means the president has vetoed the bill. "Ratification," (B), means approval. "Repeal," (C), means to put a stop to a law that has already been passed and signed at some point in the past. "Impeachment," (A), is done to a person, not a law.

16. **C** This one is tricky. When you think of impeachment, you may be thinking of Presidents Richard Nixon and Bill Clinton. Although Nixon was threatened with impeachment, he resigned before impeachment proceedings began. In Clinton's case, he was impeached, but not removed from office and did not resign.

So, impeachment is neither removal from office, (A), nor is it the act of resigning, (D). Treason, (B), is much too strong; impeachment can happen for a variety of reasons.

17. **C** The Speaker of the House is an elected position, but the Speaker is not elected directly by the American people. He or she is elected by other members of the House of Representatives.

18. **C** The Speaker of the House of Representatives is elected by other members of the House. Naturally, House members will almost always vote for a Speaker in their own political party. Democrats vote for a Democratic Speaker and Republicans vote for a Republican Speaker. Since the American people do not elect the Speaker, (A) and (B) must be wrong. Choice (D) may look tempting, but if you add up the small percentage of votes given to other Democrats in January 2011, the total percentage of Democrat votes does not reach the 55.6% assigned to John Boehner. Pelosi lost simply because there were fewer Democrats in the House. House membership can change drastically in even just two years due to changes in the sentiments of the national electorate.

19. **A** The *Magna Carta* states "No freeman shall be taken…nor will we proceed against or prosecute him, except by the lawful judgment of his peers." The Fifth Amendment states "No person shall be held to answer for a capital, or otherwise infamous crime, unless on a presentment or indictment of a Grand Jury." (The speed of the trial, (B), is not mentioned.)

20. **C** Kossuth is speaking about possible events in the future. "Your principles will conquer the world.…The respect for State rights in the Federal Government of America, and in its several States, will become an instructive example…." So, he admires the principles of the United States.

21. **A** For this question, look at the Daniel Webster quote: "I limit my aspirations for Hungary, for the present, to that single and simple point—Hungarian independence, Hungarian self-government, Hungarian control of Hungarian destinies."

22. **C** In his quote, Webster speaks only of the Lower Danube and Hungary. So, (A) is too broad. Choice (B) is wrong for the same reason. Choice (D) cannot be right, since Webster advocates for Hungarian self-government and control of its own destiny.

23. **B** The map shows a clear divide between North and South in their acceptance or rejection of slavery. All the states from Maryland to Texas south were slave states, while all other were free or mixed (popular sovereignty). This would lay the groundwork for the Civil War. Choice (A) is untrue, since the Oregon, Minnesota, and "unorganized" territories were all free. Choice (D) is too extreme and cannot be concluded based just on this map. Choice (C) may look tempting, but the map does not indicate the number of people in each region, only the size of the area.

24. **Oklahoma**

25. **B** This one is testing you on the characteristics of various Civil Right Leaders. Martin Luther King, Jr. was known for advocating nonviolent approaches to promoting change for African Americans. Malcolm X, (A), was not known for nonviolent approaches; in fact, he could be rather militant. Even President Mandela, (D), resorted to some acts of violence in his effort to end apartheid in South Africa. Choice (C) may look close, but Rosa Parks was known mostly for her role in the bus protest; she was not a widely published writer or speaker.

26. **A** Since the speaker is in favor of "nonviolent pressure," you can rule out (C) right away. Choice (B) sounds close, but the quote actually says that this is true of privileged groups, not necessarily individuals. Choice (D) contradicts Niebuhr's statement that "groups are more immoral than individuals."

27. **C** The picture of Charleston in 1865 portrays a city that used to be quite impressive which now appears to be largely abandoned and in terrible disrepair. "The year 1865" is the best hint here, since the worst of the Civil War was at this time. As you know, many Southern cities were utterly destroyed. Choice (A) may look tempting, but it does not mention the Civil War, so (C) is a better choice.

28. **Reconstruction**

29. **C** "Suffrage" is the right to vote and a "suffragette" was a female political activist. Abigail Adams, (A), was First Lady in the 1700s, before woman's suffrage was a popular issue. Abraham Lincoln, (B), was not an advocate for woman's suffrage. Eleanor Roosevelt, (D), was active in politics after women got the right to vote in 1918.

30. **B** The Gold Rush is also known as the California Gold Rush. Gold was also mined in Alaska and the Yukon Territory, but these places were not as "hot" for prospectors as California.

31. **Socialism, capitalism**

32. **D** As you can see, the dark portions of the map extend into Arabia, Mesopotamia, Assyria, and Turkey. These are part of modern-day Asia. Only Egypt and Libya are considered African countries. Eliminate (A). Choice (B) is unknown based on the map. Choice (C) is close, but, as you can see the dark portion of the map extends down a winding path in Egypt labeled the "Nile," so this was a very important waterway for Egyptians. The Mediterranean Sea was no doubt an important route for trading partners too.

33. **B** According to the passage, a candidate must win electoral votes in order to win the presidency. In order to win electoral votes, the candidate must win a state. Choice (C) is not true; Libertarians occur on the ballot in all fifty states, but have never won. Choice (A) is too extreme to be the best answer, while (D) is incorrect because third-party candidates often do appeal to people with minority political viewpoints.

34. **D** In the cartoon, a bridge is formed from the European countries that form the League of Nations. The "keystone" is the United States, but that keystone is missing from the bridge, while Uncle Sam (the symbol of the United States) sits idly next to the bridge, leaning on the keystone. Notice that the sign tells you that the League of Nations bridge was designed by the president. So, that would make the absence of the United States even more ironic.

35. **United Nations**

SCIENCE

1. **igneous, metamorphic**

   Here you need to classify both pumice and marble as igneous, metamorphic, or sedimentary rock. The passage tells you that igneous rocks are formed through the cooling and solidification of magma or lava. Since pumice is formed when molten rock is quickly expelled from the mouth of a volcano, pumice is an igneous rock. The passage also tells you that metamorphic rocks are formed below the surface of the Earth, when existing rocks are exposed to extreme heat and pressure. Since marble is formed when limestone is exposed to extreme temperature and pressure, marble is a metamorphic rock.

2. **C** This question requires you to determine the type of rock that would exist on an ocean floor. Since igneous rocks are formed through the cooling and solidification of magma, you can eliminate (A). Metamorphic rocks are formed far below the surface of the Earth, and require both high temperatures and pressure to form; thus, eliminate (B). Sedimentary rocks are those composed of layers of organic matter. In the ocean, layers of sediment are deposited; when the weight of the sediments puts enough pressure on the lower layers, sedimentary rock is created. Thus, (C) is the correct answer.

3. **37.5**

   This question requires you to use the formula provided to determine the number of minutes the kitten ran. The question tells you that the kitten ran at a speed of 8 miles per hour for 5 miles. Accordingly, you know that $S = 8$ and $D = 5$, and you will find that $S = \dfrac{D}{T}$, $8 \ mph = \dfrac{5 \ m}{T}$, and $T = \dfrac{5}{8}$ hours. Accordingly, the kitten ran for $\dfrac{5}{8}$ of an hour. Now, you must convert $\dfrac{5}{8}$ of an hour into minutes by multiplying by 60. Thus, the kitten ran for $\dfrac{5}{8} \times 60 = 37.5$ minutes.

4. **C** You're asked what would NOT be important, so eliminate answer choices that are important. For Jiajie to conduct a controlled experiment on the possible river pollution, he clearly needs water from the Zhang both near the mine and also upstream from the mine, so he can compare them to each other. This eliminates both (A) and (B). Trying to eliminate another answer choice, however, may seem tricky at first, since both (C) and (D) refer to water from somewhere other than the Zhang. But consider that you want a controlled experiment, so you need a control sample, which would mean unpolluted water. Thus, you can eliminate (D), because that unpolluted water would be important as the control sample. You're left with (C) as the best answer, because you don't need to compare pollution elsewhere to pollution in the Zhang.

5. **A** This question requires you to identify the chemical equation for photosynthesis. The passage tells you that photosynthesis is the process by which plants convert carbon dioxide, water, and energy from the Sun into glucose and oxygen. Accordingly, you need to identify the equation where carbon dioxide and water are the reactants and glucose and oxygen are the products. The only equation that shows the process of photosynthesis is (A), $6CO_2 + 6H_2O \rightarrow C_6H_{12}O_6 + 6O_2$.

6. **D** Here you need to use the information in the passage to determine the false statement. Choice (A) states that only organisms with chlorophyll can make their own food through photosynthesis; this is supported by the passage and, therefore, can be eliminated. Choice (B) states that photosynthesis depends upon energy from the Sun; this is supported by the passage and, therefore, can be eliminated. Choice (C)

states that the products of photosynthesis are glucose and oxygen; this is supported by the passage and, therefore, can be eliminated. Finally, (D) states that both plants and mammals have chlorophyll. Since photosynthesis is a process unique to plants that is triggered when the chlorophyll in leaves is activated, you know that chlorophyll is unique to plants. Thus, (D) is false and, in turn, the correct answer.

7. **cytosine, adenine**

In order to answer this question, use the information provided in the passage regarding the pairing of nucleotide bases: adenine pairs only with thymine, and cytosine pairs only with guanine. Thus, if one strand of DNA had nucleotide bases of CGATCG, the complementary strand of DNA would have nucleotide bases of **GCTAGC**.

8. This question requires you to identify the ligaments in the provided image. Based on the passage, ligaments are short, tough bands of connective tissue that connect two bones together, sometimes forming a joint. Thus, the ligaments are shown below.

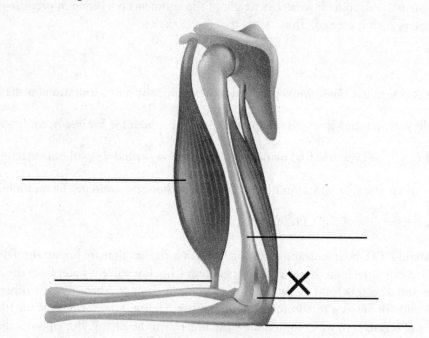

9. **B** This question requires you to identify the planet that is the fewest light minutes from Jupiter. In order to answer this question, you must consider the provided graph, on which the *x*-axis shows the distance, in both light minutes and astronomical units, from the Sun to the other planets. While this diagram places the Sun at the center of the universe, not Jupiter, you should notice that a small distance between planets indicates a small number of light minutes distance, while a large distance between planets indicates a large number of light minutes distance. Accordingly, the planet that is the fewest light minutes from Jupiter will be the planet that is closest to Jupiter. Based on our diagram, the planet closest to Jupiter is Mars, (B).

10. **Inner planets: (f) Mercury, (h) Venus, (g) Earth, (a) Mars. Outer planets: (j) Jupiter, (d) Saturn, (b) Uranus, (i) Neptune.**

This question requires you to sort the given words as inner or outer planets. The passage states that the four planets closest to the Sun are inner planets, while those farthest from the Sun are outer planets. The order of the planets from the Sun outwards can be remembered by the phrase "**M**y **V**ery **E**xcellent **M**other

Just Served Us Nachos," indicating that the order of the planets is Mercury, Venus, Earth, Mars, Jupiter, Saturn, Uranus, Neptune. Thus, the inner planets are Mercury, Venus, Earth, and Mars; the outer planets are Jupiter, Saturn, Uranus, and Neptune. The Sun is neither an inner nor outer planet, and Gandolf is not one of our planets.

11. **1** Here you need to use the diagram to find the approximate distance, in astronomical units (AUs), between Mercury and Mars. The x-axis shows the distance, in both light minutes and AUs, from the Sun to the other planets. Notice that the difference between the Sun and Mars is 1.5 AUs, and the distance between the Sun and Mercury is 0.39 AUs. Thus, the distance between Mars and Mercury is 1.5 AUs – 0.39 AUs = 1.11 AUs. Since the question asks you to round to the nearest integer, the correct answer is 1.

12. **A** This question requires you to interpret the information about atoms. The question stem tells that you that, with the exception of hydrogen, an atom must have at least one neutron for every proton. Accordingly, if the element Dubnium has 105 protons, it must have at least 105 neutrons. Thus, Dubnium may have isotopes containing 105, 157, and 163 neutrons, but it cannot have an isotope with 102 neutrons. Accordingly, the correct answer is (A).

13. **C** This question tells you that the Law of Conservation of Mass states that matter can be neither created nor destroyed, and requires you to determine the Law of Conservation of Energy. Both laws are closely related, and, like mass, energy can be neither created nor destroyed. Accordingly, the correct answer is (C); the Law of Conservation of Energy states that energy can be neither created nor destroyed in a closed system.

14. **D** In order to answer this question, you must use the image provided to determine the incorrect statement. Choice (A) states that the beginning of the Archeon Eon was approximately 3.8 million years ago. The chart provides the geologic time scale in units of millions of years, and the chart shows that the Archeon Eon spanned 3,800 – 2,500 million years before present. Accordingly, (A) is true and should be eliminated. Choice (B) states that the Cambrian Period was the first period of the Paleozoic Era. Note that the chart shows the geologic time scale where the units are shown in descending order; i.e., the Phanerozoic Eon is the most recently occurring eon and the Hadeon Eon is the oldest Eon. Accordingly, the Cambrian Period is the first of the Paleozoic Era; thus, (B) is correct and can be eliminated. Choice (C) states that there is no record regarding the eras and periods of the Hadean Eon; the last line of the chart supports this statement, so (C) can be eliminated. Choice (D) states that the Protocambrian period comprises about 87% of the geologic time scale. According to the chart, the Precambrian Epoch comprises 87% of the geologic time scale, so this statement is incorrect. Thus, (D) is the correct answer.

15. **4.6**

This question requires you to state the age of Earth in billions of years. The final line of the chart states that the origin of Earth was about 4.6 billion years ago. Accordingly, the answer is 4.6.

16. **Mesozoic; 66**

In order to answer this question correctly, you need to interpret the given chart, which shows that an eon is broken into eras, eras are split into periods, and periods are split into epochs. Accordingly, the Phanerozoic Eon is comprised of the Paleozoic, Mesozoic, and Cenozoic Eras. Next, you need to determine start and end dates of the Mesozoic Era. Note that the chart shows the approximate timeline, in units of millions of years, for the various eons, eras, periods, and epochs; for example, the Permian Period spanned from 286 million years before present to 245 million years before present. Accordingly, the Mesozoic Era spanned from 245 million years before present to 66 million years before present.

17.   **Acidic: (e) urine, (f) soda, (c) lemon juice, (h) battery acid**
       Neutral: (b) pure water
       Alkaline: (a) bleach, (d) soap, (g) antacid tablets

This question requires you to sort the given substances as acidic, neutral, or alkaline substances. The question stem tells you that a pH less than seven indicates an acidic solution, a pH of seven indicates a neutral solution, and a pH greater than seven indicates an alkaline solution. You are told the pH values for the majority of the substances: bleach has a pH of 12 and is alkaline, soap has a pH of 11 and is alkaline, urine has a pH of 6 and is acidic, soda has a pH of 3 and is acidic, and lemon juice has a pH of 2 and is acidic. Then, you have to sort the substances for which you were not given a pH measure: antacid tablets, pure water, and battery acid. Use context clues for antacid tablets; the root *ant-* means against, so antacid tablets fight acid. Accordingly, antacid tablets are alkaline. Similarly, battery acid has the word *acid* in the name, so this is an acidic substance. Finally, you are left with pure water. While you do not have any context clues here, you should know that pure water has a pH of 7, making it a neutral substance.

18. **B** Some questions on the GED® test are simply information recall questions. This question is an example of one of those questions. Human cells have 23 pairs of chromosomes, or 46 chromosomes total. Of the 23 pairs of chromosomes, one pair is made up of sex chromosomes, while the remaining 22 pairs of chromosomes are referred to as autosomes.

19.   This question requires you to identify the temporary magnets in the provided group of magnets. The question stem states that permanent magnets, which are made from highly magnetic materials such as iron, while temporary magnets can function only through the use of electricity. Accordingly, the permanent magnets in the image are those that use electricity to function, as shown below.

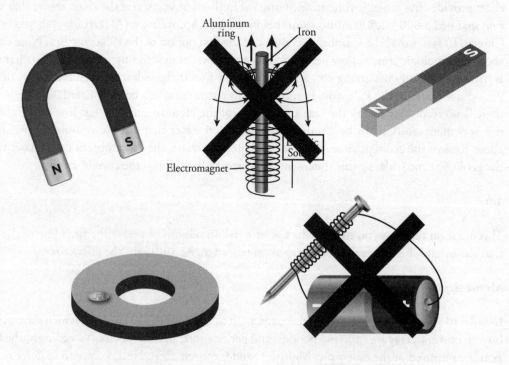

20. **50%, 50%**

The first question in this set requires you to consider the cross between a heterozygous dominant cat with a long tail and a homozygous recessive cat with a short tail. In order to answer this question, create a Punnett Square, as shown below.

	L	l
l	Ll	ll
l	Ll	ll

Accordingly, the likelihood that they will have offspring with a long tail is 50%, while the probability that they will have offspring with a short tail is 50%.

21. **A** This question requires that you have some knowledge regarding Mendel's pea plant experiments. You are told that Mendel noted that pea plants with a single dominant allele for height led the pea plant to express the trait for height. Since the explanation of Mendel's Law includes the word "dominance" in the explanation, you should be fairly confident that this exemplifies Mendel's Law of Dominance. Mendel's Law of Segregation states that alleles can segregate and recombine, and Mendel's Law of Independent Assortment states that traits can segregate and recombine independently of other traits; thus, (B) and (C) can be eliminated. Choice (D), Mendel's Law of Engendered Production, is not a law. Thus, (A) is the correct answer.

22. **0** Here you are required you to find the probability that two homozygous recessive cats will have a cat with a long tail. So, create a Punnett Square:

	l	l
l	ll	ll
l	ll	ll

You will find that the offspring of two homozygous recessive cats (ll) will result in offspring of ll, ll, ll, and ll. Thus, the likelihood that they will have offspring with a long tail is 0%.

23. **B** Here you need to identify the statement that is NOT expressed by Newton's Laws of Motion. Choice (A) states that an object at rest will remain at rest, unless acted upon by some outside force; this is supported by Newton's First Law of Motion, and can be eliminated. Choice (B) states that the work of an object is

equal to the product of the force upon that object and the distance the object travels; this is simply the definition of work and should be kept. Choice (C) states that when acted upon by an external force, an object will accelerate in proportion to that force; this is supported by Newton's Second Law of Motion, and can be eliminated. Choice (D) states that for every action there is an equal and opposite reaction; this is supported by Newton's Third Law of Motion, and can be eliminated. Thus, the correct answer is (B).

24. **C** This question requires you to identify the stage of mitosis in the given illustration. The passage states that the chromosomes do not split until anaphase; thus, eliminate both (A) and (B). The passage also states that the cell splits into two daughter cells during telophase; since the cell has not yet split, eliminate (D). The image illustrates anaphase, when the cell elongates as sister chromatids of each chromosome separate and migrate to opposite poles. Thus, the correct answer is (C).

25. **B** This question requires you to identify the temperature that is impossible for the steel ball to experience. The question stem states that temperature can be measured in Celsius, Fahrenheit, or Kelvin. Both Celsius and Fahrenheit scales can express negative temperatures, but the passage states that 0°K is absolute zero, or the point at which all molecular movement stops. Accordingly, the Kelvin scale cannot express negative values; the lowest value in the Kelvin scale is 0°K, or absolute zero. Accordingly, it is impossible for Robert to find that the steel ball has a temperature of –1°K. Thus, the correct answer is (B).

26. **107.6**

This question requires you to use the provided chart to convert 42° Celsius to the equivalent Fahrenheit temperature. The chart states that the Fahrenheit equivalent of a Celsius temperature is equal to $(C \times 1.8) + 32$. Thus, 42°C is equal to $(42 \times 1.8) + 32 = 75.6 + 32 = 107.6°$ Fahrenheit.

27. **colder, warmer**

To solve this question, one method is to convert all three temperatures to the same scale, using the formulas in the table. Another method is to carefully consider the information as presented in the passage: 0°K is absolute zero, so that is definitely colder than 0°F; water freezes at 0°C and at 32°F, so 0°C is certainly warmer than 0°F.

28. **exothermic, endothermic**

This question requires you to determine the type of reactions that occur when Liz lights a candle and when she cooks an egg. The question stem states that an exothermic reaction occurs when heat is generated in a system and released to its surroundings, while an endothermic reaction is one that absorbs heat from its surroundings. When lighting a candle, the heat from the flame is released into the atmosphere, indicating that an exothermic reaction takes place. Conversely, when cooking an egg, the egg absorbs the heat from the stove, indicating that an endothermic reaction takes place.

29. **A** This question requires you to identify the provided diagram. A food chain describes the way organisms depend upon one another in a given system; this description matches the diagram, so keep (A). A food web defines the interrelationships between organisms in an ecosystem and is, essentially, a depiction of multiple food chains; eliminate (B). A food pyramid is a way of representing a good chain based on the trophic level of each organism; eliminate (C). A phylogenetic tree shows the evolutionary relationships among organisms based on physical and genetic similarities and differences; eliminate (D).

30. **C** Here you need to identify the secondary consumer in the food chain. In a food chain, the producers, or autotrophs, are organisms that can make their own food. Accordingly, in this diagram, grass is a producer; eliminate (A). A primary consumer is one that feeds directly on producers. According to our food chain, only crickets feed directly on grass; eliminate (B). A secondary consumer is one that feeds on a primary consumer. According to our food chain, frogs eat crickets, so frogs are the secondary consumers; (C) is the correct answer. The hawk feeds upon the snake, a tertiary consumer, and is therefore a quaternary consumer.

31. **50, 5**

    This question tells you that approximately 10% of energy is transferred from one level to the next in a food chain. You need to determine how many Units of Energy are passed to both the frog and snake, if a cricket consumes 500 Units of Energy. Since the frog inherits 10% of the energy directly from the cricket, the frog will inherit 0.10 × 500 = 50 Units of Energy. Then, the snake inherits 10% of the energy directly from the frog. Thus, the snake will inherit 0.10 × 50 = 5 Units of Energy.

32. **D** In order to answer this question, refer to the provided periodic table. The question requires you to identify the element that is not an Alkali metal. According to the periodic table, Lithium (Li), Sodium (Na), and Potassium (K) are Alkali metals, while Hydrogen (H) is a nonmetal.

33. **B** Here you need to identify the element that has two protons per atom. According to the passage, from left to right and top to bottom, elements are listed in order of atomic number, which is the number of protons in each atom. Therefore, the element with two protons per atom with an atomic number of 2 is Helium (He).

34. **B** In order to answer this question, you must convert the RNA string AUGUACCGUAGU into its codon equivalent. The passage states that a codon is a string of three nucleotide bases, and the chart provides a means to identify the codon based on that three-character string. First, break the RNA string into chunks of three characters: AUG | UAC | CGU | AGU. Next, find the codon UAC in the provided chart. The codon UAC indicates the codon Tyrosine, so (B) is the correct answer.

35. **C** This question requires you to determine the nucleotide base that is *not* associated with RNA. The passage states that protein is synthesized based on the order of the nucleotide bases in a string of RNA, and provides a chart to help convert RNA to codons based on the nucleotide bases. In the chart, the only bases that can lead to protein synthesis are A, G, C, and U, or Adenine, Guanine, Cytosine, and Uracil. Accordingly, thymine is the nucleotide base not associated with RNA.

Chapter 7
Practice Test 3

Reasoning Through Language Arts

Welcome!

Here is some information that you need to know before you start this test:

- You should not spend too much time on a question if you are not certain of the answer; answer it the best you can, and go on to the next question.
- If you are not certain of the answer to a question, you can mark your answer for review and come back to it later.
- This test has three sections.
- You have **35 minutes** to complete Section 1.
- When you finish Section 1, you may review those questions.
- You may not go back to Section 1 once you have finished your review.
- You have **45 minutes** to complete the Extended Response question in Section 2.
- After completing Section 2, you may take a 10-minute break.
- You have **60 minutes** to complete Section 3.
- When you finish Section 3, you may review those questions.

Turn the page to begin.

GO ON TO THE NEXT PAGE

<u>Questions 1 through 8</u> refer to the following passage.

Excerpt from *Shifting Sands*
by Sara Ware Bassett

1   The train was ten minutes late, and while she paced the platform at Sawyer Falls, the nearest station, Marcia fidgeted.

2   She had never seen any of Jason's family. At first a desultory correspondence had taken place between him and his sister, Margaret; then gradually it had died a natural death—the result, no doubt, of his indolence and neglect. When the letters ceased coming, Marcia had let matters take their course.

3   Was it not kinder to allow the few who still loved him to remain ignorant of what he had become and to remember instead only as the dashing lad who in his teens had left the farm and gone to seek his fortune in the great world?

4   She had written Margaret a short note after his death and had received a reply expressing such genuine grief it had more than ever convinced her that her course had been the wise and generous one. What troubled her most in the letter had been its outpouring of sympathy for herself. She detested subterfuge and as she read sentence after sentence, which should have meant so much and in reality meant so little, the knowledge that she had not been entirely frank had brought with it an uncomfortable sense of guilt. It was not what she had said but what she had withheld that accused her.

5   Marcia Howe was no masquerader, and until this moment the hypocrisy she had practiced had demanded no sustained acting. Little by little, moreover, the pricking of her conscience had ceased and, fading into the past, the incident had been forgotten. Miles of distance, years of silence separated her from Jason's relatives and it had been easy to allow the deceit, if deceit it had been, to stand.

6   But now those barriers were to be broken down and she suddenly realized that to keep up the fraud so artlessly begun was going to be exceedingly difficult. She was not a clever dissembler.

7   Moreover, any insincerity between herself and Sylvia would strike at the very core of the sincere, earnest companionship she hoped would spring up between them. Even should she be a more skillful fraud than she dared anticipate and succeed in playing her role convincingly, would there not loom ever before her the danger of betrayal from outside sources?

GO ON TO THE NEXT PAGE

8   Everyone in the outlying district had known Jason for what he was. There had been no possibility of screening the sordid melodrama from the public. Times without number one fisherman and then another had come bringing the recreant back home across the channel, and had aided in getting him into the house and to bed. His shame had been one of the blots on the upright, self-respecting community.

9   It was because the villagers had helped her so loyally to shoulder a burden she never could have borne alone that Marcia felt toward them this abiding affection and gratitude. They might discuss her affairs if they chose; ingenuously build up romances where none existed; they might even gossip about her clothes, her friends, her expenditures. Their chatter did not trouble her. She had tried them out, and in the face of larger issues had found their virtues so admirable that their vices became, by contrast, mere trivialities.

1. What can the reader infer about the relationship between Marcia and Margaret?

   A.   They are complete strangers to each other.
   B.   They have met once before, at Jacob's funeral.
   C.   They confide in one another in their letters.
   D.   They show kindness to one another.

2. Which word could best replace the word "artlessly" in paragraph 6?

   A.   unconsciously
   B.   clumsily
   C.   deceptively
   D.   pragmatically

3. What can readers infer about Jason?

   A.   He died a natural death.
   B.   He kept his true self hidden from the villagers.
   C.   He left home at a young age.
   D.   His deplorable behavior was caused by estrangement from his family.

4. In this scene, Marcia's attitude toward the villagers is primarily one of

   A.   thankful respect.
   B.   hypocritical tolerance.
   C.   affection tinged with guilt.
   D.   genuine grief.

5. Read the following sentence from paragraph 1.

   > The train was ten minutes late, and while she paced the platform at Sawyer Falls, the nearest station, Marcia fidgeted.

   How does this beginning sentence affect the passage?

   A.   It reveals Marcia's character, showing that she is an impatient person.
   B.   It establishes the setting of the train station, where Marcia spends time observing the details around her.
   C.   It sets the emotional tone of the passage by revealing Marcia's emotional agitation.
   D.   It is the first glimpse the reader has into Marcia's interior dialogue.

GO ON TO THE NEXT PAGE

6. In paragraph 4, why does the author use the phrase "which should have meant so much and in reality meant so little"?

    A. to show the difference in Marcia's and Margaret's view of Jason
    B. to illustrate by contrast the difference between words and deeds
    C. to expose the hypocrisy in Margaret's character
    D. to show that what Margaret writes has no importance for Marcia

7. Which quotation from the story best supports the idea that Marcia is at the train station in order meet with one of Jason's relatives?

    A. "Miles of distance, years of silence separated her from Jason's relatives and it had been easy to allow the deceit, if deceit it had been, to stand."
    B. "But now those barriers were to be broken down and she suddenly realized that to keep up the fraud so artlessly begun was going to be exceedingly difficult."
    C. "She had never seen any of Jason's family."
    D. "When the letters ceased coming, Marcia had let matters take their course."

8. What main function does the character of Margaret serve in the passage?

    A. She acts as a contrast to Marcia.
    B. She is an example of the type of person Marcia wants to be.
    C. She represents an unresolved issue in Marcia's life.
    D. Her status as Jacob's sister highlights Marcia's distance from the family.

GO ON TO THE NEXT PAGE

Questions 9 through 16 refer to the following passage.

Excerpt from the *Protocols of the Proceedings*
International Conference Held at Washington
For the Purpose of Fixing a Prime Meridian and a Universal Day
October, 1884

Delegates of the United States:

1   Commander Sampson, Delegate of the United States, said:
From a purely scientific point of view, any meridian may be
taken as the prime meridian. But from the standpoint of
convenience and economy there is undoubtedly much room for a
choice.

2   The prime meridian should pass through some well-established
national observatory in telegraphic communication with the
whole world, in order that the differences of longitude from the
prime meridian may be determined for any point. As a matter of
economy as well as convenience that meridian should be selected
which is now in most general use. This would limit our choice
to the meridian of Greenwich, for it may fairly be stated upon
the authority of the distinguished Delegate from Canada that
more than 70 percent of all the shipping of the world uses this
meridian for purposes of navigation.

3   The charts constructed upon this meridian cover the whole
navigable globe. The cost of the plates from which these charts
are printed is probably not less than ten millions of dollars.
As a matter of economy, then, to the world at large, it would
be better to permit those plates to remain unchanged which
are engraved for the meridian of Greenwich and to make the
necessary changes in all plates engraved for other meridians.

4   Should any of us now hesitate in the adoption of a particular
meridian, or should any nation covet the honor of having the
selected meridian within its own borders, it is to be remembered
that when the prime meridian is once adopted by all it loses its
specific name and nationality, and becomes simply the Prime
Meridian.

5   Mr. Rutherfurd, Delegate of the United States, stated that
the observatory at Paris stands within the heart of a large and
populous city; that it has already been thought by many of the
principal French astronomers that it should no longer remain
there; that it has been, interfered with by the tremors of the
earth and emanations in the air, which prevent it from fulfilling
its usefulness. If a change is to be made, if sentiment should
give way to practical reason, a locality, no doubt, will be found
which may be calculated to fulfill the requirements of a prime
meridian better than that one.

GO ON TO THE NEXT PAGE

6   As to the fitness of Greenwich, he said that the observatory was placed in the middle of a large park under the control of the Government, so that no nuisance can come near it without their consent, and that it was in a position which speaks for itself.

Delegate of France:

7   Mr. Janssen, Delegate of France, said: We do not put forward the meridian of the observatory of Paris as that to be chosen for the prime meridian; but if it were chosen, and we wished to compare it with that of Greenwich as to the accuracy with which it is actually connected with the other observatories of Europe, it would not lose by the comparison.

8   National pride has led to the multiplication of geographical starting-points. Thus, as maps accumulated, the need of uniformity, especially in those that referred to general geography, was felt more and more.

9   Instead of laying down the great principle that the meridian to be offered to the world as the starting-point for all terrestrial longitudes should, have above all things, an essentially geographical and impersonal character, the question was simply asked, which one of the meridians in use among the different observatories has (if I may be allowed to use the expression) the largest number of clients? Instead of profiting by the lessons of the past, national rivalries are introduced in a question that should rally the good-will of all.

10   I can do no better than to quote from one of our most learned hydrographers. "France was the first to conceive and execute the great operations which had for their object the construction of civil and military maps and the measurement of arcs of the meridian in Europe, America, and Africa. All these operations were and are based on the Paris meridian. Nearly all the astronomical tables used at the present time by the astronomers and the navies of the whole world are French, and calculated for the Paris meridian.

11   Our actual collections amount to about 2,600 charts in use. Of this number more than half represent original French surveys, a large part of which foreign nations have reproduced. Our surveys are not confined to the coasts of France and of its colonies; there is scarcely a region of the globe for which we do not possess original work. The exclusive use of the Paris meridian by our sailors is justified by reference to a past of two centuries.

12   An immense majority of the navies of the world navigate with English charts; that is true, and it is a practical compliment to the great maritime activity of that nation.

GO ON TO THE NEXT PAGE

13   Without doubt, on account of our long and glorious past, of our great publications, a change of meridian would cause us heavy sacrifices. Nevertheless, if we are approached with offers of self-sacrifice, and thus receive proofs of a sincere desire for the general good, France has given sufficient proofs of her love of progress to make her co-operation certain.

9.   How does the argument of the Delegates of the United States relate to the argument of the Delegate of France?

A.   The Delegates of the United States introduce a guideline for establishing the Prime Meridian and the Delegate of France disagrees with that guideline.

B.   The Delegates of the United States advocate for one particular location of the Prime Meridian while the Delegate of France directly opposes that location.

C.   The Delegates of the United States criticize Paris as a possible location of the Prime Meridian while the Delegate of France defends it.

D.   The Delegate of France argues that one nation is clearly superior as a location for the Prime Meridian, while the Delegates of the United States want a location that favors all nations equally.

10.   Which quotation from the passage expresses the primary purpose of Commander Sampson's address?

A.   "It is to be remembered that when the prime meridian is once adopted by all it loses its specific name and nationality, and becomes simply the Prime Meridian."

B.   "From a purely scientific point of view, any meridian may be taken as the prime meridian."

C.   "As a matter of economy, then, to the world at large, it would be better to permit those plates to remain unchanged which are engraved for the meridian of Greenwich."

D.   "As a matter of economy as well as convenience that meridian should be selected which is now in most general use."

11.   What can readers infer about the observatory at Greenwich?

A.   The observatory is the largest one in Europe at the time of the debate.

B.   The observatory was designed with the goal of becoming the Prime Meridian.

C.   The observatory serves as a naval base for 70% of the world's shipping.

D.   The observatory is used by several sailors as a reference point in navigation.

GO ON TO THE NEXT PAGE

12. Mr. Rutherfurd mentioned the observatory in Paris in order to

    A. advocate for Paris as the site of the Prime Meridian.
    B. argue that observatories should be restricted to remote areas.
    C. introduce additional characteristics that should be considered.
    D. prove that the observatory cannot fulfill its function.

13. What approach did the Delegate of France take to counter the proposal of Greenwich as a location for the Prime Meridian?

    A. The delegate compared the two observatories to demonstrate the superiority of the Paris observatory.
    B. The delegate questioned the principle behind the selection of a meridian.
    C. The delegate offered statistics to demonstrate that more sailors depend on the French charts.
    D. The delegate argued that the motivations of the Greenwich advocates are based on national pride.

14. Read this quotation from the report:

    > "Nevertheless, if we are approached with offers of self-sacrifice, and thus receive proofs of a sincere desire for the general good, France has given sufficient proofs of her love of progress to make her co-operation certain."

    Why does the Delegate of France, in responding to the Delegates of the United States, conclude the report with this sentence?

    A. to counter the idea that the delegate for France is arguing from self-interest
    B. to endorse France as the location for the Prime Meridian that would do the most good
    C. to demonstrate that a change of the Prime Meridian would be a sacrifice for France
    D. to indicate that the delegate for France should be personally requested to co-operate

GO ON TO THE NEXT PAGE

15. Write the letters of the phrases that correspond to the opinions of the delegates into the correct locations on the chart.

Delegates from the United States	Delegate from France

(a) The selection of the prime meridian should be based in geography.

(b) The prime meridian should be that meridian which has the largest number of users.

(c) The observatory of Paris has already been evaluated by French astronomers.

(d) The selection of the Prime Meridian should involve the agreement of all nations.

16. Why does the Delegate of France discuss the "astronomical tables" (paragraph 10) and the "French surveys" (paragraph 11)?

A. to prove that the French charts are better than the English ones, even though the English charts are in wider use

B. to establish France as an authority on navigation, so that the opinion of France will be judged of more importance in deciding the Prime Meridian

C. to show that historical precedent proves that the Prime Meridian should be in Paris

D. to show how dedicated France is to cooperate with all countries in establishing a "neutral" Prime Meridian

GO ON TO THE NEXT PAGE

17. The passage below is incomplete. For each "Select" option, choose the option that correctly completes the sentence. For this practice test, circle your selection.

Ruti Chatham
Sales Supervisor
Aronco Art Supplies

Dear Ms. Chatham,

I am writing today to complain of the lamentable service I received from your company last Monday.

Select... ▼	by a representative of Aronco Art
On that day, I was visited	
On that day, I visited	
From that day, visiting	
From that day, I visited	

Supplies, Mr. Namdani, at my home.

Mr. Namdani was one hour late for his appointment and failed to apologize or even acknowledge this tardiness when he did arrive. Your representative kept his muddy coat on upon entering my house, which dirtied my furniture. Mr. Namdani then proceeded to present a variety of products to me that I was not interested in. Even though I tried to question your representative about the products I wanted to order,

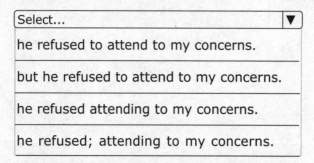

Select... ▼
he refused to attend to my concerns.
but he refused to attend to my concerns.
he refused attending to my concerns.
he refused; attending to my concerns.

We ended our meeting 30 minutes after he had arrived without him having made a sale, or me having obtained the items I needed.

It annoys me deeply that I spent a morning—a loss of half a day of work—waiting for Mr. Namdani to show up. My impression of Aronco Art Supplies was shaky before, but now my opinion

GO ON TO THE NEXT PAGE

Select... ▼	has been thoroughly tainted. If this is
of whom
of them
of it
of that

standard procedure, I wonder how any business is being accomplished by your company. Furthermore, Mr. Namdani's persistence in retaining his muddy coat

Select... ▼
has meant that I was having my furniture professionally cleaned, at no little expense.
has meant that I have had to have my furniture professionally cleaned, at no little expense.
meant that I was having my professional furniture cleaned, at no little expense.
means that I have my professional furniture cleaned, at no little expense.

I am positive that this is not the way Aronco Art Supplies wishes to treat me or any valued customer. I would welcome the opportunity to discuss this experience further and look forward to hearing from you.

Yours faithfully,

Veronica Ashtar

GO ON TO THE NEXT PAGE

THIS PAGE INTENTIONALLY LEFT BLANK.

GO ON TO THE NEXT PAGE

Reasoning Through Language Arts, Section 2

Extended Response Answer Guidelines

Please use the guidelines below as you answer the Extended Response question on the Reasoning Through Language Arts test. Following these guidelines as closely as possible will ensure that you provide the best response.

1. **Please note that this task must be completed in no more than 45 minutes.** However, don't rush through your response. Be sure to read through the passage(s) and the prompt. Then think about the message you want to convey in your response. **Be sure to plan your response before you begin writing.** Draft your response and revise it as needed.

2. As you read, think carefully about the **argumentation** presented in the passage(s). "Argumentation" refers to the assumptions, claims, support, reasoning, and credibility on which a position is based. Pay close attention to **how the author(s) use these strategies to convey his or her (their) positions.**

3. When you write your essay, be sure to
   o **determine which position presented** in the passage(s) is **better supported** by evidence from the passage(s)
   o **explain why the position you chose is the better-supported one**
   o **remember, the better-supported position is not necessarily the position you agree with**
   o **defend your assertions with multiple pieces of evidence** from the passage(s)
   o **build your main points thoroughly**
   o **put your main points in logical order** and tie your details to your main points
   o **organize your response carefully** and consider your **audience, message, and purpose**
   o **use transitional words and phrases** to connect sentences, paragraphs, and ideas
   o **choose words carefully** to express your ideas clearly
   o **vary your sentence structure** to enhance the flow and clarity of your response
   o **reread and revise your response** to correct any errors in grammar, usage, or punctuation

GO ON TO THE NEXT PAGE

Instructions

Read

- On the **page 2 tab above**, you will **read two texts** presenting **different views** on the same topic.

- **Both writers argue** that **their position** on the issue is **correct**.

Plan

- **Analyze** the two texts **to determine** which writer presents the **stronger case**.

- **Develop your own argument** in which **you explain** how one position is **better supported** than the other.

- **Include** relevant and specific **evidence** from **both sources** to support your argument.

Write

- **Type** your response in the **box on the right**.

- Your response should be approximately **4 to 7 paragraphs of 3 to 7 sentences each**.

- **Remember** to allow a few minutes **to review and edit your response**.

You have up to **45 minutes** for reading, planning, writing, and editing your response.

European Union Pros and Cons

1   The European Union is a political and economic partnership between 28 European countries in which certain decisions are negotiated through intergovernmental organizations. There has been some debate about whether membership in the EU is overall advantageous or disadvantageous to member nations.

Advantages

2   **Free trade.** The EU provides a unified market with no tariffs on imports and exports between member countries, which results in lower-priced products. Supporters of the EU maintain that, consequently, free European trade is vital to the economy of each member nation. Also, membership in the European Union allows member countries a voice in how trading rules are negotiated with other powerful nations such as the United States and China.

3   **Free movement of people.** The EU allows people to move across borders unrestricted to work or study. The European Commission has reported that more than 15 million EU citizens have relocated to other EU countries to retire or to find new job opportunities. This migration helps to make the labor markets

GO ON TO THE NEXT PAGE

of those countries more flexible. Furthermore, EU citizens have access to more scholarships for higher education. More than 1.5 million young people have completed part of their studies in another member state with the help of the Erasmus program (European Region Action Scheme for the Mobility of University Students).

4   **Louder voice**. Membership in the EU ensures that all concerns of member nations are heard internationally since the EU speaks on behalf of millions of citizens. For some, membership in the EU meant a trade of independence for influence: in return for following EU statutes, a country receives a seat around the European political table, and the concerns of that country are sounded on a global level.

5   **Security.** The collective force of the EU provides a stronger defense to aggression or terrorism. A letter by senior military figures of the UK claimed that the EU is an "increasingly important pillar of our security," especially in the face of instability, resurgent nationalism, and aggression in other countries. Through the European Union, member countries exchange criminal and passenger records, and security agencies collaborate on counter-terrorism.

Disadvantages

6   **Cost.** European Union membership has a price. According to statistics for 2013, most member countries contributed approximately 0.85% of their Gross National Income. For example, the overall cost of EU membership to the UK is £6.883 billion net, when economic returns from the EU are factored in. So even with such economic benefits, some countries wind up with net cost for EU membership.

7   **Overcrowding and net migration.** It is true that the citizens of member countries are free to move from one place to another. Unfortunately, this has led to overcrowding, notably in the major cities of the UK and it has increased prices of houses, as well as congestion on the roads. Critics observe that any member nation is unable to limit immigration because free movement of labor is a fundamental principle of the EU.

8   **Loss of sovereignty.** Few disagree that EU membership involves giving up some local control over national affairs. Critics argue that the EU has become so vast that it is too difficult to have a meaningful say on important issues. The introduction of Qualified Majority Voting means that votes can be decided against the interests and desires of a particular country. The administrative European Commission serves the European Union's interest and not the interest of the individual country.

GO ON TO THE NEXT PAGE

9   **Security.** Open borders between nations do not allow local governments to check and control immigration. Failure to exert these controls significantly increases the terrorist threat within any member nation, which endangers its citizens. For some nations, who feel it should be up to local governments to set the rules, staying out of the European Union is the only way to keep control of their borders.

You may take a 10-minute break before proceeding to Section 3.

GO ON TO THE NEXT PAGE

Questions 18 through 25 refer to the following passage.

Excerpt from "Heads Up: Stop. Think. Connect."
OnGuardOnline.gov

1   Being online—connected through some sort of device—is how you live your life. And as you spend more of your time there, it can be easy to over-share, embarrass yourself, mess up your computer and possibly get messages from creepy people.

2   Regardless of how fast your fingers fly on a keyboard, phone or tablet, the best tool you have to help avoid risks online is your brain. When you're ready to post or send a message or a photo, download a file, game or program, or shop for something—stop for a second.

3   Think about things like: Do you know and trust who you're dealing with—or what you're sharing or downloading? How will you feel if your information ends up somewhere you didn't intend? Asking a few key questions first can help you protect yourself, your friends and your computer.

Share with Care

4   Your online actions can have real-world consequences. The pictures you post and the words you write can affect the people in your life. Think before you post and share.

5   What you post could have a bigger "audience" than you think. Even if you use privacy settings, it's impossible to completely control who sees your social networking profile, pictures, videos or texts. Before you click "send," think about how you will feel if your family, teachers, coaches or neighbors find it.

6   Get someone's okay before you share photos or videos they're in. Stop and think about your own privacy—and other people's—before you share photos and videos online. It can be embarrassing, unfair and even unsafe to send or post photos and videos without getting permission from the people in them.

7   Sexting: Don't do it. Period. People who create, forward or even save sexually explicit photos, videos or messages put their friendships and reputations at risk. Worse yet, they could be breaking the law.

Protect Yourself

8   Use privacy settings to restrict who can see and post on your profile. Many social networking sites, chat rooms and blogs have privacy settings. Find out how to turn these settings on, and then do it.

GO ON TO THE NEXT PAGE

9   Learn about location-based services. Many phones have GPS technology, and there are applications that let you find out where your friends are—and let them find you. Set your privacy settings so that only people you know personally can see your location. Think about keeping location-based services off, and turning them on only when needed. Ask yourself, "Does this app need to know where I am?"

10   Do you download apps? If you do, you might be giving the app's developers access to your personal information—maybe even info that's not related to the purpose of the app. For example, say you download an app that lets you make a drawing out of a photo, but the company who made the app gets access to your entire contact list. It might share the information it collected with marketers or other companies. You can try to check what information the app collects—if it tells you—and check out your own privacy settings. Also think about whether getting that app is really worth sharing the details of your life.

11   Don't reply to text, email or pop-up messages that ask you to reply with personal information—even if the message looks like it's from a friend, family member or company you know, or threatens that something bad will happen if you don't reply. These messages may be fakes, sent to steal your information.

Interact with Tact

12   Politeness counts. Texting is just another way for people to have a conversation, and texters are just like people talking face-to-face or on the phone: they appreciate "please" and "thank you" (or pls and ty). In online conversations, using all CAPS, long rows of exclamation points or large bolded fonts is the same as shouting.

13   Avatars are people too. When you're playing a game or exploring an online world where you can create a character and interact with others, remember real people are behind those characters on the screen. Respect their feelings just like you would in person. Remember that your character or avatar is a virtual version of you—what does it tell people about you and your interests?

14   Cyberbullying is bullying that happens online. It might involve rumors or images posted on someone's profile or passed around for other people to see. Cyberbullying is a lose-lose proposition: it often makes the person being harassed feel bad—and it makes the bully look bad. It also might lead to punishment from school authorities or the police. If someone harasses you online, keep a cool head, and don't respond. Most people realize that bullying is wrong. Sometimes you can stop bullying if you ignore or block the person. If it continues, save the evidence and ask for help from an adult you trust.

GO ON TO THE NEXT PAGE

15   Speak up. If you see something inappropriate on a social networking site or in a game or chat room, let the website know and tell an adult you trust. Using Report Abuse links can help keep sites fun for everyone. Treat others the way you want to be treated—whether you're interacting with them online, on your phone or in person.

Source: Federal Trade Commission

18. What is the author's primary purpose in writing this article?

    A.   to correct common misconceptions about Internet practices
    B.   to caution readers about different ways impolite behavior can be risky
    C.   to advise readers about the possible consequences of Internet use
    D.   to enlist the help of readers in reporting cyberbullying

19. Read this sentence from paragraph 1:

    > Being online—connected through some sort of device—is how you live your life.

    Why does the author begin the article with this sentence?

    A.   to introduce the topic, showing how computers have taken over the everyday world
    B.   to engage readers' attention immediately by addressing them directly
    C.   to admonish readers for not living their lives in the real world
    D.   to call into question an attitude about online behavior that young people have

20. Throughout the article, the author directs the readers to ask themselves particular questions. How does the repeated use of questions help the author's point?

    A.   It actively encourages readers to consider concerns that they may have ignored.
    B.   It shows that there are some concerns about Internet use that are still unanswered.
    C.   It gives readers starting points for a discussion with family and friends.
    D.   It highlights the controversial nature of the sensitive issues discussed.

21. Which definition best matches the use of the word "audience" in paragraph 5?

    A.   group of receivers
    B.   formal listeners
    C.   meeting with authority
    D.   artistic appraisers

22. What can the reader infer about the article's intended audience?

    A.   The article is aimed at parents of teenagers.
    B.   The article is addressing young people who are comfortable with technology.
    C.   The article is written to people struggling to overcome Internet addiction.
    D.   The article is targeting first-time Internet users.

GO ON TO THE NEXT PAGE

23. Read this sentence from paragraph 13:

> Avatars are people too.

What can be inferred about the "avatars" in this sentence?

A. They have independent personas and intelligence.
B. They don't deserve the same respect as humans do.
C. They are reflections of their creators' personalities.
D. They are used to make online interactions easier.

24. The article claims that the reader's online actions can have real-world consequences. Write the letters of two examples the author uses to support this claim into the boxes below.

(a) Some technology reveals the user's location.

(b) People who create sexually explicit photos could be breaking the law.

(c) Cyberbullying might lead to punishment from school authorities or the police.

(d) Some email messages that look real are actually fake.

(e) Use privacy settings to restrict who can see your profile.

25. What question did the author leave unanswered in the passage?

A. Does protecting my profile keep me safe from developers of online apps?
B. How can I report improper behavior during an online game?
C. What should I do if someone is harassing me online?
D. Can I guarantee that a particular person won't see an email I sent?

GO ON TO THE NEXT PAGE

Questions 26 through 33 refer to the following article.

Excerpt from *The Almost Perfect State*
by Don Marquis

1   No matter how nearly perfect an Almost Perfect State may be, it is not nearly enough perfect unless the individuals who compose it can, somewhere between death and birth, have a perfectly corking time for a few years. The most wonderful governmental system in the world does not attract us, as a system; we are after a system that scarcely knows it is a system; the great thing is to have the largest number of individuals as happy as may be, for a little while at least, some time before they die.

2   In the Almost Perfect State every person shall have at least ten years before he dies of easy, carefree, happy living...things will be so arranged economically that this will be possible for each individual.

3   Personally we look forward to an old age of dissipation and indolence and unreverent disrepute. In fifty years we shall be ninety-two years old. We intend to work rather hard during those fifty years and accumulate enough to live on without working any more for the next ten years, for we have determined to die at the age of one hundred and two.

4   Between the years of ninety-two and a hundred and two, however, we shall be the ribald, useless, drunken outcast person we have always wished to be. We shall have a long white beard and long white hair; we shall not walk at all, but recline in a wheel chair and bellow for alcoholic beverages; in the winter we shall sit before the fire with our feet in a bucket of hot water, with a decanter of corn whiskey near at hand, and write ribald songs against organized society; strapped to one arm of our chair will be a forty-five caliber revolver, and we shall shoot out the lights when we want to go to sleep, instead of turning them off; when we want air we shall throw a silver candlestick through the front window and be damned to it; we shall address public meetings to which we have been invited because of our wisdom in a vein of jocund malice. We shall...but we don't wish to make any one envious of the good time that is coming to us...we look forward to a disreputable, vigorous, unhonored and disorderly old age.

5   We shall know that the Almost Perfect State is here when the kind of old age each person wants is possible to him. Of course, all of you may not want the kind we want...some of you may prefer prunes and morality to the bitter end. Some of you may be dissolute now and may look forward to becoming like one of the nice old fellows in a Wordsworth poem. But for our part we

GO ON TO THE NEXT PAGE

have always been a hypocrite and we shall have to continue being a hypocrite for a good many years yet, and we yearn to come out in our true colors at last. The point is, that no matter what you want to be, during those last ten years, that you may be, in the Almost Perfect State.

6   Any system of government under which the individual does all the sacrificing for the sake of the general good, for the sake of the community, the State, gets off on its wrong foot. We don't want things that cost us too much. We don't want too much strain all the time.

7   The best good that you can possibly achieve is not good enough if you have to strain yourself all the time to reach it. A thing is only worth doing, and doing again and again, if you can do it rather easily, and get some joy out of it.

8   Do the best you can, without straining yourself too much and too continuously, and leave the rest to God. If you strain yourself too much you'll have to ask God to patch you up. And for all you know, patching you up may take time that it was planned to use some other way.

9   BUT...overstrain yourself now and then. For this reason: The things you create easily and joyously will not continue to come easily and joyously unless you yourself are getting bigger all the time. And when you overstrain yourself you are assisting in the creation of a new self—if you get what we mean. And if you should ask us suddenly just what this has to do with the picture of the old guy in the wheel chair we should answer: Hanged if we know, but we seemed to sort o' run into it, somehow.

26.   Which of the following techniques does the author use to make his point about old age?

A.   The author draws an analogy between the old age of Wordsworth and the old age he plans for himself.
B.   The author uses vivid imagery to form an ironic ideal of old age.
C.   The author appeals to the authority of the governmental system to support his claims about old age.
D.   The author uses himself as a case study to illustrate the perfect old age in the Almost Perfect State.

27.   Based on the passage, which of the following reflects the author's feelings regarding public opinion?

A.   One should cultivate a good reputation in order to be asked to speak publicly later in life.
B.   In old age, one should behave as one likes without concern for what others will think.
C.   Organized society is useless and therefore public opinion should be disregarded.
D.   Gaining the support of public opinion will help bring about the Almost Perfect State.

GO ON TO THE NEXT PAGE

28. Write the letter of each word that applies to the author's characterizations of himself at old age into the character web.

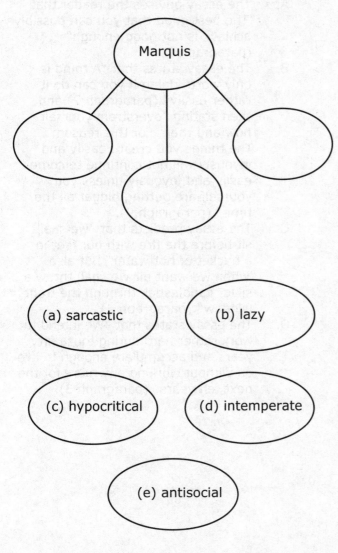

Marquis

(a) sarcastic   (b) lazy

(c) hypocritical   (d) intemperate

(e) antisocial

29. Which statement expresses a central theme of this essay?

   A. The needs of the individual are more important than the needs of the government.
   B. All people are hypocrites who sacrifice themselves to the needs of the community.
   C. One must work hard in order to enjoy a satisfying old age.
   D. The Almost Perfect State will never be perfect enough.

30. In the empty boxes, write the letters for two statements that express the author's purposes for writing the essay.

Author's Purpose

(a) to explain a mandatory system of retirement

(b) to satirize typical expectations of old age

(c) to warn readers about the dangers of straining themselves too much

(d) to advocate a specific arrangement between the state and the individual

(e) to assert that a long life depends on enjoying a ribald old age

31. Read this phrase from paragraph 3.

   "...for we have determined to die at the age of one hundred and two."

   Why does the author conclude the paragraph with this phrase?

   A. to show that the author comes from a particularly long-lived family
   B. to demonstrate that the author has carefully planned his retirement
   C. to illustrate the governmental system proposed at the end of the first paragraph with a personal example
   D. to provide a shift in tone to the sensational depictions in the following paragraph

GO ON TO THE NEXT PAGE

32. Why does the author describe himself as a "hypocrite"?

    A. because the old age he would enjoy is in direct contrast to the "nice old fellows" of the Wordsworth poem

    B. because he does not want the Almost Perfect State to apply to himself

    C. because he does not currently live the type of life he prefers

    D. because he wants things, but doesn't want them to cost too much

33. In which portions of the essay is there a contradiction in the author's reasoning?

    A. The essay advises the reader that "The best good that you can possibly achieve is not good enough" (paragraph 7).

    B. The essay states that "A thing is only worth doing if you can do it rather easily" (paragraph 7) and then stating "overstrain yourself now and then. For this reason: The things you create easily and joyously will not continue to come easily and joyously unless you yourself are getting bigger all the time" (paragraph 9).

    C. The essay predicts that "we shall sit before the fire with our feet in a bucket of hot water" but also "when we want air we shall throw a silver candlestick through the front window" (paragraph 4).

    D. The essay states that "We intend to work rather hard during those fifty years and accumulate enough to live on without working any more for the next ten years" (paragraph 3).

GO ON TO THE NEXT PAGE

Questions 34 through 41 refer to the following passage.

Excerpt from *The Quest Of The Silver Fleece*
by W.E.B. Du Bois

1   Zora, child of the swamp, was a heathen hoyden of twelve wayward, untrained years. Slight, straight, strong, full-blooded, she had dreamed her life away in willful wandering through her dark and somber kingdom until she was one with it in all its moods; mischievous, secretive, brooding; full of great and awful visions, steeped body and soul in wood-lore. Her home was out of doors, the cabin of Elspeth her port of call for talking and eating. She had not known, she had scarcely seen, a child of her own age until Bles Alwyn had fled from her dancing in the night, and she had searched and found him sleeping in the misty morning light. It was to her a strange new thing to see a fellow of like years with herself, and she gripped him to her soul in wild interest and new curiosity. Yet this childish friendship was so new and incomprehensible a thing to her that she did not know how to express it. At first she pounced upon him in mirthful, almost impish glee, teasing and mocking and half scaring him, despite his fifteen years of young manhood.

2   "Yes, they is devils down yonder behind the swamp," she would whisper, warningly, when, after the first meeting, he had crept back again and again, half fascinated, half amused to greet her; "I'se seen 'em, I'se heard 'em, 'cause my mammy is a witch."

3   The boy would sit and watch her wonderingly as she lay curled along the low branch of the mighty oak, clinging with little curved limbs and flying fingers. Possessed by the spirit of her vision, she would chant, low-voiced, tremulous, mischievous:

4   "One night a devil come to me on blue fire out of a big red flower that grows in the south swamp; he was tall and big and strong as anything, and when he spoke the trees shook and the stars fell. Even mammy was afeared; and it takes a lot to make mammy afeared, 'cause she's a witch and can conjure. He said, 'I'll come when you die—I'll come when you die, and take the conjure off you,' and then he went away on a big fire."

5   "Shucks!" the boy would say, trying to express scornful disbelief when, in truth, he was awed and doubtful. Always he would glance involuntarily back along the path behind him. Then her low birdlike laughter would rise and ring through the trees.

6   So passed a year, and there came the time when her wayward teasing and the almost painful thrill of her tale-telling nettled him and drove him away. For long months he did not meet her, until one day he saw her deep eyes fixed longingly upon him from a thicket in the swamp. He went and greeted her. But she said no word, sitting nested among the greenwood with passionate, proud silence, until he had sued long for peace; then in sudden new friendship she had

GO ON TO THE NEXT PAGE

taken his hand and led him through the swamp, showing him all the beauty of her swamp-world—great shadowy oaks and limpid pools, lone, naked trees and sweet flowers; the whispering and flitting of wild things, and the winging of furtive birds. She had dropped the impish mischief of her way, and up from beneath it rose a wistful, visionary tenderness; a mighty half-confessed, half-concealed, striving for unknown things. He seemed to have found a new friend.

34. Which word could best replace the word "fixed" in paragraph 6?

   A.   corrected
   B.   rebuilt
   C.   prepared
   D.   concentrated

35. Based on the details in the story, what can readers tell about Bles?

   A.   He lives in the swamp near Zora's house.
   B.   He feels superior to Zora because of her wild, uneducated ways.
   C.   He has a wild imagination, which causes him to be afraid of the swamp.
   D.   He feels the need to hide his feelings from Zora.

36. Write the letter for each word that describes Bles into the character web.

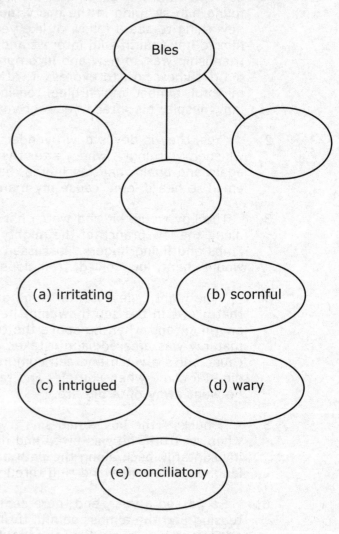

(a) irritating

(b) scornful

(c) intrigued

(d) wary

(e) conciliatory

GO ON TO THE NEXT PAGE

37. Why does the narrator describe Zora's storytelling as "almost painful" (paragraph 6)?

    A. to show that Zora chooses her words deliberately to hurt Bles

    B. to convey how intensely Bles's attention has been captured by the stories

    C. to suggest that Bles is pained because Zora doesn't return his affections

    D. to indicate that Zora's stories are so frightening that Bles is afraid to hear any more of them

38. In paragraph 5, the author states: "Then her low birdlike laughter would rise and ring through the trees." For what purpose did the author use this sentence instead of simply stating that Zora laughed at Bles?

    A. for effect, by suggesting that the volume of her laugh disturbed the surrounding animals

    B. to bring the reader back to the forest setting after a brief narrative departure

    C. to further enhance the metaphor of Zora as a wild creature

    D. to foreshadow that supernatural events will occur in the woods

39. What was Zora's aim in telling Bles about the "devils" in the swamp?

    A. She wanted to warn him about the dangers of the swamp.

    B. She wanted to confide in Bles about her frightening visions.

    C. She wanted to feel superior by exposing his fears about the swamp.

    D. She wanted to form a connection with him.

40. Which word best describes Zora's attitude toward other children in paragraph 1?

    A. ignorant

    B. fearful

    C. welcoming

    D. puzzled

41. Read the following sentence from paragraph 6:

> But she said no word, sitting nested among the greenwood with passionate, proud silence, until he had sued long for peace;

How does this sentence represent a transformation of character?

    A. It highlights a contrast to Zora's talkative behavior described in the preceding paragraphs.

    B. It shows that Bles has matured enough to want to end the fighting between them.

    C. It reveals Zora's primary character traits of passion and pride for the first time.

    D. It emphasizes Zora's connection to nature by describing her physical attitude as "nested."

GO ON TO THE NEXT PAGE

Questions 42 through 49 refer to the following excerpt.

Excerpt from
"Passive Resistance," from *Indian Home Rule*
by Mohandas K. Gandhi

1   Passive resistance is a method of securing rights by personal suffering; it is the reverse of resistance by arms. When I refuse to do a thing that is repugnant to my conscience, I use soul-force. For instance, the government of the day has passed a law which is applicable to me: I do not like it, if, by using violence, I force the government to repeal the law, I am employing what may be termed body-force. If I do not obey the law and accept the penalty for its breach, I use soul-force. It involves sacrifice of self.

2   Everybody admits that sacrifice of self is infinitely superior to sacrifice of others. Moreover, if this kind of force is used in a cause that is unjust, only the person using it suffers. He does not make others suffer for his mistakes. Men have before now done many things which were subsequently found to have been wrong. No man can claim to be absolutely in the right, or that a particular thing is wrong, because he thinks so, but it is wrong for him so long as that is his deliberate judgment. It is, therefore, meet that he should not do that which he knows to be wrong, and suffer the consequence whatever it may be. This is the key to the use of soul-force.

3   We simply want to find out what is right, and to act accordingly. The real meaning of the statement that we are a law-abiding nation is that we are passive resisters. When we do not like certain laws, we do not break the heads of law-givers, but we suffer and do not submit to the laws. That we should obey laws whether good or bad is a new-fangled notion. There was no such thing in former days. The people disregarded those laws they did not like, and suffered the penalties for their breach. It is contrary to our manhood, if we obey laws repugnant to our conscience. Such teaching is opposed to religion and means slavery. If the government were to ask us to go about without any clothing, should we do so? If I were a passive resister, I would say to them that I would have nothing to do with their law. But we have so forgotten ourselves and become so compliant, that we do not mind any degrading law.

4   A man who has realized his manhood, who fears only God, will fear no one else. Man-made laws are not necessarily binding on him. Even the government does not expect any such thing from us. They do not say: "You must do such and such a thing," but they say: "If you do not do it, we will punish you." We are sunk so low, that we fancy that it is our duty and our religion to do what the law lays down. If man will only realize that it is

GO ON TO THE NEXT PAGE

unmanly to obey laws that are unjust, no man's tyranny will enslave him. This is the key to self-rule or home-rule.

5   It is a superstition and an ungodly thing to believe that an act of a majority binds a minority. Many examples can be given in which acts of majorities will be found to have been wrong, and those of minorities to have been right. All reforms owe their origin to the initiation of minorities in opposition to majorities. If among a band of robbers, a knowledge of robbing is obligatory, is a pious man to accept the obligation? So long as the superstition that men should obey unjust laws exists, so long will their slavery exist. And a passive resister alone can remove such a superstition.

6   To use brute-force, to use gun-powder is contrary to passive resistance; for it means that we want our opponent to do by force—that which we desire but he does not. And, if such a use of force is justifiable, surely he is entitled to do likewise by us. And so we should never come to an agreement. We may simply fancy, like the blind horse moving in a circle round a mill, that we are making progress. Those who believe that they are not bound to obey laws which are repugnant to their conscience have only the remedy of passive resistance open to them. Any other must lead to disaster.

42. Why does the author use the comparison "blind horse moving in a circle round a mill" (paragraph 6)?

A. to illustrate that people should not obey unjust laws
B. to show that progress only comes with focused effort
C. to show that, without perspective, opponents cannot reconcile
D. to show the futility of an endless series of retaliations between opponents

43. Which of the following sentences from the passage exemplifies what the author means by an unjust law?

A. If the government were to ask us to go about without any clothing, should we do so?
B. But we have so forgotten ourselves and become so compliant, that we do not mind any degrading law.
C. Many examples can be given in which acts of majorities will be found to have been wrong, and those of minorities to have been right.
D. They do not say: "You must do such and such a thing," but they say: "If you do not do it, we will punish you."

GO ON TO THE NEXT PAGE

44. Write the letters of the descriptions that apply to each concept under the correct term on the chart.

Soul-force	Body-force

(a) Forcing the government to repeal a law by using violence

(b) Suffering consequences for refraining from wrong actions

(c) We shouldn't obey unjust laws.

(d) Only the person using it suffers.

(e) Leads to escalating mutual aggression justified by opponent's use of force

(f) We simply want to find out what is right.

45. Which claim by the author has the weakest support in the passage?

   A.   Everybody admits that sacrifice of self is infinitely superior to sacrifice of others.
   B.   That we should obey laws whether good or bad is a new-fangled notion.
   C.   It is a superstition and an ungodly thing to believe that an act of a majority binds a minority.
   D.   Such teaching is opposed to religion and means slavery.

46. Which of the following expresses the central theme of the passage?

   A.   Might makes right.
   B.   To thine own self be true.
   C.   If at first you don't succeed, try again.
   D.   The majority must rule.

47. Who is the author's intended audience?

   A.   the majority group in power that is oppressing less privileged people
   B.   the makers of the unjust laws in his country
   C.   the minority group representatives who want to change the social order
   D.   the makers and sellers of guns who profit from the use of violence

48. Suppose the author observed two children fighting over the same toy, and hitting each other. Based on the passage, what would be a likely course of action for the author?

   A.   Be passive and do nothing, believing that the children need to work it out for themselves.
   B.   Speak to them about how fighting wastes their time and doesn't give them what they want.
   C.   Call the children's parents so that the children can receive consequences from the proper authorities.
   D.   Physically separate the children, take the toy away, and order them both to go home.

49. Based on the use of this idea in the passage, what does the author consider the central feature of "manhood" (paragraph 3)?

   A.   personal integrity
   B.   physical strength
   C.   experience and wisdom
   D.   expression of authority

GO ON TO THE NEXT PAGE

50. The passage below is incomplete. For each "Select" option, choose the option that correctly completes the sentence. For this practice test, circle your selection.

The Honorable Richard Trotter
Chair, Ogdenville County Board

Dear Councilman Trotter,

I write to you with pleasure to endorse Mr. Shukla for the position of Ogdenville's Human Services Coordinator. For the past 8 years, Mr. Shukla has worked on various projects at different levels of hierarchy in my branch of the city administration. If praise is the measure of success,

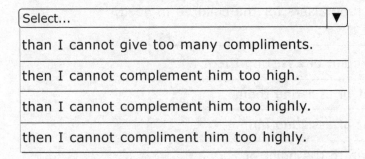

Select... ▼
than I cannot give too many compliments.
then I cannot complement him too high.
than I cannot complement him too highly.
then I cannot compliment him too highly.

He is one of the most dedicated employees in our department and he researches all aspects of a project so that there will be no loose ends upon completion. As you know, Ogdenville experienced a recent growth spurt, which almost doubled the population of the city in the space of 18 months.

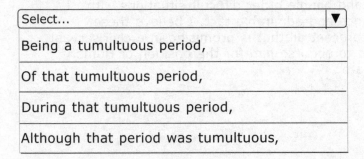

Select... ▼
Being a tumultuous period,
Of that tumultuous period,
During that tumultuous period,
Although that period was tumultuous,

Mr. Shukla tirelessly kept the files on needy populations current so there would be no delays in getting services to needy families.

Mr. Shukla brings excellent credentials to any civic service position. He holds an MA degree in Political Science from Actreaus University, has assisted the noted social work activist Ms. Sandra Diaz in the Family Resources Outreach Center

GO ON TO THE NEXT PAGE

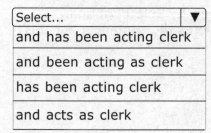

since her untimely death earlier

this year. Mr. Shukla has been a resident of Ogdenville from birth and has raised his family here.

Mr. Shukla's compassion and openheartedness are very inspiring. His first summer after college, he spent time in a historically underserved neighborhood and donated valuable hours organizing party fundraisers for the children in need,

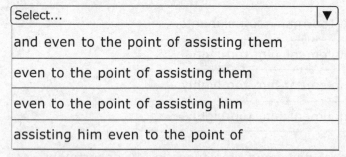

with funds from his own pocket. He also offered employment guidance to help the older ones obtain better local jobs.

I can personally verify that Mr. Shukla is an honest, hard-working leader who deserves this position. I have seen him resolve conflicts and handle other difficult situations with remarkable patience and admirable tact. I believe these characteristics represent all that is promising in a civil servant, and I am pleased to endorse him for the position of Human Services Coordinator.

Sincerely,

Edwina McGraw
Director, Family Service Division
Ogdenville Health and Resources Department

END OF TEST

Mathematical Reasoning

Welcome!

Here is some information that you need to know before you start this test:

- You should not spend too much time on a question if you are not certain of the answer; answer it the best you can, and go on to the next question.
- If you are not certain of the answer to a question, you can mark your answer for review and come back to it later.
- You have **115 minutes** to complete this test.
- This test has two parts.
- When you finish Part 1, you may review those questions.
- You may not go back to Part 1 once you have finished your review.
- You may not use a calculator in Part 1. You may use a calculator in Part 2.

Turn the page to begin.

GO ON TO THE NEXT PAGE

Mathematical Reasoning, Part 1

Mathematics Formula Sheet

Area of a:

square	$A = s^2$
rectangle	$A = lw$
parallelogram	$A = bh$
triangle	$A = \frac{1}{2}bh$
trapezoid	$A = \frac{1}{2}h(b_1 + b_2)$
circle	$A = \pi r^2$

Perimeter of a:

square	$P = 4s$
rectangle	$P = 2l + 2w$
triangle	$P = s_1 + s_2 + s_3$
Circumference of a circle	$C = 2\pi r$ OR $C = \pi d$; $\pi \approx 3.14$

Surface Area and Volume of a:

rectangular prism	$SA = 2lw + 2lh + 2wh$	$V = lwh$
right prism	$SA = ph + 2B$	$V = Bh$
cylinder	$SA = 2\pi rh + 2\pi r^2$	$V = \pi r^2 h$
pyramid	$SA = \frac{1}{2}ps + B$	$V = \frac{1}{3}Bh$
cone	$SA = \pi rs + \pi r^2$	$V = \frac{1}{3}\pi r^2 h$
sphere	$SA = 4\pi r^2$	$V = \frac{4}{3}\pi r^3$

(p = perimeter of base B; $\pi \approx 3.14$)

Data

mean	mean is equal to the total of the values of a data set, divided by the number of elements in the data set
median	median is the middle value in an odd number of ordered values of a data set, or the mean of the two middle values in an even number of ordered values in a data set

Algebra

slope of a line	$m = \dfrac{y_2 - y_1}{x_2 - x_1}$
slope-intercept form of the equation of a line	$y = mx + b$
point-slope form of the equation of a line	$y - y_1 = m(x - x_1)$
standard form of a quadratic equation	$y = ax^2 + bx + c$
quadratic formula	$x = \dfrac{-b \pm \sqrt{b^2 - 4ac}}{2a}$
Pythagorean Theorem	$a^2 + b^2 = c^2$
simple interest	$I = prt$ (I = interest, p = principal, r = rate, t = time)
distance formula	$d = rt$
total cost	total cost = (number of units) × (price per unit)

GO ON TO THE NEXT PAGE

Mathematical Reasoning, Part 1

You may NOT use a calculator in Part 1.

<u>Question 1</u> refers to the following number line.

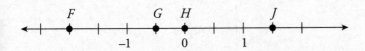

1. Which point on the number line has the greatest absolute value?

   A.　F
   B.　G
   C.　H
   D.　J

2. A list of numbers is shown from least to greatest.

   $\frac{1}{5}$　　$\frac{1}{3}$　　$\frac{1}{2}$　　☐　　$\frac{4}{5}$

   Select the correct number and write it in the box.

   | $\frac{1}{6}$ | $\frac{3}{4}$ | $\frac{2}{5}$ |

   | $\frac{5}{6}$ | $\frac{5}{4}$ |

3. Simplify.

   $$(-3)^2 - \sqrt{9}$$

   A.　−12
   B.　0
   C.　6
   D.　12

4. Which of the following is equivalent to the expression 100 × 27?

   A.　100 × 20 × 7
   B.　10 × 10 × 20 × 7
   C.　10 × 10 × 3 × 9
   D.　10 × 5 × 3 × 9

5. Simplify.

   $$2^{12} \times 2^2$$

   A.　2^6
   B.　2^{10}
   C.　2^{14}
   D.　2^{24}

GO ON TO THE NEXT PAGE

Mathematical Reasoning, Part 2

You MAY use a calculator in Part 2.

Question 6 refers to the following equation.

$$C = 3x + 7$$

6. What is the value of C when $x = \frac{1}{2}$?

   A. $\frac{17}{2}$

   B. $\frac{21}{2}$

   C. 12

   D. 13

Question 7 refers to the following scatter plot, which shows a group of students' heights and shoe sizes.

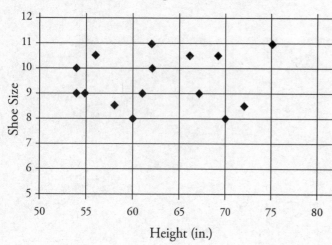

Students' Heights and Shoe Sizes

7. As the students' heights increase, their shoe sizes

   | Select... ▼ |.
   |-------------|
   | generally increase |
   | generally decrease |
   | show no relationship to their heights |

Question 8 refers to the following right triangle.

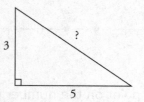

8. What is the length of the missing side?

   A. 4

   B. 5

   C. $\sqrt{34}$

   D. 34

9. Multiply.

   $$(3.0 \times 10^{12})(2.0 \times 10^{8})$$

   A. 5.0×10^{20}
   B. 5.0×10^{96}
   C. 6.0×10^{20}
   D. 6.0×10^{96}

10. Miguel has twelve hours off from work in which he plans to relax. He decides he will spend the time watching movies, which are 1.5 hours each, and playing computer games, which take 45 minutes each. Which inequality represents this situation in terms of m, the number of movies, and g, the number of computer games?

    A. $1.5m + 0.75g \le 12$
    B. $0.75m + 1.5g \le 12$
    C. $1.5m + 0.75g \ge 12$
    D. $0.75m + 1.5g \ge 12$

GO ON TO THE NEXT PAGE

| For more free content, visit <u>PrincetonReview.com</u>

Question 11 refers to the following rectangle.

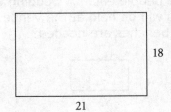

21

18

11. Find the area and perimeter of the rectangle and write them in the boxes from the options provided.

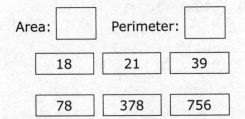

Area: [ ]   Perimeter: [ ]

| 18 | 21 | 39 |

| 78 | 378 | 756 |

12. The total cost of a snow cone with toppings can be represented by the equation $C = 1.75 + .1t$, where C is the total cost of the snow cone, in dollars, and t is the number of toppings. How many toppings did a customer order if the total cost of the order was $2.05?

A. 0
B. 1
C. 2
D. 3

13. Line k has a slope of 5 and passes through the point $(-2, 1)$. What is the equation of line k?

A. $y = 5x + 11$
B. $y = x - 2$
C. $y = 5x + 9$
D. $y = 5x + 1$

14. A teacher is making ribbons for his students to wear during an assembly. He plans to use 8 inches of ribbon for each of his 94 students. The ribbon is sold in spools of 4 yards each. How many spools of ribbon must the teacher purchase?

Note: 1 yard = 36 inches

A. 3
B. 4
C. 5
D. 6

GO ON TO THE NEXT PAGE

Question 15 refers to the following graph of a function.

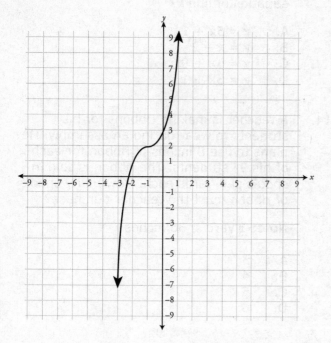

16. At a certain venue, benches can hold twelve people each. A wedding with 98 guests will be held at the venue. How many benches are needed?

17. Multiply.

$$(5x + 1)(2x - 1)$$

A. $10x^2 - 4x - 1$
B. $10x^2 - 3x - 2$
C. $10x^2 + 7x - 1$
D. $10x^2 - 3x - 1$

15. Where $x > -1$, the function is

Select... ▼
increasing
decreasing
constant

. Where $x < -1$, the

function is
Select... ▼
increasing
decreasing
constant

.

GO ON TO THE NEXT PAGE

18. Which of the following is the graph of
$y = 3x - 1$?

A.

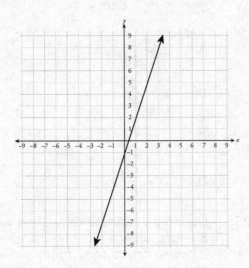

C.

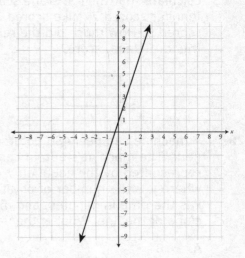

B.

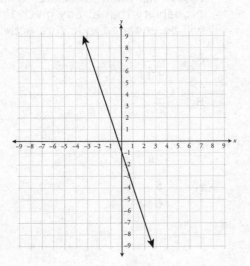

D.

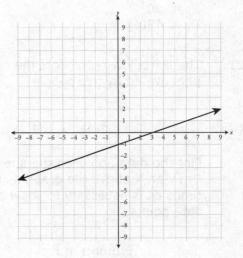

GO ON TO THE NEXT PAGE

19. A group of four friends compares their scores on a personality quiz. They calculate that their average score is 6. Jennifer scored 7, Mike scored 3, and Alec scored 9. How much did the remaining friend, Selena, score?

20. A machine can peel 480 potatoes per hour. The machine's output can be represented by the equation $y = mx$, where y is the number of potatoes peeled, x is the time in <u>minutes</u>, and m is the slope of the line. What is the value of m?

   A. 8
   B. 40
   C. 80
   D. 480

21. The list below represents the number of pets owned by five people.

   4, 0, 1, 1, 2

   Plot the data above on the line graph. Draw an X above the graph as many times as is necessary to show all the data points.

   Number of Pets

   0 1 2 3 4

22. Solve the equation for a.

   $$6ab = \frac{2}{3}$$

   A. $a = \dfrac{2}{3b}$

   B. $a = \dfrac{1}{9b}$

   C. $a = \dfrac{2b}{3}$

   D. $a = \dfrac{9}{b}$

23. During an average day, Chris works for 8 hours, sleeps for 9 hours, eats for 2 hours, drives for 1 hour, and spends the rest of his time on leisure. What is the probability that at any given time Chris will be engaged in leisure activities?

   A. $\dfrac{1}{24}$

   B. $\dfrac{1}{6}$

   C. $\dfrac{5}{24}$

   D. $\dfrac{5}{6}$

GO ON TO THE NEXT PAGE

Question 24 refers to the following scale drawing.

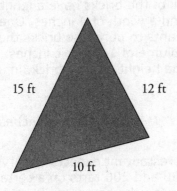

15 ft   12 ft

10 ft

Actual mural

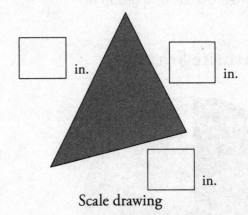

in.

in.

in.

Scale drawing

24. An artist made a scale drawing of a planned triangular mural using a scale of 2 inches = 1 foot. The full-size mural will be 15 feet by 12 feet by 10 feet. Find the side lengths of the artist's scale drawing, and mark them in the provided boxes.

| 2.5 | 5 | 5.5 | 6 |

| 7 | 7.5 | 10 | 20 |

| 24 | 30 |

25. Solve the equation for x.

$$x^2 - 6x - 11 = 4x$$

A. $x = 11$ or $x = 1$
B. $x = 11$ or $x = -1$
C. $x = -11$ or $x = -1$
D. $x = -11$ or $x = 1$

26. What is the relationship between the lines $y = 3x - 2$ and $-9x + 3y = 4$?

A. They are perpendicular.
B. They are the same line.
C. They are parallel.
D. They intersect at one point but are not perpendicular.

27. Solve for x.

$$10x - 2(3x - 1) = 5x$$

$x = $ ⬚

GO ON TO THE NEXT PAGE

Question 28 refers to the chart below, which shows the favorite seasons of a group of 325 students.

Favorite Season

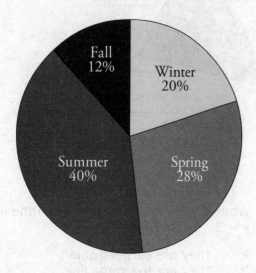

28. How many students liked fall or spring best?

    A. 39
    B. 40
    C. 91
    D. 130

29. A factory produces bricks of varying sizes. All of the bricks have a length of 8 inches and a width of 4 inches. One company wants to purchase bricks that have a volume of 160 cubic inches. What will be the height of each brick, in inches?

    [   ] inches

30. A restaurant expects to serve between 180 and 200 tarts on a certain evening. So far, the pastry chef has made 76 tarts. She solves the inequality $180 \leq 76 + t \leq 200$ to determine the number of additional tarts, t, she needs to make. What is the solution to the inequality?

    A. $104 \leq t \leq 276$
    B. $104 \leq t \leq 124$
    C. $256 \leq t \leq 276$
    D. $180 \leq t \leq 200$

31. Line n passes through the points $(0, 0)$ and $(12, 3)$. What is the equation of line n?

    A. $y = \dfrac{1}{4}x + 2$

    B. $y = x$

    C. $y = \dfrac{1}{4}x$

    D. $y = 4x$

GO ON TO THE NEXT PAGE

Mathematical Reasoning, Part 2

Question 32 refers to the following function.

$$g(x) = \frac{x}{2} + 1$$

32. Find $g(x)$ for the provided x values and write the answers in the appropriate boxes.

$$g\left(\frac{1}{2}\right) = \boxed{}$$

$$g(4) = \boxed{}$$

$$g(10) = \boxed{}$$

$\frac{1}{4}$	1	$\frac{5}{4}$	3

6	10	11

33. On Saturday, a flower shop sold 120 flowers, 80 of which were roses. The rest were tulips. What was the ratio of roses to tulips sold on Saturday?

 A. 1:2
 B. 2:3
 C. 3:2
 D. 2:1

34. Which of the following correctly represents the expression *five less than two times a number*?

 A. 2x – 5
 B. 5 – 2
 C. 5x – 2
 D. 2x + 5

Question 35 refers to the following inequality.

$$2x < 6$$

35. Which of the following represents the solution to the inequality?

 A.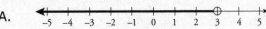

 B.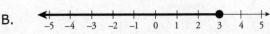

 C.

 D.

36. At the beginning of 2015, Nyema was 143 centimeters tall. After one year, she had grown 2% taller. The next year, she grew another 1% taller. To the nearest hundredth, what was Nyema's height at the beginning of 2017?

 A. 4.29 cm
 B. 147.29 cm
 C. 147.32 cm
 D. 188.76 cm

37. A circle has a diameter of 12. What is its area?

 A. 6π
 B. 12π
 C. 36π
 D. 144π

38. Casey has a $10,000 interest-free student loan. He plans to pay $50 every week until the loan is paid off. Which of the following expressions represents the amount of the loan remaining after w weeks?

 A. 10,000 + 50w
 B. 10,000w – 50
 C. 10,000 – 50w
 D. 10,000w + 50

GO ON TO THE NEXT PAGE

Question 39 refers to the following graph.

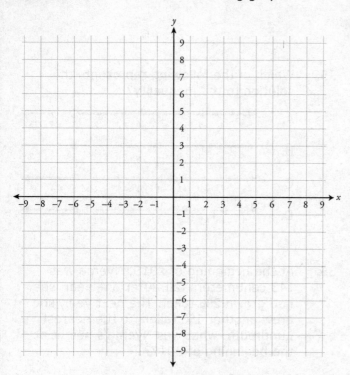

Question 40 refers to the following equation and graph.

Line A: $y = \dfrac{1}{2}x$

Line B (shown on the graph below)

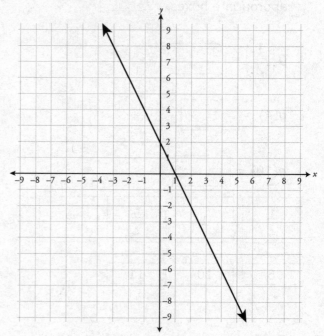

39.   Plot points A, B, C, and D on the graph.

A (−6, 1); B (0, 5); C (3, −3); D (−1, −4)

40.   The slope of line A is [Select... ▼]
       | less than |
       | greater than |
       | equal to |

the slope of line B. The *y*-intercept of

line A is [Select... ▼] the *y*-intercept
       | less than |
       | greater than |
       | equal to |

of line B.

GO ON TO THE NEXT PAGE

41. On a vacation, Michael has packed 6 shirts, 3 pairs of shorts, and 2 pairs of shoes. How many different outfit combinations consisting of one shirt, one pair of shorts, and one pair of shoes can Michael make?

   A. 3
   B. 11
   C. 18
   D. 36

Question 42 refers to the following graph of a function.

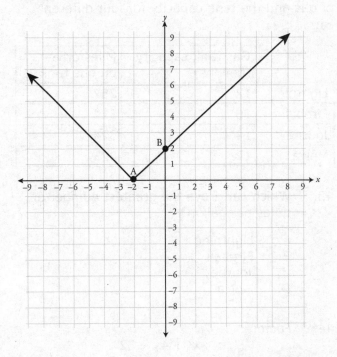

42. Write the correct options from the list below into the boxes provided.

   Point A is the [   ].

   Point B is the [   ].

   | y-intercept | midpoint | slope |
   | minimum | maximum | range |

GO ON TO THE NEXT PAGE

<u>Question 43</u> refers to the following table, which shows the number of miles driven on a full tank of gas and the tank capacity for four different cars.

	Gas tank capacity (gallons)	Miles driven on one tank
Lightning	12	287
Fireball	16	312
Journey	14	324
Metra	12	223

43. Which car drove the greatest number of miles per gallon?

    A. Lightning
    B. Fireball
    C. Journey
    D. Metra

44. Factor.
$$x^2 + 4x - 32$$

    A. $(x + 4)(x - 8)$
    B. $(x - 16)(x + 2)$
    C. $(x + 16)(x - 2)$
    D. $(x - 4)(x + 8)$

45. A test has a total of 30 questions, some worth two points, and others worth three points. The total number of points on the test is 81. How many three-point questions are on the test?

46. Subtract.
$$\left(3x^2 - 4x + \frac{1}{2}\right) - (8x^2 + x - 2)$$

    A. $11x^2 - 5x + \dfrac{5}{2}$

    B. $-5x^2 - 5x + \dfrac{5}{2}$

    C. $11x^2 - 3x - \dfrac{3}{2}$

    D. $-5x^2 - 5x - \dfrac{3}{2}$

END OF TEST

Social Studies

Welcome!

Here is some information that you need to know before you start this test:

- You should not spend too much time on a question if you are not certain of the answer; answer it the best you can, and go on to the next question.
- If you are not certain of the answer to a question, you can mark your answer for review and come back to it later.
- You have **70 minutes** to complete this test.

Turn the page to begin.

GO ON TO THE NEXT PAGE

Questions 1 through 3 refer to the following quote.

> "We will direct every resource at our command—every means of diplomacy, every tool of intelligence, every instrument of law enforcement, every financial influence, and every necessary weapon of war—to the destruction and to the defeat of the global terror network…"[W]e will pursue nations that provide aid or safe haven to terrorism…Every nation in every region now has a decision to make: Either you are with us or you are with the terrorists."
>
> –President George W. Bush, September 20, 2001

1. The above speech was most likely given directly after

   A. the Persian Gulf War.
   B. the Iraq War.
   C. the attack on the Twin Towers and Pentagon buildings.
   D. the terrorist attack on the American embassy in Benghazi, Libya.

2. Which sentiment is closest to those expressed by President Bush in the above speech?

   A. Nations that commit acts of war on American soil will be met with equal counter-force.
   B. Even nations that do not threaten the United States directly will be met with military force.
   C. Diplomacy is preferable to war in the fight against terrorism.
   D. A nation may provide financial aid to terrorists as long as it does not provide them safe haven within the nation's borders.

3. After the speech given by President Bush, the United States invaded and occupied

   A. Afghanistan.
   B. Serbia.
   C. Saudi Arabia.
   D. Pakistan.

4. A new product suddenly becomes very popular, and its initial price is quite high. Most economists would say that

   A. because demand for the product is low, the supply of that product will also be low.
   B. because demand for the product is high, the price will decrease.
   C. because demand for the product is high, producers will produce more of it.
   D. because demand for the product is low, the price will decrease.

GO ON TO THE NEXT PAGE

Social Studies

Questions 5 and 6 refer to the following graph.

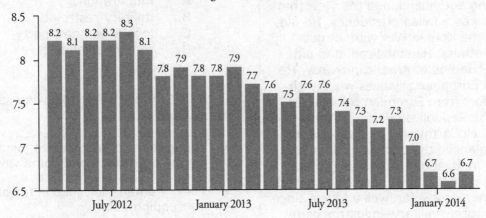

United States Unemployment Rate
Percentage of the Labor Force

Source: U.S. Bureau of Labor Statistics

5. According to the graph, the difference in the United States unemployment rate from January 2013 to January 2014 was

   [ ] percentage points.

6. In which of the following months was the unemployment rate 7.5%?

   A. January 2013
   B. May 2013
   C. June 2013
   D. July 2013

GO ON TO THE NEXT PAGE

Questions 7 and 8 refer to the following excerpt from an article by John Lewis Gaddis about the Presidency of Dwight D. Eisenhower.

"Historians long ago abandoned the view that Eisenhower's was a failed presidency. He did, after all, end the Korean War without getting into any others. He stabilized, and did not escalate, the Soviet-American rivalry. He strengthened European alliances while withdrawing support from European colonialism. He rescued the Republican Party from isolationism and McCarthyism. He maintained prosperity, balanced the budget, promoted technological innovation, facilitated (if reluctantly) the civil rights movement and warned, in the most memorable farewell address since Washington's, of a "military–industrial complex" that could endanger the nation's liberties. Not until Reagan would another president leave office with so strong a sense of having accomplished what he set out to do."

7. Write the letter(s) of the word or words that best describe the characteristics of President Eisenhower's administration in the box below.

(a) protectionism

(b) isolationism

(c) diplomacy

(d) fiscal responsibility

8. It can be inferred from Gaddis's quote that a successful presidency includes all of the following EXCEPT

A. moderation.
B. military restraint.
C. loyalty to one's party.
D. foreign alliances.

Question 9 refers to the following list of facts about World War II.

- Young men volunteered to join the military by the thousands and some were drafted.

- Many women took jobs in factories to build war equipment.

- A larger percentage of factory production was shipped to countries overseas.

- The government limited the amount of certain goods that could be purchased ("rationing").

9. Some economists claim that America's involvement in World War II brought it out of the Great Depression. Is this true?

A. Yes, because many people who had previously been unemployed were given jobs.
B. Yes, because men who joined the military could earn more than they could by working for a private company.
C. No, because shipping products overseas is harmful to the United States economy as a whole.
D. No, because rationing led to starvation and job loss.

GO ON TO THE NEXT PAGE

Questions 10 through 12 refer to the following map of regions recognized by the U.S. Environmental Protection Agency (EPA), which is a federal regulatory agency that was created for the purpose of protecting human health and the environment.

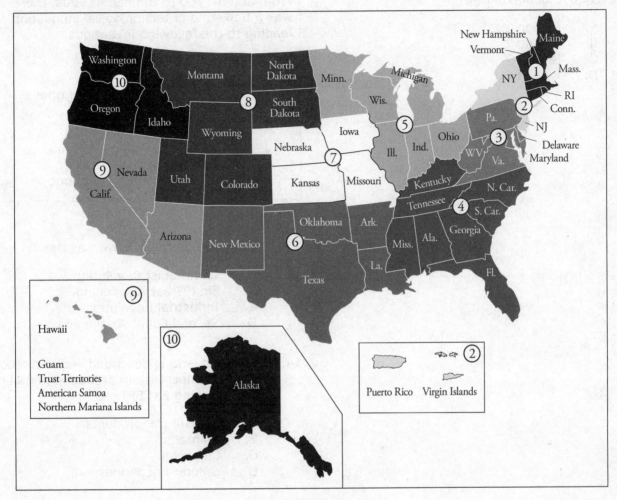

The EPA Regions

10. In which of the following regions would the EPA most frequently regulate timber rights due to concerns regarding endangered animal species?

    A. Region 2
    B. Region 6
    C. Region 7
    D. Region 10

11. In which of the following regions would the EPA be most likely to respond to frequent concerns regarding industrial air pollution?

    A. Regions 1 and 2
    B. Regions 2 and 5
    C. Regions 4 and 7
    D. Regions 8 and 10

GO ON TO THE NEXT PAGE

12. In which of the following regions would the EPA be most likely to regulate water pollution related to pesticide use in industrial agriculture?

    A. Region 1
    B. Region 2
    C. Region 7
    D. Region 8

Questions 13 and 14 refer to the following information.

From about 1760 to the early 1900s, there was a flowering of technological innovation leading to the following inventions:

- The steam engine

- Factory mass production of goods

- The cotton gin

- The use of electricity for light

- The invention of the telephone

13. This time period is known as the

    A. Communist Revolution.
    B. First Great Awakening.
    C. Industrial Revolution.
    D. Second Great Awakening.

14. The innovations described above directly led to the increase in production of all of the following EXCEPT

    A. agricultural products.
    B. railroads.
    C. textiles.
    D. cellular telephones.

GO ON TO THE NEXT PAGE

Question 15 refers to the following image.

15.   Many scientists believe in a piece of
        land they call Beringia, which may have
        served as a land bridge for prehistoric
        migrants. If the scientists' theory is true,
        Beringia served as a way to migrate from
        modern-day

        A.   China to Africa.
        B.   Africa to Europe.
        C.   Russia to Alaska.
        D.   Great Plains to Africa.

GO ON TO THE NEXT PAGE

<u>Questions 16 through 18</u> refer to the following sources.

Source 1:

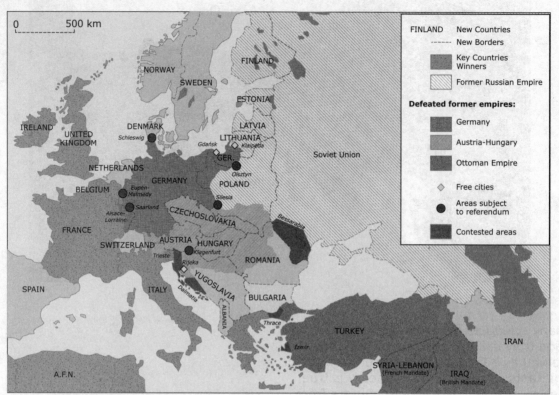

Map Reflecting Territorial Changes in Europe after World War I

Source 2:

"The 'Age of Totalitarianism' included nearly all of the infamous examples of genocide in modern history, headed by the Jewish Holocaust, but also comprising the mass murders and purges of the Communist world, other mass killings carried out by Nazi Germany and its allies, and also the Armenian Genocide of 1915. All these slaughters, it is argued here, had a common origin, the collapse of the elite structure and normal modes of government of much of central, eastern and southern Europe as a result of World War I, without which surely neither Communism nor Fascism would have existed except in the minds of unknown agitators and crackpots."

–William Rubinstein, historian

GO ON TO THE NEXT PAGE

16. Which two of the following countries were united territories immediately before World War I?

    A. Austria and Hungary
    B. Germany and the Ottoman Empire
    C. Latvia and Lithuania
    D. Norway and Sweden

17. "Totalitarianism" is a government characterized by

    A. economic prosperity.
    B. racial prejudice.
    C. a total collapse.
    D. total control.

18. All of the following countries at some time embodied the characteristics mentioned in Rubenstein's quote EXCEPT

    A. Germany.
    B. Russia.
    C. Turkey.
    D. Switzerland.

GO ON TO THE NEXT PAGE

Questions 19 and 20 refer to the following image.

The Destruction of Tea at Boston Harbor

19. In the above picture, what are the "Indians" doing on the ship?

A. throwing boxes of tea into the harbor to protest the occupation of their lands by white Bostonians
B. throwing boxes of tea into the harbor to protest the oppression of the British government
C. stealing boxes of tea from an abandoned ship
D. helping tea merchants to unload tea after a long journey across the ocean

20. In the above picture, how are the people on land reacting to the actions of the "Indians"?

A. celebrating
B. protesting
C. threatening violence
D. offering assistance

Question 21 refers to the following quote.

"We hold these truths to be self-evident, that all men are created equal, that they are endowed by their Creator with certain unalienable Rights..."

–U.S. Declaration of Independence

21. Which word could be substituted for "unalienable" without altering the meaning of the quote?

A. changeable
B. legal
C. natural
D. religious

GO ON TO THE NEXT PAGE

Social Studies

Questions 22 and 23 refer to the following source.

"To speak of popular sovereignty is to place ultimate authority in the people. There are a variety of ways in which sovereignty may be expressed. It may be immediate in the sense that the people make the law themselves, or mediated through representatives who are subject to election and recall; it may be ultimate in the sense that the people have a negative or veto over legislation, or it may be something much less dramatic. In short, popular sovereignty covers a multitude of institutional possibilities. In each case, however, popular sovereignty assumes the existence of some form of popular consent, and it is for this reason that every definition of republican government implies a theory of consent."

–Donald L. Lutz, historian

The Kansas-Nebraska Act of 1854 created the territories of Kansas and Nebraska. The initial purpose of the Kansas-Nebraska Act was to encourage more farming in the region and to eventually create a Transcontinental Railroad. The popular sovereignty clause of the law led pro- and anti-slavery elements to flood into Kansas. This surge of settlers and the result was known as "Bleeding Kansas."

22.   Why would popular sovereignty have led to a surge in pro- and anti-slavery settlers?

   A.   The settlers were seeking a more economically prosperous life.
   B.   The establishment of the Transcontinental Railroad made travel to Kansas easier.
   C.   The settlers wished to influence Kansas in matters of slavery law.
   D.   The settlers wished to start a war over slavery law.

23.   The term "Bleeding Kansas" refers to

   A.   the violent nature of the conflict between pro- and anti-slavery activists.
   B.   the loss of money resulting from political conflict in the region.
   C.   those sympathetic to the anti-slavery case, known as "bleeding hearts."
   D.   the many bloody battles fought there during the Civil War.

Question 24 refers to the following list of powerful political advocacy groups in the United States.

- American Israel Public Affairs Committee (AIPAC)—concerned with U.S. policy with Israel

- Center for Auto Safety—concerned with auto safety and quality

- Drug Policy Alliance—advocates the decriminalization of drugs

- National Rifle Association—champions the rights of gun owners

- Sierra Club—devoted to environmental causes

- U.S. Chamber of Commerce—promotes the interests of U.S. businesses

24.   "Political advocacy" is also known as

   A.   bribery.
   B.   legislating.
   C.   lobbying.
   D.   protesting.

GO ON TO THE NEXT PAGE

<u>Question 25</u> refers to the following map.

25. The map of Indiana above most likely portrays

A. treaties made between the French and English before and after the War of 1812.
B. treaties made between Indian tribes and the federal government.
C. treaties made after the Battle of Tippecanoe.
D. treaties made after the founding of Chicago.

<u>Questions 26 through 28</u> refer to the following quote.

"Antifederalists feared what Patrick Henry termed the "consolidated government" proposed by the new Constitution. They saw in Federalist hopes for commercial growth and international prestige only the lust of ambitious men for a "splendid empire" that, in the time-honored way of empires, would oppress the people with taxes, conscription, and military campaigns. Uncertain that any government over so vast a domain as the United States could be controlled by the people, Antifederalists saw in the enlarged powers of the general government only the familiar threats to the rights and liberties of the people."

–Ralph Ketchum, historian

26. The Antifederalists Ketchum refers to would have lived in which of the following time periods?

A. 1775–1800
B. 1800–1850
C. 1850–1900
D. 1900–1950

27. Antifederalists opposed "consolidated government" because they believed it promoted an increase in all of the following EXCEPT

A. commercial growth.
B. conscription.
C. taxes.
D. war.

28. Which of the following would NOT be favored by Federalists?

A. a national income tax
B. a strong federal army
C. individual liberties
D. limited federal power

GO ON TO THE NEXT PAGE

Question 29 refers to the following photograph:

Questions 31 and 32 refer to the following information.

World War I	World War II
Allied Powers: France Great Britain Italy Russia United States	Allied Powers: China France Great Britain Soviet Union (Russia) United States

31. Which of the following countries was allied with the United States in both World Wars but would later become a Cold War political opponent?

    A. France
    B. Germany
    C. Great Britain
    D. Soviet Union

32. Which of the following countries was an enemy to the Allied Powers in both World Wars but would later become a Cold War ally?

    A. China
    B. Germany
    C. Japan
    D. Soviet Union

29. These soldiers are most likely fighting in which of the following wars?

    A. Revolutionary War
    B. Civil War
    C. World War I
    D. Vietnam War

30. Which one of these foreign policy terms is NOT like the others?

    A. isolationism
    B. neutrality
    C. non-interventionism
    D. protectionism

GO ON TO THE NEXT PAGE

Questions 33 and 34 refer to the following pie chart.

Holocaust Deaths

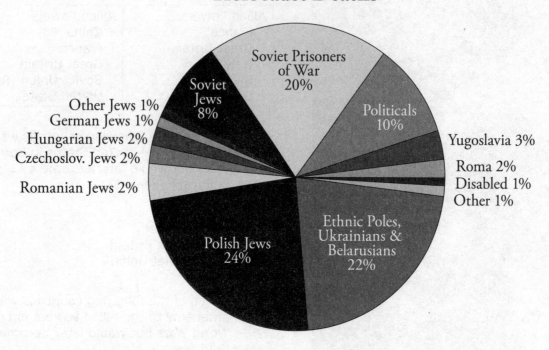

33. The chart above supports which of the following statements?

   A. Jewish people made up the majority of those killed during the Holocaust.
   B. Polish people made up the majority of those killed during the Holocaust.
   C. Soviets killed the majority of Jews during the Holocaust.
   D. More Jews from Poland were killed than Jews from all other countries combined.

34. The Holocaust occurred during which major war?

   A. Austro-Prussian War
   B. Polish-Austrian War
   C. World War I
   D. World War II

35. Suppose an economist were to make the following statement:

> "When a country's debt rises above 90% of Gross Domestic Product (GDP), it causes the growth of the economy to slow."
>
> Therefore, high debt causes slow economic growth."

Which of the following statements would best *weaken* the claim made above?

   A. The growth of a country's economy is directly correlated to its level of debt.
   B. When the growth of a country's economy slows, it causes an increase in debt.
   C. When a country's debt is below 90% of GDP, the growth of the economy can slow.
   D. Low levels of debt inevitably lead to high levels of economic growth.

END OF TEST

Science

Welcome!

Here is some information that you need to know before you start this test:

- You should not spend too much time on a question if you are not certain of the answer; answer it the best you can, and go on to the next question.
- If you are not certain of the answer to a question, you can mark your answer for review and come back to it later.
- You have **90 minutes** to complete this test.

Turn the page to begin.

GO ON TO THE NEXT PAGE

1. A [Select... ▼] occurs when the
   | lunar eclipse |
   | solar eclipse |

   Earth moves between the Moon and the Sun, resulting in a shadow cast over the Moon.

2. Which of the following correctly represents the formula for power?

   A. power = work/time
   B. power = distance/time
   C. power = momentum × speed
   D. power = mass × speed

3. Which of the following indicates the correct order of the four stages of mitosis?

   A. telophase, metaphase, prophase, anaphase
   B. anaphase, prophase, metaphase, telophase
   C. prophase, telophase, anaphase, metaphase
   D. prophase, metaphase, anaphase, telophase

GO ON TO THE NEXT PAGE

4. Write the letters of the labels below in the appropriate locations on the drawing to indicate the type of heat represented by the direction of the arrows.

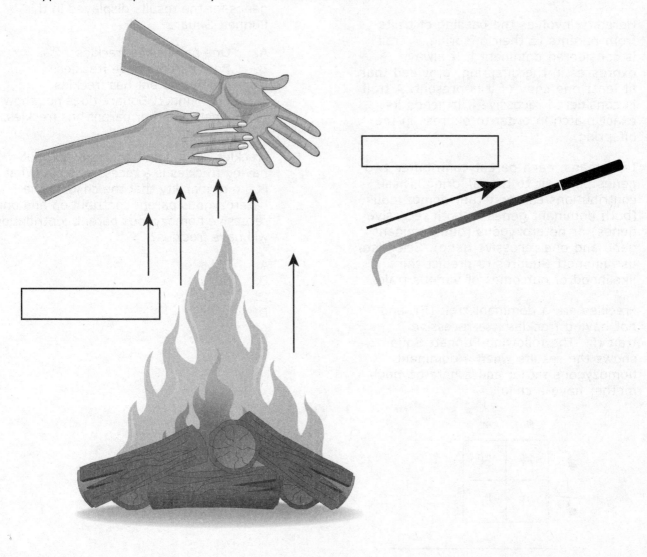

(a) convection

(b) conduction

GO ON TO THE NEXT PAGE

Questions 5 and 6 refer to the following information.

Heredity involves the passing of traits from parents to their offspring. A trait is considered dominant if it always expresses in the offspring, provided that at least one copy of it is present. A trait is considered recessive if it needs its exact match in order to express in the offspring.

In humans, each parent contributes two genes per trait to the offspring. These contributions can be either homozygous (both dominant genes or both recessive genes) or heterozygous (one dominant gene and one recessive gene). Scientists use Punnett Squares to predict the likelihood of outcomes of various traits.

Freckles are a dominant trait (F), and not having freckles is a recessive trait (f). The following Punnett Square shows the results when a dominant homozygous father and a heterozygous mother have a child.

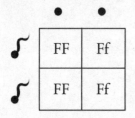

	FF	Ff
	FF	Ff

♪	sperm cell of male parent
●	egg cell of female parent
F	dominant freckles gene
f	recessive no-freckles gene

5. Which of the following is the most likely description of the parents' contributing genes for the results displayed in this Punnett Square?

A. One parent has freckles.
B. Both parents have freckles.
C. Neither parent has freckles.
D. The Punnett Square does not show whether either parent has freckles.

6. Freckles are a dominant trait, and not having freckles is a recessive trait. What is the probability that the child of one heterozygous parent contribution and one recessive homozygous parent contribution will have freckles?

A. 25%
B. 50%
C. 75%
D. 100%

GO ON TO THE NEXT PAGE

Science

Question 7 refers to the following information.

Newton's Law of Gravity states that the gravitational force that two objects exert on each other is equal to

$$F = \frac{G \times M \times m}{r^2}$$

In the equation,

F is the force of gravity;

G is a constant;

M is the mass of one of the objects;

m is the mass of the other object;

r is the distance between the centers of the objects.

7. If the mass of one object is doubled and the mass of the other object is reduced by half, the gravitational force the two objects exert on each other will

Select... ▼
increase by a factor of 4
increase by a factor of 2
remain the same
decrease by a factor of 2

Question 8 refers to the following information.

Whether a substance is classified as acidic, basic, or neutral is determined by its pH. A pH below 7 is acidic, a pH of 7 is neutral, and a pH above 7 is basic. Below is a table of common substances and their pH values.

Substance	pH
Lemon juice	2
Vinegar	3
Brown sugar	5
Coffee	5
White sugar	6
Baking soda	8
Dishwasher soap	12

8. What is the average pH of all basic substances, rounded to the nearest tenth?

A. 4.2
B. 4.8
C. 5.9
D. 10

GO ON TO THE NEXT PAGE

<u>Questions 9 and 10</u> refer to the following information.

It is estimated that in the early 20th century four sub-species of black rhinoceroses roamed the African savannas. These four sub-species comprised roughly one million animals. By the early 2000s, though, one sub-species had gone extinct, and the remaining three had a total combined population of fewer than 2,500 rhinoceroses.

The West African Black Rhinoceros was one of the three sub-species of Black Rhinoceros that survived into the early 2000s. While it had formerly roamed several countries towards the southeast region of Africa, as early as the 1980s its range had shrunk to only two countries, Cameroon and Chad. At that time, the total population was estimated to be fewer than 100 animals. By the late 1990s, it was estimated that fewer than 10 remained. Of those 10, 6 lived in total isolation, nowhere near enough to find each other, and therefore unable to mate and carry on their species.

There were many factors that contributed to the demise of the West African Black Rhinoceros. Many sports hunters sought the animals. Industrial agriculture also played a role, as humans cleared rhinoceros habitats for fields and settlements. Farmers and ranchers largely viewed the animals as pests. Others believed that the rhinoceros horn was a cure for many ailments, including cancer, which resulted in poaching. Sadly, the last West African Black Rhinoceros was seen in Cameroon in 2006. The species was officially declared extinct in 2011.

9. Which of the following can be properly inferred from the passage?

   A. Before the early 20th century, there were well over one million black rhinoceroses alive.
   B. There are only two living sub-species of black rhinoceroses.
   C. There are no more black rhinoceroses alive.
   D. Man contributed to the demise of the West African Black Rhinoceros.

10. Scientists hypothesize that powdered rhinoceros horn is not actually a cure for any human ailments. What information does this passage offer to support or refute this hypothesis?

   A. The passage provides information about what ailments powdered rhinoceros horn may cure, thus refuting the scientists' hypothesis.
   B. The passage provides no information to either support or refute the scientists' hypothesis.
   C. The passage provides information about other reasons humans killed the rhinoceroses, which supports the scientists' hypothesis.
   D. The passage provides information about other reasons humans killed the rhinoceroses, which refutes the scientists' hypothesis.

GO ON TO THE NEXT PAGE

Question 11 refers to the following information.

When an endothermic reaction takes place, the bonds between molecules are broken. This process of breaking apart molecules requires energy, so heat is absorbed from the surrounding environment. However, when an exothermic reaction takes place, bonds are created between molecules. Since molecules naturally want to stay together, this process requires far less heat than does the process of breaking bonds between molecules, so heat is actually released.

11. Based on the information above, complete the following:

When ice melts into water, bonds between molecules are [Select... ▼], which

Select...
created
broken

results in heat being [Select... ▼]

Select...
absorbed
released

[Select... ▼] reaction.

Select...
endothermic
exothermic

GO ON TO THE NEXT PAGE

Questions 12 and 13 refer to the following information.

In physics, an object's kinetic energy is the energy it possesses due to its motion. An object's potential energy is the energy it possesses by virtue of its position relative to other objects, its electric charge, stresses within the object, or other factors. Thermal energy does not have anything to do with whether an object is stationary or moving; instead, thermal energy is the energy that comes from heat, which is generated by the movement of particles within an object. The faster the particles the move, the more heat is generated.

Heat transfer occurs in three primary fashions: conduction, convection, and radiation. Conduction describes the transfer of energy between options that are physically touching each other. Convection describes the transfer of energy between an object and its environment. Radiation describes the transfer of energy via electromagnetic waves.

After driving to school, Marty notices that the brakes on his car are hot to the touch.

12. Which of the following answers gives an explanation for the temperature of the brakes?

    A.   Thermal energy was converted into kinetic energy.

    B.   Kinetic energy was converted into potential energy.

    C.   Potential energy was converted into kinetic energy.

    D.   Kinetic energy was converted into thermal energy.

13. When the brakes rub against the tire rims,

| Select... ▼ | generates heat via
| --- |
| friction |
| radiation |
| conduction |

thermal transfer. When Marty touches the brakes with his hand he fe els the

heat via

| Select... ▼ | .
| --- |
| radiation |
| conduction |
| convection |

14. Which answer provides the best explanation of this process?

$$C_6H_{12}O_6 + 6O_2 \rightarrow 6CO_2 + 6H_2O + ATP$$

    A.   Cellular respiration converts carbon, hydrogen, and oxygen into carbon dioxide, water and energy.

    B.   Cellular respiration converts glucose and oxygen into water, carbon dioxide, and energy.

    C.   Anaerobic respiration converts carbon and hydrogen into water and energy.

    D.   Anaerobic respiration converts water into carbon, hydrogen, and energy.

GO ON TO THE NEXT PAGE

Science

Questions 15 through 17 refer to the following information.

A food web is an illustration that shows which organisms prey on other organisms in an ecosystem. Lines in the illustration connect food sources to their consumers. Animals that consume exclusively plants are called herbivores, or primary consumers; animals that eat both plants and animals are called omnivores, or secondary consumers. Animals that eat only other animals are called carnivores, and are also considered secondary, tertiary, or quaternary consumers.

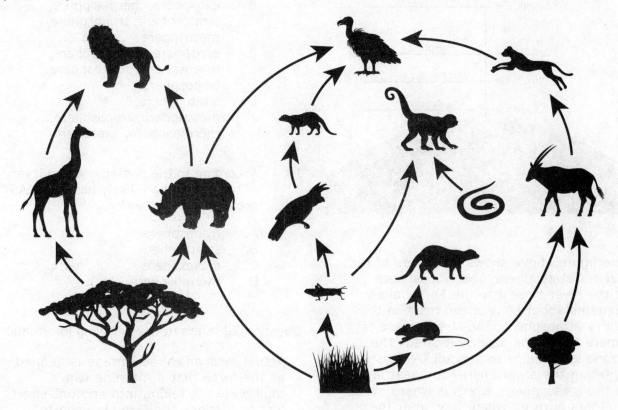

15. According to the food web, grasshoppers are

Select... ▼
carnivores
omnivores
herbivores

and monkeys are

Select... ▼
carnivores
omnivores
herbivores

.

16. According to the food web, if the rhinoceros population suddenly declined, it would likely NOT affect

A. vultures.
B. snakes.
C. lions.
D. giraffes.

17. Which organisms in the food web are secondary consumers?

A. giraffes
B. rhinoceroses
C. cheetahs
D. mice

GO ON TO THE NEXT PAGE

Science

Questions 18 and 19 refer to the following information.

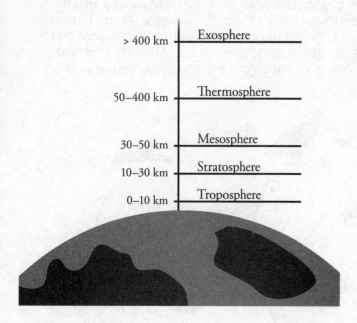

The figure above shows the layers of the Earth's atmosphere. The troposphere is the layer closest to the Earth, and contains about 80% of the mass of the entire atmosphere. The stratosphere is where the ozone layer is located. The ozone layer helps to prevent UV rays from entering the atmosphere. The next layer is the mesosphere, which is where most meteors burn up when they enter the Earth's atmosphere. The thermosphere is incredibly warm, reaching temperatures up to 1200°C. The exosphere is the outermost layer and contains mostly hydrogen and helium atoms.

18. Which of the following gives the layers of the Earth's atmosphere in the correct order from the outermost layer to the ground?

   A. stratosphere, troposphere, mesosphere, thermosphere, exosphere
   B. exosphere, thermosphere, stratosphere, troposphere, mesosphere
   C. exosphere, thermosphere, mesosphere, stratosphere, troposphere
   D. stratosphere, mesosphere, troposphere, thermosphere, exosphere

19. According to the passage, which layer of the atmosphere likely has the LEAST presence of UV rays?

   A. troposphere
   B. stratosphere
   C. mesosphere
   D. thermosphere

Question 20 refers to the following information.

Actual mechanical advantage is defined as the force that a machine can multiply while taking into account effort lost to friction. The formula used to calculate actual mechanical advantage is shown below.

$$AMA = \frac{output\ force}{input\ force}$$

20. A boulder on the side of the road requires an output force of 4000 newtons (N) to be moved. A bulldozer's engine creates 250 newtons (N) of force. What is the mechanical advantage of the bulldozer? You may use the calculator.

   A. 0.0625
   B. 16
   C. 4250
   D. 2,200,000

GO ON TO THE NEXT PAGE

Questions 21 and 22 refer to the following information.

U.S. Electricity Generation By Type (2014)

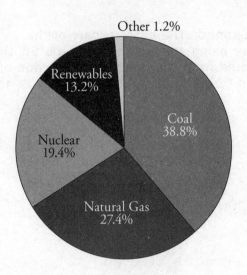

The following list indicates several sources of energy and some related advantages and disadvantages of each.

Coal

Advantages: available in abundant supply, inexpensive, generates large amounts of power

Disadvantages: dangerous work environment for miners, high negative environmental impact, emits greenhouse gases

Nuclear

Advantages: lower greenhouse emissions, inexpensive

Disadvantages: highly dangerous in the event of an accident, expensive to build power plant

Natural gas

Advantages: available in abundant supply, relatively clean

Disadvantages: high transport costs, nonrenewable, emits some pollution

21. Based on the pie chart and the information, which of the following can be inferred about the use of fuels in the United States?

A. The United States is not concerned about greenhouse emissions.

B. The United States predominantly uses an efficient, inexpensive energy source that poses danger to people involved in making the source available to the public.

C. The United States is focused on using energy sources that pose no danger to humans.

D. The United States is not concerned with finding new ways to utilize renewable sources of energy.

22. According to the pie chart, what percent of electricity came from nonrenewable sources in the United States in 2014? Type your answer in the box below. You may use a calculator.

GO ON TO THE NEXT PAGE

Question 23 refers to the following information.

The "Ring of Fire" is an area that surrounds the basin of the Pacific Ocean where a significant number of earthquake and volcanic eruptions occur. This horseshoe shape that is nearly 25,000 miles long is home to 452 volcanoes and is the source of roughly 90% of the world's earthquakes. All but three of the 25 biggest volcanic eruptions on record have occurred in the Ring of Fire.

This natural phenomenon is a direct result of plate tectonics: The eastern part of the ring resulted from the Nazca Plate and the Cocos Plate being subducted under the South American Plate. The northern portion of the ring resulted from the ongoing subduction of the Pacific Plate beneath the Aleution Islands arc. And to the west, the Pacific Plate is being subducted under the Kamchatka Peninsula arc.

23. Which of the following can be properly inferred from information presented in the map and in the passage above?

A. Volcanoes are always located toward the edge of a continent.

B. Volcanoes are equally distributed between the Eastern and Western Hemispheres.

C. Volcanoes are commonly found along the boundaries between tectonic plates.

D. The location of volcanoes is completely random across Earth.

GO ON TO THE NEXT PAGE

Science

Question 24 refers to the following graph.

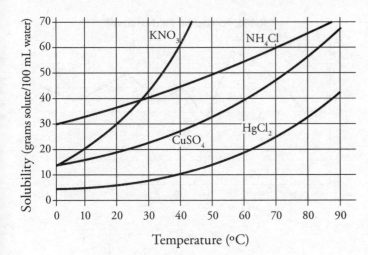

24. Which of the following can be concluded from the graph above?

    A. Solubility varies directly with temperature.
    B. At 40°C, KNO_3 and NH_4Cl have the same solubility.
    C. The solubility of $HgCl_2$ at 80°C is 20 grams solute/100mL water.
    D. There is no consistent relationship between temperature and solubility.

Question 25 refers to the following information.

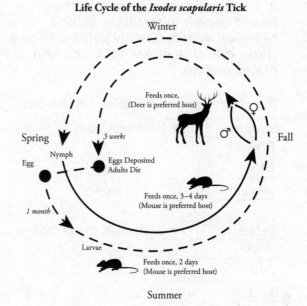

Life Cycle of the *Ixodes scapularis* Tick

25. Based on the figure above, if the deer population decreased, it would be reasonable to conclude that the tick population would [Select... ▼].

    increase

    decrease

    stay the same

GO ON TO THE NEXT PAGE

26. The central dogma of molecular biology was first presented by Francis Crick in 1956, and is an explanation of the flow of genetic information within a biological system. Simply put, the dogma states that DNA makes RNA, and RNA makes protein.

The central dogma of biology states that

Select... ▼	is made from
RNA
DNA
protein

Select... ▼	, which is made from
RNA
DNA
protein

Select... ▼	.
RNA
DNA
protein

Question 27 refers to the following graph.

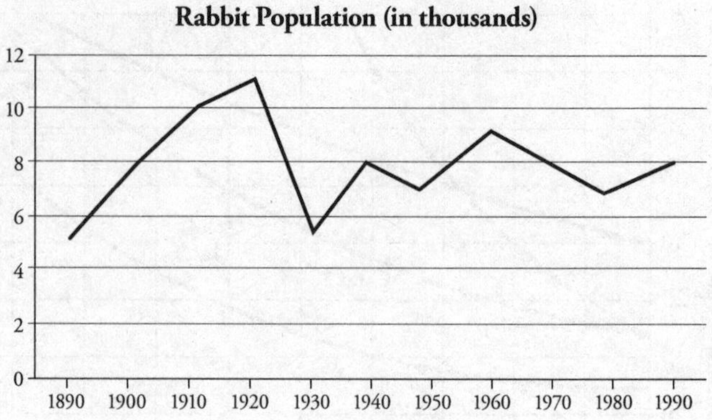

Rabbit Population (in thousands)

27. According to the graph above, what is the approximate carrying capacity, or the number of organisms an ecosystem can support, of the rabbit population?

A. 5,000
B. 7,000
C. 8,000
D. 9,000

28. The heart is part of the | Select... ▼ |
| --- |
| digestive |
| circulatory |
| respiratory |

system and the esophagus is part of the | Select... ▼ | system.
| --- |
| digestive |
| circulatory |
| respiratory |

GO ON TO THE NEXT PAGE

Science

Questions 29 and 30 refer to the following information.

Natural selection, first identified and explained by Charles Darwin, is a process in which organisms that have adapted better to their environments are more likely to survive and reproduce. It is believed that natural selection is the main driving force behind evolution. The ultimate result of evolution from natural selection is speciation, the creation of a new and distinct species.

On the other hand, artificial selection describes the targeted, intentional reproduction of individuals in a population that have specifically desirable traits. In any species that reproduces sexually, for example, two adults that both have a desirable trait are bred together.

29. Which of the following is an example of artificial selection?

    A.   Lizards with long legs can climb better to reach food and avoid floods.

    B.   Bacteria that adapt to previously fatal antibiotics and produce offspring that are also resistant to the antibiotics.

    C.   Rodents that migrated to a sandy environment changed from black to light brown to better blend in with the sand.

    D.   Dogs that are bred specifically to hunt large game.

30. Thoroughbred racehorses resulting from careful selective breeding are an example of [Select... ▼].

| natural selection |
| artificial selection |
| speciations |

Questions 31 and 32 refer to the following information.

The Law of Conservation of Energy states that energy can be neither created nor destroyed. Further, the Law of Conservation of Matter states that matter also can be neither created nor destroyed. Therefore, when a chemical change takes place, the total mass of an object stays the same.

31. When a car won't start because the battery is dead, what is the most likely explanation of what has happened to its original charge?

    A.   The charge disappeared.

    B.   The charge was converted into energy to power the car.

    C.   The charge was destroyed.

    D.   The charge leaked out of the battery.

32. When an iceberg melts, the resulting amount of water is equal to the original amount of ice. This is described by the Law of

_____

GO ON TO THE NEXT PAGE

Science

Question 33 and 34 refer to the following information.

The term "wave" is used to describe any of several different ways in which energy is transferred:

- Electromagnetic waves transfer energy via electric or magnetic field vibrations.

- Sound waves transfer energy through the vibration of air particles, or through the vibration of particles of solid matter through which sound may travel.

- Water waves transfer energy through the vibration of water particles.

Regardless of the type of wave, the greater the amplitude, or distance from the center line to the crest of the wave, the greater the energy.

33. Which of the following can be inferred from the passage?

    A.   A tsunami wave will have more energy than a wave caused by a passing thunderstorm.

    B.   Sound produced by a flute will have more energy than sound produced by a bass drum.

    C.   There are only three different kinds of waves known to man.

    D.   Tsunami waves have more energy than all other kinds of waves.

34. A sound wave with greater amplitude will [Select... ▼]

| be louder |
| travel faster |
| have a higher pitch |

than a sound wave with smaller amplitude.

Questions 35 refers to the following information.

Water Cycle

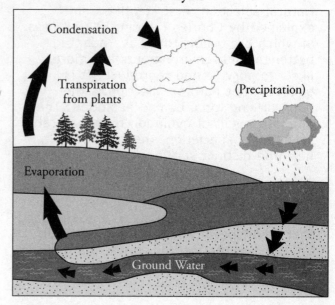

35. Select the part of the cycle that could potentially be removed from the water cycle with the least impact. Write an X on the graphic.

END OF TEST

Chapter 8
Practice Test 3:
Answers and
Explanations

REASONING THROUGH LANGUAGE ARTS

Section 1

1. **D** This question asks about the relationship between the characters, so look for clues in the text. Paragraph 4 shows Marcia's thoughts about Margaret's letter: "What troubled her most in the letter had been its outpouring of sympathy for herself." And Marcia also wonders, "Was it not kinder to allow the few who still loved him to remain ignorant of what he had become" (paragraph 3). Therefore, (D) is correct: Margaret shows sympathy for Marcia and Marcia wants to do what is kindest for Margaret. Choice (A) is incorrect because it is too strong. Although paragraph 2 states "She had never seen any of Jason's family," Margaret and Marcia are not *complete* strangers to each other, since they have exchanged letters. Because paragraph 2 notes that Margaret has not met Jason's family, (B) is also incorrect. Finally, (C) is incorrect, because while they do write letters to each other, Marcia specifically does *not* confide in Margaret: "The knowledge that she had not been entirely frank had brought with it an uncomfortable sense of guilt" (paragraph 4). The correct answer is (D).

2. **B** This language use item requires test takers to determine which word could best replace the word "artlessly" in paragraph 6, so examine how the word is used in context. The sentence states "she suddenly realized that to keep up the fraud so artlessly begun was going to be exceedingly difficult." This is followed by the line "She was not a clever dissembler." To "dissemble" means to pretend, so Marcia is not good at pretending. Thus, she is not particularly skilled at the deception she has created and anticipates that keeping it up will be "difficult." The best answer is (B), "clumsily," since Marcia is unskilled at deception. Choice (A) is incorrect since Marcia consciously made the choice to withhold information: "Was it not kinder to allow the few who still loved him to remain ignorant of what he had become" (paragraph 3). This line also proves that (D) is incorrect, because Marcia chooses the deception from emotional, not pragmatic, reasons. Finally, (C) is wrong because a fraud is a deception, so there is no need to refer to a fraud as "deceptive." The point of the emphasis of "artlessly" is Marcia's lack of skill, so the correct answer is (B).

3. **C** This question asks the reader to make an inference about Jason, who was Marcia's husband. Since Jason is referred to multiple times in the passage, check each answer against the passage, and eliminate any that don't fit with the information in the passage. Choice (A) is incorrect, since there is no information about the circumstances of Jason's death. Since paragraph 8 opens with "Everyone in the outlying district had known Jason for what he was," (B) is incorrect. Evidence for (C) can be found in paragraph 3: "to remember instead only as the dashing lad who in his teens had left the farm and gone to seek his fortune in the great world" so retain this answer. Finally, (D) is incorrect because it is too strong: There is no evidence that Jacob was *estranged* from his family, just that he did not write often (paragraph 2). The correct answer is (C).

4. **A** This development question asks about the emotional relationship between the characters, so look for words that show Marcia's attitude toward the villagers to find the answer. Paragraph 9 states "It was because the villagers had helped her so loyally to shoulder a burden she never could have borne alone that Marcia felt toward them this abiding affection and gratitude." Therefore, she feels thankful, so the answer is (A). Choices (B) and (C) are incorrect, because "hypocritical" and "guilty" refer to how Marcia feels toward Margaret, not the villagers. Choice (D) is incorrect because "genuine grief" is the emotion Marcia does *not* feel, according to paragraph 3. The correct answer is (A).

5. **C** This structure question asks about how the first sentence enhances the story. The author uses the words "paced" and "fidgeted" to indicate Marcia's nervousness, so the reader will know that all of the following internal dialogue is delivered from that emotional state. Therefore, (C) is correct. Choice (A) is incorrect: Although this first sentence does reveal something about Marcia, it does not indicate that she is an impatient person in general, just nervous at this time. Choice (B) is incorrect because Marcia spends her time in the scene lost in thought, not observing details around her. Finally, while Marcia's internal dialogue is present during the scene, it is not present in this first sentence. This first sentence reveals only her external actions of pacing and fidgeting, so (D) is incorrect. The correct answer is (C).

6. **A** This structure question asks about the author's purpose for using a specific detail: the phrase "which should have meant so much and in reality meant so little." This detail describes Marcia's reaction to Margaret's letter in paragraph 4. Margaret's sympathetic letter "should have meant so much" since Jason was Marcia's husband and Margaret's brother. However, the sympathy "meant so little" to Marcia because Marcia's opinion of Jason is low. Marcia refers to Jason as having "indolence and neglect" (paragraph 2) and refers to "his shame" (paragraph 8). Therefore, the author uses the phrase "which should have meant so much and in reality meant so little" to show the difference between how Margaret assumes Marcia feels about Jason, and how Marcia actually feels. Choice (A) is correct. Choice (B) is incorrect, because this phrase refers only to words, the words in the letter. There are no deeds from Margaret mentioned. Choice (C) is incorrect: Although Marcia does feel hypocritical, this feeling refers to her deceit of Margaret, not to her lack of emotional response to the letter, and not to her entire *character*. Finally, even though Marcia does not respond as expected to Margaret's sympathy, the letter is nevertheless of importance to Marcia, so (D) is incorrect. The correct answer is (A).

7. **B** This structure question asks which sentence from the passage supports the idea that Marcia is at the train station in order meet with one of Jason's relatives. Choice (A) is incorrect: This answer choice describes how Marcia's distance from Jason's relatives made it easy to deceive them about her emotional situation, not her physical health. Choice (B) is correct: This sentence acknowledges that the "barrier" of distance from Jason's relatives is about to be broken down. Choice (C) is incorrect because this sentence merely confirms that Marcia has never yet met any of Jason's relatives. Finally, (D) is incorrect because this sentence describes only how Marcia took no action when Jason ceased communicating with his family. The correct answer is (B).

8. **C** This structure question asks what role Margaret has in the passage. Margaret is not physically present, but her letter of sympathy initiates a personal conflict for Marcia, since Marcia feels guilty about the "fraud" (paragraph 7) of allowing Jason's family to remember him as a "dashing lad" (paragraph 3). Therefore, (C) is correct: Margaret represents an unresolved issue for Marcia. There is no information about Margaret's character aside from the letter, so there is not enough information to support (A) or (B). The fact that Margaret is Jacob's sister reflects *Jason's* distance from his own family; Marcia is distant only because she doesn't want to upset Jason's family with the truth about his character, so (D) is incorrect. The correct answer is (C).

9. **A** This comparison question asks the reader to examine the structural relationships between the two arguments, so look at the logic of each argument. The Delegate of the United States asserts that "As a matter of economy as well as convenience that meridian should be selected which is now in most general use" (paragraph 2). In response the delegate of France emphasizes instead, "the great principle that the meridian to be offered to the world as the starting-point for all terrestrial longitudes should, have above all things, an essentially geographical and impersonal character," (paragraph 9). Thus, the delegates disagree about the prime reason qualification for choosing a prime meridian, so (A) is correct. Choice (B) is incorrect because the delegate of France does not directly oppose the selection of Greenwich, but instead promises

cooperation if the other nations are sincere (paragraph 13). Furthermore, the Delegate of France denies advocating for the Paris location (paragraph 7), so (C) is incorrect. Choice (D) is incorrect because it has reversed the positions of the Delegates from the United States and France. The correct answer is (A).

10. **D** This question asks which sentence from the passage best expresses the primary purpose of the Commander Sampson's address, which is in paragraphs 1–4. According to the title, the purpose of the conference is to determine the location of prime meridian, and Commander Sampson has an opinion about what that location should be. In paragraph 2, Commander Sampson makes two points: 1) the qualifications for choosing the prime meridian, and 2) Greenwich as the location best fitting these qualifications. Thus, the correct answer will mention one of these two points. Choices (A) and (B) are incorrect, because although these are statements by Sampson, they are general points about the prime meridian, not specifics about what is the best location. Choice (C) is incorrect: This sentence is not one of Sampson's major claims, but instead offers support for the claim that the prime meridian should be Greenwich. Choice (D) is correct: This sentence expresses Sampson's core criteria for selecting the prime meridian. The correct answer is (D).

11. **D** This question asks about the observatory at Greenwich. Since different details about the observatory are discussed in different parts of the passage, use the passage to either confirm or eliminate answers based on details in the choices. Choice (A) is incorrect: There is no evidence that the Greenwich has the largest observatory, just the one in most "general use" (paragraph 2). Choice (B) is incorrect, because there is no evidence that the observatory at Greenwich was designed with the goal of becoming the Prime Meridian. The conference exists to decide the Prime Meridian because there was no such planning in the first place. Eliminate (C) because the observatory itself is not a *naval base*. Choice (D) is correct: Commander Sampson states that "more than 70 percent of all the shipping of the world uses this meridian for purposes of navigation" (paragraph 2). The correct answer is (D).

12. **C** This evaluation question asks about the reason Mr. Rutherfurd mentioned the observatory in Paris. Mr. Rutherfurd speaks in paragraph 5, to build on Commander Sampson's argument. While Commander Sampson argues that Greenwich *should* be the prime meridian, Mr. Rutherfurd bolsters the argument by providing some reasons why Paris should *not* be the prime meridian (it is at the heart of a busy city and is subject to earthquakes). Therefore, (A) is incorrect because it is a reversal of Rutherfurd's point. Choice (B) is incorrect because Rutherfurd does not argue that observatories in general should be remote; he speaks only of the Paris observatory. But this means that (C) is correct: Rutherfurd adds to Sampson's argument by mentioning the considerations of city size and vulnerability to earthquakes. Finally, (D) is too strong; Rutherfurd argues only that the Paris observatory is not ideal for the Prime Meridian, not that it cannot fulfill its function. The correct answer is (C).

13. **B** This evaluation question asks about the approach that the Delegate of France took to counter the proposal of Greenwich as a location for the Prime Meridian. Therefore, locate where the Delegate of France addresses the location of the Prime Meridian. In paragraph 9, the delegate says "Instead of laying down the great principle that the meridian to be offered to the world as the starting-point for all terrestrial longitudes should, have above all things, an essentially geographical and impersonal character, the question was simply asked, which one of the meridians in use among the different observatories has (if I may be allowed to use the expression) the largest number of clients?" Thus, the Delegate of France questions the principle for selecting the prime meridian, and the correct answer is (B). Choices (A) and (C) are incorrect because they reverse the position of the Delegate of France, who does not advocate for the Paris observatory (paragraph 7) and states that more sailors use the English charts (paragraph 12). Choice (D) is incorrect because the Delegate of France claims that national pride is responsible for *many* separate meridians, not the selection of one: "National pride has led to the multiplication of geographical starting-points" (paragraph 8). The correct answer is (B).

14. **A** This structure question asks why the Delegate of France chooses to conclude his argument in this manner, in responding to the Delegates of the United States. So, consider the role the last sentence plays in the argument. The Delegate of France believes the Prime Meridian should have "an essentially geographical and impersonal character" (paragraph 9) and emphasizes that France is *not* arguing for Paris as the location (paragraph 7). Therefore, this concluding sentence fits with the idea of impartiality and the idea that France is willing to overcome its own self-interest. Therefore, (A) is correct and (B) and (C) are incorrect because they are the reverse of the ideas stated in the Delegate of France's argument. Choice (D) is incorrect because the statement "*if* we are approached with offers of self-sacrifice" refers to the hypothetical scenario of France as a country being asked to cooperate, not a suggestion that the delegate *should be personally requested*. The correct answer is (A).

15. This item asks the reader to make specific comparisons between themes and place the correct opinions into the correct categories. The correct assignment of opinions to categories:

Delegates from the United States

(c) The observatory of Paris has already been evaluated by French astronomers. Mr. Rutherfurd states in paragraph 5 that "it has already been thought by many of the principal French astronomers that it should no longer remain there."

(b) The prime meridian should be that meridian which has the largest number of users. In paragraph 2, Commander Sampson states "that meridian should be selected which is now in most general use."

Delegate from France

(d) The selection of the Prime Meridian should involve the agreement of all nations. The Delegate from France regrets the fact that "national rivalries are introduced in a question that should rally the good-will of all" (paragraph 9). This suggests that the Delegate believes that the selection should involve the general good, and that international cooperation should result.

(a) The selection of the prime meridian should be based in geography. The Delegate from France argues that the Prime Meridian should have "an essentially geographical and impersonal character" (paragraph 9).

16. **D** This point of view question asks about the Delegate of France's reason for discussing the charts and surveys used by France, so consider how this detail relates to the Delegate's speech as a whole. The Delegate of France asserts that the selection should involve the general good, and that international cooperation should result (paragraph 9). Then there is a heavy emphasis on the "long and glorious" history of the French charts. Finally the Delegate of France concludes in paragraph 13: "Without doubt…a change of meridian would cause us heavy sacrifices," but then he immediately continues with a transition "Nevertheless, if we…receive proofs of a sincere desire for the general good, France has given sufficient proofs of her love of progress to make her co-operation certain." So why the emphasis on the history of the French charts? Not to prove that France's history with navigation is "long and glorious" (although that tone is quite evident in the speech), but that France is ready to "sacrifice" the benefits of this history and give up the use of her charts for "the general good." If France herself is ready to make such extreme sacrifices, this strengthens the Delegate of France's argument against "national rivalries" and for international cooperation (paragraph 9), so (D) is correct. Choice (A) is incorrect: The Delegate of France would not be trying to convince the others that the French charts are better, because that would not logically fit with his following offer to sacrifice France's achievements. Eliminate (B) because it reverses the Delegate of France's objective: He

would not be trying to convince the others that the opinion of France will be judged of more importance, because that would *undermine* the argument that the Prime Meridian should be "impersonal," or neutral (paragraph 9). Choice (C) can be eliminated because it directly reverses the Delegate's claim "We do not put forward the meridian of the observatory of Paris as that to be chosen for the prime meridian" (paragraph 7). The correct answer is (D).

17.   The option that correctly completes the sentence for each "Select" option:

Dropdown Item 1: Coordination and subordination, logic and clarity.

The first choice is correct for the first drop-down question:

On that day, I was visited by a representative of Aronco Art Supplies, Mr. Namdani, at my home.

Option 2 is incorrect because it incorrectly changes the voice from passive to active, resulting in the illogical sense that the letter writer was a visitor in his own home. Options 3 and 4 begin the sentence with "From" which incorrectly joins the action of "visited" in this sentence to the time period of "Monday" in the previous sentence, implying that the action of "visited" has happened continuously ("from") since Monday, instead of at just one point ("on") in time.

Dropdown Item 2: Sentence construction, coordination, and subordination

The first choice is correct for the second drop-down question:

Even though I tried to question your representative about the products I wanted to order, **he refused to attend to my concerns.**

Option 2 is incorrect: Since the sentence starts with the transition words "even though," which indicate a contrast or change in direction, using "but" (which also indicates a change in direction) to connect the two parts of the sentence is unnecessary and confusing. Option 3 is incorrect: In this option, the placement of "attending" next to "refused" is ambiguous: Did the representative refuse, and then attend? Without any punctuation in this portion, the meaning is unclear. Option 4 includes punctuation, but now the sentence definitely states that the representative refused, but simultaneously attended, which is illogical.

Dropdown Item 3: Pronouns

The third choice is correct for the third drop-down question:

My impression of Aronco Art Supplies was shaky before, but now my opinion **of it** has been thoroughly tainted.

Option 1 is incorrect: The pronouns "who" and "whom" refer only to people, and the noun in this sentence is a company, Aronco Art Supplies. Option 2 is incorrect because "them" is a plural pronoun, while the noun in the sentence refers to one company. In American English collective nouns such as *company* and *team* are treated as singular. Option 4 is incorrect because using "of that" is a bit ambiguous: "of that" what? Of that company? That impression? Although sometimes seen alone, "That" is usually used for emphasis with the emphasized noun immediately following.

Dropdown Item 4: Logic and clarity, modifiers

The second choice is correct for the fourth drop-down question:

Furthermore, Mr. Namdani's persistence in retaining his muddy coat **has meant that I have had to have my furniture professionally cleaned, at no little expense.**

Options 1 and 3 are incorrect because the time sense of the sentence is confused: "I was having" leaves the reader struggling to find out when exactly the furniture cleaning occurred: on the day of the visit, or afterward ? Option 4 is incorrect because the modifier of "professional" or "professionally" refers to the *cleaning*, not the *furniture*.

Section 2

Access your Student Tools online to read sample essays representing different score levels for the Extended Response prompts in this book.

Section 3

18. **C** This question asks about the author's primary purpose in writing the article. The article's title "Heads Up" and its identification as coming from OnGuardOnline.org indicates that the article is a warning of some kind. Paragraph 2 advises the reader to "stop for a second," and paragraph 3 states "How will you feel if your information ends up somewhere you didn't intend? Asking a few key questions first can help you protect yourself, your friends and your computer." Therefore, the author is trying to encourage the reader to pause and think about what might happen while interacting online, and (C) is correct. Choice (A) is incorrect, because there are no misconceptions listed that the author is trying to correct. Eliminate (B) because the author speaks of the necessity for politeness online, but does not address impolite behavior in general. Choice (D) is incorrect because the topic of cyberbullying is only a detail (only paragraphs 14 and 15) in the larger passage advising the need for caution online—it is not the author's primary purpose. The correct answer is (C).

19. **B** This structure question asks how this sentence relates to the article as a whole. The sentence "Being online—connected through some sort of device—is how you live your life" introduces the topic and acknowledges the importance of online interactions to the reader. The use of the second person "you" gives a sense of immediacy and familiarity to the tone. Choice (A) is incorrect: The phrase "computers have taken over the everyday world" is too negative about computers. Furthermore, this passage focuses on the readers, not the computers. Choice (B) is correct: The tone of this first sentence is meant to be engaging. Eliminate (C) because "admonish" is too negative: The writer seeks to advise, not criticize, the reader. Finally, although the author does want readers to stop and think about their actions online, that is not the function of the first sentence, so (D) is incorrect. The correct answer is (B)

20. **A** This purpose question asks you to analyze the author's rhetorical technique of asking questions throughout the passage. The author seeks to engage the reader directly by use of the second person "you"; the use of questions furthers this connection by giving the reader a signal to pause and reflect on the topic. Therefore, (A) is correct. Choice (B) is incorrect: The author is asking questions to prompt critical thinking (so that

readers find their own answers) rather than raising questions that have no answers. Choice (C) is incorrect, because, while the author does hope to inspire critical thinking, there is no indication that the author is advocating discussion with others. Furthermore, (D) is incorrect because the author doesn't indicate that the issues are "controversial." The correct answer is (A).

21. **A** This language use item requires test takers to determine which phrase matches the use of the word "audience" in paragraph 5, so look closely at the way the word is used in context. The word is used in the sentence: "What you post could have a bigger 'audience' than you think." So who is this "audience"? Whoever gets the post, so read further. Later in the paragraph is this sentence: "Before you click 'send,' think about how you will feel if your family, teachers, coaches or neighbors find it." So, the "audience" referenced is the potential receiver of the message and someone whose opinion the reader cares about. Therefore, (A), "group of receivers," is correct. Choice (B) is incorrect because the author implies that the listeners are informal: family and neighbors, for example. Choice (C) is incorrect, because although the author does include "coaches" in the list of potential recipients, the topic is online messaging, not actually meeting those in authority. Choice (D) is incorrect because this paragraph is not about artistry. The correct answer is (A).

22. **B** This is a purpose question about the author's intended audience, so use the main idea from the passage as a starting point. This author is concerned with cautioning users about online behavior. The informal tone, use of the second person "you," and mention of "coaches" and "teachers" (paragraph 5) indicate that the author is speaking to young people. Therefore, (B) is correct. Choice (A) is incorrect because there is no reference to childrearing or other parental concerns, or any other clues to signal the author is speaking to parents. Choice (C) is too strong—the author is offering guidelines for online behavior, but there is no indication of an addiction. Choice (D) is incorrect because this passage starts with the sentence "Being online—connected through some sort of device—is how you live your life," so the author is addressing regular Internet users. The correct answer is (B).

23. **C** This question asks about the "avatars" mentioned in the quotation. To answer this question, refer to the paragraph mentioned and read beyond the sentence to find out more about the "avatars." Paragraph 13 falls under the heading "Interact with tact," so this paragraph is part of the section about politeness. After the quotation "Avatars are people too," the paragraph goes on to state "Respect their feelings just like you would in person. Remember that your character or avatar is a virtual version of you—what does it tell people about you and your interests?" Therefore, the author is reminding the reader that avatars can be deeply personal and that behind an avatar is a human that needs respect. Therefore, (C) is correct, since an avatar is a "virtual version" of a person. Choice (A) is incorrect because the author is not literally claiming the avatar is an actual separate person, just that it represents a human on the other end of the Internet. Choice (B) is almost a reversal of what the author intends, because this paragraph is about giving respect to avatars. Choice (D) is incorrect; even if avatars do make online interactions easier, that is not why the author referred to them as "people." The correct answer is (C).

24. This evaluation item asks the reader to choose two examples the author uses to support the claim that online actions can have real-world consequences. The two correct answers are as follows:

(b) People who create sexually explicit photos could be breaking the law. In paragraph 7, the author cautions that sexting may "put their friendships and reputations at risk. Worse yet, they could be breaking the law."

(c) Cyberbullying might lead to punishment from school authorities or the police. The author states that cyberbullying "also might lead to punishment from school authorities or the police" (paragraph 14).

Choice (a) is incorrect because exposing one's location is a risk of some technology (paragraph 9), but is not mentioned as a consequence of the user's particular actions. Choice (c) is incorrect because there is a warning about fake email (paragraph 11), but again, it is not cited a consequence of a user's actions. Choice (d) is incorrect because privacy settings are mentioned as solution for the risks (paragraph 8), not a consequence.

25. **A** This evaluation question asks about which answer choice reflects a gap in logic or information in the passage, so check each answer against the passage. In (A) there is some uncertainty about the answer to the question, because while the passage states "You can try to check what information the app collects—if it tells you—and check out your own privacy settings" (paragraph 10), it doesn't indicate whether protecting the profile actually prevents the app from collecting information. Because there is no certain answer to this question, keep this answer choice. Choice (B) is incorrect because the passage definitely answers this question in paragraph 15: "Using Report Abuse links can help keep sites fun for everyone." Choice (C) is incorrect because the passage definitely answers this question as well: "If someone harasses you online, keep a cool head, and don't respond" (paragraph 14). Eliminate (D) because the passage does answer this question: "it's impossible to completely control who sees your social networking profile, pictures, videos or texts. Before you click 'send,' think about how you will feel if your family, teachers, coaches or neighbors find it" (paragraph 5). Because messages can be passed along, users ultimately cannot control who sees them. The correct answer is (A).

26. **B** This development question asks about the rhetorical technique the author uses to make his point about old age, so look for the paragraphs in the passage that cover this point. The author mostly discusses old age in paragraph 4, during a long exaggerated depiction of himself in later life. The author prefers this incongruous portrait of old age, "the ribald, useless, drunken outcast person we have always wished to be" in paragraph 4 to the stereotype of old age, which is shown in the "nice old fellows in a Wordsworth poem" (paragraph 5). Therefore, (B) is correct—the author uses vivid imagery to form an ironic ideal of old age. Eliminate (A) because it reverses the author's technique: An analogy is employed to show that two ideas are similar, when this author very much wants to emphasize the difference. Choice (C) is incorrect—while the author does mention a "governmental system," the author advocates for a loose system rather than invoking authority ("we are after a system that scarcely knows it is a system," paragraph 1). Choice (D) is too extreme—while the author does prefer his own type of old age, he doesn't view it as "perfect"; instead, he states "We shall know that the Almost Perfect State is here when the kind of old age each person wants is possible to him," (paragraph 5). The correct answer is (B).

27. **B** This point of view question asks about the author's feelings regarding public opinion. Since the author longs to be a "drunken outcast" (paragraph 4) in old age, his feelings about public opinion must be that whatever public opinion is, it certainly does not matter at that age. Therefore, the correct answer is (B). Choice (A) is incorrect because it reverses the author's main idea—the author feels that public opinion does *not* matter in later life. Choice (C) is incorrect because it is too extreme—the author feels that public opinion does not matter in later life, but the author does not disregard public opinion altogether. In fact, by calling himself a "hypocrite" (paragraph 5), he implies that he does act out of a concern for public opinion in the present, but "longs to come out into our true colors at last" and be able to disregard public opinion in old age. Choice (D) is incorrect, because the author never asserts that public opinion *helps* the Almost Perfect State. The correct answer is (B).

28.   This development item asks the reader to identify three adjectives that accurately match the author's depiction of himself at old age. The three correct adjectives are as follows:

(b) lazy In paragraph 4, the author states "we shall not walk at all, but recline in a wheel chair" and also "we shall shoot out the lights when we want to go to sleep, instead of turning them off; when we want air we shall throw a silver candlestick through the front window." Far from indicating the author is incapacitated in old age, the tone suggests an unwillingness to get up for even simple tasks.

(d) intemperate The author describes himself as a "drunken outcast" in old age and also asserts that he will "bellow for alcoholic beverages" (paragraph 4) which shows that he plans to indulge in drink.

(e) antisocial In addition to describing himself as an "outcast," the author imagines that he will "write ribald songs against organized society," (paragraph 4).

Choice (a) is incorrect because, although the author may display some sarcasm in writing the essay, the author does not depict himself as sarcastic in old age. Likewise, while the author describes himself as hypocritical in the present, the author plans to overcome this hypocrisy in old age, so (c) is incorrect.

29. **A** This main idea question asks about a central theme of the essay. The title of the essay is "The Almost Perfect State" and the author begins the essay by describing the preferred type of government: "it is not nearly enough perfect unless the individuals who compose it can, somewhere between death and birth, have a perfectly corking time for a few years" (paragraph 1) and develops this relationship between the individual and the government in paragraph 6: "Any system of government under which the individual does all the sacrificing for the sake of the general good, for the sake of the community, the State, gets off on its wrong foot." Therefore, (A) is correct—the author feels that what the individual wants takes priority. Choice (B) is incorrect—the author describes only himself as a "hypocrite;" he does not make this accusation of anyone else. Choice (C) is incorrect because it is too extreme: Although the author plans to "work hard" (paragraph 3), he does not assert that people *must* do so. Choice (D) is also too extreme—the author does not assert that the system will *never* be perfect. The correct answer is (A).

30.   This purpose question asks the reader to identify statements that express the author's purposes for writing this article. The two correct statements are as follows:

(b) To satirize typical expectations of old age. The author begins the essay with an assertion that individuals should be guaranteed a "carefree" old age (paragraph 2), and then launches into a description of the "unhonored" old age the author personally expects to enjoy (paragraph 4). By contrast, the author then describes, somewhat dismissively, the more traditional and literary depictions of old age: "Of course, all of you may not want the kind we want...some of you may prefer prunes and morality to the bitter end. Some of you may be dissolute now and may look forward to becoming like one of the nice old fellows in a Wordsworth poem" (paragraph 5). The author's tone (shown by "prunes" and "bitter") clearly indicates that this picture of "nice old fellows" is not the old age the author would prefer.

(d) To advocate a specific arrangement between the state and the individual. In the first paragraph, the author describes the ideal relationship between the government and the individual: "The most wonderful governmental system in the world does not attract us, as a system; we are after a system that scarcely knows it is a system; the great thing is to have the largest number of individuals as happy as may be, for a little while at least, some time before they die."

Choice (a) is incorrect because the retirement system he proposes is not *mandatory*. Choice (c) is incorrect because, while the author does caution the reader about strain, this is not the purpose behind the entire article overall. Choice (e) is incorrect because it is too extreme—the author never asserts that long life *depends* on a ribald old age.

31. **D** This structure question asks why the author uses this phrase to conclude the paragraph. Sentences at the end of paragraphs often provide a conclusion, transition, or dramatic emphasis. In this sentence the tone shifts from the preceding image of hard work ("We intend to work rather hard during those fifty years and accumulate enough to live on without working any more for the next ten years") to a rather outlandish declaration of when the author has "decided" to die—something that cannot possibly be within his control. So this sentence shows a shift from the serious to the outlandish, and this exaggerated tone is maintained in the following paragraph during the depiction of the author's imagined old age as "the ribald, useless, drunken outcast person we have always wished to be." Therefore, (D) is correct. Choice (A) is incorrect—there is no discussion of the author's family. Choice (B) is incorrect: Although the author discusses his strategy in the beginning part of the sentence ("We intend to work rather hard during those fifty years and accumulate enough to live on without working any more for the next ten years"), this is not the function of this phrase ("...for we have determined to die at the age of one hundred and two"), which shows a shift in tone. Choice (C) is incorrect: While the author does give a vivid example of his own old age, that depiction comes after this phrase, when the author states "Between the years of ninety-two and a hundred and two." The correct answer is (D).

32. **C** This language use question asks the reader to examine the author's use of the term "hypocrite" to describe himself. This is found in paragraph 5: "But for our part we have always been a hypocrite and we shall have to continue being a hypocrite for a good many years yet, and we yearn to come out in our true colors at last." The phrase "come into our true colors at last" refers to the "ribald" old age the author hopes to enjoy, suggesting that the author does not yet enjoy this "ribald" lifestyle. Therefore, (C) is correct: "hypocrite" refers to the fact that the author does not yet show his true "ribald" self to society. Choice (A) is incorrect: Although the author's ideal old age is in contrast to the "nice old fellows" described, the author does not feel this makes him a "hypocrite," since he recognizes that different people have different preferences ("We shall know that the Almost Perfect State is here when the kind of old age each person wants is possible to him"). Choice (B) is incorrect because it reverses the author's main idea—the author definitely *does* want to enjoy the old age he wants. Choice (C) is correct; the humorous story takes pretense and self-control to deliver. Choice (D) is incorrect: Although the author does state "We don't want things that cost us too much" in paragraph 6, this is not connected to his use of "hypocrite" for himself in paragraph 5. The correct answer is (C).

33. **B** This evaluation question asks about how the author's reasoning leads to a contradiction. Choice (A) is incorrect because one can do "the best good that you can possibly achieve" and still have it be "not good enough"—there is no contradiction between those two assertions. Choice (B) is correct: If the author states that only easy things are worth doing, but then advises the readers to overstrain themselves, there is a contradiction between the author recommending that the readers do only easy things, and then advising the readers do hard things. Choice (C) is incorrect, because to "sit before a fire" and then to "want air" are not contradictory, since it is possible to feel too cold and then too warm. Choice (D) is likewise incorrect because it is possible to work hard for a period of time and then stop working entirely. The correct answer is (B).

34. **D** This language use item requires test takers to determine which word could best replace the word "fixed," so examine how the word is used in context. The word occurs in the description of Bles' reunion with Zora: "For long months he did not meet her, until one day he saw her deep eyes fixed longingly upon him

from a thicket in the swamp" (paragraph 6). Zora is staring at him, so you need a meaning of "fixed" in the sense of a gaze that is steady and concentrated. Choice (D) has this meaning.

Choices (A), (B), and (C) are incorrect because, even though they all can be synonyms for "fixed," they refer to different definitions of "fixed" than the one used in the passage.

35. **D** This character development question asks about Bles's character based on the details in the story, so use the passage to either confirm or eliminate answers based on details in the choices. Choice (A) is incorrect, because while Zora tells stories of the swamp, there is no evidence in the passage that Bles lives in the swamp. Choice (B) is incorrect, because even though Zora is definitely characterized as wild, there is no evidence that Bles feels superior to her. Choice (C) is incorrect, because it is Zora who has the wild imagination, which she shares with Bles. Choice (D) is correct because paragraph 5 states Bles was "trying to express scornful disbelief when, in truth, he was awed and doubtful," showing that he felt a need to hide his true feelings. The correct answer is (D).

36. This development item asks the reader to identify three adjectives that match the author's depiction of Bles. The three correct adjectives are as follows:

(c) intrigued Paragraph 2 states that Bles is "half fascinated, half amused" by Zora and her stories.

(d) wary In paragraph 5, the narrative reveals Bles as "awed and doubtful" and goes on to say "Always he would glance involuntarily back along the path behind him," which indicates that Bles is cautious and uncertain, or wary.

(e) conciliatory After their long separation, Bles tries to reconcile with Zora: "He went and greeted her," and even after she makes no response, he persists in trying to reconcile: "he had sued long for peace" (paragraph 6).

Choice (a) is incorrect because "irritating" describes Zora rather than Bles. Also, (b) is incorrect, because while Bles tries to pretend scorn, in truth he is "awed" (paragraph 5).

37. **B** This development question asks the reader to examine the author's use of the phrase "almost painful" to describe Zora's storytelling. The phrase occurs in the sentence "So passed a year, and there came the time when her wayward teasing and the almost painful thrill of her tale-telling nettled him and drove him away." Therefore, "almost painful" suggests that the "thrill" of the storytelling was intense, and that this intensity eventually becomes uncomfortable. Therefore, (B) is correct. Choice (A) is incorrect because although Zora is described as "teasing and mocking and half scaring" (paragraph 1) and "mischievous," (paragraph 3), this is in the context of her "wildness" and does not imply that any pain she inflicts is *deliberate*. Choice (C) is incorrect because there is nothing before this phrase to indicate that Bles has *affection* for Zora. Choice (D) is incorrect because it is too extreme—the stories may be frightening, but Bles stays away not because he is *afraid* to hear more of them, but because Zora teases and the stories are too intense. The correct answer is (B).

38. **C** This structure question asks about the author's purpose for using a specific description: the sentence "then her low birdlike laughter would rise and ring through the trees." By using the adjective "birdlike" and the phrase "rise and sing through the trees," the author depicts Zora's laughter as a living wild animal, which adds to the overall depiction of her "wildness" in the passage. Therefore, (C) is correct. Choice (A) is incorrect, because there is no suggestion that her laugher *disturbed* the animals. Choice (B) is incorrect, because the author does not need to *bring back* the setting of nature, since it is present throughout the

passage. Choice (D) is incorrect, because even though previously Zora tells wild stories of "a devil," there are no *supernatural events* that occur later in the passage. The correct answer is (C).

39. **D** This purpose question asks about Zora's intention for telling Bles about "devils" in the swamp, so refer to this part of the passage and think about how this detail connects to Zora's character as a whole. This excerpt displays a development in Zora's character. In paragraph 1 she is "mischievous" and "impish" and "did not know how to express" her friendship with Bles. By paragraph 6, "she had dropped the impish mischief of her way" and "in sudden new friendship she had taken his hand." Thus, at the beginning of the narrative Zora does not know how to express friendship, but she learns how to do this by the end. The middle of the narrative depicts Zora's attempts to show friendship to Bles in the only way she knows how: storytelling, so (D) is correct. Choice (A) is incorrect: Although she speaks "warningly" (paragraph 2), Zora wants to engage Bles's attention with a fanciful tale, not warn him of literal dangers. Choice (B) is incorrect because Zora herself is not afraid of the stories she tells; instead she laughs when Bles acts warily (paragraph 5). Furthermore, (C) is incorrect because she does not want to feel *superior* to Bles; instead, she has a "wild interest" in him (paragraph 1). The correct answer is (D).

40. **A** This point of view question asks about Zora's perspective, so look for words that show Zora's attitude toward children to find the answer. In paragraph 1, the reader is introduced to Zora and told "She had not known, she had scarcely seen, a child of her own age" and "It was to her a strange new thing to see a fellow of like years with herself." Therefore, she has little experience with other children, so the answer is (A). Choice (B) is incorrect because it reverses the depiction in the passage: Instead of reacting with fear, Zora "gripped him to her soul in wild interest" (paragraph 1). Choice (C) is incorrect, because although Zora latches on to Bles, there is no way to tell whether she feels *welcoming* toward children in general. Finally, (D) is incorrect because *puzzled* expresses Zora's attitude toward her own feelings: "Yet this childish friendship was so new and incomprehensible a thing to her that she did not know how to express it" (paragraph 1). The correct answer is (A).

41. **A** This structure question asks about how the sentence represents a transformation of character. The sentence begins with the transition "But she said no word," which stands in contrast to the many vocal descriptions of Zora that come before: "teasing and mocking" (paragraph 1), "whisper" (paragraph 2), "laughter" (paragraph 5), and "tale-telling" (paragraph 6). The switch to silence indicates that something has changed in her character, which is confirmed later in the passage "She had dropped the impish mischief of her way, and up from beneath it rose a wistful, visionary tenderness." Choice (A) is correct. Choice (B) is incorrect: This sentence indicates a change in Zora, not in Bles. Choice (C) is incorrect; although she has a "passionate, proud silence" (paragraph 6), this is not the *first time* she has been depicted in such a fashion: Paragraph 1 describes her as "willful" and "full of great and awful visions." Finally, Zora has a connection to nature throughout the entire passage, so the use of "nested" does not represent a transformation of character, and (D) is incorrect. The correct answer is (A).

42. **D** This structure question asks about the author's purpose for using a specific detail: the phrase "blind horse moving in a circle round a mill." This detail follows the author's discussion of reciprocal aggression: "if such a use of force is justifiable, surely he is entitled to do likewise by us. And so we should never come to an agreement" (paragraph 6). Therefore, the comparison to a blind horse moving in a circle shows the endless nature of reciprocal aggression and its futility, and (D) is correct. Choice (A) is incorrect: Although the author does assert that people should not obey unjust laws, the image of the blind horse is not support for this assertion. Choice (B) is incorrect because it is a reversal of the author's intent: The author uses the image of a blind horse moving in a circle to show that any perception of progress is a "fancy," or imaginary. Choice (C) is also incorrect: While the author may agree that opponents need perspective, the point of the image is that the horse moves in a circle, to emphasizing the endless nature of reciprocal aggression. The correct answer is (D).

43. **A**   This structure question asks which sentence from the passage exemplifies what the author means by an unjust law. The author speaks of laws "repugnant to our conscience" so by "unjust" the author means a law that goes against personal morals. Choice (A) is correct: A law instructing people "to go about without any clothing" would be an example of an unjust law, from the author's perspective. Choice (B) is incorrect: Although this choice mentions "any degrading law," there is no specific example given. Choice (C) is incorrect because this choice refers to *acts* rather than laws. Choice (D) is incorrect because it is an example of the consequence of a law, not the unjust law itself. The correct answer is (A).

44.   This development item asks the reader to make specific comparisons between the topics of soul-force and body-force as addressed in the passage, and to place the correct details into the correct categories. The author defines these terms in paragraph 1: "the reverse of resistance by arms. When I refuse to do a thing that is repugnant to my conscience," is soul-force, so by contrast, body-force includes "resistance by arms." The correct assignment of details to categories is as follows:

Soul-force

> **(d) Only the person using it suffers.** "Moreover, if this kind of force is used in a cause that is unjust only the person using it suffers." (paragraph 2)

> **(b) Suffering consequences for refraining from wrong actions.** In paragraph 2, the author states "he should not do that which he knows to be wrong, and suffer the consequence whatever it may be. This is the key to the use of soul-force."

Body-force

> **(e) Leads to escalating mutual aggression justified by opponent's use of force** In paragraph 6, the author describes how violence leads to retaliation: "if such a use of force is justifiable, surely he is entitled to do likewise by us. And so we should never come to an agreement. We may simply fancy, like the blind horse moving in a circle round a mill, that we are making progress."

> **(a) Forcing the government to repeal a law by using violence** "If, by using violence, I force the government to repeal the law, I am employing what may be termed body-force." (paragraph 1)

45. **A**   This evaluation question asks about which claim from the passage has the weakest support, so check the answers against the passage, to determine whether each claim has any support. Choice (A) represents a claim that has no support at all—even though the author claims that "everybody admits that sacrifice of self is infinitely superior to sacrifice of others," there is no evidence in the passage to support this: no examples or additional details. Therefore, keep this answer choice. Choice (B) does have some support: Right after stating "That we should obey laws whether good or bad is a new-fangled notion," the author goes on to say "There was no such thing in former days. The people disregarded those laws they did not like" (paragraph 3). Choice (C) is incorrect because the passage definitely follows the assertion about majorities and minorities with "Many examples can be given in which acts of majorities will be found to have been wrong, and those of minorities to have been right. All reforms owe their origin to the initiation of minorities in opposition to majorities" (paragraph 5). Eliminate (D) because part of this statement does have support. The author supports the part of the assertion that such a teaching "means slavery" by asserting that obeying "laws repugnant to our conscience" is "contrary to our manhood" and that "If man will only realize that it is unmanly to obey laws that are unjust, no man's tyranny will enslave him. This is the key to self-rule" (paragraph 4). Thus, the author reasons step by step, connecting the obedience of

repugnant laws to a "loss of manhood," and then connects that idea of "manhood" to "self-rule." Also, the author offers an example: "If the government were to ask us to go about without any clothing, should we do so?" (paragraph 3). Therefore, the answer with the weakest support is (A).

46. **B** This main idea question asks about a central theme of the essay. The title of the passage is "Passive Resistance" and the author is recommending "passive resistance" as a response to "unjust laws," instead of violence, so (A) is incorrect because it reverses the main idea. Choice (B) is correct: The author believes that the individual should do what is right, not obey laws just because they are laws. The passage states "he should not do that which he knows to be wrong" in paragraph 2, and "it is contrary to our manhood, if we obey laws repugnant to our conscience" in paragraph 3. Choice (C) is incorrect: The author does not take a position on multiple attempts leading to success. Finally, the author disparages majority rule, saying "an ungodly thing to believe that an act of a majority binds a minority" (paragraph 5), so (D) is incorrect. The correct answer is (B).

47. **C** This is a purpose question about the author's intended audience, so use the main idea from the passage as a starting point. The title of the passage is "Passive Resistance" and the author is recommending "passive resistance" as a response to "unjust laws." Therefore, the author is addressing those who would resist the laws, not those who would make them, so (B) is incorrect. Furthermore, the author disparages majority rule, saying "an ungodly thing to believe that an act of a majority binds a minority" (paragraph 5). So (A) is incorrect: The author is counseling resistance to the oppressed minority, not to the majority group in power, which means (C) is correct. Choice (D) is incorrect because it reverses the author's main idea "To use brute-force, to use gun-powder is contrary to passive resistance" (paragraph 6). The correct answer is (C).

48. **B** This evaluation question asks how the author would respond to a hypothetical scenario that is relevant to the main idea, so consider the main idea and the author's point of view. The title of the passage is "Passive Resistance" and the author is recommending "passive resistance" instead of "resistance by arms" or "body-force" (paragraph 1) Therefore, (A) is incorrect: The author would not simply do nothing and allow the children to keep hitting each other because he believes "body-force" is wrong. Choice (B) is correct: By writing this essay, the author intends to recommend passive resistance as the preferred choice, and would want to communicate these views to the fighting children. Choice (C) is incorrect as it reverses the author's attitude about authority. Throughout the passage the author speaks of resisting authority, so the author would be unlikely to defer to the "proper authorities." Choice (D) is incorrect because it reverses the main idea: The author states that "To use brute-force" is "contrary to passive resistance" (paragraph 6), so the author would be unlikely to physically separate the children. The correct answer is (B).

49. **A** This point of view question asks about the author's feelings regarding "manhood." The author asserts that obeying "laws repugnant to our conscience" is "contrary to our manhood" and that "If man will only realize that it is unmanly to obey laws that are unjust, no man's tyranny will enslave him. This is the key to self-rule" (paragraph 4). Thus, the author reasons step by step, connecting the obedience of repugnant laws to a "loss of manhood," and then connects that idea of "manhood" to "self-rule." Therefore, "manhood" implies someone who doesn't obey unjust laws, someone who is moral and independent, so (A) is correct. Choice (B) is incorrect as it reverses the author's main idea: The author speaks *against* "brute-force" (paragraph 6) and "body-force" (paragraph 1). Choice (C) is incorrect because the author does not imply that *experience* is necessary for "manhood," but rather a sense of right and wrong ("We simply want to find out what is right, and to act accordingly" paragraph 3). Choice (D) is incorrect as it reverses the author's attitude about authority. Throughout the passage the author speaks of someone with manhood as someone who resists authority. The correct answer is (A).

50.   The option that correctly completes the sentence for each "Select" option:

Dropdown Item 1: Word choice.

The fourth choice is correct for the first drop-down question:

If praise is the measure of success, **then I cannot compliment him too highly.**

Options 1 and 3 are incorrect because they incorrectly use "than" which is a comparison word, instead of "then" which shows cause and effect and follows "if." Option 2 is incorrect because it uses "high," an adjective, to modify a verb; furthermore it incorrectly uses "complement" which means "to complete" instead of the correct verb "compliment" which means "praise."

Dropdown Item 2: Modifiers, coordination and subordination

The third choice is correct for the second drop-down question:

During that tumultuous period, Mr. Shukla tirelessly kept the files on needy populations current so there would be no delays in getting services to needy families.

Option 1 is incorrect: Starting the sentence with "being" means literally that "Mr. Shukla" is "being a tumultuous period," which is a misplaced modifier. Option 2 is incorrect: Starting the sentence with "of" means literally that "Mr. Shukla" is "of that tumultuous period," or belongs to that period, which is also a misplaced modifier. Option 4 begins with "although," which signals a shift of direction. However, the focus of the sentence is not that Mr. Shukla kept records *despite* the tumultuous period, but rather that Mr. Shukla kept records *while* the tumultuous period occurred, so the ideas are incorrectly joined in Option 4.

Dropdown Item 3: Parallelism, logic and clarity

The first choice is correct for the third drop-down question:

He holds an MA degree in Political Science from Actreaus University, has assisted the noted social work activist Ms. Sandra Diaz in the Family Resources Outreach Center **and has been acting clerk** since her untimely death earlier this year.

Options 2 and 4 are incorrect. The list in this sentence covers several time periods: Mr. Shukla's (current) qualifications, his (past) experience, and his (current, but began in the past) job title. Therefore, the list must be parallel, but also correctly express all these senses of time. The first two verbs are "holds" and "has assisted." The third verb, which refers to his job title, should be parallel with the first two, so "has been" is the best choice, and neither "been" nor "acts" is parallel. Option 3 is incorrect because it omits the connector "and" which is necessary in this list of items.

Dropdown Item 4: Pronouns, sentence construction

The second choice is correct for the fourth drop-down question:

His first summer after college, he spent time in a historically underserved neighborhood and donated valuable hours organizing party fundraisers for the children in need, **even to the point of assisting them** with funds from his own pocket.

Option 1 is incorrect because the conjunction "and" is unnecessary and produces a run-on of ideas. Options 3 and 4 are incorrect because they use the singular pronoun "him," which makes it seem as if Mr. Shukla is assisting himself, rather than the plural *children*.

MATHEMATICAL REASONING

Part 1

1. **A** Remember that absolute value is the distance from 0. Another way of thinking about it is that positive numbers stay positive and negative numbers become positive. Point F is at –2, so its absolute value is 2. Point G is at –0.5, which has an absolute value of 0.5. Point H is at 0, which has an absolute value of 0. Point J is at 1.5, which has an absolute value of 1.5. Therefore, point F has the greatest absolute value.

2. $\dfrac{3}{4}$ If you are comfortable with fractions, you may be able to find the answer through that knowledge and Process of Elimination. The fraction must be greater than $\dfrac{1}{2}$, and $\dfrac{1}{6}$ and $\dfrac{2}{5}$ are both smaller, since $\dfrac{1}{2}$ would be $\dfrac{3}{6}$ and $\dfrac{2.5}{5}$. Those can't be it. The fraction must also be less than $\dfrac{4}{5}$, which eliminates $\dfrac{5}{4}$, since that is greater than 1 (the same as $1\dfrac{1}{4}$). Now the question is between $\dfrac{3}{4}$ and $\dfrac{5}{6}$. You can compare each one to $\dfrac{4}{5}$ by finding common denominators: $\dfrac{3}{4} = \dfrac{15}{20}$ and $\dfrac{4}{5} = \dfrac{16}{20}$, so $\dfrac{3}{4}$ is less than $\dfrac{4}{5}$, and is the correct answer. Another option is to convert some of the fractions to decimals. If you know that $\dfrac{3}{4}$ is 0.75, $\dfrac{1}{2}$ is 0.5, and $\dfrac{4}{5}$ is 0.8, it's easy to see that $\dfrac{3}{4}$ fits between them. You can do long division to find these decimals without a calculator, but it will save time to memorize these common fractions in decimal form.

3. **C** First square –3, which is the same as (–3)(–3) = 9. Note that it is positive 9 because the two minus signs cancel out. Now take the square root of 9, which is 3 because 3 × 3 = 9. Last, subtract 9 – 3 = 6.

4. **C** Think about Process of Elimination and breaking down the numbers into factors, rather than actually doing the multiplication, which could be time-consuming. Choice (A) has the 100 part the same, which is fine, but 27 is not the same as 20 × 7, so eliminate it. Choice (B) has 10 × 10, which equals 100, but again, 20 × 7 doesn't equal 27, so it's not right. Choice (C) has 10 × 10, which equals 100, and 9 × 3, which equals 27, so it is correct. Choice (D) has 3 × 9, which equals 27, but 10 × 5 equals 50, not 100, so it is incorrect.

5. **C** The exponent rule here is that when exponents with the same base are multiplied, the powers are added. Thus, do 12 + 2 to get 14. The powers are multiplied only when there is a power to another power, such as $(2^{12})^2$.

Part 2

6. **A** Substitute $\frac{1}{2}$ for x. First multiply $\frac{1}{2}$ by 3 to get $\frac{3}{2}$. Then add 7. As a fraction, 7 is the same as $\frac{14}{2}$, so $\frac{3}{2} + \frac{14}{2} = \frac{17}{2}$. If you don't feel great about fractions, you can always use decimals with the calculator and change the answer choices to decimals as well.

7.   As the students' heights increase, their shoe sizes **show no relationship to their heights**.

   The graph does not strongly increase or decrease when looking from left to right, so there is no relationship. Consider how a line of best fit would be drawn in. In this case, it would not have a strong positive or negative slope since the data points do not follow a pattern.

8. **C** Since this is a right triangle, use the Pythagorean Theorem to find the missing side. The formula is $a^2 + b^2 = c^2$, and remember that a and b represent the two short sides and c is the long side. Thus, here it is $3^2 + 5^2 = c^2$. Next, $9 + 25 = c^2$, and $34 = c^2$. Take the square root of both sides to get $c = \sqrt{34}$.

9. **C** Since everything is multiplication, this can be rewritten as $3.0 \times 10^{12} \times 2.0 \times 10^8$, and then move the like terms closer to each other, like so: $3.0 \times 2.0 \times 10^{12} \times 10^8$. First multiply the smaller numbers: $3.0 \times 2.0 = 6.0$. Then multiply the powers of ten, but remember that when multiplying numbers with the same base, you keep the base the same and add the exponents. Thus, $10^{12} \times 10^8 = 10^{20}$. This makes the answer 6.0×10^{20}.

10. **A** The answer is (A) because 1.5 hours times the number of movies plus 0.75 hour (45 minutes) times the number of video games must be less than or equal to 12 hours, since that's the amount of time he has to relax.

11.   Area: **378**. Perimeter: **78**.

   To find the area of a rectangle, use the formula $A = L \times W$. Fill in the length and width provided. Multiplying 21 by 18 results in 378 for the area. To find the perimeter, use the formula $P = 2L + 2W$ or just add up all four sides, making sure not to forget to add the two sides that are unlabeled on the diagram: $21 + 21 + 18 + 18 = 78$.

12. **D** Put in 2.05 for C, the total cost. The equation becomes $2.05 = 1.75 + .1t$. Subtract 1.75 to get $.3 = .1t$. Then divide both sides by .1 to get $t = 3$. Another option is to guess and check numbers for t based on the answer choices.

13. **A** Use the equation of a line $y = mx + b$. Fill in m, which is the slope: $y = 5x + b$. Now fill in the x and y from the point provided: $1 = 5(-2) + b$. Next, $1 = -10 + b$, and $11 = b$. The complete formula is $y = 5x + 11$. Another good option is to eliminate any answer choice that has the slope incorrect and then plug in the point to see which equation it works in.

14. **D** First convert to the smallest units, which is inches. 4 yards × 36 inches per yard = 144 inches in each spool. Then multiply 8 inches per student × 94 students = 752 inches the teacher needs. Divide that by 144 inches in each spool to get about 5.22. This makes the answer 6 because 5 spools will not be enough.

15. Where $x > -1$, the function is **increasing.** Where $x < -1$, the function is **increasing.** The x-axis is the horizontal axis. To the right of $x = -1$, the function goes up, so it is increasing. To the left, it is also going up from left to right and is thus increasing. The function increases only from left to right.

16. **9** Divide the 98 guests into 12 guests per bench. The result is about 8.2, which means the answer is 9 because 8 benches will not be enough for all of the guests, and the problem does not indicate that anything other than whole benches can be used.

17. **D** To multiply two sets of two things in parentheses (binomials), you must use FOIL, which stands for First, Outside, Inside, Last. Start by multiplying the First term in each set of parentheses: $5x \cdot 2x = 10x^2$. Next, multiply the terms on the Outside of the parentheses: $5x \cdot -1 = -5x$. Next, multiply the terms on the Inside of the parentheses: $1 \cdot 2x = 2x$. Next, multiply the Last term in each set of parentheses: $1(-1) = -1$. Put it all together: $10x^2 - 5x + 2x - 1$. Combine like terms to get $10x^2 - 3x - 1$.

18. **A** There are many ways to solve this. One is to use the formula provided, which is in the form $y = mx + b$. In the formula, b represents the y-intercept, which is where the line crosses the y (vertical) axis. In this formula, the y-intercept is -1. Check the answer choices. Choice (A) crosses at -1, and so does (B). Choice (C) crosses at 1, so eliminate it. Choice (D) crosses at -1, so keep it. Now consider m in the equation, which represents the slope. Here the slope is 3, which means up 3 and to the right 1. A positive slope goes in the direction of up to the right, which eliminates (B). Now look at the difference between (A) and (D). From the y-intercept, (A) goes up 3 when it goes to the right 1. Choice (D) goes up 1 and to the right 3, which is the opposite—that's a slope of 1/3 because slope is rise over run. Thus, the answer is (A). Another good option to solve is to find a point on the line by plugging in an x value and then look for it in the graphs, or draw the line yourself using two or more points on the line and seeing which choice looks like your drawing.

19. **5** The average is the total divided by the number of numbers. If the average is 6 and the number of numbers is 4 (since there are four people), the total must be 24, because $24 \div 4 = 6$. The first three friends have a total of $7 + 3 + 9 = 19$, so the remaining 5 points must belong to Selena.

20. **A** Another way of referring to the slope is to say the rate of change, or just the rate here. The rate is 480 potatoes per 1 hour, but the question asks about the rate in minutes. So, think of this as 480 potatoes per 60 minutes. This can be thought of like 480 potatoes/60 minutes = 8 potatoes/minute. That is the rate. A rate is always expressed as something over something else. Another way of thinking about it is to plug in 480 for y and 60 for x and solve for m.

21. Number of Pets

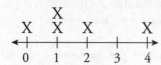

Draw an X for each number in the list, as many times as it appears.

22. **B** Get a by itself. First multiply both sides by 3 to get rid of the fraction. This results in $18ab = 2$. Now divide both sides by $18b$ to get $a = \dfrac{2}{18b}$, and divide top and bottom by 2 to simplify to $a = \dfrac{1}{9b}$.

23. **B** First find the number of hours Chris spends on leisure time. Add the four other activities mentioned: $8 + 9 + 2 + 1 = 20$. There are 24 hours in a day, so the number of hours remaining for leisure time is 4. The question asks about probability, which is written as a fraction: the thing you want over the total. The question asks about the leisure hours, which is 4, so that goes on the top. The total is 24 hours, so the answer is 4/24, which simplifies to 1/6.

24. Clockwise from top left: **30, 24, 20.** Set up a proportion using the scale provided. For the side on the left, the proportion is $\dfrac{2 \text{ inches}}{1 \text{ foot}} = \dfrac{x \text{ inches}}{15 \text{ feet}}$. Cross-multiply to get $x = 30$ inches. Set up a similar proportion for the other two sides to get 24 inches and 20 inches. Always be careful to write down the units so you have the same units on the top and bottom of both sides of the equation.

25. **B** Anytime you see an x^2 and an x in the same equation, it's a quadratic equation. Since there are answer choices, one option is to plug in each possibility and see which work and which don't. Another option is to factor the equation, and solve it that way. In order to do that, the expression must equal 0, so get everything on the left side. Here, subtract $4x$ to get $x^2 - 10x - 11 = 0$. Now factor. Draw two sets of parentheses and put x in both: $(x\ )(x\ )$. Now think of numbers that multiply together to equal 11 and add or subtract to equal 10. Since 11 is a prime number, the only option is 1 and 11. Now it is $(x\ \ 1)(x\ \ 11)$. Since it's -11, there must be one positive and one negative. To get a -10, it must be -11 and $+1$, like so: $(x - 11)(x + 1) = 0$. It's always a good idea to FOIL what you got to make sure it equals what you started with, which it does here. In order for this to equal 0, either the first set of parentheses equals 0 or the second set does. If $x - 11 = 0$, then $x = 11$. If $x + 1 = 0$, then $x = -1$. The answer is $x = 11$ or $x = -1$.

26. **C** Start by rewriting the second equation so it's in the form $y = mx + b$. Add $9x$ to both sides to get $3y = 9x + 4$. Divide both sides by 3 to get $y = 3x + 4/3$. Now compare the two equations. They both have a slope of 3 because m in the equation represents the slope. Two lines that have the same slope are parallel, meaning they never cross. Another good option is to draw both lines and see what their relationship is.

27. **2** First distribute the -2, carefully: $10x - 6x + 2 = 5x$. Now combine like terms: $4x + 2 = 5x$, and then $2 = x$.

28. **D** The question asks about the number of students who liked fall or spring. First find the percent who liked fall or spring: $12\% + 28\% = 40\%$. Keep in mind that when percents come from the same total, you can add, subtract, multiply, divide, and compare them. In a pie chart, the percents always come from the same total. So now it's 40% of the total, which the problem says is 325 students. Use the calculator to do $40/100 \times 325 = 130$.

29. **5** Use the formula for volume of a rectangular prism, since that is the shape of a brick. The formula is $V = L \times W \times H$. Fill in what is known from the problem: $160 = 8 \times 4 \times H$. Solve for H: $160 = 32H$, then $H = 5$.

30. **B** To solve an inequality, get the variable by itself. To do that here, subtract 76 from all three sections of the inequality. This results in $104 \le t \le 124$. This should make sense because if the pastry chef makes 104 more tarts, that will reach the minimum value of 180 tarts that are needed, and above that will be acceptable up to 200. With inequalities, it's always a good idea to guess and check numbers to make sure your answer makes sense.

31. **C** The equation of a line is $y = mx + b$. The first thing to find is the slope, m. Find it using the formula $m = \dfrac{y_2 - y_1}{x_2 - x_1}$. Here, that is $\dfrac{3 - 0}{12 - 0} = \dfrac{3}{12} = \dfrac{1}{4}$. Now the equation is $y = \dfrac{1}{4}x + b$. Plug in the coordinates of one of the points for x and y to solve for b. Use the easier one, $(0, 0)$: $0 = 0 + b$. Then $b = 0$. The final equation is $y = \dfrac{1}{4}x$. An equation that passes through the origin $(0, 0)$ will always look similar to this because its y-intercept is 0 and thus $b = 0$. Another, easier option is to simply plug in the points for x and y into the answer choices to find the equation in which both points work.

32. $g\left(\dfrac{1}{2}\right) = \dfrac{5}{4}$. $g(4) = 3$. $g(10) = 6$.

   To find $g\left(\dfrac{1}{2}\right)$, substitute $\dfrac{1}{2}$ for x: $\dfrac{\frac{1}{2}}{2} + 1 = \dfrac{1}{4} + 1 = \dfrac{1}{4} + \dfrac{4}{4} = \dfrac{5}{4}$. To find $g(4)$, substitute 4 for x: $\dfrac{4}{2} + 1 = 2 + 1 = 3$. To find $g(10)$, substitute 10 for x: $\dfrac{10}{2} + 1 = 5 + 1 = 6$.

33. **D** First determine the number of tulips: $120 - 80 = 40$. Thus, the ratio of roses to tulips is 80:40, which simplifies to 2:1.

34. **A** The phrase *two times a number* means to put a 2 in front of a variable. The answer choices use x, so write $2x$. Then it says *five less than* that, so subtract 5: $2x - 5$.

35. **A** Get x by itself by dividing both sides by 2. The result is $x < 3$. The correct answer is (A) because the shaded area is to the left of, less than, 3 and the 3 has an open circle. The closed circle would mean that 3 is allowed, but since it is a < sign, 3 is not allowed.

36. **C** Start by calculating her height after one year. Take 2% of 143 by doing $0.02 \times 143 = 2.86$. She grew by 2.86 cm in the first year, so add that to the 143 to get that her height at that time was 145.86. Now take 1% of that by doing $0.01 \times 145.86 = 1.4586$. Add that to the 145.86 to get her height after two years: 147.3186, which rounds to 147.32. Note that it's not allowed to add the 2% and 1% and take 3% of the original. That would result in (B), which is close but not exactly right. Since the 1% is coming from the height after one year and not the original height, it can't be added to the 2% and each step must be done individually.

37. **C** Start by writing down the formula for area of a circle: $A = \pi r^2$. To find the area, you will need to fill in the radius. That isn't provided, but the diameter is, and the diameter is always twice the radius. Thus, if the diameter is 12, the radius is 6. Now the formula is $A = \pi(6^2) = 36\pi$.

38. **C** This is written as 10,000 − 50*w* because the starting number he owes is $10,000 and that amount gets smaller as the weeks go by and he gradually pays it off, so it's subtraction. 50 is multiplied by *w* because for each week he pays $50. Also consider how you would solve this with an actual number of weeks. For instance, after three weeks, the loan amount would be 10,000 − 50 − 50 − 50, or 10,000 − 50(3). This helps show why (C) is correct.

39.

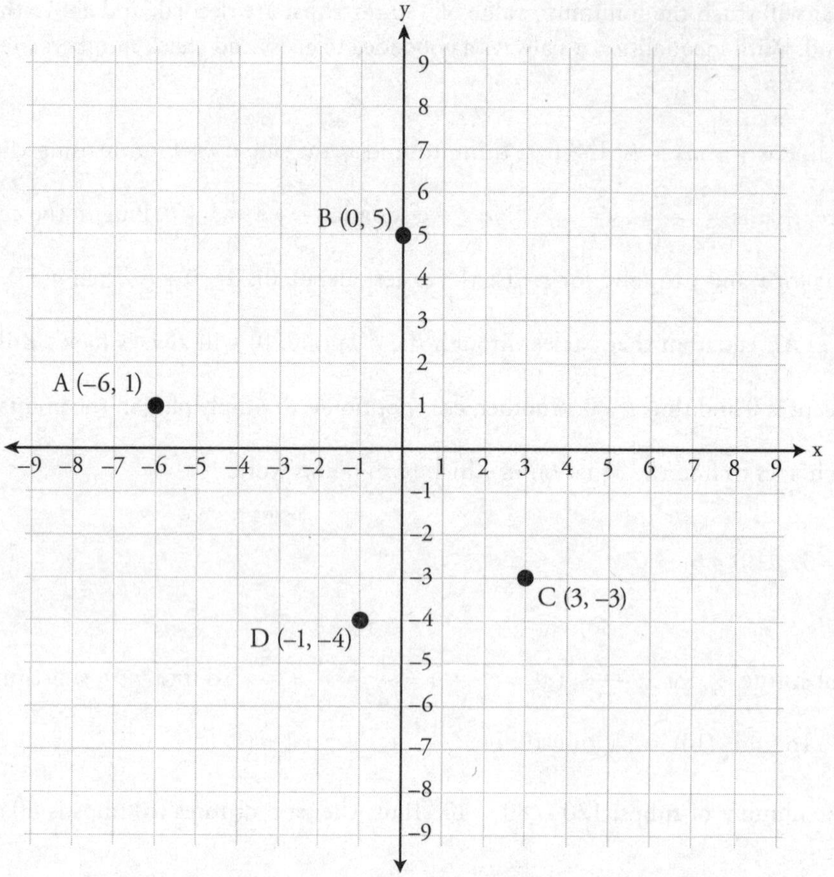

The *x*-coordinate comes first, so from the origin (0, 0) go the appropriate number of spaces to the right or left (right is positive and left is negative) and then go up or down the number of spaces in the *y*-coordinate (up is positive and down is negative).

40. The slope of line A is **greater than** the slope of line B. The *y*-intercept of line A is **less than** the *y*-intercept of line B. Determine the slope and *y*-intercept of the line shown in the graph. A good way to do this is to find two points. Try using (0, 2) and (1, 0). It's always best to look for points that clearly fall in a certain spot rather than estimating decimals. Use those two points to find the slope, using the formula $m = \dfrac{y_2 - y_1}{x_2 - x_1}$. Here, that is $\dfrac{0 - 2}{1 - 0} = \dfrac{-2}{1} = -2$. Thus, line A has a greater slope because it has a slope of $\dfrac{1}{2}$ (*m* in *y* = *mx* + *b*). The *y*-intercept is clear from the figure: The line crosses the *y*-axis at 2. Line A has a *y*-intercept of 0 because there is no *b* from the formula *y* = *mx* + *b*. Thus, the *y*-intercept of line A is less than the *y*-intercept of line B.

41. **D** The mathematical way to solve is to draw three blanks, one for each clothing item type, and put in the number of options for each one. Then simply multiply the options together: $6 \times 3 \times 2 = 36$. Another option is to write out the combinations. Since it's multiple choice and the answer choices are relatively small, it's a possible way to solve. Assign letters or numbers to the different clothing items and list the combinations in order.

42. Point A is the **minimum.** Point B is the ***y*-intercept**.

   The minimum is the lowest point on the function. Point A is the minimum because it continues in an increasing direction on both sides. It could also be described as the *x*-intercept. Point B is the *y*-intercept because the *y*-intercept is where the line crosses the *y*-axis. The words "slope" and "range" cannot describe a single point. The word "midpoint" refers to a point in the middle of a line segment. This function goes on forever in both directions, so it cannot be said to have a midpoint.

43. **A** To find the number of miles per gallon, divide the number of miles by the number of gallons for each car. Lightning is $287 \div 12 = 23.92$ miles per gallon. Do the same for the other cars to get 19.5 mpg for Fireball, 23.14 mpg for Journey, and 18.58 mpg for Metra. Thus, Lightning had the greatest number of miles per gallon.

44. **D** To factor, first set up two sets of parentheses. Since the first term is x^2, the first thing in both parentheses is x: $(x \quad)(x \quad)$. The last term is -32, and the second term includes a 4. Think of two numbers that multiply to equal 32 and add or subtract to equal 4. 32 and 1 won't work, 16 and 2 won't work, but 8 and 4 work. Fill those in: $(x \quad 8)(x \quad 4)$. Since it's a -32, there must be one plus sign and one minus sign. To get a positive 4 for the second term, it must be +8 and -4, as shown: $(x + 8)(x - 4)$. Always use FOIL to check that your answer equals the thing you started with. Another option for a multiple-choice problem such as this is to simply use FOIL on each answer choice and see which one equals the original expression. If you don't feel great about factoring but feel comfortable using FOIL, this is a great option.

45. **21** Create two equations, using two variables. Say *x* is the number of two-point questions and *y* is the number of three-point questions. Make sure to write that down so you remember which is which. Since there are 30 questions altogether, the first equation is $x + y = 30$. Then, with the other information, $2x + 3y = 81$ because 2 points for every two-point question plus 3 points for every three-point question equals 81 points. Solve using substitution. In the first equation, subtract *y* from both sides to get *x* alone: $x = 30 - y$. Now substitute that for *x* in the second equation: $2(30 - y) + 3y = 81$. Now distribute the 2: $60 - 2y + 3y = 81$. Combine like terms: $60 + y = 81$, and thus $y = 21$. That's the number of three-point questions and thus is the answer. One other option is to guess and check the numbers of two- and three-point questions, perhaps using a table.

46. **B** Carefully subtract everything in the second set of parentheses: $3x^2 - 4x + \frac{1}{2} - 8x^2 - x + 2$. Remember that two negatives turn into a positive. Now combine like terms to get $-5x^2 - 5x + \frac{5}{2}$. For the last part, $2 + \frac{1}{2} = \frac{4}{2} + \frac{1}{2} = \frac{5}{2}$. You can also use the calculator and change the fractions to decimals.

SOCIAL STUDIES

1. **C** Hopefully the date associated with this speech was helpful to you. The attacks on the Twin Towers in New York City, the Pentagon building in Washington, D.C., and the hijacking of a plane that crashed in Shanksville, Pennsylvania, all happened on September, 11, 2001, only nine days before President Bush's speech. The Persian Gulf War, (A), was in the early 1990s, while the Iraq War, (B), had not yet started. The terrorist attack on Benghazi, Libya, (D), occurred more than ten years after this speech.

2. **B** In Bush's speech, he promises to "pursue nations that provide aid or safe haven to terrorism." So, a nation need not attack the United States directly to be "pursued." Bush mentions "diplomacy," (C), but does not mention that diplomacy is preferable to other means of action.

3. **A** After 9/11, the United States would go on to invade two countries, first Afghanistan and then Iraq. We have never invaded Saudi Arabia, (C). Although the United States has had a presence in Pakistan, (D), we have never conducted a war against the government of Pakistan. Military activities in Serbia, (B), happened in the 1990s, well before 9/11.

4. **C** The GED® test may occasionally test you on the economic concept of "supply and demand." "Supply" refers to the amount of product (or service) that is available for purchase. "Demand" refers to consumers' desire for the product. In this case, you are told that the product is "popular." Therefore, demand is high. Eliminate (A) and (D). The law of supply and demand states that an increase in demand will naturally lead to an increase in supply. That matches up with (C). Choice (B) is close, but you cannot be sure if the price will decrease right away. If, for instance, the demand continued to outpace the supply, then prices could still remain high.

5. **1.1** According to the graph, January 2013 was a 7.8 and January 2014 was a 6.7. 7.8 – 6.7 = 1.1

6. **B** Count the number of bars between each labeled interval. There are six bars from January to June, so each bar must represent a month. Four bars from January must mean the 7.5 bar is at May 2013.

7. **diplomacy, fiscal responsibility**

   This question is testing you on your knowledge of some key terms. Protectionism is the desire to "protect" one's country economically and usually involves some fairly strict measures such as imposing tariffs on imported goods and limiting trade with foreign countries. There is no evidence that Eisenhower took such measures. Isolationism is also a fairly extreme approach to foreign policy which would imply that Eisenhower did not involve the United States in any foreign wars or other military entanglements. Although he did end the Korean War, the passage explicitly states that he *rescued* the Republicans from isolationism, so this cannot be a correct. (Diplomacy means that Eisenhower negotiated well with foreign countries such as "he strengthened European alliances"), while fiscal responsibility would pertain to his ability to "balance the budget."

8. **C** Eisenhower ended the Korean War "without getting into any others," so this was an example of "military restraint." He also "strengthened European alliances." The entire description suggests that Eisenhower was "moderate," since he did not mindlessly follow the more extreme members of his party ("isolationism and McCarthyism." Therefore, he was not completely loyal to his party: He rebelled against his party in certain matters.

9. **A** The Great Depression is the term given to the state of severe economic hardship that America found itself in during the 1930s, the years before World War II. One of the worst aspects of the Depression was the way it left many of the poorest Americans unemployed. The War gave many young men jobs, (B), but these were not high-paying jobs. The greatest boom in terms of employment came from private sector jobs that were created in order to support the war effort: manufacturing jobs dedicated to producing airplanes, firearms, and other military equipment. Women joined the workforce, too, so there is no question that the War enabled many Americans to increase their standard of living. Shipping products overseas, (C), was not detrimental to the economy; in fact, many companies benefitted from an increased ability to export their goods. Rationing, (D), was fairly limited and was not severe enough to cause starvation.

10. **D** This set of questions is testing you on geography. Where would the most timber be harvested? Not in New York and New Jersey (Region 2), since these are largely industrial and manufacturing areas. Region 6 includes many dry and desert areas, so rule this out. Region 7 is mostly prairie and farmland, so this cannot be right. Region 10 (the Pacific Northwest) makes sense, since there is not only lots of harvestable timber, but also endangered species such as cougars, wolves, and birds.

11. **B** Industrial air pollution would be most severe in places with many factories and a highly concentrated population. Region 2 would certainly qualify, since New York and New Jersey are very densely populated and have many factories. Regions 4, 7, 8, and 10 may have industrial areas, but they also have vast areas of wilderness and farmland. Between the two options we have left, (A) and (B), which region has more industry, Region 1 or Region 5? Notice that Region 5 includes big industrial cities such as Detroit, Michigan and Chicago, Illinois. These places are likely to be more polluted than Region 1 (New England).

12. **C** The key word in this question is "agriculture." Where is the most agriculture done in the United States? Possibly California, but Region 9 is not an option. That leaves us with the Heartland. Most corn, wheat, and soybeans are grown in states such as Nebraska, Kansas, and Iowa.

13. **C** The First and Second Great Awakenings, (B) and (D), were religious movements, while the Communist Revolution, (A), was a political movement. The Industrial Revolution, on the other hand, refers to the era of innovative technologies described in the text.

14. **D** Notice the time period: 1840 to early 1900s. Cellular telephones were not invented until the latter part of the 20th century and were not in common use until the 1990s.

15. **C** Notice that the top of the map indicates that the northern part of Beringia bordered the Arctic Sea. Africa is nowhere near the cold Arctic, so rule out (A) and (D). According to the map, the migrants are walking from Asia, so rule out (B). Therefore, they must be walking from the northeastern corner of Russia to the northwestern portion of North America, modern-day Alaska. Beringia no longer exists and is now covered in water. You might know it as the Bering Strait.

16. **A** Check the key. Austria-Hungary is listed under "Defeated Former Empires." This means that Austria and Hungary were once a united empire.

17. **D** Even if you have not heard the term "totalitarianism," the quote by William Rubenstein gives you some good clues. He mentions the Nazis, "mass murders and purges of the Communist World," and the Armenian genocide. In order to carry out such mass murders, a government would need total control, (D). Choice (A) is unknown. Choice (B) may be true in some cases, but not in all. And (C) may occur after some time, but is not what *makes* a government totalitarian.

18. **D** Rubenstein specifically mentions Germany, so rule out (A). Hopefully you remembered that Russia was Communist throughout much of the 20th century, so rule out (B). Turkey may not be familiar to you, but Switzerland is a safe choice, since it has been a neutral and stable country for centuries. (The Armenian genocide occurred in Turkey.)

19. **B** This is a painting of the Boston Tea Party. The Sons of Liberty were a radical group of American colonists in the late 1700s who wanted independence from Britain. Among their list of grievances was their unhappiness with new laws that favored the East India Tea Company and put American tea merchants at a severe disadvantage. They protested by dressing up as Indians, boarding an East India tea ship, and dumping boxes of tea into Boston Harbor.

20. **A** The onlookers are raising their hats as a sign of solidarity, praising the actions of the Sons of Liberty.

21. **C** The key phrase here is "endowed by their Creator." So, unalienable rights are those bestowed upon us by God and cannot (or should not) be altered by the actions of a government. Choice (B) may seem like a close choice, but "legal" rights would, in fact, be laws created about more minor issues, subject to change at the whims of a democracy. "Natural" rights should be *un*changeable, since they come from God. Choice (D) is too narrow, since natural rights are not limited to just freedom of religion.

22. **C** The Kansas-Nebraska Act was intended to be a novel and democratic way to deal with the issue of slavery: Let the people in individual counties decide, by popular vote, whether those regions would allow slavery or not. Unfortunately, though, the Kansas-Nebraska act made this territory a hotbed for pro- and anti-slavery activists who moved to this state to try to promote their agendas. Choice (D) is too strong, since they were not necessarily looking to start a war. Choices (A) and (B) may be true, but were not directly related to slavery issues.

23. **A** Once a number of pro- and anti-slavery factions moved into Kansas, they battled over whether to make an area slave or free. Some of these battles led to loss of life, thus the nickname "Bleeding Kansas." This was before the Civil War, not during, so rule out (D).

24. **C** Political advocacy is also known as "lobbying." Although lobbying is controversial, it can be done legally without resorting to bribery, (A). The lobbyists are advocating for the passage or stifling of certain laws, but are not themselves doing the legislating, (C).

25. **B** This is a tough question, but you might notice that a couple of the treaties include Indian names, such as Tippecanoe and Mississinwas. Michigan and Chicago were also Indian tribes (Chicago was not a city in 1821!). You might also remember that the United States government made more treaties with Indian tribes than with any other groups.

26. **A** This is testing your general knowledge of historical time periods. Although you do not need to memorize specific dates for the GED® test, it does help to know that the Revolutionary War, Articles of Confederation, and Constitution all occurred during the 1770s and 1780s.

27. **A** "Taxes, conscription, and military campaigns" are all mentioned in the second sentence of the quote. Although the Federalists hoped for economic growth, that does not mean that the Antifederalists opposed it.

28. **D** According to the end of the quote, Federalists wanted "enlarged powers of the general government." Choice (D) would directly contradict this. Federalists are not necessarily opposed to individual liberties, (C), as long as they believe the federal government has sufficient power in most situations.

29. **C** This is testing your knowledge of World War I, which was known for innovative fighting methods, including the wide use of trench warfare, especially in parts of France.

30. **D** The GED® test is testing you on some key terms. Isolationism, neutrality, and non-interventionism all pertain to foreign policy. A country practicing these principles would tend not to get involved in world conflicts. Protectionism, though, is an economic policy that has little to do with involvement in foreign wars.

31. **D** Germany is not listed as an ally in either of these lists, so rule out (B). France and Great Britain were both U.S. allies, but we have not had a confrontational relationship with either of these countries since the War of 1812—over a hundred years before World War II. The Soviet Union (listed as "Russia" during World War I), though, did become our Communist nemesis during the Cold War (the years following World War II).

32. **B** You can rule out China, (A), since it is listed as an Ally during World War II. The answer cannot be (D), since the Soviet Union was a Communist enemy after World War II. Choice (C) looks tempting, but Japan was only an enemy in the Second World War, not the First. Germany, (B), is the best answer, since it was the "bad boy" of both World Wars, but became a thriving and peaceful democracy after World War II.

33. **D** The word "majority" means "more than 50%." If you add up the percentage of Jewish people killed, it is less than 50%, (A). The same is true of Poles and Polish Jews, (B). Choice (C) is unknown from the graph and is unlikely to be true (German Nazis killed far more). That leaves (D). According to the chart, Polish Jews made up 24% of those killed. Add up the other Jewish percentages and you get 18%.

34. **D** The Holocaust occurred in the 1930s and 1940s during World War II. All the other wars listed are outside of this era.

35. **B** This is a very tricky question testing your logic. Notice that the economist's statement involves a causal relationship. In simple terms: "When the debt rises, it *causes* the economy to slow." (X caused Y). How do you weaken any causal relationship? Either show that there is some other cause (Z caused Y) or show that the causation is reversed (Y caused X). Choice (B) does the latter, so it effectively weakens the economist's statement. The other answers are meant to seem *very* close, but if you read (A) and (C) carefully, they are really strengthening the statement. (Correlation is very similar to causation.) Choice (D) is close, but keep in mind that low levels of debt are not the subject of the economist's statement. The economist is speaking of high levels of debt, so this does not weaken as effectively as (B).

SCIENCE

1. **lunar eclipse**

    A lunar eclipse occurs when the Earth moves between the Moon and the Sun, resulting in a shadow cast over the Moon. A solar eclipse occurs when the Moon moves between the Earth and the Sun, resulting in a shadow cast over the Earth.

2. **A** *Power = work/time* is the correct formula for determining power. Power is defined as the rate at which work is done to an object. Rates are always related to time. Think of the most common rate you probably know: a speed limit. It's a rate that describes how far a car can travel in a given amount of time. Power works the same way: It represents the amount of work that can be done in a certain amount of time.

3. **D** Prophase, metaphase, anaphase, telophase is the correct order of the four stages of mitosis.

4.

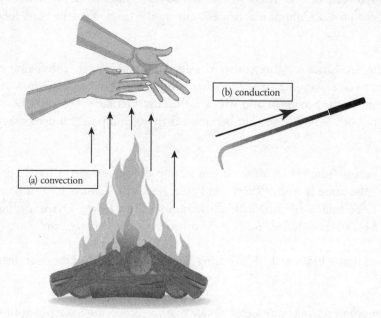

(b) conduction

(a) convection

Convection describes the heating process that causes warmer, lighter air to rise, and colder, denser air to sink, so this should be placed above the fire and below the hands that are above the fire. Conduction describes the heating process by which heat or electricity is transmitted directly through a substance or object that is a different temperature than the heat source, like the iron that is being held over the fire. Radiation describes the heating process in which energy or heat is given off in waves that move outward from the source.

5. **B** Both parents have freckles. The question indicates that freckles are a dominant trait, which is represented by a capital F. Each section of the Punnett Square combines one indicator from each parent. So the top left corner (FF) tells you that one F came from one parent and one F came from the other. On your own paper, you could write one F above the first column and one F to the left of the first row. The bottom left corner (FF) indicates exactly the same thing: one F came from each parent. Since you already have an F at the top of the first column, write an F to the left of the bottom row. The top right corner (Ff) indicates that this option has one dominant (F) and one recessive (f) trait. The label to the left of this row indicates that the F is already accounted for, so the f is coming from the top parent; label the second

column with an f. The bottom right corner confirms the same. So, one parent contributed FF and one parent contributed Ff. Since both have F, both must have freckles.

6. **B** The Punnett Square created based on the information in the question would look like this, if you placed the heterozygous parent on top and the recessive homozygous parent on the left:

	F	f
f	Ff	ff
f	Ff	ff

Based on this Punnett Square, you can see that 2 out of 4 possible results have two recessive indicators, meaning that there is a 50% chance that offspring will not have freckles ($\frac{2}{4} = \frac{1}{2} = 50\%$).

7. **remain the same**

Consider the equation: $F = \dfrac{G \times m \times M}{r^2}$. The question says that the mass of one object (M) is doubled, or multiplied by 2, and the mass of the other object (m) is reduced by half, or multiplied by $\frac{1}{2}$. If you add those in to the equation $\left(F = \dfrac{G \times 2M \times \left(\frac{1}{2}\right)m}{r^2} \right)$, you can see that we would end up multiplying $2 \times \frac{1}{2}$, which is equal to 1. Anything multiplied by 1 stays the same, so the overall gravitational force produced in this case would also stay the same.

8. **D** Read carefully! First, make sure to consider ONLY the basic substances—the ones whose pH is above 7. These include only baking soda (pH 8) and dishwasher soap (pH 12). To find the average, add these together and divide by the number of values added: $\dfrac{8 + 12}{2} = 10$.

9. **D** Man contributed to the demise of the West African Black Rhinoceros. Choice (A) is not provable—you have no way of knowing how many West African Black Rhinoceroses were alive before the early 20th century. Choice (B) is likewise not provable—the passage does not indicate about the other two sub-species that remained at the beginning of the 2000s. Choice (C) is extreme—while there are no more West African Black Rhinoceroses left, there may still be other black rhinoceroses of other sub-species alive. Choice (D), though, is provable, as hunters, farmers, and poachers are all humans who killed West African Black Rhinoceroses.

10. **B** The passage provides no information to either support or refute the scientists' hypothesis. The passage does not provide ANY information about what ailments some people believe that powdered rhinoceros horn might cure; it simply states that some people held this belief. Therefore, eliminate (A). While the passage does indicate other reasons that humans killed the rhinoceroses, this information neither supports nor refutes the scientists' hypothesis as described in this question, so eliminate (C) and (D). Choice (B) is the correct answer.

11. **broken, absorbed, endothermic**

    When ice melts, it loses its shape, which means that the bonds between the molecules have been broken apart—they're not being held as tightly together as they are when they're in the solid form of an ice cube. The temperature of the substance also changes: Ice is much colder than water! And anytime that heat is absorbed, an endothermic reaction is taking place.

12. **D** Kinetic energy was converted into thermal energy. Energy from the motion of the tires rubbing against the brakes (kinetic energy) was converted into heat (thermal energy).

13. **friction, conduction**

    Friction via thermal transfer creates heat when the brakes rub against the tire rims. When Marty touches the brakes directly, conduction allows for the transfer of heat from the rims to his hand.

14. **B** By looking at the total number of Os (oxygen) present, you can see that there are more molecules of O to start with than exist at the end. That means the process requires oxygen, so eliminate anything that says "anaerobic," meaning without oxygen. Eliminate (C) and (D). Then, looking at the result, you see that there is only water (H_2O) and ATP, so eliminate (A) because it says that carbon dioxide (CO_2) is a result of the reaction.

15. **herbivores, carnivores**

    Grasshoppers consume plants (grass), which makes them herbivores. Monkeys consume animals (grasshoppers and snakes), so they are carnivores.

16. **B** When one link in a food web experiences a population decline, any organisms that it is connected to are affected as well. Both vultures and lions feed on rhinoceroses, so they would definitely feel effects of a decreased rhinoceros population. Eliminate (A) and (C), and consider the remaining choices. Giraffes are not directly connected to rhinoceroses, but they share a food source (tree leaves) as well as a predator (lions). So, a drastic change in rhinoceros population would indirectly affect giraffes. Snakes, on the other hand, have no connection to rhinoceroses and so would not necessarily be affected by rhinoceros numbers. Eliminate (D), and (B) is the best answer.

17. **C** Cheetahs are the only secondary consumers listed, because they are the only ones that eat other animals. Giraffes, rhinoceroses, and mice all eat plants or trees, so they are considered primary consumers.

18. **C** The correct order is exosphere, thermosphere, mesosphere, stratosphere, and troposphere. These are the correct representation from the *outside in*, which is what the question asks for. Be careful not to fall for (A), which is the correct representation from the *inside out*.

19. **A** The ozone layer is found in the stratosphere, where it helps to filter out UV rays. Since this filtering process does not reduce UV rays in any layers above the stratosphere, those are likely to have significantly more UV. That means that the layer below the stratosphere will have less UV, because the UV will be filtered out. As a result, the troposphere, (A), will have the least accumulation of UV.

20. **B** Use the formula $MA = \dfrac{output\ force}{input\ force}$ to solve: $MA = \dfrac{4000}{250} = 16$.

21. **B** The United States predominantly uses an efficient, inexpensive energy source that poses danger to relatively few people. The pie chart indicates that the largest source of energy for electricity in the United States is coal (38.8%). Using that information and looking at the information about coal, the passage states that the advantages of coal include generating large amounts of power and keeping that power inexpensive. Another way to say that is to say that coal is efficient. The passage also indicates that a disadvantage of coal is that miners are exposed to risk; since it poses a danger to the miners, it's reasonable to say that it poses danger to the people responsible for bringing it to the public.

22. **86.8%**

    Subtract the percentage of electricity generated by renewals (13.2%) from the total electricity generated (100%): 100% − 13.2% = 86.8%.

23. **C** Volcanoes are commonly found along the boundaries between tectonic plates. On questions that ask about what can be inferred, be careful to stay close to what the passages says—don't make unsupported assumptions. The map shows that the volcanoes in the Ring of Fire occur along the edges of the Pacific Ocean, and the passage indicates that the Ring of Fire is a result of the Pacific Plate being subducted under other plates. Together, this leads to a conclusion that the volcanoes are common near where the plates meet.

24. **A** Solubility varies directly with temperature. Looking at the graph, the temperature increases along the x-axis and solubility increases along the y-axis. The lines within the graph that represent the six crystalline solids increase in solubility as the temperature increases.

25. **decrease**

    Based on the figure given with the question, if the deer population decreased, it would be reasonable to conclude that the tick population would decrease. Because deer is the preferred host during the winter months, it is reasonable to conclude that if there are fewer deer there would be fewer opportunities for the tick to feed during winter.

26. **protein, RNA, DNA**

    The central dogma of biology states that protein is made from RNA, which is made from DNA. Pay attention to the wording here: Protein is *made from* DNA, which is *made from* RNA. You probably know that DNA is the starting point, but this question starts from the end and works backward.

27. **C** The carrying capacity is represented by a fairly flat, horizontal line on a population graph. On this graph, the line never actually flattens out to a horizontal line. So, look for what value the graph hovers around most consistently, which is 8,000. It goes above and below 8,000 but seems to narrow in on this value.

28. **circulatory, digestive**

    The heart is part of the circulatory system and the esophagus is part of the digestive system. The heart is responsible for pumping blood through the circulatory system to transport nutrients and oxygen to all of the cells in the body and to transport waste away from the cells of the body. The esophagus connects the throat to the stomach in the digestive system.

29. **D** Natural selection occurs without human intervention: Organisms adapt to increase their odds of survival and ability to reproduce. Artificial selection, however, is caused by humans, as in the case of specifically breeding a dog with an end function in mind. Lizards adapting to grow longer legs, (A), bacteria adapting to become more resistant to antibiotics, (B), and rodents' fur changing color for better camouflage, (C), are all examples of natural selection—humans did not impact any of these changes. Humans deliberately breeding dogs for certain characteristics is an example of human intervention, which is the necessary component of artificial selection.

30. **artificial selection**

    Thoroughbred racehorses resulting from careful selective breeding are an example of artificial selection. Once again, the human impact of selective breeding indicates that this is an example of artificial selection.

31. **B** The charge was converted into energy to power the car. According to the Law of Conservation of Energy, the battery's original charge must have been converted into another type of energy. It could not have just disappeared, (A), or leaked out of the battery, (D). While the energy might have been destroyed, (C), it still would have been converted into some other kind of energy.

32. An iceberg melting is an example of **the Law of Conservation of Mass.** While the state of the liquid has changed from ice to water, it will still retain the same amount of mass as a liquid as it had as a solid.

33. **A** A tsunami wave will have more energy than a wave caused by a passing thunderstorm. Waves caused by a tsunami will have greater amplitude than will waves caused by a passing storm. Therefore, the larger amplitude will produce greater energy. This may make (D) appealing, but (D) goes too far in saying that tsunami waves have more energy than ALL other kinds of waves—that is not provable, according to the passage.

34. **be louder**

    The passage tells us that a wave's amplitude defines how much energy it has. Since this question refers to sound waves, the amount of energy of a sound wave is the volume of the sound, with greater energy meaning a louder sound. The speed at which sound travels does not depend on amplitude, and the pitch of the sound is defined by the wave's frequency, not its amplitude.

35. **Transpiration from plants**

    Transpiration from plants does not result from another part of the process, and is not an intermediate step in any of the processes. Therefore, it could potentially be removed and the remaining cycle could continue uninterrupted.

Chapter 9
Practice Test 4

Reasoning Through Language Arts

Welcome!

Here is some information that you need to know before you start this test:

- You should not spend too much time on a question if you are not certain of the answer; answer it the best you can, and go on to the next question.
- If you are not certain of the answer to a question, you can mark your answer for review and come back to it later.
- This test has three sections.
- You have **35 minutes** to complete Section 1.
- When you finish Section 1, you may review those questions.
- You may not go back to Section 1 once you have finished your review.
- You have **45 minutes** to complete the Extended Response question in Section 2.
- After completing Section 2, you may take a 10-minute break.
- You have **60 minutes** to complete Section 3.
- When you finish Section 3, you may review those questions.

Turn the page to begin.

GO ON TO THE NEXT PAGE

Questions 1 through 8 refer to the following passage.

Excerpt from *Hungry Hearts*
by Anzia Yezierska

1   Two months later, a wasted, haggard Hanneh Hayyeh stood in the kitchen, folding Mrs. Preston's wash in her basket, when the janitor—the servant of her oppressor—handed her another note.

2   "From the landlord," he said in his toneless voice.

3   Hanneh Hayyeh paled. She could tell from his smirking sneer that it was a second notice of increased rental.

4   It grew black before her eyes. She was too stunned to think. Her first instinct was to run to her husband; but she needed sympathy—not nagging. And then in her darkness she saw a light—the face of her friend, Mrs. Preston. She hurried to her.

5   "Oi—friend! The landlord raised me my rent again," she gasped, dashing into the room like a thing hounded by wild beasts.

6   Mrs. Preston was shocked by Hanneh Hayyeh's distraught appearance. For the first time she noticed the ravages of worry and hunger.

7   "Hanneh Hayyeh! Try to calm yourself. It is really quite inexcusable the way the landlords are taking advantage of the situation. There must be a way out. We'll fix it up somehow."

8   "How fix it up?" Hanneh Hayyeh flared.

9   "We'll see that you get the rent you need." There was reassurance and confidence in Mrs. Preston's tone.

10   Hanneh Hayyeh's eyes flamed. Too choked for utterance, her breath ceased for a moment.

11   "I want no charity! You think maybe I came to beg? No—I want justice!"

12   She shrank in upon herself, as though to ward off the raised whip of her persecutor. "You know how I feel?" Her voice came from the terrified depths of her. "It's as if the landlord pushed me in a corner and said to me: 'I want money, or I'll squeeze from you your life!' I have no money, so he takes my life.

GO ON TO THE NEXT PAGE

13   "Last time, when he raised me my rent, I done without meat and without milk. What more can I do without?"

14   The shudder that shook Hanneh Hayyeh communicated itself to Mrs. Preston. "I know the prices are hard to bear," she stammered, appalled.

15   "There used to be a time when poor people could eat cheap things," the toneless voice went on. "But now there ain't no more cheap things. Potatoes—rice—fish—even dry bread is dear. Look on my shoes! And I who used to be so neat with myself. I can't no more have my torn shoes fixed up. A pair of shoes or a little patch is only for millionaires."

16   "Something must be done," broke in Mrs. Preston, distraught for the first time in her life. "But in the meantime, Hanneh Hayyeh, you must accept this to tide you over." She spoke with finality as she handed her a bill.

17   Hanneh Hayyeh thrust back the money. "Ain't I hurt enough without you having to hurt me yet with charity? You want to give me hush money to swallow down an unrightness that burns my flesh? I want justice."

18   The woman's words were like bullets that shot through the static security of Mrs. Preston's life. She realized with a guilty pang that while strawberries and cream were being served at her table in January, Hanneh Hayyeh had doubtless gone without a square meal in months.

19   "We can't change the order of things overnight," faltered Mrs. Preston, baffled and bewildered by Hanneh Hayyeh's defiance of her proffered aid.

20   "Change things? There's got to be a change!" cried Hanneh Hayyeh with renewed intensity. "The world as it is is not to live in any longer. If only my Aby would get back quick. But until he comes, I'll fight till all America will have to stop and listen to me. You was always telling me that the lowest nobody got something to give to America. And that's what I got to give to America—the last breath in my body for justice. I'll wake up America from its sleep. I'll go myself to the President with my Aby's soldier picture and ask him was all this war to let loose a bunch of blood-suckers to suck the marrow out from the people?"

21   "Hanneh Hayyeh," said Mrs. Preston, with feeling, "these laws are far from just, but they are all we have so far. Give us time. We are young. We are still learning. We're doing our best."

GO ON TO THE NEXT PAGE

22   Numb with suffering the woman of the ghetto looked straight into the eyes of Mrs. Preston. "And you too—you too hold by the landlord's side?—Oi—I see! Perhaps you too got property out by agents."

23   A sigh that had in it the resignation of utter hopelessness escaped from her. "Nothing can hurt me no more—And you always stood out to me in my dreams as the angel from love and beautifulness. You always made-believe to me that you're only for democracy."

24   Tears came to Mrs. Preston's eyes. But she made no move to defend herself or reply and Hanneh Hayyeh walked out in silence.

1. The narrative implies many past and future events. Write the letters of the events into the chart to show the order in which they would occur.

Order of Events

```
┌─────────────────────────────┐
│                             │
└─────────────────────────────┘

┌─────────────────────────────┐
│                             │
└─────────────────────────────┘

┌─────────────────────────────┐
│                             │
└─────────────────────────────┘

┌─────────────────────────────┐
│                             │
└─────────────────────────────┘
```

┌─────────────────────────────┐
│ (a) Hanneh formulates her   │
│ own solution to her problem.│
└─────────────────────────────┘

┌─────────────────────────────┐
│ (b) Aby returns from his war│
│ service.   │
└─────────────────────────────┘

┌─────────────────────────────┐
│ (c) Hanneh idolizes Mrs.   │
│ Preston.   │
└─────────────────────────────┘

┌─────────────────────────────┐
│ (d) Hanneh does without   │
│ food to pay rent.   │
└─────────────────────────────┘

2. When Mrs. Preston remarks "We'll see that you get the rent you need" (paragraph 9), Hanneh's reaction to Mrs. Preston is primarily one of

A. gratitude.
B. disbelief.
C. indignation.
D. relief.

3. Which quotation from the story best supports the idea that the crisis Hanneh is experiencing is also affecting the larger community?

A. "It is really quite inexcusable the way the landlords are taking advantage of the situation."
B. "But until he comes, I'll fight till all America will have to stop and listen to me."
C. "Ain't I hurt enough without you having to hurt me yet with charity?"
D. "You always made-believe to me that you're only for democracy."

GO ON TO THE NEXT PAGE

4. What can the reader infer about the relationship between Hanneh and her husband?

   A. Hanneh's woe is partly caused by the fact that her husband is so far away.
   B. Hanneh's husband does not show compassion for Hanneh's worries.
   C. Hanneh's husband hounds her like a wild beast, which causes her distress.
   D. Talking with her husband makes Hanneh feel choked.

5. What can readers infer from the tone of the dialogue between the two women?

   A. Hanneh is just trying a ploy on Mrs. Preston's feelings in order to get Mrs. Preston to offer her money.
   B. Mrs. Preston's cool, logical reasoning cannot overcome the tide of Hanneh's emotion.
   C. Awareness of the larger social crisis gives both women a sense of urgency during the conversation.
   D. The difference in the degree of tone reveals and contributes to the unraveling of their friendship.

6. As the passage progresses, the differences in mindset between the two women become more apparent. Write the letters for the descriptions of their assumptions in the correct column, depending on whether Mrs. Preston or Hanneh holds that assumption.

Hanneh	Mrs. Preston

(a) Their friendship is one of equals.

(b) There is no reasoning with an oppressor.

(c) Help is best given in the form of direct assistance.

(d) A political system that has problems is still trustworthy.

(e) This conversation is about the climax of a problem.

GO ON TO THE NEXT PAGE

7.   What can readers infer about Hanneh's character?

   A.   She is a timid, fearful person.
   B.   She values personal tidiness and appearance.
   C.   She resents her son for leaving her to manage expenses alone.
   D.   She idealizes American life.

8.   Aside from the rise in her rent, the passage implies there is another cause of Hanneh's financial crisis. Which of the following is this other cause?

   A.   Her costs have outstripped her income.
   B.   Her wages have been lowered.
   C.   There is more competition for work, so the amount of cash she brings in has gone down.
   D.   She is having to send money overseas to support Aby.

GO ON TO THE NEXT PAGE

Questions 9 through 16 refer to the following passage.

Excerpt from "The Tyranny of Things"
by Edward Sandford Martin

1   There was a story in the newspapers the other day about
a Massachusetts minister who resigned his charge because
someone had given his parish a fine house, and his parishioners
wanted him to live in it. His salary was too small, he said, to
admit of his living in a big house, and he would not do it. He
was even deaf to the proposal that he should share the proposed
tenement with the sewing societies and clubs of his church, and
when the matter came to a serious issue, he relinquished his
charge and sought a new field of usefulness. The situation was
an amusing instance of the embarrassment of riches. Let no one
to whom restricted quarters may have grown irksome, and who
covets larger dimensions of shelter, be too hasty in deciding
that the minister was wrong. Did you ever see the house that
Hawthorne lived in at Lenox? Did you ever see Emerson's house
at Concord? They are good houses for Americans to know and
remember. They permitted thought.

2   A big house is one of the greediest cormorants which can light
upon a little income. Backs may go threadbare and stomachs
may worry along on indifferent filling, but a house will have
things, though its occupants go without. It is rarely complete,
and constantly tempts the imagination to flights in brick and
dreams in lath and plaster. It develops annual thirsts for paint
and wall-paper, at least, if not for marble and wood-carving. The
plumbing in it must be kept in order on pain of death. Whatever
price is put on coal, it has to be heated in winter; and if it is
rural or suburban, the grass about it must be cut even though
funerals in the family have to be put off for the mowing. If
the tenants are not rich enough to hire people to keep their
house clean, they must do it themselves, for there is no excuse
that will pass among housekeepers for a dirty house. Yet such
is human folly, that for a man to refuse to live in a house
because it is too big for him, is such an exceptional exhibition
of sense that it becomes the favorite paragraph of a day in the
newspapers.

3   An ideal of earthly comfort, so common that every reader
must have seen it, is to get a house so big that it is burdensome
to maintain, and fill it up so full of jimcracks that it is a constant
occupation to keep it in order. Then, when the expense of living
in it is so great that you can't afford to go away and rest from
the burden of it, the situation is complete and boarding-houses
and cemeteries begin to yawn for you. How many Americans, do
you suppose, out of the droves that flock annually to Europe, are
running away from oppressive houses?

GO ON TO THE NEXT PAGE

4   When nature undertakes to provide a house, it fits the occupant. Animals which build by instinct build only what they need, but man's building instinct, if it gets a chance to spread itself at all, is boundless, just as all his instincts are. For it is man's peculiarity that nature has filled him with impulses to do things, and left it to his discretion when to stop. She never tells him when he has finished. And perhaps we ought not to be surprised that in so many cases it happens that he doesn't know, but just goes ahead as long as the materials last.

9. What does the author mean by "jimcracks" (paragraph 3)?

A. strewn rubbish
B. necessary furniture
C. steady damage
D. useless items

10. The author uses several persuasive techniques to form his essay. Write the letters of two of the techniques the author employs into the boxes below.

(a) Using irony to emphasize a point with which he disagrees

(b) Using a metaphor by describing an inanimate object with the characteristics of a living organism

(c) Asking a rhetorical question to stimulate thought on a topic

(d) Making an appeal to the readers' emotions through nostalgic representations

(e) Citing an expert's opinion to support his argument

11. Why does the author claim that a big house "develops annual thirsts for paint and wall-paper"?

A. to show that these are the most significant expenses on a house
B. to illustrate the endless work involved in keeping a big house
C. to emphasize that the house becomes more "greedy" the longer one lives in it
D. to show how often paint and wall-paper are required in a house

12. By using the phrase "the situation is complete and boarding-houses and cemeteries begin to yawn for you" (paragraph 3), the author implies that

A. the owners of the large houses will eventually lose interest in the pointless act of house maintenance.
B. the obsession with house maintenance can consume the years and resources of the owners until they meet a destitute old age.
C. the owners of the large oppressive houses will flee to Europe to visit historic graveyards and boarding houses.
D. once the security of a large home is obtained, the owners can comfortably plan for their retirement and end of life.

GO ON TO THE NEXT PAGE

13. How does paragraph 4 relate to paragraph 3?

    A. Paragraph 4 gives an explanation for the behavior described in paragraph 3.

    B. Both paragraph 4 and paragraph 3 describe two views of the same event.

    C. Paragraph 3 provides a general claim, while Paragraph 4 provides a specific example in support of that claim.

    D. Paragraph 3 offers a view, while paragraph 4 offers a rebuttal to that view.

14. What can the reader infer about the houses of Emerson and Hawthorne?

    A. They are examples of the big houses the author describes later.

    B. They are the sorts of houses proper for ministers of the time.

    C. They are of a size that the author would not criticize.

    D. They are examples of houses that nature builds to fit the occupant.

15. The moral of this passage is

    A. the simplest approach is the best.
    B. you can't improve on nature.
    C. bigger is better.
    D. even the wealthy have problems.

16. If the author could choose his own living quarters, which of the following alternatives would he be most likely to choose?

    A. a cottage with enough room for his family's basic needs

    B. a canvas tent in the middle of the woods so that he could observe the animals

    C. a boarding-house in Europe to get away from the oppressive houses of America

    D. a small brick house with wood-carved features and decorated with many art objects

GO ON TO THE NEXT PAGE

17. The passage below is incomplete. For each "Select" option, choose the option that correctly completes the sentence. (For this practice test, circle your selection.)

Albert Sonja
Career Counselor
Manditon Adult Education Center

Dear Mr. Sonja,

I have received your letter detailing the story of Rosa R., who was born overseas to a U.S. citizen, but her birth and citizenship were not registered with the U.S. Embassy. Now Rosa wonders if she has derived U.S. citizenship.

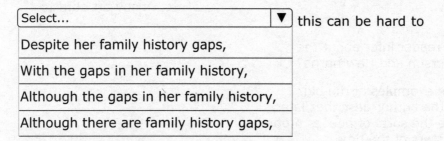 this can be hard to

Select...▼
Despite her family history gaps,
With the gaps in her family history,
Although the gaps in her family history,
Although there are family history gaps,

determine. Derivative citizenship can be quite complex and may require careful legal analysis.

If her mother was a U.S. citizen when she was born, Rosa may have derived U.S. citizenship. Whether someone born outside the United States to a U.S. citizen is herself a U.S. citizen

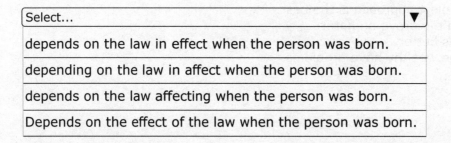

Select...▼
depends on the law in effect when the person was born.
depending on the law in affect when the person was born.
depends on the law affecting when the person was born.
Depends on the effect of the law when the person was born.

These laws have changed over the years, but usually require a consideration of whether the parent lived in the United States or its possessions for a specific period of time.

GO ON TO THE NEXT PAGE

If when Rosa was born, Rosa's mother was a U.S. citizen, but had never lived in the United States,

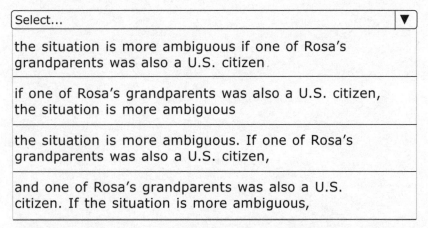

Select... ▼
the situation is more ambiguous if one of Rosa's grandparents was also a U.S. citizen
if one of Rosa's grandparents was also a U.S. citizen, the situation is more ambiguous
the situation is more ambiguous. If one of Rosa's grandparents was also a U.S. citizen,
and one of Rosa's grandparents was also a U.S. citizen. If the situation is more ambiguous,

then Rosa may still have derived U.S. citizenship. The provisions of immigration law that govern derivative citizenship are quite precise and circumstances in individual cases can be complex.

If Rosa's mother became a naturalized U.S. citizen after Rosa was born, derivative citizenship is still possible. This depends upon how many parents were naturalized, whether the naturalization happened after February 27, 2001, and whether Rosa was under 18 years old at the time. If her mother was naturalized after Rosa was 18,

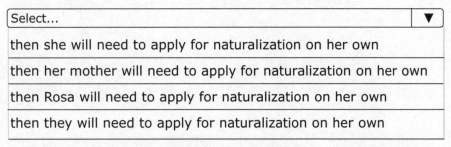

Select... ▼
then she will need to apply for naturalization on her own
then her mother will need to apply for naturalization on her own
then Rosa will need to apply for naturalization on her own
then they will need to apply for naturalization on her own

after she has been a permanent resident for at least 5 years.

To advise you further, I would need to know more information about whether Rosa's mother was a citizen when Rosa was born, whether Rosa's grandparents were citizens, and whether Rosa's mother had ever lived in the United States or its possessions.

I look forward to hearing from you.

Sincerely,

Judene Writ, esq.
Law Department
University of Manditon

GO ON TO THE NEXT PAGE

THIS PAGE INTENTIONALLY LEFT BLANK.

GO ON TO THE NEXT PAGE

Reasoning Through Language Arts, Section 2

Extended Response Answer Guidelines

Please use the guidelines below as you answer the Extended Response question on the Reasoning Through Language Arts test. Following these guidelines as closely as possible will ensure that you provide the best response.

1. **Please note that this task must be completed in no more than 45 minutes.** However, don't rush through your response. Be sure to read through the passage(s) and the prompt. Then think about the message you want to convey in your response. **Be sure to plan your response before you begin writing.** Draft your response and revise it as needed.

2. As you read, think carefully about the **argumentation** presented in the passage(s). "Argumentation" refers to the assumptions, claims, support, reasoning, and credibility on which a position is based. Pay close attention to **how the author(s) use these strategies to convey his or her (their) positions.**

3. When you write your essay, be sure to
   o **determine which position presented** in the passage(s) is **better supported** by evidence from the passage(s)
   o **explain why the position you chose is the better-supported one**
   o **remember, the better-supported position is not necessarily the position you agree with**
   o **defend your assertions with multiple pieces of evidence** from the passage(s)
   o **build your main points thoroughly**
   o **put your main points in logical order** and tie your details to your main points
   o **organize your response carefully** and consider your **audience, message, and purpose**
   o **use transitional words and phrases** to connect sentences, paragraphs, and ideas
   o **choose words carefully** to express your ideas clearly
   o **vary your sentence structure** to enhance the flow and clarity of your response
   o **reread and revise your response** to correct any errors in grammar, usage, or punctuation

GO ON TO THE NEXT PAGE

Instructions

Read

- On the **page 2 tab above**, you will **read two texts** presenting **different views** on the same topic.

- **Both writers argue** that **their position** on the issue is **correct**.

Plan

- **Analyze** the two texts **to determine** which writer presents the **stronger case**.

- **Develop your own argument** in which **you explain** how one position is **better supported** than the other.

- **Include** relevant and specific **evidence** from **both sources** to support your argument.

Write

- **Type** your response in the **box on the right**.

- Your response should be approximately **4 to 7 paragraphs of 3 to 7 sentences each**.

- **Remember** to allow a few minutes **to review and edit your response**.

You have up to **45 minutes** for reading, planning, writing, and editing your response.

Should the U.S. Retain the Electoral College?

1   In the Electoral College, a number of electors from each state (equal to its members of Congress) vote for president, usually for the candidate winning that state's popular vote. This could mean the election of a candidate who was rejected by the majority of voters nationwide: In 2000, George W. Bush got more electoral votes—and the presidency—but Al Gore won the popular vote. Many grassroots organizations advocate the dissolution of the Electoral College and the adoption of a popular election, but the system remains.

Arguments in Favor

2   **Reflects country by distribution:** No one area contains the majority (270) of electoral votes required to elect a president. So presidential candidates must work to unite states and regions rather than cater to regional differences, which is why presidential nominees tend to select vice presidential running mates from a different state.

3   **Empowers minority groups:** The Electoral College gives states with sparser, rural populations a more significant voice. The Electoral College also gives ethnic minority groups greater power, as they are more represented in States with the most

GO ON TO THE NEXT PAGE

electoral votes. A direct election of the president would damage those minority interests since their votes would be superseded by a majority of the popular vote.

4   **Stabilizes political parties:** The Electoral College reinforces the nation's two-party system, which allows for more broad campaigns instead of many parties splintering on specific issues. It encourages the proponents of vibrant but ineffective third parties to shelve their extremist views and blend into the Democrat or Republican parties, resulting in two stable, dominant parties which stay moderate on issues overall.

5   **Preserves states' importance:** The Founding Fathers choose the representative form of government to put the opinions of the individual state populations above the opinion of the total national population. The House of Representatives represents the states according to their populations, while the Senate represents each State equally regardless of population. Similarly, the Electoral College represents the states in the presidential election.

Arguments Against

6   **Allows election of disfavored candidates:** Although most citizens believe that the candidate with the most votes should win, the Electoral College allows for the election of a minority president, such as the scenario outlined in the 2000 election above. Also, a minority president could be elected if the electoral votes are split among three candidates so that no one obtained the necessary majority. In that case, one candidate could contribute electoral votes to another, or the U.S. House of Representatives would select the president.

7   **Permits "faithless" electors:** There is no guarantee that the electors' vote will mirror the state's popular vote. A "faithless elector" is one who votes for a candidate other than the one he or she promised to vote for. In the past, seven such "faithless" electors upset the votes in their states.

8   **Disproportionately represents states:** Because the minimum number of Electoral College votes for a state is three, some small states have a larger percentage of Electoral College votes than their percentage of U.S. population. Each of California's 55 Electoral College votes represents approximately 700,000 people while there are just under 200,000 people for each of Wyoming's three electoral votes.

9   **Discourages voter turnout:** A popular vote is straightforward: it's a simple majority. However, due to population changes, the Electoral College chooses delegates and reshuffles votes every 10 years. The multi-level process gives citizens the impression that an individual vote does not matter.

GO ON TO THE NEXT PAGE

Furthermore, since the number of electoral votes is independent of voter turnout, the states have no incentive to encourage voter participation.

10   **Limits voter choice:** The "popular vote winner takes all electors" mechanism means that third party or independent candidates can't make a strong showing in the Electoral College. Even if a third party candidate were to win the support of 25% of the voters nationwide, that candidate might still gain no Electoral College votes. Thus, the Electoral College reinforces a two party system and consequently limits the choices for president.

> You may take a 10-minute break before proceeding to Section 3.

GO ON TO THE NEXT PAGE

Questions 18 through 25 refer to the following passage.

Excerpt from *Three Years in Europe*
by William Wells Brown

1   During the second day we visited several of the cottages of the work people, and in these I took no little interest. The people of the United States know nothing of the real condition of the laboring classes of England. The peasants of Great Britain are always spoken of as belonging to the soil. I was taught in America that the English laborer was no better off than the slave upon a Carolina rice-field. I had seen the slaves in Missouri huddled together, three, four, and even five families in a single room not more than 15 by 25 feet square, and I expected to see the same in England. But in this I was disappointed.

2   After visiting a new house that the Doctor was building, he took us into one of the cottages that stood near the road, and gave us an opportunity, of seeing, for the first time, an English peasant's cot. We entered a low whitewashed room, with a stone floor that showed an admirable degree of cleanness. Before us was a row of shelves filled with earthen dishes and pewter spoons, glittering as if they had just come from under the hand of a woman of taste. A Cobden loaf of bread, that had just been left by the baker's boy, lay upon an oaken table which had been much worn away with the scrubbing brush; while just above lay the old family bible that had been handed down from father to son, until its possession was considered of almost as great value as its contents. A half-open door, leading into another room, showed us a clean bed; the whole presenting as fine a picture of neatness, order, and comfort, as the most fastidious taste could wish to see.

3   No occupant was present, and therefore I inspected everything with a greater degree of freedom. In front of the cottage was a small grass plot, with here and there a bed of flowers, cheated out of its share of sunshine by the tall holly that had been planted near it. As I looked upon the home of the laborer, my thoughts were with my enslaved countrymen. What a difference, thought I, there is between the tillers of the soil in England and America. There could not be a more complete refutation of the assertion that the English laborer is no better off than the American slave, than the scenes that were then before me. I called the attention of one of my American friends to a beautiful rose near the door of the cot, and said to him, "The law that will protect that flower will also guard and protect the hand that planted it." He knew that I had drank deep of the cup of slavery, was aware of what I meant, and merely nodded his head in reply. I never experienced hospitality more genuine, and yet more unpretending, than was meted out to me while at Hartwell.

GO ON TO THE NEXT PAGE

18. Which statement about the author is best supported by the passage?

    A. He is a former slave-owner who changes his mind about the institution of slavery.

    B. He has endured captivity in America.

    C. He is an English citizen who has personally witnessed slavery.

    D. He is a foreign traveler making comparisons between England and America.

19. Which of the following best expresses what the author means by "meted out" (paragraph 3)?

    A. grudgingly allowed
    B. freely bestowed
    C. gradually reduced
    D. gladly requested

20. What function does the extensive description of the cottage (paragraph 2) play in the selection as a whole?

    A. It introduces the reader to the concept of what a "tiller of the soil" is.

    B. It serves as a contrast to the images of slaves in the previous paragraph.

    C. It highlights the differences between architecture in England and in America.

    D. It proves that the description of peasants in England as "belonging to the soil" (paragraph 1) is inaccurate.

21. The sentence "But in this I was disappointed" (paragraph 1) shows the author's use of

    A. irony, because the author would not really hope to find human conditions as deplorable as those described in the previous sentence.

    B. tone, because the author wants to convey a sense of sorrow over the conditions of slaves in America described in the previous sentence.

    C. understatement, because the author is downplaying his feelings over the conditions of slaves in America.

    D. contrast, because it reveals his feelings about the difference between the real conditions and the ideal conditions of the English laborers.

22. Which statement in the passage about English peasants has the most support *against* it from the other descriptions in the passage?

    A. "The peasants of Great Britain are always spoken of as belonging to the soil."

    B. "The English laborer was no better off than the slave upon a Carolina rice-field."

    C. "The law that will protect that flower will also guard and protect the hand that planted it."

    D. "What a difference there is between the tillers of the soil in England and America."

GO ON TO THE NEXT PAGE

23. What can the reader infer about the author's intended audience?

    A. They are Americans who are unfamiliar with England.
    B. They are English peasants who have never been to America.
    C. They are former slaves who have escaped and now live in England.
    D. They are academics who have traveled both countries.

24. What does the phrase "in these I took no little interest" (paragraph 1) convey about the author's attitude?

    A. He is not very interested in the work people or their cottages.
    B. He would prefer to talk with the work people themselves, rather than just visit their cottages.
    C. He is intrigued by the possibility of examining the homes of the work people.
    D. He pretends an interest greater than he really feels, when visiting the cottages.

25. What does the author mean by "The law that will protect that flower will also guard and protect the hand that planted it" (paragraph 3)?

    A. Humans and flowers are guaranteed equal protections under English law.
    B. The gardeners have special protections under English law.
    C. English laborers have legal rights guaranteed to them.
    D. Roses are particularly protected under English law.

GO ON TO THE NEXT PAGE

Questions 26 through 33 refer to the following passage.

Excerpt from *The Underdogs:*
A Novel of the Mexican Revolution
by Mariano Azuela

1   Through the shadows of the starry night, Luis Cervantes had not yet managed to detect the exact shape of the objects about him. Seeking the most suitable resting-place, he laid his weary bones down on a fresh pile of manure under the blurred mass of a huizache tree. He lay down, more exhausted than resigned, and closed his eyes, resolutely determined to sleep until his fierce keepers or the morning sun, burning his ears, awakened him. Something vaguely like warmth at his side, then a tired hoarse breath, made him shudder. He opened his eyes and feeling about him with his hands, he sensed the coarse hairs of a large pig which, resenting the presence of a neighbor, began to grunt.

2   All Luis' efforts to sleep proved quite useless, not only because the pain of his wound or the bruises on his flesh smarted, but because he suddenly realized the exact nature of his failure.

3   Yes, failure! For he had never learned to appreciate exactly the difference between fulminating sentences of death upon bandits in the columns of a small country newspaper and actually setting out in search of them, and tracking them to their lairs, gun in hand. During his first day's march as volunteer lieutenant, he had begun to suspect the error of his ways—a brutal sixty miles' journey it was, that left his hips and legs one mass of raw soreness and soldered all his bones together. A week later, after his first skirmish against the rebels, he understood every rule of the game. Luis Cervantes would have taken up a crucifix and solemnly sworn that as soon as the soldiers, gun in hand, stood ready to shoot, some profoundly eloquent voice had spoken behind them, saying, "Run for your lives." It was all crystal clear. Even his noble-spirited horse, accustomed to battle, sought to sweep back on its hind legs and gallop furiously away, to stop only at a safe distance from the sound of firing. The sun was setting, the mountain became peopled with vague and restless shadows, darkness scaled the ramparts of the mountain hastily. What could be more logical then, than to seek refuge behind the rocks and attempt to sleep, granting mind and body a sorely needed rest?

4   But the soldier's logic is the logic of absurdity. On the morrow, for example, his colonel awakened him rudely out of his sleep, cuffing and belaboring him unmercifully, and, after having bashed in his face, deprived him of his place of vantage. The

GO ON TO THE NEXT PAGE

rest of the officers, moreover, burst into hilarious mirth and holding their sides with laughter begged the colonel to pardon the deserter. The colonel, therefore, instead of sentencing him to be shot, kicked his buttocks roundly for him and assigned him to kitchen police.

5   This signal insult was destined to bear poisonous fruit. Luis Cervantes determined to play turncoat; indeed, mentally, he had already changed sides. Did not the sufferings of the underdogs, of the disinherited masses, move him to the core? Henceforth he espoused the cause of Demos, of the subjugated, the beaten and baffled, who implore justice, and justice alone. He became intimate with the humblest private. More, even, he shed tears of compassion over a dead mule which fell, load and all, after a terribly long journey.

6   From then on, Luis Cervantes' prestige with the soldiers increased. Some actually dared to make confessions. One among them, conspicuous for his sobriety and silence, told him: "I'm a carpenter by trade, you know. I had a mother, an old woman nailed to her chair for ten years by rheumatism. In the middle of the night, they pulled me out of my house; three damn policemen; I woke up a soldier twenty-five miles away from my hometown. A month ago our company passed by there again. My mother was already under the sod!...So there's nothing left for me in this wide world; no one misses me now, you see. But, by God, I'm damned if I'll use these cartridges they make us carry, against the enemy. If a miracle happens (I pray for it every night, you know, and I guess our Lady of Guadalupe can do it all right), then I'll join Villa's men; and I swear by the holy soul of my old mother, that I'll make every one of these Government people pay, by God I will."

7   Luis Cervantes, who already shared this hidden, implacably mortal hatred of the upper classes, of his officers, and of his superiors, felt that a veil had been removed from his eyes; clearly, now, he saw the final outcome of the struggle. And yet what had happened? The first moment he was able to join his coreligionists, instead of welcoming him with open arms, they threw him into a pigsty with swine for company.

GO ON TO THE NEXT PAGE

26. Write the letters of the events below into the chart to show the order in which they occur, according to the narrative.

Order of Events

```
┌─────────────────────────┐
│                         │
│                         │
│                         │
└─────────────────────────┘

┌─────────────────────────┐
│                         │
│                         │
│                         │
└─────────────────────────┘

┌─────────────────────────┐
│                         │
│                         │
│                         │
└─────────────────────────┘

┌─────────────────────────┐
│                         │
│                         │
│                         │
└─────────────────────────┘

┌─────────────────────────┐
│                         │
│                         │
│                         │
└─────────────────────────┘
```

(a) Luis joins the army.

(b) There are news-paper reports about bandits.

(c) Luis runs away from battle.

(d) Luis is thrown into a pigpen.

(e) Luis unsuccessfully tries to sleep.

27. What does the author imply about Luis's past life?

A. He worked for a newspaper, reporting on the rebels.

B. He was drafted into the army by force.

C. He was a chaplain and heard confessions.

D. He was a carpenter.

28. How is the soldier who speaks in paragraph 6 different from his fellow soldiers?

A. He does not indulge in drinking.

B. He hates the government that he serves.

C. He ran away from combat out of self-preservation.

D. He seeks revenge against Villa's men because of his mother's death.

GO ON TO THE NEXT PAGE

29. The character of Luis undergoes several changes throughout the excerpt. Write the letter for each word into the character web that describes Luis at one point in the narrative.

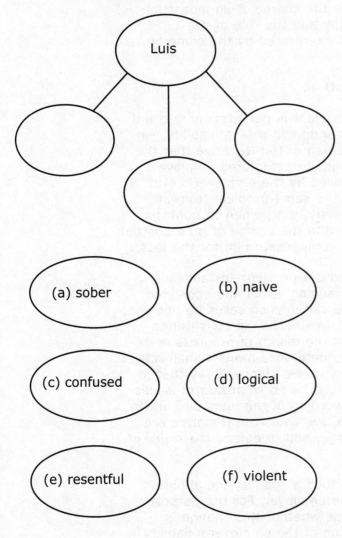

(a) sober

(b) naive

(c) confused

(d) logical

(e) resentful

(f) violent

30. Who are the "coreligionists" mentioned in paragraph 7?

   A. government soldiers
   B. people who pray to the Lady of Guadalupe
   C. the revolutionary forces
   D. the upper classes

31. What is the event that causes Luis to decide to leave the army?

   A. the death of the mule
   B. punishment for running from battle
   C. the long march on his first day
   D. seeing the sufferings of the common people

32. What is the most significant difference between Luis and the soldier who speaks in paragraph 6?

   A. The soldier is ready to use his gun against the enemy, while Luis is afraid of combat.
   B. The soldier is religious, while Luis is not.
   C. The soldier seeks revenge against Villa's men, while Luis advocates the other side.
   D. The soldier was forced to join the army, while Luis volunteered.

33. What is the "failure" Luis considers in paragraph 2?

   A. his inability to meet combat bravely
   B. his inability to be a fully logical soldier
   C. his inability to understand the nation's struggle
   D. his inability to escape his captors

GO ON TO THE NEXT PAGE

Questions 34 through 41 refer to the following passage.

Adapted and abridged from *Elements of Debating* by Leverett S. Lyon

1   Resolved, that in actions against an employer for death or injury of an employee sustained in the course of an industrial employment, the fellow-servant rule and the rule of the assumption of risk as defined and interpreted by the common law should be abolished.

Mr. Pruitt, speaking for the affirmative:

2   The question which we discuss tonight is partly economic and partly legal. Viewing it from the standpoint of legal liability, we possibly can agree with the gentlemen of the Negative that the employer should respond in damages to his injured employee, only when the injury has been caused by the employer's own fault. On the other hand, viewing the same problem from an economic standpoint, you cannot deny, that, when through no fault of his own, a worker is injured in the course of an industrial employment, that industry should compensate him for the loss.

3   Here then is the issue—the world-old-problem—established principles of law in conflict with changing social and economic conditions. As history shows, there can in such cases be but one solution. The decision of the court, yes, even the constitution of the nation, must in turn yield to the march of progress and adapt itself to changing conditions, until once more it shall reflect the sense of public justice in its own time. Hence, I say that in our discussion this evening, there can be no confusion of issues. The Affirmative, according to the wording of the question, are to advocate a change in our common law, while the Negative are to oppose the proposition for change, and to defend the order of things as they are.

4   The Affirmative are to advocate such a change, the abolition of the common-law defenses of the employer. For the purposes of this debate, it is immaterial to us whether this change is brought about by a simple extension of the employer's liability, or whether it is accompanied, as in many of our states, by a system of workman's compensation. Under any of these plans, the proposition of the Affirmative will be maintained, the employer will be deprived of his defenses at common law, and the employee will recover his damages regardless of questions of fault.

GO ON TO THE NEXT PAGE

5   Assuming then the full burden of proof, the Affirmative propose to demonstrate that the assumption of risk and the fellow-servant rule as defined and interpreted by the common law should be abolished, first, because whatever reasons may have justified these doctrines in years gone by they have no application to industrial conditions in our day; and, secondly, because the abolition of these common law defenses will but place the burden of industrial loss, as in justice it should be placed, upon the ultimate consumer of the product of the industry.

Mr. Watson, speaking for the Negative:

6   The proposed abolition of these two common-law defenses, like every change of law or any suggested reform, is brought to our attention by certain existing evils. The advocates of this reform have a definite proposition in mind and that proposition is definitely and clearly stated in the question. It is a question in which people in every walk of life are concerned. Since it is of such widespread interest, let us lift it from a plane of mere debating tactics, where a great deal of time is spent in arguing what the Affirmative or the Negative may stand for according to the interpretation of the question. Let us lift it from that plane, and consider it as practical men and women who are interested in the outcome of this great problem. It is, then, in its larger sense, a legal question and must be considered from the standpoints of justice and of expediency.

7   It is not enough for the Affirmative to point out evils that exist under these two common-law rules, for there is bound to be some evil in the administration of all law. They must further show that these evils which they have named are inherent in these two laws, and that the proposed change will remedy the existing evils. Now the Negative maintain that the evils complained of are not inherent in these laws, and we believe that the Affirmative plan is not the proper solution of the problem.

8   I will show you that these common-law rules are founded on principles of justice and that their removal would be unjust to the employer; second that it would discriminate against the smaller tradesmen, and third that the proposed remedy does not strike at the root of the evil, since it would affect only a small percentage of industrial accidents.

GO ON TO THE NEXT PAGE

34. Based on the passage, the Affirmative and the Negative share which perspective?

   A. The fundamental basis of the two laws in question is sound.
   B. Ultimately, the consumer should pay for industrial losses due to damages collected by an injured employee.
   C. The fellow-servant rule and the rule of the assumption of risk are the cause of certain social evils.
   D. If an employee is injured, employers should pay for damages when the injury is the fault of the employer.

35. The Affirmative uses the term "public justice" (paragraph 3) and the Negative uses the term "principles of justice" (paragraph 8). How do the Affirmative and Negative sides differ with respect to their interpretations of the idea of "justice"?

   A. The Negative feels that perfect justice is impossible, while the Affirmative seeks universal justice.
   B. The Affirmative sees "justice" as the protection of employees, while the Negative sees "justice" as the protection of employers.
   C. The Affirmative feels that obtaining "justice" means to remedy the evils of society, while the Negative concept of "justice" does not recognize these evils.
   D. The Affirmative seeks justice that fits the needs of the time, while the Negative advocates justice based on number of industrial accidents.

36. Which word best matches the use of the word "immaterial" in paragraph 4?

   A. unimportant
   B. incomprehensible
   C. unsolvable
   D. intangible

37. Mr. Watson, speaking for the Negative, mentioned the percentage of industrial accidents affected (paragraph 8) in order to

   A. highlight a relevant factor that the Affirmative failed to address.
   B. contend that the evils of society are not bound up in the two laws in question.
   C. show that this number has not increased despite the Affirmative's claims about industrial conditions of the day.
   D. concede that the Affirmative side is correct in maintaining that some accidents are due to industrial work.

38. In presenting the case for the abolition of the laws, Mr. Pruitt, speaking for the Affirmative, is making the assumption that

   A. employers would never voluntarily compensate an employee for injuries on the job.
   B. history shows that all laws eventually must be changed.
   C. the industrial conditions of the day cause more accidents, or more severe accidents, than did most jobs at the time the laws were created.
   D. a system of workman's compensation is preferable to the extension of employer liability.

GO ON TO THE NEXT PAGE

39. How do both the Affirmative and the Negative organize their presentations?

    A. from the interpretation of the question to the points they plan to show
    B. from the cause of the problem to the solution of the problem
    C. from specific examples to a conclusion based on those examples
    D. from the historical precedent to the present-day application

40. In making their presentations, which of the following points do the Affirmative and the Negative most disagree about?

    A. The question to be decided is a legal question.
    B. Small employers should not have to pay damages for employee-caused injuries.
    C. The Affirmative has the full burden of proof.
    D. It is a question that concerns people in every walk of life.

41. The passage provides enough information to answer which of the following questions?

    A. Is the employer responsible for compensating an employee for injuries sustained on the job?
    B. What are the evils that exist under these two common-law rules?
    C. Is this debate the first proposal of a system of workers' compensation?
    D. How will the burden of industrial loss be placed upon the ultimate consumer of the product of the industry?

GO ON TO THE NEXT PAGE

Questions 42 through 49 refer to the following passage.

Business Strategies that Work:
A Framework for Disability Inclusion
Office of Disability Employment Policy

1   What's the third largest market segment in the United States? The answer might surprise you. It's not a particular race, gender, or age group. It's people with disabilities. The size of this population—54 million strong—surpasses Hispanics, African Americans and Asian Americans. Add in their families, friends, and associates, and you get a trillion dollars in purchasing power.

2   Want a slice? Any smart business owner would. As with any customer segment, one of the best ways to tap into the growing disability market is to ensure it is represented in your workforce. What's more, research shows that consumers both with and without disabilities favor businesses that employ people with disabilities, and that people with disabilities can provide your business with the flexible, innovative thinking required for a competitive edge in the 21st century.

3   By adopting these effective and meaningful employment practices that welcome people with disabilities, you too can benefit from a vibrant, diverse workforce.

Lead the Way: Inclusive Business Culture

4   Establishing an inclusive business culture begins with leadership at the highest levels, including top executives and boards of directors. One action company leaders can take is to adopt formal expressions of commitment and intent related to the recruitment, hiring, retention, and advancement of qualified individuals with disabilities, including veterans with disabilities.

5   **Make (and publicize) the business case for employing qualified individuals with disabilities.** For example, frame the issue in communication with managers, employers, etc. in terms of return on investment and direct and indirect benefits to the company and its employees. Stress that enhancing diversity by employing people with disabilities recognizes changing demographics of the workforce, which improves employee engagement, productivity, and retention.

GO ON TO THE NEXT PAGE

Table A. Employment status of the civilian noninstitutional population by disability status and age, 2014 and 2015 annual averages [Numbers in thousands]

Characteristic	2014			2015		
	Total, 16 years and over	16 to 64 years	65 years and over	Total, 16 years and over	16 to 64 years	65 years and over
PERSONS WITH A DISABILITY						
Civilian noninstitutional population	29,219	15,612	13,606	29,752	15,771	13,981
Civilian labor force	5,699	4,717	981	5,813	4,812	1,001
Participation rate	19.5	30.2	7.2	19.5	30.5	7.2
Employed	4,985	4,062	923	5,193	4,250	942
Employment-population ratio	17.1	26.0	6.8	17.5	26.9	6.7
Unemployed	714	656	58	621	562	59
Unemployment rate	12.5	13.9	5.9	10.7	11.7	5.9
Not in labor force	23,520	10,895	12,625	23,939	10,959	12,980
PERSONS WITH NO DISABILITY						
Civilian noninstitutional population	218,728	187,375	31,353	221,049	188,521	32,528
Civilian labor force	150,223	142,847	7,376	151,317	143,517	7,800
Participation rate	68.7	76.2	23.5	68.5	76.1	24.0
Employed	141,320	134,273	7,048	143,641	136,119	7,522
Employment-population ratio	64.6	71.7	22.5	65.0	72.2	23.1
Unemployed	8,903	8,574	329	7,676	7,398	278
Unemployment rate	5.9	6.0	4.5	5.1	5.2	3.6
Not in labor force	68,505	44,528	23,977	69,732	45,004	24,728

Source: News Release, June 21, 2016. Bureau of Labor Statistics, U.S. Department of Labor.

6   **Include disability as part of all of the company's diversity policies and activities.** Establish a universal policy providing workplace flexibility and accommodations for all applicants and employees, with and without disabilities. Review personnel processes, qualification standards, and job descriptions to determine whether they facilitate or impede the hiring and advancement of qualified persons with disabilities, including veterans with disabilities.

7   **Provide training to executives and other staff** about strategies such as workforce flexibility, including customized employment around job tasks (job restructuring, job sharing, and job creation).

GO ON TO THE NEXT PAGE

Build the Pipeline: Outreach and Recruitment

8   "Where can I find qualified applicants with disabilities?" Companies have expressed concern that one of the greatest barriers they face regarding the hiring of individuals with disabilities, including veterans with disabilities, is the inability to find qualified candidates. To effectively build a pipeline of qualified applicants with disabilities, your company will need to develop relationships with a variety of recruitment sources. The investment will be well worth the effort; your company will not only secure access to talent that it otherwise may have overlooked, but also benefit from other supports that can assist in effectively integrating job candidates with disabilities into your workforce.

Recruitment Sources

9   Public recruiting sources, including One-Stop Career Centers, state and community vocational rehabilitation programs, state employment agencies, Employment Networks, independent living centers, and Department of Veterans Affairs Regional Offices.

10   Educational institutions such as community colleges, universities, and other institutions of learning, including those that offer programs for individuals with specific disabilities. For recruitment purposes, contact the college offices for students with disabilities in addition to career services. There are several internship and recruitment programs designed exclusively for students with disabilities, including the Workforce Recruitment Program for College Students with Disabilities (WRP) and Career Opportunities for Students with Disabilities (COSD).

11   Non-profit entities and social service agencies, including labor organizations, organizations for individuals with disabilities, and other such entities that may provide referrals, technical assistance, and other advice on proper placement, recruitment, and accommodations.

Recruiting Strategies

12   Use accessible online applications and recruitment and social networking sites so that job seekers with disabilities can learn about the company and its hiring initiatives. Indicate in job announcements that the company encourages applications by qualified individuals with disabilities.

13   Join employer networking groups, such as the U.S. Business Leadership Network or one of its local affiliates, that recognize and promote best practices in hiring, retention, and promoting individuals with disabilities.

GO ON TO THE NEXT PAGE

14   Post job announcements on accessible web-based "job boards" that specialize in identifying qualified individuals with disabilities, in disability-related publications, and with specific disability service organizations. Participate in career fairs targeting individuals with disabilities, including veterans with disabilities.

15   Include people with disabilities on company recruitment teams.

16   At work, it's what people CAN do that matters. On a daily basis, people with disabilities must think creatively about how to solve problems and accomplish tasks. In the workplace, this resourcefulness translates into innovative thinking, fresh ideas and varied approaches to confronting business challenges and achieving success. Employers can capitalize on these talents through inclusive employment practices that benefit everyone.

Source: United States Department of Labor

42. How does the chart support the information in the article?

A. by showing that there is a need for employment among people with disabilities
B. by validating the assertion that the disability market is growing
C. by illustrating the current inequalities in the labor market
D. by proving that the disabled market is the third largest market segment in the United States

43. What was the author's purpose for including the question "Want a slice?" (paragraph 2)?

A. to frame the prospect of gaining the purchasing power of people with disabilities in a tempting fashion
B. to suggest that the market will become further segmented as time goes on
C. to use a humorous interjection to show a sudden shift in topic
D. to urge more people with disabilities to enter the lucrative job market

44. Which quote from the article indicates that taking the steps outlined in the article will improve the workplace even before people with disabilities are hired?

A. "Establishing an inclusive business culture begins with leadership at the highest levels, including top executives and boards of directors."
B. "Use accessible online applications and recruitment and social networking sites so that job seekers with disabilities can learn about the company and its hiring initiatives."
C. "Establish a universal policy providing workplace flexibility and accommodations for all applicants and employees, with and without disabilities."
D. "People with disabilities can provide your business with the flexible, innovative thinking required for a competitive edge in the 21st century."

GO ON TO THE NEXT PAGE

45. What function does the image of the "pipeline" (paragraph 8) serve in the article?

    A. It invokes an industrial, working-class, blue collar image.
    B. It is an image of rigidity that stands in contrast to the "flexibility" mentioned previously.
    C. It is a picturesque image to represent the communications techniques discussed later.
    D. It invokes an image of a smooth and efficient delivery system.

46. Does the evidence in the article support the claim that "By adopting these effective and meaningful employment practices that welcome people with disabilities, you too can benefit from a vibrant, diverse workforce" (paragraph 3)?

    A. No. The article describes strategies for employers to hire people with disabilities, but there are no reports or examples to prove these strategies have worked or have caused benefit to the employers.
    B. Yes. The article lists a number of supportive organizations and strategies dedicated to helping people with disabilities get jobs, which is a clear indication that the practices will work.
    C. No. The chart shows that many more jobs are held by people without disabilities than people with disabilities, so the practices cannot be benefiting employers with a diverse workforce.
    D. Yes. The advice to frame the issue in communication with managers in terms of return on investment is very convincing for those in upper management.

47. What audience is the article targeting?

    A. employees of a large, diverse company
    B. managers of non-profit entities for individuals with disabilities
    C. people with disabilities who are recent college graduates
    D. executives of businesses that have very few workers with disabilities

48. What rhetorical technique does the article employ that makes its message more immediate and effective?

    A. a series of rhetorical questions
    B. a repetition of ideas for emphasis
    C. a series of direct commands
    D. an exaggerated image for emphasis

49. The article suggests that people with disabilities can provide what valuable skill?

    A. patience
    B. inventiveness
    C. traditional values
    D. diversity

GO ON TO THE NEXT PAGE

50. The passage below is incomplete. For each "Select" option, choose the option that correctly completes the sentence. For this practice test, circle your selection.

John Aruz
Director of Personnel
Wheelwright Bank

Dear Mr. Aruz:

I am writing in response to your listing in the Wheelwright Tribune for a security systems management position. I am very interested in working with your company. Please allow me to introduce myself.

This position is especially of interest to me

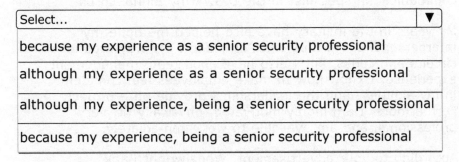

Select... ▼
because my experience as a senior security professional
although my experience as a senior security professional
although my experience, being a senior security professional
because my experience, being a senior security professional

in the Army has prepared me for a disciplined, secure work environment and the challenges associated with unexpected events. I'm looking forward to using this experience

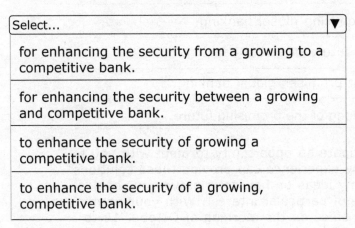

Select... ▼
for enhancing the security from a growing to a competitive bank.
for enhancing the security between a growing and competitive bank.
to enhance the security of growing a competitive bank.
to enhance the security of a growing, competitive bank.

My studies and Army service have made me a competitive IT candidate and an expert in security software specifically. After graduating with a bachelor's of science in Information Systems Management, I earned notable IT certifications and hold a current DoD Secret Security

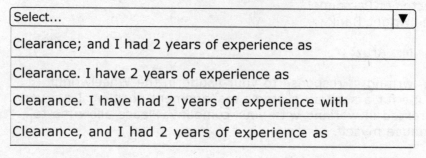

Select... ▼
Clearance; and I had 2 years of experience as
Clearance. I have 2 years of experience as
Clearance. I have had 2 years of experience with
Clearance, and I had 2 years of experience as

communication specialist in the U.S. Army Signal corps.

My years in the military have also helped me hone my interpersonal skills, thus I not only know my way around circuits and codes, but I also have good team management experience. I know how to make employees feel confident in my abilities—and the leadership I provide on a project. Furthermore, I am highly motivated, physically fit, very professional, and am available to work immediately.

According to your advertisement, Wheelwright Bank needs security solutions that will guide it into

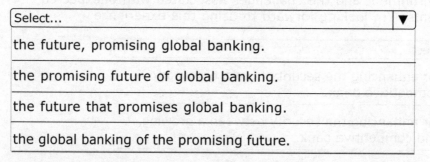

Select... ▼
the future, promising global banking.
the promising future of global banking.
the future that promises global banking.
the global banking of the promising future.

I eagerly anticipate an opportunity to meet with you to discuss how my experience can provide those solutions. You may find my ideas on how to improve your bank's security profile of particular interest. With your permission, I will call your office on the morning of October 12 to inquire if a meeting can be scheduled at a time that suits your schedule.

I look forward to meeting you.

Sincerely yours,

Jocelyn Cho

END OF TEST

Mathematical Reasoning

Welcome!

Here is some information that you need to know before you start this test:

- You should not spend too much time on a question if you are not certain of the answer; answer it the best you can, and go on to the next question.
- If you are not certain of the answer to a question, you can mark your answer for review and come back to it later.
- You have **115 minutes** to complete this test.
- This test has two parts.
- When you finish Part 1, you may review those questions.
- You may not go back to Part 1 once you have finished your review.
- You may not use a calculator in Part 1. You may use a calculator in Part 2.

Turn the page to begin.

GO ON TO THE NEXT PAGE

Mathematics Formula Sheet

Area of a:

square	$A = s^2$
rectangle	$A = lw$
parallelogram	$A = bh$
triangle	$A = \frac{1}{2}bh$
trapezoid	$A = \frac{1}{2}h(b_1 + b_2)$
circle	$A = \pi r^2$

Perimeter of a:

square	$P = 4s$
rectangle	$P = 2l + 2w$
triangle	$P = s_1 + s_2 + s_3$
Circumference of a circle	$C = 2\pi r$ OR $C = \pi d$; $\pi \approx 3.14$

Surface Area and Volume of a:

rectangular prism	$SA = 2lw + 2lh + 2wh$	$V = lwh$
right prism	$SA = ph + 2B$	$V = Bh$
cylinder	$SA = 2\pi rh + 2\pi r^2$	$V = \pi r^2 h$
pyramid	$SA = \frac{1}{2}ps + B$	$V = \frac{1}{3}Bh$
cone	$SA = \pi rs + \pi r^2$	$V = \frac{1}{3}\pi r^2 h$
sphere	$SA = 4\pi r^2$	$V = \frac{4}{3}\pi r^3$

(p = perimeter of base B; $\pi \approx 3.14$)

Data

mean	mean is equal to the total of the values of a data set, divided by the number of elements in the data set
median	median is the middle value in an odd number of ordered values of a data set, or the mean of the two middle values in an even number of ordered values in a data set

Algebra

slope of a line	$m = \dfrac{y_2 - y_1}{x_2 - x_1}$
slope-intercept form of the equation of a line	$y = mx + b$
point-slope form of the equation of a line	$y - y_1 = m(x - x_1)$
standard form of a quadratic equation	$y = ax^2 + bx + c$
quadratic formula	$x = \dfrac{-b \pm \sqrt{b^2 - 4ac}}{2a}$
Pythagorean Theorem	$a^2 + b^2 = c^2$
simple interest	$I = prt$ (I = interest, p = principal, r = rate, t = time)
distance formula	$d = rt$
total cost	total cost = (number of units) × (price per unit)

GO ON TO THE NEXT PAGE

Mathematical Reasoning, Part 1

You may NOT use a calculator in Part 1.

Question 1 refers to the following list of numbers from least to greatest.

$\frac{1}{4}$ 0.45 $\frac{2}{3}$ $\frac{9}{10}$

1. Select the number that could be correctly placed in the box.

    | 0.23 | | 0.95 | | 0.5 |
    | 0.349 | | 0.8 |

2. Which of the following is equivalent to the expression 24(4 + 5)?

    A.   24 × 4 + 24 × 5
    B.   24 × 10
    C.   24 × 20
    D.   (24 + 4) × (24 + 5)

Question 3 refers to the following number line.

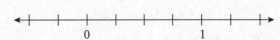

3. Select the point on the number line that represents $\frac{3}{4}$. Mark the point with an X.

4. Simplify.

    $$\sqrt[3]{-125} \times \sqrt[3]{8}$$

    A.   −10
    B.   −5
    C.   5
    D.   10

5. Simplify.

    $$\sqrt{4} + \sqrt{16}$$

    A. $\sqrt{12}$

    B. $\sqrt{20}$

    C.   6

    D.   20

GO ON TO THE NEXT PAGE

6. Multiply.

$$(x - 3)(3x - 1)$$

A. $3x^2 - 10x + 3$
B. $3x^2 - 4x - 4$
C. $3x^2 - 4x + 3$
D. $3x^2 - 10x - 3$

Question 7 refers to the following equation and graph.

Line A: $y = 4x - 1$

Line B (shown on the graph below)

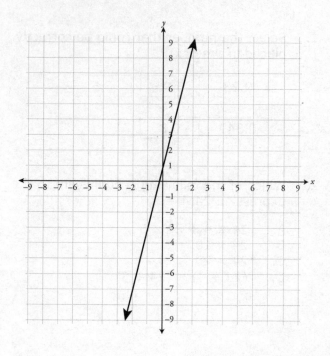

7. The slope of line A is [Select... ▼]
   | greater than |
   | less than |
   | equal to |

the slope of line B. The y-intercept of line A

is [Select... ▼] the y-intercept
   | greater than |
   | less than |
   | equal to |

of line B.

GO ON TO THE NEXT PAGE

8. A circle has an area of 225π. What is its diameter?

    A. 15
    B. 30
    C. 225
    D. 450

9. An event planner calculates that an upcoming event will require 3 flower arrangements for every 8 guests. If 72 guests are expected to attend the event, how many flower arrangements are needed?

    A. 9
    B. 27
    C. 72
    D. 216

10. A combination bike lock consists of four letters with the options A, B, and C for each letter. How many combinations are possible?

    A. 3
    B. 12
    C. 27
    D. 81

Question 11 refers to the following function.

$$h(x) = -x - 2$$

11. Find $h(x)$ for the provided x-values and write the answers in the appropriate boxes.

$h(7) =$ [ ]

$h(-2) =$ [ ]

$h(0) =$ [ ]

| -9 | -7 | -5 |

| -4 | -2 | 0 |

GO ON TO THE NEXT PAGE

Question 12 refers to the following equation.

$$P = 2y + 1$$

12. What is the value of y when $P = 6$?

    A. $\dfrac{5}{2}$

    B. 5

    C. 12

    D. 13

13. At a certain gas station, gas costs $2.79 per gallon. Maddie's car has a 14-gallon tank that is currently half full. How much will it cost to fill Maddie's tank the remaining amount at this gas station?

    $

Question 14 refers to the following triangle.

Area:

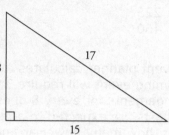

17

8

15

Perimeter:

14. Find the area and perimeter of the triangle and write them in the boxes from the options provided.

23	40	60
68	120	136

GO ON TO THE NEXT PAGE

Mathematical Reasoning, Part 2

<u>Question 15</u> refers to the following graph.

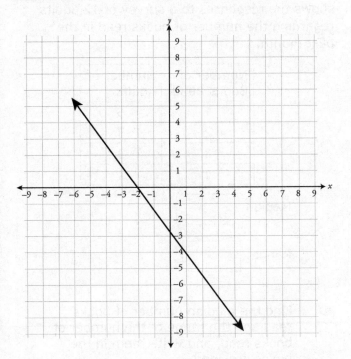

16. A restaurant has a rectangular bathroom that is 10 feet by 12 feet. The restaurant owner plans to cover the bathroom's floor with 2-inch square tiles. How many tiles will be needed to cover the bathroom floor? Note: 1 foot = 12 inches.

   A.   30
   B.   60
   C.   360
   D.   4,320

17. A fitness center charges a one-time registration fee of $50 plus a monthly membership fee of $35. Which of the following expressions shows the total cost of a gym membership after *m* months?

   A. $50m + 35$
   B. $85m$
   C. $50 + 35m$
   D. $15m$

15. What is the slope of the line?

   A. $-\dfrac{4}{3}$
   B. $-\dfrac{3}{4}$
   C. $-\dfrac{1}{2}$
   D. $\dfrac{3}{4}$

GO ON TO THE NEXT PAGE

Question 18 refers to the following chart, which shows the breakdown of one company's expenditures in the month of January.

Company Expenditures

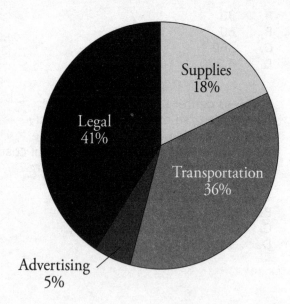

Legal 41%

Supplies 18%

Transportation 36%

Advertising 5%

18. $5,400 was spent on transportation in January. What is the total value of the company's January expenditures?

   A. $1,944
   B. $5,400
   C. $10,800
   D. $15,000

19. Divide.

$$(9.0 \times 10^9) \div (3.0 \times 10^3)$$

   A. 3.0×10^3
   B. 3.0×10^6
   C. 6.0×10^3
   D. 6.0×10^6

Question 20 refers to the following table, which shows the responses to a survey of 12 adults regarding the number of books read in the past month.

Number of Books Read	Number of Adults
1	5
2	3
3	3
4	1

Median: [   ]

Range: [   ]

20. Find the median number of books read and the range of the number of books read, and write them in the boxes provided.

1	1.5	2	2.5

3	3.5	4

21. Deyma works at an electronics store and earns an hourly wage plus commission. She earns $10.25 per hour, plus 2% of every sale she makes. On Tuesday, Deyma worked for 6 hours and sold 5 laptops, each costing $850. How much money did Deyma earn on Tuesday?

   A. $61.50
   B. $146.50
   C. $911.50
   D. $4,311.50

22. Factor.

$$x^2 + 7x - 30$$

   A. $(x - 10)(x + 3)$
   B. $(x + 5)(x - 6)$
   C. $(x - 5)(x + 6)$
   D. $(x + 10)(x - 3)$

GO ON TO THE NEXT PAGE

23. Which of the following is the graph of
    $y = -x$?

A.

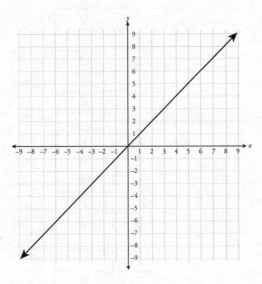

C.

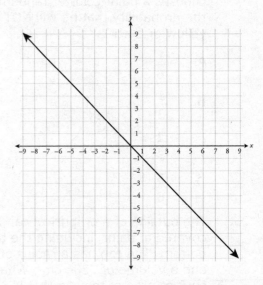

B.

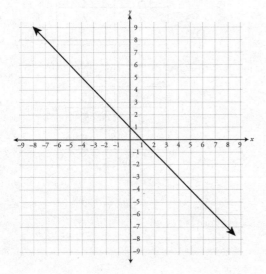

D.

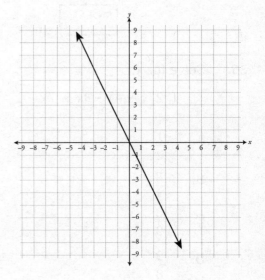

GO ON TO THE NEXT PAGE

24. Juan is working on a painting. He has red, yellow, aquamarine, fuchsia, black, and beige paints to choose from. If he chooses a paint color at random, what is the probability that he will NOT choose yellow or black?

    A. $\dfrac{1}{6}$

    B. $\dfrac{1}{3}$

    C. $\dfrac{2}{3}$

    D. $\dfrac{5}{6}$

25. The outside of a cylindrical can is fully covered in paint, including the top and bottom. The can has a radius of 6 cm and a volume of 720π cm^3. What is the surface area of the can that is covered in paint, to the nearest cm^3?

    [   ] cm^3

26. Solve for x.

    $$2(x + 4) - 3x = 7x - 1$$

    A. $\dfrac{1}{2}$

    B. $\dfrac{4}{7}$

    C. $\dfrac{8}{9}$

    D. $\dfrac{9}{8}$

27. Line p has a slope of -1 and passes through the point $(2, 0)$. What is the equation of line p?

    A. $y = x - 1$
    B. $y = -x + 2$
    C. $y = -x$
    D. $y = 2x$

28. Which table of values represents a function?

    A.

x	y
1	1
1	2
1	3
1	4

    B.

x	y
0	2
1	2
10	2
3	2

    C.

x	y
5	0
2	-2
3	3
2	7

    D.

x	y
-7	5
-8	-5
0	5
-7	-5

GO ON TO THE NEXT PAGE

Mathematical Reasoning, Part 2

Question 29 refers to the following right triangle.

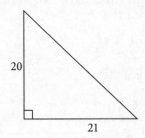

29. What is the triangle's perimeter?

    A. 29
    B. 41
    C. 70
    D. 882

30. Line *k* passes through the points (−2, −2) and (5, 1). What is the equation of line *k*?

    A. $y = \dfrac{1}{2}x - 1$

    B. $y = \dfrac{3}{7}x - \dfrac{8}{7}$

    C. $y = 3x - 14$

    D. $y = -3x + 8$

Question 31 refers to the following table, which shows four towns and their respective populations and areas.

	Population	Area (square miles)
Emersonville	43,209	24.6
Amberton	16,085	41.2
Greenshore	27,271	52.9
Bereon	50,101	30.2

31. Which town has the greatest number of people per square mile?

    A. Emersonville
    B. Amberton
    C. Greenshore
    D. Bereon

GO ON TO THE NEXT PAGE

32. Malia is tracking the temperature and the amount of precipitation in her town. The table below shows her data for the first five days.

Temperature (°F)	Precipitation (in.)
72	2
80	0
76	8
70	6
64	5

Plot the data above on the below scatter plot. Draw an X on the grid as many times as is necessary to show all the data points.

Temperature and Precipitation

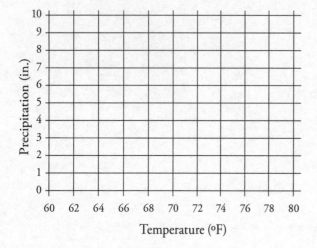

33. Which of the following correctly represents the expression *ten more than half a number*?

A. $10k + \dfrac{1}{2}$

B. $2k + 10$

C. $k + 10$

D. $\dfrac{1}{2}k + 10$

34. Jerome is selling necklaces and bracelets and charges $2 for a necklace and $1 for a bracelet. One day, he sells a total of eight items and earns $13. How many bracelets did he sell?

GO ON TO THE NEXT PAGE

Mathematical Reasoning, Part 2

<u>Question 35</u> refers to the following function.

$$k(x) = \frac{1}{2}x^3$$

35. Write your answers in the boxes below.

What is the value of $k(2)$?

What is the value of $k(4)$?

What is the value of $k(0)$?

36. What is the relationship between the lines $2y - 4x = 6$ and $y = -\frac{1}{2}x - 2$?

A. They are parallel.
B. They are the same line.
C. They intersect at one point but are not perpendicular.
D. They are perpendicular.

37. A square consists of the points (5, 2), (2, 2), (5, −1), and (x, y). Find the value of (x, y) and plot all four points on the grid.

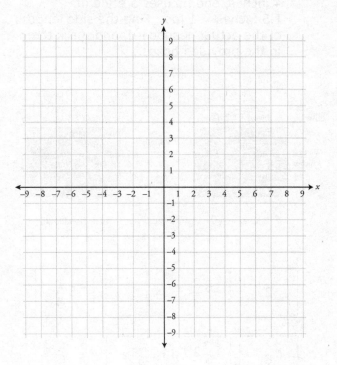

38. Lena is at a fair and wants to ride the Tilt-A-Whirl as many times as she can. She has $5.00, and the ride costs $0.75. Which inequality, when solved, expresses the number of times, t, Lena can ride the Tilt-A-Whirl?

A. $0.75t \leq 5$
B. $t \leq 0.75$
C. $0.75t \geq 5$
D. $5t \leq 0.75$

GO ON TO THE NEXT PAGE

39. Maurice is building a new rectangular headboard for his bed. He starts by drawing a scale model. His model has a length of 8 inches and a width of 4 inches, and he uses a scale of 1.5 inches = 1 foot. Find the side lengths of the actual headboard, and mark them in the provided boxes.

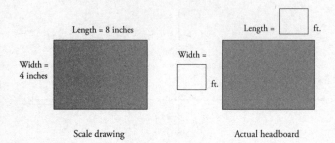

Scale drawing   Actual headboard

Question 40 refers to the following function.

$$f(x) = 2x^2 + 5$$

40. Write your answers in the boxes below.

What is the value of $f(0)$?

What is the value of $f(10)$?

What is the value of $f(-3)$?

Question 41 refers to the following equation of a line.

$$2x + 3y = x + 1$$

41. What is the slope of the line?

    A. -1

    B. $-\dfrac{1}{3}$

    C. $\dfrac{1}{3}$

    D. 2

42. Simplify.

$$\frac{x^2 + 4x + 3}{x + 1}$$

    A. $x + 3$
    B. $x + 1$
    C. $x^2 + x + 1$
    D. $x^2 + 3$

GO ON TO THE NEXT PAGE

Mathematical Reasoning, Part 2

<u>Question 43</u> refers to the following inequality.

$$3x + 1 > 13$$

43. Which of the following represents the solution to the inequality?

A.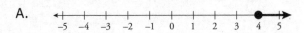

B.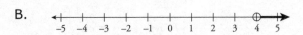

C.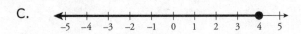

D.

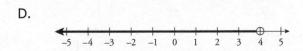

44. The amount of money on Brittany's bus pass can be represented by the equation $M = 20 - 1.25t$ where M is the amount of money on the pass and t is the number of times she rides the bus. If she currently has $3.75 left on her bus pass, how many times has she ridden the bus?

   A.   3
   B.   7
   C.   13
   D.   16

45. Solve the equation for x.

$$\frac{3y}{x} = 2$$

A. $x = \dfrac{3y}{2}$

B. $x = 6y$

C. $x = \dfrac{2}{3y}$

D. $x = \dfrac{y}{6}$

46. Will needs to weigh between 170 and 180 pounds to qualify for a certain wrestling division. He currently weighs 162 pounds. Will solves the inequality $170 < 162 + p < 180$ to determine the number of pounds, p, he needs to gain to qualify for the wrestling division. What is the solution to the inequality?

   A. $8 < p < 18$
   B. $8 < p < 342$
   C. $332 < p < 342$
   D. $170 < p < 180$

END OF TEST

THIS PAGE INTENTIONALLY LEFT BLANK.

GO ON TO THE NEXT PAGE

Social Studies

Welcome!

Here is some information that you need to know before you start this test:

- You should not spend too much time on a question if you are not certain of the answer; answer it the best you can, and go on to the next question.
- If you are not certain of the answer to a question, you can mark your answer for review and come back to it later.
- You have **70 minutes** to complete this test.

Turn the page to begin.

GO ON TO THE NEXT PAGE

Questions 1 through 3 refer to the following sources.

Source 1:

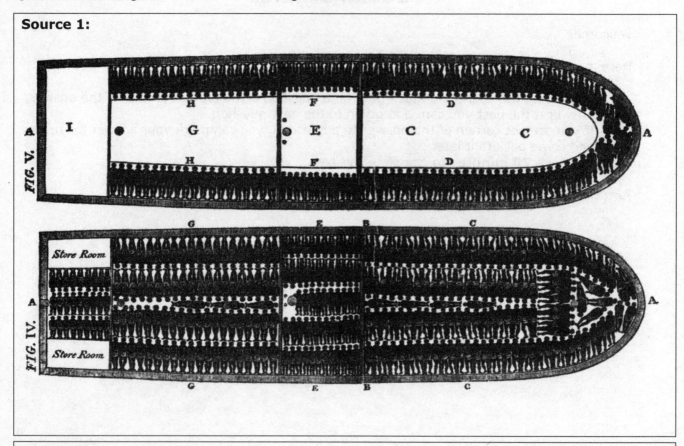

Source 2:

"Are you *a man?* Then you should have an *human* heart. But have you indeed? What is your heart made of? Is there no such principle as compassion there? Do you never *feel* another's pain? Have you no sympathy? No sense of human woe? No pity for the miserable? When you saw the flowing eyes, the heaving breasts, the bleeding sides and tortured limbs of your fellow-creatures, was you a stone, or a brute? Did you look upon them with the eyes of a tiger? When you squeezed the agonizing creatures down in the ship, or when you threw their poor mangled remains into the sea, had you no relenting? Did not one tear drop from your eye, one sigh escape from your breast? Do you feel no relenting *now?* If you do not, you must go on, till the measure of your iniquities is full. Then will the great GOD deal with *you*, as you have dealt with *them*, and require all their blood at your hands."

–John Wesley, *Thoughts Upon Slavery*, 1774

GO ON TO THE NEXT PAGE

Social Studies

1. The sentiment exhibited in Source 2 above reflects the concerns of which of the following groups?

   A. Puritans
   B. Evangelicals
   C. Freemasons
   D. Mormons

2. Which of the following most accurately depicts the historical context of the movements of goods and people (Source 1) during the centuries of transatlantic trade?

   A. slaves to the Americas; cotton, sugar, and tobacco to Africa; textiles, rum, and raw goods to Europe
   B. slaves to Africa; cotton, sugar, and tobacco to Europe; textiles, rum, and raw goods to the Americas
   C. cotton, sugar, and tobacco to the Americas; slaves to Europe; textiles, rum, and raw goods to Africa
   D. slaves to the Americas; cotton, sugar, and tobacco to Europe; textiles, rum, and raw goods to Africa

3. Which of the following correctly characterizes one consequence of the layout of transatlantic slaves shown in Source 1 above?

   A. Slave ships carried approximately equal numbers of slaves as crewmembers.
   B. Slave ships often sank due to overcrowding and imbalanced weight allotment.
   C. Slaves were forced to assist in the rowing of the slave ships.
   D. Many slaves died of disease in the crowded hulls of tightly packed ships.

GO ON TO THE NEXT PAGE

Questions 4 and 5 refer to the following source.

"Be it known, that we knowing the prosperity of these countries, and the welfare of their inhabitants depends principally on navigation and trade, which in all former times by the said Countries were carried on happily, and with a great blessing to all countries and kingdoms; and desiring that the aforesaid inhabitants should not only be preserved in their former navigation, traffic, and trade, but also that their trade may be increased as much as possible in special conformity to the treaties, alliances, leagues and covenants for traffic and navigation formerly made with other princes, republics and people, which we give them to understand must be in all parts punctually kept and adhered to."

–Charter of the Dutch
West India Company, 1621

4. What was one of the principal goals that 17th-century merchants had in setting up chartered companies such as the one whose charter is quoted in the source above?

   A. to pool resources and eliminate competition at the companies' trading posts
   B. to force governments to decrease involvement with private business affairs
   C. to encourage scientists to develop more sophisticated navigational tools
   D. to increase economic cooperation between various nations

5. From where did chartered companies such as the one quoted in the source above derive the authority to exist?

   A. ecclesiastical authorities
   B. private banks
   C. kings and other royals
   D. military leaders

Questions 6 and 7 refer to the following source.

"All of us who were engaged in the struggle must have observed frequent instances of a Superintending providence in our favor. To that kind providence we owe this happy opportunity of consulting in peace on the means of establishing our future national felicity. And have we now forgotten that powerful friend? Or do we imagine that we no longer need His assistance? I have lived, Sir, a long time and the longer I live, the more convincing proofs I see of this truth that God governs in the affairs of men. And if a sparrow cannot fall to the ground without His notice, is it probable that an empire can rise without His aid?"

–Benjamin Franklin, *Constitutional Convention
Address on Prayer,* 1787

6. In context, the word "felicity" in the source above most nearly means which of the following?

   A. common sense
   B. wisdom
   C. good fortune
   D. skill

7. In the source above, Benjamin Franklin expresses which of the following beliefs about the American Revolution?

   A. It would not have succeeded without divine aid.
   B. It was a regrettable undertaking.
   C. It demolished the American economy.
   D. It was only the first step in gaining independence from Britain.

GO ON TO THE NEXT PAGE

Social Studies

Question 8 refers to the following source.

Cuneiform tablet containing account of barley rations. Mesopotamia, ca. 2350 B.C.E.

8. Which of the following changes in human culture and behavior most directly accompanied the increase in grain production during the Neolithic Revolution?

   A.   an increase in hunter-gatherer lifestyles

   B.   an increase in monotheistic belief systems

   C.   an increase in economic equality between men and women

   D.   an increase in urban populations and organized communities

Questions 9 and 10 refer to the following source.

"Our constitution does not copy the laws of neighboring states; we are rather a pattern to others than imitators ourselves. Its administration favors the many instead of the few; this is why it is called a democracy. If we look to the laws, they afford equal justice to all in their private differences; if no social standing, advancement in public life falls to reputation for capacity, class considerations not being allowed to interfere with merit; nor again does poverty bar the way, if a man is able to serve the state, he is not hindered by the obscurity of his condition. The freedom which we enjoy in our government extends also to our ordinary life."

–Thucydides, *History of the Peloponnesian War*
II.IV. Greece, ca. 415 B.C.E.

9. According to the text above, which of the following is a characteristic of classical Greek democracy?

   A.   the weighting of individual accomplishment above financial status

   B.   the imitation of neighboring states' laws and principles

   C.   the ability of average people to overthrow leaders with whom they disagree

   D.   the justice system's protection of the injured only through explicitly written legal codes

10. The text above, like the American Constitution, promises "equal justice to all." In reality, which one of the following groups was favored within the democracies of ancient Greece and the early United States?

   A.   women

   B.   children

   C.   men

   D.   slaves

GO ON TO THE NEXT PAGE

Questions 11 through 13 refer to the following sources.

Source 1:

"You may well ask: "Why direct action? Why sit-ins, marches and so forth? Isn't negotiation a better path?" You are quite right in calling, for negotiation. Indeed, this is the very purpose of direct action. Nonviolent direct action seeks to create such a crisis and foster such a tension that a community which has constantly refused to negotiate is forced to confront the issue. It seeks so to dramatize the issue that it can no longer be ignored. My citing the creation of tension as part of the work of the nonviolent-resister may sound rather shocking. But I must confess that I am not afraid of the word "tension." I have earnestly opposed violent tension, but there is a type of con-structive, nonviolent tension which is necessary for growth."

–Martin Luther King, Jr., *Letter from a Birmingham Jail*, 1963

Source 2:

"We, men and women, who hereby constitute ourselves as the National Organization for Women, believe that the time has come for a new movement toward true equality for all women in America, and toward a fully equal partnership of the sexes, as part of the world-wide revolution of human rights now taking place within and beyond our national borders.

"The purpose of NOW is to take action to bring women into full participation in the mainstream of American society now, exercising all the privileges and responsibilities thereof in truly equal part-nership with men.

"We believe the time has come to move beyond the abstract argument, discussion and symposia over the status and special nature of women which has raged in America in recent years; the time has come to confront, with concrete action, the conditions that now prevent women from enjoying the equality of opportunity and freedom of which is their right, as individual Americans, and as human beings."

–The National Organization for Women's Statement of Purpose, 1966

Source: Reprinted with permission of the National Organization for Women. This is a historical document and may not reflect the current language or priorities of the organization.

GO ON TO THE NEXT PAGE

11. The author of Source 1 above endorses which of the following tactics as a means of achieving his aims?

    A. violent overthrow of the government
    B. nonviolent resistance
    C. appeasement
    D. legal action

12. Source 2 above suggests that which of the following was true about the women's movement in 1966?

    A. It had succeeded in achieving all of its goals.
    B. It was ready for more abstract discussions.
    C. It had not achieved full equality for all segments of society.
    D. It was not a movement supported by men.

13. Which of the following emphases do both Source 1 and Source 2 above explicitly state?

    A. the need for nonviolent resistance
    B. the need for practical steps alongside discussions
    C. the need for unity with other movements
    D. the need for new and strengthened legislation

GO ON TO THE NEXT PAGE

Questions 14 through 16 refer to the following sources.

Source 1:

"We the People of the United States, in Order to form a more perfect Union, establish Justice, insure domestic Tranquility, provide for the common defence, promote the general Welfare, and secure the Blessings of Liberty to ourselves and our Posterity, do ordain and establish this Constitution for the United States of America."

–Preamble to the Constitution of the United States

Source 2:

"The better to secure and perpetuate mutual friendship and intercourse among the people of the different States in this Union, the free inhabitants of each of these States, paupers, vagabonds, and fugitives from justice excepted, shall be entitled to all privileges and immunities of free citizens in the several States ..."

–Articles of Confederation

---

14. The Constitution as ratified in 1788 most clearly reflects the Framers' commitment to

    A. the idea of direct democracy.
    B. the principle of limited government.
    C. the abolition of slavery.
    D. protecting the rights of the accused.

15. Of the following, American federalism is most clearly exemplified by the

    A. system of checks and balances among the three branches of the national government.
    B. process by which international treaties are completed.
    C. special constitutional status of Washington, D.C.
    D. granting to states powers not granted to the national government.

16. The Constitution, as originally ratified, addressed all of the following weaknesses of the Articles of Confederation EXCEPT the

    A. lack of a chief executive office.
    B. national government's inability to levy taxes effectively.
    C. insufficiency of the government's power to raise an army.
    D. omission of a universal suffrage clause.

GO ON TO THE NEXT PAGE

Question 17 refers to the following source.

> "I want the people of America to be able to work less for the government—and more for themselves.
>
> I want them to have the rewards of their own industry. This is the chief meaning of freedom."
>
> –Calvin Coolidge, *Speech on Taxes, Liberty, and the Philosophy of Government*, August 11, 1924

17. A believer in laissez-faire economics such as U.S. President Calvin Coolidge would likely support

Select...   ▼
giving the Environmental Protection Agency greater power to fine factories that contribute to global warming
increasing taxes across higher income groups to aid the poor
the creation of a law that protects unions and grants them collective bargaining rights
the implementation of lower taxes

.

Question 18 refers to the following source.

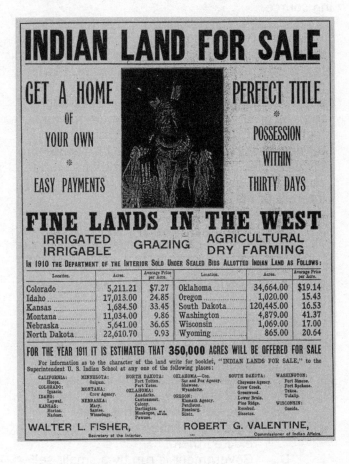

18. Which of the following laws laid the foundation for the availability of land as indicated in the source above?

    A. Indian Removal Act
    B. Sherman Antitrust Act
    C. Emergency Quota Act
    D. Kansas-Nebraska Act

GO ON TO THE NEXT PAGE

Questions 19 and 20 refer to the following source.

"Certainly, Gentlemen, it ought to be the happiness and glory of a representative to live in the strictest union, the closest correspondence, and the most unreserved communication with his constituents. Their wishes ought to have great weight with him; their opinions high respect; their business unremitted attention. It is his duty to sacrifice his repose, his pleasure, his satisfactions, to theirs,—and above all, ever, and in all cases, to prefer their interest to his own."

–Edmund Burke, *Speech to the Electors of Bristol*, November 3, 1774

19. Which of the following is a characteristic of representative democracy?

   A. Representatives are appointed to act on behalf of their geographical areas.
   B. Citizens vote directly in order to enact new laws.
   C. Elected representatives act on behalf of the people who elected them.
   D. Government is run by a small, self-appointed group of elites.

20. Edmund Burke's description of representative democracy illustrated in the passage above is most directly exemplified in which institution within the American government?

   A. cabinet
   B. judiciary
   C. Federal Bureau of Investigation
   D. legislature

GO ON TO THE NEXT PAGE

Social Studies

Questions 21 and 22 refer to the following source.

Foreign-Born Population of the United States (millions)

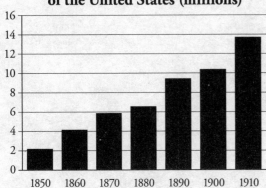

21. According to the source above, the foreign-born population of the United States in the year 1910 was approximately double the foreign-born population of the United States in the year

22. From which three of the following regions did the majority of immigrants to the United States arrive during the time period indicated in the source above? Write the letters of your selections in the boxes below.

(a) Northern Europe

(b) Australia

(c) Africa

(d) Southern Europe

(e) Eastern Europe

(f) South Asia

(g) the Middle East

Question 23 refers to the source below.

African American Slaves Using the First Cotton Gin, 1790–1800

23. Which of the following was NOT an effect of Eli Whitney's invention of the cotton gin?

A. a decrease in the value of tobacco as a cash crop

B. an increase in the number of African slaves in the southern United States

C. a decrease in the need for workers to grow and pick cotton

D. an increase in industry in the northern United States

GO ON TO THE NEXT PAGE

Question 24 refers to the source below.

GDP Per Capita, 2014 ($USD)

Afghanistan	634
Costa Rica	10,415
Finland	49,843
Greece	21,673
Kenya	1,358
Luxembourg	116,613
New Zealand	44,342
United States	54,630

24. Countries that have a high GDP per capita are also typically characterized by which of the following?

    A. high levels of secondary and post-secondary education
    B. high levels of political corruption
    C. high levels of unemployment
    D. high levels of food insecurity and malnutrition

GO ON TO THE NEXT PAGE

Questions 25 through 27 refer to the sources below.

Source 1:

"Congress shall make no law respecting an establishment of religion, or prohibiting the free exercise thereof; or abridging the freedom of speech, or of the press; or the right of the people peaceably to assemble, and to petition the Government for a redress of grievances."

–Bill of Rights, Amendment I

Source 2:

"In all criminal prosecutions, the accused shall enjoy the right to a speedy and public trial, by an impartial jury of the State and district wherein the crime shall have been committed, which district shall have been previously ascertained by law, and to be informed of the nature and cause of the accusation; to be confronted with the witnesses against him; to have compulsory process for obtaining witnesses in his favor, and to have the Assistance of Counsel for his defence."

–Bill of Rights, Amendment VI

25.   Which of the following actions would be prohibited by the First Amendment, as illustrated in Source 1 above?

    A.   the teaching of the Bible as literature in a public school

    B.   the levying of taxes in order to support a particular religious denomination

    C.   the establishment of a voluntary prayer meeting at a government agency outside of official office hours

    D.   asking a person what his or her religious affiliation is during a census interview

26.   Select the phrase within Source 1 or Source 2 that would most support the claim that a newspaper editor has the right to publish an article critical of the foreign policy agenda of the president of the United States. Write an X in the box preceding your selected phrase.

27.   An "impartial jury" as described in Source 2 above would NOT contain

Select... ▼
a juror from the same town as the accused
a juror who was influenced by negative publicity about the accused
a juror of the same race as the accused
a juror without a college degree

GO ON TO THE NEXT PAGE

Question 28 refers to the following source.

"Nearing the End of the Primaries," 1920

28. The process of holding primary elections in order to nominate American presidential candidates most clearly reflects which of the following concerns of the Progressive movement?

    A. the regulation of large corporations

    B. the shift in power from political elites to ordinary citizens

    C. the reform of child labor laws

    D. the creation of environmental regulations and national parks

GO ON TO THE NEXT PAGE

Questions 29 and 30 refer to the source below.

"Well, I Hardly Know Which to Take First!" 1898

29. The source above most clearly reflects a(n) [Select... ▼]
- imperialist
- isolationist
- nativist
- pacifist

foreign policy agenda.

GO ON TO THE NEXT PAGE

Social Studies

30. Which two of the following events in U.S. history would most exemplify the attitude depicted in the source on the preceding page? Write the letters of your selections in the boxes below.

[   ]

[   ]

(a) The overthrow of the Kingdom of Hawaii

(b) The secession of southern states prior to the Civil War

(c) The separation of Virginia and West Virginia into two states

(d) The annexation of California during the Mexican-American War

(e) The creation of the state of Tennessee out of the Southwest Territory

Question 31 refers to the following source.

"The state of nature has a law of nature to govern it, which obliges every one: and reason, which is that law, teaches all mankind, who will but consult it, that being all equal and independent, no one ought to harm another in his life, health, liberty, or possessions."

–John Locke, *The Second Treatise on Government*, 1690

31. The British author of the source above expresses the belief that natural law guarantees individuals certain rights, among them life and liberty. This notion is a prominent theme of each of the following American documents EXCEPT

   A.   the Declaration of Independence.
   B.   the Articles of Confederation.
   C.   the Bill of Rights.
   D.   the Federalist Papers.

GO ON TO THE NEXT PAGE

Social Studies

Questions 32 through 34 refer to the following source.

"Prudence, indeed, will dictate that Governments long established should not be changed for light and transient causes; and accordingly all experience hath shewn, that mankind are more disposed to suffer, while evils are sufferable, than to right themselves by abolishing the forms to which they are accustomed. But when a long train of abuses and usurpations, pursuing invariably the same Object evinces a design to reduce them under absolute Despotism, it is their right, it is their duty, to throw off such Government, and to provide new Guards for their future security. Such has been the patient sufferance of these Colonies; and such is now the necessity which constrains them to alter their former Systems of Government. The history of the present King of Great Britain is a history of repeated injuries and usurpations, all having in direct object the establishment of an absolute Tyranny over these States."

–The Declaration of Independence, 1776

32. In context, what is the best substitute for the word "prudence" at the beginning of the passage above?

   A. good judgment
   B. divine knowledge
   C. rash thinking
   D. caution

33. According to the passage, for what reason do the colonists claim independence from Great Britain?

   A. a desire to maintain their own religious traditions
   B. an opportunity to ally themselves with other nations
   C. a natural right to break free of oppressive rulers
   D. an attempt to establish their own currency

34. Each of the following laws made the American colonists unhappy with the British government EXCEPT

   A. the Stamp Act.
   B. the Tea Act.
   C. the Quartering Act.
   D. the National Bank Act.

Question 35 refers to the following source.

"All, too, will bear in mind this sacred principle, that though the will of the majority is in all cases to prevail, that will to be rightful must be reasonable; that the minority possess their equal rights, which equal law must protect, and to violate would be oppression."

–Thomas Jefferson,
First Inaugural Address, 1801

35. In the source above, Thomas Jefferson expresses which of the following?

   A. a belief that minority opinions should dominate public policy
   B. a belief that minority positions should be excluded from mainstream discourse
   C. a belief that the will of the minority is never right
   D. a belief that minority viewpoints must be safeguarded

END OF TEST

Science

Welcome!

Here is some information that you need to know before you start this test:

- You should not spend too much time on a question if you are not certain of the answer; answer it the best you can, and go on to the next question.
- If you are not certain of the answer to a question, you can mark your answer for review and come back to it later.
- You have **90 minutes** to complete this test.

Turn the page to begin.

GO ON TO THE NEXT PAGE

Questions 1 and 2 refer to the following information.

All biomes are divided into ecosystems, and ecosystems are further divided into communities, which are made up of living things that interact with one another. Members of the community are classified into three roles: producers, consumers, or decomposers.

Producers make their own food and therefore don't have to rely on other species for survival.

Consumers can't produce their own food and are forced to get it from outside sources.

- **Primary Consumers** feed on producers directly.

- **Secondary Consumers** consume primary consumers.

- **Tertiary Consumers** eat producers, primary consumers, and secondary consumers.

Decomposers break down organic matter into simple products. Decomposers are typically not considered part of the food chain.

1. Label the energy pyramid below. Write the letters of your selections in the spaces provided.

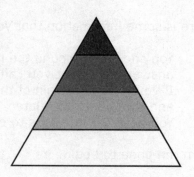

(a) Producers

(b) Primary Consumers

(c) Secondary Consumers

(d) Tertiary Consumers

2. Plants produce their own energy through photosynthesis; therefore, plants play the role of [Select... ▼] in a community.

producer

consumer

decomposer

GO ON TO THE NEXT PAGE

Science

Questions 3 and 4 refer to the following information.

In a predator-prey relationship, the predator eats the prey. While many people think about this relationship in regard to animals, like bears eating fish, the terms also apply to animals that eat plants, and the plants that are eaten. For example, rabbits eat lettuce, which makes the rabbit the predator and the lettuce the prey.

In any predator-prey relationship, the predator and prey evolve alongside each other. Consider the relationship between a tiger and a bison. The tiger needs to be able to catch the bison, or it will die. So the tiger evolves whatever capabilities it needs to be able catch its prey, like speed, camouflage, good senses (like sight and hearing), and the capacity to debilitate its prey. At the same time, though, the bison must adapt to be able to escape the tiger and survive. So it adapts and evolves capabilities that will allow it to avoid being caught and eaten. It might itself increase its ability to run quickly, or camouflage itself to avoid detection, or have some other defense mechanism that would prevent the predator from attacking. Whatever the adaptations may be, they occur relative to each other: as the tiger gets faster, so does the bison, and vice versa. Ultimately, neither one ends up getting any faster, relative to the other. This relationship takes place in all predator-prey relationships, so neither the predator nor the prey ultimately develops an evolutionary advantage.

3. Which of the following CANNOT be inferred from the passage above?

A. If an animal exhibits an evolutionary adaptation over time, the adaptation is a result of the predator-prey relationship.
B. Neither the predator nor the prey evolves to be noticeably faster than the other.
C. Both the predator and the prey adapt relative to each other.
D. Predators and prey experience adaptation in an effort to ensure their survival.

4. Which of the following is NOT an example of a predator-prey evolutionary adaptation?

A. A species of fly mimics the black and yellow stripes of common predators like bees, wasps, and hornets.
B. An inexperienced driver slows his average speed to avoid having an accident.
C. Homo sapiens developed the fight-or-flight response to prepare to run away from big animals.
D. Skunks have adapted a chemical defense mechanism in the form of spray that they can direct at potential attackers.

GO ON TO THE NEXT PAGE

Questions 5 refers to the following diagram.

In the figure below, arrows indicate the direction of cause and effect relationships. For example, primary consumers participating in cellular respiration cause a release of CO_2 into the atmosphere.

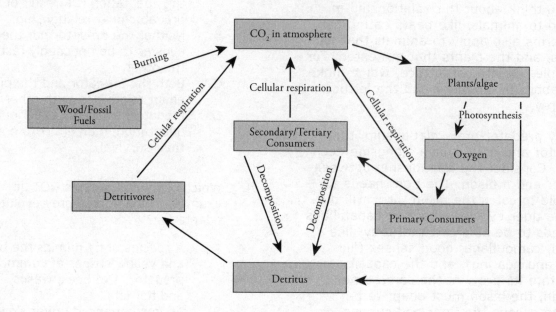

5.   The cycle above shows the interrelationship of different parts of an ecosystem. Which of the following can be inferred from the picture above?

A.   The burning of wood or fossil fuels generates CO_2, which is used by consumers.

B.   Plants and algae participate in photosynthesis that provides oxygen to consumers.

C.   Energy from the waste of one part of the ecosystem is used as fuel for another part of the ecosystem.

D.   Cellular respiration is the only means of generating CO_2 in the ecosystem.

GO ON TO THE NEXT PAGE

Questions 6 and 7 refer to the following table.

The table below shows information about the frequency and magnitude of earthquakes between 2005 and 2010.

Magnitude	2005	2006	2007	2008	2009
8.0–9.9	1	2	4	0	1
7.0–7.9	10	9	14	12	16
6.0–6.9	140	142	178	168	144
5.0–5.9	1693	1712	2074	1768	1896
4.0–4.9	13917	12838	12078	12291	6805
3.0–3.9	9191	9990	9889	11735	2905
2.0–2.9	4636	4027	3597	3860	3014
1.0–1.9	26	18	42	21	26
0.1–0.9	0	2	2	0	1

6. In the years covered by the table, the number of earthquakes of magnitude

0.1–0.9 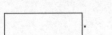 the number

Select... ▼
was less than
was equal to
was greater than
has an unknown
relationship to

of earthquakes of magnitude 9.0–9.9.

7. The mode of all earthquakes during this timeframe had a magnitude of

[   ].

Question 8 refers to the following diagram.

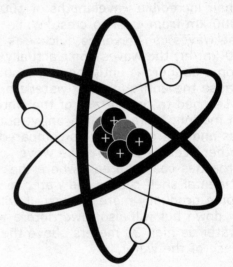

8. Write an X on the part of the atom on the diagram above that represents a proton.

GO ON TO THE NEXT PAGE

Science

Question 9 and 10 refer to the following information.

Tsunamis occur when there is a sudden displacement of massive amounts of water as a result of earthquakes on the sea bed, volcanic eruption above or below the water, meteorite impacts, or landslides. Three circumstances have to occur in order for a tsunami to result from a "seaquake":

- The quake must measure 7.0 or higher on the Richter scale.

- The sea bed must move upward or downward by the quake.

- The epicenter of the earthquake must be close to the surface of the Earth.

Tsunamis are distinct from other types of waves that occur in the ocean because of their incredible wavelengths of 100 to 300 km from crest to crest. While these waves can travel as quickly as 1000 km/hr, the waves don't actually become dangerous until they hit land. Because the entire mass of water from the sea bed to the surface of the water is in motion, there is significantly more mass and energy in play as compared to other ocean waves. As the wave approaches coastal areas, where the continental shelf causes the water to become gradually more shallow, it will slow down but will also tower into a wall of water as high 30 meters above the surface of the water.

9. Which of the following can NOT be inferred from the passage?

A. Tsunamis can be caused by underwater phenomena.
B. Wavelengths can be measured from crest to crest.
C. Tsunamis can be caused by earthquakes that cause the sea bed to move sideways.
D. Most waves in the ocean have wavelengths of less than 100 km.

10. The author says that, just before a tsunami strikes land, it will

A. travel at 1000 km/hr.
B. become more shallow.
C. slow down.
D. measure 7.0 or greater on the Richter scale.

GO ON TO THE NEXT PAGE

456 | For more free content, visit PrincetonReview.com

Science

Questions 11 through 13 refer to the following information.

11. When Block Island Southeast Lighthouse began operating on January 1, 1874, it sat 300 feet from the edge of the cliff. By 1990, that distance had been reduced to only 55 feet. To figure out how long it will be before the lighthouse sat at the edge of the cliff, engineers must calculate the

Select... ▼	loss of distance per
average
median
mode
range

year, which is

Select... ▼	feet per
2.0
2.1
2.2
2.3

year. You may use a calculator. Round to the nearest tenth.

12. Based on the calculations conducted in the question above, in approximately how many years will the edge of the cliff be at the edge of the lighthouse? Round your answer to the nearest year.

13. Which of the following is the most likely explanation for the loss of distance between the lighthouse and the cliff edge?

   A. rust
   B. oxidation
   C. erosion
   D. landslide

Questions 14 and 15 refer to the following figure.

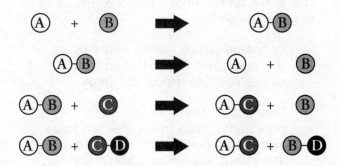

The figure above shows the four types of chemical reactions that can take place:

- synthesis
- decomposition
- single replacement
- double replacement

14. Which type of chemical reaction presented above takes place in the following reaction that describes the electrolysis of water into oxygen and hydrogen gas?

$$2H_2O \rightarrow 2H_2 + O_2$$

   A. synthesis only
   B. decomposition only
   C. single replacement
   D. double replacement

15.

Select... ▼	takes places in the
Synthesis
Decomposition
Single replacement
Double replacement

chemical reaction below.

$$2Fe(s) + O_2(g) \rightarrow 2FeO(s)$$

GO ON TO THE NEXT PAGE

Science

Question 16 refers to the following information.

There are four primary types of tissue in the human body.

- Epithelial tissue covers the surface of the body and forms the lining of most of the cavities inside the body.

- Connective tissue is the most prevalent tissue in the human body and is responsible for protection, secretion, absorption, and filtration.

- Muscle tissue is a voluntary type of muscle that is responsible for movement in the body. There are three types of muscle tissue: skeletal, smooth, cardiac.

- Nerve tissue cells receive stimuli and move nerve impulses throughout the body.

16. Write the letters of the types of tissues below into the corresponding spaces next to various organs in the body.

Organ	Tissue
brain	
heart	
skin	
elbow joint	

(a) epithelial

(b) connective

(c) muscle

(d) nerve

17. The brain is part of the [Select... ▼]
nervous
musculoskeletal
cardiovascular

system of the body; the heart is part of the [Select... ▼] system of the body.
nervous
musculoskeletal
cardiovascular

GO ON TO THE NEXT PAGE

Question 18 refers to the following figure.

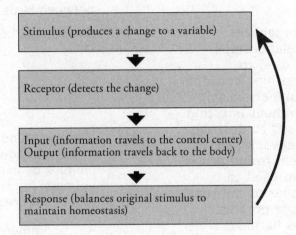

18. The figure above demonstrates a negative feedback loop, which the body uses to maintain homeostasis, internal equilibrium. Which of the following demonstrates a negative feedback loop that might occur in the body?

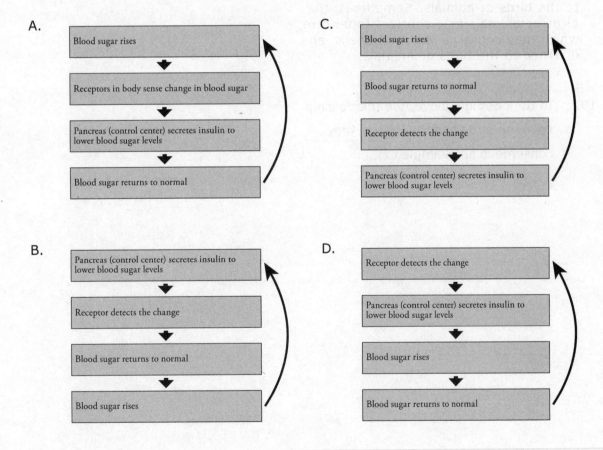

GO ON TO THE NEXT PAGE

<u>Questions 19 through 21</u> refer to the following information.

In ecosystems, multiple organisms live together in various relationships. Commensalism is a term used to describe a class of relationships between two organisms in which one organism benefits from the other without affecting it. Mutualism is a term used to describe a class of relationships between two organisms that both benefit from each other. Parasitism is a term used to describe a class of relationships between two organisms in which one organism benefits while the other is harmed.

In many ecosystems, birds prey upon insects that have been unearthed by animals that graze. Lice and fleas often live on the birds' wings or flaked-off skin of grazing animals, causing little harm to the birds or animals. Sometimes, the birds or animals may contract tapeworm, which may cause nausea, weakness, and diarrhea to the birds or animals.

19. In the passage above, the relationship between birds and the insects they consume is an example of [   ].

20. In the passage above, the relationship between birds and the grazing animals is an example of [Select... ▼].
commensalism
mutualism
parasitism

21. If it was found that the birds mentioned in the passage above helped the grazing animals by eating parasitic insects off the animals' fur, what term would describe this kind of relationship?

A. commensalism
B. mutualism
C. parasitism
D. amensalism

GO ON TO THE NEXT PAGE

Questions 22 and 23 refer to the following table.

Meiosis	Mitosis
2 successive cell divisions	1 cell division
4 genetically different, haploid daughter cells	2 genetically identical, diploid daughter cells
Occurs only in animals, plants, and fungi	Occurs in all organisms except viruses
Creates germ cells (eggs and sperm) only	Creates all body cells
Longer prophase than mitosis prophase	Shorter prophase than meiosis prophase
Prophase I involves recombination/crossing over of chromosomes	Prophase I does not involve recombination/ crossing over of chromosomes
Metaphase I involves line-up of chromosomes along the equator	Metaphase involves line-up of chromosomes along the equator
Anaphase I sees sister chromatids move together to the same pole	Anaphase sees sister chromatids move to opposite poles
Anaphase II sees sister chromatids separate to opposite poles	

22. Based on the table above, the following figure represents [Select... ▼].

| meiosis |
| mitosis |

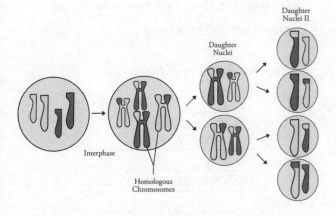

Interphase

Homologous Chromosomes

Daughter Nuclei

Daughter Nuclei II

23. In Experiment 3 in the table below, the cell undergoes [Select... ▼] and

| meiosis |
| mitosis |

each resulting cell has [Select... ▼]

| 23 |
| 46 |

chromosomes.

Experiment	Number of Initial Chromosomes	Number of Chromosomes in Each Resulting Cell	Number of Final Cells
1	10	10	4
2	8	8	4
3	46	?	2

GO ON TO THE NEXT PAGE

Science

Question 24 refers to the following figure.

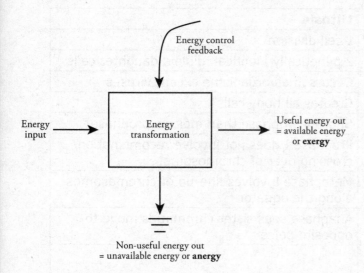

24. Energy transformation describes the process of changing one form of energy into another form of energy. The Law of Thermodynamics states that energy cannot be created or destroyed, and can only change form. Which of the following is NOT a type of machine that facilitates energy transformation?

A. hydroelectric dam
B. microphone
C. electric heater
D. running water

Questions 25 through 27 refer to the following information.

Jeanne decides to rearrange the living room and wants to move the entertainment center to a different wall. Jeanne pushes the entertainment center, which weighs 80 kg, for 10 minutes, exerting an average force of 50 N, but it just will not move. When Deb, her daughter, arrives home, Jeanne asks Deb for help moving the entertainment center. Together, they exert 90N of force for 5 minutes and are able to move the piece of furniture to its new location across the room 15 feet from where it began. While they are in the process of moving it, the remote control falls off the unit and onto the floor.

25. Write the letter of the correct force into the box that describes it. You might need to use a force more than once.

Jeanne being unable to move the entertainment center by herself ☐.

Jeanne and Deb together moving the entertainment center ☐.

The remote control falling to the floor ☐.

(a) Gravity

(b) Potential energy

(c) Kinetic energy

(d) Friction

(e) Air resistance

GO ON TO THE NEXT PAGE

26. If work is defined as $W = F \times d$, how much work did Jeanne do before Deb arrived?

    A. 0
    B. 400
    C. 800
    D. 1350

27. If work is defined as $W = F \times d$, how much work did Jeanne and Deb exert, in Joules, to move the entertainment center?

    A. 0
    B. 450
    C. 720
    D. 1350

Questions 28 and 29 refer to the following information.

The space in between the two walls of a thermos is vacuum-sealed so there is no air in the space. As a result, there is little to no transfer of heat into or out of the thermos.

28. Bryan's thermos is broken, and there is air between the walls of the thermos. If he pours hot coffee into the thermos, which term best describes the resulting situation?

    A. endothermic reaction
    B. exothermic reaction
    C. convection
    D. conduction

29. Based on the information above, which of the following must be true?

    A. A cold liquid in a sealed thermos would never warm up.
    B. If not for the vacuum seal, heat would be lost from the inside of a thermos to the outside world.
    C. Heat transfers more readily in the presence of air than it does in a vacuum.
    D. Heat transfers more readily in a vacuum than it does in the presence of air.

Question 30 refers to the following information.

Acceleration of gravity indicates that an object in free-fall will accelerate at 9.8 m/s². If the time and velocity for an object in free-fall were calculated, the following pattern emerges:

Time	Velocity
0 seconds	0 m/s
1 second	−9.8 m/s
2 seconds	−19.6 m/s
3 seconds	−29.4 m/s
4 seconds	−39.2 m/s

30. What would the velocity of an object in free-fall be after 10 seconds? You may use a calculator.

    A. −9.8 m/s
    B. −39.2 m/s
    C. −38.8 m/s
    D. −98 m/s

GO ON TO THE NEXT PAGE

Questions 31 and 32 refer to the following figure.

1. Geospiza magnirostris.
3. Geospiza parvula.

2. Geospiza fortis.
4. Certhidea olivasea.

The figure above represents Darwin's Finches, a collection of fourteen species of birds that Darwin studied while traveling in the Galapagos Islands. From his study of these birds, Darwin developed the term "adaptive radiation," in reference to patterns of macroevolution in which one species of an animal branches off into other, different species in order to better fit into a particular niche or habitat in an ecosystem. "Adaptive radiation" is also known as "divergent evolution," and describes how the tree of life branches off, resulting in our planet's wide range of biodiversity.

GO ON TO THE NEXT PAGE

Science

31. A recent study shed light on the evolutionary history of Darwin's Finches and has identified a gene that explains variation in beak shape within and among the various species of the birds.

    All of the following might have contributed to adaptation among the birds' beaks, EXCEPT

    A. rainfall impacting the size of seeds upon which the birds feed
    B. a change in the ecosystem resulted in a change in dietary intake
    C. a new land-dwelling predator entered the ecosystem, causing birds to nest higher in trees and use different materials to build their nests
    D. a species of bird becoming extinct

32. Which of the following does NOT contribute to natural selection?

    A. overpopulation
    B. popularization
    C. adaptation
    D. reproduction of adaptations

Questions 33 through 35 are based on the following information.

Hereditary traits are encoded by genes that are located on chromosomes. Chromosomes come in pairs, and the pair of genes for a particular feature determines the characteristics of that trait. Traits are identified as either dominant, which always express when they are present, or recessive, which express only when they show up in pairs.

Dimples are recognized as a dominant trait, D; a lack of dimples is a recessive trait, d. The following Punnett Square shows the results when two parents have a child. Punnett Squares predict the likelihood of a specific gene combination presenting in the offspring.

	d	d
D	?	Dd
d	dd	dd

D	dominant dimples trait
d	recessive no-dimples trait

33. What is the probability that the child will have dimples?

    A. 25%
    B. 50%
    C. 75%
    D. 100%

GO ON TO THE NEXT PAGE

34. According to the information given in the Punnett Square, what genotype should replace the "?" in the Punnett Square?

    A. DD
    B. Dd
    C. dD
    D. dd

35. The genotypic ratio of this Punnett Square is best expressed as Select... ▼ .

Select... ▼
1:1
1:2
2:1
3:1

END OF TEST

Chapter 10
Practice Test 4:
Answers and
Explanations

REASONING THROUGH LANGUAGE ARTS

Section 1

1. This plot development item asks the reader to arrange the sequence of implied past and future events in the order they would occur. The correct order from first to last is as follows:

    (c) Hanneh idolizes Mrs. Preston. This is indicated in paragraph 23 when Hanneh says "you always stood out to me in my dreams as the angel from love and beautifulness." Before the conversation in this passage, therefore, Hanneh idolized Mrs. Preston.

    (d) Hanneh does without food to pay rent. This is revealed in paragraph 13 when Hanneh says "Last time, when he raised me my rent, I done without meat and without milk." So, before the conversation in this passage, she had to go without food to pay rent.

    (a) Hanneh formulates her own solution to her problem. This occurs in paragraph 20 when Hanneh declares "I'll wake up America from its sleep. I'll go myself to the President with my Aby's soldier picture and ask him was all this war to let loose a bunch of blood-suckers to suck the marrow out from the people?"

    (b) Aby returns from his war service. This does not occur within the passage, but Hanneh anticipates it happening in the future, when she says "If only my Aby would get back quick" and follows this with "until he comes," (paragraph 20). Therefore, Aby's return, whenever it occurs, must occur after the events of this passage.

2. **C** This character development question asks about Hanneh's response to Mrs. Preston. Use the dialogue that occurs right before the sentence in paragraph 9, and read beyond paragraph 9, to get a sense of the entire exchange between the characters. In paragraph 8, Hanneh is already agitated, indicated by the word "flared." This is developed in paragraph 10, as "Hanneh Hayyeh's eyes flamed. Too choked for utterance, her breath ceased for a moment." Therefore, (C) is correct: Hanneh is indignant and outraged. Choices (A) and (D) are incorrect, because they reverse Hanneh's attitude: She shows the opposite of relief and gratitude! Choice (B) is incorrect, because she definitely believes that she is being given charity, which is what makes her so angry (paragraph 11). The correct answer is (C).

3. **A** This structure question asks which sentence from the passage supports the idea that the crisis Hanneh is experiencing is also affecting the larger community. Choice (A) is correct: Mrs. Preston mentions that "landlords are taking advantage of the situation," which implies that there is a "situation" and that landlords, plural, are involved, meaning that the problem is not limited to Hanneh. Choice (B) is incorrect, because although this sentence claims she will make "all America" listen, this does not indicate whether "all America" is experiencing the same hardship. Choices (C) and (D) are incorrect, because they use "I," "you," and "me," and so refer just to the relationship between the two women, not a larger community. The correct answer is (A).

4. **B** This development question asks about the emotional relationship between the characters, so look for words that show Hanneh's attitude about her husband. Although her husband is never seen in the excerpt, he exerts influence: "Her first instinct was to run to her husband; but she needed sympathy—not nagging" (paragraph 4). Thus, Hanneh does *not* expect sympathy, but *does* expect nagging, from her husband. Go through the answers, eliminating any that do not reflect this idea. Choice (A) is incorrect: If her husband

were "far away," Henneh would not think to "run to her husband" (paragraph 4). Choice (B) is correct: Since Hanneh does *not* expect sympathy from her husband, he does not "show compassion" for her worries. Choice (C) is incorrect: It is not her husband whom Hanneh feels is a "wild beast," but rather the threat of rent (paragraph 5). Paragraph 10 indicates that what makes Hanneh feel "choked" is the thought of being offered charity, so (D) is incorrect. The correct answer is (B).

5. **D** This character development question asks about the tone of the dialogue between the two women, so check each answer against the passage to see whether the details and the tone match the passage. Choice (A) is incorrect, because it reverses Hanneh's feelings about receiving money ("Ain't I hurt enough without you having to hurt me yet with charity?" paragraph 17). Choice (B) is incorrect because Mrs. Preston does not remain cool and logical; instead, she is "distraught" (paragraph 16) and winds up in tears (paragraph 24). Choice (C) is incorrect because only Hanneh expresses a sense of urgency; by contrast, Mrs. Preston says "Give us time" (paragraph 21). Choice (D) is correct: It's the difference in a sense of urgency that shows the emotional distance between the women, and as the women begin to realize this difference, it separates them further. At the end, they both give up the conversation and, to an extent, their friendship: Hanneh is in "resignation" (paragraph 23), while Mrs. Preston "made no move to defend herself or reply" (paragraph 24). The correct answer is (D).

6. This item asks the reader to make specific comparisons between themes and place the correct opinions into the correct categories. The correct assignment of opinions to categories is as follows:

Hanneh

(b) There is no reasoning with an oppressor. Hanneh feels she has utterly no options available to reason with the landlord; she feels as if "the landlord pushed me in a corner and said to me: 'I want money, or I'll squeeze from you your life!' I have no money, so he takes my life" (paragraph 12) The depictions of the landlord as a "persecutor" (paragraph 12) and a "blood-sucker" (paragraph 20) reinforce the idea of the landlord as an oppressor. Hanneh ultimately resolves to have the government intervene (paragraph 20), further supporting the idea that the landlord cannot be reasoned with directly.

(e) This conversation is about the climax of a problem. For Hanneh, this conversation shows that a preexisting problem has reached a breaking point, since she says "What more can I do without?" in paragraph 13, and then declares in paragraph 20 "Change things? There's got to be a change!" By contrast, this conversation is the *first* time Mrs. Preston realizes how bad things are: "For the first time she noticed the ravages of worry and hunger" (paragraph 6), so for Mrs. Preston this conversation is the revelation of a problem.

Mrs. Preston

(d) A political system that has problems is still trustworthy. In paragraph 21, Mrs. Preston states "these laws are far from just, but they are all we have so far. Give us time. We are young. We are still learning. We're doing our best." By contrast, Hanneh firmly believes the system should change (paragraph 20) because it is unjust, an "unrightness that burns my flesh" (paragraph 17).

(c) Help is best given in the form of direct assistance. Mrs. Preston wants to give Hanneh money directly, or immediately (paragraphs 9 and 16), but Hanneh recoils from this idea (paragraph 11). Instead, Hanneh wants "justice," which is a more indirect and longer pursuit (paragraph 20).

7. **B** This character development question asks about Hanneh's character based on the details in the story, so use the passage to either confirm or eliminate answers based on details in the choices. Choice (A) is incorrect, because while Hanneh is afraid of her powerlessness to pay rent ("She shrank in upon herself, as though to ward off the raised whip of her persecutor." paragraph 12), she is far from timid, as shown by the use of "flared" (paragraph 8) and her shouting that she will go to the President (paragraph 20). Choice (B) is correct; there is evidence that Hanneh likes to be tidy and mourns her shabby appearance: "And I who used to be so neat with myself." (paragraph 15). Choice (C) is incorrect because it reverses Hanneh's emotion of missing her husband, which is shown in paragraph 20: "If only my Aby would get back quick" and "I'll go myself to the President with my Aby's soldier picture." Choice (D) is incorrect because, while Hanneh's feelings about American life before this passage is unknown, she definitely does not idealize American life during the passage. She speaks of America as sleeping and also states "The world as it is is not to live in any longer" (paragraph 20). The correct answer is (B).

8. **A** This structure question asks what specific details in the passage imply another cause for Hanneh's financial crisis. Hanneh speaks of the declining financial situation in paragraph 15: "There used to be a time when poor people could eat cheap things," she complains "But now there ain't no more cheap things. Potatoes—rice—fish—even dry bread is dear." And she continues "I can't no more have my torn shoes fixed up." Therefore, the prices of groceries and clothes have also risen, not just the rents, and (A) is correct. Choice (B) is incorrect, because while Hanneh does have difficulty making ends meet, this is because costs are high; there is no evidence that her *wages have been lowered*. Choice (C) is incorrect because there is no information about *competition for work*. Finally, (D) is incorrect because there is no evidence that she must send money overseas. The correct answer is (A).

9. **D** This language use question requires test takers to determine what the author means by his use of "jimcracks" in paragraph 3, so examine how the word is used in context. The passage talks of "a house so big that it is burdensome to maintain, and fill it up so full of jimcracks that it is a constant occupation to keep it in order." The other part of the passage that speaks of "filling" a house is in paragraph 2: "Backs may go threadbare and stomachs may worry along on indifferent filling, but a house will have things." So it is clear that "jimcracks" refers to physical items that people would purposely obtain, but the tone of the passage is disparaging toward big houses and all the complexities associated with them. Therefore, eliminate (A) because these items are obtained, not discarded. Eliminate (B) because "necessary" does not match the disparaging tone of the passage. Eliminate (C) because "damage" is not a collection of physical objects. Keep (D) because "useless items" reflects both the physical nature of the context and the disparaging tone of the author. The correct answer is (D).

10. This development question asks about the rhetorical technique the author uses to make his point. The two correct statements are as follows:

(b) Using a metaphor by describing an inanimate object with the characteristics of a living organism. The author describes a big house as a "one of the greediest cormorants" and as having "thirsts" (paragraph 2).

(c) Asking a rhetorical question to stimulate thought on a topic. The author questions the reader directly to encourage thought on the topic: "How many Americans, do you suppose, out of the droves that flock annually to Europe, are running away from oppressive houses?" (paragraph 3).

Choice (a) is wrong because there is a specific point with which the author disagrees; instead, the author begins the essay by *agreeing* with the minister's choice to give up his big house. Choice (d) is wrong because, even though the author asks the reader "did you ever see" the houses of Hawthorne and Emerson, there are no detailed romantic representations or wistfulness that would indicate nostalgia. Choice (e) is incorrect because the author never cites an expert's opinion.

11. **B** This structure question asks about the author's purpose for using a specific detail: the phrase "develops annual thirsts for paint and wall-paper," so locate the detail and think about how it relates to the author's argument as a whole. This detail is found in paragraph 2 following the sentence that describes the continual work needed to keep up a big house: "It is rarely complete, and constantly tempts the imagination to flights in brick and dreams in lath and plaster." Thus, the author uses "annual thirsts" to further emphasize this continual work, and the correct answer is (B). Choice (A) is incorrect because it is extreme: The author doesn't imply that paint and wall-paper are the *most significant* expenses. Choice (C) is incorrect, because there is no assertion that the "thirsts" become more developed over time, just that they occur on a regular basis. Choice (D) is incorrect: Although "annual" does imply that paint and wall-paper are required on a regular basis, this is not the *reason* the author uses that phrase. The author uses the phrase to strengthen the main point of the second paragraph, which is the endless work of a big house. The correct answer is (B).

12. **B** This structure question asks about what the author means by using the detail that "the situation is complete and boarding-houses and cemeteries begin to yawn for you" in paragraph 3, so locate the detail and consider the author's purpose. In paragraph 3, the author continues his argument that big houses are more work than they are worth, concluding with "Then, when the expense of living in it is so great that you can't afford to go away and rest from the burden of it, the situation is complete and boarding-houses and cemeteries begin to yawn for you." Therefore, the author implies that the continual work of a big house will be "complete" only when the owners "can't afford to go away" and are at the end of life, when "cemeteries begin to yawn for you," and (B) is correct. Choice (A) is incorrect: The "cemeteries" are what "yawn," not the owners! Choice (C) is incorrect, because while the author does suggest that some Americans "flock to Europe" to run away from their houses, there is no evidence that they do so to visit *graveyards*. Eliminate (D) because this reverses the author's point: The big house doesn't make the owners *comfortable* but instead drains their resources. The correct answer is (B).

13. **A** This development question asks about how two parts of the passage relate to each other, so examine paragraphs 3 and 4, looking for the logical progression between them. Paragraph 3 details a "common" behavior of humans: to get a big house and fill it with "jimcracks" so that it is a "constant occupation." Paragraph 4 begins with a transition to nature "When nature undertakes to provide a house, it fits the occupant," and then makes a contrast: "Animals which build by instinct build only what they need, but man's building instinct, if it gets a chance to spread itself at all, is boundless, just as all his instincts are." This depiction of human instincts explains the filling the house up with "jimcracks" and the "constant occupation" described in paragraph 3, so (A) is correct. Choice (B) is incorrect: The two paragraphs do not provide two different views of the maintenance of a big house, but one such view and paired with one general observation of "man's building instinct." Eliminate (C) because this reverses the relationship of the paragraphs: Paragraph 3 contains the specific example (obtaining a big house), while paragraph 4 provides the general claim about "man's building instinct." Choice (D) is incorrect because paragraph 4 does not contain a *rebuttal*. The correct answer is (A).

14. **C** This structure question asks what conclusions the reader can make about specific details in the passage, so refer to these details and consider how they relate to the author's purpose. The author's purpose in the essay is to criticize the purchase of houses so big that they are continual work. In contrast, author speaks of the houses of Emerson and Hawthorne in paragraph 1, saying "They are good houses for Americans to know and remember. They permitted thought." Therefore, these houses are "good houses," unlike the "big

houses" the author criticizes, and the correct answer is (C). Choice (A) is incorrect because this reverses the author's purpose: He approves of the houses of Emerson and Hawthorne, so they are *not* examples of the big houses. Choice (B) is incorrect, because even though this detail appears in the same paragraph as the story about the minister, it is not the author's intent to recommend houses *proper for ministers*. Finally, (D) is incorrect because these are not houses that *nature builds*. The correct answer is (C).

15. **A** This main idea question asks about a central theme of the essay, so consider the author's primary purpose. The author's purpose in the essay is to criticize the purchase of houses so big that they are continual work, and to criticize "things"—both the "things" that fill the house, and the houses themselves—as "oppressive" (paragraph 3). Thus, the author would agree with (A), and advocate a simple approach. Choice (B) is incorrect because it is too extreme—the author simply says a house by nature "fits the occupant" (paragraph 4), not that it can't be improved. Choice (C) is incorrect because "bigger is better" reverses the author's main idea. Finally, while the author is speaking of expensive houses, the author make a statement about which kind of people have problems so (D) is incorrect. The correct answer is (A).

16. **A** This evaluation question asks how the author would respond to a hypothetical scenario that is relevant to the main idea, so consider the main idea and the author's point of view. The author's purpose in the essay is to criticize the purchase of houses so big that they are continual work. Therefore, the author would likely prefer a *small* house. Choice (A) definitely depicts a small house, so retain this answer. Choice (B) is incorrect: Although a *tent* is definitely not a big house, the author does not advocate living in the woods. Rather, the author uses the houses of Hawthorne and Emerson as examples in paragraph 1). Even though there are no details about these houses, they are indeed houses, not tents, that the author uses as prime examples. Choice (C) is incorrect: The author speaks of the boarding-house as a place of last resort, along with the grave (paragraph 3), so the author would not want to live in one. Choice (D) does contain the idea of a small house, but since the title of this essay is "The Tyranny of Things," the author would not want to fill his house with many objects (or "jimcracks" as he disparagingly calls them in paragraph 3). The correct answer is (A).

17. The option that correctly completes the sentence for each "Select" option:

Dropdown Item 1: Coordination and subordination

The second choice is correct for the first drop-down question:

With the gaps in her family history, this can be hard to determine.

Option 1 is incorrect because it begins the sentence with "despite," which signals a shift of direction. However, the focus of the sentence is not that citizenship will be hard to determine *despite* there are gaps in her family history, the focus of the sentence is that citizenship will be hard to determine *because* there are gaps in her family history; so the ideas are incorrectly joined in Option 1. Options 3 and 4 make a similar error by beginning the sentence with "although," which signals a shift of direction, so the ideas are incorrectly joined in Options 3 and 4.

Dropdown Item 2: Word choice, sentence construction, capitalization

The first choice is correct for the second drop-down question:

Whether someone born outside the United States to a U.S. citizen is herself a U.S. citizen **depends on the law in effect when the person was born.**

Option 2 is incorrect: Starting the sentence with "depending" changes the main verb to a participle (a modifier), resulting in a sentence fragment. Option 3 incorrectly uses "affect" (a verb) instead of "effect" (a noun), resulting in the illogical meaning that the law determines when a person was born. Option 4 incorrectly capitalizes "Depends" in the middle of a sentence.

Dropdown Item 3: Punctuation, logic and clarity, sentence construction

The third choice is correct for the third drop-down question:

If when Rosa was born, Rosa's mother was a U.S. citizen, but had never lived in the United States, **the situation is more ambiguous. If one of Rosa's grandparents was also a U.S. citizen,** then Rosa may still have derived U.S. citizenship.

Option 1 and Option 2 are incorrect, because the placement of the period leaves the following "then" to begin a new sentence with no capitalization. Option 4 incorrectly uses "and," which forms a list of two items: 1) if Rosa's mother was a U.S. citizen, and 2) if one of Rosa's grandparents was also a U.S. citizen. However, this list is all part of one subordinate clause beginning with "if"—a sentence fragment.

Dropdown Item 4: Pronouns, logic, and clarity

The third choice is correct for the fourth drop-down question:

If her mother was naturalized after Rosa was 18, **then Rosa will need to apply for naturalization on her own** after she has been a permanent resident for at least 5 years.

Option 1 is incorrect because it is unclear who is meant by the pronoun "she"—Rosa or her mother? Option 2 is illogical because it is Rosa who needs to apply for naturalization, not her mother. Option 4 is incorrect because the pronoun "they" refers to both Rosa and her mother needing to apply for naturalization—which is not the case.

Section 2

Access your Student Tools online to read sample essays representing different score levels for the Extended Response prompts in this book.

Section 3

18. **B** This development question asks about the author's character based on the details of the passage, so examine the passage for places in which the author talks about himself, and eliminate any answers that don't fit with the information in the passage. The author mentions himself in paragraph 1, stating "I had seen the slaves in Missouri huddled together" and again in paragraph 3, stating "my thoughts were with my enslaved countrymen" and "He knew that I had drank deep of the cup of slavery," so this indicates the author has been a slave in the past, and (B) is correct. Choice (A) is incorrect because it reverses the description of the author: He was definitely not a slave-owner. Choice (C) is incorrect because the author's perspective on the English is that of an *outsider*, not an insider, so the author is not an English citizen. Finally, eliminate (D) because the statement "I had seen the slaves

in Missouri huddled together" in paragraph 1 suggests that the author is *not* foreign to America. The correct answer is (B).

19. **B** This language use question requires test takers to determine what the author means by his use of "meted out" in paragraph 3, so examine how the phrase is used in context. The full sentence states "I never experienced hospitality more genuine, and yet more unpretending, than was meted out to me while at Hartwell." Here the author's tone is affectionate and grateful; eliminate answers that don't match this tone, such as (A). Choice (B) is correct: The tone is positive and the sense of hospitality being "bestowed" is sound. Choice (C) is incorrect, as the idea of hospitality being *reduced* does not fit the tone of the passage. Finally, eliminate (D) because, while the tone of this choice is positive, the sense of "hospitality that was gladly requested of me" doesn't make sense with the depiction of the author as a visitor: The author is receiving hospitality, not having it *requested* from him. The correct answer is (B).

20. **C** This structure question asks about how the extensive description of the cottage in paragraph 2 enhances the story, so read this part of the passage while considering the author's purpose. The author visits the cottage to find how the English "tillers of the soil" actually live, and to truthfully compare the state of workers in England and America. He states: "What a difference, thought I, there is between the tillers of the soil in England and America" (paragraph 3), so (C) is correct. Choice (A) is incorrect: While this passage does introduce the concept of what a "tiller of the soil" is, this is not the function of the *cottage*. Finally, eliminate (D) because the description of the cottage is there to highlight a difference "between the tillers of the soil in England and America " (paragraph 3), not to refute the description of them as "belonging to the soil. The correct answer is (C).

21. **A** This purpose question asks you to analyze the author's rhetorical technique as shown through the use of the phrase "But in this I was disappointed." This sentence immediately follows the description of the author's expectations: "I had seen the slaves in Missouri huddled together, three, four, and even five families in a single room not more than 15 by 25 feet square, and I expected to see the same in England." Would the author *really* be "disappointed" to not see such a miserable image in England? Of course not. Here, the author is employing irony, or the invoking of a state that seems deliberately contrary to what's expected, for effect. Therefore, (A) is correct. Choice (B) is incorrect: The author is dismayed over the conditions of slaves in America, but "disappointed" would not convey this feeling. Choice (C) is incorrect, because "disappointed" refers to the author's feelings upon seeing the cottage, not about the slaves in America. Furthermore, eliminate (D) because the contrast the author makes is not between real conditions and ideal conditions of the English laborers, but between the English laborers and the American slaves. The correct answer is (A).

22. **B** This evaluation question asks about which claim from the passage has the most support against it, so check the answers against the passage, to determine whether each claim has any support against it. Choice (A) is a claim found in paragraph 1, and there is no evidence either against or for this claim. Therefore, eliminate this answer choice. Choice (B) is another claim found in paragraph 1, but this is the claim the author refutes by using the appearance of the cottage as evidence against this claim. Therefore, keep this answer choice. Choice (C) is a claim found in paragraph 3, and there is slight support for this claim, since the "American friend" nods his head in agreement. Eliminate (C). Also eliminate (D) as this is another claim found in paragraph 3, and it is the claim the author defends by using the appearance of the cottage as evidence for this assertion. Therefore, the claim that has the most support against it is (B).

23. **A** This is a purpose question about the author's intended audience, so use the main idea from the passage as a starting point. The author's primary purpose is to expose and refute the claim that "the English laborer was no better off than the slave" (paragraph 1). So the author is speaking to Americans like himself, who are unaware of "the real condition of the laboring classes of England (paragraph 1)." Therefore, (A) is correct. Choice (B) is incorrect because English peasants would already know "the real condition of the laboring classes" and would not need to read this essay. Similarly, (C) is incorrect: Slaves who have escaped and live in England can observe the condition of the laboring classes firsthand; they do not need this essay. Finally, (D) is incorrect because if the readers have already traveled in England, they may have observed the condition of the laboring classes firsthand. The correct answer is (A).

24. **C** This structure question asks about the author's purpose for using a specific detail: the phrase "no little interest" in paragraph 1. The phrase occurs in the introductory sentence: "During the second day we visited several of the cottages of the work people, and in these I took no little interest." And it is followed by one of the author's key points: "The people of the United States know nothing of the real condition of the laboring classes of England." The primary purpose of the author is to expose and refute the claim that "the English laborer was no better off than the slave." Since the author uses the cottage as evidence for that refutation, the author is actually *very* interested in the cottages, so his interest is literally "not little," in other words, "great." Thus, (A) is incorrect. Choice (B) is incorrect, because there is no evidence that he wants to talk with the workers themselves. In (C), "intrigued" means "great interest," so keep this answer. Finally, eliminate (D) since there is no evidence that the author is *pretending*. The correct answer is (C).

25. **C** This structure question asks what the author means by "The law that will protect that flower will also guard and protect the hand that planted it" (paragraph 3), so think about how this detail relates to the author's primary purpose, which is to refute the claim that "the English laborer was no better off than the slave" (paragraph 1). The author makes this specific observation about the flower at the very end of the excerpt, after he has examined the cottage and found that English laborers are indeed very much better off than slaves. Therefore, the image of the flower further supports the author's conclusion. Choices (A) and (B) are incorrect; the author is not trying to suggest that humans and flowers have *equal* protection, or that gardeners have *special protections*. Choice (C) is correct; this answer highlights how English laborers are better off than American slaves—English laborers have legal protections—so keep this answer. Eliminate (D) because the author is making a point about the *hand* that planted the flower (the human), not the flower itself. The correct answer is (C).

26. This plot development item asks the reader to arrange the sequence of events in the excerpt in the order in which they occur, according to the narrative. In this passage, the main character begins in the "shadows," and thinks back over recent events. Therefore, the events are not revealed to the reader in a linear time sequence; instead, the reader has to reconstruct the order from past to present. The correct order of events from first to last is as follows:

(b) There are newspaper reports about bandits. The sentence "he had never learned to appreciate exactly the difference between fulminating sentences of death upon bandits in the columns of a small country newspaper and actually setting out in search of them" (paragraph 3) strongly suggests that Luis was a newspaper reporter fulminating, or ranting against, the "bandits" he later chases as a soldier.

(a) Luis joins the army. The next sentence shows Luis in the army: "During his first day's march as volunteer lieutenant, he had begun to suspect the error of his ways" (paragraph 3).

(c) Luis runs away from battle. However, Luis doesn't stay on the march long: "some profoundly eloquent voice had spoken behind them, saying, 'Run for your lives'…What could be more logical then, than to seek refuge behind the rocks?" (paragraph 3).

(d) Luis is thrown into a pigpen. Almost as soon as Luis escapes the army, he is captured and thrown into a pigpen: "They threw him into a pigsty with swine for company" (paragraph 7).

(e) Luis unsuccessfully tries to sleep. Sleeping in the pigsty is impossible for Luis: "All Luis's efforts to sleep proved quite useless," (paragraph 2).

27. **A**   This character development question asks about Luis's past life based on the details of the passage. Since Luis's character is discussed throughout the excerpt, check each answer against the passage, eliminating those that do not match the information about Luis. Choice (A) is correct, since the sentence "he had never learned to appreciate exactly the difference between fulminating sentences of death upon bandits in the columns of a small country newspaper and actually setting out in search of them" (paragraph 3) strongly suggests that Luis was a newspaper reporter fulminating, or ranting against, the "bandits" he later chases as a soldier. Choice (B) is incorrect because Luis volunteered for the army: "During his first day's march as volunteer lieutenant, he had begun to suspect the error of his ways" (paragraph 3). Choice (C) is incorrect because even though paragraph 6 states "Some actually dared to make confessions," this does not prove that Luis was a chaplain. Finally, eliminate (D) because the person who was a carpenter is the soldier who speaks to Luis, not Luis himself (paragraph 6). The correct answer is (A).

28. **A**   This character development question asks about how the soldier in paragraph 6 is different, so go to this part of the passage and look for words that highlight a unique quality about this soldier. Paragraph 6 describes this soldier as "conspicuous for his sobriety and silence," so the correct answer will reflect at least one of these qualities. Choice (A) is correct: "sobriety" means the soldier does not drink. Choice (B) is incorrect: Although this soldier does indeed hate the government ("I'll make every one of these Government people pay"), this does not make him different from the other soldiers, who also "dared to make confessions" (paragraph 6). Choice (C) is incorrect: The person who ran away from combat was Luis, not this soldier (paragraph 3). Finally, eliminate (D) because it reverses the direction of the narrative: The soldier wants revenge on the government, not Villa's men (who are the revolutionaries). The correct answer is (A).

29.   This development item asks the reader to identify three adjectives that match the author's depiction of Luis. The three correct adjectives are as follows:

(b) Naive Paragraph 3 reveals that Luis is ignorant, or naïve, about army life, at first. He had to learn "to appreciate exactly the difference between fulminating sentences of death upon bandits in the columns of a small country newspaper and actually setting out in search of them" and also "he had begun to suspect the error of his ways" during the march. Finally, he naively fails to anticipate the consequences of running away from battle: "What could be more logical then, than to seek refuge behind the rocks?"

(c) Confused In paragraph 7, Luis is puzzled by the outcome of his seeking to join the revolutionaries: "And yet what had happened? The first moment he was able to join his coreligionists, instead of welcoming him with open arms, they threw him into a pigsty with swine for company."

(e) Resentful After being punished for running from battle, Luis is resentful: "This signal insult was destined to bear poisonous fruit. Luis Cervantes determined to play turncoat; indeed, mentally, he had already changed sides."

Choice (a) is incorrect because "sober" describes the soldier who speaks to Luis, not Luis himself (paragraph 6). Also, (f) is incorrect, because while Luis is resentful, there are no depictions of him being violent in the excerpt.

30. **C** This language use item asks about an unusual word, "coreligionists," so return to the passage and see how this word is used in context. Paragraph 7 describes Luis's change of perspective: He "felt that a veil had been removed from his eyes; clearly, now, he saw the final outcome of the struggle. And yet what had happened? The first moment he was able to join his coreligionists, instead of welcoming him with open arms, they threw him into a pigsty with swine for company." In this paragraph Luis has finally escaped the army and seeks to "change sides" (as he determined in paragraph 5). Therefore, the "coreligionists" (paragraph 7) he seeks are the revolutionaries, and (C) is correct. Choice (A) is incorrect because it reverses the roles of the characters: Luis is fleeing the government soldiers, not seeking them out. Choice (B) is incorrect because even though the word in question is "coreligionists," Luis is not seeking religious practitioners, but rather comrades of a political stance. Choice (D) is incorrect because it reverses Luis's perspective: He identifies with the lower classes "Did not the sufferings of the underdogs, of the disinherited masses, move him to the core?" (paragraph 5). The correct answer is (C).

31. **B** This plot development item asks the reader to consider which event caused Luis to decide to leave the army, so locate the place in the passage where Luis makes this decision. During the march in paragraph 3, "he had begun to suspect the error of his ways," but Luis doesn't decide to leave the army until after he flees battle, specifically after he is punished for doing so: "Luis Cervantes determined to play turncoat" (paragraph 5). Therefore, (B) is correct and (C) is incorrect. Choice (A) is incorrect because the death of the mule happens after he makes this decision. Likewise, (D) is incorrect because Luis reflects on the "sufferings of the underdogs" (paragraph 5) only after he has decided to "play turncoat" and escape the army. The correct answer is (B).

32. **D** This comparison question asks the reader to contrast the soldier in paragraph 6 with Luis, so check each answer choice against the passage and eliminate those answers that reverse the characters or show a similarity instead of a difference. Choice (A) is incorrect: While Luis is afraid of combat (paragraph 3), there is no evidence about whether the other soldier is afraid or not. Choice (B) is incorrect because this is a similarity: The soldier in paragraph 6 states "I pray for it every night, you know," and Luis in paragraph 3 "would have taken up a crucifix and solemnly sworn." Choice (C) is incorrect because both Luis and the soldier want revenge on the government forces. Therefore, (D) is correct: Luis is a "volunteer lieutenant" (paragraph 3) but the soldier in paragraph 6 was taken by force: "In the middle of the night, they pulled me out of my house." The correct answer is (D).

33. **C** This structure question asks about the author's meaning of a specific detail: the "failure" Luis considers in paragraph 2, so locate the detail and think about how it relates to the narrative as a whole. This "failure" is further explored in paragraph 3: "Yes, failure! For he had never learned to appreciate exactly the difference between fulminating sentences of death upon bandits in the columns of a small country newspaper and actually setting out in search of them." Thus, Luis realizes he has failed to comprehend the difference between how the revolution appears when writing about it in a newspaper, and how it appears to those who must actually fight. Choice (A) is incorrect; even though Luis runs from battle,

he does not seem to regret this or see it as a "failure"; instead it seems "logical" to him (paragraph 3). Choice (B) is incorrect because it is extreme: The passage doesn't indicate that Luis strives to be a *fully* logical soldier. Choice (C) is correct: Before he was a soldier, Luis failed to understand the nature of army life, and once he deserted the army, he failed to understand that the revolutionaries would be suspicious, not welcoming (paragraph 7). Eliminate (D) because, while Luis does remain captive, he does not view this as a "failure." The correct answer is (C).

34. **D** This is a comparison question about a perspective the two sides share. Check each answer choice against the passage and eliminate those answers that have no support, that reverse the sides, or that show a difference instead of a similarity. Choice (A) is incorrect because the Affirmative seeks to change these laws while the Negative wants to retain them (paragraph 3). Choice (B) is incorrect because only the Affirmative thinks the consumer should pay (paragraph 5). Choice (C) is incorrect, because the Negative asserts that the evils *bring* the calls for change to attention, not that the laws *cause* the evils. Choice (D) is correct: The Affirmative states that "Viewing it from the standpoint of legal liability, we possibly can agree with the gentlemen of the Negative that the employer should respond in damages to his injured employee, only when the injury has been caused by the employer's own fault" (paragraph 2). Therefore, the two sides agree that an employee should be compensated when the employer is at fault (the difference between the sides is whether that should be the *only* case). The correct answer is (D).

35. **B** This is a comparison question about how the two sides differ in their concepts of "justice." First find these ideas in the passage to gather context for how they are used. The Affirmative in paragraph 3 states "The decision of the court, yes, even the constitution of the nation, must in turn yield to the march of progress and adapt itself to changing conditions, until once more it shall reflect the sense of public justice in its own time." Thus, the Affirmative sees "public justice" as something to which the "constitution of the nation" must yield due to "changing conditions." These changing conditions are earlier specified as "economic and social" conditions; so the Affirmative sees "public justice" as the government and laws yielding to social conditions. Conversely, the Negative in paragraph 8 states "I will show you that these common-law rules are founded on principles of justice and that their removal would be unjust to the employer." Therefore, the Negative sees "principles of justice" as essential to the employer. Now check each answer choice and eliminate those answers that have no support, that reverse the sides, or that show a similarity instead of a difference. Choice (A) is incorrect because it is too extreme: There is no evidence that the sides are seeking justice that is *perfect* or *universal*. Choice (B) is correct: The Negative sees "justice" as protecting employers, while Affirmative is more interested in justice that protects employees. Choice (C) is incorrect, because it reverses the position of the Negative; the Negative *does* recognize these evils (paragraph 6). Choice (D) is incorrect because the Negative never asserts that justice should be *based on the number* of industrial accidents. The correct answer is (B).

36. **A** This language use item requires test takers to determine which word best matches the word "immaterial" in paragraph 4, so examine how the word is used in context. The Affirmative states "For the purposes of this debate, it is immaterial to us whether this change is brought about by a simple extension of the employer's liability…. Under any of these plans, the proposition of the Affirmative will be maintained." Therefore, the Affirmative does not feel that "how the change is brought about" is important, and the answer is (A). Choices (B) and (C) are incorrect because there is nothing in this sentence that indicates that the Affirmative doesn't understand this aspect. Finally, (D) is wrong because while it may be true that the concern of "how the change is brought about" does not have physical presence, that does not fit the logic of the sentence. The correct answer is (A).

37. **A** This point of view question asks about Mr. Watson's reason for mentioning the percentage of industrial accidents affected, so consider how this detail relates to the Negative's argument as a whole. Here is the statement: "The proposed remedy does not strike at the root of the evil, since it would affect only a small percentage of industrial accidents." So why does Mr. Watson mention the percentage of industrial accidents? The Negative's argument as a whole is concerned with responding to the Affirmative, and in paragraph 5, the Affirmative states "whatever reasons may have justified these doctrines in years gone by they have no application to industrial conditions in our day." The Negative can either choose to deny this statement about "industrial conditions" entirely, or argue around this point from another angle. Thus, (A) is correct: The Negative is tackling the subject of industrial conditions, but chooses the as-yet-unexplored angle about percentages rather than to directly attack the state of "industrial conditions in our day." Eliminate (B) because the statement about percentage of industrial accidents is completely unrelated to the Negative's other point about the evils of society. Choice (C) is incorrect: The argument that the percentage is *small* does not allow for a conclusion that the number has not *increased*. There could have been an increase from a very small percentage to a not-as-small percentage, and the point of the Negative would still be that this is a tiny fraction of affected accidents overall. Eliminate (D) because the Negative does not raise this point in order to *concede* to the Affirmative. The correct answer is (A).

38. **C** This is evaluation question asks about the speaker's assumptions. Check each answer choice against the passage and eliminate those answers that are not assumptions for the Affirmative or that reverse the sides. Choice (A) is incorrect because the argument does not address whether employers *voluntarily* compensate; the argument is only about the law that affects compensation. Choice (B) is incorrect because *all laws* is too extreme: The Affirmative does speak of what "history shows," but only specifically "in such cases" of "principles of law in conflict with changing social and economic conditions" (paragraph 3). Choice (C) is correct: Because the Affirmative states "whatever reasons may have justified these doctrines in years gone by they have no application to industrial conditions in our day" (paragraph 5); the law is assuming that "conditions in our day" are different from those in years gone by. Eliminate (D) because the Affirmative is not concerned with the precise system to be put in place: "For the purposes of this debate, it is immaterial" (paragraph 4). The correct answer is (C).

39. **A** To reach the correct answer for this structure question, examine how the arguments as a whole are built. Both the Affirmative and the Negative begin their arguments by defining what the question is they are debating: the "interpretation of the question" (paragraph 6). Both the Affirmative and the Negative conclude their arguments by listing several points they will address (paragraph 5 and paragraph 8). Therefore, (A) is correct. Choice (B) is incorrect because the Affirmative advocates a "solution" (a change in law), but the Negative argues against such a change. Choice (C) is incorrect because this is a reversal of the structure: The specifics are at the end, not the beginning. Choice (D) is incorrect because only the Affirmative is concerned with present-day applications (paragraph 3). The correct answer is (A).

40. **B** This is a comparison question about a perspective the two sides disagree about. Check each answer choice against the passage and eliminate those answers that have no support, that reverse the sides, or that show a similarity instead of a difference. Choice (A) is incorrect because both sides recognize that this question has legal aspects: The Affirmative states "The question which we discuss tonight is partly economic and partly legal" in paragraph 2, and the Negative states "It is, then, in its larger sense, a legal question" in paragraph 6. Choice (B) is correct: The Negative feels that "the employer should respond in damages to his injured employee, only when the injury has been caused by the employer's own fault" (paragraph 2), while the Affirmative feels that "the employer will be deprived

of his defenses at common law, and the employee will recover his damages regardless of questions of fault" (paragraph 4). Choice (C) is incorrect, because both sides agree that the Affirmative has the burden of proof (paragraph 5 and paragraph 7). Choice (D) is incorrect, because the sides more agree than disagree on this issue: The Negative states "It is a question in which people in every walk of life are concerned" (paragraph 6), while the Affirmative is concerned that the laws fit "social conditions." The correct answer is (B).

41. **C** This evaluation question asks about which questions could logically be answered from information in the passage, so check each answer against the passage and eliminate those that are not supported. In (A) there is some uncertainty about the answer to the question, because there is no explanation of what the current law specifies. Because there is no certain answer to this question, eliminate this answer choice. Choice (B) is incorrect because while the Negative recognizes that there are "evils" in paragraph 7, it fails to specify what those evils are. Choice (C) is correct: The Affirmative states "whether it is accompanied, as in many of our states, by a system of workman's compensation" (paragraph 4), meaning that a system of worker's compensation is already in place in some states, so this is not the *first* proposal of such a system. Choice (D) is incorrect, because the Affirmative recognizes that a change could be accomplished by workman's compensation or by an extension of the employer's liability, but does not specify which, and does not say *how* this will ultimately place the burden on the consumer. The correct answer is (C).

42. **B** This structure question asks about how a figure relates to the overall purpose of the article by the Office of Disability Employment Policy, which covers strategies for disability inclusion. The chart gives data about the percentage of total population that is disabled, and corresponding employment figures for 2014 and 2015. The chart follows the description of "the growing disability market" in paragraph 2. Because the total on the chart for the Persons with a Disability (civilian noninstitutional population) is larger in 2015, this supports the claim that the market is growing, so (B) is correct. Choices (A) and (C) are incorrect: Even if the data in the chart seem to indicate a *need* for employment, or *inequalities*, there is no such corresponding assertion in the article about a *need* or *inequalities* in employment for the chart to support. Finally, (D) is incorrect because the chart does not break down other market segments, so there is no way to tell from the chart whether the disabled market is third largest. The correct answer is (B).

43. **A** This structure question asks about the author's purpose for using a specific detail: the question "Want a slice?" so locate the detail and think about how it relates to the author's argument as a whole. The article's title "Business Strategies that Work: A Framework for Disability Inclusion" and its identification as coming from the Office of Disability Employment Policy indicates that the article's purpose is to encourage business owners to offer employment opportunities to disabled people. The question "Want a slice?" which is usually a way of offering tempting food, emphasizes the purpose of the article by making the prospect of disability employment, and the corresponding market share, even more attractive, so (A) is correct. Choice (B) is incorrect, because there is no indication that the market will become *more segmented*. Choice (C) is incorrect because, while the interjection may be humorous, there is no *shift* in topic, but rather a development of the topic. Choice (D) is incorrect: Although the purpose of the article is to get more jobs for those with disabilities, the article is addressed to the employer, not the potential employee. The correct answer is (A).

44. **C** This structure question asks which sentence from the passage supports the idea that taking the steps outlined in the article will improve the workplace even before people with disabilities are hired. This would mean that improvements in the workplace to facilitate hiring people with disabilities would be useful even before the hiring took place, so the improvements would be useful to the previous,

presumably nondisabled employees. Check each answer choice to see whether it supports this idea. Choice (A) is incorrect: Establishing inclusive leadership at the *highest levels* will not necessarily translate into improvements for nondisabled people. Choice (B) is incorrect, because while it is clear how this recommendation benefits people with disabilities, there is no suggestion that it improves the workplace before those people are hired. Choice (C) is correct: Providing "accommodations for all applicants and employees, with and without disabilities" indicates that the improvements will benefit the other employees as well. Choice (D) is incorrect because this sentence discusses benefits that will improve the workplace *after* people with disabilities are hired. The correct answer is (C).

45. **D** This structure question asks about the author's purpose for using a specific detail: the image of the "pipeline" (paragraph 8). This detail follows the question at the beginning of the paragraph: "Where can I find qualified applicants with disabilities?" Since the article's purpose is to persuade employers to hire people with disabilities, the writers want to smooth over any problems the employers anticipate. The recommendation to "build a pipeline of qualified applicants" gives the reader an impression of an easy, abundant delivery system, so (D) is correct. Choice (A) is incorrect, because the article isn't specifying "blue-collar" employment. Choice (B) is incorrect because this image is the reverse of the author's purpose: The author wants to present an attractive image of the hiring process. Eliminate (C) because the pipeline definitely refers to a smooth delivery of candidates from various sources, not the communications techniques discussed later. The correct answer is (D).

46. **A** This evaluation question asks whether the article supports the claim that "By adopting these effective and meaningful employment practices that welcome people with disabilities, you too can benefit from a vibrant, diverse workforce"? The article clearly wants employers to believe this, but is there evidence that such a "vibrant, diverse workforce" will actually result from the "employment practices"? As there are no case studies or testimonials, there is no direct evidence that the strategies work. They may be very plausible and very *likely* to work; however, there is simply no evidence in the passage that they *do* work, so the answer is (A), and (B) and (D) are incorrect. Choice (C) is incorrect because the fact that fewer jobs are held by people with disabilities doesn't indicate one way or the other whether the strategies work. It could be that without the strategies, there would be an even lower figure on the chart; or it could be that the strategies have no effect. The correct answer is (A).

47. **D** This is a purpose question about the author's intended audience, so use the main idea from the passage as a starting point. The article's title "Business Strategies that Work: A Framework for Disability Inclusion" and its identification as coming from the Office of Disability Employment Policy indicates that the article's purpose is to encourage business owners to offer employment opportunities to disabled people. This is confirmed in paragraph 2, when the article states "Want a slice? Any smart business owner would." Choice (A) is incorrect, because the article's intended audience is the employers, not the employees. Choice (B) is incorrect as well because the article begins with a discussion of market share, implying that the audience is very much for-profit. Choice (C) is incorrect because the article is instead written for the future employers of these recent graduates. Choice (D) is correct: The article hopes to reach and teach executives who don't already know how to make the hiring process inclusive. The correct answer is (D).

48. **C** This development question asks about the rhetorical technique the article uses to make its message more immediate and effective, so check each answer against the passage, and eliminate any that don't fit with the style and techniques in the passage. Eliminate (A), because although the author does use some questions in paragraphs 1, 2, and 8, these are not *rhetorical* questions, since the author immediately answers them. Choice (B) is incorrect because the author divides ideas neatly into categories instead of repeating them throughout the passage. Choice (C) is correct—the author uses a series of direct commands (in bold),

directly guiding the reader through the process of increasing disability inclusion. Eliminate (D) because there is no exaggerated image used in the article, just a friendly business tone. The correct answer is (C).

49. **B** This point of view question asks about the author's perspective on people with disabilities as revealed through the details of the passage, so examine the passage for places in which the author discusses the skills that people with disabilities can provide. The final paragraph of the article states "On a daily basis, people with disabilities must think creatively about how to solve problems and accomplish tasks. In the workplace, this resourcefulness translates into innovative thinking, fresh ideas and varied approaches." Therefore, (B) is correct. Choice (A) is incorrect; although patience may be a quality people with disabilities have, it is not indicated as a skill in the article. Choice (C) is incorrect, since the article never suggests that traditional values are connected to employee skills. Choice (D) is incorrect, because "diversity" is a social characteristic, not a skill. The correct answer is (B).

50. The option that correctly completes the sentence for each "Select" option:

Dropdown Item 1: Coordination and subordination, modifiers

The first choice is correct for the first drop-down question:

This position is especially of interest to me **because my experience as a senior security professional** in the Army has prepared me for a disciplined, secure work environment and the challenges associated with unexpected events.

Options 2 and 3 are incorrect because they incorrectly use "although," which signals a shift of direction. However, the focus of the sentence is not that the writer is prepared *despite* the experience as a senior security professional, but *because of* the experience as a senior security professional. Option 4 is incorrect because it uses the construction "my experience, being a senior security professional" which makes it seem as if the "experience" is the "senior security professional," which is a modifier error.

Dropdown Item 2: Coordination and subordination, modifiers

The fourth choice is correct for the second drop-down question:

I'm looking forward to using this experience **to enhance the security of a growing, competitive bank.**

Option 1 is incorrect: Connecting the parts of the sentence with "from" and "to" makes it seem as if the bank is progressing from "growing" to "competitive," when really both modifiers apply to the bank simultaneously. Option 2 has a similar error: By using "between" and "and" to connect the parts of the sentence, there now seem to be two banks. Option 3 has changed the modifier "growing" to the verb "growing," which now seems as if the writer wants to enhance the security of the "growing" rather than to enhance the security of the bank.

Dropdown Item 3: Sentence construction, logic, and clarity

The second choice is correct for the third drop-down question:

I earned notable IT certifications and hold a current DoD Secret Security **Clearance. I have 2 years of experience as** Communication Specialist in the U.S. Army Signal corps.

Options 1 and 4 are incorrect. Since there is already a conjunction "and" joining two items in the first part of the list, joining the second part with "and" as well creates a run-on sentence. Option 3 is incorrect, since for the writer to say she has 2 years of experience *with* Communication Specialist is unclear—it leaves the reader asking "with whom?" The writer means to say she has 2 years of experience *as* Communication Specialist, not *with* Communication Specialist.

Dropdown Item 4: Modifiers, logic, and clarity

The second choice is correct for the fourth drop-down question:

According to your advertisement, Wheelwright Bank needs security solutions that will guide it into **the promising future of global banking.**

Option 1 is incorrect because the construction "solutions that will guide it into the future, promising" is a modifier error. This construction seems to imply that it's either the future or the solutions that are "promising," which is illogical. Options 3 has a similar error with the construction "the future that promises." Option 4 has the construction "solutions that will guide it into the global banking," which is unclear: Are the solutions meant to guide into "banking" or into "future"? This lack of clarity is an error.

MATHEMATICAL REASONING

Part 1

1. **0.8** Consider Process of Elimination. The answer must be greater than 2/3, which is about 0.66. This eliminates 0.23, 0.5, and 0.349. It must also be less than 9/10, which is the same as 0.9. This eliminates 0.95 since it is a little greater than 0.9, which can be written as 0.90. Thus, only 0.8 remains. While you can change the fractions to decimals using long division, it's best to memorize these common fractions in their decimal forms to save time.

2. **A** When a number or variable is just to the left of the parentheses, the Distributive Property applies. Distribute the number outside to all of the terms inside. Choice (A) does this correctly. Choices (B) and (C) are incorrect because adding the numbers on the inside results in 9, so another way of writing this expression is 24 × 9, not 10 or 20. Choice (D) gets the Distributive Property backward. The number outside needs to be multiplied by everything inside.

3.

First see how many spaces are between the 0 and the 1. There are four spaces, so the lines are counting fourths. The first line to the right of the 0 is 1/4, then 2/4, and then 3/4. Always be sure to count the spaces, not the lines.

4. **A** First take the cube root of –125. Consider what number cubed could equal 125. $3 \times 3 \times 3 = 27$, which is too small. $4 \times 4 \times 4 = 64$, also too small. $5 \times 5 \times 5 = 125$, so the cube root of 125 is 5, and the cube root of –125 is –5 because $(-5) \times (-5) \times (-5) = -125$. Next take the cube root of 8. Because $2 \times 2 \times 2 = 8$, the cube root of 8 is 2. Now multiply –5 by 2 to get an answer of –10.

5. **C** First find the square root of 4, which is 2 because $2 \times 2 = 4$. Then find the square root of 16, which is 4 because $4 \times 4 = 16$. Last, add together $2 + 4 = 6$.

Part 2

6. **A** To multiply two sets of two things in parentheses (binomials), you must use FOIL, which stands for First, Outside, Inside, Last. Start by multiplying the First term in each set of parentheses: $x \cdot 3x = 3x^2$. Next, multiply the terms on the Outside of the parentheses: $x \cdot -1 = -x$. Next, multiply the terms on the Inside of the parentheses: $-3 \cdot 3x = -9x$. Next, multiply the Last term in each set of parentheses: $-3(-1) = 3$. Put it all together: $3x^2 - x - 9x + 3$. Combine like terms to get $3x^2 - 10x + 3$.

7. The slope of line A is **equal to** the slope of line B. The y-intercept of line A is **less than** the y-intercept of line B. Determine the slope and y-intercept of the line shown in the graph. A good way to do this is to find two points. Try using $(-1, -3)$ and $(0, 1)$. It's always best to look for points that clearly fall in a certain spot rather than estimating decimals. Use those two points to find the slope, using the formula $m = \dfrac{y_2 - y_1}{x_2 - x_1}$. Here, that is $\dfrac{1 - (-3)}{0 - (-1)} = \dfrac{1 + 3}{0 + 1} = \dfrac{4}{1} = 4$. Thus, the slopes are equal because line A also has a slope of 4 (m in $y = mx + b$). The y-intercept is clear from the figure: The line crosses the y-axis at 1. Line A has a y-intercept of –1 because –1 is in the spot of b in the formula $y = mx + b$. Thus, the y-intercept of line A is less than the y-intercept of line B.

8. **B** Since the problem mentions area, use the formula for area of a circle: $A = \pi r^2$. Fill in 225π for A and solve for r by canceling out the π on both sides and then taking the square root of 225 to get $r = 15$. However, the question asks for the diameter, not the radius, so double 15 to get a diameter of 30, since the diameter is always twice the radius.

9. **B** Set up a proportion with the same units on both sides: $\dfrac{3 \text{ arrangements}}{8 \text{ guests}} = \dfrac{x \text{ arrangements}}{72 \text{ guests}}$. Cross-multiply to get $8x = 216$ and divide by 8 to get $x = 27$.

10. **D** The quickest way to solve is to draw four blanks for the four letters in the combination. Write the number of options for each blank: 3, the letters A, B, and C. Then multiply together: $3 \times 3 \times 3 \times 3$ to get 81. Notice that it is 3 every time because there could be a combination like BBBB or CCAA, so the letters can repeat. Another option is to write out all the combinations: AAAA, AAAB, AABB, and so on. Since the answer choices are not close together and most are relatively small, it is not difficult to get the answer this way as long as you are methodical about writing down the combinations in order. Once you got past 27, you would know the answer is (D).

11. $h(7) = -9.\ h(-2) = 0.\ h(0) = -2.$

To find $h(7)$, substitute 7 for x: $-7 - 2 = -9$. To find $h(-2)$, substitute -2 for x: $2 - 2 = 0$. To find $h(0)$, substitute 0 for x: $0 - 2 = -2$.

12. **A**   Substitute 6 for P. Be careful not to substitute it for y. The equation is $6 = 2y + 1$. Subtract 1 from both sides to get $5 = 2y$. Then divide by 2 to get $y = 5/2$.

13.   **$19.53**

Start by determining how much gas is needed. If a 14-gallon tank is half full, then 7 gallons of gas are needed. Multiply the 7 gallons by $2.79 per gallon to get $19.53.

14.   **Area: 60. Perimeter: 40.**

To find the area of a triangle, use the formula $A = 1/2\,bh$. The base is 15 and the height is 8. Remember that the height must always be perpendicular to (make a right angle with) the base, so 17 cannot be the height. $1/2 \times 15 \times 8 = 60$, so the area is 60. To find the perimeter, just add all the sides. $15 + 8 + 17 = 40$.

15. **A**   First find two points on the line by looking at the figure. Two points that definitely appear to be on the line are $(-2, 0)$ and $(1, -4)$. Use those points in the slope formula, which is $\dfrac{y_2 - y_1}{x_2 - x_1}$. Here, that is $\dfrac{-4 - 0}{1 - (-2)} = \dfrac{-4}{1 + 2} = -\dfrac{4}{3}$. Another option is to use the two points you've located to count how many spaces up/down and over the line goes. Starting at $(-2, 0)$, it goes down 4 spaces and to the right 3 spaces to get to $(1, -4)$, so the slope is $-\dfrac{4}{3}$.

16. **D**   The question asks about covering a two-dimensional space, so you need to find the area of the space. Since the tile measurements are given in inches, start by converting room measurements from feet to inches. The floor is $10 \times 12 = 120$ inches by $12 \times 12 = 144$ inches. Then multiply 120×144 to get a total of 17,280 square inches. Each tile is $2 \times 2 = 4$ square inches. Divide 17,280 square inches by 4 square inches to get 4,320 tiles. Note that if you start with 10×12 to get an area of 120 square feet, you can't just multiply that by 12 inches in a foot because each square foot is $12 \times 12 = 144$ square inches. Be careful with the difference between units and square units. It's normally best to convert to the smallest units before doing area calculations.

17. **C**   This is written as $50 + 35m$ because the $50 is a flat, one-time rate—it's not multiplied by anything else. The 35 must be multiplied by m because it costs $35 for each month. Another way to make this type of problem easier is to make up a number. Ask yourself how much it would cost after two months. It would be $50 + 35 + 35$ or $50 + 35(2)$, which helps show why (C) is correct.

18. **D** First find transportation in the pie chart: It's 36% of the total. The question asks for the total and states that transportation is \$5,400. Another way to say this is \$5,400 is 36% of the total. Rewrite this in math: $5,400 = \dfrac{36}{100}x$, because "is" means =, % means $\dfrac{}{100}$, "of" means to multiply, and the total is the missing number. Now solve for x. Multiply both sides by 100 to get $540,000 = 36x$ and divide by 36 to get \$15,000. Also consider Process of Elimination. \$5,400 is JUST the amount for transportation, so the total amount must be greater than that, eliminating (A) and (B).

19. **B** It may be helpful to write this as a fraction: $\dfrac{9 \times 10^9}{3 \times 10^3}$. Divide 9 by 3 to get 3, then divide 10^9 by 10^3 to get 10^6. Remember that when you divide exponents, you subtract the powers. Thus, the answer is 3.0×10^6.

20. **Median: 2. Range: 3.**

The median is the middle number when the list is in order. Start by writing out the list. Five people read 1 book each, so write down 1, 1, 1, 1, 1. Continue the same way to get a list of 1, 1, 1, 1, 1, 2, 2, 2, 3, 3, 3, 4. Find the number in the middle by crossing out the first and last numbers until you get to the middle. In this case, there is an even number of numbers, so 2 and 2 are left in the middle. Ordinarily, take the average of them, but since they are both 2, it is easy to see that the median must be 2. The range refers to the difference between the greatest number and the least number. The most books read was 4 and the least books read was 1, so the difference, and the range, is 3.

21. **B** First calculate how much Deyma earns for her regular wage over six hours by doing $10.25 \times 6 = 61.50$. Then find the total amount she sold by multiplying the 5 laptops by \$850 to get \$4,250. Deyma earns 2% of that amount, so multiply \$4,250 by 0.02 or 2/100. This equals \$85 for her commission. Last, add together her wage, \$61.50, and her commission, \$85, to get \$146.50.

22. **D** To factor, first set up two sets of parentheses. Since the first term is x^2, the first thing in both parentheses is x: $(x\quad)(x\quad)$. The last term is -30, and the second term includes a 7. Think of two numbers that multiply to equal 30 and add or subtract to equal 7. 15 and 2 won't work, and neither will 5 and 6 or 30 and 1, but 10 and 3 work. Fill those in: $(x\quad 10)(x\quad 3)$. Since it's a -30, there must be one plus sign and one minus sign. To get a positive 7 for the second term, it must be $+10$ and -3, as shown: $(x + 10)(x - 3)$. Always use FOIL to check that your answer equals the thing you started with. Another option for a multiple-choice problem such as this is to simply use FOIL on each answer choice and see which one equals the original expression. If you don't feel great about factoring but feel comfortable using FOIL, this is a great option.

23. **C** There are many ways to solve this. One is to use the formula provided, which is in the form $y = mx + b$. In the formula, b represents the y-intercept, which is where the line crosses the y (vertical) axis. In this formula, the y-intercept is 0 because there is no number by itself in the problem. Check the answer choices. Choice (A) crosses at 0, so keep it. Choice (B) crosses at 1, so eliminate it. Choices (C) and (D) cross at 0, so keep them as well. Now consider m in the equation, which represents the slope. Here, the slope is -1, which means down 1 and to the right 1. Eliminate (A) because a line that goes up to the right has a

positive slope. For (C), notice that (0, 0) and (1, –1) are both on the line. The line goes down 1 and to the right 1, so this is the correct slope. For (D), the line goes down 2 and right 1, which is a slope of –2. Another good option to solve is to find a point on the line by plugging in an x value and then look for it in the graphs, or draw the line yourself using two or more points on the line and seeing which choice looks like your drawing.

24. **C** The question asks about probability, which is written as a fraction: the thing you want over the total. What you want is for it to not be yellow or black, so that leaves 4 options that would be acceptable. That goes on the top of the fraction. The total number of colors is 6. Thus, the answer is 4/6, which simplifies to 2/3.

25. **980**

Use the formula for surface area of a cylinder, which is $SA = 2\pi rh + 2\pi r^2$. The radius is provided, but the height is not. The volume is, however, so use the formula for volume of a cylinder: $V = \pi r^2 h$. Fill in what you know: $720\pi = \pi(6^2)h$. Cancel out the π on both sides to get $720 = 6^2 h$, then $720 = 36h$, then $h = 20$. Now plug in those numbers to the surface area formula: $SA = 2\pi(6)(20) + 2\pi(6^2) = 2\pi(120) + 2\pi(36) = 240\pi + 72\pi = 312\pi$. Use the button on the calculator or 3.14 to get an answer that rounds to 980. Keep in mind it's always a good idea to leave π in, rather than converting to a decimal, until the very end to get the most accurate result.

26. **D** First distribute the 2: $2x + 8 – 3x = 7x – 1$. Now combine like terms: $-x + 8 = 7x – 1$, and then $9 = 8x$, and thus $x = 9/8$.

27. **B** Use the equation of a line $y = mx + b$. Fill in m, which is the slope: $y = -x + b$. Now fill in the x and y from the point provided: $0 = -2 + b$, and thus $b = 2$. The complete formula is $y = -x + 2$. Another good option is to eliminate any answer choice that has the slope incorrect and then plug in the point to see which equation it works in.

28. **B** The rule for a function is it cannot repeat x-values with different y-values. Choices (A), (C), and (D) all do this, so they are not functions. Choice (B) has four distinct x-values. It is fine that the y-values are the same.

29. **C** Perimeter is the distance around the figure, so first find the missing side. Since this is a right triangle, use the Pythagorean Theorem: $a^2 + b^2 = c^2$. a and b represent the two short sides and c is the long side. Here, the formula is $20^2 + 21^2 = c^2$. Calculate the left side to get $841 = c^2$ and take the square root of both sides to get $c = 29$. Now find the perimeter by adding $20 + 21 + 29 = 70$.

30. **B** The equation of a line is $y = mx + b$. The first thing to find is the slope, m. Find it using the formula $\frac{y_2 - y_1}{x_2 - x_1}$. Here, that is $\frac{1 - (-2)}{5 - (-2)} = \frac{1 + 2}{5 + 2} = \frac{3}{7}$. Now the equation is $y = \frac{3}{7}x + b$. Plug in the coordinates of one of the points for x and y to solve for b. Use the easier one, (5, 1): $1 = \frac{3}{7}(5) + b$. Then $1 = \frac{15}{7} + b$ and $b = 1 - \frac{15}{7} = \frac{7}{7} - \frac{15}{7} = -\frac{8}{7}$. The final equation is $y = \frac{3}{7}x - \frac{8}{7}$. Another, easier option is to simply plug in the points for x and y into the answer choices to find the equation in which both points work.

31. **A** To find the number of people per square mile, divide the population by the number of miles for each town. Emersonville is 43,209 ÷ 24.6 = 1,756.46 people per square mile. Do the same for the other towns to get 390.41 for Amberton, 515.52 for Greenshore, and 1,658.97 for Bereon. Thus, Emersonville has the greatest number of people per square mile.

32.

Temperature and Precipitation

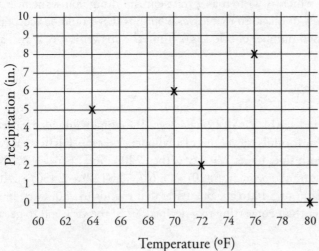

Plot a point for the temperatures and precipitations in the table, as shown above.

33. **D** The phrase *half a number* means to put a 1/2 in front of a variable (or divide by 2). The answer choices use *k*, so write 1/2*k*. Then it says *10 more than* that, so 1/2*k* + 10.

34. **3** Create two equations, using two variables. To keep it simple, use *b* for the number of bracelets and *n* for the number of necklaces. The total number of bracelets and necklaces is 8, so one equation is *b* + *n* = 8. The other information has to do with the amount of money. The second equation is 2*n* + 1*b* = 13 because $2 for every necklace and $1 for every bracelet adds up to $13. There are two good ways to solve. One is through substitution. Subtract *n* from both sides of the first equation to get *b* alone: *b* = 8 − *n*. Now, substitute that into the second equation for *b*: 2*n* + (8 − *n*) = 13. Then simplify: 2*n* + 8 − *n* = 13, then *n* + 8 = 13, and *n* = 5. That's the number of necklaces, so subtract it from 8 to get that there were 3 bracelets. Thus, the answer is 3. The second good way to solve is to stack the equations and subtract:

$$
\begin{array}{l}
n + b = 8 \\
\underline{-(2n + b = 13)} \\
-n \quad\quad = -5
\end{array}
$$

And thus *n* = 5. One other option is to guess and check. Since there are only 8 pieces of jewelry total, it would be fairly easy to guess and check numbers of bracelets.

35. **$k(2) = 4.$ $k(4) = 32.$ $k(0) = 0.$**

To find $k(2)$, put in 2 for *x*. This results in $\frac{1}{2}(2^3) = \frac{1}{2}(8) = 4$. To find $k(4)$, put in 4 for *x*. This results in $\frac{1}{2}(4^3) = \frac{1}{2}(64) = 32$. To find $k(0)$, put in 0 for *x*. This results in $\frac{1}{2}(0^3) = 0$.

36. **D** Start by rewriting the first equation so it's in the form $y = mx + b$. Add $4x$ to both sides to get $2y = 4x + 6$. Divide both sides by 2 to get $y = 2x + 3$. Compare the slopes of the equations, which are represented by m. The first one has a slope of 2 and the second one has a slope of $-1/2$. Lines whose slopes are negative reciprocals of each other are perpendicular, meaning they intersect at a right angle. Another good option is to draw both lines and see what their relationship is.

37.

Plot the three given points first. The x-coordinate comes first, so from the origin (0,0) go the appropriate number of spaces to the right or left (right is positive and left is negative) and then go up or down the number of spaces in the y-coordinate (up is positive and down is negative). Then locate the missing point. The problem states that the coordinates form a square. Since they go from 2 to 5 on the x-axis, the side of the square is 3. Count down 3 spaces from (2, 2) and left 3 spaces from (5, -1) to find that the missing point is (2, -1)

38. **A** The correct answer is (A) because 0.75 times the number of times she rides the ride must be less than or equal to 5, since she only has $5.00.

39. **Width: $2\frac{2}{3}$. Length: $5\frac{1}{3}$.**

    Start by setting up a proportion. For the width, it is $\dfrac{1.5 \text{ inches}}{1 \text{ foot}} = \dfrac{4 \text{ inches}}{x \text{ feet}}$. Cross-multiply to get $1.5x = 4$, and divide by 1.5 to get $x = 2\frac{2}{3}$ feet. Do the same for the length to get $5\frac{1}{3}$ feet, or consider that 8 is twice 4, so the actual length will be twice $2\frac{2}{3}$.

40. **$f(0) = 5$. $f(10) = 205$. $f(-3) = 23$.**

    To find $f(0)$, put in 0 for x. This results in $2(0)^2 + 5 = 0 + 5 = 5$. To find $f(10)$, put in 10 for x. This results in $2(10)^2 + 5 = 2(100) + 5 = 200 + 5 = 205$. To find $f(-3)$, put in -3 for x. This results in $2(-3)^2 + 5 = 2(9) + 5 = 18 + 5 = 23$. Always be sure to follow order of operations.

41. **B** To find the slope, put the line into the form $y = mx + b$. Subtract $2x$ from both sides to get $3y = -x + 1$. Then divide by 3 to get $y = -1/3x + 1$. Since m represents the slope, the slope here is $-1/3$.

42. **A** Start by factoring the quadratic on the top. Draw two sets of parentheses and put an x in the beginning of each: $(x\ \ )(x\ \ )$. Consider what multiplies to equal 3 and adds to equal 4: 3 and 1. Everything is positive here, so that makes it easier. The result is $(x + 3)(x + 1)$. Since $x + 1$ is on the top and the bottom, it cancels out and all that is left is $x + 3$.

43. **B** Get x by itself by subtracting 1 from both sides to get $3x > 12$ and then dividing by 3 to get $x > 4$. Choice (B) shows this correctly because the line is shaded to the right of 4 and the 4 has an open circle because it is a $>$ sign and 4 is not included in the solution. A closed circle would be used for $\geq$.

44. **C** Put in 3.75 for M, the amount on the pass. The equation becomes $3.75 = 20 - 1.25t$. Subtract 20 from both sides to get $-16.25 = -1.25t$. Multiply both sides by -1 to get $16.25 = 1.25t$. Last, divide by 1.25 to get $t = 13$.

45. **A** Get x by itself. First, multiply both sides by x to get rid of the fraction. This results in $3y = 2x$. Then, divide both sides by 2 to get $\dfrac{3y}{2} = x$.

46. **A** To solve an inequality, get the variable by itself. To do that here, subtract 162 from all three sections of the inequality. This results in $8 < p < 18$. This should make sense because if Will gains 8 pounds, he will be at the lower limit of 170. If he gains more than that but less than 18, he will be within the range he is looking for. With inequalities, it's always a good idea to guess and check numbers to make sure your answer makes sense.

SOCIAL STUDIES

1. **B** There had always been anti-slavery sentiments among certain religious groups, particularly in England and the United States, but the date of the passage in question (1774) indicates that the author was probably associated with the growing evangelical movement in the late 18th century. In addition to their religious fervor, evangelical groups historically supported many social justice movements such as the fight against slavery. Therefore, (B) is the best answer. Choice (A) is too early chronologically; (C) is an okay option, but the Freemasons were not generally known for their abolitionist views. Mormonism was not founded until the 1820s, so (D) is chronologically too late.

2. **D** The networks and movements of goods and people around three continents are often referred to as the "Triangular Trade." The classical understanding of this theory holds that slaves were brought from Africa to the Americas, where the use of African slaves was essential to growing cash crops, which were then shipped to Europe, where those goods themselves or products made from those goods were used to purchase more slaves in Africa. Therefore, (D) is the best answer.

3. **D** The owners of slave ships involved in the transatlantic passage wanted to make their voyages as profitable as possible, which meant cramming as many slaves as possible into the boats. For the slaves themselves, this meant a minimum of space in which to move and unbearable conditions that bred disease and death. Choice (D) is the best answer.

4. **A** During the 17th century, European nations greatly increased their commercial endeavors. As part of this process, merchants sometimes banded together into companies, in part because they could do things more efficiently and cheaply, and thus earn more profits, when they worked together. In the case of the Dutch West India Company mentioned in the source text, one primary goal was to monopolize trade in the Caribbean and eliminate competition from the Spanish and Portuguese. The best answer is (A).

5. **C** Chartered companies in Europe during the early modern period were typically formed under the authority of a king or other royal figure, who would shape the company, define its parameters, and lay out the terms under which the company could conduct its business ventures. The best answer is (C).

6. **C** In the quote, Franklin is addressing the Constitutional Convention about a decade after the American Revolution. He is commenting upon the success of the colonists in gaining independence from Great Britain, and in context the word "felicity" must mean something like "luck" or "fortune," (C).

7. **A** In the quote, Franklin clearly expresses his religious belief and states that "God governs in the affairs of men." He further asks, "is it probable that an empire can rise without [God's] aid?"—implying that "the struggle" (i.e., the American Revolution) would not have succeeded without God's help, (A).

8. **D** As ancient civilizations developed more sophisticated methods of farming, there was an accompanying increase in the number of and populations of cities. As food production increased through advances in agriculture, societies became more well-organized, with distinct cultural identities, making (D) the best answer. Choice (A) is backward (as agriculture increased over the course of human history, hunter-gatherer lifestyles declined). Choice (B) is incorrect because the ancient Mesopotamians were polytheistic. Choice (C) is incorrect because women had very few economic (or other) opportunities during the time period in question.

9. **A** The text states "class considerations not being allowed to interfere with merit; nor again does poverty bar the way, if a man is able to serve the state," which in plain English means that a citizen's ability was more important than his wealth or status in classical Greek democracy, making (A) the best answer. Choice (B) is incorrect because the first sentence of the text contradicts the idea that the Greeks were imitating their neighbors. Choice (C) is incorrect because the text does not mention overthrowing leaders. Choice (D) is incorrect because the text does not state that all laws or codes are actually written down.

10. **C** In both ancient Greece and the early United States, the only people allowed to participate in the democratic process were adult males, (C).

11. **B** In the context of this discussion about "direct action," Martin Luther King states that "there is a type of constructive, nonviolent tension which is necessary for growth." Unlike some other civil rights leaders, Martin Luther King did not endorse violent action, (A). In this speech, he never mentions appeasement, (C), or legal action, (D). Therefore, (B) is the best answer.

12. **C** Source 2 states that there are "conditions that now prevent women from enjoying the equality of opportunity and freedom of which is their right," making (C) the best answer. Choice (A) is incorrect for the same reason, and (B) and (D) are both contradicted by the source text.

13. **B** Source 1 states that sit-ins, marches, and other forms of direct action serve "to dramatize the issue that it can no longer be ignored." Source 2 states that "the time has come to move beyond the abstract argument, discussion and symposia." Therefore, these two sources agree that practical action is needed, making (B) the best answer.

14. **B** The term "limited government," (B), refers to the concept of defining government powers by means of a constitution. A constitution specifies what the government is allowed to do and also what it may not do. In setting distinct limits on government power, the Framers of the U.S. Constitution hoped to prevent the government from achieving the same level of power as had the British monarchy. Direct democracy, (A), refers to a form of democratic government in which all citizens vote on all issues. The Constitution established a representative democracy, in which citizens vote for representatives who, in turn, act on their behalf and assume the nation's legislative and executive duties. The abolition of slavery, (C), did not occur until 1865 with the ratification of the Thirteenth Amendment. The Framers of the Constitution did not seriously consider abolition. As ratified in 1788, the Constitution did not yet have a Bill of Rights. The Bill of Rights was ratified in 1791; only then did the Constitution reflect a concern for protecting the rights of the accused, (D).

15. **D** Federalism is a system under which the federal government shares power with the states. The Tenth Amendment to the Constitution reserves to the states all powers not granted the national government by the Constitution, (D). Therefore, it is instrumental in defining the relationship between the two levels of government, which is the essence of federalism. The system of checks and balances, (A), among the three branches of the federal government concerns the national government only. International treaties, (B), are the sole responsibility of the federal government, and do not relate to the states in any way. Washington, D.C. Choice (C) does have special constitutional status as the nation's capital. The federal government plays a role in governing the city, and the city is not represented in Congress. However, Washington's constitutional status has little influence on American Federalism.

16. **D** Each of the answer choices correctly identifies a weakness of the Articles of Confederation. However, neither the Articles nor the original Constitution had a universal suffrage clause, (D). Under both, blacks and women were among those who had no right to vote. Many states allowed only property owners to

vote, as you can see from Source 2. Under the Articles of Confederation, the national government was entirely dependent on the states to enforce national law, as it had no executive powers of its own. The Constitution rectified this problem by establishing the executive branch of government, (A). Under the Articles of Confederation, state governments held the power to impose trade tariffs. The Constitution grants this power to Congress, (B). Under the Articles of Confederation, the national government was dependent on the states to provide soldiers for national defense. This system proved unreliable at best. The Constitution grants Congress the power to raise an army, (C).

17. A believer in laissez-faire economics such as U.S. President Calvin Coolidge would likely support **the implementation of lower taxes.**

A supporter of laissez-faire economic policy would be in favor of "letting things be" in the free market, less regulation, and fewer taxes. For these reasons, **giving the Environmental Protection Agency greater power to fine factories that contribute to global warming** and **increasing taxes across higher income groups to aid the poor** is incorrect. Free-marketers are traditionally skeptical of labor unions for controlling the labor supply, so **the creation of a law that protects unions and grants them collective bargaining rights** would not be supported by a believer in laissez-faire economics. The idea of "letting things be" would mean applying the same treatment to everyone rather than manipulating the law based on individual circumstances—**the implementation of lower taxes** does exactly that.

18. **A** The Indian Removal Act of 1830, (A), authorized the president to remove Native Americans from their ancestral homelands to federal territory in locations west of the Mississippi River. This Act and many laws that followed were part of a broader movement of white settlers to expand westward within the continental United States and settle lands that were previously inhabited by Native American tribes. The Sherman Antitrust Act of 1890, (B), was designed to prohibit business monopolies; the Emergency Quota Act of 1921, (C), restricted immigration into the United States; the Kansas-Nebraska Act of 1854, (D), created the territories of Kansas and Nebraska and was a controversial piece of legislation in the debates over the abolition of slavery.

19. **C** In a representative democracy, such as that of the United States, citizens vote to elect representatives who act on behalf of the voters' interests and concerns, (C). Representatives are not appointed, (A). Citizens do not vote directly to enact laws, (B), but rather the citizens' representatives enact laws on their behalf (in the United States, the enactment of laws is one of the roles of Congress). A government consisting of a small group of self-appointed elites, (D), is known as an oligarchy.

20. **D** The legislature, (D), is the branch of the American government in which congressmen and congresswomen, elected by citizens, represent their constituents by enacting laws (among other tasks). Members of the cabinet, (A), are appointed by the president; federal judges of the judiciary branch, (B), are also appointed by the president; employees of the Federal Bureau of Investigation, (C), are part of a broader law enforcement community and are neither elected nor considered representatives of the American citizenry in any political sense.

21. **1880**

According to the graph, the 1910 foreign-born population was just under 14 million. The foreign-born population in 1880 was just under 7 million, which is about half of the 1910 number.

22. **a**, **d**, and **e**

Between the mid-19th century and the early 20th century, the majority of immigrants to the United States came from Europe. In the early part of the time period indicated in the chart, most immigrants came from England, Ireland, Germany, and Scandinavia. Beginning in the later part of the 19th century, there was a massive increase in immigrants from southern and eastern Europe (Italy and Greece, among other countries).

23. **C** The invention of the cotton gin, which was used to drastically reduce the time needed to separate seeds from cotton (making it easier to produce goods), led to cotton becoming the dominant cash crop of the United States. Farmers and plantation owners in the southern states increased their use of slave labor in the cotton fields during the early 19th century, so (C) is not true (and thus the correct answer). The rise of cotton led to a decrease in the value of tobacco, (A), and an increase in the number of slaves, (B), as just described. As the production of cotton grew in the southern United States, industry grew in the north, (D), as there was an increased need for factories to produce the cotton-based goods that were to be exported to Britain and elsewhere.

24. **A** There are many things that correlate with a country's high level of GDP; among the most prominent of those is the correlation between citizens' education levels and the economic robustness of those citizens' countries. Choices (B), (C), and (D) are all characteristics that correlate with countries that have low GDPs per capita.

25. **B** The First Amendment is typically understood as prohibiting anything that either advances or hinders the practice of a particular religion. Since the government is responsible for levying taxes, it would be a violation of the First Amendment for the government to levy taxes that would specifically benefit a particular religious group, (B).

26. "Congress shall make no law respecting an establishment of religion, or prohibiting the free exercise thereof; or abridging the freedom of speech, or of the press; or the right of the people peaceably to assemble, and to petition the Government for a redress of grievances."

The First Amendment provides protection for free speech and freedom of the press. While there are, at times, limitations to these freedoms, in general an American newspaper editor is well within his or her rights to critique the government in published articles.

27. An "impartial jury" as described in Source 2 would NOT contain **a juror who was influenced by negative publicity about the accused**.

There are many things that can constitute a reason for someone to be prohibited from serving on a jury, such as being a victim of a similar crime, a personal relationship with the accused, a connection to law enforcement, etc. In order to be impartial, it is important that jury members not have preconceived opinions about the case at hand, and thus someone who was **influenced by negative publicity about the accused** would be considered potentially biased.

28. **B** A large number of Republicans entered the race during the buildup to the election of 1920. Beginning in 1901, states increasingly began to use a primary process in order to select nominees for elected office, whereas previously party leaders and political insiders were responsible for choosing nominees. The new primary process reflected the concerns of the Progressive Era, in particular the Progressive Movement's concerns about political corruption. Holding primaries, it was thought, would bring the process to the

people and take it out of the hands of elites, (B). Choices (A), (C), and (D) reflect Progressive ideals, but do not relate to the topic of elections.

29.   The source most clearly reflects a(n) **imperialist** foreign policy agenda.

The cartoon pictured shows Uncle Sam ordering from a restaurant menu (taking his orders from President McKinley) in which the menu items are Cuba, Puerto Rico, the Philippines, and the Sandwich Islands. The title of the cartoon, "Well, I Hardly Know Which to Take First!" reflects the attitude of **imperialism** that was dominant in some quarters at the end of the 19th century (i.e., the United States, as a superior power, has the right to "take" and colonize less powerful lands). **Isolationist** refers to a foreign policy stance in which a country tries to stay out of other countries' affairs; **nativist** refers to a domestic policy that favors native-born citizens over immigrants; **pacifist** refers to a belief in non-violence.

30.   **a, d**

As described in the explanation for the previous question, the cartoon depicts an imperialist ideology. The United States was instrumental in the overthrow of the Kingdom of Hawaii, (a), and was heavily involved in Hawaiian politics, exerting American influence long before Hawaii became a state in 1959. What is now California used to be part of Mexico, but American military forces seized the territory, (d), during the early part of the Mexican-American War (1846–1847). Both of these actions can be classified as imperialist in nature.

31. **B** After the Revolutionary War, the colonists came together and drafted the Articles of Confederation, (B), whose main purpose was to unify the states and come to a consensus about how to manage American independence and sovereignty. The natural rights philosophy expressed in the source quoted is not a prominent theme of this text. The texts of (A), (C), and (D) all espouse natural rights philosophy as a foundation of government.

32. **A** "Prudence" in the modern context typically means "wisdom" or "caution." In the context of the source, it means something like "good judgment," (A). The authors of the Declaration of Independence believed that it was self-evident to reasonable people that the cause of independence was just.

33. **C** The passage mentions the "despotism" and "tyranny" of Great Britain, (C), as reasons for pursuing independence and a new form of government. The colonists believed that "it is their right, it is their duty, to throw off such Government." Choices (A), (B), and (D) are not mentioned in the source.

34. **D** The National Bank Act, (D), was passed in 1863 and thus has nothing to do with the lead-up to the American Revolution. Choices (A) and (B) were tax acts created by the British to build up Britain's economy after the French and Indian Wars. The colonists viewed these tax policies as oppressive. The Quartering Act, (C), required colonists to house British soldiers, sparking widespread resentment among the colonists.

35. **D** In the quote, Jefferson emphasizes that it is important that the "minority possess their equal rights." He acknowledges that the majority opinion dominates and should drive action, but only if minority viewpoints are respected and not oppressed, (D).

SCIENCE

1. Producers are the foundation of any community, because they can create their own food. Primary consumers eat exclusively producers, so they should be one level up from producers. Secondary consumers come next, with tertiary consumers at the top of the energy pyramid.

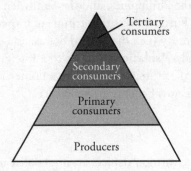

2. **producer**

    Plants produce their own energy through photosynthesis; therefore, plants play the role of producer in a community.

3. **A** If an animal exhibits an evolutionary adaptation over time, the adaptation is a result of the predator-prey relationship. The passage indicates that adaptation occurs in the predator-prey relationship, but there is no indication that the predator-prey relationship is the ONLY cause of evolution. There could be other causes of adaptation that occur outside of the predator-prey relationship.

4. **B** An inexperienced driver slows his average speed to avoid having an accident. While this is an example of an adaptation to preserve life, it is not an adaptation that results from a predator-prey relationship. A species adapting coloring of another species that is less likely to be attacked (fly that looks like a bee), a species adapting a response that aids in escaping attack (homo sapiens developing fight-or-flight), and a species adapting a defense mechanism that prevents attack (skunks developing chemical spray mechanism) are directly related to prey changing in order to avoid being killed and eaten by the indicated predators.

5. **B** Plants and algae participate in photosynthesis that provides oxygen to consumers. Arrows from plants and algae to primary consumers are labeled "photosynthesis." This process converts CO_2 into oxygen, which is used by the primary consumers. The burning of wood/fossil fuels does create carbon dioxide, but there are no arrows on the diagram that indicate the carbon dioxide being used by consumers, so eliminate (A). There is likewise no indication that the waste from one part of the ecosystem is used as fuel for another part of the ecosystem, so eliminate (C). While cellular respiration is one way of producing carbon dioxide, the arrow from the burning of wood and fossil fuels also indicates another means of producing carbon dioxide, so eliminate (D).

6. **has an unknown relationship to**

    This is a tricky question, because while the table tells you that there were 5 earthquakes of magnitude 0.1–0.9, it doesn't actually tell you how many there were of magnitude 9.0 and above, since those are grouped in with 8.0–8.9. While it would be reasonable to assume that, of the 8 quakes of 8.0 or higher, probably more were 8.0–8.9 since that is the general trend, you cannot know this for sure given the information you have.

7. **4.0–4.9**

   Look for the largest number representing frequency in the chart—that is the mode of all earthquakes. It occurred in 2005, with a total of 13,917 earthquakes having a magnitude between 4.0–4.9.

8.

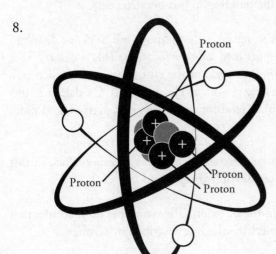

   There are four protons in this image, as shown by the callouts.

9. **C** Tsunamis cannot be caused by earthquakes that cause the sea bed to move sideways. The bullet points clearly state that one of the three circumstances that must happen in order for a tsunami to occur is that the sea bed must move upward or downward—it does not indicate that sideways movement will cause a tsunami. All three other statements are proven in the passage.

10. **C** While all the answer choices appear in the text, you need to find the one that describes a tsunami's behavior just before it strikes land. Eliminate (A) because it refers to the wave's speed in the open water rather than when reaching the coast. Choice (B) describes the general state of the ocean by a continental shelf, not a tsunami specifically, so that, too, can be eliminated. The Richter scale referred to in (D) measures earthquake magnitude, not tsunami waves, so that, too, is incorrect. You are left with (C), which does describe the tsunami accurately.

11. **average, 2.1**

    To figure out how long it will be before the lighthouse sat at the edge of the cliff, engineers must calculate the average loss of distance per year, which is 2.1 feet per year. Average feet lost per year = $\dfrac{1990 - 1874}{300 - 55}$ = 2.11 feet per year.

12. **26** Using the calculation from question 11, take the average already determined (2.11 feet per year) and set

that equal to the remaining distance (50 feet) over the number of years (unknown): $2.11 = \dfrac{50}{c}$. Solve

and determine that the cliff edge will be at the edge of the building in just over 26 years.

13. **C** Erosion is defined as the surface processes, like wind or water flow, that remove soil, rock, or dissolved material from one location on Earth's surface and transport it to another location. This is exactly what happens when a cliff is worn away—both water and wind eat away at the cliff. Rust occurs when iron or an iron alloy is exposed to oxygen and moisture for a long period, so eliminate (A). Oxidation results when an element combines with oxygen, so eliminate (B). A landslide occurs when a mass of land slides down a hill, so eliminate (D).

14. **B** Decomposition takes place whenever a compound is broken into smaller chemical components. In this case, the water molecules are separated into distinct molecules of hydrogen and oxygen.

15. **Synthesis** takes places in the chemical reaction shown in the question. The two types of molecules that are originally separate combine to create one kind of molecule, which is described by synthesis.

16.

Organ	Tissue
Brain	(d) Nerve
Heart	(c) Muscle
Skin	(a) Epithelial
Elbow Joint	(b) Connective

The brain is made up of nerve tissue, as are the other components of the nervous system. The heart is made up of cardiac muscle tissue—it's the only organ in the body that is made up of this tissue! The skin is entirely epithelial tissue, covering the surface of the body. All joints in the body, including the elbow, contain connective tissue to hold the bones and muscles together.

17. **nervous, cardiovascular**

The brain is part of the **nervous** system of the body; the heart is part of the **cardiovascular** system of the body.

18. **A** Blood sugar rises; receptors in body sense change in blood sugar; pancreas (control center) secretes insulin to lower blood sugar levels; blood sugar returns to normal. An increase in blood sugar is a stimulus, and receptors in the body detect this change. When information of this change reaches the brain, it signals the pancreas to respond by secreting insulin in order to lower blood sugar levels. When enough insulin has been released, the body is able to regulate blood sugar and return to homeostasis.

19. **parasitism**

The birds benefit in this relationship, but the insects do not—they die! The relationship that describes a situation in which one organism benefits as a result of another organism's death is a parasitism.

20. **commensalism**

    The birds benefit from the grazing animals, which unearth insects for the birds to eat, and the grazing animals are unaffected. This describes a commensalist relationship, which exists between two organisms that benefit from each other.

21. **B** The passage has already established that the grazing animals benefit the birds. The new information in the question indicates that the grazing animals will now benefit from the birds, as well. This describes mutualism, a relationship in which both organisms benefit from each other.

22. **meiosis**

    Based on the table above question 23, the figure given in that question represents meiosis. The drawing shows crossing over of chromosomes, two steps of cell division, and four genetically different daughter cells, which all indicate meiosis.

23. **mitosis, 46 chromosomes**

    In Experiment 3 in the table given, the cell undergoes mitosis and each resulting cell has 46 chromosomes. Based upon the number of final cells—2—it can be determined that the cell undergoes mitosis. Because mitosis creates identical copies of cells, each resulting new cell will also have 46 chromosomes.

24. **D** A hydroelectric dam converts water energy into electric energy, so eliminate (A); a microphone converts sound energy into electric energy, so eliminate (B); an electric heater converts electric energy into thermal energy, so eliminate (C); running water does not convert one form of energy into any other without an outside entity, so select (D).

25. **(b) friction, (c) kinetic energy, (a) gravity**

    Jeanne tries in vain to move the entertainment center, but she cannot exert enough force to overcome friction. However, with Deb's help, they're able to actually move the unit by producing kinetic energy. Gravity causes the remote control to fall off the entertainment center.

26. **A** The equation for work requires that the object move a distance. Since the entertainment unit did not move, Jeanne did not do any work. Therefore, eliminate (B), (C), and (D).

27. **D** As defined in the question, *work = force applied × distance moved*. Therefore, the total force applied (90N) times the distance moved (15 feet) yields 1350, or (D). Eliminate (A), (B), and (C).

28. **C** Convection describes the process by which heat moves from a warmer area to a cooler one, which is what happens when Bryan's coffee cools in his broken thermos. It's convection because the heat moves through a fluid (the air) rather than conduction, (D), which would require direct contact. Both endothermic, (A), and exothermic, (B), are incorrect, because energy is not released (exothermic) or absorbed (endothermic) in a chemical reaction.

29. **C** Use Process of Elimination to find the correct answer. You can get rid of (A) because "never" is too strong. You can also eliminate (D) because the passage states that the thermos's vacuum seal slows heat transfer, whereas it would be faster if there were air between the thermos walls. That leaves (B) and (C), which initially seem to say very similar things. However, (B) specifies that without the vacuum seal heat would be *lost*—in other words, that a hot liquid in the thermos would cool. That's true, according to the passage—but what if the thermos contained a cold liquid? In that case, the vacuum seal would keep the liquid cold. So, (B) is not always the case, and (C) is the best answer.

30. **D** Simply multiply the value for acceleration of gravity (9.8 m/s²) by the time elapsed (10 seconds) and the result is –98 m/s.

31. **D** All of the options indicated would impact the way a bird feeds except for the last option, another bird going extinct. Survival or extinction of another species would not likely have an impact on the shape of another species' beaks.

32. **B** Overpopulation often forces species to self-select in order to retain the strongest genes in the gene pool. Along the way, species adapt to new situations and gradually begin to produce offspring who inherit these adaptations. Popularization is not a step in the process of natural selection.

33. **B** This Punnett Square describes one homozygous recessive parent gene (dd) and one heterozygous dominant parent gene. When determining the offspring genetic combinations, the top left corner will be Dd, the top right will be Dd, the bottom left will be dd and the bottom right will be dd. Since dimples is a dominant trait, represented by D, you can see that two out of four resulting expressions contain D. Therefore, two out of four, or 50%, of the resulting expressions are likely to have dimples.

34. **B** This Punnett Square describes one homozygous recessive parent gene (dd) and one heterozygous dominant parent gene. When determining the offspring genetic combinations, the top left corner will be Dd, the top right will be Dd, the bottom left will be dd and the bottom right will be dd.

35. **1:1** Genotypic ratio represents the likelihood of different genotypes. In this Punnett Square, there are two genotypes expressed: Dd and dd. Since there are two of each, the resulting ratio is 1:1.

Chapter 11
Practice Test 5

Reasoning Through Language Arts

Welcome!

Here is some information that you need to know before you start this test:

- You should not spend too much time on a question if you are not certain of the answer; answer it the best you can, and go on to the next question.
- If you are not certain of the answer to a question, you can mark your answer for review and come back to it later.
- This test has three sections.
- You have **35 minutes** to complete Section 1.
- When you finish Section 1, you may review those questions.
- You may not go back to Section 1 once you have finished your review.
- You have **45 minutes** to complete the Extended Response question in Section 2.
- After completing Section 2, you may take a 10-minute break.
- You have **60 minutes** to complete Section 3.
- When you finish Section 3, you may review those questions.

Turn the page to begin.

GO ON TO THE NEXT PAGE

Questions 1 through 8 refer to the following article.

Adapted from "Prevention and Control of Stress Among Emergency Workers"
National Institute of Mental Health

1   This pamphlet discusses approaches that have been found helpful to workers in dealing with disaster-related stress. It suggests interventions that may be helpful before, during, and after a disaster.

2   The suggestions presented here are guidelines. No single suggestion will work for all people at all times. However, these ideas are based on a wealth of experience and wisdom from disaster workers.

Predisaster Interventions: Prevention

3   Some of the most important stress management interventions for disaster workers take place predisaster. These activities are important in preparing workers for what they will likely encounter in the disaster situation. Preparation can help minimize the effects of stress when it occurs and can help individuals cope with stress in a more efficient manner. The following are some useful predisaster interventions.

Orientation and Training

4   Training on the mental health aspects of emergency workers' jobs, both routine and during disasters, should be provided as part of workers' initial on-the-job orientation and ongoing service training. Such education can prepare workers for the stresses they may experience in their work, decrease their vulnerability, and increase their effectiveness in dealing with job-related stresses when they occur.

Predisaster Personal Emergency Preparedness Plans

5   Having a personal and family emergency plan will help individuals to cope with whatever emergencies may occur while they are at home. Every emergency worker should be familiar with hazards and potential emergencies inherent in the local geographic area and should have contingency plans for self and family. This is important not only to the safety of the family but also to the availability of the worker for disaster assignment. The more quickly things can be taken care of at home, the more quickly the worker can report to work relatively free of family worries. Similarly, if the worker is at work when a disaster occurs, peace of mind and concentration will be enhanced if the person's family is prepared and able to cope.

GO ON TO THE NEXT PAGE

6   Every family emergency plan should include the following:

- A home inspection to identify hazards and eliminate them

- A plan for different types of emergencies that might occur in the area, such as tornado, hurricane, earthquake, or hazardous materials spill; training for what to do before, during, and after each emergency

- An evacuation plan: what to take, where to go, where to meet or reunite

- A plan to care for children, individuals needing assistance (the ill or those with disabilities), and pets

- Training of every capable family member in how to turn off utilities and in first aid

- Prominent posting of emergency phone numbers

7   Emergency supplies and equipment should include the following:

- Food and water for 72 hours, include special diets, infant formula, and pet food

- Portable radio, flashlight, and batteries

- An adequate supply of prescription medications, prescription eyeglasses, extra batteries for hearing aid, etc.

- First aid kit

- Blankets or sleeping bags

- Sanitation supplies

- Fire extinguisher

- Personal hygiene supplies

- Alternate lighting, camping lantern, candles, matches

- Safety equipment, hose for firefighting, heavy shoes and gloves, work clothes

- Tools

- Cooking supplies, charcoal, camp stove

GO ON TO THE NEXT PAGE

8   It is a good idea to establish a mutual aid system within the neighborhood. With a bit of preplanning, neighbors can arrange to look out for and assist one another in times of emergency, pooling supplies as well as skills. Many neighborhoods develop emergency preparedness plans as part of the Neighborhood Crime Alert network. Such a mutual aid arrangement can give emergency workers increased peace of mind about their families' welfare.

9   In addition, every worker who is likely to be called out on emergency assignment on short notice is wise to have an emergency bag prepacked. Supplies should be tailored to the nature of the worker's usual type of assignment. If the assignment is likely to entail any length of time away from home, the bag should include the following:

- Clothes, including sturdy shoes and clothes for inclement weather

- Eyeglasses and medications (including over-the-counter remedies for personal stress reactions—antacids, aspirin, antidiarrheal medicine, etc.)

- Personal hygiene supplies

- Paper and pens

- Forms or supplies necessary to the worker's disaster assignment

Interventions During the Disaster

10   The following are suggestions for workers for management of stress during a disaster operation:

- Develop a "buddy" system with a coworker. Agree to keep an eye on each other's functioning, fatigue level, and stress symptoms. Tell the buddy how to know when you are getting stressed ("If I start doing so-and-so, tell me to take a break"). Make a pact with the buddy to take a break when he or she suggests it, if the situation and command officers allow.

- Encourage and support coworkers. Listen to one another's feelings. Don't take anger too personally. Hold criticism unless it's essential. Tell each other "You're doing great" and "Good job." Give each other a pat on the back. Bring each other a snack or something to drink.

- Try to get some activity and exercise.

- Try to eat frequently, in small quantities.

GO ON TO THE NEXT PAGE

- Humor can break the tension and provide relief. Use it with care, however. People are highly suggestible in disaster situations, and victims or coworkers can take things personally and be hurt if they are the brunt of "disaster humor."

- Use positive "self-talk," such as "I'm doing fine" and "I'm using the skills I've been trained to use."

- Take deep breaths, hold them, then blow out forcefully.

Source: National Institute of Mental Health

1. What can the reader infer about the article's intended audience?

   A. The article is written to provide preventative measures for disasters.
   B. The article is written for people dealing with disaster-related grief.
   C. The article is written for people working disaster relief.
   D. The article is written for people with stressful jobs.

2. Read these sentences from the article.

   > Training on the mental health aspects of emergency workers' jobs, both routine and during disasters, should be provided as part of workers' initial on-the-job orientation and ongoing service training.

   Based on these details from the article, what can the readers infer about emergency training?

   A. Mental health of emergency workers is an important element of emergency training.
   B. Mental health dictates a person's ability to perform the necessary task at hand.
   C. Emergency workers do not need ongoing service training if they have good mental health.
   D. Mental preparation is key to surviving natural and man-made disasters.

3. What inference can the reader make based on the predisaster emergency preparedness recommendations mentioned in paragraph 5?

   A. Having a personal plan can alleviate stress for emergency workers and allow them to focus on their jobs.
   B. Caring for their families is more important than aiding in disaster relief.
   C. A neighborhood is stronger as a group than an individual family in preparing for disasters.
   D. Having a buddy system can keep workers accountable to each other and help monitor fatigue or stress.

GO ON TO THE NEXT PAGE

4. The author claims that disaster workers can take steps to maintain calm during a disaster. Write the letters of the two actions that support this claim into the boxes below.

(a) Take deep breaths and exhale forcefully.

(b) Scream loudly to release tension.

(c) Take anger out on another coworker to relieve stress.

(d) Have a "buddy system" to be accountable for another coworker.

5. Based on the details of the article, what is the author's purpose for including the checklist at the end?

   A. to offer advice for a person undergoing trauma
   B. to help victims cope with loss and disaster
   C. to help aid workers cope while on the job
   D. to help aid workers intervene and end the disaster

6. The author suggests steps for disaster workers to take in order to intervene during the disaster. Write letters of the two actions that support this claim into the boxes below.

(a) Avoid wide-open fields.

(b) Get some exercise.

(c) Encourage your coworkers verbally and mentally.

(d) Work through the fatigue until it subsides.

(e) Carry paper and pens for necessary paperwork.

GO ON TO THE NEXT PAGE

7. Read this sentence from paragraph 5.

> Every emergency worker should be familiar with hazards and potential emergencies inherent in the local geographic area and should have contingency plans for self and family.

According to these details in the passage, why is it important to have a contingency plan for an emergency worker's family?

A. It is important to have a contingency plan to relieve stress while on disaster jobs.

B. It is important to evacuate workers' families first and then others the workers are trying to save.

C. It is important to be involved in the Neighborhood Crime Alert network.

D. It is important for emergency workers' families to have a plan so that the workers can worry less about them and complete their jobs.

8. Which sentence expresses the primary purpose of the article?

A. "The suggestions presented here are guidelines. No single suggestion will work for all people at all times."

B. "Preparation can help minimize the effects of stress when it occurs and can help individuals cope with stress in a more efficient manner."

C. "It is a good idea to establish a mutual aid system within the neighborhood."

D. "The more quickly things can be taken care of at home, the more quickly the worker can report to work relatively free of family worries."

GO ON TO THE NEXT PAGE

Questions 9 through 16 refer to the following passage.

Excerpt from *At the Earth's Core*
by Edgar Rice Burroughs

II: A Strange World

1   I glanced at the chronometer.

2   "Half after twelve. We have been out seventy-two hours, so it must be midnight. Nevertheless I am going to have a look at the blessed sky that I had given up all hope of ever seeing again," and so saying I lifted the bars from the inner door, and swung it open. There was quite a quantity of loose material in the jacket, and this I had to remove with a shovel to get at the opposite door in the outer shell.

3   In a short time I had removed enough of the earth and rock to the floor of the cabin to expose the door beyond. Perry was directly behind me as I threw it open. The upper half was above the surface of the ground. With an expression of surprise I turned and looked at Perry—it was broad daylight without!

4   "Something seems to have gone wrong either with our calculations or the chronometer," I said. Perry shook his head—there was a strange expression in his eyes.

5   "Let's have a look beyond that door, David," he cried.

6   Together we stepped out to stand in silent contemplation of a landscape at once weird and beautiful. Before us a low and level shore stretched down to a silent sea. As far as the eye could reach the surface of the water was dotted with countless tiny isles—some of towering, barren, granitic rock—others resplendent in gorgeous trappings of tropical vegetation, myriad starred with the magnificent splendor of vivid blooms.

7   Behind us rose a dark and forbidding wood of giant arborescent ferns intermingled with the commoner types of a primeval tropical forest. Huge creepers depended in great loops from tree to tree, dense under-brush overgrew a tangled mass of fallen trunks and branches. Upon the outer verge we could see the same splendid coloring of countless blossoms that glorified the islands, but within the dense shadows all seemed dark and gloomy as the grave.

8   And upon all the noonday sun poured its torrid rays out of a cloudless sky.

9   "Where on Earth can we be?" I asked, turning to Perry.

GO ON TO THE NEXT PAGE

10   For some moments the old man did not reply. He stood with bowed head, buried in deep thought. But at last he spoke.

11   "David," he said, "I am not so sure that we are ON Earth."

12   "What do you mean Perry?" I cried. "Do you think that we are dead, and this is heaven?" He smiled, and turning, pointing to the nose of the prospector protruding from the ground at our backs.

13   "But for that, David, I might believe that we were indeed come to the country beyond the Styx. The prospector renders that theory untenable—it, certainly, could never have gone to heaven. However I am willing to concede that we actually may be in another world from that which we have always known. If we are not ON Earth, there is every reason to believe that we may be IN it."

14   "We may have quartered through the Earth's crust and come out upon some tropical island of the West Indies," I suggested. Again Perry shook his head.

15   "Let us wait and see, David," he replied, "and in the meantime suppose we do a bit of exploring up and down the coast—we may find a native who can enlighten us."

9. The initial setting of this story is

    A.   outside in the woods.
    B.   underground in a tunnel.
    C.   inside a dark cabin.
    D.   overlooking the sea.

10. Based on the story, why are the men surprised by the daylight outside?

    A.   They either made an incorrect calculation or their equipment broke.
    B.   They are unfamiliar with the terrain.
    C.   They disagreed with each other's navigation.
    D.   They in fact were correct in their expectations.

11. Write the letters for two items that describe the landscape the men discover in the boxes below.

    (a) A calm shoreline extending toward the sea

    (b) Strong waves lapping against the rocks

    (c) Tiny islands in the distance

    (d) An open peninsula with lush vegetation

GO ON TO THE NEXT PAGE

12. Read this sentence from the passage.

> Together we stepped out to stand in silent contemplation of a landscape at once weird and beautiful.

The description of the landscape contributes to the story by

A. highlighting the discrepancy between the dark of the cabin and the lightness of the outside.
B. showing the uncertainty in the men's voices.
C. setting a foreign scene before the two men.
D. portraying how the setting is at once beautiful and dangerous.

13. Read these sentences from the passage.

> "What do you mean Perry?" I cried. "Do you think that we are dead, and this is heaven?"

Which attribute does the narrator reveal about himself?

A. He is delirious from lack of sleep.
B. He is fearful for his life.
C. He is flabbergasted by Perry's remarks.
D. He is amused by Perry's innocence.

14. Read these sentences from the passage.

> For some moments the old man did not reply. He stood with bowed head, buried in deep thought. But at last he spoke.

What inference can be made about Perry?

A. He is amused by David's naivety.
B. He strongly disapproves of David's suggestion.
C. He fears for their safety in this new place.
D. He is deep in thought about how to say what he thinking.

15. Which word describes Perry's behavior in paragraph 12?

A. hysterical
B. wise
C. amusing
D. fearful

16. Write the letters of two items to describe the narrator's attitude toward Perry in the boxes below.

[ ]

[ ]

(a) Respectful

(b) Intimidated

(c) Amicable

(d) Begrudging

GO ON TO THE NEXT PAGE

17. The passage below is incomplete. For each "Select" option, choose the option that correctly completes the sentence. For this practice test, circle your selection.

Welcome to the Treble Music Academy!

We look forward to working with you as you embark on your music learning experience. In the academy, you will engage in

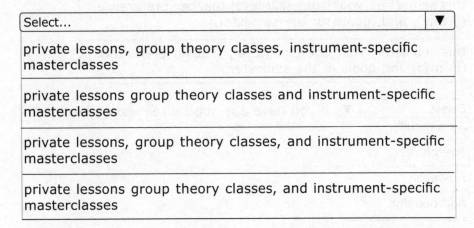

Select... ▼

private lessons, group theory classes, instrument-specific masterclasses

private lessons group theory classes and instrument-specific masterclasses

private lessons, group theory classes, and instrument-specific masterclasses

private lessons group theory classes, and instrument-specific masterclasses

to refine your skills. Our instructors are very experienced with all types of skill levels and ages, and we do our best to match our

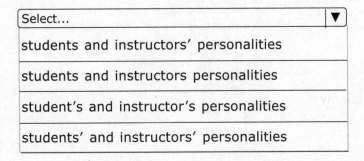

Select... ▼

students and instructors' personalities

students and instructors personalities

student's and instructor's personalities

students' and instructors' personalities

for the best learning environment possible. Please reply to us with the following information so that we can best serve you

GO ON TO THE NEXT PAGE

Select... ▼
this semester: your age, skill level, teacher preference (if any), and goals for the semester.
this semester, your age, skill level, teacher preference (if any), and goals for the semester.
this semester: your age, skill level teacher preference (if any), and, goals for the semester.
this semester, your age, skill level, teacher preference (if any), and goals of the semester.

Select... ▼	if you have any special requests, please let
As a result,	
Therefore,	
However,	
Additionally,	

us know. Our goal is to deliver the greatest services possible to you. Enjoy the rest of the summer, and we look forward to working with you in the fall.

Sincerely,

The Staff
Treble Music Academy

GO ON TO THE NEXT PAGE

Reasoning Through Language Arts, Section 2

Extended Response Answer Guidelines

Please use the guidelines below as you answer the Extended Response question on the Reasoning Through Language Arts test. Following these guidelines as closely as possible will ensure that you provide the best response.

1. **Please note that this task must be completed in no more than 45 minutes.** However, don't rush through your response. Be sure to read through the passage(s) and the prompt. Then think about the message you want to convey in your response. **Be sure to plan your response before you begin writing.** Draft your response and revise it as needed.

2. As you read, think carefully about the **argumentation** presented in the passage(s). "Argumentation" refers to the assumptions, claims, support, reasoning, and credibility on which a position is based. Pay close attention to **how the author(s) use these strategies to convey his or her (their) positions.**

3. When you write your essay, be sure to
   - **determine which position presented** in the passage(s) is **better supported** by evidence from the passage(s)
   - **explain why the position you chose is the better-supported one**
   - **remember, the better-supported position is not necessarily the position you agree with**
   - **defend your assertions with multiple pieces of evidence** from the passage(s)
   - **build your main points thoroughly**
   - **put your main points in logical order** and tie your details to your main points
   - **organize your response carefully** and consider your **audience, message, and purpose**
   - **use transitional words and phrases** to connect sentences, paragraphs, and ideas
   - **choose words carefully** to express your ideas clearly
   - **vary your sentence structure** to enhance the flow and clarity of your response
   - **reread and revise your response** to correct any errors in grammar, usage, or punctuation

GO ON TO THE NEXT PAGE

Instructions

Read

- On the **page 2 tab above**, you will **read two texts** presenting **different views** on the same topic.

- **Both writers argue** that **their position** on the issue is **correct**.

Plan

- **Analyze** the two texts **to determine** which writer presents the **stronger case**.

- **Develop your own argument** in which **you explain** how one position is **better supported** than the other.

- **Include** relevant and specific **evidence** from **both sources** to support your argument.

Write

- **Type** your response in the **box on the right**.

- Your response should be approximately **4 to 7 paragraphs of 3 to 7 sentences each**.

- **Remember** to allow a few minutes **to review and edit your response**.

<u>You have up to **45 minutes** for reading, planning, writing, and editing your response.</u>

Interview with Dr. Nils-Axel Mörner

Dr. Nils-Axel Mörner is the head of the Paleogeophysics and Geodynamics department at Stockholm University in Sweden. Dr. Mörner has been studying the sea level and its effects on coastal areas for some 35 years. He was interviewed by Gregory Murphy on June 6 for EIR.

1   **EIR:** What is the real state of the sea-level rising?

2   **Mörner:** You have to look at that in a lot of different ways. That is what I have done in a lot of different papers, so we can confine ourselves to the short story here. One way is to look at the global picture, to try to find the essence of what is going on. And then we can see that the sea level was indeed rising, from, let us say, 1850 to 1930–40. And that rise had a rate in the order of 1 millimeter per year. Not more. 1.1 is the exact figure.

3   That ended in 1940, and there had been no rise until 1970; and then we can come into the debate here on what is going on, and we have to go to satellite altimetry, and I will return to that. But before doing that: There's another way of checking it, because if the radius of the Earth increases, because sea level is rising, then immediately the Earth's rate of rotation would slow down. That is a physical law, right? You have it in figure-skating: when they rotate very fast, the arms are close to the body; and

GO ON TO THE NEXT PAGE

then when they increase the radius, by putting out their arms, they stop by themselves. So you can look at the rotation and the same comes up: Yes, it might be 1.1 mm per year, but absolutely not more. It could be less, because there could be other factors affecting the Earth, but it certainly could not be more. Absolutely not! Again, it's a matter of physics.

"Americans in Danger From Rising Seas Could Triple"
by Marianne Lavelle

4   The number of Americans who could be displaced by rising seas will triple by the end of this century. That's the stark new conclusion of scientists who studied the impact of climate change on coastal areas.

5   As many as 13.1 million people in the United States will be in the path of flooding by 2100, three times the current population that resides in low-lying coastal areas, according to the paper published online Monday in *Nature Climate Change*. The researchers took into account rapid population growth along the coasts in a way never done before.

6   The U.S. National Oceanic and Atmospheric Administration predicts sea levels will rise 8 inches (0.3 meter) to 6.6 feet (2 meters) by 2100, depending on the speed and extent of polar ice melt.

7   The new study underscores the challenge facing U.S. coastal cities as they grapple with global warming's impact on a landscape that happens to be the nation's most sought-after real estate.

8   But the study, which took land elevation into account, also predicts "catastrophic impacts" for a handful of sparsely populated low-lying counties, such as Tyrell County, North Carolina. Tyrell, which bills itself as "nature's buffer zone" between the popular seashore resorts of the Outer Banks and the state's urban mainland, boasts the only mainland population of red wolves in the wild, as well as more than two dozen groups of endangered red cockaded woodpeckers. But 92 percent of its human population—about 6,000 people by 2100—will live on land at risk of inundation in the high sea-level rise scenario.

You may take a 10-minute break before proceeding to Section 3.

GO ON TO THE NEXT PAGE

Questions 18 through 25 refer to the following article.

Excerpt from "Car-Size Stingray May Be World's Largest Freshwater Fish"
by Brian Clark Howard

1   Scientists working in Thailand's Mae Klong River made a *big* find last week: an enormous stingray that they think is a contender for the largest freshwater fish ever documented by researchers.

2   The ray was caught and released in about 65 feet (20 meters) of water in the Amphawa District, about an hour outside Bangkok.

3   Nantarika Chansue, a veterinarian and professor at Chulalongkorn University in Bangkok, helped catch and measure what she calls the "big one." The ray (*Himantura polylepis* or *H. chaophraya*) was 7.9 feet (2.4 meters) across and 14 feet (4.3 meters) long and weighed an estimated 700 to 800 pounds (318 to 363 kilograms), she said via email.

4   The team was unable to get an exact weight because "it's really hard to weigh these things without hurting them, because they are such big, awkward animals," says Zeb Hogan, a National Geographic fellow and a professor of biology at the University of Nevada, Reno.

5   "Certainly [this] was a huge fish, even compared to other giant freshwater stingrays, and definitely ranks among the largest freshwater fish in the world," he says.

6   Hogan has a connection to this particular ray: The same animal was caught and tagged in 2009 under a program he runs with Nantarika.

7   Nantarika performed a portable ultrasound on the ray while it was held in a cage in the river, revealing that the animal was pregnant with two fetal rays. Records show that she was also pregnant when caught in 2009.

8   "That indicates it was found in an area that is likely a nursery ground," Hogan says.

9   In 2009, the ray was 6.5 feet (2 meters) across and 15 feet (4.58 meters) long. "Her tail might have been shortened by some accident," says Nantarika. The ray also had bite marks that may have come from a male ray.

GO ON TO THE NEXT PAGE

10   By knowing how much time had elapsed since the ray was last studied, scientists now have a better idea about how fast rays can grow. Like most fish, they keep growing as long as they live and can find enough food. Giant stingrays are bottom feeders, preying on fish, prawns, mussels, clams, and whatever else they can find. Scientists don't know how long the rays can live, but Nantarika estimates this one is between 35 and 40 years old, based on its size.

Record Catch?

11   Hogan keeps track of freshwater fish size records through his Megafish Project, which studies the world's biggest freshwater fish, and says the previous size record for a freshwater fish was an estimated 693 pounds (314 kilograms), for a Mekong giant catfish. The largest freshwater ray he has measured was about 400 pounds (180 kilograms). Unconfirmed reports have suggested sizes for the rays as big as 1,100 to 1,300 pounds (500 to 600 kilograms).

12   The Guinness Book of World Records lists the Mekong giant catfish, which also lives in Thailand, as the "world's largest freshwater fish," weighing up to 660 pounds (300 kilograms). The 2015 edition of the book breaks out the largest saltwater ray as a separate category from bony fish, even though rays are technically a type of fish. Anthony Yodice, a spokesperson for Guinness World Records North America, said the organization would not comment on whether this catch constitutes a new record until a formal application had been submitted and reviewed.

13   The ray was the seventh that has been re-caught by Hogan and Nantarika over the course of their ten-year program.

14   The animals are hard to find, so the scientists work with partners such as Fishsiam Ltd, a company that offers guided catch-and-release fishing trips to tourists and that caught last week's huge ray.

15   Fishsiam's guides measure rays that are caught and attach tags and microchips, which Nantarika and Hogan use to track growth rates and movements. The company uses a special net and cage to keep the animals in the water and to reduce stress while they are being studied.

16   The catch was filmed for an upcoming episode of the ABC TV show *Ocean Mysteries*, hosted by Jeff Corwin. "For the most part they are a gentle giant," Corwin says of the rays.

17   The giant freshwater stingray has the longest spine of any species of ray, up to 15 inches, and carries powerful venom. The animal uses its spine for defense and it can be lethal, but injuries to people are quite rare.

GO ON TO THE NEXT PAGE

A Threatened Species

18   Giant freshwater stingrays are listed as endangered by the International Union for the Conservation of Nature, in part due to Hogan's and Nantarika's work. "These rays are decreasing rapidly since there is no national law to protect them," Nantarika says.

19   Other large fish in the region, including the Mekong giant catfish, are in worse shape because they are easier for fishermen to catch. Freshwater rays are so large and strong that they break most fishing gear that isn't specially designed to catch them. And since they aren't a popular food item, there isn't much commercial fishing pressure.

20   The rays are threatened by pollution, oil spills, and dams that have fragmented their habitat, however.

21   The fact that the big ray found this week was pregnant again is good news for the species, Hogan says, and proves that the animals can survive the catch-and-release process.

Source: "Car-Size Stingray May Be World's Largest Freshwater Fish," Brian Clark Howard, National Geographic News, March 15, 2015. Reprinted with permission from National Geographic Creative.

18. What is the main idea of the article?

    A.   Scientists say giant freshwater rays will go extinct in the coming years.

    B.   It is very difficult to weigh giant freshwater stingrays.

    C.   The giant freshwater stingray has the longest spine of any species of ray.

    D.   The largest giant freshwater stingray to-date has been found, which has implications about their endangered status.

19. According to the article, which of the following is correct according the passage?

    A.   The Mekong giant catfish is the largest fish in the region.

    B.   The Guinness Book of World Records lists the Mekong giant catfish as the world's largest freshwater fish.

    C.   Giant freshwater rays are bottom dwellers that eat krill and other algae.

    D.   Giant freshwater rays live to be about ten years old.

GO ON TO THE NEXT PAGE

20. In the boxes below, write the letters of the two details that the author mentions about the Mekong giant catfish.

```
┌─────────────────────────┐
│                         │
└─────────────────────────┘

┌─────────────────────────┐
│                         │
└─────────────────────────┘
```

┌─────────────────────────────────┐
│ (a) The Mekong giant catfish   │
│ weighs about 1,100 to   │
│ 1,300 pounds.   │
└─────────────────────────────────┘

┌─────────────────────────────────┐
│ (b) The Mekong giant catfish   │
│ currently holds the world record│
│ for largest freshwater fish.   │
└─────────────────────────────────┘

┌─────────────────────────────────┐
│ (c) The giant freshwater   │
│ stingray preys upon the Mekong │
│ giant catfish.   │
└─────────────────────────────────┘

┌─────────────────────────────────┐
│ (d) The Mekong giant catfish also│
│ lives in Thailand.   │
└─────────────────────────────────┘

21. According to the article, why are some rays tagged and microchipped?

    A. Researchers can track population growth by adding more and more tags.
    B. Researchers can track the rays' growth and movement.
    C. Researchers can study genetic diversity throughout the population.
    D. Researchers can study stress levels of the rays.

22. What can be inferred about the "Fishsiam Ltd" mentioned in paragraphs 14–15?

    A. Fishsiam conducts research for the scientists who study the giant freshwater stingray.
    B. Fishsiam has the technology scientists need to study the giant freshwater stingray.
    C. Fishsiam has caught a giant freshwater stingray.
    D. Fishsiam has contributed to overfishing in the area that has contributed to the giant freshwater stingray's endangered status.

23. Read the following sentence from the article.

    ┌─────────────────────────────────────┐
    │ "For the most part they are a gentle │
    │ giant," Corwin says of the rays.   │
    └─────────────────────────────────────┘

    Based on the details of the article, why does the author mention this quotation by Corwin?

    A. Their giant size makes them predators to other equally sized animals.
    B. While the giant freshwater stingray is large, they are not usually aggressive toward humans.
    C. Their long spines are extremely venomous.
    D. The giant freshwater stingray is the size of a car, making them extremely dangerous.

GO ON TO THE NEXT PAGE

24. The author claims that the freshwater rays are endangered. In the box below, write the letters for two pieces of evidence that support this claim.

> [ ]

> [ ]

> (a) Giant stingrays are venomous, though they rarely injure people.

> (b) There are no laws to protect the stingrays.

> (c) The rays are threatened by pollution and oil spills.

> (d) Stingrays often become pregnant, so they produce a lot of offspring.

25. Read the following sentence from the article.

> The fact that the big ray found this week was pregnant again is good news for the species, Hogan says, and proves that the animals can survive the catch-and-release process.

Why does the author choose to conclude the article with this sentence?

A. to provide the reader with optimism that the giant freshwater stingray may be able to repopulate

B. to illustrate the effects of dwindling populations and overfishing the giant freshwater stingray

C. to suggest that giant freshwater stingrays reproduce more often than previously thought

D. to conclude that most giant freshwater stingrays are unintentionally caught and then released by fishermen

GO ON TO THE NEXT PAGE

Questions 26 through 33 refer to the following passage.

Excerpt from *Worlds Within Worlds: The Story of Nuclear Energy*
by Isaac Asimov

The Energy of the Sun

1   As it happens, though, nuclear fission is not the only route to useful nuclear energy.

2   Aston's studies in the 1920s had shown that it was the middle-sized nuclei that were most tightly packed. Energy would be given off if middle-sized nuclei were produced from either extreme. Not only would energy be formed by the breakup of particularly massive nuclei through fission, but also through the combination of small nuclei to form larger ones ("nuclear fusion").

3   In fact, from Aston's studies it could be seen that, mass for mass, nuclear fusion would produce far more energy than nuclear fission. This was particularly true in the conversion of hydrogen to helium; that is, the conversion of the individual protons of 4 separate hydrogen nuclei into the 2-proton—2-neutron structure of the helium nucleus. A gram of hydrogen, undergoing fusion to helium, would deliver some fifteen times as much energy as a gram of uranium undergoing fission.

4   As early as 1920, the English astronomer Arthur Stanley Eddington (1882–1944) had speculated that the Sun's energy might be derived from the interaction of subatomic particles. Some sort of nuclear reaction seemed, by then, to be the most reasonable way of accounting for the vast energies constantly being produced by the Sun.

5   The speculation became more plausible with each year. Eddington himself studied the structure of stars, and by 1926 had produced convincing theoretical reasons for supposing that the center of the Sun was at enormous densities and temperatures. A temperature of some 15,000,000 to 20,000,000°C seemed to characterize the Sun's center.

6   At such temperatures, atoms could not exist in earthly fashion. Held together by the Sun's strong gravitational field, they collided with such energy that all or almost all their electrons were stripped off, and little more than bare nuclei were left. These bare nuclei could approach each other much more closely than whole atoms could (which was why the center of the Sun was so much more dense than earthly matter could be). The bare nuclei, smashing together at central-sun temperatures, could cling together and form more complex nuclei. Nuclear reactions brought about by such intense heat (millions of degrees) are called "thermonuclear reactions."

GO ON TO THE NEXT PAGE

7   As the 1920s progressed further studies of the chemical structure of the Sun showed it to be even richer in hydrogen than had been thought. In 1929 the American astronomer Henry Norris Russell (1877–1957) reported evidence that the Sun was 60% hydrogen in volume. (Even this was too conservative; 80% is considered more nearly correct now.) If the Sun's energy were based on nuclear reactions at all, then it had to be the result of hydrogen fusion. Nothing else was present in sufficient quantity to be useful as a fuel.

8   More and more was learned about the exact manner in which nuclei interacted and about the quantity of energy given off in particular nuclear reactions. It became possible to calculate what might be going on inside the Sun by considering the densities and temperatures present, the kind and number of different nuclei available, and the quantity of energy that must be produced. In 1938 the German-American physicist Hans Albrecht Bethe (1906–) and the German astronomer Carl Friedrich von Weizsäcker (1912–) independently worked out the possible reactions, and hydrogen fusion was shown to be a thoroughly practical way of keeping the Sun going.

9   Thanks to the high rate of energy production by thermonuclear reactions and to the vast quantity of hydrogen in the Sun, not only has it been possible for the Sun to have been radiating energy for the last 5,000,000,000 years or so, but it will continue to radiate energy in the present fashion for at least 5,000,000,000 years into the future.

26.   Which sentence expresses the primary purpose of the article?

A.   "In fact, from Aston's studies it could be seen that, mass for mass, nuclear fusion would produce far more energy than nuclear fission."

B.   "Eddington himself studied the structure of stars, and by 1926 had produced convincing theoretical reasons for supposing that the center of the Sun was at enormous densities and temperatures."

C.   "Held together by the Sun's strong gravitational field, they collided with such energy that all or almost all their electrons were stripped off, and little more than bare nuclei were left."

D.   "More and more was learned about the exact manner in which nuclei interacted and about the quantity of energy given off in particular nuclear reactions."

27.   According to the passage, which is the most effective way of producing energy?

A.   nuclear fusion
B.   thermodynamics
C.   nuclear fission
D.   hydrogen fusion

28.   According to the passage, the Sun is mostly comprised of

A.   hydrogen.
B.   helium.
C.   oxygen.
D.   protons.

GO ON TO THE NEXT PAGE

29. Which definition best matches the use of the word "conversion" in paragraph 3?

    A. overhaul
    B. renovation
    C. exchange
    D. transformation

30. The author mentions which of the following facts about the Sun? In the boxes below, write the letters for two true statements.

    ┌─────────────────────────────┐
    │   │
    └─────────────────────────────┘

    ┌─────────────────────────────┐
    │   │
    └─────────────────────────────┘

    (a) The Sun contains approximately 5,000,000,000 hydrogen atoms at its core.

    (b) The Sun is approximately 15,000,000 to 20,000,000°C at its center.

    (c) Atoms on the Sun should not exist at such high temperatures.

    (d) Multiple sources have shown that hydrogen fusion is a practical way of keeping the Sun going.

31. Which definition best matches the use of the word "conservative" in paragraph 7?

    A. conformist
    B. cautious
    C. established
    D. traditional

32. Read these sentences from the article.

    > Thanks to the high rate of energy production by thermonuclear reactions and to the vast quantity of hydrogen in the Sun, not only has it been possible for the Sun to have been radiating energy for the last 5,000,000,000 years or so, but it will continue to radiate energy in the present fashion for at least 5,000,000,000 years into the future.

    Why does the author choose to conclude the article with this sentence?

    A. to illustrate how very old the Sun is
    B. to show how often thermonuclear reactions exist in the solar system
    C. to depict how this process will continue long into the future
    D. to show that thermonuclear radiation is the strongest form of energy

GO ON TO THE NEXT PAGE

33. In the boxes below, write the letters of the phrases that represent details from the article.

```
┌─────────────────────────────┐
│                             │
│                             │
└─────────────────────────────┘
```

```
┌─────────────────────────────┐
│                             │
└─────────────────────────────┘
```

```
┌─────────────────────────────┐
│ (a) Atoms could not exist in │
│ the same way as they do on   │
│ Earth because of the Sun's   │
│ extreme temperatures.        │
└─────────────────────────────┘
```

```
┌─────────────────────────────┐
│ (b) The Sun's extreme        │
│ temperatures cause electrons │
│ to disappear through         │
│ nuclear fission.             │
└─────────────────────────────┘
```

```
┌─────────────────────────────┐
│ (c) Arthur Stanley           │
│ Eddington's speculations     │
│ that the Sun's energy might  │
│ be derived from the          │
│ interaction of subatomic     │
│ particles proved too         │
│ conservative in his          │
│ estimations.                 │
└─────────────────────────────┘
```

```
┌─────────────────────────────┐
│ (d) The Sun is approximately │
│ 60% comprised of hydrogen.   │
└─────────────────────────────┘
```

```
┌─────────────────────────────┐
│ (e) Physicist Hans Albrecht  │
│ Bethe and astronomer Carl    │
│ Friedrich von Weizsäcker     │
│ independently worked out     │
│ the possible reactions that  │
│ occur in the Sun.            │
└─────────────────────────────┘
```

GO ON TO THE NEXT PAGE

Questions 34 through 41 refer to the following article.

Excerpt from "Climate Change Is Making Your Allergies Even Worse" by Becky Little

1   When one tree loves another tree very much, it releases pollen to fertilize the ovules of that tree, plus whatever other trees happen to be around (you know how it goes). But when the pollen begins to blow, you're probably not marveling at the miracle of tree reproduction—you're dreading the allergies that accompany it.

2   The reason that pollen makes some people sniffle and sneeze is because their immune systems attack it like a parasite, says Leonard Bielory, professor and allergy specialist at Rutgers University Center of Environmental Prediction.

3   That's because certain people's immune systems recognize the protein sequence in pollen as similar to the protein sequence in parasites. When this happens, their bodies attempt to expel the "parasite" through sneezing and other symptoms. This attack on the pollen, Bielory says, "is the reaction we call *allergy*."

4   The fact that some people's bodies react this way is actually kind of weird, since pollen "is rather innocuous," he says. Our immune system "really should not be reacting to it, because pollen is nothing more than the male reproductive component of plants."

So Hot in Here

5   Reports of pollen allergies first appeared around the time of the industrial revolution. Whether that means that these allergies were the product of pollution, new diets, or changes in hygiene isn't clear. What *is* clear, writes Charles W. Schmidt in this month's issue of *Environmental Health Perspectives*, is the role of climate change in contemporary pollen allergies.

6   "When exposed to warmer temperatures and higher levels of CO_2, plants grow more vigorously and produce more pollen than they otherwise would," writes Schmidt.

7   Warming temperatures in some areas, like the northern United States, extend the periods during which plants release pollen. The combined effect of warming temperatures and more CO_2 means that the amount of pollen in the air has been increasing and will continue to increase as climate change worsens. (According to a study presented by Bielory, pollen counts could double by 2040.)

GO ON TO THE NEXT PAGE

8   This is bad news not just for people who have allergies, but also for people who don't.

9   "In general, the longer you're exposed to an allergen, the more likely you are going to be sensitized to that allergen," Bielory says. People who have pollen allergies may experience intensified symptoms, and people who don't normally have pollen allergies may start to.

10   Already, Schmidt writes, there "is evidence suggesting that hay fever prevalence is rising in many parts of the world."

Does Honey Help?

11   With the increase in the number of pollen allergy-sufferers, it's understandable that people have begun to seek natural ways to alleviate their symptoms. Some have even argued that consuming honey will build up your resistance because it contains pollen.

12   But as Rachel E. Gross points out at *Slate*, that theory's just *honey bunches of lies*; mainly because the pollen that makes you sneeze doesn't come from flowers.

13   In the spring, the pollen that gives humans allergies comes from trees. In the summer, people have allergic reactions to grass pollen; and at the end of summer and beginning of fall, people begin to suffer from pollinating weeds—especially ragweed, which has spread from the United States to Europe and the Middle East.

14   Really, the "natural" ways to deal with pollen allergies are to stay clean, keep your windows closed, and go outside when pollen counts are lower, such as after it rains. If your symptoms are bad enough, take over-the-counter medication or see an allergist. And if you don't mind the risk of malnutrition or life-threatening diseases, there's always hookworms.

Source: "Climate Change Is Making Your Allergies Even Worse," Becky Little, National Geographic News, April 8, 2016. Reprinted with permission from National Geographic Creative.

GO ON TO THE NEXT PAGE

34. Which sentence expresses the primary purpose of the article?

    A.   "'When exposed to warmer temperatures and higher levels of CO_2, plants grow more vigorously and produce more pollen than they otherwise would,' writes Schmidt."

    B.   "The combined effect of warming temperatures and more CO_2 means that the amount of pollen in the air has been increasing and will continue to increase as climate change worsens."

    C.   "Some have even argued that consuming honey will build up your resistance because it contains pollen."

    D.   "Really, the 'natural' ways to deal with pollen allergies are to stay clean, keep your windows closed, and go outside when pollen counts are lower, such as after it rains."

35. In the boxes below, write the letters of the two sentences that represent details from the article.

(a) Reports of pollen allergies first appeared around the time of the industrial revolution.

(b) Bees are a major carrier of allergens that cause symptoms for people.

(c) Warming temperatures will inevitably cause pollen levels to double by 2040.

(d) Current numbers of pollen may increase along with increased climate change.

(e) Hookworms are a potential naturopathic way of treating allergies.

GO ON TO THE NEXT PAGE

36. Read this sentence from paragraph 8:

> This is bad news not just for people who have allergies, but also for people who don't.

Based on these details from the article, what can readers infer about allergens in the future?

- A. Allergens will inevitably spread to those who do not currently have allergies.
- B. Pollen allergies first appeared around the time of the industrial revolution.
- C. Increased temperatures may cause an increase in the amount and timespan of pollen spread.
- D. Consuming honey will help guard against future increases in allergy symptoms.

37. Which definition best matches the use of the word "contemporary" in paragraph 5?

- A. fashionable
- B. trendy
- C. current
- D. ongoing

38. Read this sentence from paragraph 4:

> Our immune system "really should not be reacting to it, because pollen is nothing more than the male reproductive component of plants."

The author includes this detail in order to

- A. emphasize that pollen is an unlikely irritant to the immune system.
- B. argue against the body's reaction to pollen.
- C. contrast the earlier argument that pollen is innocuous.
- D. show how pollen levels have contributed to increased allergy symptoms.

39. In the boxes below, write the letters of the two phrases that represent details from the article about CO_2 levels.

```
┌─────────────────────┐
│                     │
└─────────────────────┘

┌─────────────────────┐
│                     │
└─────────────────────┘
```

(a) Plants grow more heartily when exposed to warmer temperatures and higher levels of CO_2.

(b) CO_2 levels have decimated the ozone layer and have overheated the vegetation.

(c) The combined effect of warming temperatures and more CO_2 means that the amount of pollen in the air has been increasing and will continue to increase as climate change worsens.

(d) The increased amount of CO_2 means that more people will have difficulty breathing.

GO ON TO THE NEXT PAGE

40. Read this sentence from paragraph 12.

> But as Rachel E. Gross points out at *Slate*, that theory's just *honey bunches of lies*.

Based on the details of the article, what is the author's purpose for including this sentence?

A. to show the opposite side of the argument that eating honey will improve allergy symptoms

B. to include a credible source stating that eating honey will not improve allergy symptoms

C. to mock those who believe that honey will make them immune to allergies

D. to allude to a product and help advertise in the middle of the article

41. Read this sentence from paragraph 14.

> And if you don't mind the risk of malnutrition or life-threatening diseases, there's always hookworms.

Why does the author choose to conclude the article with this sentence?

A. The author believes hookworms could possibly help boost the immune system.

B. Malnutrition and life-threatening diseases are really not as bad as they seem.

C. Hookworms could play a role in fighting the effects of allergies.

D. The author makes a joke by offering an alternative natural method of combating allergies.

GO ON TO THE NEXT PAGE

Questions 42 through 49 refer to the following passage.

Excerpt from *Theodore Roosevelt's Letters to His Children* by Theodore Roosevelt

White House, Oct. 15, 1904

Darling Kermit:

1   The weather has been beautiful the last week—mild, and yet with the true feeling of Fall in the air. When Mother and I have ridden up Rock Creek through the country round about, it has been a perpetual delight just to look at the foliage. I have never seen leaves turn more beautifully. The Virginia creepers and some of the maple and gum trees are scarlet and crimson. The oaks are deep red brown. The beeches, birches and hickories are brilliant saffron. Just at this moment I am dictating while on my way with Mother to the wedding of Senator Knox's daughter, and the country is a blaze of color as we pass through it, so that it is a joy to the eye to look upon it. I do not think I have ever before seen the colorings of the woods so beautiful so far south as this. Ted is hard at work with Matt. Hale, who is a very nice fellow and has become quite one of the household, like good Mademoiselle. I am really fond of her. She is so bright and amusing and now seems perfectly happy, and is not only devoted to Archie and Quentin but is very wise in the way she takes care of them. Quentin, under parental duress, rides Algonquin every day. Archie has just bought himself a football suit, but I have not noticed that he has played football as yet. He is spending Saturday and Sunday out at Dr. Rixey's. Ted plays tennis with Matt. Hale and me and Mr. Cooley. We tried Dan Moore. You could beat him. Yesterday I took an afternoon off and we all went for a scramble and climb down the other side of the Potomac from Chain Bridge home. It was great fun. To-morrow (Sunday) we shall have lunch early and spend the afternoon in a drive of the entire family, including Ethel, but not including Archie and Quentin, out to Burnt Mills and back. When I say we all scrambled along the Potomac, I of course only meant Matt. Hale and Ted and I. Three or four active male friends took the walk with us.

2   In politics things at the moment seem to look quite right, but every form of lie is being circulated by the Democrats, and they intend undoubtedly to spring all kinds of sensational untruths at the very end of the campaign. I have not any idea whether we will win or not. Before election I shall send you my guess as to the way the different States will vote, and then you can keep it and see how near to the truth I come. But of course you will remember that it is a mere guess, and that I may be utterly mistaken all along the line. In any event, even if I am beaten

GO ON TO THE NEXT PAGE

you must remember that we have had three years of great enjoyment out of the Presidency and that we are mighty lucky to have had them.

3   I generally have people in to lunch, but at dinner, thank fortune, we are usually alone. Though I have callers in the evening, I generally have an hour in which to sit with Mother and the others up in the library, talking and reading and watching the bright wood fire. Ted and Ethel, as well as Archie and Quentin, are generally in Mother's room for twenty minutes or a half hour just before she dresses, according to immemorial custom.

4   Last evening Mother and I and Ted and Ethel and Matt. Hale went to the theatre to see "The Yankee Consul," which was quite funny.

42. The detailed description of Roosevelt's travels enhances the letter by

    A.   contrasting the lies the Democrats are spreading.
    B.   describing the scenery while traveling to a the wedding he is attending.
    C.   show the vastness of the country.
    D.   show evidence that he is going to win the election.

43. Which definition best matches the use of the phrase "a blaze" in paragraph 1?

    A.   aglow
    B.   inferno
    C.   on fire
    D.   shining

44. Why does the author use the phrase "You could beat him" in paragraph 1?

    A.   to encourage Kermit to beat Dan Moore
    B.   to betray Dan Moore's trust
    C.   to analyze and rank the tennis players' abilities
    D.   to include an offhand comment to Kermit

45. What can readers infer about Roosevelt?

    A.   He is a kind husband who devotes himself solely to his wife.
    B.   He is a pragmatic diplomat on his reelection campaign.
    C.   He enjoys time with his wife in between visitors.
    D.   He is tired from campaigning for his reelection.

46. Read this sentence from paragraph 3.

> I generally have people in to lunch, but at dinner, thank fortune, we are usually alone.

According to the article, who is "we" who are usually alone?

    A.   Theodore Roosevelt and Archie
    B.   Theodore Roosevelt and Archie and Quentin
    C.   Theodore Roosevelt and Mother
    D.   Theodore Roosevelt and Mother and Quentin

GO ON TO THE NEXT PAGE

47. The author claims that he is uncertain about the results of the election. In the boxes below, write the letters of two supporting quotations that the author mentions.

[   ]

[   ]

(a) "I do not think I have ever before seen the colorings of the woods so beautiful so far south as this."

(b) "Yesterday I took an afternoon off and we all went for a scramble and climb down the other side of the Potomac from Chain Bridge home."

(c) "In politics things at the moment seem to look quite right, but every form of lie is being circulated by the Democrats, and they intend undoubtedly to spring all kinds of sensational untruths at the very end of the campaign."

(d) "Before election I shall send you my guess as to the way the different States will vote, and then you can keep it and see how near to the truth I come."

(e) "I generally have people in to lunch, but at dinner, thank fortune, we are usually alone."

48. Read this sentence from paragraph 2.

> In any event, even if I am beaten you must remember that we have had three years of great enjoyment out of the Presidency and that we are mighty lucky to have had them.

Based on the details of the article, what is the author's purpose for including this sentence?

A. to show how fortunate the family is to have enjoyed the company of such esteemed diplomats
B. to illustrate his enjoyment of his tennis partners
C. to concede the election to the Democrats since they have been spreading untrue propaganda
D. to recognize that their experiences have been positive, even if they are to come to a close soon

49. In the boxes below, write the letters of the two sentences that represent details from the letter.

[   ]

[   ]

(a) Kermit is not with the Roosevelts traveling.

(b) Roosevelt and his wife are traveling through the countryside by the Potomac.

(c) Archie and Quentin are older siblings of Kermit.

(d) The Republicans lie just as much as the Democrats.

GO ON TO THE NEXT PAGE

50. The passage below is incomplete. For each "Select" option, choose the option that correctly completes the sentence. For this practice test, circle your selection.

Mr. Adam Smith, owner
Fit and Fun Gyms
123 Main Street
Columbia, MO 65203

Dear Mr. Smith,

I have very much enjoyed my membership at your

Select... ▼
gym Fit and Fun,
gym Fit and Fun
gym, Fit and Fun
gym, Fit and Fun,

for the past four years. In the past,

Select... ▼
it has been well cared for and clean, and the staff has been very friendly.
it has been well cared for, clean, and very friendly.
the staff was very friendly, clean, and well cared for.
the staff has been very friendly, it was clean and it was well cared for.

I know the challenges of running a small business, and I appreciate your efforts.

It has come to my attention recently that, since the new supervisor started, the equipment has not been as well cared for. I am concerned for my safety and the safety of others in using the machines if the machines are not taken care of properly.

Select... ▼
Therefore,
However,
Similarly,
Sure,

the yoga mats and free weights have not been as

well cared for recently, and they are beginning to show dirt and wear.

GO ON TO THE NEXT PAGE

I do not know if this problem is because of the new supervisor's carelessness or regular wear and tear, but I would like to request that this matter be attended to.

Select... ▼
I would like to reiterate that
I will reiterate
I would have reiterated that
I would reiterate

I have enjoyed going to your

gym, though I will consider cancelling my membership and joining elsewhere if this issue is not resolved.

Sincerely,

James Terry

END OF TEST

Mathematical Reasoning

Welcome!

Here is some information that you need to know before you start this test:

- You should not spend too much time on a question if you are not certain of the answer; answer it the best you can, and go on to the next question.
- If you are not certain of the answer to a question, you can mark your answer for review and come back to it later.
- You have **115 minutes** to complete this test.
- This test has two parts.
- When you finish Part 1, you may review those questions.
- You may not go back to Part 1 once you have finished your review.
- You may not use a calculator in Part 1. You may use a calculator in Part 2.

Turn the page to begin.

GO ON TO THE NEXT PAGE

Mathematics Formula Sheet

Area of a:

square	$A = s^2$
rectangle	$A = lw$
parallelogram	$A = bh$
triangle	$A = \frac{1}{2}bh$
trapezoid	$A = \frac{1}{2}h(b_1 + b_2)$
circle	$A = \pi r^2$

Perimeter of a:

square	$P = 4s$
rectangle	$P = 2l + 2w$
triangle	$P = s_1 + s_2 + s_3$
Circumference of a circle	$C = 2\pi r$ OR $C = \pi d$; $\pi \approx 3.14$

Surface Area and Volume of a:

rectangular prism	$SA = 2lw + 2lh + 2wh$	$V = lwh$
right prism	$SA = ph + 2B$	$V = Bh$
cylinder	$SA = 2\pi rh + 2\pi r^2$	$V = \pi r^2 h$
pyramid	$SA = \frac{1}{2}ps + B$	$V = \frac{1}{3}Bh$
cone	$SA = \pi rs + \pi r^2$	$V = \frac{1}{3}\pi r^2 h$
sphere	$SA = 4\pi r^2$	$V = \frac{4}{3}\pi r^3$

(p = perimeter of base B; $\pi \approx 3.14$)

Data

mean	mean is equal to the total of the values of a data set, divided by the number of elements in the data set
median	median is the middle value in an odd number of ordered values of a data set, or the mean of the two middle values in an even number of ordered values in a data set

Algebra

slope of a line	$m = \dfrac{y_2 - y_1}{x_2 - x_1}$
slope-intercept form of the equation of a line	$y = mx + b$
point-slope form of the equation of a line	$y - y_1 = m(x - x_1)$
standard form of a quadratic equation	$y = ax^2 + bx + c$
quadratic formula	$x = \dfrac{-b \pm \sqrt{b^2 - 4ac}}{2a}$
Pythagorean Theorem	$a^2 + b^2 = c^2$
simple interest	$I = prt$ (I = interest, p = principal, r = rate, t = time)
distance formula	$d = rt$
total cost	total cost = (number of units) × (price per unit)

GO ON TO THE NEXT PAGE

Mathematical Reasoning, Part 1

You may NOT use a calculator in Part 1.

1. Which of the following is equivalent to the expression $\frac{1}{5} + \frac{3}{4}$?

   A. $\frac{1}{20} + \frac{3}{20}$

   B. $\frac{5}{20} + \frac{15}{20}$

   C. $\frac{3}{5} + \frac{1}{4}$

   D. $\frac{4}{20} + \frac{15}{20}$

Question 2 refers to the following number line.

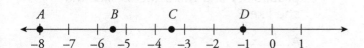

2. What is the distance, in units, from point B to point D on the number line?

   A. −5.5
   B. −4.5
   C. 4.5
   D. 5.5

3. The value of $\frac{1}{4}^{2}$ is [Select... ▼]
   | greater than |
   | equal to |
   | less than |

   the value of $\sqrt{\frac{1}{4}}$.

Question 4 refers to the following list of numbers from least to greatest.

   0.4   0.421   [   ]   0.45   0.455

4. Select the correct number and write it in the box above.

   | 0.43 | | 0.54 | | .034 |

   | 0.4121 | | 0.451 |

5. Simplify.

   $$4^2 + \sqrt{9} =$$

   A. 5
   B. 11
   C. 19
   D. 47

GO ON TO THE NEXT PAGE

Mathematical Reasoning, Part 2

You MAY use a calculator in Part 2.

Question 6 refers to the following inequality.

$$\frac{x}{2} \le 1$$

6. Which of the following represents the solution to the inequality?

   A.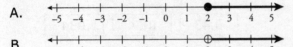
   B.
   C.
   D.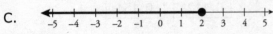

7. Line m has a slope of $-\frac{1}{3}$ and passes through the point $(0, 5)$. What is the equation of line m?

   A. $y = 3x + 5$

   B. $y = -\frac{1}{3}x$

   C. $y = -\frac{1}{3}x - 5$

   D. $y = -\frac{1}{3}x + 5$

Question 8 refers to the following expression.

$$2(x + 3)^2$$

8. All of the following are equivalent to the above expression EXCEPT

   A. $2(x + 3)(x + 3)$
   B. $2x^2 + 12x + 18$
   C. $2(x^2 + 6x + 9)$
   D. $2x^2 + 18$

9. A pizza consists of eight slices. Three slices are mushroom, two are green pepper, one is pineapple, and the rest are plain cheese. Amanda likes only mushroom and plain cheese. If she selects a slice at random, what is the probability she will select a slice that she likes?

   A. $\frac{3}{8}$

   B. $\frac{1}{2}$

   C. $\frac{3}{5}$

   D. $\frac{5}{8}$

GO ON TO THE NEXT PAGE

<u>Question 10</u> refers to the following graph, which shows the number of grams of sugar per serving in each of five different cereals.

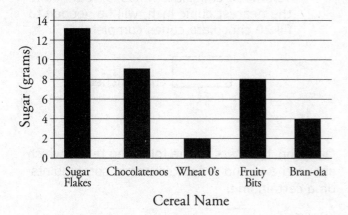

10. Write your answers to the questions below in the boxes provided.

What is the range of grams of sugar in the five cereals?

What is the average number of grams of sugar among the five cereals?

[ ]

| 2 | 5.5 | 7.2 |
| 11 | 13 | 36 |

11. The total number of books Kyle read in the last year can be represented by the equation $B = 12 + 2L$ where B is the total number of books he read and L is the number of trips he took to the library. If Kyle read 76 books last year, how many trips to the library did he take?

A. 6
B. 32
C. 64
D. 164

12. A restaurant anticipates that it will need 80 two-ounce dinner rolls for a special event. The rolls are purchased from a local bakery in bags that weigh 3 pounds each. How many bags of rolls must the restaurant purchase for the event? Note: 1 pound = 16 ounces.

A. 3
B. 4
C. 5
D. 53

GO ON TO THE NEXT PAGE

Question 13 refers to the following right triangle.

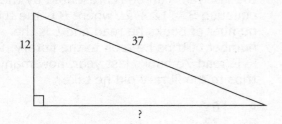

13. What is the length of the missing side?

    A. 12
    B. 30
    C. 35
    D. 38.9

14. Multiply.

    $$(2x + 2)(x - 3)$$

    A. $2x^2 - x - 6$
    B. $2x^2 - 4x - 6$
    C. $2x^2 - 6$
    D. $2x - 4x - 6$

15. Line m passes through the points $(1, 6)$ and $(-3, 8)$. What is the equation of line m?

    A. $y = -x + 5$

    B. $y = -\frac{1}{2}x + \frac{11}{2}$

    C. $y = 2x + 4$

    D. $y = -\frac{1}{2}x + \frac{13}{2}$

16. A pastry chef is making a dessert that involves a chocolate cone filled with chocolate mousse. The cone has a radius of 1/2 inch and a height of 3 inches. What volume of chocolate mousse, rounded to the nearest cubic inch, will be needed to fill 20 chocolate cones completely?

    [   ] cubic inches

Question 17 refers to the following table, which shows the x- and y-coordinates of some points on a certain line.

x	y
0	2
2	5
4	8
8	14

17. What is the slope of the line?

    A. 0

    B. 1

    C. $\frac{3}{2}$

    D. 3

18. Solve the equation for z.

    $$y + 2 = 4zy$$

    A. $z = \frac{1}{2}$

    B. $z = \frac{4y}{y + 2}$

    C. $z = \frac{y + 2}{4y}$

    D. $z = \frac{1}{2}y + 2$

GO ON TO THE NEXT PAGE

Mathematical Reasoning, Part 2

Question 19 refers to the following list of numbers.

$$9, 2, 0, 12, 4, 1, 7$$

19. Find the median and mean of the list of numbers and write them in the boxes provided.

Median: ⬚

Mean: ⬚

2	4	5

7	9	35

20. Janelle is going to the gym to run, lift weights, and stretch. In how many different orders could she complete the three activities?

A.   1
B.   3
C.   6
D.   27

21. A circle has an area of 256π. What is its radius?

A.   16
B.   16π
C.   256
D.   65,536

22. Jamal is taking money for food and souvenirs on his school trip. He has brought $80, but his teacher tells him students are allowed to take a maximum of $65. He knows he will need at least $40 for the things he definitely wants to buy. Jamal solves the inequality $40 \leq 80 - d \leq 65$ to determine the number of dollars, d, he must leave behind. What is the solution to the inequality?

A. $40 \leq d \leq 80$
B. $65 \leq d \leq 80$
C. $15 \leq d \leq 40$
D. $40 \leq d \leq 65$

GO ON TO THE NEXT PAGE

23. Which of the following is the graph of
    $y = \frac{1}{2}x + 4$?

A.

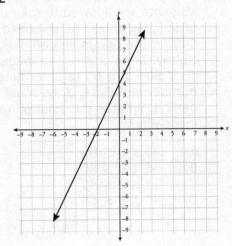

C.

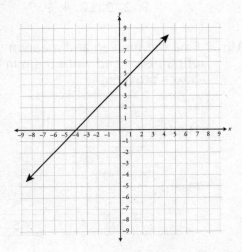

B.

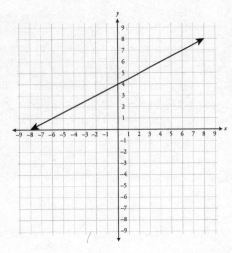

D.

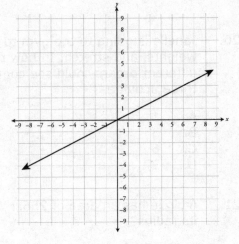

GO ON TO THE NEXT PAGE

24. A store sells diapers in both crates and bags. 10 crates and 6 bags together contain 276 diapers, and 5 crates and 2 bags together contain 117 diapers. How many diapers are in one crate?

[ ]

Question 25 refers to the following rectangle with an area of 208cm².

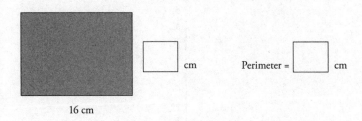

16 cm

[ ] cm   Perimeter = [ ] cm

25. Find the width and perimeter of the rectangle and write them in the boxes from the options provided.

13	14	16
29	58	208

26. Add.

$$(5.4 \times 10^{12}) + (6.3 \times 10^{12})$$

A. 1.17×10^{12}
B. 1.17×10^{13}
C. 1.17×10^{24}
D. 1.17×10^{144}

27. Solve the equation for x.

$$x^2 - 4x = 32$$

A. $x = -8$ or $x = 4$
B. $x = 8$ or $x = 4$
C. $x = 8$ or $x = -4$
D. $x = -8$ or $x = -4$

28. So far, Marina has read 168 pages of her book. She plans to read 40 pages every day. Which of the following expresses the number of pages Marina has read after d days?

A. $168d + 40$
B. $168 - 40d$
C. $168 + 40d$
D. $168d - 40$

29. In a certain classroom, the ratio of boys to girls is 4:5. If there are 20 girls in the class, how many boys are there?

A. 4
B. 16
C. 20
D. 25

GO ON TO THE NEXT PAGE

<u>Question 30</u> refers to the following function.

$$f(x) = 2x + 5$$

30. Find $f(x)$ for the provided x-values and write the answers in the appropriate boxes.

$f(5) = $ ⬚

$f(0) = $ ⬚

$f(-2) = $ ⬚

| -2 | 0 | 1 | 2 |

| 5 | 15 | 20 |

<u>Question 31</u> refers to the following list of corresponding x- and y-coordinates.

x	y
0	2
-2	0
6	-1
-2	-3

31. Plot the points on the graph.

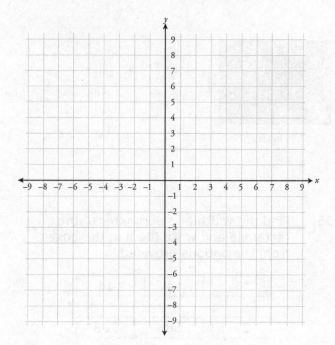

32. Ariella is trying to save up to buy a concert ticket, which costs $35.00. She decides to offer services to her neighbors. She will mow lawns for $2.50 per lawn and babysit for $7.50 per hour. Which inequality represents this situation in terms of m, the number of lawns she mows, and b, the number of hours she babysits?

A. $7.5m + 2.5b \leq 35$
B. $2.5m + 7.5b \leq 35$
C. $7.5m + 2.5b \geq 35$
D. $2.5m + 7.5b \geq 35$

GO ON TO THE NEXT PAGE

Mathematical Reasoning, Part 2

33. Factor.

$$x^2 - 4x - 45$$

A. $(x + 8)(x - 5)$
B. $(x + 9)(x - 5)$
C. $(x - 8)(x + 5)$
D. $(x - 9)(x + 5)$

34. Michelle created a scale drawing of her home in order to make renovations. She plans to add a rectangular patio that is 18 feet long by 8 feet wide. In the scale drawing, the patio is 6 inches long. Find the scale Michelle used in her drawing and the width of the patio that she drew, and mark them in the provided boxes.

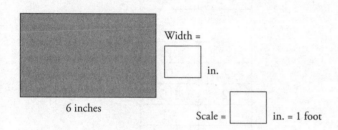

Width =

[   ] in.

6 inches

Scale = [   ] in. = 1 foot

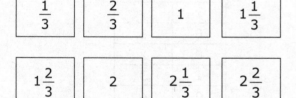

$\frac{1}{3}$	$\frac{2}{3}$	1	$1\frac{1}{3}$
$1\frac{2}{3}$	2	$2\frac{1}{3}$	$2\frac{2}{3}$

35. Which of the following correctly represents the expression *three times the quantity of a number minus one*?

A. $3(a - 1)$
B. $a + 3$
C. $3a - 1$
D. $3(-1)$

Question 36 refers to the following equation and graph.

Line A: $y = \dfrac{2}{3}x + 5$

Line B (shown on the graph below)

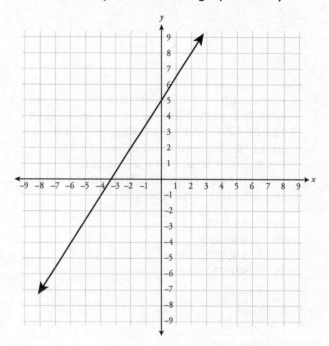

36. The slope of line A is [Select... ▼] the

| greater than |
| less than |
| equal to |

slope of line B. The *y*-intercept of line A is

[Select... ▼] the *y*-intercept of line B.

| greater than |
| less than |
| equal to |

GO ON TO THE NEXT PAGE

Question 37 refers to the following equation.

$$Z = 8 - 2q$$

37.   What is the value of Z when $q = -4$?

   A.   −8
   B.   0
   C.   8
   D.   16

38.   Airrick inherits $5,000 from his grandparents. First he must pay a state tax of 12% on his inheritance. Then he puts the remaining amount into an account that earns 2% interest, compounded annually. How much is in the account after one year?

   A. $12.00
   B. $88.00
   C. $4,488.00
   D. $5,712.00

39.   Which table of values represents a function?

   A.

x	y
4	1
2	7.5
1	3
1	2

   B.

x	y
−1	−1
−2	−2
−3	−3
−1	−2

   C.

x	y
−2.5	0
2	1.6
−9	−1
3.7	5

   D.

x	y
0	1
0	2
1	3
0	4

40.   A square with a side of 4 units has its top edge on the line $y = 8$. What is the equation of the line that includes the bottom edge of the square?

   A. $y = 4$
   B. $x = 8$
   C. $y = 12$
   D. $x = 4$

GO ON TO THE NEXT PAGE

Mathematical Reasoning, Part 2

Question 41 refers to the following graph of a function.

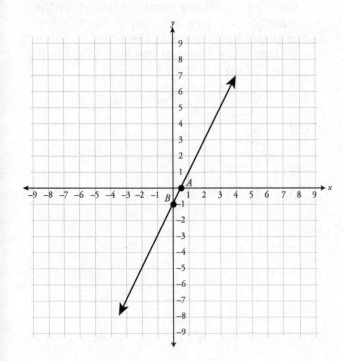

41. Write the correct options from the list below into the boxes provided.

Point A is the [＿＿＿＿＿].

Point B is the [＿＿＿＿＿].

slope		y–intercept		range

maximum		x-intercept		minimum

42. A box of spaghetti costs 87 cents and a jar of tomato sauce costs $1.12. What is the total cost of four boxes of spaghetti and four jars of tomato sauce?

$[＿＿＿＿]

43. Solve for x.

$$12 - 2x = 8x - 3(x + 1)$$

A. $\dfrac{1}{5}$

B. $\dfrac{3}{7}$

C. $\dfrac{4}{5}$

D. $\dfrac{15}{7}$

Question 44 refers to the following table, which shows four different sizes of laundry detergent offered by one brand and their costs.

	Size (fluid ounces)	Price
Mini	8	$3.99
Regular	16	$5.99
Large	24	$7.99
Jumbo	32	$9.99

44. Which size of detergent costs the least amount per fluid ounce?

A. mini
B. regular
C. large
D. jumbo

GO ON TO THE NEXT PAGE

45. Solve the equation for x.

$$x^2 + 4x = 21$$

A. $x = 7$ or $x = 3$
B. $x = -7$ or $x = 3$
C. $x = -7$ or $x = -3$
D. $x = 7$ or $x = -3$

46. A printer can print 50 sheets of paper every 10 minutes. The printer's output can be graphically represented using the equation $y = mx$, where y is the number of papers printed, x is the time in minutes, and m is the slope of the line. What is the value of m?

A. $\dfrac{1}{5}$

B. $\dfrac{1}{2}$

C. 1

D. 5

END OF TEST

Social Studies

Welcome!

Here is some information that you need to know before you start this test:

- You should not spend too much time on a question if you are not certain of the answer; answer it the best you can, and go on to the next question.
- If you are not certain of the answer to a question, you can mark your answer for review and come back to it later.
- You have **70 minutes** to complete this test.

Turn the page to begin.

GO ON TO THE NEXT PAGE

Questions 1 and 2 refer to the following source.

> "An elective despotism was not the government we fought for; but one which should not only be founded on free principles, but in which the powers of government should be so divided and balanced among several bodies of magistracy, as that no one could transcend their legal limits, without being effectually checked and restrained by the others.
>
> For this reason, that convention which passed the ordinance of government, laid its foundation on this basis, that the legislative, executive, and judiciary departments should be separate and distinct, so that no person should exercise the powers of more than one of them at the same time."
>
> –James Madison, *Federalist* 48, 1788

1. Which foundational principle of American government is illustrated in the source above?

   A. popular sovereignty
   B. checks and balances
   C. federalism
   D. judicial review

2. In which of the following ways is the American system of separation of powers different from the structure of a parliamentary system of government?

   A. In a parliamentary system, the head of state is part of the judicial branch.
   B. In a parliamentary system, all decisions made by the executive branch are subject to popular referendum.
   C. In a parliamentary system, there is no judiciary.
   D. In a parliamentary system, the executive derives its legitimacy from the legislature.

GO ON TO THE NEXT PAGE

Social Studies

Questions 3 through 5 refer to the following sources.

Source 1:

"The alternate domination of one faction over another, sharpened by the spirit of revenge, natural to party dissension, which in different ages and countries has perpetrated the most horrid enormities, is itself a frightful despotism. But this leads at length to a more formal and permanent despotism. The disorders and miseries which result gradually incline the minds of men to seek security and repose in the absolute power of an individual; and sooner or later the chief of some prevailing faction, more able or more fortunate than his competitors, turns this disposition to the purposes of his own elevation, on the ruins of public liberty."

–George Washington, *Farewell Address,* 1796

Source 2:

"It is now well understood that two political sects have arisen within the U.S. The one believing that the Executive is the branch of our Government which the most needs support: the other that, like the analogous branch in the English government, it is already too strong for the republican parts of the Constitution, and therefore, in equivocal cases, they incline to the Legislative powers. The former of these are called Federalists, sometimes Aristocrats or Monocrats and sometimes Tories, after the corresponding sect in the English government, of exactly the same definition: the latter are styled Republicans, Whigs, Jacobins, Anarchists, Disorganizers, etc. These terms are in familiar use with most persons."

–Thomas Jefferson, *Letter to John Wise,* 1798

---

3. The author of Source 1 would most likely have which of the following attitudes toward the situation described in Source 2?

   A. approval
   B. apathy
   C. exuberance
   D. dismay

4. According to Source 2, the two main political parties in 1798 disagreed about which of the following?

   A. the appropriate amount of power that should be given to the Executive branch
   B. whether the Executive branch should be a separate entity from the Legislative branch
   C. whether the Legislative branch should be subservient to the Judicial branch
   D. the constitutionality of the separation of powers among the three branches of government

5. Based on your understanding of American political parties in the late 18th century, drag and drop the political positions below into the correct column.

Federalists	Democratic-Republicans

(a) favored a limited central government

(b) favored a strong central government

(c) favored a national bank

(d) opposed a national bank

(e) strict interpretation of the Constitution

(f) loose interpretation of the Constitution

GO ON TO THE NEXT PAGE

Question 6 refers to the following source.

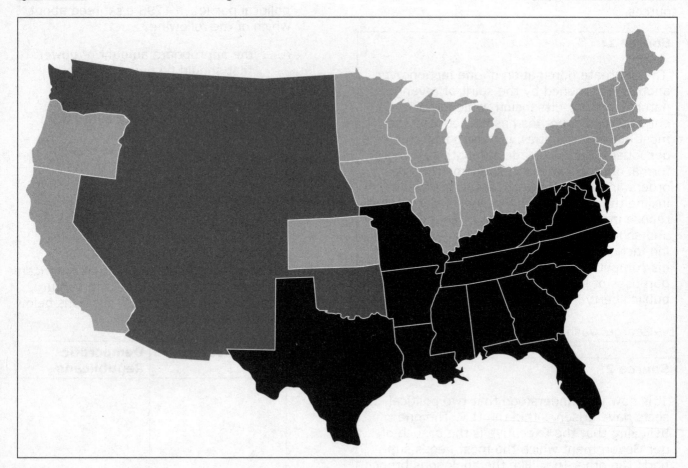

6. The map shown above most likely indicates which of the following?

   A. Loyalist and patriot states in 1775
   B. cotton-growing and non-cotton-growing states in 1832
   C. Democratic and Free-Soil states in 1850
   D. free and slave states in 1861

GO ON TO THE NEXT PAGE

Social Studies

Question 7 refers to the following source.

> "Good afternoon. On my orders, the United States military has begun strikes against Al Qaeda terrorist training camps and military installations of the Taliban regime in Afghanistan. These carefully targeted actions are designed to disrupt the use of Afghanistan as a terrorist base of operations and to attack the military capability of the Taliban regime.
>
> "We are joined in this operation by our staunch friend, Great Britain. Other close friends, including Canada, Australia, Germany and France, have pledged forces as the operation unfolds. More than 40 countries in the Middle East, Africa, Europe, and across Asia have granted air transit or landing rights. Many more have shared intelligence. We are supported by the collective will of the world.
>
> "More than two weeks ago, I gave Taliban leaders a series of clear and specific demands: Close terrorist training camps; hand over leaders of the Al Qaeda network; and return all foreign nationals, including American citizens, unjustly detained in your country. None of these demands was met. And now, the Taliban will pay a price."
>
> –George W. Bush, *Address to the Nation*, October 7, 2001

7. One of the events that immediately followed the start of the American war in Afghanistan was

| Select... ▼ | .

    the opening of the Guantanamo Bay detention camp in Cuba

    the killing of Osama bin Laden

    the creation of the terrorist group ISIS

    the election of Barack Obama

GO ON TO THE NEXT PAGE

<u>Questions 8 and 9</u> refer to the following sources.

Source 1:

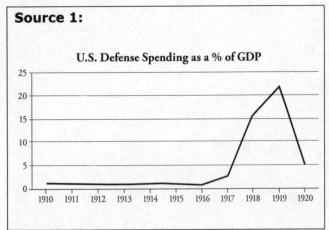

U.S. Defense Spending as a % of GDP

Source 2:

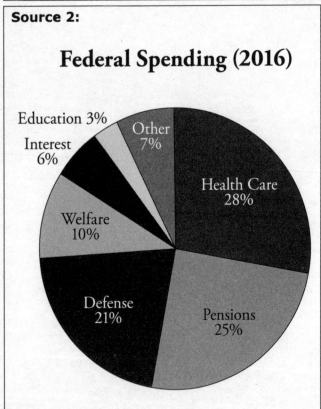

8. In Source 1 above, what is the most likely explanation for the massive increase in defense spending in 1917–1919?

    A.   the need to protect the continental United States from foreign invaders
    B.   the buildup to conflict between the United States and Mexico
    C.   the entry of the United States into World War I
    D.   the desire to establish American colonies in Africa

9. According to Source 2, what percent of the American government's spending in 2016 was devoted to health care?

10. Each of the following is responsible for a key component of establishing the Federal budget EXCEPT

Select... ▼
the House of Representatives
the Senate
the Supreme Court
the President

GO ON TO THE NEXT PAGE

Social Studies

Question 11 refers to the following source.

"If woman would fulfill her traditional responsibility to her own children; if she would educate and protect from danger factory children who must find their recreation on the street; if she would bring the cultural forces to bear upon our materialistic civilization; and if she would do it all with the dignity and directness fitting one who carries on her immemorial duties, then she must bring herself to the use of the ballot—that latest implement for self-government."

–Jane Addams, *Why Women Should Vote*, 1915

11. The sentiment expressed by Jane Addams in the source above most clearly reflects the aspirations of

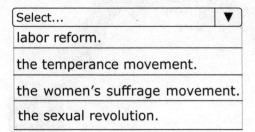

Select... ▼
labor reform.

the temperance movement.

the women's suffrage movement.

the sexual revolution.

Question 12 refers to the following source.

"Representatives and direct Taxes shall be apportioned among the several States which may be included within this Union, according to their respective Numbers, which shall be determined by adding to the whole Number of free Persons, including those bound to Service for a Term of Years, and excluding Indians not taxed, three fifths of all other Persons."

–*The Constitution of the United States*, Article I, Section 2

12. The debate that led to the so-called "Three-Fifths Compromise" illustrated in the source above concerned which of the following?

A. whether women would be counted equally to men when determining a state's population for representative and taxation purposes

B. whether and how slaves would be counted when determining a state's population for representative and taxation purposes

C. the appropriate minimum age for a person to be counted when determining a state's population for representative and taxation purposes

D. the appropriate term length for elected representatives relative to state populations

GO ON TO THE NEXT PAGE

Questions 13 and 14 refer to the following source.

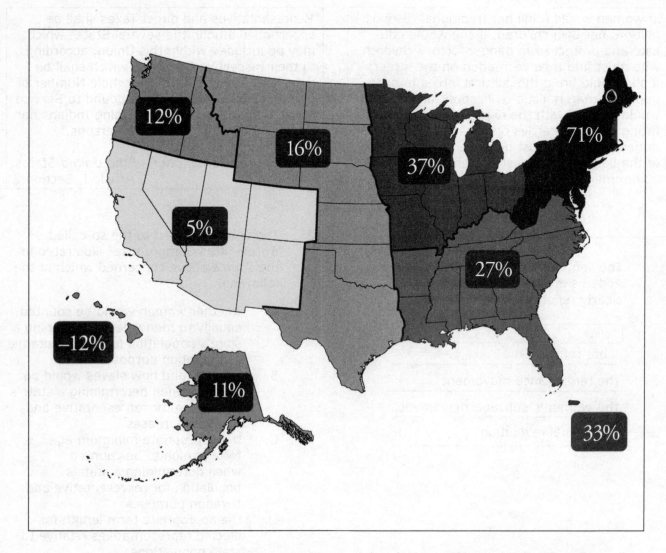

Very Heavy Precipitation Change in the United States (1958–2012)

13. According to the source above, which of the following regions experienced the most dramatic increase in very heavy precipitation in the time period indicated?

    A. Southwest
    B. Midwest
    C. Northeast
    D. Southeast

14. Each of the following is a threat to humans posed by an increase in heavy precipitation events EXCEPT

    A. earthquakes.
    B. flooding.
    C. landslides.
    D. crop damage.

GO ON TO THE NEXT PAGE

Social Studies

Question 15 refers to the following source.

> "The purpose of protecting the life of our nation and preserving the liberty of our citizens is to pursue the happiness of our people. Our success in that pursuit is the test of our success as a nation. For a century we labored to settle and to subdue a continent. For half a century we called upon unbounded invention and untiring industry to create an order of plenty for all of our people. The challenge of the next half century is whether we have the wisdom to use that wealth to enrich and elevate our national life, and to advance the quality of our American civilization.
>
> "Your imagination and your initiative, and your indignation will determine whether we build a society where progress is the servant of our needs, or a society where old values and new visions are buried under unbridled growth. For in your time we have the opportunity to move not only toward the rich society and the powerful society, but upward to the Great Society. The Great Society rests on abundance and liberty for all. It demands an end to poverty and racial injustice, to which we are totally committed in our time. But that is just the beginning."
>
> –Lyndon Johnson, *The Great Society,* 1964

15. The law that best exemplifies Lyndon Johnson's Great Society program is

Select... ▼
the Sherman Antitrust Act.
the Interstate Commerce Act.
the Civil Rights Act.
the Endangered Species Act.

GO ON TO THE NEXT PAGE

Social Studies

Questions 16 through 18 refer to the following sources.

Source 1:

"No Person except a natural born Citizen, or a Citizen of the United States, at the time of the Adoption of this Constitution, shall be eligible to the Office of President; neither shall any Person be eligible to that Office who shall not have attained to the Age of thirty five Years, and been fourteen Years a Resident within the United States.

In Case of the Removal of the President from Office, or of his Death, Resignation, or Inability to discharge the Powers and Duties of the said Office, the Same shall devolve on the Vice President, and the Congress may by Law provide for the Case of Removal, Death, Resignation or Inability, both of the President and Vice President, declaring what Officer shall then act as President, and such Officer shall act accordingly, until the Disability be removed, or a President shall be elected.

The President shall, at stated Times, receive for his Services, a Compensation, which shall neither be increased nor diminished during the Period for which he shall have been elected, and he shall not receive within that Period any other Emolument from the United States, or any of them."

–The Constitution of the United States, Article II, Section 1

Source 2:

"The Senate shall have the sole Power to try all Impeachments. When sitting for that Purpose, they shall be on Oath or Affirmation. When the President of the United States is tried, the Chief Justice shall preside: And no Person shall be convicted without the Concurrence of two thirds of the Members present.

"Judgment in Cases of Impeachment shall not extend further than to removal from Office, and disqualification to hold and enjoy any Office of honor, Trust or Profit under the United States: but the Party convicted shall nevertheless be liable and subject to Indictment, Trial, Judgment and Punishment, according to Law."

–The Constitution of the United States, Article II, Section 3

---

16. The word "compensation" in Source 1 would best be replaced by which of the following?

    A. concealment
    B. penalty
    C. contract
    D. salary

17. Who was the only American president to be impeached in the twentieth century (enter last name only)?

    [   ]

GO ON TO THE NEXT PAGE

Social Studies

18. Drag and drop the items below into the appropriate box to indicate whether they are constitutional or unconstitutional.

Constitutional	Unconstitutional

(a) The Speaker of the House presiding over a presidential impeachment hearing

(b) An impeachment hearing resulting in a prison sentence for the accused

(c) The Vice President taking up the presidency after the President's death

(d) A 37-year-old who has lived in the United States for nine years becoming President

(e) An impeachment conviction occurring with three fourths of the members present agreeing

Question 19 refers to the following source.

Types of Credit

Secured	The borrower puts up an asset, which the creditor is entitled to seize if the borrower violates the credit agreement
Unsecured	The borrower gives word to the creditor that he or she will repay what is borrowed
Revolving	Payments fluctuate based on how much credit the borrower has used and how much the borrower wishes to repay in a given time period
Non-Revolving	The borrower is required to pay a fixed amount per payment period

19. A borrower whose car is repossessed after he or she fails to pay his or her monthly bill of $300 would most likely be a borrower with which type of credit?

   A. unsecured, revolving
   B. unsecured, non-revolving
   C. secured, revolving
   D. secured, non-revolving

GO ON TO THE NEXT PAGE

Social Studies

Questions 20 through 22 refer to the following sources.

Source 1:

"We the General Assembly of Virginia do enact that no man shall be compelled to frequent or support any religious worship, place, or ministry whatsoever, nor shall be enforced, restrained, molested, or burdened in his body or goods, nor shall otherwise suffer, on account of his religious opinions or belief; but that all men shall be free to profess, and by argument to maintain, their opinions in matters of religion, and that the same shall in no wise diminish, enlarge, or affect their civil capacities."

–Thomas Jefferson, *Virginia Statute for Religious Freedom,* 1779

Source 2:

"We hold it for a fundamental and undeniable truth, "that Religion or the duty which we owe to our Creator and the manner of discharging it, can be directed only by reason and conviction, not by force or violence." The Religion then of every man must be left to the conviction and conscience of every man; and it is the right of every man to exercise it as these may dictate. This right is in its nature an unalienable right. It is unalienable, because the opinions of men, depending only on the evidence contemplated by their own minds cannot follow the dictates of other men: It is unalienable also, because what is here a right towards men, is a duty towards the Creator. It is the duty of every man to render to the Creator such homage and such only as he believes to be acceptable to him."

–James Madison, *Memorial and Remonstrance Against Religious Assessments,* 1785

---

20. The two sources above contain principles that would later be reflected in

Select... ▼
the Declaration of Independence.
the First Amendment.
the Jay Treaty.
the Emancipation Proclamation.

21. The word "frequent" in Source 1 above could be replaced by each of the following EXCEPT

   A. visit habitually.
   B. disassociate from.
   C. associate with.
   D. go often to.

22. Which of the following was one reason that Thomas Jefferson and James Madison were proponents of religious freedom?

   A. They were concerned that the new nation did not have adequate safeguards preventing the establishment of a national religion.
   B. They wanted to make sure that Americans did not deviate from the Anglican Church.
   C. They hoped to ensure that elected officials in the United States would always be Christians.
   D. They believed that the best government is one founded upon Christian principles.

GO ON TO THE NEXT PAGE

Social Studies

Questions 23 and 24 refer to the following source.

Population of the United States

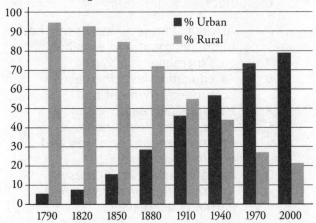

Questions 25 and 26 refer to the following source.

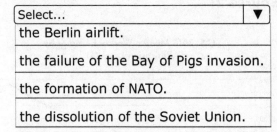

"This Government, as promised, has maintained the closest surveillance of the Soviet military buildup on the island of Cuba. Within the past week, unmistakable evidence has established the fact that a series of offensive missile sites is now in preparation on that imprisoned island. The purpose of these bases can be none other than to provide a nuclear strike capability against the Western Hemisphere."

–John F. Kennedy, *Address to the Nation*, October 22, 1962

25. The Cuban Missile crisis discussed by President Kennedy in the source above was directly preceded by

Select... ▼
the Berlin airlift.
the failure of the Bay of Pigs invasion.
the formation of NATO.
the dissolution of the Soviet Union.

23. According to the data above, in which time period did the urban population of the United States surpass the rural population of the United States?

A. 1790–1820
B. 1850–1880
C. 1910–1940
D. 1970–2000

24. Each of the following is a reason for the historical increase in American urbanization over time EXCEPT

A. the Industrial Revolution.
B. increased agricultural efficiency.
C. new technologies in construction.
D. global warming and sea level rise.

26. The United States government's concern about communism in Cuba during the Cold War period reflected which of the following policy ideas?

A. containment
B. libertarianism
C. decentralization
D. pacifism

GO ON TO THE NEXT PAGE

Questions 27 and 28 refer to the following sources.

Source 1:

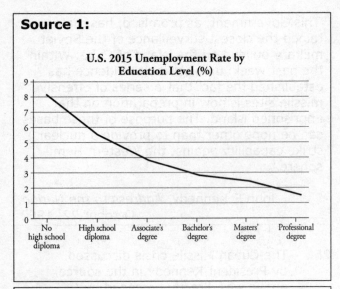

U.S. 2015 Unemployment Rate by Education Level (%)

Source 2:

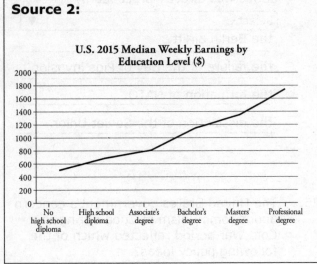

U.S. 2015 Median Weekly Earnings by Education Level ($)

27. According to Sources 1 and 2, what can be said about the correlation between education level on the one hand and unemployment and earnings on the other?

   A. As education level increases, both unemployment and earnings also increase.
   B. As education level increases, both unemployment and earnings decrease.
   C. As education level increases, unemployment decreases and earnings increase.
   D. As education level increases, unemployment increases and earnings decrease.

28. According to Source 2 above, what is the approximate median weekly earning of a person with a bachelor's degree?

   A. $500
   B. $800
   C. $1,100
   D. $1,700

GO ON TO THE NEXT PAGE

Question 29 refers to the following source.

> "The United States of America on the one part, and His Imperial Majesty the Sultan of the Ottoman empire on the other part, being equally animated by the desire of extending the commercial relations between their respective countries, have agreed, for this purpose, to conclude a treaty of commerce and navigation, and have named as their respective plenipotentiaries, that is to say: The President of the United States of America, Edward Joy Morris, minister resident at the Sublime Porte and His Imperial Majesty the Sultan of the Ottoman empire, his highness Mehemed Emin Aali Pacha, minister of foreign affairs, decorated with the imperial orders of the Ottomanich in Brilliants, Majidich, and order of Merit of the First Class, and the grand crosses of several foreign orders; who, after having communicated to each other their respective full powers, found in good and due form, have agreed upon the following articles."
>
> *–Treaty of Commerce and Navigation between the United States and the Ottoman Empire* (1862)

29. To whom does the Constitution grant the power to make treaties such as the one above?

    A. the president alone
    B. the president, with the advice and consent of the Senate
    C. the president, with the advice and consent of the House of Representatives
    D. the president, with the advice and consent of both the Senate and the House of Representatives

GO ON TO THE NEXT PAGE

Question 30 refers to the following source.

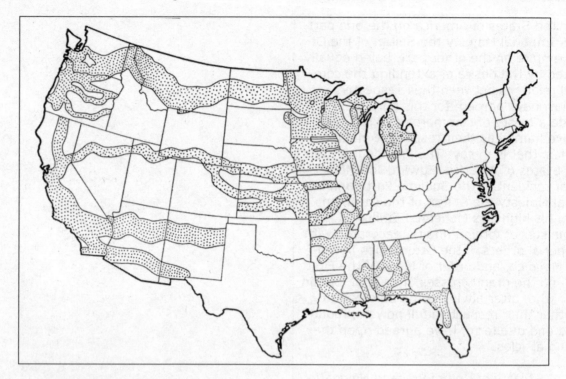

30.   The shaded portions of the map above most likely indicate which of the following?

    A.   major American river systems
    B.   primary migration routes for displaced Native Americans
    C.   areas of extreme drought
    D.   U.S. government land grants to railroad companies

Questions 31 and 32 refer to the following source.

> "Neither slavery nor involuntary servitude, except as a punishment for crime whereof the party shall have been duly convicted, shall exist within the United States, or any place subject to their jurisdiction."

31. The passage above is an excerpt from the

Select... ▼	Amendment to the
2nd
7th
13th
21st

United States Constitution.

32. The constitutional amendment quoted in the passage to the left was ratified by Congress during which time period in American history?

A. Revolutionary Era
B. Era of Good Feelings
C. Reconstruction Era
D. Progressive Era

GO ON TO THE NEXT PAGE

Questions 33 through 35 refer to the following sources.

Source 1:

"The civil law, as well as nature herself, has always recognized a wide difference in the respective spheres and destinies of man and woman. Man is, or should be, woman's protector and defender. The natural and proper timidity and delicacy which belongs to the female sex evidently unfits it for many of the occupations of civil life. The constitution of the family organization, which is founded in the divine ordinance, as well as in the nature of things, indicates the domestic sphere as that which properly belongs to the domain and functions of womanhood."

–Justice Bradley concurring in the opinion of the court, *Bradwell v. Illinois,* 1873

Source 2:

Party Affiliation: Women in Congress, 95th–109th Congresses (1977–2006)*

This chart shows the party breakdown only for women Members for this time period.

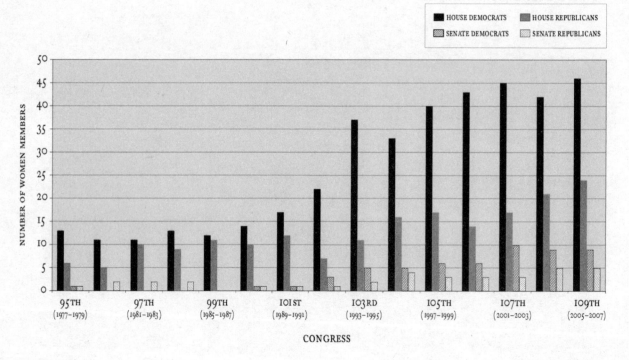

*As of August 1, 2006

GO ON TO THE NEXT PAGE

33. The author of Source 1 above would most likely disagree that

Select... ▼
there are naturally separate spheres for men and women.
men and women should have equal opportunities in employment.
a woman's primary role is domestic.
a man's role is to protect and defend women.

34. According to Source 2 above, women have historically been represented in the greatest numbers among which group in Congress?

    A.   House Democrats
    B.   House Republicans
    C.   Senate Democrats
    D.   Senate Republicans

35. Which of the following statements was true about the 109th Congress?

    A.   Women accounted for more than 30% of the total number of senators.
    B.   Women accounted for less than 30% of the total number of senators.
    C.   Women accounted for about 50% of all congresspeople.
    D.   The number of Republican women in the House was lower than the number of Republican women in the Senate.

END OF TEST

THIS PAGE INTENTIONALLY LEFT BLANK.

GO ON TO THE NEXT PAGE

Science

Welcome!

Here is some information that you need to know before you start this test:

- You should not spend too much time on a question if you are not certain of the answer; answer it the best you can, and go on to the next question.
- If you are not certain of the answer to a question, you can mark your answer for review and come back to it later.
- You have **90 minutes** to complete this test.

Turn the page to begin.

GO ON TO THE NEXT PAGE

Science

Questions 1 through 3 refer to the following information.

A reaction is an object's response to stimuli that leads to physical or chemical changes. While a physical change may alter the form and properties of an object, it will not alter the object's chemical composition. Conversely, a chemical change occurs when bonds between atoms are broken to form new molecules with new properties.

Chemists use chemical equations to show the molecules that are present both before and after a chemical reaction. The molecules that are present before a chemical reaction are referred to as reactants, while the molecules that are present after a chemical reaction are referred to as products. Note that atoms cannot be created or destroyed, so the chemical equation must be balanced; i.e., the same number of atoms must be present both before and after a chemical reaction.

The chemical equation that shows the chemical reaction in which fluorine and sulfur molecules are converted into sulfur hexafluoride is shown as follows:

$$3F_2 + S \rightarrow SF_6$$

1. As water changes from a liquid to a solid, it undergoes a(n)

   A. reaction.
   B. chemical change.
   C. physical change.
   D. alteration.

2. How many molecules of sulfur are present both before and after the chemical reaction?

   [ ]

3. In the chemical equation provided, fluorine and sulfur are the

   [Select... ▼], while sulfur
   products
   reactants

   hexafluoride is the [Select... ▼].
   product
   reactant

4. A place where many organisms live and depend upon other organisms for survival is a(n)

   A. biome.
   B. ecosystem.
   C. food web.
   D. habitat.

GO ON TO THE NEXT PAGE

Science

Questions 5 and 6 refer to the following information.

The table below shows the mass and speed of five different animals.

	Mass (lbs)	Speed (m/s)
Cat	10	34
Dog	30	28
Fox	40	45
Giraffe	450	80
Wolf	160	60

5. Given that the speed of an object is given

    by the equation $speed = \dfrac{distance}{time}$,

    how long will it take a dog to travel

    112 meters?

    A. 1 second
    B. 3.73 seconds
    C. 4 seconds
    D. 3,136 seconds

6. The amount of force an object has can be found with the equation $force = mass \times acceleration$. If a wolf accelerates at a rate of 44 m/s, what is the force of the wolf?

     N

Question 7 refers to the following image.

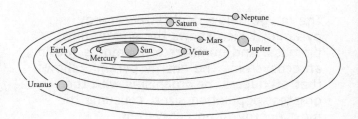

7. Terrestrial planets are those that have solid surfaces, and are located closest to the Sun. Accordingly, which of the following is NOT a terrestrial planet?

    A. Mercury
    B. Earth
    C. Mars
    D. Saturn

GO ON TO THE NEXT PAGE

Questions 8 through 10 refer to the following information.

The image below depicts the energy pyramid, which shows the energy flow, biomass, and numbers of members within an ecosystem. The energy pyramid shows that producers, or organisms with the greatest population sizes, consume the most energy in an ecosystem.

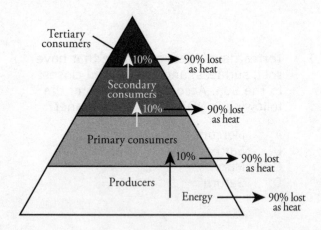

8. Write an X on the level on the energy pyramid that represents organisms with the smallest population sizes.

9. If the producers consume 100 units of energy, how many of those units of energy will be received by the secondary consumers?

    A. 1
    B. 9
    C. 10
    D. 90

10. Arrange the following groups in order from greatest to least, in terms of population size, energy consumption, and biomass. Write the letters of your selections in the boxes below.

    ☐ → ☐ → ☐ → ☐

    (a) Tertiary Consumers

    (b) Primary Consumers

    (c) Producers

    (d) Secondary Consumers

11. What type of mutation occurs when chromosomes fail to separate properly during meiosis?

    A. conjunction
    B. non-disjunction
    C. echolocation
    D. translocation

GO ON TO THE NEXT PAGE

Science

Questions 12 and 13 refer to the following information.

The rock cycle shows the effects of time, pressure, and the Earth's heat on the creation of igneous rock, metamorphic rock, and sedimentary rock.

The Rock Cycle

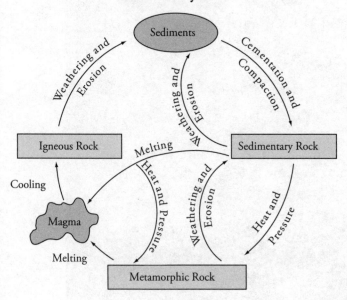

12. Which are formed as a direct result of weathering and erosion?

    A. igneous rocks
    B. magma
    C. sediments
    D. metamorphic rocks

13. Unlike | Select... ▼ | rocks, which are
    | igneous |
    | metamorphic |
    | sedimentary |

    formed from the Earth's heat and

    pressure, | Select... ▼ | rocks are
    | igneous |
    | metamorphic |
    | sedimentary |

    formed by the cooling of magma.

14. The management or regulation of a resource so that its use does not exceed the capacity of the resource to regenerate itself is known as

    A. conservation.
    B. management.
    C. preservation.
    D. sustainability.

GO ON TO THE NEXT PAGE

Question 15 refers to the following image.

15. The landform shown in the image above, which depicts a large area of flat land, is known as a

    A. desert.
    B. mountain.
    C. plain.
    D. valley.

GO ON TO THE NEXT PAGE

16. The city of La Grange, Texas, is a small town located miles from any major city. In an effort to bring business to La Grange, the town is contemplating allowing a commercial fishing business, Bait-n-Hook, to set up a large fishing and processing plant along the Colorado River. While the commercial fishing business would bring a substantial cash flow to La Grange, some citizens are concerned about the negative environmental effects of allowing Bait-n-Hook to establish business in La Grange.

    All of the following are reasons that citizens of La Grange would be concerned about Bait-n-Hook's environmental impact EXCEPT

    A.   overfishing may lead to species decline in the Colorado River.
    B.   population growth can cause loss of existing open spaces and animal habitats.
    C.   increased pollution from commercial manufacturing waste could negatively affect both water and air quality.
    D.   new jobs created by commercial fishing would be filled by outsiders who do not respect La Grange's ecology the way that longtime residents do.

Questions 17 through 19 refer to the following information.

In horses, the trait for hard hooves is dominant, expressed if a horse is either homozygous dominant, having alleles HH, or heterozygous, having alleles Hh. Conversely, horses that are homozygous recessive, having alleles hh, have soft hooves.

17. If two heterozygous horses mate, what percent of the offspring will also be heterozygous?

    A.   25%
    B.   50%
    C.   75%
    D.   100%

18. What percent of the offspring of two homozygous dominant horses will be homozygous recessive?

    [   ] %

19. All offspring of a mating of two homozygous dominant horses would have

    [Select...   ▼] , and 25% of the
    | soft hooves |
    | hard hooves |

    offspring of a mating of two heterozygous

    horses would have [Select...   ▼] .
    | soft hooves |
    | hard hooves |

GO ON TO THE NEXT PAGE

20. Which of the following proposes that the Earth began approximately 13.8 billion years ago as a small singularity that inflated, expanded, and cooled to form our solar system.

    A. Theory of Evolution
    B. Hubble's Law
    C. Photoelectric Effect
    D. Big Bang Theory

Question 21 refers to the following image.

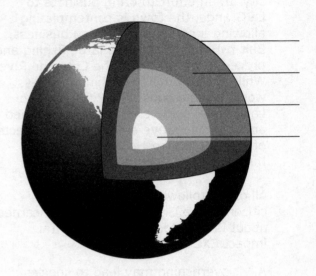

21. The lithosphere contains a rigid upper mantle and the surface of the Earth. Write an X on the line that identifies the lithosphere on the diagram above.

GO ON TO THE NEXT PAGE

<u>Questions 22 and 23</u> refer to the following information.

The following table shows the Average Heart Rate at 50% Maximum Activity and Average Maximum Heart Rate for individuals of varying ages.

Age (years)	Average Heart Rate at 50% Maximum Activity	Average Maximum Heart Rate
20	100 beats per minute	200 beats per minute
30	95 beats per minute	190 beats per minute
40	90 beats per minute	180 beats per minute
50	85 beats per minute	170 beats per minute
60	80 beats per minute	160 beats per minute
70	75 beats per minute	150 beats per minute

22. The average heart rate at 50% maximum activity for a 25-year-old would be

approximately [Select... ▼] beats
| 95 |
| 97.5 |
| 100 |

per minute, while the average maximum heart rate of a 55-year-old would be

approximately [Select... ▼] beats
| 160 |
| 165 |
| 170 |

per minute.

23. Age and average heart rate have a(n)

[Select... ▼] relationship.
| constant |
| direct |
| indirect |
| unknown |

GO ON TO THE NEXT PAGE

Questions 24 through 26 refer to the following information.

Visible Spectrum of Light

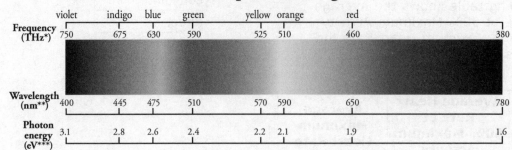

* In terahertz (THz); 1 THz = 1 × 10^{12} cycles per second
** In nanometers (nm); 1nm = 1 × 10^{-9} meter
*** In electron volts (eV)

24. As frequency increases,

    A. photon energy increases, but
       wavelength decreases.
    B. wavelength increases, but photon
       energy decreases.
    C. wavelength and photon energy
       also increase.
    D. photon energy increases, but
       wavelength stays the same.

25. The color with the greatest frequency,
    measured in Terahertz (THz), is

    A. violet.
    B. blue.
    C. orange.
    D. red.

26. The color red has a wavelength of

    | Select... ▼ | nanometers (nm), and
    | 460 |
    | 650 |
    | 750 |

    photon energy of | Select... ▼ |

    | 1.9 |
    | 2.1 |
    | 3.1 |

    electronvolts (eV).

27. Which of the following is an example of
    survival of the fittest?

    A. Since elephants are bigger than
       mice, the elephants outlive
       the mice.
    B. Over a week-long period, dogs aged
       10 years or older were not adopted
       at a shelter.
    C. Orangutans at a local zoo have
       determined that they receive
       human food when they hit a lever in
       their cage.
    D. Over a few centuries, a species of
       cat has experienced changes in fur
       color that allow it to blend into its
       native land.

GO ON TO THE NEXT PAGE

Science

Questions 28 and 29 refer to the following information.

The transfer of heat can occur in multiple ways. For example, conduction occurs when excited molecules come into direct contact with nearby molecules, transferring some of their heat energy to neighboring particles. Conversely, convection occurs when warmer air or liquid rises, as it has more excited molecules, and the cooler air or liquid drops down. Finally, radiation is the transfer of energy through empty space; unlike conduction and convection, no direct transfer occurs.

28. The Greenhouse Effect, which is the trapping of the Sun's warmth in the planet's atmosphere, is an example of

    A. conduction.
    B. convection.
    C. radiation.
    D. homeostasis.

29. An ice cube melting in your hand is an

    example of [Select... ▼], while the

    | conduction |
    | convection |
    | radiation |

    Sun warming the Earth is an

    example of [Select... ▼].

    | conduction |
    | convection |
    | radiation |

30. In order to treat an individual suffering from strep throat, which is caused by the bacteria *streptococcus pyogenes*, one must determine the strain of bacteria that is causing the infection. Once the specific bacteria strain is identified, what can be done for the individual?

    A. Antibiotics can be administered to combat the viral infection.
    B. Nothing can be done because bacterial infections cannot be treated.
    C. Antibiotics can be administered to combat the bacterial infection.
    D. Nothing can be done because viral infections cannot be treated.

31. If every atom must have at least one neutron for every existing proton, what is the minimum number of neutrons that exist in an atom with 32 protons?

    [   ]

GO ON TO THE NEXT PAGE

Questions 32 through 34 refer to the following information.

Resource	Renewable (Y/N)	U.S. Consumption (%)	Benefits	Drawbacks
Biomass	Y	3.9%	• abundant • low setup and maintenance costs • cleaner than fossil fuels • reduces waste	• pollution • high setup and maintenance costs • very inefficient • not easily scalable
Coal	N	22.6%	• abundant • low setup and maintenance costs • high energy density • current infrastructure supports coal	• acid mine drainage • ecosystem damage • subsidence • pollution • limited
Geothermal	Y	0.4%	• low setup and maintenance costs • environmentally friendly • extremely efficient	• can cause earthquakes • high setup costs • location specific • only renewable if managed properly
Hydropower	Y	2.5%	• environmentally friendly • world's most renewable energy	• high setup cost • unreliable during droughts • can be used only near water
Natural Gas	N	24%	• abundant • cleanest of fossil fuels • current infrastructure supports natural gas • extremely efficient	• ecosystem damage through fracking • releases greenhouse gases • potentially dangerous
Nuclear	N	8.5%	• low pollution • low cost to maintain • extremely efficient	• radioactive waste • nuclear meltdown • unknown risks
Oil	N	37.4%	• low setup and maintenance costs • current infrastructure supports oil • high energy density	• ecosystem damage • high pollution • limited supply
Solar	Y	0.1%	• environmentally friendly • low cost to maintain • government subsidies • unlimited supply	• can be unreliable • low efficiency • high setup cost • requires large area of land
Wind	Y	0.5%	• environmentally friendly • extremely efficient	• bird deaths • high setup cost • can be unreliable

GO ON TO THE NEXT PAGE

32. Based on the chart above, all of the following resources are abundant EXCEPT

    A. coal.
    B. natural gas.
    C. oil.
    D. solar.

33. Arrange the following resources in order from least to greatest consumption in the United States. Write the letters of your selections in the boxes below.

    ☐ → ☐ → ☐ → ☐

    → ☐ → ☐

    (a) wind

    (b) oil

    (c) coal

    (d) biomass

    (e) solar

    (f) natural gas

34. Fossil fuels, which include coal, oil, and natural gas, are examples of

    | Select... ▼ | resources, while
    | nonrenewable |
    | renewable |

    biomass, solar, and wind are examples of

    | Select... ▼ | resources.
    | nonrenewable |
    | renewable |

35. The process that occurs when a sugar is combined with oxygen and water to produce carbon dioxide, water, and ATP is known as

    A. cellular respiration.
    B. photosynthesis.
    C. oxidation.
    D. transcription.

END OF TEST

Chapter 12
Practice Test 5:
Answers and
Explanations

REASONING THROUGH LANGUAGE ARTS

Section 1

1. **C** The article is titled "Prevention and Control of Stress Among Emergency Workers," meaning it is aimed toward emergency workers. Eliminate (A) and (B) since the article doesn't deal with prevention, nor does it address grief. Choice (D) is incorrect because the article is not about all workers with stressful jobs, but rather about those working in disaster areas. Therefore, (C) is correct.

2. **A** Based on the sentence in the box, it is important to have initial training as well as ongoing training; this supports (A). Choice (B) goes beyond the passage since it does not say that mental health dictates, or totally controls, a worker's abilities. Choice (C) is incorrect because workers need ongoing training regardless of their mental health status, and (D) is not supported by the passage with regard to mental preparation.

3. **A** Paragraph 5 encourages emergency workers to have a plan for their families, making (A) correct. Choice (B) doesn't work because the passage doesn't compare caring for one's own family and aiding others. Choice (C) is stated in another paragraph, but it is not mentioned in paragraph 5, making this choice incorrect. Similarly, (D) is a true statement, but it is not the main point of paragraph 5.

4. **(a), (d)**

   Look at the numbered points at the end of the passage. Only (a) and (d) are listed in these suggestions. Choices (b) and (c) are not found anywhere in the passage.

5. **C** The checklist at the end is intended to help the emergency workers manage stress while on the job. Choice (A) is too general because the passage addresses emergency workers specifically, not anyone dealing with trauma. Choice (B) is similarly incorrect because the passage is not intended for victims. Choice (D) might seem tempting, but the list is not intended to help emergency workers end the disaster, but rather to manage stress. Therefore, (C) is the best choice.

6. **(b), (c)**

   Like Question 4, this question pertains to the bullets in paragraph 10. This section describes ways in which disaster workers can monitor and alleviate their own stress, as well as that of their fellow workers and of disaster victims. The passage does not mention (a) or recommend (d), and (e) refers to a bullet in paragraph 9. That leaves (b) and (c), both of which are bulleted items listed in paragraph 10.

7. **D** The boxed sentence talks about having a contingency plan for themselves and their families. This sentence is included because if workers' families are safe, the workers will be less worried about them. Choice (A) is tempting, but it misunderstands what the contingency plan is for: such a plan is for logistics and practical matters of safety, not directly for stress relief. You can eliminate this answer choice. Choice (B) is also incorrect because it is not mentioned in the passage. Choice (C) is a true statement mentioned in the passage, but it is not the reason for the boxed sentence. Therefore, (D) is correct since it is specific to the workers' families.

8. **B** The main point of this article is to offer stress management tips to emergency workers. Choice (A) is not specific to any subject, making it incorrect. Choice (B) works because preparation can minimize the stress levels. The mutual aid system mentioned in (C) is not the main point of the article, nor is the worker's family in (D). Therefore, the correct answer is (B).

9. **C** The initial, or beginning, setting of the story is definitely somewhere covered and dark, eliminating (A) and (D). Choice (C) is correct because the cabin is mentioned in the third paragraph.

10. **A** The men are surprised that it is daylight because they were expecting something else based on their calculations. This supports (A). They were not correct in their expectations, eliminating (D). While they are unfamiliar with the terrain as in (B), the question asks us about the daylight, not the landscape, so you can eliminate this answer choice. Choice (C) is not mentioned in the passage.

11. **(a), (c)**

    Paragraph 6 gives a description of the landscape. There is a "low and level shore stretched down to a silent sea," which supports (a). The passage also states that "the water was dotted with countless tiny isles," supporting (c). The passage describes a "silent sea," rather than the strong and noisy waves indicated by (b). Choice (d) is not mentioned in the passage.

12. **C** This sentence offers a description of new, strange scenery. The men find this scenery surprising, but not because of how it contrasts with the cabin's darkness; therefore, you can eliminate (A). The men are not speaking, which eliminates (B) as well. Choice (D) is partially right that it is beautiful, but there is no mention of it being dangerous. Choice (C) is correct.

13. **C** The narrator is surprised in a negative way, which eliminates (D). There is no evidence that he is sleep deprived, eliminating (A). Choice (B) is too strong that he is actually fearful for his life, though he is confused. Therefore, (C) is correct.

14. **D** In these sentences, Perry is thinking about how to say what he wants, which supports (D). Choices (A), (B), and (C) are all unsupported by the text, as there is no evidence that Perry is laughing at David, nor disapproving of him, nor feeling fearful about their environment.

15. **B** In this paragraph, David is confused and questioning, while Perry seems to know the answers. This supports (B). The other choices do not describe Perry's behavior, since he is not, (A), uncontrolled, or (C), funny, or (D), afraid.

16. **(a), (c)**

    David respects Perry and his opinions, supporting (a). He does not seem overwhelmed by Perry's wisdom, so eliminate (b). David also has a positive relationship with Perry, which supports (c) and eliminates (d).

17. Drop-Down Item 1: **private lessons, group theory classes, and instrument-specific masterclasses**

    Here you have a list, so you need to make sure that the items in the list are separated properly. Because there are three items, you need a comma between the first two items, and an "and" between the second and third items. Option 1 is incorrect because it is missing the "and," which is crucial to making the list complete and final. Option 2 does not contain any commas, and there must be a comma between the first and second items; so, Option 2 is incorrect. Option 4 is missing a comma after "lessons." Therefore, Option 3 is correct and contains all the necessary commas.

Drop-Down Item 2: **students' and instructors' personalities**

Option 4 is correct here because the letter refers to all students and all instructors. Therefore, there must be plural possessive forms to refer to their personalities. As such, the apostrophes must be placed after the *s* instead of in front of the *s*, which is used for the singular possessive form.

Drop-Down Item 3: **this semester: your age, skill level, teacher preference (if any), and goals for the semester**

Option 1 is correct here. There must be a colon rather than a comma to set up this list, eliminating options 2 and 4. Option 3 includes an unnecessary comma after "and."

Drop-Down Item 4: **However,**

Option 3 is correct because there must be a contrast between the previous sentence and the next sentence. "However" is a transition word that indicates contrasting statements, whereas all of the other connecting words link to related sentences.

Section 2

Access your Student Tools online to read sample essays representing different score levels for the Extended Response prompts in this book.

Section 3

18. **D** The article is about the largest giant freshwater stingray that has been found so far, which supports (D). Scientists are actually quite optimistic about the species' reproductive future, which eliminates (A). Choice (B) is a true statement but is not the main idea. Choice (C) is also a true statement, but again is not the main idea of the passage.

19. **B** This question asks for a true statement based on the passage. The Mekong giant catfish is listed in the Guinness Book of World Records as the largest freshwater fish, though the freshwater stingray is also technically a fish. This makes (A) incorrect, but supports (B). Choice (C) is incorrect because rays eat other fish, not algae. Similarly, giant freshwater stingrays live to be 30–40 years old, not 10 years old, eliminating (D).

20. **(b), (d)**

    The Mekong giant catfish does not weigh 1,100 to 1,300 pounds, eliminating (a). The Guinness world record is true in (b). There is no support in the passage to state that the stingray preys upon the catfish specifically, eliminating (c), though it is stated in the ninth paragraph that the Mekong giant catfish lives in Thailand.

21. **B** Paragraph 15 talks about tagging and microchipping the stingrays. It states the scientists can track the ray's growth and movement, supporting (B). Neither (A) or (C) are mentioned in the text, and while the researchers try to reduce the rays' stress, their tags do not measure that stress, as (D) states.

22. **C** Paragraphs 14 and 15 state that Fishsiam has caught giant freshwater stingrays since the company partners with the scientists to catch and release the rays for research purposes, as (C) says. The passage does not say that Fishsiam does research, (A), or contributes technology, (B), or overfished the rays, (D).

23. **B** The passage states that the stingrays are not aggressive toward humans. This supports (B). Choice (A) is not stated in the passage. Choice (C) is a true fact, but it is not the reason for the quote in the box above question 23. Choice (D) is also true that the stingray is the size of a car, but that is not the reason for them being dangerous.

24. **(b), (c)**

The last three paragraphs talk about the endangered stingrays. They are threatened by pollution and there are no rules or regulations to protect them. The fact that they are venomous is not a contributing factor, eliminating (a). Choice (d) is not stated in the passage.

25. **A** This last statement is an optimistic piece of information to suggest that the species may bounce back. This supports (A). It does not illustrate the dwindling populations mentioned in (B). Choice (C) is not supported by the text, making it incorrect. Choice (D) is not supported by the text, even though it is not usually the desired catch of the fishermen.

26. **A** The article is focused on the way the sun produces energy, using the process of nuclear fusion. Choice (A), from paragraph 3, best summarizes this main idea. Choices (B), (C), and (D) are all details of the passage, but they do not communicate the main point of the passage.

27. **A** This detail question asks us to find a piece of information from the passages. As seen in the previous question, the author notes that nuclear fusion produces more energy than fission, which supports (A) and eliminates (C). Neither (B) nor (D) are cited as energy sources in the article.

28. **A** Paragraph 7 states that the Sun is primarily comprised of hydrogen, as in (A).

29. **D** In paragraph 3, the word "conversion" is being used in the sense of changing something into something else. In the answer choices, "renovation" and "overhaul" both describe only surface changes, not the deep change that converting hydrogen to helium entails, so you can eliminate both (A) and (B). Choice (C), "exchange," means a switching of one for the other, which is not what the text shows. So, (D) is the best answer.

30. **(b), (d)**

Choice (a) is not mentioned in the passage, and (c) is extreme. Choices (b) and (d) are both supported by the passage.

31. **B** The passage says the 60% hydrogen estimate was "too conservative," so you need a word that means moderate, or timid, or not excessive. Choice (B) has this meaning, whereas the other options refer to other definitions of "conservative," instead of the one used here.

32. **C** The last sentence predicts that the Sun will continue to burn with these types of reactions into the future. Choice (A) shows that the Sun is old, but that is not the purpose of the sentence. Choice (B) is too broad and is not supported by the sentence, which is about length of time rather than frequency. Choice (C) is supported. Choice (D) is not supported, because the sentence doesn't refer to strength of energy.

33. **(a), (e)**

    Choice (a) is found in paragraph 6, making it a true statement. Choices (b), (c), and (d) are not supported by the passage. Choice (e) is found in paragraph 8.

34. **A** The passage talks about how the climate change is causing more pollen to be produced, which means more allergic reactions in humans. This supports (B). Choice (A) is close, noting that the plants grow more vigorously, but it lacks any reference to climate change, which is a key part of the main idea. Choice (C) is incorrect because the article argues the opposite. Choice (D) offers advice on how to deal with pollen but has nothing to do with why that pollen is produced, so it is not the main point of the passage.

35. **(a), (d)**

    Choice (a) is mentioned in paragraph 5. Choice (b) is not true because the passage states that the pollen bees carry (that is, the pollen from flowers) does not generally trigger allergy symptoms (paragraph 12). Choice (c) is too strong and predicts the future. Choice (d) is supported in paragraph 7. Hookworms are introduced as a joke at the end of the passage, making (e) incorrect.

36. **C** Paragraphs 7 to 9 predict what may happen in the future to the increase of pollen spread and its effects on people in the future. Choice (A) is too strong because it contains "inevitably." Choice (B) is a true statement, but it is not the reason for the author to include the boxed sentence in the passage. Choice (D) is incorrect according to the passage.

37. **C** In the paragraph, "contemporary" refers to what's happening at the present, so (C), current is a good fit. Choices (A) and (B) refer to style choices, but you're looking for the scientific reality, so you can eliminate these. Choice (D), ongoing, doesn't work because the present pollen situation is different than previous ones.

38. **A** The boxed sentence states that the immune system should not really react to pollen the way that it does. This supports (A), that it is an unlikely irritant. It does not argue against the body's reaction, eliminating (B). There is not an earlier argument as in (C), and (D) is off topic.

39. **(a), (c)**

    Choice (a) is supported in paragraph 6. Choice (b) is not supported by the article. Choice (c) is also supported by paragraph 6. Choice (d) is not mentioned by the passage.

40. **B** The author includes another credible source to add validity to her claims. This supports (B). Choice (A) is incorrect because the passage does not show the opposite side to the argument. Choice (C) is not mentioned anywhere in the passage, nor is there a product mentioned in the passage as in (D).

41. **D** The author concludes with an ironic joke that a hookworm would potentially alleviate allergy symptoms, even though it is a terrible idea! Choice (A) takes this suggestion seriously, so it is incorrect. Choice (B) is an incorrect statement and is unsupported by the article. Choice (C) is true, but it is a very dangerous option that the author does not recommend, and not the reason for including that sentence.

42. **B** Roosevelt includes his travel descriptions to describe the beauty and scenery he is passing. This does not support (A), though it is mentioned later in the passage. Choice (B) works. Choice (C) is not supported by the passage, since Roosevelt's descriptions don't involve the size of the nation. Choice (D) is incorrect because he is uncertain he is going to win the election.

43. **A** The phrase "a blaze" is being used to describe the bright colors of the foliage, as if the yellows and reds of the flowers and leaves were a fire. This supports (A), aglow. The other choices refer to an actual fire, but Roosevelt is using a metaphor rather than talking about a literal "blaze."

44. **D** The phrase "You could beat him" is a side comment to Kermit about Dan Moore's tennis abilities. This supports (D). Choice (A) is too literal and therefore incorrect. Choice (B) is incorrect because it is not betraying anyone's trust. Choice (C) is incorrect because Roosevelt does not compare all the other players' abilities, only Moore's.

45. **C** The first sentence of paragraph 3 supports (C), that they are alone between visitors. Choice (A) is too strong, since Roosevelt devotes some time and energy to people other than his wife, even if he prefers her. While (B) is an assumption one might make, there are no references to actual diplomacy explicitly stated in the passage, so this choice is incorrect. Finally, there is no support for (D), making it incorrect as well.

46. **C** When Roosevelt refers to *we* in paragraph 3, he is referring to himself and Mother. He mentions other people who come to visit, but when they leave and he is alone with someone else, it is mother. Choice (C) is correct.

47. **(c), (d)**

Roosevelt is uncertain about the election, so the options must be about the election, eliminating (a), (b), and (e). Therefore, (c) and (d) are correct.

48. **D** The boxed sentence acknowledges the good times the family has had in the White House thus far, and that Roosevelt is thankful for those experiences, which supports (D). Choice (A) is correct until "enjoyed the company of such esteemed diplomats" which are not mentioned in the passage. Since it is partially wrong, the entire choice must be eliminated. Choice (B) is off topic with his tennis partners, who are only mentioned as part of his travels, not his stay in the White House. Choice (C) is unsupported because it does not say that Roosevelt will concede the election. Therefore, (D) is correct.

49. **(a), (b)**

Since the letter is addressed to Kermit, he is not with Roosevelt, supporting (a). Choice (b) is true since it states that Mother is travelling with Roosevelt, Mother being Kermit's mother and Roosevelt's wife. Choices (c) and (d) are both unsupported by the text.

50. Drop-Down Item 1: **gym, Fit and Fun,**

Option 4 is correct because the gym's name is unnecessary information, as it is stated in the address and the sentence would still be understood without the name inclusion. When unnecessary information is included, it must be offset with a pair of commas. If it is necessary, then no commas are needed.

Drop-Down Item 2: **it has been well cared for and clean, and the staff has been very friendly.**

This question tests the intended meaning of a sentence. Option 1 is correct because it distinguishes the staff as being friendly and the gym as being clean and well cared for. Option 2 omits the staff from the sentence and therefore refers to the gym as being friendly instead of the people who work there. Option 3 is incorrect because the staff is also clean and well cared for instead of the gym, which changes the original meaning of the sentence. Option 4 contains tense issues because it should not be in the past.

Drop-Down Item 3: **Similarly,**

The previous sentence and the current sentence are similar in nature, so the transitional word should suggest similarity. Option 1 would be a cause and effect relationship. Option 2 would instead offer a contrast. Finally, option 4 is a concession or transition to allow an exception.

Drop-Down Item 4: **I would like to reiterate that**

Option 1 is correct because it continues with the present tense and is in keeping with the polite tone of the letter. It should not be in the future tense, and *that* needs to be included in the answer.

MATHEMATICAL REASONING

Part 1

1. **D** To add fractions, they must have the same denominator. Start by finding a common denominator using the least common multiple. The LCM of 5 and 4 is 20. Think: $\frac{1}{5} = \frac{?}{20}$. $5 \times 4 = 20$, so do 1×4 on the top row to get $\frac{1}{5} = \frac{4}{20}$. Do the same for the other fraction: $\frac{3}{4} = \frac{?}{20}$. Since $4 \times 5 = 20$, multiply the top by 5 to get $\frac{15}{20}$. Thus, add $\frac{4}{20} + \frac{15}{20}$ to get the answer, which is (D).

2. **C** Distance is always positive units, even when the numbers themselves are negative. Therefore, (A) and (B) can't be correct. Point B is at –5.5 and point D is at –1. Since distance is positive, you can think about it like the distance, or difference, between 1 and 5.5, which is 4.5. Or, do $-1 - (-5.5)$, which equals 4.5. One other option is to consider that from point B to 0 is 5.5 units, so to –1 it must be less than that.

3. The value of $\left(\frac{1}{4}\right)^2$ is **less than** the value of $\sqrt{\frac{1}{4}}$.

Start by finding the value of $\left(\frac{1}{4}\right)^2$, which is the same as $\frac{1}{4} \times \frac{1}{4} = \frac{1}{16}$. Simply multiply straight across the top and bottom. Next find the value of $\sqrt{\frac{1}{4}}$. To take the square root of a fraction, square root the top and bottom. The square root of 1 is 1 and the square root of 4 is 2, so the result is $\frac{1}{2}$. Since $\frac{1}{2}$ is greater than $\frac{1}{16}$, the first expression is less than the second. Note that unlike positive whole numbers, positive fractions become smaller when put to a power and greater when put under a root.

4. **0.43**

Consider Process of Elimination. The decimal must be greater than 0.421, so that eliminates 0.34, since it has a 3 in the tenths place, and 0.4121, since it has a 1 in the hundredths place. Keep in mind that unlike whole numbers, a longer decimal isn't necessarily bigger. You have to compare the numbers in each place. The decimal must also be less than 0.45, which eliminates 0.54, since it has a 5 in the tenths place, and 0.451 because it has a 1 in the thousandths place, making it just a bit greater than 0.45, which has a 0 in the thousandths place. 0.43 is the only decimal remaining.

5. **C** First square 4, which is $4 \times 4 = 16$. Then take the square root of 9, which is 3, because $3 \times 3 = 9$. Now add $16 + 3$ to get 19.

Part 2

6. **C** Get x by itself by multiplying both sides by 2 to get $x \le 2$. Choice (C) shows this correctly because the line is shaded to the left of 2 and 2 has a closed circle, which is used for $\le$, showing that 2 is allowed. An open circle would be used for $<$.

7. **D** Use the equation of a line $y = mx + b$. Fill in m, which is the slope: $y = -\frac{1}{3}x + b$. Now fill in the x and y from the point provided: $5 = -\frac{1}{3}(0) + b$, and thus $b = 5$. Now the complete formula is $y = -\frac{1}{3}x + 5$. Another good option is to eliminate any answer choice that has the slope incorrect and then plug in the point to see which equation it works in.

8. **D** First expand the expression: $(x + 3)^2$ is the same as $(x + 3)(x + 3)$. Always write this out first and do not just square the first term and square the second term—that will result in an incorrect answer. Thus, (A) is equivalent because it's the expanded form. Now use FOIL on the two sets of parentheses to get $x^2 + 6x + 9$. Everything is still being multiplied by 2, so (C) is equivalent. Now multiply everything by 2 to get $2x^2 + 12x + 18$, so (B) is equivalent. Choice (D) is the odd one out that is not equivalent.

9. **D** The question asks about probability, which is written as a fraction: the thing you want over the total. What you want is plain cheese or mushroom, since that's what Amanda likes. First find the number of plain cheese. Add the numbers provided: $3 + 2 + 1 = 6$, so that leaves 2 plain cheese. Add that to the mushroom, 3, to get a total of 5 slices that Amanda likes out of 8 total, resulting in an answer of 5/8.

10. **Range: 11. Average: 7.2.**

   The range refers to the difference between the greatest and least numbers. Make sure to use the numbers that are actually represented on the graph. The highest bar goes to 13, and the lowest goes to 2, so the range is $13 - 2 = 11$. To find the average, add up all the numbers and divide by the number of numbers. $13 + 9 + 2 + 8 + 4 = 36$, and $36 \div 5 = 7.2$.

11. **B** Put in 76 for B, the total number of books he read. The equation becomes $76 = 12 + 2L$. First subtract 12 from both sides to get $64 = 2L$. Now divide by 2 to get $L = 32$.

12. **B** First convert to the smallest units, which is ounces. 3 pounds $\times$ 16 ounces in a pound = 48 ounces in each bag. Now find the number of ounces needed: 2 ounces per roll $\times$ 80 rolls = 160 ounces. Lastly, divide 160 ounces needed by 48 ounces in each bag to get about 3.33 bags. This makes the answer 4 bags because 3 bags will not be enough.

13. **C** Since this is a right triangle, use the Pythagorean Theorem to find the missing side. The formula is $a^2 + b^2 = c^2$, and remember that a and b represent the two short sides and c is the long side. Thus, here it is $12^2 + b^2 = 37^2$. It's fine to switch a and b but just make sure that 37 is in place of c since it's the long side. Then calculate: $144 + b^2 = 1,369$. Subtract 144 to get $b^2 = 1,225$ and take the square root of both sides to get $b = 35$.

14. **B** To multiply two sets of two things in parentheses (binomials), you must use FOIL, which stands for First, Outside, Inside, Last. Start by multiplying the First term in each set of parentheses: $2x \cdot x = 2x^2$. Next, multiply the terms on the Outside of the parentheses: $2x \cdot -3 = -6x$. Next, multiply the terms on the Inside of the parentheses: $2 \cdot x = 2x$. Next, multiply the Last term in each set of parentheses: $2(-3) = -6$. Put it all together: $2x^2 - 6x + 2x - 6$. Combine like terms to get $2x^2 - 4x - 6$.

15. **D** The equation of a line is $y = mx + b$. The first thing to find is the slope, m. Find it using the formula $m = \dfrac{y_2 - y_1}{x_2 - x_1}$. Here, that is $\dfrac{8 - 6}{-3 - 1} = \dfrac{2}{-4} = -\dfrac{1}{2}$. Now the equation is $y = -\dfrac{1}{2}x + b$. Plug in the coordinates of one of the points for x and y to solve for b. Use the easier one, $(1, 6)$: $6 = -\dfrac{1}{2}(1) + b$. Then $6 = -\dfrac{1}{2} + b$ and $b = 6.5$ or $\dfrac{13}{2}$. The final equation is $y = -\dfrac{1}{2}x + \dfrac{13}{2}$. Another, easier option is to simply plug in the points for x and y into the answer choices to find the equation in which both points work.

16. **16** Use the formula for volume of a cone, which is $V = \dfrac{1}{3}r^2h$. Fill in what is provided: $V = \dfrac{1}{3}\left(\dfrac{1}{2}\right)^2(3)$. Simplify to get $V = \dfrac{1}{4}$. That's the volume of one cone, but the problem asks about the volume of 20 cones, so multiply $\dfrac{1}{4}$ by 20 to get a total volume of 5. Using the button on the calculator or 3.14 results in about 15.7, which rounds up to 16.

17. **C** Calculate slope by using the formula $m = \dfrac{y_2 - y_1}{x_2 - x_1}$, using any two of the points provided. Try $(0, 2)$ and $(2, 5)$. The formula is $\dfrac{5 - 2}{2 - 0} = \dfrac{3}{2}$.

18. **C** Get z by itself. Simply divide both sides by $4y$ to get $z = \dfrac{y + 2}{4y}$.

19. **Median: 4. Mean: 5.**

The median is the middle number when the list is in ascending order. Start by writing the list in order: 0, 1, 2, 4, 7, 9, 12. Find the number in the middle, which is 4. That's the median. Now find the mean, which is another name for the average. Add up all the numbers and divide by 7, the number of numbers. The total of the numbers is 35, and 35 divided by 7 is 5, so the mean is 5.

20. **C** There are two good ways to do this. One is numerical: Draw blanks for each event, which here means three blanks. There are three options for her first exercise, so put 3 in the first blank. Then she's not going to do

the same exercise over again, so there are 2 options left for the second blank, and by the same reasoning, 1 for the third blank. This kind of problem always uses multiplication, so multiply $3 \times 2 \times 1 = 6$. Another easier way is to simply write out the combinations, since there are only 3 events. Use R for run, L for lift weights, and S for stretch. The combinations are RLS, RSL, LRS, LSR, SRL, and SLR. Just be sure to write down the combinations in order so you know you aren't forgetting any.

21. **A** Since the problem mentions area, use the formula for area of a circle: $A = \pi r^2$. Fill in 256π for A and solve for r by canceling out the π on both sides and then taking the square root of 256, which is 16. This makes the radius 16.

22. **C** To solve an inequality, get the variable by itself. To do that here, subtract 80 from both sides to get $-40 \le -d \le -15$. Now, multiply everything by -1 to make the $-d$ positive. The key rule to remember is that with inequalities, when you multiply or divide by a negative number, the greater than or less than signs flip to the other direction. Thus, this becomes $40 \ge d \ge 15$, or as would more commonly be written, $15 \le d \le 40$. This should make sense because if Jamal leaves behind \$15, he will be left with \$65, the maximum he is allowed to take. Any number between 15 and 40 inclusive will allow him to have an acceptable amount of money left. With inequalities, it's always a good idea to guess and check numbers to make sure your answer makes sense.

23. **B** There are many ways to solve this. One is to use the formula provided, which is in the form $y = mx + b$. In the formula, b represents the y-intercept, which is where the line crosses the y-axis (vertical) In this formula, the y-intercept is 4. Check the answer choices. Choice (A) crosses at 4, so keep it. Same with (B) and (C). Choice (D) crosses at 0, so eliminate it. Now consider m in the equation, which represents the slope. Here the slope is 1/2, which means up 1 and to the right 2 since slope is rise over run. For (A), look at the x-intercept, $(-2, 0)$. You have to go to the right 2 and up 4 to get to the next easy point, which is $(0, 4)$. That is a slope of 4/2 (rise over run), which equals 2, not 1/2. Eliminate it. For (B), look at the points $(0, 4)$ and $(2, 5)$. The graph goes right 2 and up 1, which is a slope of 1/2. This makes (B) correct. Choice (C) has a slope of 1 because going from $(-4, 0)$ to $(0, 4)$ goes up 4 and right 4, resulting in a slope of $4/4 = 1$. Another good option to solve is to find a point on the line by plugging in an x-value and then looking for it in the graphs, or draw the line yourself using two or more points on the line and seeing which choice looks like your drawing.

24. **15** Create two equations, using two variables. To keep it simple, use c for the number of crates and b for the number of bags. The first equations is $10c + 6b = 276$, and the second is $5c + 2b = 117$. The simplest way to solve this system of equations is to stack them and add or subtract to get rid of one of the variables. Notice that the first equation has $10c$ and the second has $5c$, so multiply everything in the second equation by 2: $10c + 4b = 234$. Now both equations have $10c$ and you can subtract them to get rid of the variable c, like so:

$$
\begin{array}{r}
10c + 6b = 276 \\
- \underline{(10c + 4b = 234)} \\
0 + 2b = 42
\end{array}
$$

Next, if $2b = 42$, divide by 2 to get $b = 21$. That's the number of diapers in a bag. The question asks for how many in a crate, so substitute 21 for b in one of the equations: $10c + 6(21) = 276$. Solve normally to get $c = 15$, which is the answer. It is also possible to solve the system of equations using substitution rather than stacking, but in this case, neither equation makes it easy to get either c or b alone, so it's the

25. **Width: 13. Perimeter: 58.**

First start with the area of a rectangle formula, $A = L \times W$, since the area is provided. Fill in the area and the length: $208 = 16 \times W$. Now divide by 16 to find that the width is 13. Then to find the perimeter, add all the sides or use the formula $P = 2L + 2W$. $16 + 16 + 13 + 13 = 58$.

26. **B** Since both terms have the 10 to the same power, the terms may be added together. $5.4 + 6.3 = 11.7$. Thus, this equals 11.7×10^{12}. Note that the power does not change because this is addition, not multiplication. However, scientific notation requires the first number to have only one digit before the decimal point, which means the decimal point must be moved one place to the left to get 1.17, but this means the 10^{12} increases to 10^{13} to absorb the 10 that was divided out by the first term. This makes the answer 1.17×10^{13}.

27. **C** Anytime you see an x^2 and an x in the same equation, it's a quadratic equation. Since there are answer choices, one option is to plug in each possibility and see which work and which don't. Another option is to factor the equation, and solve it that way. In order to do that, the expression must equal 0, so get everything on the left side. Here, subtract 32 to get $x^2 - 4x - 32 = 0$. Now factor. Draw two sets of parentheses and put x in both: $(x\ )(x\ )$. Now think of numbers that multiply together to equal 32 and add or subtract to equal 4. 16 and 2 won't work, but 8 and 4 do. Now it is $(x\ 8)(x\ 4)$. Since it's -32, there must be one positive and one negative. To get a -4, it must be -8 and $+4$, like so: $(x - 8)(x + 4) = 0$. It's always a good idea to FOIL what you got to make sure it equals what you started with, which it does here. In order for this to equal 0, either the first set of parentheses equals 0 or the second set does. If $x - 8 = 0$, then $x = 8$. If $x + 4 = 0$, then $x = -4$. The answer is $x = 8$ or $x = -4$.

28. **C** This is written as $168 + 40d$ because 168 is the number she's already read—it doesn't change. She reads more of the book, so it's addition, and it's 40 pages for every d days. Also consider how you would solve this with an actual number. After three days, she's read $168 + 40 + 40 + 40$ or $168 + 40(3)$. This helps show why (C) is correct.

29. **B** Set up a proportion with the same units on both sides: $\dfrac{4 \text{ boys}}{5 \text{ girls}} = \dfrac{x \text{ boys}}{20 \text{ girls}}$. Cross-multiply to get $5x = 80$, and divide by 8 to get $x = 16$ boys.

30. **$f(5) = 15. f(0) = 5. f(-2) = 1.$**

To find $f(5)$, substitute 5 for x: $2(5) + 5 = 10 + 5 = 15$. $f(0) = 2(0) + 5 = 0 + 5 = 5$. $f(-2) = 2(-2) + 5 = -4 + 5 = 1$.

31.

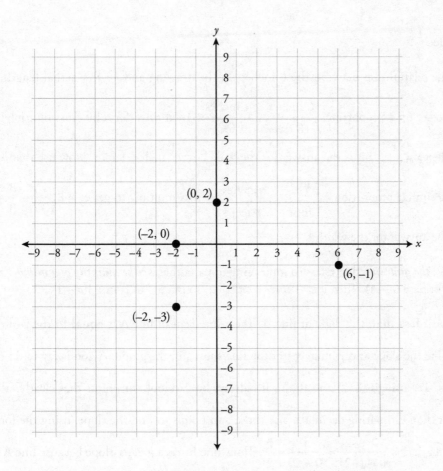

A table is just another way of writing the coordinates. The points are (0, 2), (–2, 0), (6, –1), and (–2, –2). The *x*-coordinate comes first, so from the origin (0,0) go the appropriate number of spaces to the right or left (right is positive and left is negative) and then go up or down the number of spaces in the *y*-coordinate (up is positive and down is negative).

32. **D** The answer is (D) because $2.50 times the number of lawns she mows plus $7.50 times the number of hours she babysits must equal at least $35, since that is the amount that she needs for her ticket. Thus, it must be greater than or equal to 35.

33. **D** To factor, first set up two sets of parentheses. Since the first term is x^2, the first thing in both parentheses is x: $(x\ \ )(x\ \ )$. The last term is –45, and the second term includes a 4. Think of two numbers that multiply to equal 45 and add or subtract to equal 4. 45 and 1 won't work, but 9 and 5 work. Fill those in: $(x\ \ 9)(x\ \ 5)$. Since it's a –45, there must be one plus sign and one minus sign. To get a negative 4 for the second term, it must be –9 and +5, as shown: $(x – 9)(x + 5)$. Always use FOIL to check that your answer equals the thing you started with. Another option for a multiple-choice problem such as this is to simply use FOIL on each answer choice and see which one equals the original expression. If you don't feel great about factoring but feel comfortable using FOIL, this is a great option.

34. **Width:** $2\frac{2}{3}$. **Scale:** $\frac{1}{3}$.

First determine the relationship between the 6 inches on the drawing and 18 feet actual length. One good strategy is to set up a proportion: $\dfrac{6 \text{ inches}}{18 \text{ feet}} = \dfrac{x \text{ inches}}{1 \text{ foot}}$. Then solve for x by cross-multiplying to get $6 = 18x$ and then $x = \dfrac{1}{3}$. This is the answer for the scale box: $\dfrac{1}{3}$ inch = 1 foot. Now use that to find the width, using a similar proportion: $\dfrac{\frac{1}{3} \text{ inch}}{1 \text{ foot}} = \dfrac{x \text{ inches}}{8 \text{ feet}}$. Cross-multiply to get $x = 8\left(\dfrac{1}{3}\right) = \dfrac{8}{3} = 2\dfrac{2}{3}$ inches, which is the answer for the width.

35. **A** When a phrase says *the quantity*, that refers to something in parentheses. *The quantity of a number minus one* means $(x - 1)$ or here $(a - 1)$. Then it says *three times* that, so put a 3 in front: $3(a - 1)$.

36. The slope of line A is **less than** the slope of line B. The y-intercept of line A is **equal to** the y-intercept of line B. Determine the slope and y-intercept of the line shown in the graph. A good way to do this is to find two points. Try using $(-2, 2)$ and $(0, 5)$. It's always best to look for points that clearly fall in a certain spot rather than estimating decimals. Use those two points to find the slope, using the formula $m = \dfrac{y_2 - y_1}{x_2 - x_1}$. Here, that is $\dfrac{5 - 2}{0 - (-2)} = \dfrac{3}{0 + 2} = \dfrac{3}{2}$. Thus, line B has a greater slope because line A has a slope of $\dfrac{2}{3}$ (m in $y = mx + b$). The y-intercept is clear from the figure: The line crosses the y-axis at 5. Line A also has a y-intercept of 5 because 5 is in the spot of b in the formula $y = mx + b$. Thus, the y-intercepts are equal.

37. **D** Substitute -4 for q. First find $2q$ or $2(-4) = -8$. Now the problem is $8 - (-8)$. Be very careful with the negatives. Two negatives equal a positive, so this is actually $8 + 8 = 16$.

38. **C** Start by calculating how much is left after the state tax. Take 12% of 5,000 by doing $5{,}000 \times 0.12 = \$600$. Subtract that amount since it is paid in taxes to get that there is \$4,400 left. That goes into the account and earns 2% interest after one year, so calculate the interest by doing $0.02 \times 4{,}400$ to get \$88 in interest. This is added to the amount in the account, so $\$4{,}400 + \$88 = \$4{,}488.00$.

39. **C** The rule for a function is it cannot repeat x-values with different y-values. Choices (A), (B), and (D) all do this, so they are not functions. Choice (C) has four distinct x-values.

40. **A** The key here is to know that a square has sides that are parallel. It may be helpful to draw the line $y = 8$. It's a horizontal line. If that's the top of the square, the bottom of the square is also a horizontal line. Since the side of the square is 4, the bottom of the square is 4 units down, so it is at $y = 4$.

41. **Point A is the *x*-intercept. Point B is the *y*-intercept.**

The *x*-intercept is where the line crosses the *x*-axis, and the *y*-intercept is where the line crosses the *y*-axis. The words "slope" and "range" cannot describe a single point, and maximum and minimum cannot describe anything on a straight line because a line goes on forever in two directions.

42. **7.96**

Start by calculating the cost of 4 packs of spaghetti by doing $0.87 × 4, which equals $3.48. Then, do $1.12 × 4 to find the cost of 4 jars of sauce, which equals $4.48. Then add $3.48 + $4.48 to get an answer of $7.96.

43. **D** First carefully distribute the –3: $12 - 2x = 8x - 3x - 3$. Now combine like terms: $12 - 2x = 5x - 3$, and then $15 = 7x$, so $x = 15/7$.

44. **D** To find the cost per fluid ounce, divide the cost by the number of fluid ounces for each detergent size. Mini is about $3.99 ÷ 8 = $0.50 per fluid ounce. Do the same for the other sizes to get $0.37 for Regular, $0.33 for Large, and $0.31 for Jumbo. Thus, Jumbo costs the least per fluid ounce.

45. **B** Anytime you see an x^2 and an x in the same equation, it's a quadratic and you should factor it. In order to do that, the expression must equal 0, so get everything on the left side. Here, subtract 21 to get $x^2 + 4x - 21 = 0$. Now factor. Draw two sets of parentheses and put x in both: $(x\ \ )(x\ \ )$. Now think of numbers that multiply together to equal 21 and add or subtract to equal 4. 21 and 1 won't work, but 7 and 3 do. Now it is $(x\ \ 7)(x\ \ 3)$. Since it's –21, there must be one positive and one negative. To get a +4, it must be +7 and –3, like so: $(x + 7)(x - 3) = 0$. It's always a good idea to FOIL what you got to make sure it equals what you started with, which it does here. In order for this to equal 0, either the first set of parentheses equals 0 or the second set does. If $x + 7 = 0$, then $x = -7$. If $x - 3 = 0$, then $x = 3$. The answer is $x = -7$ or $x = 3$. One other option is to plug in the numbers from the answer choices to see which ones will solve the equation correctly. This could even be a faster option.

46. **D** Another way of referring to the slope is to say the rate of change, or just the rate here. The rate is 50 sheets per 10 minutes, or $\frac{50}{10}$ sheets/minute, which equals 5 sheets/minute. That is the rate. A rate is always expressed as something over something else. Another way of thinking about it is to plug in 50 for *y* and 10 for *x* and solve for *m*.

SOCIAL STUDIES

1. **B** In the quote, James Madison discusses the importance of the separation of powers within the government so that "no one could transcend their legal limits, without being effectually checked and restrained by the others." This principle is referred to as "checks and balances," (B). Popular sovereignty, (A), refers to the principle that the government's authority is derived from the people; federalism, (C), refers to the relationship between the federal government and the states; judicial review, (D), refers to the process by which the Supreme Court reviews the legality of congressional acts.

2. **D** One of the major differences between the American form of government and the parliamentary systems of countries such as the United Kingdom is that in parliamentary systems, the executive derives its authority from the legislature, (D). Choices (A), (B), and (C) are not true statements.

3. **D** In Source 1, George Washington warns of the dangers of factionalism and political parties and states that such divisions can lead to despotism. In Source 2, Thomas Jefferson notes that political parties have arisen in the United States and that the relationship between those parties is quite contentious. Washington would therefore have a very negative view of the situation described by Jefferson. The only answer choice with a negative connotation is (D).

4. **A** In Source 2, Jefferson states that one party believes that "the Executive is the branch of our Government which the most needs support," i.e., that the Executive should be strengthened, while the other party believes that the Executive branch "is already too strong." It can be inferred, therefore, that the two parties described by Jefferson disagree about the amount of power that should be given to the Executive branch, (A).

5.

Federalists	Democratic-Republicans
(b) favored a strong central government	(a) favored a limited central government
(c) favored a national bank	(d) opposed a national bank
(f) loose interpretation of the Constitution	(e) strict interpretation of the Constitution

In the late 18th century, the Federalists were the party that favored a strong central government, (b), a national bank, (c), and a loose interpretation of the Constitution, (f). The Democratic-Republicans, on the other hand, favored a limited central government (a), opposed a national bank, (d), and held the view that the Constitution must be interpreted strictly, (e). There are many differences, but in general it can be said that in their own ways, both the modern Republican party and the modern Democratic party grew out of what used to be called the Democratic-Republican party.

6. **D** The map clearly indicates a division between the northern (and west coast) states and the southern states. This division must be related to differences over slavery in the years immediately preceding the Civil War, (D).

7. One of the events that immediately followed the start of the American war in Afghanistan was **the opening of the Guantanamo Bay detention camp in Cuba**.

Following the terrorist attacks of September 11, 2001, the Bush administration along with American allies launched a war in Afghanistan, with the aim of defeating the Taliban and denying Al Qaeda a territory in which to organize and train. Prisoners from this war were often transferred from Afghanistan to **the Guantanamo Bay detention camp in Cuba**, which was opened in 2002. The **killing of Osama bin Laden** occurred in 2011. The **creation of the terrorist group ISIS** occurred when members broke off from Al Qaeda in 2004. The **election of Barack Obama** occurred in 2008.

8. **C** The United States entered World War I in April of 1917, (C). Because of the war effort, the government needed to spend a huge sum of money on supplies, weapons, etc. The government's spending on defense (i.e., the military) jumped in 1917 and only began to drop again in 1919 after the war had ended.

9. **28** The pie chart in Source 2 indicates that the U.S. government spending on health care in 2016 accounts for 28% of all federal spending.

10.   Each of the following is responsible for a key component of establishing the federal budget EXCEPT **the Supreme Court**.

The process by which the federal government creates a budget is that the president submits a budget request to Congress, after which the House and Senate must approve the president's budget. The House and Senate try to come to an agreement over any disputes about how the money should be spent, and then the president signs off on the finished budget and it becomes law. The **Supreme Court** is not involved in this process.

11.   The sentiment expressed by Jane Addams in the source given in the question most clearly reflects the aspirations of **the women's suffrage movement**.

The demand for increased political rights for American women began in earnest in the middle of the 19th century, but it was not until the early 20th century that women in the United States began to see widespread tangible results of their movement. Efforts of activists such as Jane Addams and her peers in **the women's suffrage movement** eventually resulted in the 1920 passing of the 19th Amendment to the Constitution, which forbade voting discrimination on the basis of sex.

12. **B** During the Constitutional Convention in 1787, northern and southern states debated whether and how to include slaves in the population count (which would then determine how many representatives each state would have in Congress and how those states would be taxed), (B). The so-called "three-fifths compromise" meant that a slave would be counted as three fifths of a person rather than as a whole person.

13. **C** According to the graph, the area with the greatest change in very heavy precipitation is the northeast, (C), with a 71% increase.

14. **A** An increase in heavy precipitation events, which is currently occurring in all areas of the United States except Hawaii, presents the threat of flooding, (B), which can lead to landslides, (C), and crop destruction, (D). Earthquakes, (A), are caused by shifts in tectonic plates under the surface of the Earth and are not affected by rain or snow.

15.   The law that best exemplifies Lyndon Johnson's Great Society program is **the Civil Rights Act**.

Prior to his assassination in 1963, President John F. Kennedy had called for sweeping civil rights legislation. Despite a lot of resistance from Congress, Johnson was successfully able to push the legislation forward, resulting in **the Civil Rights Act** of 1964. This act prohibited segregation in public places and businesses, employment discrimination, and many other of the so-called Jim Crow laws that oppressed African Americans throughout the United States (and in particular in the south).

16. **D** Source 1 states that the president shall receive a "compensation" "for his services," meaning that the compensation is the president's payment or salary, (D), while he or she is in office.

17.   **Clinton**

President Bill Clinton was impeached in 1998 on the charges of perjury (lying before a federal grand jury) and obstruction of justice. He was ultimately not removed from office because the Senate failed to garner support from at least two thirds of the members present as required by the Constitution.

18.

Constitutional	Unconstitutional
(c), (e)	(a), (b), (d)

Source 2 states that in the event of a presidential impeachment hearing, the Chief Justice (of the Supreme Court) shall preside, making (a) unconstitutional. Source 2 states that the impeachment process shall only result in the removal of the accused from office and the prevention of the accused from holding future offices, making (b) unconstitutional (although criminal trials after the impeachment trial are allowed). Source 1 states that the vice president shall take up the office of the president in the event of the president's death, resignation, or incapacity, making (c) constitutional. Source 1 states that no one can be president without having lived in the United States for fourteen years, making (d) unconstitutional. Source 2 states that only two thirds of the members present at an impeachment trial must agree on the outcome, making (e) constitutional.

19. **D** If the person in question has his or her car seized for violating a contract, then the person must have put up his or her car as an asset—this is a form of secured credit. If the borrower is obligated to pay a fixed monthly amount, then this person has a non-revolving type of credit. The answer, therefore, must be (D).

20. The two sources given in the question contain principles that would later be reflected in **the First Amendment**.

The statute in Source 1 guarantees freedom of religion for the people of Virginia. The proclamation in Source 2, originally published as part of a campaign against a statewide tax in Virginia to fund Christian teachers and ministers, similarly suggests a concern for freedom of religion. These principles of freedom of religion are reflected in **the First Amendment**, particularly the so-called "Establishment Clause," which states that "Congress shall make no law respecting an establishment of religion, or prohibiting the free exercise thereof." **The Declaration of Independence** was adopted in 1776 and thus cannot be the correct answer. **The Jay Treaty** (1795) between the United States and England concerned trade. **The Emancipation Proclamation** (1863) changed the legal status of all African Americans from slave to free.

21. **B** Source 1 states that no one shall be forced to be a part of any particular religious belief or practice, nor shall anyone be prohibited from being a party of any particular religious belief or practice. Thus, in context, to "frequent" "any religious worship, place, or ministry" means to "visit habitually," (A), "associate with," (C), or "go often to," (D). To "disassociate from," (B), has the opposite meaning, and thus is the correct answer.

22. **A** Both Thomas Jefferson and James Madison were very active in the post-Revolution debates about the role of religion in the new nation. Jefferson was instrumental in disassociating Virginia from the Anglican Church. Both wanted to make sure that there were safeguards in place so that the United States would not establish any sort of state religion, (A), as was common in many parts of the world in the 18th century.

23. **C** The darker line on the graph represents the urban population of the United States, while the lighter line on the graph represents the rural population of the United States. In 1910, the lighter line is taller than the darker line, whereas in 1940 the darker line is taller than the lighter line. Therefore, the urban population must have surpassed the rural population sometime between 1910 and 1940, (C).

24. **D** The Industrial Revolution, (A), led to, among other things, mechanization and the emergence of the factory system. Since most factories needed a lot of employees, businesses typically based themselves in urban areas. Increased agricultural efficiency, (B), closely related to industrialization, meant that farms needed fewer workers. In the late 19th and early 20th century, many African Americans in particular moved to cities. New technologies in construction, (C), meant that taller buildings could be built, thus making it easier for large numbers of people to live in the same geographic area. Global warming and sea level rise, (D), have historically had nothing to do with trends in rural vs. urban populations.

25. The Cuban Missile crisis discussed by President Kennedy in the source given in the question was directly preceded by **the failure of the Bay of Pigs invasion**.

    The **Bay of Pigs invasion** was a failed attempt by the United States government to overthrow the regime of the Cuban communist leader Fidel Castro. In response to this invasion, the Soviet Union agreed to Cuba's request to station nuclear missiles in Cuba to deter American aggression, the events surrounding which were the closest the United States and the USSR came to nuclear confrontation during the Cold War. The **Berlin airlift** and the **formation of NATO** occurred in the years immediately following World War II; the **dissolution of the Soviet Union** occurred in 1991.

26. **A** Containment, (A), refers to the notion that one country can use diplomatic or military strategies to prevent another country from expanding its territory or ideology. Within the context of the Cuban Missile Crisis, the American government was concerned about the spread of communism in Cuba under Fidel Castro and therefore attempted to overthrow his regime in 1961. Libertarianism, (B), is a political philosophy that emphasizes freedom of choice; decentralization, (C), is a policy that favors moving power away from a centralized authority; pacifism, (D), is an ideology that espouses non-violence.

27. **C** In Source 1, as education levels increase, unemployment decreases. In Source 2, as education levels increase, so too do median weekly earnings. Therefore, the answer is (C).

28. **C** Source 2 clearly indicates that the median weekly earnings of a person with a bachelor's degree is somewhere between $1,000 and $1,200, making (C) the best answer.

29. **B** Article II of the Constitution states that "The President...shall have Power, by and with the Advice and Consent of the Senate, to make Treaties, provided two thirds of the Senators present concur," (B).

30. **D** At the end of the 19th century, the U.S. government transferred public land all over the country to major railroad companies in order to promote railroad construction for transportation of goods as well as people, (D). The fact that the shaded portions of the map primarily follow and east-west route for extremely long distances (mainly in the less heavily populated western half of the country) should be a hint that (D) is the best answer.

31. The passage in the question is an excerpt from the **13th** Amendment to the United States Constitution.

    The source provides a quotation regarding the abolition of slavery in the United States, part of the **13th** Amendment to the Constitution (1865). The **2nd** Amendment (1791) concerns the right to keep and bear arms; the **7th** Amendment (1791) concerns an individual's right to trial by jury; the **21st** Amendment (1933) repealed the prohibition on alcohol implemented by the 18th Amendment (1919).

32. **C** The fact that the source concerns the abolition of slavery and involuntary servitude indicates that it must have been written in the period immediately following the Civil War known as the Reconstruction Era, (C). The Revolutionary Era, (A), in the late 18th century was much too early for any discussion of the abolition of slavery. The Era of Good Feelings, (B), refers to the period of optimism and unity that followed the end of the War of 1812, long before the abolition of slavery. The Progressive Era, (D), refers to the period of social and political reform that occurred in the late 19th and early 20th centuries, several decades after the abolition of slavery.

33. The author of Source 1 would most likely disagree that **men and women should have equal opportunities in employment**.

    Justice Bradley, the author of Source 1, holds a very traditionalist and patriarchal view regarding the respective roles of men and women in American society. He states that nature has decreed that women are timid and gentle, need protection, and should stay within the domestic sphere. Therefore, he would most likely disagree that **men and women should have equal opportunities in employment** (he explicitly notes his opinion that women are "unfit" "for many of the occupations of civil life").

34. **A** The black line on the chart, which shows the number of House Democrats, (A), in Congress in the years noted, is the tallest line in each of the years shown.

35. **B** According to the chart, there were 9 Democratic women senators and 5 Republican women senators in the 109th Congress. Since there are 100 senators total, these 14 women made up far less than 30% of the total number of senators, (B).

SCIENCE

1. **C** The first question requires you to determine what occurs when water moves from a liquid to a solid state. The passage states that a physical change may alter the form and properties of an object, but it will not alter the object's chemical composition. Thus, since water is still water (H_2O) regardless of its physical state, no chemical change has occurred.

2. **1** This question asks you to determine the number of sulfur molecules present both before and after the chemical reaction provided. According to the chemical equation $3F_2 + S \rightarrow SF_6$, one molecule of sulfur exists in both the reactants and products.

3. **reactants, product**

    The passage states that the molecules that are present before a chemical reaction are referred to as reactants, while the molecules that are present after a chemical reaction are referred to as products. Therefore, in the chemical equation provided, fluorine and sulfur are the reactants, while sulfur hexafluoride is the product.

4. **B** This question requires you to know definitions related to ecology, or the branch of biology that deals with the relations of organisms to one another and to their physical surroundings. A biome is a large, naturally occurring community of flora and fauna occupying a major habitat; eliminate (A). An ecosystem is a place where many organisms live and depend upon other organisms for survival; keep (B). A food web is a chart that shows the way that organisms pass energy from one to another; eliminate (C). A habitat is the natural home or environment of an animal, plant, or other organism; eliminate (D).

5. **C** This question requires you to use the equation given, $speed = \dfrac{distance}{time}$, to determine the time it will take a dog to travel 112 meters. Based on the chart provided, the speed of a dog is 28 m/s. Accordingly, the time it will take a dog to travel 112 meters is 28 m/s $= \dfrac{112\ m}{time}$, $time = \dfrac{112\ m}{28\ m/s}$, and $time = 4\ s$.

6. **7,040**

   This question requires you to use the equation given, *force = mass × acceleration*, to find the force of a wolf that accelerates at a rate of 44 m/s and has a mass of 160 lbs. Thus, the force of the wolf is *force* = 160 lbs × 44 m/s = 7,040 N.

7. **D** Here, the question stem states that terrestrial planets are those that have solid surfaces, and are located closest to the Sun. Your job is to identify the non-terrestrial planet. Given the graph of the planets, you will see that the planets closest to the Sun are Mercury, Venus, Earth, and Mars. Accordingly, Saturn is not a terrestrial planet.

8. This question requires you to identify the level on the energy pyramid that represents organisms with the smallest population sizes.

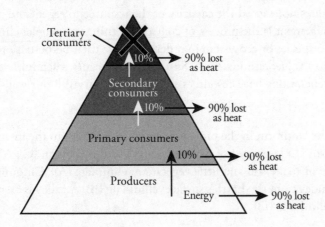

9. **A** This question requires you to use the energy pyramid to determine the amount of energy received by secondary consumers, if the producers consume 100 units of energy. According to the energy pyramid, 90% of the energy is lost as heat between levels, with only 10% moving onward as energy. Thus, if producers consume 100 units of energy, 10 units of energy will pass to the primary consumers. Of those 10 units the primary consumers consume, only 10% will pass to the secondary consumers. Therefore, if the producers consume 100 units of energy, only 1 unit of energy will be passed to the secondary consumers.

10. Here you are asked to arrange the groups of producers, primary consumers, secondary consumers, and tertiary consumers, in order from greatest to least, in terms of population size, energy consumption, and biomass. The passage states that producers are organisms with the greatest population sizes, and that the energy pyramid shows the flow of energy from greatest to least energy consumption. Accordingly, in order from greatest to least, in terms of population size, energy consumption, and biomass, you have **(c) producers, (b) primary consumers, (d) secondary consumers, and (a) tertiary consumers**.

11. **B**   Unlike many of the GED® questions, which require you to use provided information to answer questions, this GED® question requires that you have some background knowledge regarding chromosomal mutations. The question requires you to identify the type of mutation that occurs when chromosomes fail to separate properly during meiosis. First, you can eliminate (A) and (C), as they are not types of mutations. A non-disjunction mutation occurs when chromosomes fail to separate properly during meiosis, while a translocation mutation occurs when a chromosome breaks and the segment moves to another chromosome; thus, the correct answer is (B), and (D) can be eliminated.

12. **C**   This question requires you to identify the substance formed as a direct result of weathering and erosion. According to the image of the rock cycle, weathering and erosion directly leads to the creation of both sediments and sedimentary rocks. Accordingly, the correct answer is (C), sediments.

13.   **metamorphic, igneous**

In order to answer this question, you need to identify two types of rocks: those that are formed from the Earth's heat and pressure, and those that are formed by the cooling of magma. Based on the rock cycle graph, rocks that are formed from the Earth's heat and pressure are metamorphic rocks, while igneous rocks are formed by the cooling of magma.

14. **A**   This question requires you to identify the concept defined in the question stem. The management or regulation of a resource so that its use does not exceed the capacity of the resource to regenerate itself is known as conservation; keep (A). Management is the process of controlling things or people; eliminate (B). Preservation is the maintenance of a species or ecosystem in order to ensure their perpetuation, with no concern as to their potential monetary value; eliminate (C). Sustainability occurs when humans and nature exist in harmony, and future generations have resources necessary for survival and well-being; eliminate (D).

15. **C**   This question requires you to identify the landform in the provided image. In addition to the image, the question stem tells you that the landform is a large area of flat land; this describes a plain, (C). A desert is a large, dry, barren region with sandy or rocky soil and little vegetation; eliminate (A). A mountain is a large, tall rocky area of land that extrudes from the Earth's surface; eliminate (B). A valley is an area of low land between mountains or hills; eliminate (D).

16. **D**   Use your understanding of how humans affect ecosystems to answer this question. Eliminate all the good reasons La Grange's citizens might object to Bait-n-Hook's environmental impact, so use Process of Elimination and consider each answer choice. As La Grange is a small town, it is probable that overfishing has not occurred, but that would change when Bait-n-Hook sets up shop. Therefore, eliminate (A). A big business moving to town would cause population growth and bring with it more houses and commercial buildings, which would cause a loss of what had been open spaces. You can eliminate (B) as well, since this, too, is a valid concern. It's further likely that when Bait-n-Hook establishes itself on the Colorado River there would be increased pollution levels, both in town (associated with commercial manufacturing waste) and in the Colorado River (due to the waste drainage associated with commercial businesses). This lets you get rid of (C). Finally, while Bait-n-Hook's arrival in town would open up new jobs, and at least some of those jobs might be filled by people moving to La Grange, there's no solid reason to assume that any such newcomers would not respect the local ecology. So (D) is the strongest answer.

17. **B** In order to determine the percent of offspring that will be heterozygous when two heterozygous horses mate, construct a Punnett Square, as shown below.

	H	h
H	HH	Hh
h	Hh	hh

Based on the Punnett Square, you can see that the mating of two heterozygous horses (Hh) result in offspring of HH, Hh, Hh, and hh. Thus, 50% of the offspring from the mating of two heterozygous horses will be heterozygous.

18. **0** In order to determine the percent of offspring that will be homozygous recessive when two homozygous dominant horses mate, construct a Punnett Square, as shown below.

	H	H
H	HH	HH
H	HH	HH

Based on the Punnett Square, you can see that the mating of two homozygous dominant horses (HH) result in offspring of HH, HH, HH, and HH. Thus, 0% of the offspring from the mating of two homozygous dominant horses will be homozygous recessive.

19. **hard hooves, soft hooves**

In order to answer this question, consider the information that you found in the previous two questions. The first part of the question requires you to determine if all offspring of a mating of two homozygous dominant horses have hard or soft hooves. Based on the Punnett Square constructed in question 18 (above), all of the horses have alleles HH, indicating hard hooves. Similarly, you need to determine the hoof type for all offspring of a mating of two heterozygous horses. Based on the Punnett Square constructed in question 17 (above), the mating of two heterozygous horses results in 75% of the offspring having hard hooves and 25% of the offspring having soft hooves.

20. **D** This question requires that you have some knowledge regarding the age of the universe, which is approximately 13.8 billion years old. Accordingly, the Big Bang Theory proposes that the Earth began approximately 13.8 billion years ago as a small singularity that inflated, expanded, and cooled to form our solar system; (D) is the correct answer. If you didn't recognize the theory, look at the answer choices. The Theory of Evolution relates to the process by which organisms change over time as a result of changes in heritable traits; eliminate (A). Hubble's Law states that galaxies are expanding at speeds proportional to their distance from Earth; eliminate (B). The Photoelectric Effect is the production of excited electrons when light is shone onto a material; eliminate (C).

21. This question requires that you mark the lithosphere on the provided diagram, and informs you that the lithosphere contains a rigid upper mantle and the surface of the Earth. If the lithosphere contains the surface of the Earth, it must be the outermost layer of the Earth, as shown below.

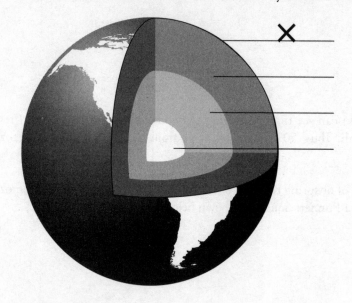

22. **97.5, 165**

In order to answer this question, you need to use the table provided to find the average heart rate at 50% maximum activity for a 25-year-old. The average heart rate at 50% maximum activity for a 25-year-old will be equal to the average heart rate at 50% maximum activity for both a 20-year-old and a 30-year-old. Since the average heart rate at 50% maximum activity for a 20-year-old and 30-year-old is 100 beats per minute and 95 beats per minute, respectively, the average heart rate at 50% maximum activity for a 25-year-old is $\frac{100 + 95}{2} = 97.5$ beats per minute. Next, find the average maximum heart rate of a 55-year-old. Since the average maximum heart rate for a 50-year-old and 60-year-old is 170 beats per minute and 160 beats per minute, respectively, the average maximum heart rate for a 55-year-old is $\frac{170 + 160}{2} = 165$ beats per minute.

23. **indirect**

This question requires you to determine the relationship between age and average heart rate. Based on the table provided, as age increases, average heart rate decreases. Accordingly, age and heart rate have an indirect relationship.

24. **A** Check the table to figure out this question. As frequency increases, for example, from orange (510 THz) to blue (630 THz), photon energy also increases (from 2.1 eV to 2.6 eV). At the same time, wavelength decreases (from 590 nm to 475 nm). Choice (A) accurately describes both relationships.

25. **A** This question requires you to look at the graph of the visible light spectrum and find the color with the greatest frequency, measured in THz. Based on the graph provided, violet has the greatest frequency, at 750 THz, while Red has the least frequency, at 460 THz. Thus, the correct answer is (A), violet.

26. **650, 1.9**

    This question requires that you identify the wavelength size and photon energy of the color red. Based on the graph provided, red has a wavelength of 650 nm, and a photon energy of 1.9 eV.

27. **D** In order to answer this question, you must know the definition of survival of the fittest. Survival of the fittest is the idea that, over a period of many generations, species will acquire adaptations that are favorable for the environment, and will pass these adaptations on to offspring. Choice (A) states that because elephants are bigger than mice, the elephants outlive the mice; this is not survival of the fittest, so eliminate (A). Choice (B) states that over a week-long period, dogs older than 10 years were not adopted at a shelter; this is not survival of the fittest, so eliminate (B). Choice (C) states that orangutans at a local zoo have determined that they receive human food when they hit a lever in their cage; this is not survival of the fittest, so eliminate (C). Finally, (D) states that over a few centuries, a species of cat has experienced changes in fur color that allow it to blend into its native land; this is an adaptation over time, and, therefore, is an example of survival of the fittest.

28. **B** This question requires you to identify the type of heat transfer that occurs in the Greenhouse Effect, which is the trapping of the Sun's warmth in the planet's atmosphere. Based on the information in the passage, convection occurs when warmer air or liquid rises, as it has more excited molecules, and the cooler air or liquid drops down. In the Greenhouse Effect, the warmer air rises and is trapped in the atmosphere. Accordingly, the Greenhouse Effect is an example of convection, or (B).

29. **conduction, radiation**

    Here you need to determine the type of heat transfer that occurs when an ice cube melts in your hand. Based on the passage, conduction occurs when excited molecules come into direct contact with nearby molecules, transferring some of their heat energy to neighboring particles. By holding an ice cube in your hand, heat will transfer from your hand to the ice cube, causing the ice cube to melt. Thus, an ice cube melting in your hand is an example of conduction. Conversely, the Sun warming the Earth is an example of radiation, as the passage states that radiation is the transfer of energy through empty space.

30. **C** This question requires you to have some knowledge of bacterial and viral infections. In particular, you should know that bacterial infections can be treated with antibiotics, while viral infections cannot be treated with antibiotics. Accordingly, once the specific strain of *streptococcus pyogenes* bacteria is identified, antibiotics can be administered to combat the bacterial infection.

31. **32** Here you are told that every atom must have at least one neutron for every existing proton, and you need to determine the minimum number of neutrons that exist in an atom with 32 protons. Thus, if there must be one neutron for every proton, an atom with 32 protons will have a minimum of 32 neutrons.

32. **C** This question requires you to use the provided chart to determine the resource that is not in abundant supply. According to the given chart, coal and natural gas are abundant; eliminate (A) and (B). The chart states that oil has a limited supply, while solar has an unlimited supply. Thus, (D) can be eliminated, and the correct answer is (C).

33.   **(e) solar, (a) wind, (d) biomass, (c) coal, (f) natural gas, (b) oil**

Here you need to arrange the provided resources in order from least to greatest consumption in the United States. The resources you have to sort are wind (0.5%), oil (37.4%), coal (22.6%), biomass (3.9%), solar (0.1%), and natural gas (24%). Thus, the correct order of resources, in order from least to greatest consumption in the United States is (e) solar, (a) wind, (d) biomass, (c) coal, (f) natural gas, and (b) oil.

34.   **nonrenewable, renewable**

This question requires that you classify coal, oil, and natural gas as either renewable or nonrenewable. Based on the chart provided, coal, oil, and natural gas are nonrenewable resources. Conversely, the chart indicates that biomass, solar, and wind are examples of renewable resources.

35. **A**   This question requires that you have knowledge of both photosynthesis and cellular respiration. Here you are required to identify the process that occurs when a sugar is combined with oxygen and water to produce carbon dioxide, water, and ATP; this process is cellular respiration, (A). Photosynthesis is the process by which plants use sunlight to synthesize carbon dioxide and water, producing oxygen as a byproduct; eliminate (B). Oxidation is the chemical combination of a substance with oxygen; eliminate (C). Transcription is the process by which the information on a strand of DNA is copied to a mRNA; eliminate (D).

NOTES

NOTES

NOTES

NOTES

NOTES

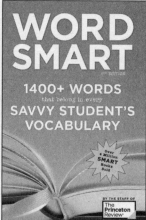